SECOND EDITION

POLITICS
IN
STATES
AND
COMMUNITIES

THOMAS R. DYE

Prentice-Hall, Inc., Englewood Cliffs, New Jersey

Library of Congress Cataloging in Publication Data

DYE, THOMAS R.
    Politics in States and communities.

    Includes bibliographical references.
    1. State governments.   2. Local government—
United States.   I. Title.
JK2408.D82 1973   320.4'73   72–11912
ISBN 0–13–686154–7

© 1973, 1969 by Prentice-Hall, Inc., Englewood Cliffs, N. J.

10   9   8   7   6   5

PRINTED IN THE UNITED STATES OF AMERICA

Prentice-Hall International, Inc., London
Prentice-Hall of Australia, Pty. Ltd., Sydney
Prentice-Hall of Canada, Ltd., Toronto
Prentice-Hall of India Private Limited, New Delhi
Prentice-Hall of Japan, Inc., Tokyo

to Joann

Contents

Foreword

If this book has a theme, it is that states and communities in America play an important role in the political life of the nation. State and local governments do more than merely provide certain services such as education, road building, or fire protection. They also perform a vital political function by helping to resolve conflicts of interest in American society. The concern of this book is with "politics," that is, conflicts over public policy in American states and communities and the structures and processes designed to manage these conflicts.

This book not only attempts to *describe* politics and public policy in American states and communities, but, more important, it attempts to *explain* differences that are encountered from state to state and community to community by means of comparative analysis. In the past the phrase "comparative government" applied to the study of foreign governments, but the American states and communities provide an excellent opportunity for genuine comparative study. By that we mean the comparison of political institutions and behavior from state to state and community to community for the purpose of identifying and explaining existing similarities or differences. Only by comparing politics and public policies in different states and communities can we arrive at any explanation of political life.

No longer is the field of state and local government a "lost world" to students of politics. Today, some of the most intellectually exciting and theoretically significant research in political science is focused on American states and communities. This book tries to summarize the results of recent systematic, comparative research in political science and incorporate these results into a comprehensive analysis of politics in states and communities.

The author of a textbook is deeply indebted to the research scholars whose labors produce the insight and understanding that a text tries to convey to its readers. There is no way to adequately express this indebtedness.

ONE

Politics
in
States and Communities

A POLITICAL APPROACH TO STATES
AND COMMUNITIES

States and communities do more than provide public services such as education, highways, and police protection. They also play an important role in managing conflicts of interest in American society. It is appropriate for a book on "politics" in states and communities to consider important conflicts in American life, for "Politics arises out of conflicts, and it consists of the activities—for example, reasonable discussion, empassioned oratory, balloting, and street fighting—by which conflict is carried on."[1] The concern of this book is therefore with "politics," that is, conflicts over public policy in American states and communities, and the structures and processes designed to manage these conflicts.

There are various approaches to the study of state and local government. Many books emphasize basic structure, organization, and practice of government; other books suggest that the key to understanding lies in the mastery of the constitutional relationships between national, state, and local governments; still other books concentrate on the administration of state and local governments. No one denies that the organizational, constitutional, or administrative aspects of state and local govern-

[1]Edward C. Banfield and James Q. Wilson, *City Politics* (Cambridge: Harvard–M.I.T. Press, 1963), p. 7.

ment are important, but the really critical problems facing American communities, such as education, welfare, racial hatred, slum housing, financial crises, and transportation, cannot be solved through organizational reform, constitutional change, or administrative efficiency. The obstacles to the solution of these problems are primarily *political* in character; that is, people have different ideas about what should be done, or if anything should be done at all. Only when everyone agrees on a solution can the problem be entrusted to lawyers, accountants, or technicians. In American politics, this agreement seldom exists. Even if there is "only one way to pave a street," political questions remain, "Whose street shall be paved?" "Who will get the paving contract?" "Who will bear the cost?" "Why not build a school gym instead of paving the street?"

The management of conflict in society is one of the basic purposes of government. The Founding Fathers were very much aware that the control of "factions" was the principal function of government. Moreover, they defined faction as a number of citizens united by common interests that oppose the interests of a number of other citizens. James Madison thought that regulating such conflict was "the principal task of modern legislation."[2] To paraphrase Madison, the management of conflict is a principal task of state and local government.

A political approach to states and communities does not ignore the organization of state and local government, the constitutional limitations upon them, or their administrative problems, for the principal responsibility for managing conflict falls upon government institutions. Governments manage conflict by establishing and enforcing general rules by which conflict is to be carried on, by arranging compromises and balancing interests in public policy, and by imposing settlements which the parties in the disputes must accept. In other words, governments must lay down "the rules of the game" in political activity; they must make decisions which allocate values among competing interests and then see that these decisions are carried out. The organization of a government, its constitutional limitations, and the administrative arrangements under which it operates all vitally affect the way it performs political functions. In considering the constitutional, organizational, and administrative aspects of state and local government, we should focus our attention on their impact on political questions.

A COMPARATIVE APPROACH TO STATES
AND COMMUNITIES

The task of political science is not only to *describe* politics and public policy in American states and communities but, more importantly, to *explain* differences encountered from state to state and community to

---

[2]James Madison, *The Federalist*, No. 10.

ONE

Politics
in
States and Communities

2James Madison, *The Federalist*, No. 10.

community by means of comparative analysis. We want to know "what" is happening in American politics, but we also want to know "why" it is happening. In the past, the phrase "comparative government" applied to the study of foreign governments, but American states and communities provide an excellent opportunity for genuine comparative study, that is, the comparison of political institutions and behavior from state to state and community to community for the purposes of identifying or explaining the similarities or differences that are found. Studies that merely describe governmental agencies or political events, without identifying or explaining their similarities or differences, cannot really contribute to the explanation of politics and public affairs. Even the most insightful descriptions of political events do not provide explanations of their significance that rise above the level of hunches. Comparison, in other words, is a vital part of explanation. Only by comparing politics and public policy in different states and communities with different socioeconomic and political environments can we arrive at any comprehensive explanations of political life. Comparative analysis can help us answer the question "why."

The American states provide an excellent opportunity for applying comparative analysis. These fifty separate political systems share a common institutional framework and cultural background. All states operate under written constitutions, which divide authority between executive, legislative, and judicial branches. The structure and operations of these branches are quite similar from state to state. All states function within the common framework of the American federal system. All states share a national language, national symbols, and a national history. Thus, some important institutional and cultural factors can be treated as constants in the comparative study of state politics.

Of course, American states and communities are not entirely alike in their social and economic environments, the nature of their political systems, or their public policies. These differences, however, are important assets in comparative study because they enable us to search for relationships between different socioeconomic environments, political system characteristics, and policy outcomes. For example, if differences among states and communities in educational policies are closely associated with differences in social or economic environments or in party systems, then we may assume that socioenvironments or party systems help "explain" educational policies.

By way of example, let us pose some specific questions about state and community politics which a comparative approach will help us answer. Are single-industry states more likely to have powerful pressure groups dominating the state legislature than multi-industry states? Are governors generally more powerful in the urban industrial states than in the rural agricultural states? What effect does urbanization have on party competition in the states? Is one-partyism a product of ruralism, poverty, or a lack of industrial development? What is the impact of educational levels on voter participation rates? Do states with competitive parties and high voter turnout have more generous welfare programs than one-party states with low voter turnout? What factors affect crime rates in states and cities, and what forces operate to shape state prison and parole programs? How do income levels in the states affect spending for education, welfare, highways, and so forth? Are tax burdens significantly heavier in some states than in others? Do some states shift the burden of taxation onto the poor more than other states, and, if so, what factors affect this process? Does a large black population improve the chances for civil rights legislation and desegregation, or does it strengthen the position of political forces resisting social change? What differences exist between cities that have experienced serious rioting among black populations and those that have not? What kinds of cities are likely to have strong political party organizations ("machines") dominating local government in contrast to reform-minded, "do-good" administrations? Are "machine" cities more responsive to the demands of ethnic or black populations than "reformed" cities? Is city-manager government more common among middle-sized cities than big cities, and, if so, why? Where has metropolitan government been successful and what factors contribute to its success or failure? What is the impact of federal programs on states and cities? Do federal grants-in-aid operate to reduce inequalities among the states in educational opportunities? What is the effect of federal money on housing, urban renewal, planning, transportation, and poverty programs in the nation's cities? These are the kinds of questions that can be approached from a comparative viewpoint.

SETTINGS FOR STATE POLITICS

State politics are often affected by unique historical circumstances. (See Figure 1–1, Table 1–1.) Louisiana is distinctive because of its French-Spanish colonial background, and the continuing influence of this backgroud on its politics today. For nine years Texas was an independent republic (1836–45) before it was annexed as a state by Congress. California was the scene of a great gold rush in 1849. Eleven southern states were involved in a bloody war against the federal government from 1861 to 1865. Hawaii has a unique history and culture, combining the influence of Polynesian, Chinese, Japanese, and hoalie civilizations. Alaska's rugged climate and geography and physical isolation set it apart. Wisconsin and Minnesota reflect the Scandinavian influences of their settlers. The states of the Deep South—South Carolina, Georgia, Alabama, Mississippi, Louisiana—still reflect their plantation cultures. Life in Florida is more tourist oriented than anywhere else. Michigan is noted for its

FIGURE 1-1

Source: U.S. Bureau of the Census.

TABLE 1-1
The States of the Union—Historical Data

State or Other Jurisdiction	Capital	Source of State Lands	Date Organized as Territory	Date Admitted to Union	Chronological Order of Admission to Union
Alabama	Montgomery	Mississippi Territory, 1798(a)	March 3, 1817	Dec. 14,1819	22
Alaska	Juneau	Purchased from Russia, 1867	Aug. 24, 1912	Jan. 3, 1959	49
Arizona	Phoenix	Ceded by Mexico, 1848(b)	Feb. 24, 1863	Feb. 14, 1912	48
Arkansas	Little Rock	Louisiana Purchase, 1803	March 2, 1819	June 15, 1836	25
California	Sacramento	Ceded by Mexico, 1848	(c)	Sept. 9, 1850	31
Colorado	Denver	Louisiana Purchase, 1803(d)	Feb. 28, 1861	Aug. 1, 1876	38
Connecticut	Hartford	Royal charter, 1662(e)		Jan. 9, 1788(f)	5
Delaware	Dover	Swedish charter, 1638; English charter 1683(e)		Dec. 7, 1787(f)	1
Florida	Tallahassee	Ceded by Spain, 1819	March 30, 1822	March 3, 1845	27
Georgia	Atlanta	Charter, 1732, from George II to Trustees for Establishing the Colony of Georgia(e)		Jan. 2, 1788(f)	4
Hawaii	Honolulu	Annexed, 1898	June 14, 1900	Aug. 21, 1959	50
Idaho	Boise	Treaty with Britain, 1846	March 4, 1863	July 3, 1890	43
Illinois	Springfield	Northwest Territory, 1787	Feb. 3, 1809	Dec. 3, 1818	21
Indiana	Indianapolis	Northwest Territory, 1787	May 7, 1800	Dec. 11, 1816	19
Iowa	Des Moines	Louisiana Purchase, 1803	June 12, 1838	Dec. 28, 1846	29
Kansas	Topeka	Louisiana Purchase, 1803(d)	May 30, 1854	Jan. 29, 1861	34
Kentucky	Frankfort	Part of Virginia until admitted as State	(c)	June 1, 1792	15
Louisiana	Baton Rouge	Louisiana Purchase, 1803(g)	March 26, 1804	April 30, 1812	18
Maine	Augusta	Part of Massachusetts until admitted as State	(c)	March 15, 1820	23
Maryland	Annapolis	Charter, 1632, from Charles I to Calvert(e)		April 28, 1788(f)	7
Massachusetts	Boston	Charter to Massachusetts Bay Company, 1629(e)		Feb. 6, 1788(f)	6
Michigan	Lansing	Northwest Territory, 1787	Jan. 11, 1805	Jan. 26, 1837	26
Minnesota	St. Paul	Northwest Territory, 1787(h)	March 3, 1849	May 11, 1858	32

State/Territory	Capital	Acquisition/Settlement	Organized/Territory	Admitted/Ratified	No.
Mississippi	Jackson	Mississippi Territory(i)	April 7, 1798	Dec. 10, 1817	20
Missouri	Jefferson City	Louisiana Purchase, 1803	June 4, 1812	Aug. 10, 1821	24
Montana	Helena	Louisiana Purchase, 1803(j)	May 26, 1864	Nov. 8, 1889	41
Nebraska	Lincoln	Louisiana Purchase, 1803	May 30, 1854	March 1, 1867	37
Nevada	Carson City	Ceded by Mexico, 1848	March 2, 1861	Oct. 31, 1864	36
New Hampshire	Concord	Grants from Council for New England, 1622 and 1629. Made royal province, 1679(e)		June 21, 1788(f)	9
New Jersey	Trenton	Dutch settlement, 1618; English charter, 1664(e)		Dec. 18, 1787(f)	3
New Mexico	Santa Fe	Ceded by Mexico, 1848(b)	Sept. 9, 1850	Jan. 6, 1912	47
New York	Albany	Dutch settlement, 1623; English control, 1664(e)		July 26, 1788(f)	11
North Carolina	Raleigh	Charter, 1663, from Charles II(e)		Nov. 21, 1789(f)	12
North Dakota	Bismarck	Louisiana Purchase, 1803(k)	March 2, 1861	Nov. 2, 1889	39
Ohio	Columbus	Northwest Territory, 1787	(c)	March 1, 1803	17
Oklahoma	Oklahoma City	Louisiana Purchase, 1803	May 2, 1890	Nov. 16, 1907	46
Oregon	Salem	Settlement and treaty with Britain, 1846	Aug. 14, 1848	Feb. 14, 1859	33
Pennsylvania	Harrisburg	Grant from Charles II to William Penn, 1681(e)		Dec. 12, 1787(f)	2
Rhode Island	Providence	Charter, 1663, from Charles II(e)		May 29, 1790(f)	13
South Carolina	Columbia	Charter, 1663, from Charles II(e)		May 23, 1788(f)	8
South Dakota	Pierre	Louisiana Purchase, 1803	March 2, 1861	Nov. 2, 1889	40
Tennessee	Nashville	Part of North Carolina until admitted as State	(c)	June 1, 1796	16
Texas	Austin	Republic of Texas, 1845	(c)	Dec. 29, 1845	28
Utah	Salt Lake City	Ceded by Mexico, 1848	Sept. 9, 1850	Jan. 4, 1896	45
Vermont	Montpelier	From lands of New Hampshire and New York		March 4, 1791	14
Virginia	Richmond	Charter, 1609, from James I to London Company (e)	(c)	June 25, 1788(f)	10
Washington	Olympia	Oregon Territory, 1848	March 2, 1853	Nov. 11, 1889	42
West Virginia	Charleston	Part of Virginia until admitted as State	(c)	June 20, 1863	35
Wisconsin	Madison	Northwest Territory, 1787	April 20, 1836	May 29, 1848	30
Wyoming	Cheyenne	Louisiana Purchase, 1803(d,j)	July 25, 1868	July 10, 1890	44
American Samoa	Pago Pago		Became a Territory, 1899		—
Guam	Agana	Ceded by Spain, 1898	Aug. 1, 1950		—
Puerto Rico	San Juan	Ceded by Spain, 1898		July 25, 1952(l)	—

TABLE 1-1 (Cont.)

The States of the Union—Historical Data

State of Other Jurisdiction	Capital	Source of State Lands	Date Organized as Territory	Date Admitted to Union	Chronological Order of Admission to Union
TTPI	Saipan	Administered as trusteeship for the United Nations, July 18, 1947			—
Virgin Islands	Charlotte Amalie	Purchased from Denmark, January 17, 1917			—

(a) By the Treaty of Paris, 1783, England gave up claim to the thirteen original Colonies, and to all land within an area extending along the present Canadian border to the Lake of the Woods, down the Mississippi River to the 31st parallel, east to the Chattahoochie, down that river to the mouth of the Flint, east to the source of the St. Mary's, down that river to the ocean. Territory west of the Alleghenies was claimed by various States, but was eventually all ceded to the Nation. Thus, the major part of Alabama was acquired by the Treaty of Paris, but the lower portion from Spain in 1813.

(b) Portion of land obtained by Gadsden Purchase, 1853.

(c) No territorial status before admission to Union.

(d) Portion of land ceded by Mexico, 1848.

(e) One of the original thirteen Colonies.

(f) Date of ratification of U.S. Constitution.

(g) West Feliciana District (Baton Rouge) acquired from Spain, 1810, added to Louisiana, 1812.

(h) Portion of land obtained by Louisiana Purchase, 1803.

(i) See footnote (a). The lower portion of Mississippi was also acquired from Spain in 1813.

(j) Portion of land obtained from Oregon Territory, 1848.

(k) The northern portion and the Red River Valley were acquired by treaty with Great Britain in 1818.

(l) On this date Puerto Rico became a self-governing Commonwealth by compact approved by the United States Congress and the voters of Puerto Rico as provided in U.S. Public Law 600 of 1950.

SOURCE: THE BOOK OF THE STATES 1972-73 (Lexington, Ky.: Council of State Governments, 1972).

automobile industry, Pennsylvania for its steel industry, and West Virginia for its depleted coal mines. Nevada is most conspicuous for its legalized gambling.

These unique historical and cultural settings help to shape state political systems and public policies; however, students of state politics must search for social and economic conditions that appear most influential in shaping state politics over time in all the states. Despite the uniqueness of history and culture in many of our states, we must still search for generalizations which will help to explain why state governments do what they do. Since it is impossible to consider all the environmental conditions that might influence state politics, we must focus our attention on a limited number of environmental variables.

Economic development is one of the most influential environmental variables affecting state politics. Economic development is defined here to include three closely related components; urbanization, income, and education. *Urbanization* is an integral part of economic development. Industrial activities require the concentration of people in urban centers, whereas agricultural activities spread population over larger land areas. It is possible for a population center to grow without industrialization, but industrialization requires urbanization. A common definition of urbanization is the percentage of population living in urban areas, that is, in incorporated cities of twenty-five hundred or more or the urban fringe of cities of fifty thousand or more. This is the standard Census Bureau definition. In 1790 the urban population of the United States was only 5 percent of the total population. By 1900 this figure had grown to 40 percent, and in 1970, 73.5 percent of the population lived in urban areas. Yet here again not all the states share this high degree of urbanization. Vermont has the smallest proportion of urban residents of any state in the nation (32.2 percent), and California has the highest proportion (90.9 percent). The distribution of states according to the percentage of their population living in urban areas is shown in Figure 1–2.

Rising *income* is also a basic component of economic development. An industrial economy means increased worker productivity and the creation of surplus wealth. Per capita personal income in the United States grew from $1,500 in 1950 to $2,200 in 1960 and to $3,900 in 1970. This wealth was not evenly distributed throughout the states (see Figure 1–2). Per capita personal income in Connecticut was over $4,800, but it was only $2,500 in Mississippi.

An economically developed society requires educated, rather than uneducated, workers. Many economists have asserted that economic growth involves an upgrading of the quality in the work force, the development of professional managerial skills, and an increase in the volume of research. These developments obviously involve a general increase in the

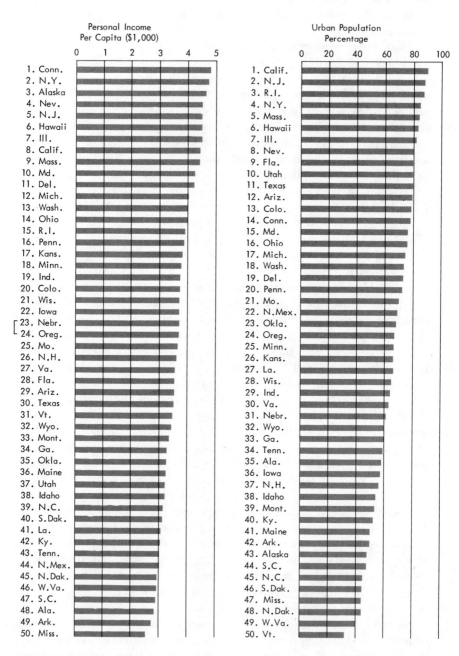

FIGURE 1–2 Rankings of the States: Income, Urbanization, and Education

Median School Year
Completed by Adult Population

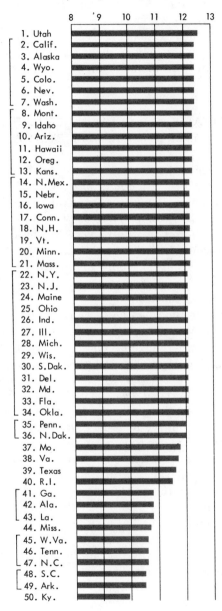

```
        8    '9   10   11   12   13
 1. Utah
 2. Calif.
 3. Alaska
 4. Wyo.
 5. Colo.
 6. Nev.
 7. Wash.
 8. Mont.
 9. Idaho
10. Ariz.
11. Hawaii
12. Oreg.
13. Kans.
14. N.Mex.
15. Nebr.
16. Iowa
17. Conn.
18. N.H.
19. Vt.
20. Minn.
21. Mass.
22. N.Y.
23. N.J.
24. Maine
25. Ohio
26. Ind.
27. Ill.
28. Mich.
29. Wis.
30. S.Dak.
31. Del.
32. Md.
33. Fla.
34. Okla.
35. Penn.
36. N.Dak.
37. Mo.
38. Va.
39. Texas
40. R.I.
41. Ga.
42. Ala.
43. La.
44. Miss.
45. W.Va.
46. Tenn.
47. N.C.
48. S.C.
49. Ark.
50. Ky.
```

FIGURE 1–2 (Cont.)

11

educational levels of the adult population. In 1940 the median school year completed by the adult population of the United States was 8.6. By 1970 the median school year had advanced to 12.0. This generally high level of educational attainment did not prevail uniformly throughout the states (see Figure 1–2).

The extent to which economic development—urbanization, income, and education—affects the politics of the states is an important question, which we will return to again and again in the chapters that follow.

STATES AND COMMUNITIES IN THE AMERICAN POLITICAL SYSTEM

At the beginning of the twentieth century, most government activity in America was carried on at the *local* level. Table 1–2 reveals that local governments once made about 59 percent of all government expenditures in the United States, compared to 35 percent for the federal government and 6 percent for state governments. Yet by the 1970s centralization in the American federal system had proceeded to the point where local governments were making only 23 percent of all government expenditures, compared to 64 percent for the federal government and 13 percent for state governments.

Wars and the depression had a great deal to do with the shift away from local reliance in American government. During national emergencies, both foreign and domestic, Americans have turned to the federal government for help. After the emergency, federal activity decreases somewhat in relation to state and local activity, but federal activity never returns to the precrisis level. Thus, during World War I and World War II, and the Korean and Vietnamese wars, the federal government increased its percentage of total government activity, while local and state government percentages declined. Since the federal government has the primary responsibility for national defense, this is what we would expect to occur during wartime. But the federal government also expands its activities in response to domestic crisis; it was during the 1930s that federal expenditures surpassed the combined expenditures of all states and communities.

While foreign and domestic crises have brought about increasing centralization in American government, it should be noted that expanded federal activity has *not* come at the expense of state and local activity. Federal power and state-local power are not at the opposite ends of a seesaw; the growth of federal power has not necessarily curtailed the power of states and localities. National activity has expanded in the twentieth century, but so has the activity of state and local governments.

TABLE 1-2

A Comparison of the Expenditures of Federal, State, and Local Governments over Seven Decades

	PERCENTAGES OF TOTAL GENERAL EXPENDITURES OF GOVERNMENTS IN THE U.S.[3]		
	Federal[1]	State[2]	Local[2]
1902	35%	6%	59%
1927	31	13	56
1936	50	14	36
1944	91	3	7
1950	64	12	24
1960	62	13	25
1970	64	13	23

[1] Figures include social security and trust fund expenditures.

[2] State payments to local governments are shown as local government expenditures; federal grants-in-aid are shown as federal expenditures.

[3] Figures may not total correctly because of rounding.

SOURCE: Standard sources of data on American states and communities in tables throughout include: U.S. Bureau of the Census, STATISTICAL ABSTRACT OF THE UNITED STATES, published annually by the U.S.Government Printing Office, Washington, D.C.; U.S. Bureau of the Census, CENSUS OF GOVERNMENTS, published after each five-year governmental census (1967, 1972, etc.) by the U.S. Government Printing Office, Washington, D.C.; U.S. Bureau of the Census CENSUS OF POPULATION 1970, including individual state volumes on "Numbers of Inhabitants," "General Population Characteristics," and "General Social and Economic Characteristics," as well as individual reports on Standard Metropolitan Statistical Areas, published by the U.S. Government Printing Office, Washington, D.C.; THE BOOK OF THE STATES, published biennially by the Council of State Governments, Lexington, Kentucky; MUNICIPAL YEARBOOK, published annually by the International City Managers Association, Washington, D.C.; U.S. Bureau of the Census, CITY-COUNTY DATA BOOK, published every five years by the U.S. Government Printing Office, Washington, D.C.; and AMERICA VOTES, edited by Richard Scammon, and published periodically by the Governmental Affairs Institute, Washington, D.C. Unless otherwise indicated, the social, economic, governmental, and electoral data presented in this volume are drawn from these sources.

The extent of centralization of government activity in the American federal system varies widely according to policy area (see Table 1–3). In the fields of national defense, space research, and postal service, the federal government assumes almost exclusive responsibility. In all other fields, state and local governments share responsibility and costs with the federal government. State and local governments assume the major share of the costs of education, highways, health and hospitals, sanitation, and fire and police protection. Welfare costs are gradually being shifted to the federal government, and the federal government assumes the major share of the costs of natural resource development and social security.

States and communities in America operate the world's largest public

TABLE 1-3

Federal and State-Local Shares of Expenditures
by Policy Areas, 1927-70

	1927		1938		1970	
	Federal[1]	State and Local	Federal[1]	State and Local	Federal[1]	State and Local
National defense	100%	0%	100%	0%	100%	0%
Space research	100	0	100	0	100	0
Postal service	100	0	100	0	100	0
Education	1	99	6	94	10	90
Highways	1	99	23	77	29	71
Welfare	6	94	13	87	58	42
Health and hospitals	18	82	19	81	33	67
Natural resources	31	69	81	19	80	20
Housing and urban renewal	-	-	-	-	82	18

[1] Federal grants-in-aid are shown as federal expenditures.

school system and highway network. They operate most of the nation's judicial, welfare, police, health, correctional, and recreational facilities. Most regulation of industry, banking, commerce, utilities, labor, and protection of public safety is in the hands of state and local governments. Their programs in conservation, sanitation, social work, housing, and urban planning are vital to the day-to-day lives of all Americans. Even when the national government is involved in these programs, states and communities must decide whether to participate in national programs, and if they participate, they must administer the programs within their jurisdictions. Despite the glamour of national politics, states and communities carry on the greatest volume of public business, settle the greatest number of political conflicts, make the majority of policy decisions, and direct the bulk of public programs. They have the major responsibility for maintaining domestic law and order, for educating the children, for moving Americans from place to place, and for caring for the poor and the ill. They regulate the provision of water, gas, electric, and other public utilities, share in the regulation of insurance and banking enterprise, regulate the use of land, and supervise the sale and ownership of property. Their courts settle by far the greatest number of civil and criminal cases. In short, states and communities are by no means unimportant political systems.

Education. Education is the most important responsibility of state and local governments and the most costly of all state-local functions. States and communities are responsible for decisions about what should be taught in the public schools, how much should be spent on the education of each child, how many children should be in each classroom, how much teachers should be paid, how responsibilities in education should be divided between state and local governments, what qualifications teachers must have, what types and rates of taxes shall be levied for education, and many other decisions which affect the life of every child in America. Support for higher education, including funds for state colleges and universities, is one of the most rapidly increasing expenditures of state governments. The promise of equal access to a college degree for all qualified students is proving to be a heavy burden on states and communities. The federal government is currently contributing about 10 percent of the total expenditures for education.

Transportation. Transportation—more particularly highways—is the second most costly function of state and local governments. There are over two million miles of surface roads in America, and nearly one hundred million registered motor vehicles in the nation, almost one for every two persons. States and communities must make decisions about the allocation of money for streets and highways, sources of funds for highway revenue, the extent of gasoline and motor vehicle taxation, the regulation of traffic on the highways, the location of highways, the determination of construction policies, the division of responsibility between state and local governments for highway financing administration, the division of highway funds between rural and urban areas, and other important issues in highway politics. While the federal government is deeply involved in highway construction, federal grants for highways amount to less than 30 percent of all expenditures for highways.

Health and welfare. States and communities continue to carry a heavy burden in the field of health and welfare—despite an extensive system of federal grants-in-aid for this purpose—and spend about as much as the federal government. States and communities must make decisions about participation in federal programs and allocate responsibilities among themselves for health and welfare programs. Within the broad outlines of federal policy, states and communities decide the amount of money appropriated for health and welfare purposes, the benefits to be paid to recipients, the rules of eligibility, and the means by which the programs will be administered. States and communities may choose to grant assistance beyond the limits supported by the national government, or they may choose to have no welfare programs at all. Moreover, states and communities must maintain institutions for the care of persons who are so destitute, alone, or ill that federal payments are not sufficient. These are the state orphanages, homes for the aged, and state and county hospitals and homes for the physically and mentally ill.

Crime. States and communities have the principal responsibility for public safety in America. Crime is increasing at a much greater rate than the population. The federal government, through the Federal Bureau of Investigation, has limited jurisdiction over certain crimes, such as kidnapping, bank robbery, and espionage. State police have important high-way safety responsibilities and cooperate with local authorities in the apprehension of criminals. But community police forces continue to be the principal instrument of law enforcement and public safety. Local governments employ over a quarter of a million policemen in the United States today, and approximately the same number of firemen. The sheriff and his deputies are still the principal enforcement and arresting officers in rural counties. States and communities also have the principal responsibility for maintaining prisons and correctional institutions. Each year, over two million Americans are prisoners in jails, police stations, juvenile homes, or penitentiaries. More than 90 percent of these prisoners are at state and local rather than federal institutions.

Civil rights. The national government has defined a national system of civil rights, but these rights cannot become realities without the support of state and local authorities. States and communities must deal directly with racial problems, such as desegregation in the public schools, job discrimination, and the existence of segregated housing patterns or ghettos in the cities. They must deal with the consequences of racial tension, including violence. Some states have gone much further than the federal government in guaranteeing civil rights, for example, by bussing students out of segregated neighborhoods to avoid de facto segregation in the schools. Other states and communities have resisted federal attempts to desegregate their public schools, hospitals, and recreation facilities.

Physical environment. Local governments have the principal responsibility for our physical environment. They must plan streets, parks, and commercial, residential, and industrial areas and provide essential public utilities for the community. The waste materials of human beings—rubbish, garbage, and sewage—exceed one ton every day per person. The task of disposal is an immense one; the problem is not only collecting it but finding ways to dispose of it. If it is incinerated, it contributes to air pollution; and if it is carried off into streams, rivers, or lakes, it contributes to water pollution. Thus, communities are largely responsible for two of the nation's most pressing problems—air and water pollution.

Taxation. To pay for these programs, states and communities must make important decisions about taxation: they must decide about levels of taxation and what tax burdens their citizens can carry. They must determine what reliance shall be placed upon income, sales, or property taxation. States and communities must raise over $100 billion per year and at the same time compete with each other to attract industry and commerce.

While it is true that the decisions of states and communities are at times heavily influenced by decisions made at the national level, states and communities continue to bear the major responsibility for policy making and finance in domestic affairs. States and communities are important political systems with the legal authority, money, manpower, and policies and programs which touch the lives of all Americans.

THE CONSTITUTIONAL FRAMEWORK OF
STATE GOVERNMENT

Probably no other people in the world are more devoted than the American people to the idea of written constitutions. This devotion has deep roots in American national traditions. In 1215 a group of English lords forced King John to sign a document, later known as the Magna Carta, which guaranteed them certain feudal rights and set a precedent for constitutional government. Although the British political tradition eventually rejected the formal written constitutions, the idea of a written constitution was strongly reinforced by the experience in the American colonies. The American colonies were legally established by charters given to companies establishing settlements here. These charters became more elaborate as the colonial ventures succeeded, and the habit of depending upon a written code for the regulation of governmental organization and operation became strongly entrenched in the American colonies.

The charters, or "constitutions," were granted by royal action, either by recognizing proprietary rights, as in Maryland, Delaware, and Pennsylvania, or by granting royal commissions to companies to establish governments, as in Virginia, Massachusetts, New Hampshire, New York, New Jersey, Georgia, and North and South Carolina. Only in Connecticut and Rhode Island was there much popular participation in early constitution making. In these two colonies, royal charters were granted directly to the colonists themselves, who participated in drawing up the charter for the submission to the Crown. The important point is that these charters, whatever their origin, were present in all the colonies, and many political traditions and expectations grew up around them. All the colonies and charters were subject to royal control. Colonists looked to these charters for protection against British interference in colonial affairs. This was particularly true in Connecticut and Rhode Island, which were organized along popular principles with elected governors and legislatures whose acts were not subjected to a royal governor's veto, nor sent to England for approval. The political importance of these early charters is illustrated by the conflict over the Fundamental Orders of Connecticut. In 1685 King James issued an order for the repeal of Connecticut's charter. The colony offered its submission, and in 1687 Sir Edmund Androse went to Hartford and in the name of the Crown declared the government dissolved. The charter was not surrendered, however, but secreted in an oak tree, which is now displayed for sightseers. Immediately after the English revolution of 1688, people returned to exercising all the powers of the original charter. Succeeding British monarchs silently permitted this without struggle or resistance. After the Declaration of Independence, new constitutions were written in eleven colonies; Connecticut retained her charter as the fundamental law until 1818, and Rhode Island kept her charter until 1842. The colonial experience, together with the earlier English heritage, had firmly implanted the tradition of written constitutions.

Constitutions govern governments. They prescribe the essential structure and organization of government, and they distribute powers among the various branches of government. Constitutions both authorize governments to exercise power and place prohibitions on the exercise of governmental power. Constitutions provide for stability and continuity in government by providing for terms of offices and for orderly replacement of political leaders. They provide the opportunity for orderly change. Since constitutions govern the activities of governments themselves, they are considered more fundamental than the ordinary laws and statutes passed by governments. State *constitutions* take precedence over any state *law* in conflict with them. Since constitutions are more fundamental than ordinary law, they cannot be changed by the routine methods employed to amend ordinary laws. Amendments generally require some special legislative procedures together with popular referendum. (See Table 1–4.)

State constitutions take precedence over state law, but they are subordinate to the U.S. Constitution and the laws of the United States. The United States Constitution mentions state constitutions only once, and it does so to assert the supremacy of the U.S. Constitution and the laws and treaties of the United States. Article VI states:

> This constitution, and the laws of the United States which shall be made in pursuance thereof; and all treaties made, or which shall be made, under the authority of the United States, shall be the supreme law of the land; and the judge in every state shall be bound thereby, anything in the constitution or laws of any state to the contrary notwithstanding.

All state constitutions have preambles, most of which begin with "We the people," as one might expect. In contrast to our Founding Fathers and their unholy belief in separation of church and state, most state constitutions make specific reference to divine authority. For example: "We the people of the state of Arizona, grateful to almighty God for our liberties, do ordain this constitution . . ."; "We the people of the state of New Jersey, grateful to almighty God for the civil and religious liberties which he hath so long permitted us to enjoy . . .". Several state constitutions are in probable violation of the First Amendment of the U.S. Constitution prohibiting the "establishment of religion": Massachusetts insists that "all persons should worship the Supreme Being"; Delaware that "all persons should assemble to public worship"; and several states prohibit "nonbelievers" from holding public office.

All state constitutions have a bill of rights, which asserts the basic freedoms of speech, press, religion, and assembly. There are frequent references to basic procedural rights, such as the writ of habeas corpus, trial by jury, protection against double jeopardy and self-incrimination, prohibitions against ex post facto laws, imprisonment for debt, unreasonable searches and seizures, and excessive bail. Frequently one finds in the state constitutions interesting "rights," which are not found in the national Constitution. The right of private clubs and fraternal organizations to sell alcoholic beverages is specifically enumerated in the Oregon Constitution. Management interests have incorporated a "right to work" provision barring union shops in the Florida Constitution.

All state constitutions reflect the American political tradition of separation of powers, with separate legislative, executive, and judicial articles establishing these separate branches of government. Generally, however, state constitutions emphasize legislative power over executive power. The historical explanation for this is that governors were appointed by the king in most colonies and the early constitutions reflected the colonists' distaste for executive authority. Yet the fact that constitutions are usually written by legislatures, legislative commissions, or constitutional conventions which resemble legislatures may also explain why legislative power is emphasized. Finally, the curtailment of executive power may reflect the desires of important interest groups in the states, who would prefer to deal with independent boards and commissions in the executive branch rather than a strong governor. (See Chapter 6 for further discussion of this point.)

Whether the reasons are historical or political, the executive branches of most state governments are weakened and divided by state constitutions. Executive powers are divided between the governor and many separately elected executive officers—attorney general, secretary of state, treasurer, auditor, lieutenant governor, state school superintendent, and others. State constitutions also curtail executive authority by establishing a multitude of boards or commissions to head executive departments. Membership on these boards and commissions is generally for long overlapping terms, which are not coextensive with the term of the governor.

Only the Nebraska Constitution provides for a unicameral legislature. All other state legislatures are divided into an upper and a lower chamber—making a total of ninety-nine state legislative bodies. In many states the basis for apportioning these bodies is set forth in the state constitution. However, since the guarantee of the U.S. Constitution that no state shall deny to any person the "equal protection of the laws" takes pre-

TABLE 1-4
General Information On State Constitutions

State or Other Jurisdiction	Number of Constitutions	Dates of Adoption	Effective Date of Present Constitution	Estimated Length (Number of words)	Number of Amendments	
					Proposed	Adopted
Alabama	6	1819; 1861; 1865; 1868; 1875; 1901	1901	106,000	474	320
Alaska	1	1956	1959	14,400	96(a)	7(b)
Arizona	1	1911	1912	16,000	132	69
Arkansas	5	1836; 1861; 1864; 1868; 1874	1874	40,170	(c)	53
California	2	1849; 1879	1879	68,000	646	375
Colorado	1	1876	1876	40,190	(c)	74
Connecticut	4	1818(d); 1965	1965	7,959	4	3(e)
Delaware	4	1776; 1792; 1831; 1897	1897	22,000	(c)	81
Florida	6	1839; 1861; 1865; 1868; 1885; 1968	1969	21,286	8	4
Georgia	8	1777; 1789; 1798; 1861; 1865; 1868; 1877; 1945	1945	500,000	921	691
Hawaii	1	1950	1959	11,882	35	32
Idaho	1	1889	1890	22,280	125	85
Illinois	4	1818; 1848; 1870; 1970	1971	17,500	0	0
Indiana	2	1816; 1851	1851	11,120	45	25
Iowa	2	1846; 1857	1857	11,200	38	35(f)
Kansas	1	1859	1861	14,500	86	58
Kentucky	4	1792; 1799; 1850; 1891	1891	21,500	45	20
Louisiana	10	1812; 1845; 1852; 1861; 1864; 1868; 1879; 1898; 1913; 1921	1921	255,450	724	496
Maine	1	1820	1820	15,000	135	116(g)
Maryland	4	1776; 1851; 1864; 1867	1867	35,500	181	143
Massachusetts	1	1780	1780	26,000	108	91
Michigan	4	1835; 1850; 1908; 1963	1964	19,867	8	4
Minnesota	1	1858	1858	20,080	182	96
Mississippi	4	1817; 1832; 1869; 1890	1890	25,742	104	35
Missouri	4	1820; 1865; 1875; 1945	1945	33,260	45	28
Montana	1	1889	1889	28,000	57	37
Nebraska	2	1866; 1875	1875	23,170	197	129
Nevada	1	1864	1864	17,160	110	65
New Hampshire	2	1776; 1784(h)	1784	12,200	135(h)	61(h)
New Jersey	3	1776; 1844; 1947	1947	16,040	21	16

State	Number of constitutions	Dates of adoption	Date of present constitution	Estimated number of words	Number of amendments submitted to voters	Number of amendments adopted
New Mexico	1	1911	1912	26,136	175	82
New York	6	1777; 1801; 1821; 1846; 1868; 1894	1894	47,000	240	179
North Carolina	3	1776; 1868; 1970	1971	17,000	0	0
North Dakota	1	1889	1889	31,470	(c)	86
Ohio	2	1802; 1851	1851	29,110	184	103
Oklahoma	1	1907	1907	63,213	184	79
Oregon	1	1859	1859	23,000	256	127
Pennsylvania	4	1776; 1790; 1838; 1873; 1968(i)	1873; 1968	24,750	122	92
Rhode Island	1	1843(d)	1843	21,040	70	36
South Carolina	6	1776; 1778; 1790; 1865; 1868; 1895	1895	45,740	401	398
South Dakota	1	1889	1889	30,290	156	78
Tennessee	3	1796; 1835; 1870	1870	15,150	34	18
Texas	5	1845; 1861; 1866; 1869; 1876	1876	52,270	321	201
Utah	1	1896	1896	20,990	99	56
Vermont	3	1777; 1786; 1793	1793	7,600	200	44
Virginia	6	1776; 1830; 1851; 1868; 1902; 1970	1971	8,000	0	0
Washington	1	1889	1889	26,930	95	54
West Virginia	2	1863; 1872	1872	22,970	67	40
Wisconsin	1	1848	1848	17,900	121(j)	93(k)
Wyoming	1	1890	1890	23,170	61	33
Puerto Rico	1	1952	1952	9,000	7	6

(a) Total number of measures proposed by the Legislature, including duplications.

(b) Total number of proposed measures adopted by the Legislature, six of which require voter approval.

(c) Data not available.

(d) Colonial charters with some alterations, in Connecticut (1638, 1662) and Rhode Island (1663), served as the first constitutions for these States.

(e) 47, 1, and 12 prior amendments were incorporated in the constitution in 1955, 1961, and 1965 respectively.

(f) Three amendments were adopted but were nullified on procedural grounds by the Iowa Supreme Court.

(g) One adopted amendment will not become effective until the Legislature enacts further legislation.

(h) The constitution of 1784 was extensively amended, rearranged and clarified in 1793. Figures show proposals and adoptions since 1793.

(i) Limited convention.

(j) Separate ballot proposals, some concerning more than one section.

(k) Two of the ratified amendments were later invalidated by the Wisconsin Supreme Court.

SOURCE: THE BOOK OF THE STATES 1972-73 (Lexington, Ky.: Council of State Governments, 1972).

cedence over state constitutions, malapportionment embodied in a state constitution is no more acceptable to federal courts than malapportionment by state law. (See Chapter 5.)

Unlike the U.S. Congress, state legislatures do not need specific constitutional delegations of power to pass particular kinds of laws. Congress must justify every law it passes as part of its enumerated powers, according to Article I, Section 8, of the Constitution; but the states originated as governments of general sovereignty and therefore did not need to enumerate their powers. Yet as state constitutions have grown more lengthy and complex, thus giving state courts greater opportunity to limit legislative power, the practice of inserting constitutional authorization for specific state programs has grown. In other words, although state legislatures have *general* rather than *enumerated* powers, the practice of specific constitutional authorization for state power has grown as a safeguard against court interpretations limiting legislative authority.

On the whole, state courts are far more likely to find that the acts of state legislatures are in violation of the state's constitution than the Supreme Court is to find the acts of Congress in violation of the U.S. Constitution. Lengthy constitutions with an abundance of detail invite litigation in the courts and the nullification of legislation. Lengthy, complex state constitutions, then, are a source of political strength for state courts. Supposedly, it is not the wisdom of legislation but its constitutionality that concerns the courts. But obviously the power to interpret state constitutions gives the courts a great deal of political power. As Duane Lockard notes, there are many instances of court invalidation of legislation because of the "we-don't-think-it-is-a-good-idea" rule.[3]

All state constitutions have articles on suffrage and elections. These provisions set the times of elections and the qualifications for voting and office holding. (See Chapter 3 for further discussion.)

All state constitutions have articles on taxation and finance. These articles often place severe restrictions and limitations upon the taxing power of state and local governments. They reflect a distrust of state legislatures, and they testify to the political power of interest groups seeking to avoid taxation. State constitutions generally provide that state taxation shall be uniform and equal upon the same classes of subjects. The power of municipalities to collect taxes is also set forth in restricted terms. Certain classes of property may be exempted from taxation: property devoted to religious, educational, or charitable purposes; municipal and public property; certain agricultural and forest land; public utilities; and even "homesteads," that is, low-priced owner-occupied homes. Some state constitutions exempt new industries from certain kinds of taxation in order to stimulate industrial growth.

[3]Duane Lockard, *The Politics of State and Local Government* (New York: The Macmillan Company, 1963), p. 88.

Another common limitation on taxing and spending powers of state governments is the constitutional earmarking of certain state revenues for specific programs. For example, constitutional provisions may require that all gasoline taxes be spent for highway purposes. Approximately half of all state revenues cannot be used for other than earmarked purposes. Some states have gone so far as to specify particular tax rates in their constitutions.

Debt limitations represent another constitutional restriction on fiscal powers. All but five states have constitutional limitations on debt. Some constitutions prevent a state from contracting any debt at all, requiring it to operate officially in the black each year. Other constitutions set specific dollar limits, usually very low sums, on the amount of debt that can be incurred. This forces many states to resort to constitutional amendment when they wish to borrow money for specific purposes. More commonly, however, it means that states must issue "revenue bonds" for specific projects which are backed by revenue produced by the project rather than the general tax revenues of the state. Since these revenues are less secure, they carry a higher interest rate; thus, states are forced to pay higher interest rates simply because of their constitutional limitations on debt. State constitutions also limit the debt of local governments: it may not exceed a certain percentage of the property tax base; the purposes for which local government debt may be incurred are limited; bond referendums must be submitted for approval of the local electorate. These provisions also force local governments to finance specific projects on a revenue basis at higher cost, rather than through obligations on general tax and revenues. In general, constitutional limitations on debt force both state and local governments to devise ingenious methods of working their way out of their fiscal straitjacket.

Typical state constitutions will also have provisions on education, highways, natural resources, corporations, and public utilities. Many of these provisions go into great detail about regulation, administration, and financial management—details that would ordinarily be left to legislatures if voters and organized interests had much confidence in them. Many interest groups are not satisfied with writing their preferences into law but seek instead to write their preferences into state constitutions. The result is that many constitutions contain a wide range of guarantees and prohibitions to protect interests powerful enough to push their way into the fundamental law of the state. Their preferences are thus protected from ordinary legislative majorities; therefore, extraordinary procedures of constitutional amendment are required to alter this protection.

All state constitutions provide for revision by amendment, but the difficulty of amending constitutions varies widely. (See Table 1–5.) Some states require a constitutional amendment to be passed by not one but

TABLE 1-5
Amending State Constitutions

State	Legislative Vote Required for Proposal	Approval by Two Sessions	Ratification by Electorate
Alabama	3/5	No	MA
Alaska	2/3	No	MA
Arizona	Maj.	No	MA
Arkansas	Maj.	No	MA
California	2/3	No	MA
Colorado	2/3	No	MA
Connecticut	(g)	(g)	MA
Delaware	2/3	Yes	None
Florida	3/5	No	MA
Georgia	2/3	No	MA
Hawaii	(f)	(f)	MA
Idaho	2/3	No	MA
Illinois	3/5	No	ME
Indiana	Maj.	Yes	MA
Iowa	Maj.	Yes	MA
Kansas	2/3	Yes	MA
Kentucky	3/5	No	MA
Louisiana	2/3	No	MA
Maine	2/3	No	MA
Maryland	3/5	No	MA
Massachusetts	Maj.	Yes	MA
Michigan	2/3	No	MA
Minnesota	Maj.	No	ME
Mississippi	2/3	No	MA
Missouri	Maj.	No	MA
Montana	2/3	No	MA
Nebraska	3/5	No	MA
Nevada	Maj.	Yes	MA
New Hampshire	3/5	No	2/3MA
New Jersey	(b)	(b)	MA
New Mexico	Maj.(c)	No	MA(c)
New York	Maj.	Yes	MA
North Carolina	3/5	No	MA
North Dakota	Maj.	No	MA
Ohio	3/5	No	MA
Oklahoma	Maj.	No	ME

two successive legislatures, in addition to being submitted to the electorate for its approval in a referendum. In the states requiring only one legislative session to propose an amendment, some permit a constitutional amendment to be proposed by a simple majority vote but others require either a two-thirds or a three-fifths vote. Every state except Delaware requires constitutional amendments proposed by the legislature to be submitted to the voters for approval in a referendum. Some states require an approval by a majority of all voters participating in the general election, rather than a majority of those voting on the amendment.

TABLE 1-5 (Cont.)

State	Legislative Vote Required for Proposal	Approval by Two Sessions	Ratification by Electorate
Oregon	Maj.	No	MA
Pennsylvania	Maj.	Yes	MA
Rhode Island	Maj.	Yes	3/5MA
South Carolina	2/3	Yes	MA
South Dakota	Maj.	No	MA
Tennessee	(d)	Yes	ME
Texas	2/3	No	MA
Utah	2/3	No	MA
Vermont	(e)	Yes	MA
Virginia	Maj.	Yes	MA
Washington	2/3	No	MA
West Virginia	2/3	No	MA
Wisconsin	Maj.	Yes	MA
Wyoming	2/3	No	ME

Key: MA—Majority vote on Amendment; ME—Maiority vote in election.

(a) No provision for proposal of amendments by legislature. Consititution amended only by consititutional convention.

(b) Three-fifths of all members of each house; or majority of all members of each house for two successive sessions.

(c) Amendments dealing with certain sections on elective franchise and education must be proposed by 3/4 vote of the legislature and ratified by 3/4 vote of the electorate and 2/3 vote in each county.

(d) Majority members elected, first passage; 2/3 members elected, second passage.

(e) Two-thirds vote Senate, majority vote House. first passage; majority both houses, second passage. Since 1910, amendments may be submitted only at 10-year intervals.

(f) Approval at two successive sessions required if votes in each house are majority but less than 2/3.

(g) Majority vote in each house in two sessions or 3/4 vote in each house in one session.

SOURCE: THE BOOK OF STATES 1972-73 (Lexington, Ky.: Council of State Governments, 1972).

This presents a genuine obstacle to ratification of constitutional amendments, since voter interest and participation in the choice of candidates is generally greater than interest or participation in constitutional amendments. The most common means of amending state constitutions is to provide for approval by a two-thirds vote in the legislature and then by a majority of the people voting on it in the next election. In all but a few states, constitutions can also be changed by calling a constitutional convention. This is a very cumbersome procedure, although it can result in more extensive rewriting than the process of single amendments would achieve. Generally, the legislature must first submit to the voters the issue of calling a convention; if the voters approve, the convention must convene, draw up its revisions, and submit its revisions again to the electorate in a referendum.

All state constitutions have provisions regarding the organization and powers of local government. Local governments are really subdivisions of state governments; they are not legally independent governmental bodies. State constitutions generally describe the organization of counties, cities, towns, townships, boroughs, school districts, and special districts. They may delegate responsibilities to them for public safety, police, fire, sanitation, sewage and refuse disposal, hospitals, streets, and public health. State constitutions may establish tax and debt limits for local governments, describe the kinds of taxes they may levy, and prescribe a way in which their funds may be spent. In the absence of constitutional provisions governing local governments, these subordinate units must rely upon state legislatures for their organization and powers. In recent years there has been a movement toward greater home rule for communities. More than half the states have provided for some semblance of home rule, which removes some of the internal affairs of communities from the intervention of state legislatures. Of course, when a "home rule" charter is granted to a community by an act of the legislature, it can be readily withdrawn or revised by the legislature. But when the authorization for municipal home rule is part of the state's constitution, it is somewhat less subject to state legislative intervention. Constitutional home rule is a more secure grant of power to communities than legislative home rule. There is still much opposition to home rule for communities. Rural interests may hesitate to relinquish their influence over city governments. Legislators elected from cities may prefer to exercise local power themselves through special legislation rather than grant power over communities to mayors and councils. (See Chapter 8 for further discussion.)

THE POLITICS OF STATE CONSTITUTIONS

The U.S. Constitution is a relatively brief document, which sets forth the fundamental structure of the government and the important limitations placed upon its power. It is simple and brief; it leaves to the Congress, the president, and the courts the power to determine public policy. But very few state constitutions are simple or brief, and most of them set forth many details of public policy. The California Constitution limits the power of the legislature with regard to setting time limits on the length of wrestling matches.[4] The Georgia Constitution announces a

---

[4]See Robert B. Dishman, *State Constitutions: The Shape of the Document*, rev. ed. (New York: National Municipal League, 1968).

$250,000 reward for the first person to strike oil in the state. The Louisiana Constitution proclaims Huey Long's birthday an annual state holiday. Such constitutional detail makes the need for amendment quite frequent. Unlike the U.S. Constitution, state constitutions are too detailed and specific to permit much change through interpretation. Hence, most existing constitutions have been amended many times, and few elections are held in which voters are not asked to vote on constitutional amendments.

What is the political significance of these constitutional restraints on state power? Duane Lockard explains:

> Substantially, the reason the complexity is important is that it allots an advantage to some contestants in the political process and a handicap for others. By inviting litigation the wealth of detail plays into the hands of those who want to prevent a particular law from going into effect, and although a legislative majority may have approved it, and the governor's signature may be authentic, there are always possibilities that the courts can be persuaded to invalidate a law on grounds that some minute aspect of constitutional procedure was not properly complied with. If so, dissenters to a law may carry the day, and the legislation be cancelled, for it may be impossible to mount once again the necessary peak of interest that pushed through the legislation in the first place. At least, delay of from one to two years is likely since re-enactment must wait until the next legislative session.[5]

Thus, it appears that lengthy detailed constitutions tend to *strengthen the position of conservative interests*, those who wish to preserve the status quo. As we have already noted, it also tends to *strengthen the role of the courts*, since an abundance of constitutional detail leads to decision making through court litigation.

Professor Lewis A. Froman has argued convincingly that lengthy and detailed state constitutions reflect the strength of organized interest groups in the states.[6] He reasons that in states where interest groups are stronger, a larger number of special privileges and advantages will be granted in state constitutions. The stronger the interest groups in the state, the greater the length of the state constitution, the greater the number of proposed amendments, and the greater the number of amendments adopted. To test his theory about state constitutions, he used the judgments of political scientists about which states had strong, moderately strong, or weak interest groups, and he then compared the constitutions of each of these three groups of states. The results are shown in Table 1–6. States with strong interest groups tend to have long constitu-

---

[5]Lockard, *The Politics of State and Local Government*, p. 86.
[6]Lewis A. Froman, Jr., "Some Effects of Interest Group Strength in State Politics," *American Political Science Review*, 60 (December 1966), 952–62.

TABLE 1-6
Relationships Between Strength of Interest Groups
and Three Dependent Variables

Strength of Interest Groups	Average Length of Constitution	N^1	Average No. of Proposed Amendments per Year	N^2	Average No. of Adopted Amendments per Year	N^3
Strong	33,233	24	2.97	19	1.58	22
Moderate	17,985	14	1.14	12	.76	14
Weak	14,828	7	.68	5	.41	7

[1] Alaska and Hawaii are excluded from this table. In addition, Idaho, New Hampshire, and North Dakota were not classified by strength of interest groups.

[2] Arkansas, Colorado, Connecticut, Delaware, Iowa, Michigan, North Carolina, Utah, and Washington are excluded for lack of data.

[3] Michigan and North Carolina are excluded for lack of data.

SOURCE: Lewis A. Froman, Jr., "Some Effects of Interest Group Strength in State Politics," AMERICAN POLITICAL SCIENCE REVIEW, 60 (December 1966), 956.

tions, which deal directly with questions of public policy (labor practices, regulation of utilities, transportation problems, and so on). Typically interest groups press for constitutional provisions to protect their interests because they are unwilling to trust future legislatures in matters of public policy. Thus, strong interest group states are likely to have lengthy constitutions, which, among other things, specify public utility tariffs and charges, limit the taxing powers of the states and communities, place restrictions on state debt, specify the duties and powers of public service commissions and the regulation of utilities, set forth regulations on insurance companies, specify the duties of local government officials, set the salaries of the state and local officeholders, exempt certain industries from taxation, regulate school systems, and so on. He concludes that constitutions are one of the means by which advantages and disadvantages are distributed in political systems and that the strength of interest groups in gaining special constitutional advantages can be observed in the length of state constitutions and in amending activity.

Important political interests are at stake in constitutional revision. Legislatures are understandably hesitant about calling constitutional conventions. A "runaway" convention may rearrange the balance of political power in the state. It may strengthen the governor at the expense of the legislature, establish new bases for legislative apportionment, authorize new taxes, eliminate the earmarking of certain revenues, or allocate greater power over urban affairs to cities. In other words, a constitutional convention may seriously alter the status quo. Interest groups that presently enjoy special privileges or exemptions from taxation in the state constitution have reason to fear a constitutional convention. They may stress the expense involved in such a convention or the danger that "radical reformers" may foist their dangerous ideas upon an unsuspecting public. Taxpayer groups may fear that constitutional limitations on taxing powers may be removed. Public officials may be concerned that their offices will be abolished. In other words, constitutional revision is a political thicket which discourages all but the most courageous of men.

Reform interests—good-government groups, the League of Women Voters, and political science professors—argue that the constitution and the structure of state and local government should be simple, brief, and understandable. It should permit the legislature and the governor to make public policy. It should allocate power to the governor and the legislature commensurate with their responsibilities, and it should enable the voters to hold elected officials clearly accountable for public decisions. It should permit local governmental consolidation and community home rule. The need for frequent amendment should be eliminated.

These ideas are not received with enthusiasm by organized interests in the states, but they do appeal to many voters. The idea of successful constitutional revision appeals to an ambitious governor with aspirations to higher office. A favorite device for constitutional revision is the establishment of a constitutional revision commission. A typical commission is created by an act of a legislature, and its membership usually includes legislators, executive officials, and prominent citizens. Legislatures generally prefer such a commission to a constitutional convention, because a commission can only study and report to a legislature on the changes it deems necessary. Such recommendations are usually handled like regular constitutional amendments, although they may be more sweeping than ordinary amendments.

POLITICS IN CONSTITUTIONAL CONVENTIONS

While there has been only one national Constitutional Convention, in 1787, there have been many state constitutional conventions—more than a dozen in the last decade alone.[7] These conventions generally come into being in response to demands by reform-oriented "good-government" interest groups, often with the assistance of aspiring politicians who are seeking higher office and want to use the convention as a stepping-stone. But the activities of constitutional reformers usually spark counteractivities from interests desiring to preserve the status quo—political office-holders, party politicians, bureaucrats, and business interests, particularly those subject to state regulation.

[7]See *Book of the States, 1970–71* (Lexington, Ky.: Council of State Governments, 1970), pp. 3–47.

Participants in state constitutional conventions can be categorized as follows:[8]

Reformers, who are active in civic organizations and are generally recruited from upper-class segments of society. Their motivation is ideological—they are interested primarily in "good government."

Aspirants for higher political office, who are often young lawyers seeking a reputation for reform and innovation. Their motivation is career advancement—they are generally but not always on the side of reform.

Chieftains with high public office in the state, who frequently exercise internal convention leadership. Their motivation is the preservation of their leadership in state affairs—they are generally fluid on the issue of reform.

Statesmen, who have previously held high public office (ex-governors, senators, etc.) or who currently hold judgeships. Their motivation is prestige—they are to be found on either side of major issues.

Stand-ins for party leaders or officeholders, who are selected for their past party loyalty and who generally follow the advice of those who selected them. They are motivated by recognition they receive by being there—they are likely supporters of the status quo.

Standpatters are middle-level or minor officeholders or bureaucrats, who enter the convention to protect a present position in the government structure. They are motivated by a desire to preserve their political position—they are consistent opponents of major reforms.

Membership in constitutional conventions is generally weighted in the direction of reform, since the calling of the convention itself indicates the strength of reformers in the state political system. There is a relationship, however, between the type of election for delegate and the type of delegate selected. Partisan elections (delegates run under party labels) with small-size districts maximize the selection of party activists, current officeholders, and bureaucrats interested in preserving the status quo. Nonpartisan elections (delegates run without party designation) with at-large or multimember constituencies maximize the number of "blue-ribbon," "disinterested," "good-government" types.

The basic division within the convention itself is frequently between reformers versus preservers of the status quo. This line of division is often more pronounced than the division between Republicans versus Democrats, urban versus rural, a governor's supporters versus his opponents, legislators versus nonlegislators, and so forth. Reformers in recent state conventions have pressed for many of the same provisions— shorter constitution, lower voting age, reduced size of the legislature, removal of limitation of legislative activity, fewer separately elected

[8]For a test of these categories in Maryland, Rhode Island, and New York, see Elmer E. Cornwell, Jr., Jay S. Goodman, and Wayne R. Swanson, "State Constitutional Conventions: Delegates, Roll Calls and Issues," *Midwest Journal of Political Science,* 14 (February 1970), 105–30.

executive officials, municipal home rule, removal of limitations on taxing authority, removal of special constitutional provisions dealing with business and industry, court reform, and so forth.[9]

Despite the influence of reformers at constitutional conventions, the final outcome of constitutional revision through the convention method has been mixed. While new constitutions have generally moved states closer to the "reform model," the extent of change has not been very great.[10] Since new constitutions must go to the voters for approval, reform-oriented constitution makers must be careful not to offend voters with controversial innovations. They must also try to satisfy all major blocs at the convention in order to avoid their leaving the convention only to work against ratification. New constitutions are very vulnerable at the polls. Generally voters must vote yes or no on the whole document; voters who are offended by a single provision may vote no even when all other provisions are acceptable. Different voters may be voting no for different reasons, but a cumulation of specific no votes on separate provisions may spell defeat for the whole document. Provisions that frequently prove controversial include state aid to parochial schools (see Chapter 14), legislative pay increases (see Chapter 5), state civil rights guarantees (see Chapter 13), and welfare reform (see Chapter 16). (In the past voters also tended to defeat constitutional clauses aimed at lowering the voting age; but now that this reform has been incorporated into the Twenty-sixth Amendment of the U.S. Constitution, the issue has been largely removed from state politics. See Chapter 3.)

Of course, reform interests have not yet succeeded in simplifying state constitutions or in eliminating the special privileges and exemptions contained in them. Newer constitutions, however, are somewhat shorter and more streamlined than the average state constitution. All the newer documents tend to strengthen the executive, provide for more equitable apportionment, and remove limitation on legislative power. But most state constitutions are still very conservative documents. There is not much hope that state constitutions will be simplified in the near future or that special exemptions and privileges will be eliminated.

[9]For an excellent political analysis of constitutional conventions in Maryland, Rhode Island, and New York, see Cornwell *et al.*, "State Constitutional Conventions."

[10]Reformers do not always agree on what the "ideal" state constitution should look like. For a close approximation of the reform model, see *Model State Constitution* (New York: National Municipal League, 1968).

TWO

States, Communities, and American Federalism

THE POLITICS OF DECENTRALIZATION

Why have state and local governments anyway? Why not have a central-ized political system with a single responsible government accountable to national majorities in national elections—a government capable of implementing uniform policies throughout the country?

Over a century ago Alexis de Tocqueville, in a haunting, perhaps prophetic, passage in his *Democracy in America,* described a nation of people "equal and alike," totally dependent upon a single centralized government. His melancholic vision is worth quoting at length:

> I seek to trace the novel features under which despotism may appear in the world. The first thing that strikes the observation is an innumera-ble multitude of men, all equal and alike, incessantly endeavoring to procure the petty and paltry pleasures with which they glut their lives. Each of them, living apart, is as a stranger to the fate of all the rest; his children and his private friends constitute to him the whole of mankind. As for the rest of his fellow citizens, he is close to them, but does not see them; he touches them, but does not feel them; he exists only in himself and for himself alone; and if his kindred still remain to him, he may be said at any rate to have lost his country.
>
> Above this race of men stands an immense and tutelary power, which takes upon itself alone to secure their gratifications and to watch over their fate. That power is absolute, minute, regular, provident, and mild.

It would be like the authority of a parent if, like that authority, its object was to prepare men for manhood; but it seeks, on the contrary, to keep them in perpetual childhood: it is well content that the people should rejoice, provided they think of nothing but rejoicing. For their happiness such a government willingly labors, but it chooses to be the sole agent and the only arbiter of that happiness; it provides for their security, forsees and supplies their necessities, facilitates their pleasures, manages their principal concerns, directs their industry, regulates the descent of property, and subdivides their inheritances: what remains, but to spare them all the care of thinking and all the trouble of living? . . .

After having thus successively taken each member of the community in its powerful grasp and fashioned him at will, the supreme power then extends its arm over the whole community. It covers the surface of society with a network of small complicated rules, minute and uniform, through which the most original minds and the most energetic characters cannot penetrate, to rise above the crowd. The will of man is not shattered, but softened, bent, and guided; men are seldom forced by it to act, but they are constantly restrained from acting. Such a power does not destroy, but it prevents existence; it does not tyrannize, but it compresses, enervates, extinguishes, and stupefies a people, till each nation is reduced to nothing better than a flock of timid and industrious animals, of which the government is the shepherd.[1]

Let us describe some of the political advantages in decentralized government.

1. Political decentralization frequently reduces the severity of conflict in a society. Decentralization is a classic method by which disparate peoples can be brought together in a nation without engendering irresolvable conflict. Conflicts beween geographically defined groups in America are resolved by allowing each to pursue its own policies within the separate states and communities; this avoids battling over a single national policy to be applied uniformly throughout the land. As Robert Dahl explains:

> American local governments have, then, permitted an important measure of local variety and heterogeneity. In so doing, doubtless they have reduced the strain on national institutions. People are able to work out many of their problems in their states and localities, finding solutions which would lead to interminable debate and conflict if they were imposed uniformly throughout the United States. Even though the most pressing questions of the day cannot be de-nationalized, the existence of local autonomy helps to free the national arena for precisely these "national" issues.[2]

[1] Alexis de Tocqueville, *Democracy in America*, trans. by Reeve, Bowen and Bradley (New: York: Random House—Vintage Books, 1955), II, 336–37.
[2] Robert A. Dahl, *Pluralist Democracy in the United States: Conflict and Consent* (Chicago: Rand McNally & Co., 1967), p. 183.

Thus, state and local governments in America have probably reduced the severity of conflict that a wholly national system of government would encounter. It is particularly important to denationalize conflicts in a large country like the United States where there is great diversity in people, problems, and resources. Of course, denationalizing conflicts sometimes maintains the stability of the national political system at the price of "sweeping under the rug" very serious conflicts. Certainly this was the case with regard to the questions of slavery and segregation. For long periods of American history these issues were cast out of national politics in an effort to reduce conflict and achieve unity between North and South. For more than sixty years after the Constitutional Convention, national conflict over slavery was reduced by denationalizing the conflict. When the question of slavery did emerge as a national issue in the 1850s, nationalization of the conflict led directly to Civil War. A decade after the end of the Civil War the issue of segregation was denationalized, and for another sixty years or more national conflict over the issue was avoided. When the question was nationalized again in the 1950s and 1960s, it turned into one of the most explosive issues in American politics.

2. Decentralization distributes power more widely among different sets of leaders. The widespread distribution of power is generally thought to be a protection against tyranny; a plurality of leadership is generally believed to be more democratic than a single set of all-powerful leaders. To the extent that pluralism exists in America, state and local governments have undoubtedly contributed to it. Robert Dahl observes that "state and local governments have provided a number of centers of power whose autonomy is strongly protected by Constitutional and political traditions. A governor of a state or the mayor of a large city may not be the political equal of a president (at least not often); but he is most assuredly not a subordinate. In dealing with a governor or mayor, a president rarely if ever commands; he negotiates; he may even plead. Here then is a part of the intermediate stratum of leadership that Tocqueville looked to as a barrier to tyranny."[3] It should be added that state and local governments provide a political base of offices for the opposition party when it has lost national elections. In this way state and local governments contribute to party competition in America by helping to tide over the losing party after electoral defeat so that it may remain strong enough to challenge incumbents at the next election. And finally, of course, state and local governments provide a channel of recruitment for national political leaders. National leaders can be drawn from a pool of leaders experienced in state and local politics.

3. Decentralization allows more people to participate in the political system. There are nearly ninety thousand governments in America—

[3]*Ibid.*, p. 189.

states, counties, townships, municipalities, towns, special districts, and school districts. Nearly a million people hold some kind of public office in America. The opportunity to participate doubtlessly contributes to popular support of the political system. Many people are given the opportunity to exercise political leadership; moreover, state and local governments are widely regarded as being "closer to the people." Survey data reveal that Americans look upon local governments as being more manageable and more responsive to individual desires than the national government. Thus, by providing more opportunities for direct citizen involvement in government, state and local governments contribute to the popular sense of political effectiveness and well-being.

4. Decentralization makes government more manageable and efficient. Frequently we are told that our present system of multiple state and local governments is inefficient and unmanageable and in need of reform. And certainly there is much room for improvement. But imagine the bureaucracy, red tape, and confusion if every government activity in every local community in the nation—police, schools, roads, fire fighting, garbage collection, sewage disposal, and so forth—were controlled by a centralized administration in Washington. In practical terms, it would not be possible to govern a nation as large as the United States without decentralizing much of the decision making. If local governments did not exist, they would have to be invented. Even in the Soviet Union— where centralized discipline and policy control are a matter of political ideology—national leaders have been forced to resort to decentralization simply as a matter of practical expediency. Government becomes arbitrary when a bureaucracy far from the scene directs a local administrator to proceed with the impossible—local conditions notwithstanding. Decentralization softens the rigidity of law and makes unpopular laws more tolerable.

EXPERIMENT IN THE STATES— LEGAL ABORTIONS

Seldom in its history has the United States embarked upon a more important and emotion-charged experiment in social reform than it has done recently with new state laws liberalizing abortion. It is not our purpose here to debate the merits of these laws, but to point out how the actions of state governments can profoundly affect the lives of individuals and the future of the nation.

Until recently, abortions for any purpose other than saving the life of the mother were criminal offenses under state law. About a dozen states acted in the late 1960s to permit abortions in cases of rape or incest, or to protect the physical health of the mother, and in some cases her mental health as well. Relatively few abortions were performed under these laws, however, because of the red tape involved—review of each case by several concurring physicians, approval of a hospital board, and so forth. Then, in 1970, New York, Alaska, Hawaii, and Washington enacted laws that in effect permitted abortion at the request of the woman involved and the concurrence of a physician. New York, unlike the other states enacting such laws, did *not* establish a state residency requirement for patients. New York law now permits abortion on request. Considerable controversy surrounded this abortion law, and it passed by a very close vote in the legislature. In 1972, the legislature reversed itself and passed a repeal bill, but Governor Rockefeller vetoed the repeal bill and left standing the original liberal abortion law.

The New York experience was instructive for the nation. New York City quickly became a national center for abortion. The number of abortions rose above the number of live births. The number of criminal abortions in the city fell to near zero, and there was a substantial decline in the number of children placed up for adoption. About half of the abortions performed on city residents involved black or Puerto Rican women; nonresident abortions have largely involved white middle-class women who could afford to travel to the city.

Abortion is a highly sensitive issue. It is not an issue that can be compromised. The arguments touch on fundamental moral and religious principles. Proponents of abortion argue that a woman should be permitted to control her own body and should not be forced by law to have unwanted children. They cite the heavy tolls in lives lost in criminal abortions and the psychological and emotional pain of an unwanted pregnancy. Opponents of abortion generally base their belief on the sanctity of life, including the life of the unborn child which they believe deserves the protection of law—"the right to life." Many believe that the killing of an unborn child for any reason other than the preservation of the life or health of the mother is murder.

National opinion on abortion has changed rapidly in recent years. As late as 1969 the Gallup poll reported a majority of Americans opposed to abortion for any reason other than the health of the mother, rape or incest. But by 1972 for the first time national opinion supported the statement: "The decision to have an abortion should be made solely by a woman and her physician." The results were:

	Agree	Disagree	No Opinion
Total	64%	31%	5%
Men	63	32	5
Women	64	31	5
Protestants	65	31	4
Catholics	56	39	5
College	74	22	4
High School	65	30	5
Grade School	47	45	8

Interestingly, there are no major differences between men and women on this topic. Moreover, a majority of Catholics also support this statement although the Catholic Church itself strongly opposes abortion.

The movement for liberal abortion in America was rewarded in 1973 with a very important decision by the U.S. Supreme Court striking down state laws preventing abortion in the first three months of pregnancy. The Supreme Court ruled that the Constitutional guarantee of personal liberty in the First and Fourteenth Amendments included a woman's decision to bear a child, and that the state's power to protect health and safety could not justify *any* restriction on early abortion. Between the third and sixth month of pregnancy, the state could set standards for how and when abortion can be performed, in order to protect the health of the mother; but the state cannot prohibit abortions in this period. Only in the final three months of pregnancy, the Supreme Court said, can the state ban all abortions to safeguard the life and health of the mother and unborn infant. Opponents of abortion had argued that the word "person" in the Constitution included the unborn child, and that the First and Fourteenth Amendments to the Constitution protected his "right to life." But the Supreme Court rejected this argument.

The Supreme Court has now established a national policy on abortion to replace varied state laws. Nonetheless, it was the centralization, variety, and experimentation in public policy in the states which led to change in abortion laws. That is the advantage of federalism.

THE STRUCTURE OF AMERICAN FEDERALISM

In deciding in 1869 that a state had no constitutional right to secede from the union, Chief Justice Salmon P. Chase described the legal character of American federalism:

> The preservation of the states and the maintenance of their governments, are as much within the design and care of the constitution as the preservation of the union and the maintenance of the national government. The constitution, in all of its provisions, looks to an indestructible union, composed of indestructible states.[4]

What is meant by "an indestructible union, composed of indestructible states"? The American federal union is an indissoluble partnership

[4]Texas v. White, 7 Wallace 700 (1869).

between the states and the national government. The Constitution of the United States allocated power between two separate authorities, the nation and the states, each of which was to be independent of the other. Both the nation and the states were allowed to enforce their laws through their own officials and courts directly on individuals. Legally, neither the Congress nor any single state or group of states could determine for itself whose authority was legitimate in a disputed area, nor could either level of government change the constitutional division of power without the approval of the other. The Constitution itself was the only legal source of authority for the division of powers between the states and the nation. American federalism differs from a "decentralized" political system in that the central government is not constitutionally authorized to determine itself the extent to which powers are to be exercised by the states. The national government has no legal authority to alter or abolish the power of the states. At the same time, American federalism differs from a "confederation" of states in which the national government is dependent upon the states for its power. The American federal system is a strong national government, coupled with a strong state government, in which authority and power are shared, constitutionally and practically.

The framework of American federalism is determined by (1) the powers delegated by the Constitution to the national government; (2) the constitutional guarantees given to the states; (3) the powers denied by the Constitution to the national goverment and to the states; (4) the constitutional provisions giving the states a role in the composition of the national government; (5) the subsequent interpretation of these constitutional provisions by the courts; and (6) the practices that evolved for the settlement of disputes between the nation and the states.

Article I, Section 8, of the U.S. Constitution lists eighteen grants of delegated power to Congress, including authority over matters of war and foreign affairs, the power to declare war, raise armies, equip navies, establish uniform rules for naturalization, and so on. Another series of delegated powers are related to control of the economy, including the power to coin money, to control its value, and to regulate foreign and interstate commerce. The national government has been given independent powers of taxation "to pay the debts and provide for the common defense and general welfare of the United States." It has the power to establish its own court system, to decide cases arising under the Constitution and the laws and treaties of the U.S. and cases involving certain kinds of parties. The national government was given the authority to grant copyright patents, establish post offices, enact bankruptcy laws, punish counterfeiting, punish crimes committed on the high seas, and govern the District of Columbia. Finally, after seventeen grants of express power, came the power "to make all laws which shall be necessary and proper for carrying into execution the foregoing powers, and all other powers vested by this constitution in the government of the United States or in any department or officer thereof." This is generally referred to as the Necessary and Proper Clause.

These delegated powers, when coupled with the National Supremacy Clause of Article VI, insured a powerful national government. The National Supremacy Clause was quite specific regarding the relationship between the national government and the states. In questions involving conflict between the state laws and the Constitution, laws, or treaties of the U.S.:

> This constitution, and the laws of the United States which shall be made in pursuance thereof; and all treaties made or which shall be made under the authority of the United States shall be the supreme law of the land; and the judges in every state shall be bound thereby, anything in the constitution or laws of any state to the contrary notwithstanding.

Despite these broad grants of power to the national government, the states retained a great deal of authority over the lives of their citizens. The constitutional provisions specifically guaranteeing or limiting state powers are outlined in Table 2–1. The Tenth Amendment reaffirmed the idea that the national government had only certain delegated powers and that all powers not delegated to it were retained by the states:

> The powers not delegated to the United States by the constitution, nor prohibited by it to the states, are reserved to the states respectively, or to the people.

The states retained control over the ownership and use of property; the regulation of offenses against persons and property (criminal law and civil law); the regulation of marriage and divorce; the control of business, labor, farming, trades, and professions; the provision of education, welfare, health, hospitals, and other social welfare activities; and provision of highways, roads, canals, and other public works. The states retained full authority over the organization and control of local government units. Finally, the states, like the federal government, possessed the power to tax and spend for the general welfare.

The Constitution denies some powers to both national and state governments; these denials generally safeguard individual rights. Both nation and states were forbidden to pass ex post facto laws or bills of attainder. The first eight amendments to the Constitution, "the Bill of Rights," originally applied to the federal government, but the Fourteenth Amendment, passed by Congress in 1866, provided that the states must also adhere to fundamental guarantees of individual liberty. "No state

TABLE 2-1

Federal Constitutional Provisions
Specifically Limiting or Guaranteeing State Powers

GUARANTEES TO STATES	LIMITS ON STATES
A. State Integrity and Sovereignty	
No division or consolidation of states without state legislative consent (IV-2)[a]	States cannot enter into treaties, alliances, or confederations (I-10)
Republican form of government (IV-2)	No separate coinage (I-10)
Protection against invasion (IV-2)	No grants of titles of nobility (I-10)
Protection against domestic violence on application of proper state authorities (IV-2)	No interstate or foreign compacts without Congressional consent (I-10)
Powers not delegated to the U.S. by the Constitution, nor prohibited by it to the states, are reserved to the states (Amendment X)	U.S. Constitution, all laws and treaties made under it to be supreme law of the land, binding on every state (VI)
	Slavery forbidden (Amendment XIII)
States cannot be sued by citizens of another state or a foreign nation (Amendment XI)	All state legislative, executive, and judicial officers, and state Representatives in Congress to be bound by U.S. Constitution (VI)
	No abridgement of privileges and immunities of the U.S. Citizens (Amendment XIV)
	Reduction of representation in U.S. House of Representatives for denial of franchise to citizens (Amendment XIV)
	No payment of debts incurred in aid of insurrection or rebellion against U.S. or for emancipation of slaves (Amendment XIV)
	No abridgement of right to vote on account of race, color, or previous condition of servitude (Amendment XV)
	Popular election of Senators (Amendment XVII)
	No abridgement of right to vote on account of sex (Amendment XIX)
	No poll taxes in federal elections (Amendment XXIV)
	No denial of the right to vote to persons 18 years of age or older (Amendment XXVI)

[a] Numbers in parentheses refer to the Article and Section of the Constitution containing the provision.

SOURCE: Daniel J. Elazar, AMERICAN FEDERALISM: A VIEW FROM THE STATES, 2nd Ed., Table 6. Copyright © 1972 by Thomas Y. Crowell, Inc. Reprinted by permission of the publisher.

TABLE 2-1 (Cont.)

GUARANTEES TO STATES	LIMITS ON STATES
	B. Military Affairs and Defense
Power to maintain militia and appoint militia offers (I-8, Amendment II)	No letters of marque and reprisal (I-10)
	No maintenance of standing military forces in peacetime without Congress' consent (I-10)
	No engaging in war without Congress' consent, except to repel invations (I-10)
	C. Commerce and Taxation
Equal apportionment of federal direct taxes (I-2, 9)	No levying of duties on vessels of sister states (I-9)
No federal export duties (I-9)	No legal tender other than gold or silver (I-10)
No preferential treatment for ports of one state (I-9)	No impairment of obligations of contracts (I-10)
Reciprocal full faith and credit among states for public acts, records, and judicial proceedings (IV-1)	No levying of import or export duties without consent of Congress except reasonable inspection fees (I-10)
Reciprocal privileges and immunities for citizens of the several states (IV-2)	No tonnage duties without Congress's consent (I-10)
Intoxicating liquor may not be imported into states where its sale or use is prohibited (Amendment XXI-2)	
	D. Administration of Justice
Federal criminal trials to be held in state where crime was committed (III-2)[b]	No bills of attainder (I-10)
	No ex post facto laws (I-10)
Extradition for crimes (IV-2)	U.S. Supreme Court has original jurisdiction over all cases in which a state shall be a party (III-2)
Federal criminal juries to be chosen from states and district in which crime was committed (Amendment VI)[b]	Judges in every state bounded by U.S. Constitution and all laws and treaties made under it, notwithstanding the constitution or laws of any state (VI)
Federal judicial power to extend to controversies between two or more states, a state or citizens of another state when state is plaintiff, and between foreign nation or its citizens with original jurisfiction vested in the Supreme Court (III-2)	No denial of life, liberty, or property without due process of law (Amendment XIV)
	No denial of equal protection of state laws to persons within its limits (Amendment XIV)

[b] This provision insures the integrity of the state's common law in federal cases.

TABLE 2-2

Federal Constitutional Provisions Specifically Giving the
States a Role in the Composition of the National Government

GUARANTEES TO STATES	LIMITS ON STATES
A. National Legislature	
Members of House of Representatives chosen by people of several states based on those qualified to vote for most numerous house of state legislature (I-2)	Representatives must be 25 years old and citizens of the U.S. for 7 years (I-2)
Representatives must be inhabitants of states from which they are elected at time of election (I-2)	Senators must be 30 years old and citizens of the U.S. for 9 years (I-3)
Representatives to be apportioned among the states according to population every ten years (I-2)	Congress may make or alter regulations as to the times, places, and manner of holding elections for Senators and Representatives (I-4)
State executive has authority to fill vacancies (I-2)	Each house shall be the judge of the elections, returns, and qualifications of its own members, punish its members for disorderly behavior, and expel a member by two-thirds vote (I-5)
Each state shall have at least one Representative (I-2)	
Senate shall be composed of two Senators from each state (I-3) chosen by the people qualified to vote for the most numerous house of the state legislature (Amendment XVII) with vacancies to be filled as prescribed by states legislation (Amendment XVII)	Basis for apportionment of representation in House of Representatives may be reduced proportionate to state deprivation of the right to vote of otherwise qualified citizens (Amendment XIV-2)
Senators must be inhabitants of the states from which they are chosen at time of election (1-3)	States cannot be represented by persons who have taken an oath to support Consitution and since engaged in insurrection, without express consent of two-thirds of Congress (Amendment XIV-3)
Times, places, and manner of holding elections for Senators and Representatives shall be prescribed for each state by its legislature (I-4)	
No state to be deprived of equal representation in the Senate without its consent (V)	

SOURCE: Daniel J. Elazar, AMERICAN FEDERALISM: A VIEW FROM THE STATES, 2nd Ed., Table 7. Copyright © 1972 by Thomas Y. Crowell, Inc. Reprinted by permission of the publisher.

shall make or enforce any law which shall abridge the privileges or immunities of the citizens of the United States; nor shall any state deprive any person of life, liberty or property without due process of law; nor deny to any person within its jurisdiction equal protection of the laws."

Some powers were denied only to the states, generally as a safeguard to

TABLE 2-2 (Cont.)

GUARANTEES TO STATES	LIMITS ON STATES
B. National Executive	
To be selected by the electors of the several states with each state allotted a number of electors equal to the total number of its Senators and Representatives (II-1)	Congress may determine the time of choosing electors and a uniform day on which they shall cast their votes (II-1)
Each state to have one vote if Presidential election is decided in House of Representatives (II-1)	
Approval of Presidential appointees by the Senate as Congress shall prescribe (II-2)	
C. Amendment of Constitution	
Amendments must be ratified by three-fourths of the states (V)	
Amendments must be proposed by two-thirds of the states (V)	
D. Voting Rights	
	Cannot be denied or abridged on grounds of race, color, or previous condition of servitude (Amendment XV-1)
	Cannot be denied or abridged on account of sex (Amendment XIX-1)
	No poll tax may be levied as requirement to vote in federal elections (Amendment XXIV)
	Cannot be denied to persons 18 years of age or older (Amendment XXVI)
E. Foreign Affairs	
Treaties must be ratified by two-thirds of Senate (II-2)	Treaties binding on states as supreme law of the land (VI)
Appointment of foreign service officers subjected to Senate confirmation (II-2)	
F. Military Affairs and Defense	
Power to appoint the officers of and train the militia when not in federal service reserved to the states (I-8)	Congress may provide for organizing, arming, and disciplining the militia when it is not in federal service and for governing it when it is (I-8)

national unity, including the powers to coin money, enter into treaties with foreign powers, interfere with the obligations of contracts, levy duties on imports or exports without congressional consent, maintain military forces in peacetime, engage in war, or enter into compacts with foreign nations or other states. These limitations are outlined in Table 2–1.

The states also play an important role in the composition of the national government. U.S. representatives must be apportioned among the states according to their population every ten years. Governors have the authority to fill vacancies in Congress, and every state must have at least one representative regardless of population. The Senate of the United States is composed of two senators from each state regardless of the state's population. The times, places, and manner of holding elections for Congress are determined by the states. The president is chosen by electors, allotted to each state on the basis of its senators and representatives. Amendments to the U.S. Constitution must be ratified by three-fourths of the states. The states' role in the composition of the national government is outlined in Table 2–2.

THE EVOLUTION OF AMERICAN FEDERALISM

The importance of formal constitutional arrangements should not be underestimated; however, the American federal system is a product of more than formal constitutional provisions. It is also shaped by the interpretations placed upon constitutional principles and the way in which disputes over state and national authority have been resolved.

The real meaning of American federalism has emerged in the heat of political conflict between states and nation. In the formulative days of the new Republic, Chief Justice John Marshall, who presided over the Supreme Court from 1801 to 1835, became a major architect of American federalism. Under John Marshall, the Supreme Court assumed the role of arbiter in disputes between state and national authority. It was under John Marshall that the Supreme Court in *Marbury* v. *Madison* assumed the power to interpret the U.S. Constitution authoritatively. Nothing in the Constitution explicitly vested the Supreme Court with the power to render authoritative interpretations of the Constitution; from time to time Congress, the president, and the states have laid claim to this power. But John Marshall argued forcefully that Article III of the Constitution, which says that "the judicial power of the United States shall be vested in one Supreme Court," made the Court the final arbiter in conflicts over the meaning of the Constitution. Marshall argued that the "the judicial power" historically meant the power to interpret the meaning of the law, and since the Constitution was the supreme *law* of the land, it was the legitimate duty of the Supreme Court to interpret that law. This meant that the Supreme Court assumed the role of umpire of the federal system and referee of conflicts between nation and states.

The fact that the referee of disputes between state and national authority has been the *national* Supreme Court has had a profound influence on the development of American federalism. Since the Supreme Court is a *national* institution, organized and staffed by national authority, one might say that in disputes between nation and states, one of the members of the two contending teams is also serving as umpire. Constitutionally speaking, then, there is really no limitation on national as against state authority *if* all three branches of the national government —the Congress, the President, and the Court—act together to override state authority. The Constitution and the laws of the United States "made in pursuance thereof" are the supreme laws of the land, "anything in the constitution or laws of any state to the contrary notwithstanding." And the Supreme Court, a national institution, through its "judicial power" interprets the Constitution and decides what laws are "made in pursuance thereof." Thus, *Marbury* v. *Madison* paved the way for the development of national power.

Chief Justice John Marshall was also responsible for making the *Necessary and Proper Clause* the most significant grant of constitutional power to the national government. Political conflict over the scope of national power arose before the new Republic had been in operation for a year. In 1790 Alexander Hamilton, as secretary of the treasury, proposed the establishment of a national bank. Congress acted on Hamilton's suggestion in 1791, establishing a national bank to serve as a depository for national money and to facilitate federal borrowing. Jeffersonians considered the national bank dangerous centralization in government and objected that the power to establish a national bank was nowhere to be found in the enumerated powers of Congress. Thomas Jefferson contended that Congress had no constitutional authority to establish a bank because a bank was not "indispensably necessary" in carrying out its delegated functions. Hamilton replied that Congress could easily deduce the power to establish a bank from grants of authority in the Constitution relating to currency and other aspects of national finance, backed by the clause authorizing Congress "to make all laws which will be necessary and proper for carrying into execution the foregoing powers." Jefferson interpreted the word "necessary" to mean "indispensable," but Hamilton argued that the national government had the right to choose the manner and means of performing its delegated functions and was not restricted to employing only those means considered indispensable in the performance of its functions. The question eventually reached the Supreme Court in 1819 when Maryland levied a tax on the national bank and the bank refused to pay it. In the case of *McCulloch* v. *Maryland*, Chief Justice John Marshall accepted the broader Hamiltonian version of the Necessary and Proper Clause:

> This government is acknowledged by all to be one of enumerated powers. The principle that it can exercise only the powers granted to it is now universally admitted. But the question respecting the extent of the powers actually granted is perpetually arising and will probably continue to arise as long as our system shall exist . . . The powers of the government are limited, and its powers are not to be transcended. But we think the sound construction of the Constitution must allow the national legislature that discretion with respect to the means by which the powers it confers are to be carried into execution, which will enable that body to perform the high duties assigned to it in a manner most beneficial to the people. Let the end be legitimate, let it be within the scope of the Constitution, and all means which are appropriate, which are plainly adopted to that end, which are not prohibited but consistent with the letter and the spirit of the Constitution, are constitutional.[5]

The *McCulloch* case firmly established the principle that the Necessary and Proper Clause gives Congress the right to choose its means for carrying out the enumerated powers of the national government. Even the Jeffersonians found themselves invoking the Necessary and Proper Clause to support the annexation of Louisiana in 1803. Today Congress can devise programs, create agencies, and establish national laws on the basis of long chains of reasoning from the most meager phrases of the constitutional text because of the broad interpretation of the Necessary and Proper Clause. The Supreme Court has generally, although not universally, acceded to broad exercises of congressional power under the Necessary and Proper Clause.

Another major contribution of the Marshall Court was its interpretation of the *National Supremacy Clause*. In *McCulloch* v. *Maryland*, the Court held Maryland's tax on the national bank to be unconstitutional on the grounds that the state tax interfered with a national activity which was being carried out under the Constitution and laws "made in pursuance thereof." Maryland's state taxing law was declared unconstitutional because it conflicted with the federal law establishing the national bank. From Marshall's time to the present, the National Supremacy Clause has meant that states could not refuse to obey federal laws. States have no right to disobey or resist the application of valid federal laws.

Of course it was one thing to announce that the state had no constitutional right to resist federal authority, but it was quite another thing to establish this principle as a political reality. In the famous Virginia and Kentucky Resolutions, the early Jeffersonians devised a doctrine of state

[5]McCulloch v. Maryland, 4 Wheaton 316 (1819).

"interposition" to resist enforcement of the national government's Alien and Sedition Acts of 1798 which were passed by a Federalist Congress. The Jeffersonians argued, rightly no doubt, that the Alien and Sedition Acts violated the Constitution's guarantees of free speech and press. But the "interposition" argument went on to assert that when the national government acted "unconstitutionally" in the eyes of the state, the state was empowered to "interpose" itself between its people and the operation of an unconstitutional federal law. Since the Jeffersonians captured the presidency in 1800, and a Jeffersonian Congress repealed the Alien and Sedition Acts in 1801, the interposition argument in the Kentucky and Virginia Resolutions was never formally challenged in the courts.

The *Civil War* was, of course, the greatest crisis of the American federal system. Did a state have the right to oppose national law to the point of secession? In the years preceding the Civil War, John C. Calhoun argued that the Constitution was a compact made by the *states* in a sovereign capacity rather than by the *people* in their national capacity. Calhoun contended that the federal government was an agent of the states, that the states retained their sovereignty in this compact, and that the federal government must not violate the compact, under the penalty of state nullification or even secession. Calhoun's doctrine was embodied in the Constitution of the Confederacy, which begins with the words "We, the people of the Confederate States, each state acting in its sovereign and independent character, in order to form a permanent federal government . . ." This wording contrasts with the preamble of the United States Constitution, "We, the people of the United States, in order to form a more perfect union . . ." The difference emphasizes Calhoun's thesis that the central government should be an agency of the states rather than of the people.

The issue was decided in the nation's bloodiest war. What was decided on the battlefield between 1861 and 1865 was confirmed by the Supreme Court in 1869: "Our is an indestructible union, composed of indestructible states."[6] Yet the states' rights doctrines, and political disputes over the character of American federalism, did not disappear with Lee's surrender at Appomattox. The Thirteenth, Fourteenth, and **Fifteenth** Amendments, passed by the Reconstruction Congress, were clearly aimed at limiting state power in the interests of individual freedom. The Thirteenth Amendment eliminated slavery in the states, the Fifteenth Amendment prevented states from discriminating against Negroes in the right to vote; and the Fourteenth Amendment declared that "No State shall make or enforce any law which shall abridge the privileges or immunities of citizens of the United States; nor shall any state deprive any per-

[6]Texas v. White, 7 Wallace 700 (1869).

son of life, liberty, or property without due process of law; nor deny to any person within its jurisdiction the equal protection of the laws." These amendments delegated to Congress the power to secure their enforcement. Yet for several generations these amendments were narrowly construed and added little, if anything, to national power. By tacit agreement, after southern states demonstrated their continued political importance in the disputed presidential election of 1876, the federal government refrained from using its power to enforce these civil rights. But beginning slowly in the 1920s, the Supreme Court began to build a national system of civil rights based upon the Fourteenth Amendment. In early cases, the Court held that the Fourteenth Amendment prevented states from interfering with free speech, free press, or religious practices. But not until 1952, in the Supreme Court's desegregation decision in *Brown* v. *Board of Education* in Topeka, Kansas, did the Court begin to call for the full assertion of national authority on behalf of civil rights.[7] When the Court decided that the Fourteenth Amendment prohibited the states from segregating the races in public schools, it was asserting national authority over deeply held beliefs and long-standing practices in many of the states.

The Supreme Court's use of the *Fourteenth Amendment* to insure a national system of civil rights supported by the power of the federal government is an important step in the evolution of the American federal system. Of course, the controversy over federally imposed desegregation in the southern states renewed the debate over states' rights versus national authority. The vigorous resistance of southern states to desegregation in the decade following *Brown* v. *Board of Education* testified to the continued strength of the states in the American federal system. Despite the clear mandate of the Supreme Court, the southern states succeeded in avoiding all but token integration for more than ten years.[8] Yet only occasionally did resistance take the form of "interposition." Governor Faubus used the Arkansas National Guard to prevent the desegration of Little Rock Central High School in 1957, but this "interposition" was ended quickly when President Eisenhower ordered the National Guard removed and sent units of the United States Army to enforce national authority. In 1962 President Kennedy took similar action when Governor Ross Barnett of Mississippi personally barred the entry of a black student to the University of Mississippi, despite a federal court order requiring his admission. Governor George Wallace of Alabama "stood in the doorway" to prevent desegregation but left his post at the doorway several hours later when federal marshals arrived. These actions

---

[7] Brown v. Board of Education of Topeka, Kansas, 347 U.S. 483 (1954).
[8] See Chapter 13, "Black Politics, Civil Rights, and Public Order."

failed to alter the principle of national supremacy in the American political system.

The growth of national power under the *Interstate Commerce Clause* is also an important development in the evolution of American federalism. The Industrial Revolution in America created a national economy with a nationwide network of transportation and communication and the potential for national economic depressions. In response to the growth of the national economy, Congress progressively widened the definition of "interstate commerce" to include the regulation of interstate transportation (particularly the railroads) and of communication (particularly telephone and telegraph). Industrialization created interstate businesses, which could only be regulated by the national government; this was recognized in the passage of the Sherman Anti-Trust Act in 1890. Yet for a time, the Supreme Court placed obstacles in the way of national authority over the economy, and by so doing created a "crisis" in American federalism. For many years, the Court narrowly construed interstate commerce to mean only the movement of goods and services across state lines, and until the late 1930s, the Supreme Court insisted that agriculture, mining, manufacturing, and labor relations were outside the reach of the delegated powers of the national government. But when confronted with the depression of the 1930s and the threat of presidential attack on the membership of the Court itself, the Court yielded. In *National Labor Relations Board* v. *Jones and Laughlin Steel Corporation* in 1937, the Court recognized the principle that production and distribution of goods and services for a national market could be regulated by Congress under the Interstate Commerce Clause. The effect was to give the national government effective control over the national economy, and today few economic activities are not within the reach of congressional power.

THE GROWTH OF POWER IN WASHINGTON

A common myth about American federalism is that it resembles a layer cake with local governments at the base, state governments in the middle, and the national government at the top. This view suggests that the state and local governments are "closer" to the people than the national government. Another common fallacy is that governmental activities in the American system are parceled out to either the states or the communities, or to the national government.

While the layer cake theory of federalism and the notion of separation of national and state powers have been very popular, there is ample evidence that in practice American federalism never really operated in this fashion.[9] American federalism has been characterized by far more cooperation, coordination, and sharing of responsibilities than by separation. At all times in our history, the national government and the states have shared powers. Actually, it is very difficult to identify programs of states and communities in which the national government does not participate. Whatever the field of government activity, federal-state-local relations are usually characterized by frequent conferences, joint planning, continuous consultation, exchange of facilities and information, and awareness of common efforts on behalf of the public. As for the myth that the national government is not very "close" to the people, in terms of proximity, communication, and the provision of direct services, one may simply consult a local telephone directory to see how many *local* phone numbers are listed under "United States Government." Even modest-size communities have extensive listings under the Departments of Agriculture, Commerce, Justice, and the Interior, the Weather Bureau, Federal Bureau of Investigation, Federal Aviation Agency, General Services Administration, Social Security Administration, the Internal Revenue Service, and, of course, the Post Office. Often federal listings outnumber state or local government listings.

In practice, then, federalism has come to mean the sharing of power between the nation and the states, rather than a sharp separation between national and state responsibilities.

Professor Morton Grodzins has suggested that a marble cake, rather than a layer cake, is a better image of American federalism:

> The American form of government is often, but erroneously, symbolized by a three-layer cake. A far more accurate image is the rainbow or marble cake, characterized by an inseparable mingling of differently colored ingredients, the colors appearing in vertical and diagonal strands and unexpected whorls. The colors are mixed in the marble cake, so functions are mixed in the American federal system.[10]

Over the years the national government has acquired much greater power in the federal system than the Founding Fathers originally envisioned. The growth of power in Washington has not necessarily meant a reduction in the powers of states and local governments—in fact, *all* governments have vastly increased their powers and responsibilities in the twentieth century. But today the national government is no longer really a government with only "delegated" or "enumerated" powers. The delegated powers of the national government are now so broadly defined

---

9See Daniel J. Elazar, *The American Partnership: Inter-governmental Cooperation in Nineteenth-Century United States* (Chicago: University of Chicago Press, 1962).

10Morton Grodzins, "The Federal System," in The American Assembly, *Goals for Americans* (Englewood Cliffs, N.J.: Prentice-Hall, Inc., 1960), p. 265.

—particularly the power to tax and spend for the general welfare and the interstate commerce power—that the government in Washington is involved in every aspect of American life. There are really no segments of public activity "reserved" to the states or the people.

It is possible to argue that even in the earliest days of the Republic, the national government was deeply involved in public activities that were not specifically delegated to it in the Constitution. The first Congress of the United States in the famous Northwest Ordinance, providing for the government of the territories to the west of the Appalachian Mountains, authorized grants of federal land for the establishment of public schools, and, by so doing, showed a concern for education, an area "reserved" to the states by the Constitution. Again, in 1863 in the Morrill Land Grant Act, Congress provided grants of land to the states to promote higher education.

Many commentators feel that the date 1913, when the Sixteenth Amendment gave the federal government the power to tax incomes directly, was the beginning of a new era in American federalism. Congress had been given the power to tax and spend for the general welfare in Article I of the Constitution. But the Sixteenth Amendment helped to shift the balance of financial power from the states to Washington, when it gave Congress the power to tax the incomes of corporations and individuals on a progressive basis. The income tax gave the federal government the power to raise large sums of money, which it proceeded to spend for the general welfare as well as for defense. It is no coincidence that the first major grant-in-aid programs (agricultural extension in 1914, highways in 1916, vocational education in 1917, and public health in 1918) all came shortly after the inauguration of the federal income tax. Many conservative commentators have recognized the financial power that the progressive income tax has given the national government, and they have frequently proposed its elimination.

The federal "grant-in-aid" has become a principal instrument in the expansion of national power. It should be noted that there is no general grant of power to the national government in the Constitution to protect and advance the public health, safety, welfare, or morals. Theoretically, the national government may not enact laws dealing directly with housing, streets, zoning, schools, health, police protection, fire fighting, crime, vice, and so on, simply because such a law might contribute to the general welfare. However, it may *tax* or *borrow* or *spend money* for the general welfare, even though it has no power in the Constitution to regulate welfare activities directly. This is a subtle distinction, but it is an important one. For example, Congress cannot outlaw billboards on highways, because billboard regulation is not among the enumerated powers of Congress in the U.S. Constitution. But the federal government, through its power to tax and spend, can provide financial assistance to the states to build highways and then pass a law threatening to withdraw financial aid if the states do not outlaw billboards themselves. Thus, the federal government can involve itself in highways and even billboard regulation through its taxing power and financial resources, even though these fields are "reserved" to the states.

The Great Depression of the 1930s brought pressure upon the national government to use its tax and spending powers in a wide variety of areas formerly reserved to states and communities. The federal government initiated grant-in-aid programs to states and communities for public assistance, unemployment compensation, employment services, child welfare, public housing, urban renewal, and so on; it also expanded federal grant-in-aid programs in highways, vocational education, and rehabilitation. The inadequacy of state and local revenue systems to meet the financial crisis created by the depression contributed significantly to the expansion of federal power. States and communities called upon the superior taxing powers of the national government to assist them in many fields in which the federal government had not previously involved itself.

During World War II and the cold war that followed, federal grant-in-aid programs contrived to expand while taking on labels that made

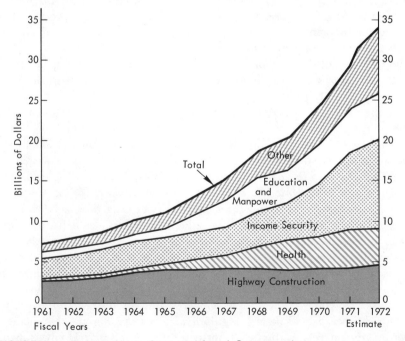

FIGURE 2–1   Federal Aid to State and Local Governments

them appear to be part of the defense effort. Aid to public schools came in a program to assist school districts experiencing rapid population growth because of military bases, defense industries, or federal installations. In 1956 the Interstate and *Defense* Highway Act greatly expanded federal aid for the construction of the interstate highway system. In the National *Defense* Education Act of 1957, federal grants and loans were authorized for higher education. How important these highway and education programs were to the defense effort is debatable, but identifying them with defense made them more attractive to Congress and expanded future federal activity in domestic affairs. The 1960s brought a myriad of new federal grant programs in urban affairs, education, economic development, manpower, and education, including the Elementary and Secondary Education Act of 1965, the Economic Development Act of 1965, the Manpower Training and Development Act of 1962, the Economic Opportunity Act of 1964, and the Model Cities Act of 1965. Figure 2–1 shows the expansion of federal grant programs in a single decade.

FEDERAL GRANTS-IN-AID: PROS AND CONS

Today grant-in-aid programs are the single most important source of federal influence over state policy. Approximately one-sixth of all state and local government revenues are from federal grants. This money is paid out through a staggering number and variety of programs. There are probably five hundred different federal grant programs in existence today. So numerous and diverse are federal aid programs that a substantial information gap surrounds their availability, purpose, and requirements. Learning about the availability of federal grants, and mastering the art of grant application, places a heavy burden on state and local officials. Moreover, the problem of program coordination, not only between levels of government but also among federal agencies, is a difficult one.

Federal grants are available in nearly every major category of state and local government activity. (See Table 2–3.) Federal grants may be obtained to assist in everything from the celebration of the American Revolution Bicentennial to the drainage of abandoned mines, riot control, and school milk. Federal aid for welfare and highways, however, accounts for over two-thirds of total federal aid money.

Not only have federal grants-in-aid to the states expanded rapidly in terms of the number of programs and the dollar amounts involved; states and communities have also come to *rely* on the national government for an ever-increasing share of their total revenues (see Table 2–4).

TABLE 2-3

Federal Grant-In-Aid Programs to State
and Local Governments by Major Category

Income security
Funds appropriated to the President:
Disaster relief
Public assistance:
Income maintenance payments
Social services for welfare recipients
Juvenile delinquency
Vocational rehabilitation
Administration on Aging
Food stamp
Child nutrition program and special milk
Community services

Veterans benefits and services
Veterans Administration:
Aid to State homes
Grants for construction of State nursing
homes
Administrative expenses

Health
Department of Health, Education, and
Welfare
Hospital construction
(Portion to private, nonprofit
institutions)
Health manpower
Comprehensive health planning services
Regional medical programs
Construction of health educational and
mental health facilities
Mental health services and development
Health services
Environmental health
Indian health services and facilities
Patient care and health services
Communicable and chronic diseases
Maternal and child health
Medical assistance

National defense
Executive Office of the President; Office
Emergency Preparedness—
Federal contributions to
State and local planning
Department of Defense—Military:
Civil defense shelters and financial
assistance
Construction of Army National Guard
centers
Atomic Energy Commission

Education and manpower
Funds appropriated to the President: Office
of Economic Opportunity
Department of Health, Education, and
Welfare:
Elementary and secondary education
Office of Child Development
Assistance to schools in federally
affected areas
Education of the handicapped
Civil rights education
Higher education activities
(Portion to private institutions)
Vocational education
Libraries and community services
Special institutions for the blind and
deaf
Education professions development
Work incentive activities
Emergency school assistance
Department of Labor:
Manpower development and training
activities
Grants to States for administration of
employment security programs (trust
fund)
Department of Interior: Bureau of Indian
Affairs:
Education and welfare services
National Foundation the Arts and the
Humanities
Corporation for Public Broadcasting
Equal Employment Opportunities
Commission

Agricultural and rural development
Department of Agriculture:
Commodity Credit Corporation and
Consumer and Marketing Service:
Removal of surplus agricultural
commodities and value of commodities
donated
Rural water and waste disposal facilities
Mutual and self-help housing
Rural housing for domestic farm labor
Resource conservation and development
Consumer protective programs
Cooperative agricultural extension
service
Water Bank Act Program

TABLE 2-3 (Cont.)

General government
Department of the Interior:
Grants to territories
Internal revenue collection, Virgin.
Islands (shared revenue)
Department of Justice: Law enforcement
assistance
Treasury Department: Tax collections for
Puerto Rico (shared revenue)
National Capital region:
Federal payment to District of
Columbia
Washington Metropolitan Transit Agency

Commerce and transportation
Funds appropriated to the President:
Public works acceleration
Appalachian development
Department of Commerce:
State marine schools
Regional development
Promotion of tourism
National Bureau of Standards
National Oceanic and Atmospheric
Administration
Economic development assistance
Department of the Interior: Resources
management
Department of Transportation:
Forest and public lands highways
Highway beautification
Highway safety
Federal aid highways (trust fund)
Urban mass transportation facilities
Federal aid for airports and airways

International affairs and finance
Department of State:
East-West Cultural and Technical
Interchange Center
International Center, Washington, D.C.

Natural resources
Department of Agriculture:
Watershed protection and flood
prevention
Grants for forest protection, utilization,
and basic scientific research
National forest and grassland funds:
payments to States and counties (shared
revenue)
Assistance to States for tree planting
Department of Defense—Civil. Corps of
Engineers:
Flood control
Payments to States, Flood Control Act
of 1954 (shared revenue)

Department of the Interior:
Payment to States and counties (shared
revenue)
Bureau of Reclamation
Mine drainage and solid waste disposal
Fish and wildlife restoration and
management
Outdoor recreational areas (Land and
Water Conservation Fund)
Preservation of historic properties
Federal Power Commission: Payments to
States (shared revenue)
Tennessee Valley Authority: Payments in
lieu of taxes (shared revenue)
Water Resources Council
Environmental Protection Agency

SOURCE: BUDGET OF THE UNITED STATES GOVERNMENT 1973 (Washington: Government Printing Office, 1972).

Before the New Deal, federal grants amounted to only 2 or 3 percent of total state-local revenue. The New Deal itself, in spite of all of its innovations in federal aid programs, only raised this proportion to 7 or 8 percent. State-local reliance on federal aid has continued to increase, from 8 percent over total state-local revenues in 1946 to over *17* percent today. Thus, no matter how it is measured—increased numbers of programs, increased dollar amounts, increased reliance by states and communities—federal aid has grown into a major influence over state and local governmental activity.

TABLE 2-4
Federal Grants-in-Aid and State-Local Finances

	Total Federal Grants-in-Aid (In Millions)	Federal Grants as a Percentage of State Local Revenue
1902	$ 7	*
1913	12	*
1922	118	2.1
1927	123	1.6
1932	232	2.9
1938	800	7.2
1940	945	8.1
1944	954	6.8
1948	1,861	8.6
1950	2,486	9.7
1955	3,131	8.3
1960	6,974	11.6
1962	7,871	11.3
1967	15,366	14.0
1970	25,029	14.8
1972	36,080	16.6

*Less than 1 percent.

There are several reasons for this growth of federal aid. First of all, these grants permit the federal government to single out and support those state and local government services in which it has a particular interest. Grants permit the national government to set national goals and priorities in all levels of government without formally altering the federal structure. Thus, as problems of public assistance, urban renewal, highway construction, education, poverty, and so on acquire national significance, they can be dealt with by the application of national resources.

Second, the grant-in-aid system helps to overcome the inadequacies of state-local revenue resources. Contrary to the political rhetoric charging the states with fiscal conservatism, the states have actually demonstrated a great deal of fiscal courage, effort, and ingenuity in trying to cope with money problems. In the last two decades state-local expenditures have risen at a faster *rate* than federal expenditures. These fiscal efforts have meant increased income or sales tax rates in nearly every state in the past ten years as well as increased liquor and gasoline tax rates. Yet in spite of these near herculean efforts by states, their fiscal problems continue to multiply.

States and communities must raise revenue and at the same time carry on interstate and interlocal competition for industry and wealth. While the influence of tax considerations on industrial locations decisions may be overstated by most lawmakers, this overstatement itself is part of the political lore at statehouses and courthouses and operates to impede revenue raising. Competitive considerations not only inhibit state-local taxing efforts but also tend to push them in regressive directions.

Debates over finances in state capitals invariably include references to the "preemption" of income taxes by the national government. While there are no compelling economic reasons why the federal income tax preempts this source of revenue (particularly since the federal government permits the deduction of state income taxes from total taxable income), nonetheless most state lawmakers, and probably their constituents as well, believe that the federal government already takes all the income taxes they wish to pay. This means states are stuck with sales taxes and localities with property taxes, and these taxes respond sluggishly to rises in the GNP in contrast to income taxes.

A third general argument on behalf of federal grants-in-aid centers about the greater progressivity of the federal tax structure. If a particular government program is funded through state and local taxes, it is funded on a tax structure that is regressive or only mildly progressive. In contrast, if a particular program is funded out of federal taxes, it is funded on a more progressive basis. This may help to explain the "liberal" predisposition for federal financial involvement.

Finally, grants-in-aid provide an opportunity for the national government to insure a uniform level of public service throughout the nation as a minimum or foundation program—for example, federal grants-in-aid to help achieve equality in educational opportunity in all parts of the nation or to help insure a minimum level of existence for the poverty stricken regardless of where they live.[11] This aspect of federal policy assumes that in some parts of the nation, state and local governments are

[11]The meaning of *equalization* in federal policy is more complex than it appears at first glance. Basically, equalization means some policy recognition of differences in the states' relative capacities to raise funds from their own resources, in order to achieve more uniform program standards throughout the nation. This means, first of all, equal federal grants per unit of need, whether the unit of need is defined as pupils, poverty-stricken families, ill-housed families, medically indigent, aged, etc. But exclusive reliance upon equal allocations per unit of need is likely to mean unequal program expenditures when state-local matching funds are required. A grant offering Mississippi two dollars per person which has to be matched on a fifty-fifty basis requires a larger state tax effort relative to personal income from Mississippi citizens than a similar grant of two dollars per person offered to New York's wealthier citizens. In view of unequal tax resources of the states, grants must take into account both program needs and fiscal resources. Equalization policy must also include a deliberate varying of the amount of federal funds directly with program needs and inversely with fiscal resources. Finally, equalization policy must also consider what minimum program level is desired, and then larger amounts of federal funds must go in support of minimum program levels and lesser amounts in support of programs exceeding minimum levels.

unable, or perhaps unwilling, to devote their resources to raising public service levels to minimum national standards.

Whenever the national government contributes financially to state or local programs, state and local officials are left with less freedom of choice than they would have had otherwise. Federal grants-in-aid are invariably accompanied by federal standards or "guidelines," which must be adhered to if states and communities are to receive their federal money. The national government gives money to states and communities only if they are willing to meet conditions specified by Congress. Often Congress delegates to federal agencies the power to establish the "conditions" that are attached to grants.

No state is required to accept a federal grant-in-aid. Thus, states are not required to meet federal standards or guidelines, which are set forth as conditions for federal aid; states and communities have the alternative of rejecting the federal money, and they have sometimes done so. But it is very difficult for states and communities to resist the pressure to accept federal money. It is sometimes said that states are "bribed and blackmailed" into federal grant-in-aid programs. They are "bribed" by the temptation of much needed federal money, and they are "blackmailed" by the thought that other states and communities will get the federal money if they do not, money contributed in part by their own citizens through federal taxation.

In short, through the power to tax and spend for the general welfare, and through "conditions" attached to federal grants-in-aid, the national government has come to exercise great powers in many areas originally "reserved" to the states—highways, welfare, education, housing, natural resources, employment, health and so on. Of course, federal grants-in-aid have also enabled many states and communities to provide necessary and desirable services that they could not have afforded had it not been for federal aid. Federal guidelines have often improved standards of administration, personnel policies, and fiscal practices in states and communities. More importantly, federal guidelines have helped to insure that states and communities do not engage in racial discrimination in federally aided programs.

Yet the centralization of power in Washington has created some serious problems in the implementation of public policy. First of all, federal grant programs frequently work at cross-purposes, reflecting fragmentation of federal programs. For example, urban renewal grants attempt to save central cities from deterioration and population loss, while federal highway grants have built expressways to make possible the suburban exodus. The federal public housing programs have tried to increase the supply of low-rent housing for the poor, but federally funded urban renewal and highway programs have torn down low-rent housing.

Second, the federal government has never set any significant priorities among its hundreds of giant programs. The result is that too few dollars chase too many goals. Cities are pressured to apply for funds for projects they do not really need, simply because federal funds are available, while they may receive little or no federal assistance for more vital programs. Federal grant money is frequently provided for "new" or "innovative" or "demonstration" programs, when the real crisis facing states and communities may be in traditional public services—police, sewage, sanitation, and so forth.

Third, the administrative quagmire created by the maze of separate federal grant programs threatens to drown state and local officials in red tape. The five hundred separate federal grant programs with separate purposes and guidelines are uncoordinated and bureaucratic. State and local officials spend a great deal of their time in "grantmanship"—learning where to find federal funds, how to apply, and how to write applications in such a way as to appear to meet purposes and guidelines.

Finally, the current grant-in-aid system assumes that federal officials are better judges of goals and priorities at all levels of government than state or local officials. State and local officials do not determine what activities in their states and communities will receive federal money—federal officials determine these priorities. Moreover, federal officials must approve each federally funded project—a public housing project in Des Moines, an airport in Pittsburgh, a new set of welfare regulations in California, a sewage disposal system in Baton Rouge, an urban renewal project in Atlanta, a highway in North Dakota, and so forth. Whether federal officials or state and local officials are better judges of public goals and priorities is of course a political question.

REVENUE SHARING—A NEW DIRECTION IN FEDERALISM

The many dissatisfactions with the conditional grant-in-aid system led to appeals for a new approach to federal financial assistance to state and local governments—unrestricted federal grants with no strings attached. For many years Congress debated the idea of "revenue sharing"— the turnover of federal tax dollars to state and local governments for use as they see fit. The idea of revenue sharing assumes that the federal government is better at *collecting* revenue than state or local governments, but state and local governments are better at *spending* it. Consequently, revenue sharing was said to combine the best features of each level of government. More importantly, revenue sharing promised to reverse the flow of money and power to Washington, to end excessive red tape, and to revitalize state and local governments. The Nixon Administration made revenue sharing a top priority program in its requests to Congress.

The State and Local Fiscal Assistance Act of 1972 is a true landmark in American federalism. This Act establishes general revenue sharing and provides for the distributon of over five billion dollars per year of federal monies to states and communities with very few restrictions on its use. This Act was strongly supported by state and local goverment officials. Two-thirds of these shared revenues go to local governments and one-third to state governments. The formula for allocation to states and cities is based on three factors: population, tax effort, and the income level of the population. These revenues may be used for police and fire protection, sewage and garbage disposal, pollution abatement, transportation, physical facilities, parks and recreation, and many other recognized state-local functions; but the Act denied use of these funds for welfare or education, because these functions were already heavily supported with federal monies. Revenue sharing under this Act does *not* replace any existing grant-in-aid programs, but does provide states and communities with new unrestricted revenues.

Revenue sharing promises to reverse the trend toward centralization of power in Washington. Of course, it still is too early to judge whether revenue sharing will accomplish such a bold objective. Congress will always be under pressure to attach restrictions to the use of any money coming out of the federal treasury. We will return to the specific issues posed by revenue sharing in the final chapter of this book (Chapter 18). But revenue sharing may mark the beginning of a new phase of American federalism—one in which states and communities acquire new resources and new power to cope with the challenges of the 1970s.

POLITICS OF FEDERALISM

What political interests are likely to support the rights of states in contrast to national authority? Are arguments over states' rights versus national authority merely sham arguments which hide deeper political cleavages?

Debate over federalism can never be removed from the political context in which it takes place. The concept of federalism itself was born in the political environment that surrounded the Constitutional Convention. Federalism was a political compromise between those "anti-federalists" who wanted to retain the full sovereignty of the individual states by not allowing the national government to act directly on individuals and those "federalists" who wanted a strong national government capable of acting directly on individuals. It was a political com-promise which eased the way to reconciliation of the interests of the larger and smaller states. It stifled the objections of many small farmers, "Jefferson's men," and others, who would later form the Democratic party, to a national government with real power. For the conservatives, or "Hamilton's men," and those who would later form the Federalist party, the most important aspect of federalism was that it removed polit-ical power from the states where democratic tendencies were most marked and where, sometimes, small farmers captured control from the "men of principle and property."

The Jeffersonians continued to criticize the national government and to argue in favor of a strict interpretation of its powers. When the Fed-eralists passed the Alien and Sedition Acts of 1798 to stifle newspaper criticism of the new government by Jeffersonian newspaper editors, Jef-fersonians responded with the most extreme states' rights arguments, that is, the doctrines of "nullification" and "interposition." Yet, when Jeffer-son himself became president in 1801, he seemingly reversed his earlier position of strict interpretation of national power and proceeded to purchase the Louisiana Territory, even though there was no expressed authorization in the Constitution to do so. Later, the New England states, long the backbone of the Federalist party, threatened to secede from the Union because of harm suffered by shipping interests in the War of 1812 against England. Thus, even in the early days of the American Republic, the shifting position of the Federalists and Democrats over the question of states' rights and national authority suggests that the question of fed-eralism is not wholly divorced from the question of which political in-terests are stronger in Washington and which political interests are stronger in the states.

Interests that constitute a majority at the national level assert the supremacy of the national government and extol the virtues of national regulation. Interests that are minorities in national politics, but compose local or statewide majorities in one or more states, continue to see merit in the preservation of the rights of states.

The states' rights argument has been most vigorously defended in recent years by the southern states seeking to preserve traditional pat-terns of race relations. So closely tied was the states' rights argument with the question of segregation that it became almost synonymous with bigotry, prejudice, and racial hatred. Yet the right to "interpose" state sovereignty and "nullify" federal laws has been claimed at one time or another by states in every section of the country. On the eve of the Civil War, many northern states affirmed their right to interpose themselves between federal fugitive slave laws and the immorality of returning escaped Negroes to the bonds of slavery. Yet in recent years the states' rights argument became a thin cover for southern states to remain free from the national enforcement of civil rights. States' rights became the antithesis of civil rights. The Supreme Court's desegregation decision in *Brown* v. *Board of Education* in Topeka, Kansas, prompted one hundred southern congressmen to draw up the "Southern Manifesto" in March of 1956, which bitterly attacked the Supreme Court for "the clear abuse of judicial power" that "encroaches upon the reserved rights of the states and the people." It even commended the motives of "those states which have declared the intention to resist forced integration by any lawful means." Of course, the federal courts quickly disposed of the doctrine of "interposition" as they had done so many times in the past: "The conclusion is clear that interposition is not a constitutional doctrine. If taken seriously, it is illegal defiance of constitutional authority."[12]

States' rights have also been argued by conservative and rural political interests, which oppose big government and big spending and do not feel the necessity of extensive public services in education, health, welfare, housing and transportation, or urban renewal. Their argument for states' rights may stem from the fact that the states are unable or unwilling to undertake new public programs, and the states' rights argument may be merely a way of avoiding *any* public programs in these areas. Often their arguments against the activities of the national government are really arguments against governmental activities in general.

In contrast, urban interests, low-income groups, blacks, ethnic groups, and labor organizations frequently turn to the national government for help. States' rights arguments have little appeal to these groups, which are important in the national electorate but do not constitute majorities in the large number of sparsely settled states of New England, the Midwest, the Rocky Mountains, and the South. They are heavily concentrated in the large, urban, industrial states—states that are of critical importance in presidential elections and hence must be reckoned with by the national parties. Since these interests are unable to gain satisfaction at one level of government, they naturally turn to another in an effort to better their fortunes.

Business interests have generally been opposed to centralization in Washington. State governments appear to be more favorably inclined toward business than is the federal government. States and communities are not in a very good position to regulate a business or a corporation that is national in organization and scope. States and communities compete with one another to attract business and industry. The success of their efforts often depends on whether they can offer a "favorable climate" for business. This means that in addition to the availability of

---

[12]Bush v. New Orleans School Board, 364 U.S. 500 (1960).

transportation, land, and a skilled labor force, states and communities attempt to provide a "favorable" tax structure, with correspondingly low levels of expenditure for public services not deemed essential by business interests. Moreover, states and communities that are in competition with one another cannot afford regulatory systems which are inimical to business interests. In contrast, the national government does not face these competitive pressures. It is coextensive with the economy, and it can avoid being divided and ruled by economic interests. It is capable of regulating the economy on behalf of interests other than those of business. Consequently, those who identify with business interests are likely to invoke the slogan of states' rights when faced with the prospect of federal regulation.

Federal aid programs have created a vast bureaucracy in Washington which has acquired great power over a wide variety of public activities in America—education, welfare, health, transportation, natural resources, housing, urban affairs, civil rights. This bureaucracy, together with the congressional committee members who oversee its activities and appropriate its funds, has come to believe that it knows more about national needs than do state and local officials. This bureaucracy has become the important force in the movement toward centralization in the American federal system. As federal programs expand, the bureaucracy expands, which in turn provides a thrust for further program expansion.

The prevailing philosophy of America's liberal leadership includes a commitment to use governmental power to correct perceived wrongs done to others. It is a philosophy of reform, public-regardingness, and do-goodism. The liberal believes that men's lives can be changed by the exercise of governmental power—end discrimination, abolish poverty, eliminate slums, insure employment, uplift the poor, educate the masses, cure the sick. The government in Washington has more power and resources than state and local governments have, and the liberal has turned to it, rather than to state and local governments, to cure America's ills. State and local governments are regarded as too slow, cumbersome, weak, and unresponsive. The government in Washington is seen as the principal instrument for liberal social and economic reform. Thus liberalism and centralization are closely related in American politics.

PUBLIC ATTITUDES TOWARD STATE AND LOCAL GOVERNMENT

Public confidence in state and local government is very high. Most Americans believe that state governments spend taxpayers' dollars "more wisely" than the federal government. This preference for state spending

TABLE 2-5
Government Spending

Question: "Which do you think spends the taxpayer's dollar more wisely—
the State government or the Federal Government?"
(in percent)

	State	Federal	Neither	No Opinion
National	49	18	17	16
Sex				
Men	52	18	19	11
Women	47	16	16	21
Education				
College	57	19	18	6
High School	51	17	16	16
Grade School	40	18	18	24
Occupation				
Professional and				
business	56	15	17	12
White collar	52	20	16	12
Farmers	59	6	20	15
Manual	45	21	16	18
Age				
21 to 29 years	49	23	14	14
30 to 49 years	49	17	17	17
50 and over	49	15	19	17
Religion				
Protestant	52	15	16	17
Catholic	44	24	18	14
Jewish	X	X	X	X
Politics				
Republican	60	11	17	12
Democrat	46	21	14	19
Independent	44	19	22	15
Region				
East	37	27	19	17
Midwest	54	16	18	12
South	58	10	14	18
West	46	16	19	19
Income				
$10,000 and over	53	18	18	11
$7,000 and over	50	18	19	13
$5,000 to $6,999	54	19	14	13
$3,000 to $4,999	44	16	16	24
Under $3,000	44	15	18	23
Community size				
1,000,000 and				
over	36	24	19	21
5000,000 and over	41	23	17	19
50,000 to 499,999	46	19	18	17
2,500 to 49,999	57	13	14	16
Under 2,500, rural	56	12	19	13

SOURCE: CONGRESSIONAL RECORD, February 15, 1967.

over federal spending was evidenced in all segments of the population, although the proportion of support for federal spending was slightly higher among Democrats, Catholics, Easterners, low-income earners, and big-city dwellers. Public opinion appears to support the notion that states and communities are better at spending money, even if the federal government is better at collecting it. Of course, public opinion may or may not be "right" about which level of government spends money "more wisely," but the confidence expressed in state government is itself a source of power for the states in their relations with the national government. (See Table 2–5.)

What kind of people pay the most attention to state and local politics? Jennings and Zeigler studied the characteristics of people who indicated in a national survey that they "pay more attention" to state politics than to national or international affairs.[13] Although the "attentive public" for state and local politics "is not particularly large," these authors speculate that state and local politics may tend to reflect the values of these attentive people more than the values of the public at large. Jennings and Zeigler found that the attentive public for state politics was concentrated in small-town and rural environments, possessed less education than the attentive public for national politics, and had lived in the same state or county for most of their lives. Southerners and westerners were more attentive to state politics than midwesterners or easterners. Moreover, the attentive public for state politics evidenced somewhat more conservative values than the attentive public for national politics. The former were less trusting and more suspicious of people and governments, particularly the government in Washington.

INTERSTATE RELATIONS

The U.S. Constitution provides that "full faith and credit shall be given in each state to the public acts, records, and judicial proceedings of every other state." As more Americans move from state to state, it becomes increasingly important that the states recognize each other's legal instruments. This constitutional clause is intended to protect the rights of individuals who move from one state to another, and it is also intended to prevent individuals from evading their legal responsibilities by crossing state lines. Courts in Illinois must recognize decisions made by courts in Michigan. Contracts entered into in New York may be enforced in Florida. Corporations chartered in Delaware should be permitted to do business in North Dakota. One of the more serious problems in interstate relations today is the failure of the states to meet

[13]M. Kent Jennings and Harmon Zeigler, "The Salience of American State Politics," *American Political Science Review* (June 1970), 64, 523–35.

their obligations under the Full Faith and Credit Clause in the area of domestic relations, including divorce, alimony, child support, and custody of children. Nevada's divorce laws are quite liberal, and one need only live in that state six weeks to establish residence. When Mr. Williams left North Carolina to go to Reno to obtain a divorce, then married and returned home to North Carolina, his home state convicted him of bigamy and refused to recognize his Nevada divorce. The Supreme Court said that Mr. Williams had not established a bona fide residence in Nevada and the Nevada court had no jurisdiction over his divorce.[14] This decision opened the door to challenging the validity of divorces granted by other states where the divorce had been preceded only by temporary residence. States have also begun to evade the intent of the Full Faith and Credit Clause in cases involving alimony payments, child support, and custody of children. The result is now a complex and confused situation in domestic relations law.

The Constitution also states: "The citizens of each state shall be entitled to all privileges and immunities of citizens in the several states." Apparently the Founding Fathers thought that no state should discriminate against citizens from another state in favor of its own citizens. To do so would seriously jeopardize national unity. This clause also implies that citizens of any state may move freely about the country and settle where they like, with the assurance that as newcomers they will not be subjected to unreasonable discrimination. The newcomer should not be subject to discriminatory taxation, he should be permitted to engage in lawful occupations under the same conditions as other citizens of the state, he should not be prevented from acquiring and using property, or denied equal protection of the laws, or refused access to the courts. However, states have managed to compromise this constitutional guarantee in several important ways. States establish residence requirements for voting and holding office, which prevent newcomers from exercising the same rights as older residents. States often require periods of residence as a prerequisite for holding a state job or for admission into professional practice such as law, medicine, and so on. States discriminate against out-of-state students in the tuition charged in public schools and colleges.

The Constitution also provides that "A person charged in any state with treason, felony, or other crime who shall flee from justice and be found in another state, shall on the demand of the executive authority from the state from which he fled, be delivered up, to be removed to the state having jurisdiction of the crime." In other words, the Constitution requires governors to extradite fugitives from another state's justice. But the Supreme Court conceded that it has no power to compel the governor of a state to fulfill this constitutional obligation. Governors have not always honored requests for extradition, but since no state wants to harbor

14Williams v. North Carolina, 325 U.S. 226 (1945).

criminals of another state, extradition is seldom refused. Among reasons advanced for the occasional refusals are (1) the individual has become a law-abiding citizen in his new state; (2) a northern governor did not approve of the conditions in Georgia chain gangs; (3) a black returned to a southern state would not receive a fair trial; (4) the governor did not believe that there was sufficient evidence against the fugitive to warrant his conviction in the first place.

The Constitution provides that "No state shall without the consent of Congress . . . enter into any agreement or compact with another state." Over one hundred interstate compacts now serve a wide variety of interests, such as interstate water resources; conservation of natural resources, including oil, wildlife, fisheries; the control of floods; the development of interstate toll highways; the coordination of civil defense measures; the reciprocal supervision of parolees; the coordination of welfare and institutional care programs; the administration of interstate metropolitan areas; and the resolution of interstate tax conflicts. In practice, Congress has little to do with these compacts; the Supreme Court has held that congressional consent is required only if the compact encroaches upon some federal power. Only once did Congress refuse consent to an interstate compact. In 1947 Congress refused to authorize a regional agreement between southern governors for the establishment of the Southern Regional Education Board. This board was to plan a regional program for higher education in the southern states, but the congressional debates centered upon segregation in southern colleges and universities. When Congress failed to give its consent, the southern states formed the board anyhow, and its constitutionality has never been challenged in the courts. One of the most notable interstate compacts is the Port Authority of New York and New Jersey which was established by New York and New Jersey in 1921. The Port Authority is a giant organization which operates a wide variety of port and transportation enterprises. A new pattern of interstate compacts was established with the Delaware Basin River Compact in 1961. This compact included Delaware, New York, New Jersey, and Pennsylvania, and, in a new departure, the U.S. government. This was the first interstate compact in which the federal government itself became a signatory and a party to the compact. The Delaware River Basin Commission is authorized to deal with water resource problems in the Delaware River, in hopes of resolving long conflicts between the four states over the use of water in the river.

States are not supposed to make war on each other, although they did so from 1861 to 1865. They are supposed to take their conflicts to the Supreme Court. The constitution gives the Supreme Court the power to settle all cases involving two or more states. In recent years the Supreme Court has heard disputes between states over boundaries, the diversion of water, fishing rights, and the disposal of sewage and garbage.

THREE

Participation
in
State Politics

THE NATURE OF POLITICAL PARTICIPATION

Popular participation in the political system is the very definition of democracy. There are many ways that individuals can participate in politics. They may run for, and win, public office; participate in marches, demonstrations, and sit-ins; make financial contributions to political candidates or causes; attend political meetings, speeches, and rallies; write letters to public officials or to newspapers; wear a political button or place a bumper sticker on a car; belong to organizations that support or oppose particular candidates or take stands on public issues; attempt to influence friends while discussing candidates or issues; vote in elections; or merely follow an issue or a campaign in the mass media. This listing probably constitutes a ranking of the forms of political participation in their ascending order of frequency. Only a small proportion of the population ever runs for office or participates in demonstrations, while a much larger proportion votes in elections and follows campaigns in newspapers or on television.

The first activities listed involve greater expenditure of time and energy and require greater personal commitment than the more common activities. Less than 1 percent of the American adult population runs for public office. Only about 5 percent are active in parties and campaigns, and about 10 percent make financial contributions. Less than 20 percent wear political buttons or display bumper stickers. About one-third of the population belongs to organizations that could be classified as interest groups, and only a few more ever try to convince their friends to vote for a certain candidate. About 65 percent of the American people will vote in a hard-fought presidential campaign; but far fewer vote in state and local elections. Fully one-third of the population is politically apathetic: they do not vote at all, and they are largely unaware of the political life of the nation.

VOTING IN THE STATES

Voting is the central form of popular participation in a democracy. Voting requires an individual to make not one, but two decisions. He must choose between rival parties or candidates, and he must choose whether or not to cast his vote at all. This latter decision is just as important as his selection of parties or candidates, because his selection is not effective if he fails to vote. Decisions about whether or not to vote can clearly influence the outcome of elections, yet nonvoting is widespread. Presidential elections inspire about two-thirds of the voting age population to go to the polls, while elections to statewide offices turn out less than half of the eligible voters. State elections held in nonpresidential years inspire even fewer voters, and only a very small minority cast votes in local elections held at times other than national or statewide elections. The idea behind "off-year" elections was to separate state and local issues from matters of national concern. Such off-year elections may succeed in insulating state and local politics from national trends, but they also significantly reduce the number of voters participating in state and local elections.

There is a great deal of variation among the states in voter participation rates (see Figure 3–1). The turnout in presidential elections ranges from less than 50 percent of the voting population in several southern states to over 75 percent in Utah. Voter participation is significantly related to educational levels (see Figure 3–2). Participation is notably higher in states with higher median family incomes and well-educated adult populations. The states with the lowest turnouts are the Deep South states; the next lowest turnouts are found in the border states. Midwestern, New England, and Mountain states rank very high in voter turnout. The urban industrial states, with large metropolitan populations, tend to cluster around the middle of the rankings.

Region, income, and education levels are not the only variables affecting voter turnout. Turnout figures are also affected by the laws of the states, which define registration procedures, residency requirements, vot-

Percentage of Voting Age Population Casting Votes

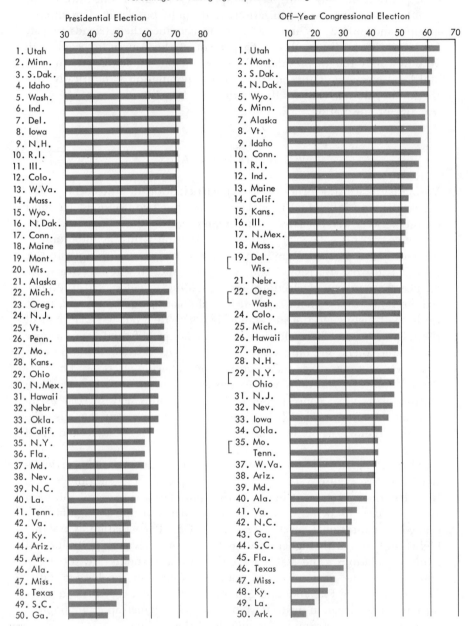

FIGURE 3-1   Rankings of the States: Voter Participation

FIGURE 3–2 The Fifty States Arranged According to Education and Voting Turnout

1 Ala.	11 Hawaii	21 Mass.	31 N.M.	41 S.D.
2 Alaska	12 Idaho	22 Mich.	32 N.Y.	42 Tenn.
3 Ariz.	13 Ill.	23 Minn.	33 N.C.	43 Tex.
4 Ark.	14 Ind.	24 Miss.	34 N.D.	44 Utah
5 Calif.	15 Iowa	25 Mo.	35 Ohio	45 Vt.
6 Colo.	16 Kan.	26 Mont.	36 Okla.	46 Va.
7 Conn.	17 Ky.	27 Neb.	37 Ore.	47 Wash.
8 Del.	18 La.	28 Nev.	38 Pa.	48 W.Va.
9 Fla.	19 Me.	29 N.H.	39 R.I.	49 Wis.
10 Ga.	20 Md.	30 N.J.	40 S.C.	50 Wyo.

Note: This figure is a "scatter diagram" or "plot" of the relationship between education and voter turnout in the states. Education is placed on the horizontal axis, and voter turnout on the vertical axis. Then each state is plotted on the graph according to its individual scores in education and voter turnout, as if these scores were coordinates on a map. Each state is represented by a dot. The result is a visual portrayal of the relationship between these two variables in the fifty states. The broken line represents the proposition that educational levels "explain" or "account for" voter turnout levels; as educational levels increase, voter turnout should increase. The closer the dots (states) hug the line, the closer the relationship between education and voter turnout. States that are far away from the line do not conform to the proposition that education affects voter turnout.

ing hours, absentee ballot rules, and so on. Voter participation rates can also be affected by the degree of interparty competition in a state. The more vigorous the competition between the parties, the greater the interest of citizens in elections, and the larger the voter turnout. When parties and candidates compete vigorously, they make news and are given a large play via the mass media. Thus a setting of competitive politics tends to have a greater amount of political stimuli available in the environment than does a setting with weak competition. People are also more likely to perceive that their votes count in a close, competitive contest, and thus they are more likely to cast them. Moreover, when parties are fighting in a close contest, their workers tend to spend more time and energy campaigning and getting out the vote.

Finally, voter behavior in some states is a product of unique political history. West Virginia has experienced considerable poverty in recent years—its adult educational level is one of the lowest in the nation and its registration and voting laws are similar to those of most states. Yet West Virginia voters insist upon going to the polls in large numbers. For many years this apparent inconsistency defied political analysts. But a recent intensive study of West Virginia politics suggests that the bloody history of organizing miners' unions in that state established a tradition of active political participation among West Virginians. "Contrary to what was taking place in other border and southern states, in West Virginia that group that was least likely to participate in politics—the lower socio-economic status group, the 'working man'—was being motivated and 'organized' to participate [by the United Mine Workers]."[1]

WHO VOTES AND WHO DOESN'T

Nonvoting does not occur uniformly throughout all segments of the population. National surveys conducted by the University of Michigan's Survey Research Center produced percentages for nonvoting for various groups in presidential elections as shown in Table 3–1. The exact per-

---

This particular scatter diagram suggests that education *does* affect voter turnout, because in general we can see that states with higher educational levels have higher voter turnouts. But the relationship is not very close because a number of states lie far away from the broken line. Arizona and Nevada have lower voter turnouts than one would expect, given their education levels: while North Dakota and West Virginia have higher voter turnout levels than one would expect given their educational levels.

This type of figure will be used throughout the text to show relationships between socioeconomic conditions and political characteristics in the fifty states.

[1]Gerald W. Johnson, "Research Note on Political Correlates of Voter Participation: A Deviant Case Analysis," *American Political Science Review*, 65 (September 1971), 768–76.

TABLE 3-1

Characteristics of Nonvoters

	Percentage of Nonvoters in Presidential Elections		
	1960	1964	1968
Education			
Grade school	33	32	37
High school	19	22	21
College	10	11	16
Occupation			
Professional and managerial	12	14	12
Other white collar	18	15	13
Skilled and semi-skilled	24	26	29
Unskilled	31	32	35
Farm	18	19	13
Community			
Metropolitan area	19	18	21
Towns and cities	22	20	21
Rural areas	22	26	26
Race			
White	19	21	22
Black	47	35	32
Labor			
Union	23	17	24
Nonunion	20	24	23
Religion			
Protestant	23	24	24
Catholic	13	16	19

SOURCE: Data drawn from elections studies of the Survey Research Center, University of Michigan.

centages as listed may change from one election to another, but the general pattern remains very stable. Nonvoting is associated with lower educational levels, unskilled occupations, rural living, nonmembership in organizations, and the especially deprived status in which large numbers of blacks find themselves. High voter turnout is related to college education; professional, managerial, or other white-collar occupations; metropolitan residence; and membership in voluntary associations. On the whole, Catholics and Jews vote more frequently than Protestants. Although these figures pertain only to voting, other forms of participation follow substantially the same pattern.

Actually, the percentages of nonvoters shown in public opinion surveys are lower than the real percentages of nonvoters. For example, actual votes cast in presidential elections indicate that nearly 40 percent of the population fail to vote, yet the percentages of nonvoters shown in

Table 3–1 are generally lower than this figure. The main reason for this discrepancy is that many respondents lie to interviewers and exaggerate their political activity.

Nonvoting is sometimes viewed as a reflection of "alienation" from the political system. Political alienation involves a feeling that voting and other forms of participation are useless, that nothing is really decided by an election, and that the individual cannot personally influence the outcome of political events. The fact that nonvoting occurs most frequently among those at the bottom of the income, occupation, and education ladder in America tends to substantiate this view. Alienation occurs more frequently among those groups who have not shared in the general affluence of society. This interpretation is discouraging for those who cherish the democratic ideal, because it suggests that not all groups in society place a high value on democratic institutions.

SECURING THE RIGHT TO VOTE

The only mention of voting requirements in the Constitution of the United States as it was originally adopted is in Article I: "The electors in each state shall have the qualifications requisite for electors for the most numerous branch of the state legislature." Of course, "electors" (voters) for the most numerous branch of the state legislature are determined by *state* laws and constitutions. The effect of this constitutional provision was to leave to the states the power to determine who is eligible to vote in both state and federal elections. Over the years, however, a combination of constitutional amendments, congressional actions, and Supreme Court decisions have largely removed control over voting from the states and made it a responsibility of the national government.

Early in American history, the states chose to enact very restrictive voter eligibility standards: suffrage was limited to males over twenty-one years of age, who resided in the voting district for a certain period and owned a considerable amount of land or received a large income from other investments. So great was the fear that "the common man" would use his franchise to attack the rights of property that only about 120,000 persons out of 2 million were permitted to vote in the 1780s. Men of property felt that only other men of property had sufficient "stake in society" to exercise their franchise in a "responsible" fashion. But Jeffersonian and Jacksonian principles of democracy, including confidence in the reason and integrity of the common man, spread rapidly in the new Republic. Soon property qualifications were eliminated, and suffrage was extended to great masses of people by state law.

The first important limitation on state powers over voting came with the ratification of the Fifteenth Amendment: "The right of the citizens of the United States to vote shall not be denied or abridged by the United States or any state on account of race, color, or previous condition of servitude." The object of this amendment, passed by the Reconstruction Congress and adopted in 1870, was to extend suffrage to former Negro slaves and prohibit voter discrimination on the basis of race. The Fifteenth Amendment also gives Congress the power to enforce Negro voting rights "by appropriate legislation." Thus, the states retained their right to determine voter qualifications, *so long as they do not practice racial discrimination*, and Congress was given the power to pass legislation insuring Negro voting rights.

It is a tribute to the ingenuity of southern politicians that they were able to defeat the purpose of this amendment for almost a century. While social·and economic pressures and threats of violence succeeded in intimidating many thousands of would-be voters, there were also many "legal" methods of disenfranchisement.

For many years the most effective means of banning black voting was a technique known as the "white primary." So strong was the Democratic party throughout the South that the Democratic nomination for public office was tantamount to election. This meant that *primary* elections to choose the Democratic nominee were the only elections in which real choices were made. If blacks were prevented from voting in Democratic primaries they could be effectively disenfranchised. Thus southern state legislatures resorted to the simple device of declaring the Democratic party in southern states a private club and ruling that only white persons could participate in its elections, that is, in *primary* elections. Blacks would be free to vote in "official," general elections, but all whites tacitly agreed to support the Democratic, or "white man's" party, in general elections, regardless of their differences in the primary. Not until 1944, in *Smith* v. *Allright*, did the Supreme Court declare this practice unconstitutional: "When primaries become part of the machinery in choosing officials, state and national, as they have here, the same tests to determine the character of discrimination . . . should be applied to the primary as are applied to the general election."[2] The white primary was declared to be a violation of the Fifteenth Amendment.

Black voting in the South increased substantially after World War II. From an estimated 5 percent of voting age blacks registered in southern states in the 1940s, black registration rose to an estimated 20 percent in 1952, 25 percent in 1956, 28 percent in 1960, and 39 percent in 1964.

[2]Smith v. Allright, 321 U.S. 649 (1944).

This last figure was a little more than half of the comparable figure for white registration in the South. However, most of this increase in black registration occurred in urban areas of the South. Prior to 1965, in hundreds of rural counties throughout the South, no Negroes had ever been permitted to vote. Despite the Fifteenth Amendment, local regis- trars in the South succeeded in barring Negro registration by means of an endless variety of obstacles, delays, and frustrations. Application forms for registration were lengthy and complicated; even a minor error would lead to rejection, like underlining rather than circling in the "Mr.- Mrs.-Miss" set of choices as instructed. Literacy tests were the most com- mon form of disenfranchisement. Many a black college graduate failed to interpret "properly" the complex legal documents that were part of his test. In the unlikely event that a black succeeded in passing such tests, he would then be required to convince the registrar that he was of "good character" and that he had paid his poll taxes. Often the law required that an applicant's name be published in the newspaper for two weeks. Needless to say, white applicants for voter registration were seldom asked to go through these lengthy procedures.

The Civil Rights Act of 1964 made it unlawful for registrars to apply unequal standards in registration procedures, or to reject applications because of immaterial errors. It required that literacy tests be in writing and made a sixth-grade education a presumption of literacy. The Twenty- fourth Amendment to the Constitution was ratified in 1964, making poll taxes unconstitutional as a requirement for voting in national elec- tions. In 1965 the Supreme Court declared poll taxes unconstitutional in state and local elections as well.[3] Yet in Selma, Alabama, in early 1965, civil rights organizations effectively demonstrated that local registrars were still keeping large numbers of blacks off the voting rolls. Registrars closed their offices for all but a few hours every month, placed limits on the number of applications processed, went out to lunch when black applicants appeared, delayed months before processing black applica- tions, and discovered a variety of other methods to keep blacks disen- franchised. It became apparent that a registrar who wanted to keep blacks from voting could always find a way to do so if he tried hard enough, regardless of the law.

In response to the Selma episode, Congress enacted a strong Voting Rights Act in 1965 designed to fulfill the Fifteenth Amendment's prom- ise that the right to vote shall not be denied because of race. The act applied to any state or county where (1) the literacy test or similar qualifying device was enforced as of November 1, 1964, and (2) fewer

3Harper v. Virginia State Board of Elections, 383 U.S. 663 (1966).

than 50 percent of voting age residents either were registered or cast ballots in the 1964 presidential election. In these areas, the Attorney General upon evidence of voter discrimination was empowered to replace local registrars with federal registrars, abolish literacy tests, and register voters under simplified federal procedures. Opponents of the new law argued that it interfered with the historic right of states to determine voter qualifications. However, a constitutional amendment by definition takes precedence over earlier language in a constitution. The Fifteenth Amendment prohibited racial discrimination in voting and gave Congress the power to enforce this prohibition "by appropriate legislation." In 1966 the Supreme Court took notice of the long history of discrimination by southern voting registrars and upheld the Voting Rights Act of 1965 as "appropriate legislation" in the fight against voter discrimination.[4] It turned out that federal registrars were sent to only a small number of southern counties. Many southern counties which had previously discriminated in voting registration hurried to sign up black voters just to avoid the imposition of federal registrars.

The black voter is now very important in southern state and local politics. By 1970 it was estimated that 65 percent of eligible blacks in the southern states were registered to vote, compared with 70 percent of eligible whites.[5] Most of the remaining difference between blacks and whites is attributable to the generally lower economic and educational levels of black populations in the South rather than to race itself. Blacks and whites at the same socioeconomic level register and vote with the same frequency.[6] Blacks sit in every southern state legislature and hold important political office in local governments throughout the South. There are many southern towns and counties where blacks outnumber whites, and where in recent years black local officials have replaced traditional white leadership. Perhaps the best known example of black success in local southern politics is Fayette, Mississippi, where a black majority elected Charles Evers (brother of the slain civil rights leader Medgar Evers) mayor, as well as an all-black city council.

It is important to remember, however, that blacks are a minority in every state in the nation. Unless black candidates can win some white support, they cannot achieve success in statewide elections. In any statewide election in which blacks and whites divide strictly along racial lines, the black candidate will be defeated. (See Table 3–2.) Thus, black separatism offers little hope of acquiring real power in America, but

[4]South Carolina v. Katzenbach, 383 U.S. 301 (1966).
[5]U.S. Bureau of the Census, *Statistical Abstract of the United States, 1970*, p. 369.
[6]Anthony M. Orum, "Social and Political Participation of Negroes," *American Journal of Sociology*, 72 (July 1966), 44.

TABLE 3-2

The Black Potential for Electoral Influence in the South

	Black Percentage of Total Population	Registered Voters		Percent Black
		White	Black	
Alabama	26.4	1,311,000	315,000	19.4
Arkansas	18.6	728,000	153,000	17.4
Florida	15.5	2,495,000	302,000	10.8
Georgia	25.9	1,615,000	395,000	19.7
Louisiana	29.9	1,143,000	319,000	21.8
Mississippi	36.8	690,000	286,000	29.3
North Carolina	22.4	1,640,000	305,000	15.7
South Carolina	30.5	668,000	221,000	24.9
Tennessee	16.1	1,600,000	242,000	13.1
Texas	12.7	3,599,000	550,000	13.3
Virginia	18.6	1,496,000	269,000	15.2

SOURCE: U.S. Bureau of the Census, STATISTICAL ABSTRACT OF THE UNITED STATES, 1971, p. 365.

increased black participation in coalitional politics offers a path to black political influence in the South and in the nation. We will return to the topic of black politics and the struggle for equality in Chapter 13.

VOTING AND AMERICAN YOUTH

Before 1970 only three of the fifty states permitted persons eighteen to twenty-one years of age to vote—Georgia, Kentucky, and Alaska. All other states, in the exercise of their constitutional responsibility to determine the qualifications of "electors," had set the voting age at twenty-one. The movement for eighteen-year-old voting had received its original impetus in Georgia in 1944 under the leadership of Governor Ellis Arnal, who argued successfully that eighteen-year-olds were then being called upon to fight and die for their country in World War II and therefore deserved to have a voice in the conduct of government. But this argument failed to convince adult voters or leaders in other states; qualifications for military service were not regarded as the same as qualifications for rational decision making in elections. In state after state, voters rejected state constitutional amendments designed to extend the vote to eighteen-year-olds.

In the Voting Rights Act of 1970, Congress intervened on behalf of eighteen-year-old voting. In this act, Congress asserted very far-reaching authority over the conduct of elections in America by (1) extending the suffrage to persons eighteen to twenty-one years of age regardless of state law, (2) abolishing residency requirements of more than thirty days for voting in national elections, and (3) suspending all literacy tests. This action by Congress immediately raised serious constitutional questions about the extent of congressional power over voting. There was no doubt that Congress could, under the Fifteenth Amendment, end *racial* discrimination in state electoral laws or practices, but extending the suffrage by act of Congress to young people was another matter. The Constitution vests the authority to determine general voter qualifications in the states, and all previous restrictions on state power over the suffrage had come by constitutional amendment—the Fifteenth Amendment barring racial discrimination (1870), the Nineteenth Amendment dealing with women's voting rights (1920), and the Twenty-fourth Amendment eliminating poll taxes (1964).

The constitutional question of congressional power to determine voter qualifications came before the Supreme Court in *Oregon* v. *Mitchell* in 1971. In a controversial five to four decision, the Court held that Congress had acted constitutionally in extending the vote to eighteen-year-olds in *federal* elections, but not in *state* or *local* elections. The reasoning of the judges was complex, and no one was really satisfied with the outcome of the case.[7] Granting eighteen-year-olds the right to vote in federal but not in state and local elections promised to create a good deal of confusion and frustration in the administration of state election laws.

The constitutional debate prompted Congress to pass and send to the states the Twenty-sixth Amendment to the Constitution extending voting rights to all persons over eighteen years of age in all federal, state, and local elections. The legislatures of three-fourths of the states promptly ratified the amendment, perhaps more out of a desire to end confusion than out of a genuine enthusiasm for eighteen-year-old voting. Thus

---

[7]Five separate opinions were written, by different justices in this book-length Court decision. Justice Black argued that federal authority over voter qualifications could be derived from the sentence in Article I, Section 4, of the Constitution which provided that "The times, places, and manner of holding elections for senators and representatives shall be prescribed in each state by the legislature thereof; but the Congress may at any time by law make or alter such regulations." Black said, "I believe that Congress has the final authority over federal elections," but he added, "I would hold that Congress has exceeded its powers in attempting to lower the voting age in state and local elections." Of course, dissenting justices pointed out that determining "times, places, and manner of holding elections" was not the same as determining voter eligibility and that elsewhere in Article I the Constitution gives the states the power to determine voter qualifications. In contrast to the five to four division over eighteen-year-old voting, the Supreme Court was nearly unanimous in upholding the congressional ban on residency requirements in national elections, and unanimous in upholding the prohibition on literacy tests.

Congress succeeded in extending the vote to America's youth, although the states had declined to do so themselves.

VOTING LAWS IN THE STATES

Voting laws in the states are now heavily circumscribed by national authority:

Fifteenth Amendment—No denial of voting because of race
Nineteenth Amendment—No denial of voting because of sex
Twenty-fourth Amendment—No poll taxes
Twenty-sixth Amendment—No denial of voting to persons eighteen or over
Civil Rights Act of 1964—No discrimination in the application of voter registration laws
Voting Rights Act of 1965—Attorney general may replace local voting officials with federal examiners on evidence of voter discrimination in southern states
Voting Rights Act of 1970—No denial of voting to persons eighteen or over; no residency requirements in national elections; no literacy tests

The states, however, continue to administer and finance national, state, and local elections. All but four states (Alaska, Arkansas, North Dakota, and Texas) have established a system of voting registration. Presumably, registration helps to prevent fraud and multiple voting in elections. Registration may be either permanent (once a voter is on a registration list, he remains there until he leaves the district) or periodic (voters must register at periodic intervals ranging from one to ten years). Some states will accept a record of having voted sometime during the registration period as a substitute for reregistration. This system requires no initiative on the part of the voter in keeping his name on the list of eligibles. As a matter of practice, registration lists are usually out of date whether registration is permanent or periodic. Registration procedures can be employed to facilitate or to hinder voting. In many localities registration is inconvenient. It may require a trip to the county courthouse, and registration forms may be complicated. In contrast, many communities have adopted mobile registration systems, where registrars canvass door to door or booths are conveniently established in shopping centers on well-publicized days preceding elections.

PUBLIC OPINION AND PUBLIC POLICY

The problem in assessing the independent effect of public opinion on the actions of decision makers is that the actions of decision makers help to mold mass opinion. Public policy may accord with mass opinion, but we can never be sure whether mass opinion shaped public policy or public policy shaped mass opinion.

In V. O. Key's most important book, *Public Opinion and American Democracy*, he wrote:

> Government, as we have seen, attempts to mold public opinion toward support of the programs and policies it espouses. Given that endeavor, perfect congruence between public policy and public opinion could be government *of* public opinion rather than government *by* public opinion.[8]

While V. O. Key himself was convinced that public opinion did have some independent effect on public policy, he was never able to demonstrate this in any systematic fashion.

There is very little *direct* evidence in the existing research literature to support the notion that public opinion is an important influence over public policy. Many surveys reveal the absence of any knowledge or opinion about public policy on the part of masses of citizens. This suggests that mass opinion has little influence over the content of public policy. How can mass opinion be said to affect public policy when there *is* no mass opinion on a great many policy questions? Studies suggesting that the masses of people have little knowledge of, or interest in, or opinion about, a great many policy questions clearly imply that public opinion has little impact on the content of public policy. Likewise studies indicating that public opinion is unstable and inconsistent also imply that public opinion has little policy impact.

Let us begin our examination of the impact of public opinion on state policy by considering five state policies about which most people have opinions of some kind—legal lotteries, capital punishment, right-to-work laws, antidiscrimination laws, and gun controls. Professor Frank Munger converted national survey data about public opinion on these topics into estimates of opinion within the separate electorates.[9] He was able to designate the states in which a majority supported legislation on these topics and the states in which a majority opposed such legislation. Then he examined the laws of the states to ascertain the congruence between majority opinion and public policy. The results are shown in Table 3–3.

The really startling fact about public policy in these five issues is the

[8]V. O. Key, Jr., *Public Opinion and American Democracy* (New York: Alfred A. Knopf, Inc., 1967), pp. 422–23.

[9]Frank J. Munger, "Opinions, Elections, Parties, and Policies: A Cross-State Analysis," paper delivered at annual meeting of the American Political Science Association, New York, 1969.

TABLE 3-3
Public Opinion and Public Policy in the States

	In States Where Majority Supports			In States Where Majority Opposes			Index of Agreement (States in Which Preference and Policies Coincide)	
	N	Have Statute	No Statute	N	Have Statute	No Statute	N	Percent
State Lotteries: Would you favor or oppose lotteries (or sweepstakes) in this state run by the state government to help pay the cost of government (AIPO 672 and AIPO 688)	20	2	18	30	0	30	32	64
Capital Punishment: Are you in favor of the death penalty for persons convicted of murder? (AIPO 704 and AIPO 729)	21	18	3	29	22	7	25	50
Right-to-Work: Do you think a person should or should not be required to join a union if he works in a unionized factory or business? (AIPO 711, AIPO 717, AIPO 718, AIPO 723). An Affirmative "should," has been treated as a negative right-to-work legislation.	31	17	14	19	2	17	34	68
Public Accommodations: How would you feel about a law which would give all persons—Negroes as well as whites—the right to be served in public places such as hotels, restaurants, theaters, and similar establishments? Would you like to see Congress pass such a law or not? (AIPO 674, AIPO 676, AIPO 683)	34	32	2	16	2	14	46	92
Gun Controls: Would you favor or oppose a law which would require a person to obtain a police permit before he or she could buy a gun? (AIPO 681, AIPO 704, AIPO 717, AIPO 733)	50	8	42	0	0	0	8	16
Total	156	77	79	94	26	68	145	58

SOURCE: Data from Frank J. Munger, "Opinions, Elections, Parties, and Policies: A Cross-State Analysis," paper delivered at annual meeting of the American Political Science Association, New York, 1969.

general lack of congruence between public policy and public opinion. Munger concludes: "There are substantial discrepancies between electoral preferences and state policies; and there are great variations among the five policy areas in the closeness of fit between opinions and actions." The overall figure for policy-opinion congruence is only 58 percent; this means that the chances of a state's policy matching the preferences of its citizens are only a little better than the fifty-fifty ratio generated by chance! Of course, it is true that these five policy areas are by no means a representative sample of all public policy. And it is also interesting to note that in the area of civil rights—where many studies have suggested that public opinion is generally well defined and intense—state policy is in conformity with public opinion in the states. But on such seemingly important questions as lotteries, capital punishment, right-to-work laws, and gun controls, public opinion has little relationship to public policy. Certainly we have no evidence to support the assertion that public opinion is an *important* independent influence over public policy.

When V. O. Key wrestled with the same problem confronting us— namely, the determination of the impact of popular preferences on public policy—he concluded that "the Missing Piece of the Puzzle" was "that thin stratum of persons referred to variously as the political elite, the political activists, the leadership echelons, or the influentials."

> The longer one frets with the puzzle of how democratic regimes manage to function, the more plausible it appears that a substantial part of the explanation is to be found in the motives that activate the *leadership echelon*, the values that it holds, the rules of the political game to which it adheres, in the expectations which it entertains about its own status in society, and perhaps in some of the objective circumstances, both material and institutional, in which it functions.[10]

In short, it is not really the opinions of the *general* public that influence public policy, but rather the opinions of state and community leaders, inside and outside of government.

When state legislators are asked to name individuals whom they regard as knowledgeable about public affairs, and whose advice they might seek out about public issues or problems, they tend to name wealthy, well-educated, and prestigiously employed individuals who are politically active in their states and communities.[11] They name individuals who meet frequently with public officials, who understand public issues, who hold public office, and who tend to believe that the state legislature and other

[10]Key, *Public Opinion and American Democracy*, p. 537.

[11]R. Boynton, Samuel C. Patterson, and Ronald D. Hedlund, "The Missing Links in Legislative Politics: Attentive Constituents," *Journal of Politics*, 31 (August 1969), 700–721.

governing bodies are doing a "good job." In brief, state legislators interact *with people like themselves*, and not with the general public. The "attentive constituents" differed from the general public in their awareness of public issues, their activity and experience in politics, and in their loyalty to, and support for, governing institutions.

INTEREST GROUPS IN STATE POLITICS

Membership in a political interest group is an important form of political participation, and interest group activity is an important aspect of political life.[12] Political interest groups arise when individuals with a common interest decide that by banding together and by consolidating their strength, they can exercise more influence over public policy than they could as individuals acting alone. The impulse toward organization and collective action is particularly strong in a society of great size and complexity. As societies become more urban and industrial, individual action in politics gives way to collective action by giant organizations of businessmen, farmers, professionals, and laborers, as well as racial, religious, and ideological groups. As Earl Latham explained: "Organization represents concentrated power, and concentrated power can exercise dominating influence when it encounters power which is diffused and not concentrated and therefore weaker."[13]

Groups may be highly organized into formal organizations with offices and professional staffs within the state capitals of every state: the National Association of Manufacturers, the AFL–CIO, and the National Education Association are examples of highly organized interest groups that operate in every state. Other groups have little formal organization and have been unable to organize themselves very effectively for political action: an example of such a group would be American consumers. Political interest groups may be organized around occupational or economic interests (for example, the American Farm Bureau Federation, the National Association of Real Estate Boards, the United States Chamber of Commerce), or on racial or religious bases (for example, the National Association for the Advancement of Colored People, the National Council of Churches, the Anti-Defamation League of B'nai B'rith), or around shared experiences (for example, the American Legion, the Veterans of Foreign Wars, the League of Women Voters, the Automobile Association of America), or around ideological positions (for example, Americans for

12See Harmon Zeigler, *Interest Groups in American Society* (Englewood Cliffs, N.J.: Prentice-Hall, Inc., 1964).
13Earl Latham, "The Group Basis of Politics," *American Political Science Review*, 46 (June 1952), 387.

Democratic Action, Americans for Constitutional Action). Government officials and governments themselves organize to help exert pressure on higher levels of government (for example, the National Governors' Conference, the Council of State Governments, the National League of Cities, U.S. Conference of Mayors, and National Association of Counties). Even the recipients of government services are organizing themselves (for example, the National Welfare Rights Organization).

Many scholars believe that economic interests tend to exercise more influence in American politics than noneconomic interests. Nearly 175 years ago James Madison in *The Federalist*, No. 10, spoke about the power of "a land interest, a manufacturing interest, a mercantile interest, a moneyed interest, and many lesser interests" in the new American nation. But certainly the proliferation of active noneconomic groups in America, from the American Legion to the Sierra Club, the League of Women Voters and the National Society for the Prevention of Cruelty to Animals, testifies to the importance of organization in all phases of political life. Particularly active at the state level are the businesses subject to extensive regulation by state governments. The truckers, railroads, insurance companies, and liquor interests are consistently found to be among the most highly organized groups in state capitals. State chapters of the National Education Association are active in state capitals, presenting the demands of educational administrators and teachers. Even local governments and local government officials organize themselves to present their demands at state capitals.

It is very difficult to get a comprehensive picture of interest group activity in state capitals. Many organizations, businesses, legal firms, and individuals engage in interest group activity of one kind or another, and it is difficult to keep track of their varied activities. Many states require the registration of "lobbyists" and the submission of reports about their membership and finances. These laws do not restrain lobbying (that would probably violate the First Amendment freedom to "petition the government for redress of grievances"). Rather they are meant to spotlight the activities of lobbyists. However, many hundreds of lobbyists never register under the pretext that they are not *really lobbyists*, but, instead, businesses, public relations firms, lawyers, researchers, or educational people. Thus, only the larger, formal, organized interest groups are officially registered as lobbyists in the states.

Many smaller businesses maintain part-time lobbyists or contract with law firms that specialize in representing businesses in government. These lobbyists and business representatives help to sell their company's services or products to government agencies, handle their company's relations with administrative and regulatory agencies, and attempt to influence legislation in which their company has an interest. In almost every state, there are hundreds of professional organizations, from accountants to undertakers, and most of these have engaged in lobbying activity from time to time. State chapters of the National Education Association and the American Medical Association are perhaps the most influential of these professional groups. In addition to the activities of the AFL–CIO, individual labor unions—United Automobile Workers, United Steel Workers, International Association of Machinists, International Brotherhood of Teamsters, United Mine Workers, and so on—are also active in state capitols on behalf of working men and women. American farmers generally have a number of trade associations speaking for them in specialized fields—cattlemen, sheepmen, poultry producers, and citrus growers, for example—and three organizations attempt to speak for all farmers at both the state and the national level—the American Farm Bureau Federation, the National Grange, and the National Farmers Union. State chapters of the Sierra Club and the Audubon Society have

TABLE 3-4

Interest Groups in Four States Most Frequently Mentioned
by State Legislators

California	New Jersey
California Teachers Association	New Jersey Education Association
AFL-CIO	Chamber of Commerce
California Farm Bureau	AFL-CIO
California Medical Association	New Jersey Municipal League
Leauge of California Cities	New Jersey Taxpayer Association
Chamber of Commerce	New Jersey Manufacturer's Association
PTA(s)	League of Women Voters
League of Women Voters	New Jersey Farm Bureau
California State Grange	PTA(s)
Legislative Committee	
California Taxpayers Association	

Ohio	Tennessee
Ohio Farm Bureau	Tennessee Education Association
Ohio Education Association	Tennessee Municipal League
Chamber of Commerce	Tennessee Manufacturer's Association
Ohio State Grange	Tennessee County Services Association
AFL-CIO	Tennessee Farm Bureau
Ohio Manufacturer's Association	"Trading Stamps"
Ohio Council of Retail Merchants	AFL-CIO
Ohio Medical Association	Tennessee Taxpayers Association
League of Women Voters	PTA(s)
PTA(s)	

SOURCE: John C. Wahlke et al., THE LEGISLATIVE SYSTEM (New York: John Wiley & Sons, Inc., 1962), pp. 318-19.

become increasingly influential as issues in pollution, ecology, and environmental protection have become popular.

One way to assess interest group activity is to ask state legislators what groups, if any, they perceive as being powerful in state politics. This was the approach of the authors of *The Legislative System*. In the course of their interviews, California state legislators referred to fifty-six specific organizations; New Jersey legislators named thirty-eight or more organizations; Ohio legislators mentioned sixty organizations; and Tennessee lawmakers mentioned forty organizations.[14] Some of the more frequently mentioned interest groups are listed in Table 3–4. Thus, there seems to be little doubt that most elected officials are aware of interest group activity.

There is also considerable agreement among the state legislators about which types of interest groups are most powerful. Business interests were named in *The Legislative System* study as "most powerful groups" more often than any other interests in all four states. Educational interests rank second in three states and tie for third in the fourth, and labor interests rank third in all four states. Agricultural interests, government interests (the associations of city, county, and township governments and government employee associations), ethnic and demographic interests, and religious, charitable, and civic interests were given some mention as powerful interests.

FUNCTIONS AND TACTICS OF INTEREST GROUPS

Both interest groups and political parties organize individuals to make claims upon government, but these two forms of political organizations differ in several respects. An interest group seeks to influence specific policies of government—it does not seek to achieve control over government as a whole. A political party concentrates on winning public office in elections and is somewhat less concerned with policy questions. An interest group does not ordinarily run candidates for public office under its own banner, although it may give influential support to candidates running under a party banner. Finally, the basic function of a political party in a two-party system is to organize a *majority* of persons for the purpose of governing. In contrast, an interest group gives political expression to the interests of *minority* groups.

In a democracy, where decisions are made by majority rule, it is par-

14John C. Wahlke et al., *The Legislative System* (New York: John Wiley & Sons, Inc., 1962), pp. 311–42.

ticularly important that minorities have a means of expressing themselves. Organized interest group activity offers a form of protection for
minorities when the faint preferences of a majority threaten the vital
interest of a minority. The threatened minority can be expected to engage in intense political activity and, in so doing, ward off the threat to
its vital interest. In short, interest group activity can function to represent intensity of feelings in minorities and to blunt the effects of majori-
tarianism.

Interest groups are also essential in representing interests that are not
geographically defined in American society. The formal structure of
American government does not recognize functional interest groupings—
such as businessmen, laborers, farmers, blacks, Catholics, and so on—but
territorial divisions instead—such as cities, counties, legislative districts,
and states. Interest groups supplement the formal system of territorial
representation in American government by providing for an internal
system of functional representation.

Interest groups also function to stimulate interest and participation in
politics among their members. They often pressure candidates to clarify
their stands on issues in an election, and they perform an important
information and education function for public officials and citizens alike.

Interest group techniques are as varied as the imaginations of their
leaders. Groups are attempting to advance their interests when a liquor
firm sends a case of bourbon to a state legislator; when the John Birch
Society distributes its books to public school children; when the League
of Women Voters distributes biographies of political candidates; when
an insurance company argues before a state insurance commission that
insurance rates must be increased; when the National Education Association provides state legislators with information comparing teachers'
salaries in the fifty states; when railroads ask state highway departments
to place weight limitations upon trucks; when the American Civil Liberties Union supplies lawyers for civil rights demonstrators; or when
theater owners testify in legislative committee hearings against the adoption of daylight savings time. Let us try to classify the many techniques
of interest groups under three major headings—public relations, electioneering, and lobbying.

Most people think of interest group tactics as direct attempts to influence decision makers, but these groups spend more of their time,
energy, and resources in general public relations activities than anything else. The purpose of a continuing public relations campaign is to create an environment favorable to the interest group and its program. It is
hoped that a reservoir of public goodwill can be established, which can
be relied on later when a critical issue arises. Generally, business interests have a distinct advantage over nonbusiness interests in public

relations. Business interests already have at their disposal public relations skills of their advertising departments. The cost of business public relations campaigns can be regarded as tax-deductible operating costs.

Electioneering is a common practice among interest groups. If a candidate who is already favorably inclined toward a particular interest can be elected, the group is reassured that its interests will be protected once he has taken office. On the whole, it is a good strategy for interest groups to remain in the background during campaigns—making monetary contributions to their favorite candidates, offering their public relations skills to them, or exhorting their own members to support them. Political campaigns are very expensive, and it is always difficult for a candidate to find enough money to finance his campaign. This is true for officeholders seeking reelection as well as new contenders. It is perfectly legal for an interest group to make a large contribution to a candidate's campaign fund. Ordinarily, a respectable lobbyist would not be so crude as to exact any specific pledges from a candidate in exchange for a campaign contribution. He simply makes a contribution and lets the candidate figure out what he should do when in office to assure further contributions for his next campaign.

It is considered bad taste for an interest group to make a campaign contribution to a state legislator at the very time that a bill in which the group is interested is being considered. However, interest group activity in state capitals may be somewhat cruder—if not actually corrupt—than interest group activity in Washington. In interviewing lobbyists and legislators in Washington, Lester Milbrath found that they considered state lobbying much more corrupt than national lobbying: "Lobbying is very different before state legislators; it is much more individualistic. Maybe this is the reason they have more bribery in state legislatures than in Congress." "In the state legislatures, lobbying is definitely on a lower plane. The lobbyists are loose and hand out money and favors quite freely." "Lobbying at the state level is cruder, more basic, and more obvious." "Lobbying at the state level is faster and more freewheeling and less visible; that is why it is more open to corruption."[15]

Needless to say, it is difficult to document such activity. However, it seems reasonable to believe that state legislators are more subject to the pressures and appeals of organized interest groups than congressmen. State legislators meet less often and for shorter periods of time than Congress, and, consequently, most state legislatures have not developed the formal and informal rules governing their behavior that exist in the

[15]Lester Milbrath, *The Washington Lobbyists* (Chicago: Rand McNally & Co., 1963), pp. 241–43; also cited by Harmon Zeigler, "Interest Groups in the States," in *Politics in the American States*, ed. Herbert Jacob and Kenneth Vines (Boston: Little, Brown and Company, 1965), p. 104.

U.S. Congress. State legislators are less likely to assume the "professional" attitude that characterizes many congressmen; state legislators are more likely to regard their legislative careers as secondary aspects of their lives. Moreover, state legislators make less money than congressmen and may therefore be more vulnerable to the appeals of interest groups offering financial support.

Lobbying is defined as any communication, by someone acting on behalf of a group, directed at a government decision maker with the hope of influencing his decision. Direct persuasion is usually more than just a matter of argument or emotional appeal to the lawmaker. Often it involves the communication of useful technical and political information. Many public officials are required to vote on, or decide about, hundreds of questions each year. It is impossible for them to be fully informed about the wide variety of the bills and issues they face. Consequently, many decision makers come to depend upon the skilled lobbyists to provide technical information about matters requiring action and to inform them of the policy preferences of important segments of the population. A state legislator or administrator may call upon the Chamber of Commerce, the AFL–CIO, or the National Education Association to inform him about the views of businessmen, labor, or teachers on a particular issue.

A CASE OF PRESSURE POLITICS: THE RAILROADS VERSUS THE TRUCKERS

A classic example of pressure politics was the dispute in Pennsylvania in the early 1950s over the weight limitations on trucks.[16] The weight load a truck may carry is a matter of state law. For many years Pennsylvania had one of the lowest permissible truck weights in the country. For three-quarters of a century, the Pennsylvania Railroad had virtually undisputed power in Pennsylvania. This did not result so much from bribery or overt pressure as from a widespread feeling that "what is good for the Pennsylvania Railroad is good for Pennsylvania." But the accelerated growth of the trucking industry after World War II created serious competition for the railroads. By the 1950s the truckers had become a sizable political force in their own right. Pennsylvania is the keystone state in east-west traffic in the nation, and the weight limitation seriously affected truck transportation. Democratic victories in the early 1950s encouraged the truckers to believe that the time had arrived for

[16]The following case study is taken from Andrew Hacker, "Pressure Politics in Pennsylvania: The Truckers v. The Railroads," in *The Uses of Power*, ed. Alan F. Westin (New York: Harcourt, Brace & World, Inc., 1962).

raising the permissible truck weights. Democratic legislators in Pennsylvania generally owed very little to the Pennsylvania Railroad, since "the Pennsy" had long been a bulwark of the Republican party in that state.

The "Pennsy," sensing that the truckers were about to make their move, formed an Eastern Railroads Presidents' Conference and hired a professional public relations firm to plan and execute a countercampaign against the truckers. Carl Bryor and Associates, Inc., planned a grassroots campaign of suspicion and resentment against heavy trucks that travel the roads. The campaign tried to take advantage of motorists' hostility toward large trucks and to emphasize the theme that large trucks are destroying the roads and taxpayers are forced to pay for these damages. Bryor insisted that the railroads remain in the background in his public relations campaign and used other groups—motorists, property owners, taxpayers, farmers, or women's groups—to circulate their antitruck propaganda. Shortly after the Bryor firm was hired, the following articles appeared in national magazines: *Everybody's Digest* contained an article entitled "The Giants That Wreck Our Highways." The message: "Heavy trucks are making their runs on your tax dollars." *The Reader's Digest* contained an article entitled "The Rape of Our Roads." The message: "Overloaded trucks are breaking up our highways faster than we can find money to repair them." *Harper's* contained an article entitled "Our Roads Are Going to Pot." Its message: "Trucks have apparently been a large factor in hastening highway destruction." *The Saturday Evening Post*'s article, entitled "Are Trucks Destroying Our Highways?" contained the message: "Giant trailer rigs, some weighing close to 80 tons, speed overland by night hitting back roads to dodge weight inspectors." *Argosy* contained an article entitled "Hell on Wheels," and its message was: "Gunning his big trailer-truck up to 60, often driving 24 hours without a rest, breaking the law, and risking his life, Butch Watson is typical of the tough breed of gypsy truckers."

The Bryor organization took credit for these articles, saying that they were better than straight advertising since readers suspect that the advertiser has some self-serving ax to grind. Readers are more likely to accept ideas they find in news stories or feature articles.

The trucking industry, however, had its own resources. The Pennsylvania Motor Truck Federation had members in every Pennsylvania county, and these owners or operators of trucking firms were relatively wealthy men, who were often prominent locally and could exert influence on the legislators throughout the state. The federation collected a large war chest from its members and proceeded to make generous campaign contributions to Democrats and Republicans alike. The federation was nonpartisan in its cultivation of votes, and news of its generosity toward candidates spread rapidly. One state legislator wrote to the federation: "I am again a candidate for the legislature. What, if any, assistance can I expect from your association? I can assure you that I do not forget my friends." Needless to say, the federation saw to it that this aspiring legislator's campaign fund was generously increased. The truckers invested a great deal of money throughout the state, but this expenditure would be more than recouped by the new profits that would result from increasing the weight limit.

While the Bryor organization was recruiting support of the automobile association, business groups, and county and township officials, and placing articles and stories attacking the truckers, the Pennsylvania legislature was considering its bill to raise truck rates. The Pennsylvania Motor Truck Association had done an effective lobbying job with legislators. Despite the climate of opinion created by the antitruck messages, the Pennsylvania legislators paid their campaign debt to the truckers by voting through the increase in weight limits. Both houses of the legislature gave large majorities to the bill and the scene quickly shifted to the office of Governor John S. Fine. He had the power to veto the bill, and in Pennsylvania, the legislature seldom overrides a governor's veto. The governor, a Republican, was more in debt to the Pennsylvania Railroad than he was to the truckers. He took the unusual step of holding a public hearing, which one hundred individuals from ninety-four organizations attended. Speaking against the bill were representatives from the Pennsylvania Federation of Women's Clubs, the Keystone Auto Club, the Pittsburgh Auto Club, the Brotherhood of Railway Trainmen, the Brotherhood of Locomotive Firemen and Engineers, the Brotherhood of Railroad Conductors, the United Mine Workers, the Pennsylvania Grange, the Association of Township Supervisors, and, of course, the Associated Railroads of Pennsylvania. Speaking for the bill were twenty-four persons representing the Teamsters' Union, the major gasoline companies, the automobile industry, the cement industry, several construction unions, and the Pennsylvania Motor Truck Association.

To the dismay of the truckers, Governor Fine vetoed the bill. The truckers immediately proceeded to launch a devastating counterattack. At very modest expense, they secured the services of Miss Sonya Saroyan, a disgruntled employee of the Bryor firm, who defected to the enemy's camp and brought with her a complete file of the antitruck campaign. Armed with the Saroyan documents, the Pennsylvania Motor Truck Association and thirty-seven trucking firms sued the Eastern Railroad Presidents' Conference, thirty-one railroads, and Carl Bryor and Associates for the sum of $250 million. Counsel for the truckers claimed that the railroads, in alliance with Bryor, had conspired to put the truckers out of the long-haul freight business in violation of the Sherman and Clayton antitrust laws. The truckers contended that the railroads, by means of a public relations campaign and the corruption of public officials, had caused them to lose the goodwill of their customers and the general public. The complete record of the Bryor activity was exposed. It was also argued that the railroads and Bryor had tried to damage the truckers by securing, through illegitimate means, statutory restrictions that would do them economic harm. The railroads were also accused of using unfair techniques to exert political pressure.

The railroads, in their defense, contended that they had retained Bryor to give them expert assistance in effectively exercising their rights under the First Amendment. The Association of Railroads, just like any other group, has the constitutional rights of free speech and petition. Free speech, they argued, gave them the right to point out the shortcomings of the trucking industry. As for working through other groups and publications instead of conducting the antitruck campaign in the name of the railroads, they argued that these organizations and publications agreed with the railroad position of their own free will. Railroad money and Bryor talent, in short, only subsidized groups that favored the railroad cause. The railroads claimed that the whole controversy was a political rather than an economic one. The entire campaign was one of political persuasion: bringing one's case to the general public is a legitimate and time-honored practice. Moreover, they argued that the application of pressure on lawmakers and executive officials was a necessary and desirable component of the democratic process.

The case reached the Supreme Court in 1961. In a unanimous opinion, Justice Hugo Black supported the position of the railroads:

> In a representative democracy such as this, these branches of government act on behalf of the people, and to a very large extent, the whole concept of representation depends upon the ability of the people to make their wishes known to their representatives. . . . It is neither unusual nor illegal for people to seek action on laws in the hope that they may bring about an advantage to themselves and a disadvantage to their competitors. . . . Indeed it is quite probably people with just such a hope of personal advantage who provide much of the information upon which governments must act. . . . We have restored what seems to have been the true nature of the case—a "no holds barred" fight between two industries both of which are seeking a profitable source of income. Inherent in such fights, which are commonplace in the halls of legislative bodies, is the possibility, and in many instances even the probability, that one group or the other will get hurt by the arguments that are made. In this particular instance, each group appeared to have utilized all the political powers it could muster in an attempt to bring about the passage of laws that would help it or injure the other. But the contest itself appears to have been conducted along the lines normally accepted in our political system, except to the extent that each group has deliberately deceived the public and public officials.[17]

[17]Hacker, "Pressure Politics in Pennsylvania," p. 365.

In the meantime, even before the case was decided, Pennsylvania elected a new governor, George Leader, a Democrat. The railroads did not support Leader in his campaign for the governorship, but instead gave their customary heavy support to the Republican candidate. Again, the legislature passed a bill raising truck weights, but this time the governor signed the bill into law.

INTEREST GROUPS IN THE STATES:
A COMPARATIVE VIEW

How can states be compared in terms of the strength of their interest groups? Some measure of "strength" must be developed by which the states can be ranked. But it is very difficult to measure the "strength" of interest groups, since this is a function of many factors including size, resources, organization, leadership, prestige, unity or "cohesion," and "access" (contacts) to decision makers. Thus, a strictly objective measure of interest group strength in each state is exceedingly difficult to obtain. However, some years ago the American Political Science Association sent questionnaires to political scientists located in several states, asking them to judge whether interest groups in their respective states were strong, moderately strong, or weak.[18] These judgments by political scientists are open to challenge, but they are probably the best available estimate of interest group strength in the states.

Harmon Zeigler used this "classification" to show that states with stronger interest groups are also more likely to be (1) one-party states in contrast to competitive two-party states, (2) states in which parties in the legislature show little cohesion or unity, and (3) states that are poor, rural, and agricultural.[19] Zeigler notes that states that are wealthy, urban, and industrial have *more* interest groups, but it is in these states that interest groups are more likely to balance each other and less likely to dominate the political scene. Poor, rural, agricultural states may have *fewer* interest groups, but it is in these states with relatively backward economies that strong interest groups exercise considerable power over public policy. (See table 3-5.)

Zeigler also identified several "pressure group patterns" in the states.[20] The first pattern, "an alliance of dominant groups," was the typical pattern in rural, agricultural states with one party politics and weak

---

[18]Belle Zeller, ed., *American State Legislatures* (New York: Thomas Y. Crowell Company, 1954), pp. 190-91.
[19]Harmon Zeigler, "Interest Groups in the American States."
[20]*Ibid.*, pp. 117-28.

TABLE 3-5
The Strength of Pressure Groups in Varying Political
and Economic Situations

Social Conditions	Types of Pressure System[a]		
	Strong[b]	Moderate[c]	Weak[d]
Party competition	(24 states)	(14 states)	(7 states)
One-party	33.3%	0%	0%
Modified one-party	37.5%	42.8%	0%
Two-party	29.1%	57.1%	100.0%
Cohesion of parties in legislature			
Weak cohesion	75.0%	14.2%	0%
Moderate cohesion	12.5%	35.7%	14.2%
Strong cohesion	12.5%	50.0%	85.7%
Socio-economic variables			
Urban	58.6%	65.1%	73.3%
Per capita income	$1900	$2335	$2450
Industrialization index	88.8	92.8	94.0

[a] Alaska, Hawaii, Idaho, New Hampshire, and North Dakota are not classified or included.

[b] Alabama, Arizona, Arkansas, California, Florida, Georgia, Iowa, Kentucky, Louisiana, Maine, Michigan, Minnesota, Mississippi, Montana, Nebraska, New Mexico, North Carolina, Oklahoma, Oregon, South Carolina, Tennessee, Texas, Washington, Wisconsin.

[c] Delaware, Illinois, Kansas, Maryland, Massachusetts, Nevada, New York, Ohio, Pennsylvania, South Dakota, Utah, Vermont, Virginia, West Virginia.

[d] Colorado, Connecticut, Indiana, Missouri, New Jersey, Rhode Island, Wyoming.

SOURCE: Harmon Zeigler, "Interest Groups in the American States," in
POLITICS IN THE AMERICAN STATES, ed. Herbert Jacob and Kenneth Vines
(Boston: Little, Brown and Company, 1965), p. 114.

legislative unity among the parties. This pattern was descriptive of the
southern states and of nonsouthern states without industrial economies,
such as Maine.

A good sample of this pattern is Maine, of which Lockhard writes: "In
few American states are the reins of government more openly or more
completely in the hands of a few leaders of economic interest groups than
in Maine." Specifically, power, timber, and manufacturing—the big three
—have proven to be the catalysts for much of the controversy in the state.
While other interests occasionally voice demands, the big three clearly outdistance any rivals in political activity and power. Certainly the key position of these interests in the economy of the state contributes to their crucial position in the decision making process of the state. Over three-fourths
of the state is woodland and most of this land is owned by a handful of

timber companies and paper manufacturers. These interests, combined with power companies and textile and shoe manufacturers, are able—in so far as their well-being is directly involved—to "control Maine politics."[21]

A second pattern of "a single dominant interest" is found in rural nonindustrial states, but states with two-party politics and moderate legislative unity, such as Montana. About Montana, Zeigler writes:

> In a state in which the extraction of minerals is the major nonagricultural source of personal income, Anaconda is the largest employer. While "the company," as it is known in Montana, began its operations in mining for copper, it now owns mills, aluminum companies, railroads, fabricating plants, and forests. The enormity of the Anaconda empire is described by Thomas Payne: "Its strength rests not only in its wealth and resources, but also with its elaborate network of relationships with key citizens, banks, legal firms, and business organizations throughout the state. Rare is that unit of local government—county, city, or school district—that does not have among its official family an associate, in some capacity, of the Anaconda Company."[22]

The position of Anaconda in Montana is not much different from the position of oil companies in Texas or Du Pont in Delaware. Of course, there is a difference between reputation for control and actual control of public policy. No doubt the reputation for control exceeds the actual control that these interests exercise over public policy. Undoubtedly, in large areas of state policy, these dominant groups have little interest and exercise little influence.

A third pattern described by Zeigler was that in which there is a "conflict between two dominant groups." This pattern is found in a nondiversified industrial economy with strong two-party politics and legislative unity within the parties. Michigan is a prime example of this bipolar interest group pattern. Joseph LaPalombara writes: ". . . No major issues of policy (taxation, social legislation, labor legislation, and so on) are likely to be decided in Michigan, without the intervention, within their respective parties and before agencies of government, of automotive labor, and automotive management."[23] The United Automobile Workers union is deeply involved in the affairs of the Democratic party, while the automobile manufacturers are deeply involved in the Republican party. In other words, labor and management in Michigan each have "their" political parties.

21*Ibid.*, p. 118.

22*Ibid.*, pp. 119–20; quotation from Thomas Payne, "Under the Copper Dome: Politics in Montana," in Frank Jonas, *Western Politics* (Salt Lake City: University of Utah Press, 1961), pp. 197–98.

23Joseph LaPalombara, *Guide to Michigan Politics* (East Lansing: Michigan State University Press, 1960), p. 104; also cited by Zeigler, "Interest Groups in the American States," p. 123.

Another pattern of interest group activity was described by Zeigler as the "triumph of many interests." This pattern is found in urban states with industrial economies but relatively weak political parties. Party loyalty has never been strong in California, with many legislators and voters crossing party lines in their political activity. The lack of any effective and disciplined party organization in California paved the way for interest groups to exercise relatively unchecked influence in California politics. No one interest group dominated California politics, but especially during the "lobby era" of 1942–53, the initiation of public policy appeared to be largely the responsibility of organized groups in that state. The railroads, especially the Southern Pacific, the California State Brewers Institute, the race tracks, motion pictures, citrus growers, airplane manufacturers, insurance companies, utilities, and a host of other interests maintained large offices in Sacramento, financially supported many state legislators, and largely dominated legislative affairs.

In states with strong party systems, one usually finds that interest groups are vigorous and active, but dependent upon parties for access to governmental decision makers. Strong parties appear to act as a check upon interest group influence. Interest groups must channel their contributions to candidates through the party organization, and, as a consequence, candidates feel more in debt to their parties. Interest groups direct their appeals not to individual legislators so much as to party leaders. While the parties in such states come to represent coalitions of interest groups, the intervention of parties appears to free candidates and officeholders from direct dependence upon interest groups.

What is the impact of interest groups on the structure of state government? Lewis A. Froman used the same classification of states by interest group strength that Zeigler employed in an interesting attempt to answer this question.[24] He found that the stronger the interest groups, the greater the number of state-elected officials, and the greater the likelihood that state agencies would be headed by elected rather than appointed officials. He concluded that states with stronger interest groups are better able to isolate government agencies and officials from executive and legislative influence than states with weaker interest groups. Interest groups strive to isolate administrative agencies from the governor and the legislature in order to strengthen their own influence with these agencies. By weakening gubernatorial and legislative control over state administration, interest groups feel that they are more likely to be successful in exercising influence in administrative agencies.

[24]Lewis A. Froman, "Some Effects of Interest Group Strength in State Politics," *American Political Science Review*, 60 (December 1966), 952–62.

FOUR

Parties
in
State Politics

PARTIES IN THE FIFTY STATES

Federalism has had a profound effect on the organization of American parties. Decentralization of power is the most important characteristic of American party organizations. These organizations are built around important public offices at the federal, state, and local level. Organizationally, the Democratic and Republican parties consist of a national committee; a House and Senate party conference; various national clubs, such as Young Democrats and Young Republicans, and Democratic and Republican Women's Federations; and fifty state parties, which in turn are composed of state committees and county and city organizations. This structure is tied together very loosely. State parties are not very responsive to national direction, and in most states, city and county organizations operate quite independently of the state committees. State committees are generally involved in important statewide elections—governors, U.S. senators, and congressmen in the smaller states. City and county committees are generally responsible for county and municipal offices, state legislative seats, and congressional seats in the larger states. The Democratic and Republican National Committees exist primarily for the purpose of holding national conventions every four years to select the presidential candidate. Since each level of party organization has "its own fish to fry," each operates quite independently of the other levels.

State parties are by no means merely local representatives of national firms. In fact, the national Democratic and Republican parties are often described as confederations of fifty distinct party organizations. It is not surprising in the American system of federalism—where only the president and the vice-president have *national* constituencies, and senators, congressmen, governors, state legislators, county and municipal officials all have *local* constituencies—that the American parties would be decentralized in their organization. Parties function to capture control of public office for their nominees, and most elective offices in the American political system are chosen by state and local constituencies rather than national constituencies. (One might say *all* elected offices in the U.S. are chosen by state or local constituencies, since the president and the vice-president are really elected by the electoral votes of the states rather than the popular vote of the nation.) Elections in the United States are regulated and administered mainly by the fifty states, rather than the national government.

Party affairs are largely governed by the laws of the states. Each state sets forth the conditions that an organization must meet to qualify as a political party and to get its candidates' names printed on the official election ballots. Each state sets the qualifications for membership in a party, and the right to vote in the party's primary election. State laws determine the number, method of selection, and duties of various party officials, committees, and conventions. The states, rather than the parties themselves, decide how the parties shall go about nominating candidates for public office. Most states require that party nominations be made by direct primaries, but several states still nominate by party caucuses or conventions. Most states also attempt to regulate party finances, although with little success.

Since party organizations in the states are relatively autonomous from the national Democratic and Republican parties, we can expect a great deal of variation in party systems from state to state. First of all, the comparative strength of the Republican and Democratic parties obviously differs from state to state. States can also be differentiated by the level of interparty competition and by the strengths and functions of their party organizations. Some states can be characterized as one-party states, while in other states more competitive situations exist. In some states, the Republican and Democratic parties offer substantially different policy positions on education, welfare, taxation, highways, and other important public issues. In other states, it is more difficult to distinguish a clear party position on these issues. In some states, the Democratic and Republican parties represent separate social and economic groups in the states: the Democratic party may be composed of central-city, low-income, ethnic, and racial constituencies, while the Republican party represents middle-class, suburban, small-town, and rural constituencies. However, in other states both parties may attempt to represent the same groups, and it is then difficult to detect any socioeconomic differences between Democrats and Republicans.

The wide range of differences between state party systems means that state party organizations with the same party label may be quite different from one another. Often, state Democratic parties are further apart on policy matters from each other than from Republicans. The Minnesota and Mississippi Democratic parties, for example, have little in common except the party label. Variations in state Republican parties may be just as great: certainly the New York and Arizona Republicans are quite different from one another, not to mention the Alabama Republicans. Each of these Republican and Democratic state parties is more a product of its statewide constituency than of any national Democratic or Republican organization. State parties are more inclined to fit their programs to popular demands within their states than to offer significantly different policy alternatives derived from national party differences. Democratic and Republican parties within a state are competing in the same vote market, and hence their policy positions have more in common with each other than with those of their counterparts in different states. In short, parties in each state tailor their policies to local conditions.

In this chapter we will endeavor not only to describe the structure and activities of state party systems but also to compare state party systems and identify some of the causes and consequences of variations among the states.

ONE-PARTY AND TWO-PARTY STATES

Interparty competition has received a great deal of attention from political scientists studying state politics. Many political scientists have contended that competitive, responsible parties are necessary for effective democratic control of government in modern society. The ideal party system is said to be one in which competitive parties present alternative programs in election campaigns, and the party winning the majority of votes captures all the power it needs to write its program into law. Moreover, in the ideal party system, the party's elected officials act cohesively, so the voters can hold the party collectively responsible for public affairs at the end of its term of public office. The key to this ideal party system is the existence of competitive parties, which are roughly balanced in strength.

In reality, however, the degree of party competition among the states varies a great deal. In the past, the Republican party in the Deep South states was practically nonexistent, and even today, despite the recent Republican upsurge in the South, the Republican party frequently fails to run candidates for governor, U.S. senator, Congress, and the state legislature. Even though these southern states may be competitive in presidential elections, Democrats have continued to win state office by wide margins and dominate southern state legislatures by heavy majorities. The party systems in these states have been termed "one-party Democratic." Republican domination in the midwestern and upper New England states has never been so complete that it warrants the designation of a "one-party system."

There are several important differences between one-party states and two-party states. Voters in two-party states use party labels to help them identify the politics of candidates. The fact that a candidate runs under a Republican or Democratic label does not guarantee his stand on every public issue, but it indicates with which broad coalition in American politics a candidate has associated himself. Party labels carry meaning for most voters, even though individual candidates may be "disloyal" to their party on occasion. At the very least, a party label in a two-party state tells more about a candidate's politics than a strange name on a ballot with no party affiliation indicated.

A party label in a competitive state is a very conspicuous attribute of a candidate. One-party states may have important "liberal" or "conservative" factions of some durability. But in two-party states, the party label can be seen by every voter on election day. A party label is not so obscure as an alignment with a liberal or conservative faction. Most students of state politics feel that it is more difficult to hold factions responsible. Factions are even more fluid, and change personality and policies more frequently than parties. V. O. Key argues that southern factional systems obscure politics for most voters and permit conservative interests to manipulate the voters.[1] A large number of people who have very little knowledge about the policies or memberships of various factions are easily misled. This does not mean that many voters are not confused about party policies in competitive states or that competitive parties can always hold their legislators responsible, but it does mean that party competition is more likely to clarify things for the voter than factional politics. Even if policy differences between the parties are vague, there is at least an "inparty" and an "out-party," which can be identified

---

[1]V. O. Key, Jr., *Southern Politics in State and Nation* (New York: Alfred A. Knopf, Inc., 1949). See also Alan P. Sindler, "Bifactional Rivalry as an Alternative to Two-Party Competition in Louisiana," *American Political Science Review*, 46 (1955), 641.

at election time. Finally, in one-party states, and even in states with limited competition, the minority party often fails to run candidates for many offices. Under these circumstances, the party out of office is unable to perform the important role of criticizing officeholders. The existence of a competitive party *outside* of government, a party that has a real chance of replacing officeholders at the next election, can help to make officeholders more aware of their responsibilities to the voters. In a competitive two-party system, the party out of power has the strongest kind of incentive for exposing the weaknesses of the ruling party.

In recent years political scientists have developed various ways of measuring interparty competition in the states.[2] Figure 4–1 shows the distribution of the fifty states by levels of interparty competition in lower and upper houses of state leigslatures and in governors' elections. This distribution of states by level of party competition focuses upon *state* offices and not upon a state's congressional delegation, its U.S. senators, or its vote in presidential elections. Other students of state politics have included a wider range of offices in their measures of party competition, but these measures of party competition are directly related to the study of *state* government.

CAUSES AND CONSEQUENCES OF PARTY COMPETITION

Why do some states have competitive two-party systems and others do not? Slavery and the subsequent status of the Negro in society had a great deal to do with one-partyism in the South.[3] A majority of white southerners were Democrats before the Civil War, and the Republican party was founded to resist the spread of slavery. A Republican president wrote the Emancipation Proclamation and a Republican Congress wrote the Thirteenth, Fourteenth, and Fifteenth Amendments and supervised the military occupation of the South. Also, one-partyism is characteristic of political systems in which large numbers of people are united in opposition to a perceived serious threat. One overriding sentiment in the South, which united both rich and poor, farmers and laborers, and all other groups of southern whites, was the desire to keep Negroes "in their place." One-partyism helped to exclude Negroes from effective political participation. Whites would handle their own squabbles within the Democratic party primary and unite behind the "white man's party" in the general election.

---

[2]See David G. Pfeiffer, "The Measurement of Inter-Party Competition and Systemic Stability," *American Political Science Review*, 61 (1967), 457–67.
[3]See Key, *Southern Politics in State and Nation.*

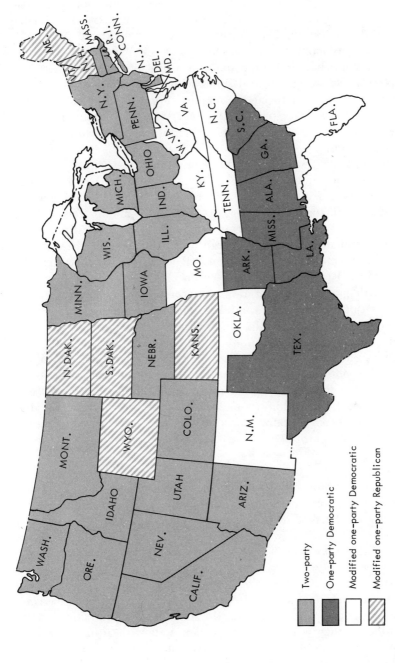

FIGURE 4-1 Democratic and Republican Success in State Offices, 1954–70

Two-party

One-party Democratic

Modified one-party Democratic

Modified one-party Republican

Note: Hawaii and Alaska, not shown, are two-party states.

But this explanation, while helpful in understanding southern politics, fails to explain the lack of effective party competition in many states outside the South. Party competition also appears to be closely related to socioeconomic conditions in the states. Party competition is greater in those urban, industrial states in which separate socioeconomic groups reside. Rural agricultural states with homogeneous populations do not provide enough social division to support well-organized, disciplined, and competitive parties. It is not surprising, then, that competitive states tend to be those urban and industrial states with heterogeneous populations.

In large states, such as New York, Pennsylvania, and Illinois, the parties are first divided along rural-urban lines, and, within urban areas, they are further divided on socioeconomic bases. Republicans dominate in rural areas and in the wealthier urban areas (upper-middle-class suburbs and several "silk-stocking" districts in the cities). Democratic districts are found predominantly in the less wealthy, urban areas of the state. A similar pattern emerges if occupational, religious, or racial characteristics are considered. Republican districts within urban areas prove to be the districts with greater concentrations of professional, managerial, sales, and clerical jobs. Republican candidates fare badly among black voters. The Democrats dominate in the ethnic districts with southern and eastern European, Irish, and Catholic voters. These are frequently the big-city, mining, and mill districts. The Republicans draw heavily in the Anglo-Saxon, northern and western European, Protestant districts of these states. A high degree of party competition results from these socioeconomic conditions within a state's electorate. In contrast, the less competitive states—for example, Maine, Kansas, Vermont, New Hampshire, North and South Dakota—are more homogeneous in their social composition.

Table 4–1 confirms our reasoning that party competition is related to urbanization, income, and education in the states. The two-party states are more urban, wealthy, and well educated than either the one-party Democratic or the modified one-party Republican states. It is also interesting to note that the two-party states and the Republican states have much smaller proportions of blacks in their populations. In contrast, the one-party Democratic states have larger proportions of blacks in their populations.

What difference does it make in public policy whether a state has competitive or noncompetitive parties? Do states with a competitive party system differ in their approach to education, welfare, health, taxation, or highways from states with noncompetitive party systems? This is not an easy question to answer. Since competitive states tend to be wealthy, urban, industrial states, and noncompetitive states poorer, rural, agricul-

TABLE 4-1

Social and Economic Characteristics of the States
and Party Competition

	One-Party Democratic[1] (7 states)	Modified One-Party Democratic[2] (10 states)	Two-Party[3] (26 states)	Modified One-Party[4] (7 states)
Urbanization	53%	57%	69%	49%
Income	$1,501	$1,841	$2,360	$1,972
Education	9.1 yrs.	9.7 yrs.	11.2 yrs.	10.9 yrs.
Black Population	29%	15%	4%	1%

[1] Alabama, Arkansas, Georgia, Louisiana, Mississippi, South Carolina, Texas.

[2] Florida, Kentucky, Maryland, Missouri, Oklahoma, New Mexico, North Carolina, Tennessee, Virginia, West Virginia.

[3] Alaska, Arizona, California, Colorado, Connecticut, Delaware, Hawaii, Idaho, Illinois, Indiana, Iowa, Massachusetts, Michigan, Minnesota, Montana, Nebraska, Nevada, New Jersey, New York, Ohio, Oregon, Pennsylvania, Rhode Island, Utah, Washington, Wisconsin.

[4] Kansas, Maine, New Hampshire, North Dakota, South Dakota, Vermont, Wyoming.

tural states, it is difficult to sort out the effects of party competition from these other socioeconomic variables. Several scholars have asserted that a competitive party system leads to more liberal education, welfare, and taxation policies and that one-partyism strengthens conservative views; however, available evidence suggests that interparty competition does not play a really influential role in determining public policies in these fields. As we shall see in later chapters, education, welfare, taxation, and highway programs appear to be more closely related to socioeconomic factors in the states than to the degree of party competition itself.[4] How-

[4]The traditional assumption that party competition had an important liberalizing effect on public policy is found in V. O. Key, Jr., *American State Politics: An Introduction* (New York: Alfred A. Knopf, Inc., 1956); Duane Lockard, *The Politics of State and Local Government* (New York: The Macmillan Company, 1963); John H. Fenton, *People and Parties in Politics* (Glenview: Scott, Foresman & Company, 1966). The effect of party competition on public policy was shown in statistic analysis to be *less* influential than economic conditions in Thomas R. Dye, *Politics, Economics, and the Public* (Chicago: Rand McNally & Co., 1966); Richard E. Dawson and James A. Robinson, "Inter-Party Competition, Economic Variables, and Welfare Policies in the American States," *Journal of Politics*, 25 (May 1963), 265–89; Richard I. Hofferbert, "The Relation between Public Policy and Some Structural and Environmental Variables in the American States," *American Political Science Review*, 60 (March 1966), 78–82. However, party competition combined with voter participation was found to have *some* effect on certain welfare policies in Ira Sharkansky and Richard I. Hofferbert, "Dimensions of State Politics, Economics and Public Policy," *American Political Science Review*, 63 (September 1969), 867–79. For a full discussion of the impact of economic and political variables in shaping public policy, see Thomas R. Dye, *Understanding Public Policy* (Englewood Cliffs, N.J.: Prentice-Hall, Inc., 1972), Chap. 11.

ever, as we have already observed, a lack of party competition can seriously affect the degree of popular control over state government and the ability of individuals to hold public officials responsible for the state of public affairs. Also, as we observed in Chapter 3, the lack of party competition appears to reduce voter participation in state politics.

The "ideal" party model, with its emphasis on responsibility, unity, and discipline, may be ill suited to a complex, pluralistic society such as the United States. A large nation with many diverse interests might not be accommodated by a two-party system in which the parties were highly centralized and disciplined. It is the relative irresponsibility of our parties, and the generality and ambiguity of their party platforms, that makes compromise possible in this nation. Neither party is so different from the other that members of the losing party will fail to support candidates of the winning party after they are elected to office. Austin Ranney has argued that an increase in responsibility, discipline, and unity in American parties might destroy the system rather than improve it: "To the extent that this [party irresponsibility] is an accurate description of our present national party system, it results, not from any mere organizational deficiency in our national party machinery, but rather from the diversity and multiplicity of our interest groups and the heterogeneity and complexity of the political conflict they express. As long as the basic nature of the American community remains the same, therefore, centralizing and disciplining our national parties would very likely result in a multiple party rather than a two party system."[5]

REPUBLICAN AND DEMOCRATIC PARTY FORTUNES IN STATES

In recent years the Democratic party has held a slight edge in American state politics. Table 4–2 shows the number of upper and lower houses in state legislatures controlled by Democrats and Republicans from 1954 through 1970, with the number of Democratic and Republican governors. For most of this period the Democratic party has held control of a majority of state legislatures and governorships.

Because of these Democratic successes, any distribution of states according to the degree of Democratic or Republican party success will be skewed toward the Democratic party. A state's political coloration in national politics may be quite different from its statewide political affiliations. In 1964 five Democratic states of the Old Confederacy (Alabama,

[5]See Austin Ranney, *The Doctrine of Responsible Party Government* (Urbana: University of Illinois Press, 1954).

TABLE 4-2
Governorships and State Legislative Chambers Controlled
By Democrats and Republicans, 1954-1970

	Upper Houses			Lower Houses			Governorships	
	Dem.	Rep.	Tie	Dem.	Rep.	Tie	Dem.	Rep.
1970	26	21	1	22	25	1	29	21
1968	25	22	1	23	25	0	16	34
1966	29	18	1	25	22	1	24	26
1964	34	12	2	39	9	0	33	17
1962	28	20	0	27	29	1	33	17
1960	30	18	0	31	17	0	34	16
1958	31	17	0	28	9	1	35	15
1956	25	21	2	28	20	0	31	19
1954	20	25	1	26	20	0	27	21

SOURCE: U.S. Bureau of the Census, STATISTICAL ABSTRACT OF THE UNITED STATES, 1970, pp. 366-67.

Georgia, Louisiana, Mississippi, and South Carolina) voted for Republican presidential candidate Barry Goldwater, largely on the basis of his vote against the Civil Rights Act of 1964. Yet in these states, over 90 percent of both houses of the legislature were Democratic. In 1968 only one (Texas) of the eleven southern states cast its electoral votes for the Democratic presidential nominee, Hubert Humphrey. Five states cast their vote for George C. Wallace (Alabama, Arkansas, Georgia, Louisiana, and Mississippi), and the remainder for Republican Richard Nixon (Florida, North Carolina, South Carolina, Tennessee, and Virginia). And in 1972, every southern state gave the Republican President a heavy majority. Yet all these states were strongly (although not exclusively) Democratic in state and local politics.

Historically, southern states have accounted for much of the Democratic party's strength in state politics, while midwestern and New England states have accounted for many of the Republican party's victories. It is not really surprising that this regional factor is reflected in Democratic and Republican party successes. The Republican party was founded in 1854 to resist the spread of slavery, which, at the time, was the principal labor source in the southern region. The Civil War was the deepest political cleavage in American history; seventeen states fought for the Union and eleven states for the Confederacy. A Republican president led the Union to victory in the war against the Confederacy, and presided over the military occupation of the southern states. Of course, the Civil War ended over a century ago, but these party identifications linger on in state politics as a product of the way in which individuals acquire party affiliations from their parents. A few individuals change party affiliation as a result of changes in their social or economic position in life, or a move to another community. But massive party switches take place only under crises circumstances, such as the Civil War, the Great Depression, or, perhaps, the civil rights revolution of the 1960s.

Democratic and Republican states differ significantly with respect to income and educational levels. Democratic states tend to have lower income and educational levels than Republican states. This relationship between Democratic success and state politics in lower income and educational levels depends upon the eleven southern states, which are both Democratic and at the bottom of state rankings on income and education. If we remove the eleven southern states, we find that there is really no relationship in the thirty-nine nonsouthern states between Democratic or Republican party success and urbanization or income or education. There is, however, a significant relationship between Democratic success and industrialization in nonsouthern states: an increase in industrialization leads to an increase in Democratic success.[6]

Perhaps the most noteworthy trend in party fortunes in recent years has been the rise of Republican party strength in a number of southern and border states. Table 4–3 reveals the increasing success of the Republican party in the South in presidential and gubernatorial voting. Before the Eisenhower years, both southern and border states merited the phrase "the Solid South." Eisenhower made the original inroads into the Solid South by carrying Texas, Virginia, and Florida. Yet for a while it did not appear that these isolated Republican victories in presidential elections would result in any significant Republican inroads into state capitals. When Barry Goldwater cast his vote against the Civil Rights Act of 1964, Republican party fortunes soared in the Deep South states. While it is true that a majority of both Republicans and Democrats in Congress supported the Civil Rights Act, many Deep South voters held the Democratic party responsible, since the act was passed by a Democratic Congress with the support of a Democratic president. Goldwater won electoral votes of five Deep South states—Alabama, Georgia, Louisiana, Mississippi, and South Carolina. George C. Wallace blunted Republican hopes of winning over the entire region in 1968 by winning five Deep South states (Alabama, Arkansas, Georgia, Louisiana, and Mississippi). (Republican Senator Strom Thurmond was generally credited with keeping South Carolina out of the Wallace bloc.) But Republican Richard Nixon won five southern states and four of the six border states. In 1972, the Republican Presidential majorities in the southern states were far greater than the national majority (61 percent). Indeed, the southern states led the Nixon landslide.

[6]Dye, *Politics, Economics, and the Public,* p. 53.

TABLE 4-3
The Rise of Republicanism in the South

	Presidential Voting					Vote for Governor			
	1944	1956	1964	1968	1972	1954-56	1964-66	1968-70	1972
Southern States									
Alabama	D81	D56	R69	W66	R76	D73	D63	D75	—
Arkansas	D70	D52	R56	W40	R69	D81	R54	R51	D76
Florida.	D70	R57	D51	R40	R72	D74	R55	D57	—
Georgia	D82	D66	R54	W42	R70	D100	R47*	D54	—
Louisiana	D81	D53	D57	W48	R69	D100	D61	D100	—
Mississippi	D88	D58	R88	W64	R80	D100	D62	D70	—
North Carolina	D67	D51	D56	R40	R71	D67	D57	D53	R51
South Carolina	D88	D45	R59	R38	R72	D100	D58	D51	—
Tennessee	D60	R49	D55	R39	R70	D87	D80	R52	—
Texas	D71	R55	D63	D41	R66	D78	D73	D56	D48
Virginia	D62	R55	D53	R43	R69	D55	D48	R52	—
Border States									
Delaware	D54	R64	D61	R45	R60	R52	D51	R51	D51
Kentucky	D54	R54	D64	R44	R65	D58	D51	R51	—
Maryland	D52	R60	D65	D43	R62	D54	R50	D66	—
Missouri	D51	D50	D64	R46	R62	D52	D62	D61	R55
Oklahoma	D55	R55	D56	R46	R75	D59	R56	D48	—
West Virginia	D55	R54	D68	D50	R63	R54	D55	R51	R55

* Republican candidate Howard Calloway won the popular vote but failed to obtain the necessary majority; Democratic candidate Lester Maddox was elected by the state legislature.

The increasing Republicanism of the South is not confined exclusively to presidential elections. Republicans have increased their representation in southern state legislatures in recent years, and several Republicans have been elected to important statewide offices. Republican Claude Kirk was elected governor of Florida in 1966, and Republican Winthrop Rockefeller was elected governor of Arkansas. (Republican Howard "Bo" Calloway won a plurality of votes in the Georgia gubernatorial election of 1966, although he failed to win a majority, and, as prescribed by the state constitution in such cases, the Georgia legislature picked the winner —a conservative Democrat, Lester Maddox.) The Republican gains in the South reflect the region's increasing disenchantment with the policies of the federal government. The apparent conservatism of the Republican party in recent years appeals to many southern voters.

Yet the influence of traditional party ties in state and local politics remains strong. Today it appears that the South will continue to remain Democratic in state and local politics. In the early 1970s most southern governors' chairs were held by Democrats, and Democrats continued to control every southern state legislature.

NATIONAL TIDES AND STATE POLITICS

National political tides have an important bearing on party fortunes in states and communities. National issues, personalities, and party loyalties will affect voting for state and local offices, particularly in presidential election years. Of course, one way of trying to insulate state elections from national influences is to hold state elections at times other than the dates of national elections. About half of the states elect their governors in off years, that is, years in which no presidential election takes place. Eleven states elect their governors for two-year terms in even-numbered years and alternate gubernatorial elections between presidential years and off years. Twelve states elect their governors for four-year terms in presidential years, and, theoretically, these states are most subject to national tides in their gubernatorial politics. It is difficult to measure the effect of a president's "coattails" in state politics. Eisenhower did not appear to help Republican officeholders in the states in 1956; yet in 1958, without Eisenhower at the head of the Republican ticket, Republicans fared even worse. In 1960 the Kennedy-Nixon battle was so close that no national trends were apparent, although Kennedy helped many local Democratic candidates in big-city, Catholic areas. Johnson was influential in sweeping many state and local candidates into office in 1964 (although it may have been that Goldwater was influential in keeping many

TABLE 4-4
Governorships Won by Democrats and Republicans

Eisenhower v. Stevenson 1956		Off- Year 1958		Kennedy v. Nixon 1960		Off- Year 1962	
Dem	Rep	Dem	Rep	Dem	Rep	Dem	Rep
17	14	30	9	16	12	25	14

Johnson v. Goldwater 1964		Off- Year 1966		Nixon v. Humphrey 1968		Off- Year 1970		Nixon v. McGovern 1972	
Dem	Rep	Dem	Rep	Dem	Rep	Dem	Rep	Dem	Rep
18	8	13	24	8	13	22	13	11	7

Republican candidates out of office). Republicans fared much better in the off years 1962 and 1966 when Johnson was not a candidate (and Goldwater was not leading the Republican ticket). Nixon appeared to help GOP candidates for governor in 1968. In 1970 Nixon campaigned for Republican candidates, but they fared badly nonetheless; Nixon's landslide in 1972 provided little or no help to State GOP candidates.

On the whole, states that vote Democratic in presidential elections tend to vote Democratic in gubernatorial elections, and, of course, there is a correlation between Republican voting in presidential and gubernatorial elections.[7] Before 1964 southern states not only elected Democrats to their state houses but also provided electoral votes for Democratic presidential candidates. Midwestern and New England states tended to vote for Republican presidential as well as gubernatorial candidates. Thus, a state's partisan preferences in national and state politics are not totally divorced. However, it is possible to identify those states that are more Democratic in presidential elections than in gubernatorial elections, and those states that are more Democratic in gubernatorial elections than in presidential elections. Certainly the southern states have been more Democratic in gubernatorial than in presidential elections—this was true even before the Goldwater candidacy in 1964. Interestingly, fewer states have been more Democratic in presidential than in gubernatorial elections; however, New York and California have treated Republican gubernatorial candidates better than Republican presidential aspirants.

[7]See M. Kent Jennings and Richard G. Niemi, "Party Identification at Multiple Levels of Government," *American Journal of Sociology*, 72 (July 1966), 86–101.

DEMOCRATS AND REPUBLICANS—WHAT'S
THE DIFFERENCE?

It is sometimes difficult to define the meaning of party labels in state politics. The Democratic and Republican party organizations in the fifty states are devoid of any common ideology and very often lacking in clear and consistent policy positions. The Democratic and Republican parties within a state are competing in the same vote market, and, hence, both must tailor their policies to local conditions.

Does this mean that there are no real differences between Republican and Democratic parties in the states? Certainly at the national level, it is not difficult to see the different coalitions of groups that compose the Democratic and Republican parties. While the moderate viewpoints of American parties insure that major social groups are seldom wholly within one party or the other, differences between the Democratic and Republican parties at the national level are revealed by different proportions of votes given by major groups in the electorate to the Democratic and Republican parties.[8] The Democratic party receives a disproportionate amount of support from Catholics and Jews; blacks; lower educational and income groups; younger people; skilled, semiskilled, and unskilled laborers; union members; and big-city residents. The Republican party receives disproportionate support from Protestants; whites; higher educational and income groups; older people; professional, managerial, and other white-collar workers; nonunion members; and rural and small-town residents. (See Table 4–5.)

The differing group bases of the Democratic and Republican parties at the national level are reflected in the policy positions of Democratic and Republican leaders. Herbert J. McCloskey and his associates presented a series of policy questions to over three thousand delegates at the Democratic and Republican National Convention.[9] McCloskey found that there were substantial differences between Democrats and Republicans on important public issues, including public ownership of natural resources, government regulation of economy, equalitarianism, tax policy, and foreign policy. McCloskey concluded:

> Although it has received wide currency, especially among Europeans, the belief that the two American parties are identical in principle and doctrine

[8]See Fred I. Greenstein, *The American Party System and the American People* (Englewood Cliffs, N.J.: Prentice-Hall, Inc., 1965).

[9]Herbert J. McCloskey et al., "Issue Conflict and Consensus among Leaders and Followers," *American Political Science Review*, 54 (1960), 426.

TABLE 4-5

Republican and Democratic Division of Major Social Groups

	Vote Republican	Vote Democratic	Vote Other (Inc. Wallace—1968)
Education			
1960			
Grade school	44%	54%	2%
High school	46	52	2
College	63	35	2
1964			
Grade school	20	78	2
High school	31	68	1
College	45	53	2
1968			
Grade school	30	51	19
High school	44	41	15
College	57	35	8
Occupation			
1960			
Professional and Managerial	54	44	2
Other white collar	52	48	0
Skilled and semiskilled	40	57	3
Unskilled	41	59	0
Farm operators	67	33	0
1964			
Professional and Managerial	41	57	2
Other white collar	35	63	2
Skilled and semiskilled	23	76	1
Unskilled	16	81	4
Farm operators	35	63	2
1968			
Professional and Managerial	60	34	6
Other white collare	48	40	12
Skilled and semiskilled	39	44	17
Unskilled	32	55	13
Farm operators	45	36	19
Union Affiliation			
1960			
Member	35	62	3
Nonmember	55	44	1
1964			
Member	16	83	1
Nonmember	37	61	2
1968			
Member	37	47	16
Nonmember	49	39	12

TABLE 4-5 (cont'd)

	Vote Republican	Vote Democratic	Vote Other (Inc. Wallace—1968)
Community			
1960			
Metropolitan areas	41	57	2
Towns and cities	59	60	1
Rural areas	51	47	2
1964			
Metropolitan areas	28	71	1
Towns and cities	39	60	1
Rural areas	30	67	3
1968			
Metropolitan areas	46	46	8
Towns and cities	45	41	14
Rural areas	50	31	19
Religion			
1960			
Protestant	62	36	2
Catholic	17	82	1
1964			
Protestant	36	61	2
Catholic	21	79	.5
1968			
Protestant	51	35	14
Catholic	36	55	9
Race			
1960			
White	52	47	1
Black	27	66	7
1964			
White	35	63	2
Black	0	98	2
1968			
White	49	36	15
Black	3	96	1

has little foundation in fact. Examination of the opinions of Democratic and Republican leaders shows them to be distinct communities of co-believers who diverge sharply on many important issues. Their disagreements, furthermore, conform to an image familiar to most observers and are generally consistent with differences turned up by studies of congressional rollcalls. Republican and Democratic leaders stand furthest apart on issues that grow out of their group identification and support—out of the managerial, proprietary, and high status connections of the one, and the labor, minority, low status, and intellectual connections of the other.[10]

McCloskey went on to identify the different policy positions of his Democratic and Republican leaders:

> Democratic leaders typically display the strongest urge to elevate the low-born, the uneducated, the deprived minorities, and the poor in general; they are more disposed to employ the nation's collective power to advance humanitarian and social welfare goals (for example, social security, immigration, racial integration, a higher minimum wage, and public education). They are more critical of wealth and big business and more eager to bring them under regulation. Theirs is the greater faith in the wisdom of using legislation for redistributing the national product and for furnishing social services on a wide scale. Of the two groups of leaders, the Democrats are the more "progressively" oriented toward social reform and experimentation. Republican leaders, while not uniformly differentiated from their opponents, subscribe in greater measure to the simple practices of individualism, laissez faire, and national independence. They prefer to overcome humanity's misfortunes by relying upon personal effort, private incentives, frugality, hard work, responsibility, self denial (for both men and government), and the strengthening rather than the diminution of the economic and status distinctions that are the "natural" rewards of the differences of human character and fortunes.[11]

These differences between the Democratic and Republican parties at the national level can be observed in the politics of some states but not in others. Certainly, differences between the Democratic and Republican parties in the large urban industrial states tend to resemble the differences between the national Democratic and Republican parties. William J. Keefe reported that Democratic and Republican parties in the Pennsylvania and Illinois state legislatures differed substantially in questions involving labor minorities, social legislation, and the role of government in the economy.[12] On the other hand, the Democratic party in the southern states has *not* typically represented the "lowborn, the uneducated, the deprived minorities, and the poor in general," nor has it advocated the use of national power to advance racial integration. While it is true that the Democratic party in the southern states has supported national efforts to redistribute wealth and furnish social services on a national scale, one suspects that the southern Democrats have done so for the very practical reason that the southern states stand to gain the most by such

[10]*Ibid.*, p. 426.
[11]*Ibid.*, p. 428.
[12]William J. Keefe, "Comparative Study of the Role of Political Parties in State Legislatures," *Western Political Quarterly*, 9 (1956), 535–41.

redistribution. Nor has the Republican party in New York always conformed to the symbols and practices of individualism and laissez faire to
the same extent as the national Republican party. New York Republicans have rather consistently supported social welfare measures at both
the state and the national level. In short, the national images of the Democratic and Republican parties are not always the images that these parties reflect in the politics of individual states.

State Republican and Democratic parties resemble the national Republican and Democratic parties only in those states where each party
represents separate socioeconomic constituencies. Party conflict over policy questions is most frequent in those states in which the Democratic
party represents central-city, low-income, ethnic, and racial constituencies, and the Republican party represents middle-class, suburban, small-
town, and rural constituencies.[13] In these larger urban industrialized
states, the Democratic and Republican parties will tend to disagree over
taxation and appropriations, welfare, education, and regulation of business and labor—that is, the major social and economic controversies that
divide the national parties.

In contrast, state parties do not necessarily reflect national party differences in homogeneous states, where there are no major social divisions in
the electorate. For example, the Democratic party does not fully reflect the
views of labor groups, Catholic voters, and racial and ethnic minorities
in those midwestern and New England states that do not have large
numbers of these kinds of voters. In these states the Democratic party
will tend to be atypical of the national Democratic party and will tend
to represent the attitudes of small-town and rural residents, farmers, and
shopkeepers. Similarly, the Republican party in New York cannot afford
the image of a party devoted to the interests of white, Protestant, middle-
class, small-town, rural people. New York's large number of Catholics
and Jews, ethnic groups, Negroes and Puerto Ricans, low-income, urban
dwellers make the New York state Republican party something different
from the national Republican party. The Democratic party in southern
states has not been associated with urban, ethnic, or racial minorities;
quite the contrary, it has been the party of the "establishment." The fact
that the national Democratic party has been associated at various times
with the aspirations of minorities in America, including the black, has
caused quite a bit of confusion and frustration among the ranks of traditional southern Democrats. "I am a *Georgia* Democrat" is a common

[13]See Thomas A. Flinn, "Party Responsibility in the States: Some Causal Factors,"
American Political Science Review, 58 (1964), 60–71; Duncan MacRae, Jr., "The Rela-
tion between Roll Call Votes and Constituencies in the Massachusetts House of
Representatives," *American Political Science Review*, 46 (1952), 1046–55; and Thomas
R. Dye, "A Comparison of Constituency Influences in the Upper and Lower Chambers
of a State Legislature," *Western Political Quarterly*, 14 (1961), 473–80.

phrase by which Georiga Democrats disassociate themselves from the national image of their party.[14] In the long run, however, the influence of mass communication, and the concentration of attention on national affairs, may cause state parties to reflect increasingly the views of the national parties.

STATE PARTY ORGANIZATIONS

State party organizations generally consist of a "state committee," a "state chairman," and perhaps a small office staff working at the state capitol. Democratic and Republican state committees vary from state to state in composition, organization, and functions; they are generally controlled by state law. Membership on the state committee may range from about a dozen up to several hundred. The members may be chosen through party primaries or by state party conventions. Generally, representation on state committees is allocated to counties, but occasionally other units of government are recognized in state party organization. A state party chairman generally serves at the head of the state committee; state chairmen are generally selected by the state committee, but their selection is often dictated by the party's candidate for governor.

State committees are supposed to direct the campaigns for important statewide elections—governors and U.S. senators, and congressmen in the smaller states. They are supposed to serve as central coordinating agencies for these election campaigns and to serve as the party's principal fundraising organization in the state. However, the role of the state committee very often depends upon the preferences of the party's statewide candidates regarding the handling of their campaigns. Often candidates have their own campaign organizations to plan and execute campaign strategy. State party organizations may or may not play an effective role in the candidate's campaign, depending upon the candidate's preferences. State committees are not very responsive to the direction of the national committee, and in most states, city and county party organizations operate quite independently of the state committees. In other words, there is no real hierarchy of authority in state party systems. As V. O. Key explained: "The party organization is sometimes regarded as a hierarchy, based upon the precinct executive, and capped by the national committee, but it may be more accurately described as a system of layers of organization. Each successive layer—county or city, state, national—has an independent concern about elections in its geographical jurisdiction. Yet each higher level

[14]For a description of contrasting views of the national Democratic party and the Mississippi Democratic party, see F. Glenn Abney, "Partisan Realignment in a One-Party System," *Journal of Politics*, 31 (November 1969), 1102–6.

of organization, to accomplish its ends, must obtain the collaboration of the lower layer or layers of organization. That collaboration comes about, to the extent that it does come about, through a sense of common cause rather than by the exercise of command."[15]

Party organizations at the city and county level are probably the most cohesive organizations within the parties. The nation's three thousand Republican and three thousand Democratic county chairmen probably constitute the most important building blocks in party organization in America. City and county party officers and committees are chosen locally and cannot be removed by any higher party authority. City and county committees are elected by the voters in their constituency, and they cannot be removed by state committees or national committees of their party, even if they decide to campaign for the opposition party. For example, many Democratic party officials in the South openly campaigned for Goldwater (1964), Wallace (1968), and Nixon (1972), yet there was little the state or national Democratic party organizations could do about it. In short, authority is not concentrated in any single statewide organization but is divided among many city and county party organizations.

State party organizations have also been weakened by our system of primary elections for determining the party's nominee for statewide office. State party organizations were very powerful in the nineteenth century, when state party conventions made the nominations for statewide office. But with the advent of the primary system, support from party leaders was no longer a prerequisite for a party nomination, and anyone who wished to run for governor, senator, or other statewide offices could organize a group of supporters to place his name on the party's primary ballot.[16] The state party organization or convention may give an "official" endorsement to a candidate in the primary, but such an endorsement may or may not carry weight with the party's rank-and-file voters.

Although state party organizations are weakened by decentralization, state party chairmen are by no means political hacks. Most state chairmen have been successful businessmen, lawyers, or public officials, who

15V. O. Key, Jr., *Politics, Parties, and Pressure Groups* (New York: Thomas Y. Crowell Company, 1964), p. 316.

16Every state except Connecticut by law requires that party candidates for public office be nominated by direct primaries. Even southern states, which once permitted their weak Republican parties to nominate candidates by convention, now hold Republican primaries. Under a unique "challenge primary" law, Connecticut allows party candidates to be selected by party conventions, *but* anyone who wins 20 percent of the vote of convention delegates and fails to win the nomination may choose to "challenge" the convention winner in a party primary election. If no one "challenges" the convention's choice, he becomes the party's nominee in the general election and no primary is held. See Duane Lockard, *Connecticut's Challenge Primary* (New York: Henry Holt and Co., 1959).

serve in their posts without salaries to satisfy their interest in politics and public affairs.[17] Republican chairmen are more likely to have held important positions in business and management, while Democratic chairmen are more likely to be lawyers who have previously held political office. Most state parties have small paid staffs operating under a full-time executive director who is responsible to the state chairman and the state committee.

City and county, rather than state, party organizations are the most cohesive level of organization. City machines and bosses are discussed at length in Chapter 9, together with the reform movements which have attempted to counter their power. There are very few *state-wide* machines headed by *state* bosses that command the loyalties of their county chairmen and direct party affairs from a statewide perspective. Ed Crump, from Memphis, Tennessee, was said to manage governors and legislators in the same way he managed mayors. Huey Long's organization in Louisiana in the 1920s and 1930s and the Harry Byrd organization in Virginia from the 1930s to the 1960s could be classified as statewide machines. They were tightly disciplined party organizations, held together and motivated by a desire for tangible benefits rather than by principle or ideology. They established a system of rewards and punishments in which votes were obtained by trading off social services, patronage jobs, and petty favors; these were, in turn, paid for by kickbacks from public contractors, bribes from holders of business franchises, contributions from persons with an interest in specific public policies, and other proceeds from the sale of government benefits. It is not a coincidence that most statewide machines developed in the poor rural states, particularly in the South. It is in these states, with their rural economies, lower family income, and poorly educated work forces, that patronage looks most attractive, and local pork barrel projects are most important. "Ole Gene" Talmadge found that Georgia's county chairmen could be bought relatively cheaply; all that was required was a firm grip on the state highway department, which acted as the chief dispenser of patronage and pork in the Talmadge organization. It is also in the poorer rural states where demagoguery can be an important instrument of power, supplementing the use of patronage and pork. A demagogue plays upon racial and religious prejudice and fear to attract uneducated masses to his cause. However, statewide political machines are highly exceptional, and on the whole, state party organizations are quite decentralized. (See Chapter 9 for further discussion.)

[17]See Charles W. Wiggins and William L. Turk, "State Party Chairmen: A Profile," *Western Political Quarterly*, 23 (June 1970), 321–32.

FIVE

Legislators
in
State Politics

FUNCTIONS OF STATE LEGISLATURES

If you were to ask state legislators what the job of the legislature is, they might say: "Our job is to pass laws," or "We have to represent the people," or "We have to make policy." All the answers are correct. But none by itself tells the whole story of the role of the legislature in state politics.

It is true that, from a legal viewpoint, the function of state legislatures is to "pass laws," that is, the enactment of statutory law. In the early 1950s American state legislators considered about 25,000 bills a year, but by the 1970s this figure had grown to over 150,000. The total number of state legislative enactments grew from approximately 15,000 to over 50,000 in that same twenty-year period.[1] As our society grows more complex and becomes increasingly urban and industrial, the need for formal statutory control seems to grow. Legislatures in urban industrial states will enact more than 1,000 laws in a legislative session, while legislatures in rural agricultural states will enact fewer than 500.

The range of subject matter of bills considered by a legislature is

---

[1]Council of State Governments, *Book of the States*. Published biennially by the Council of State Governments, Chicago.

enormous. A legislature may consider the authorization of a billion dollars of state spending, or it may debate the expansion of the hunting season on raccoons, or it may increase teachers' salaries, or it may argue over an appropriate color for automobile license plates. Obviously, these considerations range from the trivial to the vital; yet every bill that comes into the legislature is important to someone. In addition to the enactment of statutory law, legislatures share in the process of state constitutional revision, approve many of the governor's appointments, establish U.S. congressional districts, and consider amendments to the U.S. Constitution. But perhaps their single most important legal function is the passage of the appropriation and tax measures in the state budget. No state monies may be spent without a legislative appropriation, and it is difficult to think of any governmental action that does not involve some financial expenditure. Potentially, a legislature can control any activity of the state government through its power over appropriations, but as a practical matter, this legal power over fiscal affairs does not amount to political control.

From a political viewpoint, the function of state legislatures is to resolve conflicts over public policy. But it is misleading to say merely that the legislature "makes policy." Obviously, the legislature is not the only group that helps to make policy. The governor, the courts, executive agencies, interest groups, the press, political parties, and many other groups of individuals share in the making of public policy. How, then, do we distinguish the role of the legislature from that of other groups? For example, does the legislature merely "rubber stamp" the decisions of a strong governor or of the influential leaders of powerful interest groups? Or are legislatures themselves an important part of the process of proposing and deciding public policy? Does the legislature merely referee political struggles between organized interests in the state, recording the terms of surrender, compromises, or conquests in the form of statutes, or does the legislature exercise independent influence over policy? Are legislatures "initiators" of public policy, or do they merely express public sentiment in favor of or in opposition to policies initiated by others? These are the critical questions about the function of legislatures in state politics.

It is true, from the point of view of representation, that the legislature functions to "represent the people." But the question remains, "How does a state legislature go about representing the people?" Do legislators simply "mirror" the views of their constituents, or do they exercise independent judgment in determining policy judgments? Do legislators follow public opinion, or do they try to educate the people about the public issues and change their opinion before the next election? And exactly who are "the people" the legislator represents? Does the legislator represent the views of the state's population, his own constituents, or particular groups within his constituency? How does he respond to the appeals of the governor, influential party leaders, or important interest groups in his state? Does he vote along party lines to uphold the party platform with which he is affiliated, or does he ignore party labels in legislative issues? What role do liberal or conservative ideologies play in determining a state legislator's behavior. In short, in "representing the people," does a legislator reflect the views of his state, his constituency, groups within his constituency, his party, or his own conscience? We hope in this chapter to explore some of the forces influencing the way in which legislatures "represent the people."

THE MAKING OF A STATE LEGISLATOR

People need not be physically represented in a legislature in order for their interests to be recognized. State legislators are not "representative" of the population of their states in the sense of being typical cross sections of them. On the contrary, state legislators are generally selected from the better-educated, more prestigiously employed, middle-class segments of the population. Yet our system of popular elections requires these legislators to "represent" the interests of their constituents, even though they do not share the same social background as their constituents.

However, evidence indicates that legislators generally mirror their constituents in certain "birthright" characteristics—race, religion, and ethnic and national background. In a thorough study of the Pennsylvania state legislature, for example, Frank Sorauf found that religious composition of constituencies had a distinct impact on both Democratic and Republican candidates.[2] Protestant candidates came from Protestant districts, and Catholics tended to win in Catholic districts. These religious differences parallel ethnic differences. Catholic candidates seldom won in the Protestant "Bible Belt" counties of Pennsylvania, nor did Lutherans or Presbyterians win in the Irish and Italian wards of Philadelphia.

Another social characteristic in which the constituencies demand conformity is race. Of the nearly eight thousand state legislators in the nation, no more than two hundred are black. Blacks are reasonably well represented in the legislatures of northern urban industrial states (see Table 5–1) where the black population is concentrated in core areas of large cities. Blacks are seriously underrepresented in the legislatures

[2]Frank J. Sorauf, *Party and Representation* (New York: Atherton Press, 1963), pp. 89–94.

TABLE 5-1

Social Background of State Legislators, Selected States

	Percent College Graduate	Percent Professional, Managerial, or Sales	Percent Farmers and Farm Laborers	Percent Catholic	Percent Black (1970)
California					
Population	10	48	2	22	7.0
Legislators (1957)	54	86	13	17	5.8
New Jersey					
Population	8	45	1	37	10.7
Legislators (1957)	63	92	2	36	3.4
Ohio					
Population	7	40	3	18	9.1
Legislators (1957)	58	88	10	23	9.8
Tennessee					
Population	5	35	10	1	16.1
Legislators (1957)	46	84	13	2	6.1
Pennsylvania					
Population	6	39	2	27	8.6
Legislators (1958)	32	76	5	34	4.3
Georgia					
Population	6	35	8	0.9	25.9
Legislators (1961)	57	78	22	0.4	6.0
Wisconsin					
Population	7	37	11	29	2.9
Legislators (1953)	40	68	22	33	0.8

SOURCE: Figures are derived from the following: John C. Wahlke et. al., THE LEG-ISLATIVE SYSTEM (New York: John Wiley & Sons, Inc., 1962), pp. 486-91; Frank J. Sorauf, PARTY AND REPRESENTATION (New York: Atherton Press, 1963), pp. 69-71; THE WISCONSIN BLUE BOOK 1954; GEORGIA OFFICIAL AND STAT-ISTICAL REGISTER 1961; National Council of Churches of Christ, CHURCHES AND CHURCH MEMBERSHIP IN THE U.S. (New York, 1956); U.S. Bureau of the Census, U.S. CENSUS OF POPULATION 1960, "United States Summary" PC1-1C (Washington, D.C.: Government Printing Office, 1962); Congressional Quarterly Service, REVOLUTION IN CIVIL RIGHTS, 4th ed.(Washington, D.C., 1968), p. 114; and U.S. Bureau of the Census, STATISTICAL ABSTRACT OF THE UNITED STATES 1971 (Washington: Government Printing Office, 1971), p.363.

of southern and border rural states. This underrepresentation occurs primarily because blacks are spread out in rural areas rather than concentrated in black urban constituencies. The vast majority of the nation's black state legislators are Democrats elected from ghetto areas of large cities. At present this is true in the South as well as in the North; for example, all Georgia's black legislators are from Atlanta's ghetto area. (There are some predominantly black rural constituencies in the Deep South states, particularly Mississippi, which soon may elect some black legislators.) For the near future, it is very likely that all, or nearly all, black state legislators in the nation will come from majority black constituencies. From the viewpoint of representation, the ghettos, with their concentration of black voters, grant blacks an advantage in capturing legislative seats. This advantage is lost when the black vote is spread out and diluted. For the same reason, single-member legislative districts grant blacks an advantage in capturing legislative seats over multimember districts which dilute the black vote to the point where it is less than a majority.

Legislators are far less mobile than the population as a whole. They tend to have deep roots in their constituencies. One study reported that 83 percent of the state legislators of New Jersey had been born in the district they represented or had lived there over thirty years; in Tennessee this figure was 76 percent and in Ohio it was 88 percent. Even in California, one of the states with the highest population mobility, 56 percent of the legislators had been born in their district or had lived there thirty years, and only 10 percent had lived in their districts less than ten years.[3]

Certain social characteristics, however, escape the constituencies' demand for conformity. More than three-quarters of the nation's state legislators have been exposed to a college education, a striking contrast to the educational level of the total population. Legislators are also concentrated in the occupations with more prestige. A great majority of legislators are either engaged in the professions or are proprietors, managers, or officials of business concerns. Farmers constitute a sizable minority of legislators in all but the most urban states. Lawyers are the largest single occupational group.

Women in our population are seldom represented by more than 5 percent of the members of any state legislature. Sorauf reports that the legislative chambers bear the signs of the male club—highly burnished cuspidors, for example; the lady legislator "may be viewed as an intruder in the smoking-room company."[4] Women are somewhat better represented (up to 18 percent) in the less populous New England and western states with less "professional" legislatures; the large urban industrial states with more "professional" legislatures have few female representatives.[5]

Since the populations of the fifty states vary in ethnic and religious composition, it can be expected that state chambers will reflect ethnic

[3] John C. Wahlke et al., *The Legislative System* (New York: John Wiley & Sons, Inc., 1962), p. 488.

[4] Sorauf, *Party and Representation*, p. 67.

[5] For an excellent survey of women in state legislatures from 1921 to 1964, see Emmy F. Werner, "Women in State Legislatures," *Western Political Quarterly*, 21 (March 1968), 40–50.

and religious attributes in varying proportions. Table 5–1 indicates that the educational and occupational levels of legislators in every state will tend to be higher than the general population in those states. There is, however, a tendency for legislatures to reflect their states in certain characteristics. The Catholic percentage of the population in New Jersey, Pennsylvania, and Wisconsin is higher than in the other states, and there are more Catholics in these legislatures. There are very few Catholics in the population or the legislature of Tennessee and Georgia. The farm populations of Tennessee, Georgia, and Wisconsin are larger than those of the other states, and there are correspondingly more farmers in their legislatures.

Social background information on state legislators also indicates that legislators tend to come from the "upwardly mobile" sectors of the population.[6] This places many of them among the "second-rung" elites in the status system rather than the established wealth. Although the sons and grandsons of distinguished old families of great wealth are increasingly entering presidential and gubernatorial politics in the states, they seldom run for the state legislature. In contrast, state legislators have tended to take up occupations with more prestige than their fathers. Legislators are frequently among the middle or upper-middle status groups for whom politics is an avenue of upward mobility. Constituencies accept higher educated, more "prestigiously" employed candidates in the name of success, status, and the popular conceptions of "qualifications" for the legislative job. In general, constituencies seek gregarious, socially rising men from the prevailing racial, religious, and nationality groups of the district. Candidates should be "respectable" in whatever ways the local mores define that term. The voters seem to want candidates typical of themselves in religion, race, and ethnic background, but with education, occupation, and social status above the average. In short, constituents seem to prefer that their legislators be "local boys made good."[7]

Occupational data also clearly indicate that the state legislator's job is a part-time one with a salary that is not self-supporting. Legislators must come from occupational groups with flexible work responsibility.

---

[6]The data on social characteristics of state legislators are voluminous. More useful studies include Charles S. Hyneman, "Who Makes Our Laws," *Political Science Quarterly*, 55 (1940), 556–81; Paul Beckett and Celeste Sunderland, "Washington State Lawmakers," *Western Political Quarterly*, 10 (1957), 180–202; Joseph A. Schlesinger, "Lawyers and American Politics," *Midwest Journal of Political Science*, 1 (1957), 26–39; David Derge, "The Lawyer as Decision-Maker in American State Legislatures," *Journal of Politics*, 21 (1959), 408–33; Victor S. Hjelm and Joseph P. Pisciotte, "Profiles and Careers of Colorado State Legislators," *Western Political Quarterly*, 21 (December 1968), 698–722; Wahlke et al., *The Legislative System*, pp. 489–90; and Sorauf *Party and Representation*, pp. 75–81.

[7]Sorauf, *Party and Representation*, p. 91.

The lawyer, the farmer, or the business owner can adjust his work to the legislative schedule, but the office manager cannot. The overrepresented occupations are those involving extensive public contact. The lawyer, insurance agent, farm implement dealer, tavern owner, and undertaker establish in their businesses the wide circle of friends necessary for political success. In short, the legislator's occupation should provide free time, public contacts, and social respectability.

The overrepresentation of lawyers among state legislators is particularly marked. It is sometimes argued that the lawyer brings a special kind of skill to politics. The lawyer's occupation is the representation of clients, so he makes no great change in occupation when he moves from representing clients in private practice to representing constituents in the legislature. A lawyer is trained to deal with public policy as it is reflected in the statute books, so he may be reasonably familiar with public policy before entering the legislature. Also, service in the legislature can help a lawyer's private practice through free public advertising and opportunities to make contacts with potential clients.[8]

The state legislature is a convenient starting place for a political career. About one-half of the state legislators in the nation had never served in public office before their election to the legislature, and a greater percentage of new members are in the lower rather than upper chambers. The other half had only limited experience on city councils, county commissions, and school boards. The record of turnover of state legislators suggests that returning to office is not particularly important to many of them. Thus, in many ways the state legislatures appear "amateurish" in comparison with Congress, where turnover is low and members acquire more parliamentary skills. The high turnover clearly is *not* a product of competition for the job; only a very small proportion of state legislators are rejected at the polls. Most simply do not seek reelection and quit because of dissatisfaction: "Being in the legislature has hurt my law practice and cost me money"; "Any way you look at it, the job means a sacrifice to you, your home, and your business"; "It's a nervous life"; "The more service a man has, the more enemies he makes."[9]

Why does a legislator decide to run for office in the first place? It is next to impossible to determine the real motivations of political office seekers—they seldom know themselves. Legislators will usually describe their motivations in highly idealistic terms: "I felt that I could do the community a service"; "I considered it a civic duty."[10] Only seldom are

<hr />

[8]Schlesinger, "Lawyers and American Politics," pp. 26–39; Derge, "The Lawyer as Decision-Maker in American State Legislatures," pp. 408–33.

[9]Quotations from state legislators interviewed by Wahlke et al., *The Legislative System*, pp. 95–134.

[10]*Ibid.*

reasons for candidacy expressed in personal terms: "Oh, I just think it's lots of fun." Occasionally a state legislator admits that legislative service is an alternative to unemployment. Gregariousness and the desire to socialize no doubt contribute to the reasons for some office seekers. Politics can have a special lure of its own: "It gets into your blood and you like it." Particular issues may mobilize a political career but ideological involvement occupies a relatively unimportant place in a candidate's motives. Activity in organizations that are deeply involved in politics often leads to candidacy: "When I decided to run, I was quite active in the union."

An individual faces two important obstacles when he decides to run for the state legislature: the primary and the general election. His seat in the legislature depends on how much competition he meets in these elections. First let us consider competition in the primary elections. Available evidence indicates that more than half of the nation's state legislators are unopposed for their party's nomination in primary elections. Many legislators who do face primary competition have only token opposition. V. O. Key has shown that most primary competition occurs in a party's "sure" districts, some competition occurs in "close" districts, and there is a distinct shortage of candidates in districts where thae party's chances are poor."[11] In other words, primary competition is greater where the likelihood of victory in the general election is greater. Exceptions to this generalization are found in districts where the incumbent legislator is so strong that he discourages prospective competitors, even though chances for the party's success in the general election may be good.

The culmination of the recruitment process is in the general election, yet in many legislative constituencies one party is so entrenched that the voters have little real choice at the general election. In many one-party states, the minority party is so weak that it fails to run candidates for many legislative seats. In the southern and border states where the legislatures are heavily Democratic, there often is no competition in the general election for legislative seats. (Of course, in these states primary competition in the majority party is frequent.) More seats are contested in states with close two-party competition, but even in a hotly contested state such as Pennsylvania, nominations to the state legislature occasionally will not be filled because of a collapse in local party organization in certain districts. "Competition" implies more than a name filed under the opposition party label. Generally a competitive election is one in which the winning candidate wins by something less than two to one. In light of this more realistic definition of competition, the

---

[11]V. O. Key, Jr., *American State Politics: An Introduction* (New York: Alfred A. Knopf, Inc., 1956), pp. 171–81.

absence of truly competitive politics in state legislative elections is striking. Even in Pennsylvania, over half of the state legislators are elected by margins in excess of two to one.[12] Similar findings are reported for competitive Massachusetts and Michigan.[13]

LEGISLATORS REPRESENT PEOPLE, NOT TREES OR ACRES

The politics of representation center about the size and composition of legislative districts and who gains and who loses from the variations. Inequality of representation, or "malapportionment," is claimed when there are differing numbers of people in districts that receive the same number of representatives in the legislature. For example, if one legislator represents a district of ten thousand inhabitants and another a district of forty thousand, it is said that the right to vote in the smaller districts is worth four times as much as it is in the larger district.

Prior to 1962 malapportionment was widespread in American state legislatures. Small minorities of the population could elect a majority of the house or senate or both in most of the states (see Table 5–2). Generally it was the rural voters in a state who controlled a majority of legislative seats, and it was the urban voters who were discriminated against in the value of their vote.[14]

For many years the federal courts avoided the distasteful task of compelling legislative reapportionment by asserting that this was a legislative rather than a judicial function. Underrepresented populations were told by the courts that their remedy was to elect a legislature that would do its duty, a worthless prescription, of course, since electing a legislature was the very thing underrepresented populations could not do.[15] The position of the courts changed radically, however, after the U.S. Supreme Court decision in *Baker* v. *Carr.*[16] This case involved the complaint of urban residents in Tennessee where the largest district in the lower house was twenty-three times larger than the smallest district. Petitioners argued that such inequalities in state apportionment

---

[12]Sorauf, *Party and Representation*, p. 117.

[13]Duncan MacRae, "The Relations between Roll-Call Votes and Constituencies in the Massachusetts House of Representatives," *American Political Science Review,* 46 (1952), 1046–55; Robert W. Becker et al., "Correlates of Legislative Voting," *Midwest Journal of Political Science,* 6 (1962), 384–96.

[14]Paul T. David and Ralph Eisenberg, *Devaluation of the Urban and Suburban Vote* (Charlottesville: Bureau of Public Administration, University of Virginia, 1961). See also Manning J. Dauer and Robert G. Kelsay, "Unrepresentative States," *National Municipal Review,* 44 (1955), 551–75.

[15]Colegrove v. Green, 328 U.S. 549 (1946).

[16]Baker v. Carr, 369 U.S. 186 (1962).

TABLE 5-2
Changes in Representation Resulting from Reapportionment of Legislatures
1962-1968

| | Minimum Percent of Population Which Could Elect a Majority | | | |
| | Senate | | House | |
	1962	1968	1962	1968
Alabama	25	48	26	48
Alaska	35	51	49	48
Arizona	13	52	NA	51
Arkansas	44	49	33	48
California	11	49	45	49
Colorado	30	50	32	54
Connecticut	33	48	12	44
Delaware	22	53	19	49
Florida	12	51	12	50
Georgia	23	48	22	43
Hawaii	23	50	48	43
Idaho	17	47	33	47
Illinois	29	50	40	49
Indiana	40	49	35	49
Iowa	35	45	27	45
Kansas	27	49	19	49
Kentucky	42	47	34	45
Louisiana	33	48	34	47
Maine	47	51	40	43
Maryland	14	47	25	48
Massachusetts	45	50	45	46
Michigan	29	53	44	51
Minnesota	40	48	35	47
Mississippi	35	49	29	48
Missouri	48	52	20	49
Montana	16	47	37	48
Nebraska	37	49	—	—
Nevada	8	50	35	48
New Hampshire	45	52	44	46
New Jersey	19	50	47	50
New Mexico	14	46	27	46
New York	41	49	33	49
North Carolina	37	49	27	48
North Dakota	32	47	40	47
Ohio	41	50	30	47
Oklahoma	25	49	30	49
Oregon	48	47	48	48
Pennsylvania	33	50	38	47
Rhode Island	18	50	47	49
South Carolina	23	48	46	46
South Dakota	38	47	39	47
Tennessee	27	49	29	47
Texas	30	49	39	47
Utah	21	48	33	48
Vermont	47	49	12	49
Virginia	38	48	37	47
Washington	34	48	35	47
West Virginia	47	47	40	46
Wisconsin	45	48	40	45
Wyoming	27	47	36	46

SOURCE: BOOK OF THE STATES 1968-69 (Lexington, Ky.: Council of State Governments, 1968), pp. 66-67.

laws denied them "equal protection of the laws" guaranteed by the Fourteenth Amendment and that the federal courts should grant relief from these inequalities. The Supreme Court decided (1) that even though apportionment is a legislative function, the federal courts can accept jurisdiction where a constitutional question is involved; (2) that voters in underrepresented areas are entitled to judicial relief from apportionment laws that violate constitutional mandates; and (3) that discriminatory and arbitrary state apportionment laws can violate the Fourteenth Amendment's prohibition against laws that deny citizens equal protection. The Supreme Court returned the Tennessee case to a lower federal court which ordered reapportionment.

Reaction to the decision was immediate and widespread. Underrepresented voters throughout the nation petitioned federal courts to order state legislative reapportionment on the basis of the equal protection clause of the Fourteenth Amendment. Federal courts found themselves struggling with the mathematics of apportionment. The courts did not decide on any firm mathematical standard of correct apportionment, holding only that "as nearly as practicable, one man's vote should be equal to another's."[17] State after state was induced to reapportion its legislature under the threat of judicial intervention. Federal courts generally allowed legislatures time to reapportion themselves, but token reapportionment was found unacceptable. The courts threatened to bar legislative elections by districts in states that failed to meet constitutional standards of apportionment. In addition to requiring population equality in legislative districting, the Supreme Court also required population equality in congressional districting by state legislatures[18] and threw out the county unit system of voting in statewide elections.[19] The philosophy underlying all these decisions was expressed by the Court: "The conception of political equality from the Declaration of Independence to Lincoln's Gettysburg Address, to the Fourteenth, Fifteenth, Seventeenth, and Nineteenth Amendments can mean only one thing— one person, one vote."[20] The Court made no distinction between malapportionment that was a product of state law and malapportionment that was embodied in state constitutions; both forms of malapportionment were declared to be in violation of the Fourteenth Amendment.

Two years after *Baker* v. *Carr*, the Supreme Court decided that representation in the second house of a state legislature also had to be based on population. Most state constitutions based representation in the upper chamber upon some unit of local government, rather than upon

[17]Westberry v. Sanders, 84 S. Ct. 526 (1964).
[18]*Ibid.*
[19]Gray v. Sanders, 83 S. Ct. 801 (1963).
[20]*Ibid.*, p. 809.

population. The justifications for such an arrangement are rooted deep in American democratic theory. The idea of bicameralism was based in part upon the advantages of having two separate systems of representation in a legislature. *The Federalist papers* vigorously defend a second chamber capable of checking the popular majority which was represented in the lower chamber and protecting interests which may be threatened by that majority. In 1964, however, the Supreme Court in *Reynolds* v. *Sims,* a case involving Alabama's attempt to base representation in its senate on counties, the Court decided that *both* houses of a state legislature must be fairly apportioned according to population.[21] In the words of Chief Justice Earl Warren, writing for the Court: "Legislators represent people, not trees or acres. Legislators are elected by voters, not farms or cities or economic interests. . . . The complexions of societies and civilizations change, often with amazing rapidity. A nation once primarily rural in character becomes predominantly urban. Representation schemes once fair and equitable became archaic and outdated."[22] The Court dismissed the federal analogy as "irrelevant" because "political subdivisions of states . . . never have been considered as sovereign entities."[23] The court argued that requiring both houses to have the same basis of representation did not make bicameralism meaningless, because differences between the houses in numbers, terms of office, and size of constituencies would still remain.

By 1968 every state had reapportioned one or both houses of its legislature, generally in response to a federal court order to do so. The results have been startling: Today there is very little malapportionment in any state, and "one man, one vote" is the prevailing style of representation (see Table 5–3).

THE IMPACT OF REAPPORTIONMENT

What has been the impact of reapportionment on state legislative politics? Reapportionment has significantly increased the representation afforded urban interests. Of course this is what reapportionment was

[21]Reynolds v. Sims, 84 S. Ct. 1362 (1964).
[22]*Ibid.*, p. 1381.
[23]Apparently representational schemes once fair and equitable can grow archaic very rapidly, for it was as late as 1948 that Earl Warren, the governor of California, wrote: "The agricultural counties of California are far more important in the life of our state than the relationship their population bears to the entire population of the state. It is for this reason that I never have been in favor of redistricting their representation in our state senate on a strictly population basis. It is the same reason that the founding fathers of our country gave balanced representation to the states of the Union, equal representation in one house and proportionate representation based on population in the other." Quoted in *Time*, June 26, 1962, p. 22.

TABLE 5-3

The Effects of Reapportionment on the
Representation Afforded Urban Communities in Georgia

	Percentage of State Population	Percentage of Representation			
		Senate		House	
		"Before"	"After"	"Before"	"After"
Atlanta metropolitan area	20.0	6.0	24.3	6.3	12.2
All metropolitan areas	39.0	14.3	44.3	15.1	29.1
All non-metropolitan areas	61.0	85.7	55.7	84.9	70.9
Urban counties (over 50% urban population)	53.3	28.7	52.0	24.9	43.8
Rural counties (less than 50% urban population)	46.7	71.3	47.9	75.1	51.2
Counties with cities over 50,000	28.2	11.2	37.0	10.2	28.1
Counties with cities 10,000 to 50,000	22.3	21.4	22.1	19.5	22.1
Counties with cities 10,000 or less	49.4	67.4	40.8	70.3	49.8

expected to do. But it is still interesting to observe the full impact of reapportionment in increasing the representation afforded urban constituencies and decreasing rural representation. Table 5–3 is illustrative of what happened in many states. The percentage of the state's population living in various types of urban communities is shown in the left column; these figures are compared with the percentage of house and senate seats afforded these communities "before" and "after" reapportionment. Georgia's urban counties, which contain 53.3 percent of the state's population, increased their representation in the Senate from 28.7 to 52.0 percent and in the House from 24.9 to 48.8 percent. Rural counties, which contain 46.7 percent of the state's population, decreased their representation from 71.3 to 47.9 percent in the Senate and from 75.1 to 51.2 percent in the House.

Finally, there is evidence that reapportionment has a significant impact on the kinds of people who are winning seats in state legislatures. Reapportionment seems to bring younger, better-educated, more prestigiously employed men into the legislature. It also brings many "new" people into legislative politics—men who have had little or no previous experience in public office. This, however, may be a temporary effect which will disappear after reapportionment legislatures have been functioning over time.

What has been the impact of reapportionment on the policy choices of state legislatures? There is no doubt that significant political differences exist between big-city and small-town or rural legislators and that malapportionment granted a real political advantage to the latter. If the perceptions of state legislators themselves about legislative conflict are to be given any weight, then rural-urban conflict not only is discernible but is the most important conflict in American state legislatures. Rural-urban conflict was the only type of conflict rated "important" by over half of the legislators interviewed in four separate states.[24] It seems safe to say that legislators from large central cities and those from rural areas and small towns differ over the following: housing and welfare measures, aid for urban renewal and mass transit, the division of the state's tax dollar, state aid to schools, the location of highways, and the regulating authority granted cities.[25] In some southern states, urban legislators represent a "moderate" approach to race relations, while segregationists remain strong in rural areas. According to the Advisory Commission on Intergovernmental Relations, the unrepresentativeness of state legislatures forced big cities to take their cause to the federal government where they felt cities could obtain a fairer hearing.[26] It was claimed that the rural character of state legislatures resulted in a bypassing of the states by cities requesting direct federal-to-local grants-in-aid, such as the federal public housing and urban renewal programs.

One must be cautious, however, in estimating the policy consequences of reapportionment. In the past proponents of reapportionment were overly enthusiastic about its expected consequences. Having attributed a lack of party competition, unfair distribution of state funds, conservative tax schemes, unprogressive education policies and penny-pinching welfare programs to rural overrepresentation, they naturally expected to see these policies change significantly with reapportionment. Yet there is little in the way of empirical evidence to support such hopes.

In the first place, even before *Baker* v. *Carr* there was no evidence that the policy choices of well-apportioned states differed significantly from the policy choices of malapportioned states. There were no significant differences between well-apportioned and malapportioned states in the levels of expenditures for welfare and education, the quality of public education, the tax burden, the revenue structure, the liberality of welfare benefits, or the extent of state participation in education, health, and welfare.[27] Most of the differences among the states in these

24Wahlke et al., *The Legislative System*, p. 425.

25See Malcolm Jewell, *The State Legislature* (New York: Random House, Inc., 1962), pp. 17–33; Loren P. Beth, *The Politics of Misrepresentation* (Baton Rouge: Louisiana University Press, 1962); and Gordon E. Baker, *Rural versus Urban Political Power* (New York: Doubleday & Co., Inc., 1955).

26Advisory Commission on Intergovernmental Relations, *A Report to the President for Transmittal to Congress* (Washington, D.C.: Government Printing Office, 1955), p. 39.

27Thomas R. Dye, "Malapportionment and Public Policy in the States," *Journal of Politics*, 27 (August 1965), 586–601; Herbert Jacob, "The Consequences of Malapportionment: A Note of Caution," *Social Forces* (Winter 1965), 256–61; and David kinds of policies were accounted for by differences in socioeconomic environment; apportionment practices seem to have little direct impact on these policies. Of course, it is possible that the policy impact of reapportionment will be subtle and diverse and that reapportionment will have a greater impact on the rural-urban division of *marginal increases* in public expenditures, in contrast to *overall levels* of public expenditures, sources, or benefits. But there is little evidence that the "one man, one vote" movement will dramatically change the nature or extent of state involvement in urban problems, and reapportionment certainly is not likely to solve any of the pressing problems of the nation's cities—poverty, racial tension, slum housing, congestion, and so forth.

If reapportionment does increase urban representation, why does it not lead to major policy changes? Within urban areas there are many real conflicts of interest between city and suburbs based upon the different attributes of persons living in each area. Crowded slum dwellers living in the central city have different opinions about public policy than inhabitants of suburban split-levels on half-acre lots. Blacks in ghettos have different policy positions than whites in suburbs. Often there are differences between the residents of medium-sized cities and the residents of a large central city in a metropolitan area. In contrast, rural legislators are much more likely to agree on policy issues and to vote in a bloc. On some issues we find a conservative coalition of suburban and rural legislators. Several studies of legislative voting have indicated that urban legislators have difficulty in agreeing on policy positions and voting as a bloc.[28]

Before reapportionment, Florida was one of the most malapportioned states in the nation, and many observers expected dramatic changes with reapportionment. There were many policy changes in Florida in the 1960s, perhaps even some that could be attributed to reapportionment. But as one Florida solon explained:

> The fellows from the upstate counties control the state's politics, no matter what happens with the one-man one-vote law. Those fellows work together and vote together whenever there's something really important coming up. They can stop the big cities cold whenever they want to.

Brady and Douglas Edmonds, *The Effects of Malapportionment on Policy Outputs in the American States* (Iowa City: Laboratory for Political Research, University of Iowa, 1966).

[28]David Derge, "Metropolitan and Outstate Alignments in the Illinois and Missouri Legislative Delegations," *American Political Science Review*, 52 (1958), 1052–65; Richard T. Frost, "On Derge's Metropolitan and Outstate Legislative Delegations," *American Political Science Review*, 53 (1959), 792–95; and Robert S. Friedman, "The Urban Rural Conflict Revisited," *Western Political Quarterly*, 14 (1961), 495.

Here's why: Take Dade County [Miami] for example. They've got 22 representatives in Tallahassee and you'd think that would give them a lot of power, but they're always fighting among themselves. When they split down the middle, they end up with a majority of one. That gives Dade County one vote while the Porkchoppers [rural legislators] are putting up a couple of dozen solid votes all one way.[29]

LEGISLATIVE ORGANIZATION AND PROCEDURE

The formal rules and procedures by which state legislatures operate are primarily designed to make the legislative process fair and orderly. Without established customs, rules, and procedures it would be impossible for fifty, one hundred, or two hundred men to arrive at a collective decision about the thousands of items submitted to them at a legislative session. State legislatures follow a fairly standard pattern in the formal process of making laws. Table 5–4 provides a brief description of some of the more important procedural steps in lawmaking.

What are the political consequences of the legislative procedures described in Table 5–4? Obviously, it is a very difficult process for a bill to become a law—legislative procedures offer many opportunities to defeat legislation. Formal rules and procedures of state legislatures lend themselves easily to those who would delay or obstruct legislation. Table 5–4 illustrates the deliberative function of legislatures and the consequent procedural advantages given to "conservative" forces; that is, those who would defend the *status quo*. Moreover, these procedures imply that the legislature is structured for deliberation, destruction, and delay in decision making, rather than speed and innovation. This suggests that the legislature functions as an arbiter, rather than an initiator, of public policy, since its procedures are designed to maximize deliberation, even at the expense of granting advantage to those who oppose change.

INFORMAL RULES OF THE GAME

Partly to counteract the impact of formal rules and procedures, legislatures have developed a number of informal "rules of the game." These unwritten rules are not merely quaint and curious folkways. They support the purposes and functions of the legislature by helping to maintain the working consensus among legislators so essential to legislative output. Some rules contribute to the legislative task by promoting group

[29]Tallahassee *Democrat*, October 26, 1969, p. B1.

TABLE 5-4

Summary of Legislative Procedure for Bill Passage

1. INTRODUCTION OF BILL	One or more members file bill with Clerk or presiding officer who gives it a number and refers it to a committee. This constitutes the first reading.
2. COMMITTEE HEARINGS	Important bills may be given public hearings at which all interested persons or groups may testify. Committee may speed or delay hearings.
3. COMMITTEE REPORT	Committee meets in executive (closed) session. Bills may be amended or pigeonholed or reported favorably or unfavorably.
4. BILL PLACED ON CALENDAR	Bills reported by committee are placed on calendar for floor consideration. Urgent or favorite bills may get priority by unanimous consent or informal maneuvering; other bills may be delayed, sometimes indefinitely.
5. FLOOR DEBATE, AMENDMENT, VOTE	The second reading of the bill before the entire chamber is usually accompanied by debate and perhaps amendments from the floor. Often the crucial vote is on an amendment or on second reading.
6. THIRD READING AND PASSAGE	Usually a bill is delayed one calendar day before it is brought to the floor for third reading. On third reading debate is not customary and amendments usually require unanimous consent. After final vote, bill is certified by presiding officer and sent to second house.
7. REFERRAL TO SECOND CHAMBER	Bill is sent to second chamber where steps 1 through 6 must be repeated. Bills must pass both chambers in identical form before going to governor.
8. CONFERENCE COMMITTEE	If there are differences in wording in the bills passed by each house, one or the other house must accept the wording of the other house or request a conference committee. This committee is made up of members of both houses and it arrives at a single wording for the bill.
9. VOTE ON CONFERENCE COMMITTEE REPORT	Both houses must vote to approve conference committee wording of bill. Bills may be shuttled back and forth and eventually die for lack of agreement between both houses.

TABLE 5-4 (Cont.)

10. GOVERNOR'S SIGNATURE OR VETO	An identical bill passed by both houses becomes law with the governor's signature. It may also become law without his signature after a certain lapse of time (e.g., 10 days) if the legislature is still in session. If the legislature has adjourned during this time, the governor's failure to sign is the same as a veto. A governor may formally veto a bill and return it to the house of origin for reconsideration. An unusual majority is generally required to override a veto.

cohesion and solidarity. In the words of legislators themselves: "Support another member's local bill if it doesn't affect you or your district"; "Don't steal another's bill"; "Accept the author's amendments to a bill"; "Don't make personal attacks on other members."[30] Other informal rules promote predictability of behavior: "Keep your word"; "Don't conceal the real purpose of bills or amendments"; "Notify in advance if you cannot keep a commitment." Other rules try to put limits on interpersonal conflict: "Be willing to compromise"; "Accept half a loaf"; "Respect the seniority system"; "Respect committee jurisdiction." Finally, other rules are designed to expedite legislative business: "Don't talk too much"; "Don't fight unnecessarily"; "Don't introduce too many bills and amendments"; "Don't point out the absence of a quorum"; "Don't be too political."

A most important informal device is unanimous consent for the suspension of formal rules; this permits a legislature to consider bills not on the calendar, pass bills immediately without the necessary three readings, dispense with time-consuming formalities, permit nonmembers to speak, and otherwise alter procedure. Another informal rule is the practice in many states of passing "local bills" that would affect only one area of a state without debate or opposition when the delegation in that area unanimously supports that bill.

Most of these rules are enforced by informal sanctions. The most frequently mentioned sanction involves obstructing the bills of an errant legislator by abstaining or voting against him, keeping his bills in committee, and amending his bills; or more personal sanctions, such as using the "silent treatment," not trusting him and removing patronage and good committee assignments. Other sanctions include denial of legislative courtesies and occasionally even overt demonstrations of displea-

[30]Quotations from state legislators interviewed by Wahle, *The Legislative System,* pp. 146–61.

sure, such as ridicule, hissing, or laughing. The observance of rules, however, is not obtained primarily through fear of sanction so much as the positive recognition by legislators of the usefulness of rules in helping the legislature perform its chores.

LEGISLATIVE COMMITTEES

While it is most convenient to study legislative decision making by observing floor actions, particularly the devision of ayes and nays, the floor is not the only locus of important legislative devisions. Many observers and legislators feel that committee work is essential to the legislative process. It is here that public hearings are held, policies pleaded and debated, legislation amended and compromised, bills rushed to the floor or pigeonholed. Harmon Zeigler writes: "The committee hearing is generally the most important source of information for legislators, and lobbyists tend to flock to the committee rooms as the focal point of their contact with legislators.[31] The function of the committee system is to reduce legislative work to manageable proportions by providing for a division of labor among legislators. But by so doing the committees themselves often come to exercise considerable influence over the outcome of legislation. Another opportunity is provided for delay and obstruction by less than the majority of legislators, sometimes by a single committee chairman. Duane Lockard reports, "What a new legislator soon finds is that there is no choice but to depend upon his colleagues to inform him about issues assigned to their committees, and, like it or not, he is reduced to following their advice unless he knows the subject well enough to have an opinion. It is a source of surprise to many new members how many issues they are too ignorant to have an opinion about. . . ."[32]

A typical legislative chamber will have between twenty and thirty standing committees which consider all bills in a particular field, such as revenue, appropriations, highways, welfare, education, labor, judiciary, or local government. Many houses operate with a rules committee which governs house proceedings and determines the priority given the bills on the legislative calendar. Committees may prevent the bill from coming to the floor for vote by inaction ("pigeonholing"), although twenty states require every committee to report on every bill either favorably or unfavorably.

The importance of committee systems seems to vary from state to

[31]Harmon Zeigler and Michael Baer, *Lobbying: Interaction and Influence in American State Legislatures* (Belmont: Wadsworth Publishing Co., 1969), p. 126.

[32]Duane Lockard, *The Politics of State and Local Government* (New York: The Macmillan Company, 1963), p. 28.

state. Yet Malcolm Jewell argues effectively that state legislative committees do not exercise the independent influence over legislation that congressional committees enjoy. He offers several reasons "why legislative standing committees are but pale shadows of their Congressional counterparts.[33] Most state legislatures meet only a few months every other year, giving committees very little time for any careful review of bills. Committees seldom have any staff assistance, legislative turnover is high, a seniority system is not as prevalent as it is in Congress, and committee members seldom acquire the experience and expertise of their congressional counterparts. In most state legislatures the rules committee does not have the power to determine what bills will reach the floor as does the rules committee of the U.S. House of Representatives. The committee system, in short, does not offer the state legislator an independent source of power separate from party or factional basis of power. Of course, the fact that legislative committees are not independent sources of power does not mean that they are never used as important instruments of party or factional control.[34]

These among other studies suggest the following explanations for variations among the several states and the strength of their committee system: (1) Committees exercise less independent influence over legislation in two-party states where party discipline is high; (2) committees exercise less influence in two-party states when the governor and the legislature are of the same party but exercise more influence under divided government; (3) in states where the governor, the party, or a faction exercises strong influence over the legislature, committees are not likely to play an independent role; and (4) in contrast, committees are more likely to be influential in one-party states where the governor does not exert strong leadership.

LEGISLATIVE PROFESSIONALISM

Some state legislatures are highly professional, while others are not. By *professional* we mean that in some legislatures the members are well-paid and tend to think of their jobs as full-time ones; members and committees are well staffed and have good informational services available to them; and a variety of legislative services, such as bill drafting and statutory revision, are well supported and maintained. In other

[33] Jewell, *The State Legislature*, p. 93.
[34] See Loren P. Beth and William C. Havard, "Committee Stacking and Political Power in Florida," *Journal of Politics*, 23 (1961), 57–83. In contrast, see Gilbert Y. Steiner and Samuel K. Gove, *Legislative Politics in Illinois* (Urbana: University of Illinois Press, 1960), pp. 12–13.

legislatures, members are poorly paid and regard their legislative work as part time; there is little in the way of staff for legislators or committees; and little or nothing is provided in the way of legislative assistance and services.

The Citizens Conference on State Legislatures has undertaken to rank the states according to their idea of legislative professionalism. This organization is a reform-oriented good-government group which has studied and evaluated various aspects of legislative life in the states, as described in Table 5–5. Note that this tables does *not* rank state legislatures according to the wisdom of their legislation, but only according to their institutional character.

The pay, perquisites, and working conditions of legislators vary a great deal from state to state. In general, the more populous urban industrial states provide more comfortable environments for their legislators than do the smaller rural states. California legislators receive an annual salary of $16,000, and legislators in Massachusetts, Michigan, and New York receive compensation in excess of $10,000 per year. In contrast, New Hampshire pays its legislators $200 for the biennium. It is not surprising that turnover is higher among legislators in rural than in the urban states. The larger urban states, however, tend to consider more legislation, remain in session longer, and demand more time of their legislators. This means that their legislators probably devote a smaller proportion of their time to private business and become more dependent on their legislative salary.

ROLE PLAYING IN LEGISLATURES

Roles are expectations about the kind of behavior people ought to exhibit. Expectations are placed upon a legislator by his fellow legislators, his party, the opposition party, the governor, his constituents, interest groups, and his friends, as well as by himself.

Perhaps the most distinctive roles in the legislative process are those of the leadership. A typical legislative chamber has a presiding officer, a majority and a minority floor leader, a number of committee chairmen, and a steering committee. These leaders perform functions similar to the functions of rules. First of all, leaders are expected to help make the legislative system stable and manageable. They are expected to maintain order, to know the rules and procedures, to follow the rules, and to show fairness and impartiality. Leaders are also expected to help focus the issues and resolve conflict by presenting issues clearly, narrowing the alternatives, organizing public hearings, and promoting the party or administrative point of view on bills. The majority leader is supposed to "get the administrative program through," while the minority leader "tries to develop criticism," "find party issues," and "develop a con-

TABLE 5-5
Rankings of State Legislatures

Major factors considered under the five categories:

Functional—time and its utilization, availability of staffing physical facilities such as office space, size of the legislature, number of committees, organization, and procedures.

Accountable—districting, method of leadership selection, adequacy of information necessary for lawmaking, public access to voting records and actual deliberations, character and quality of bill drafting, leadership constraints, and treatment of minority party.

Informed—amount of time devoted to legislative process, number of standing committees, handling of testimony, staffing between sessions, reports filing, form and character of bills, and professional staff resources.

Independent—independence of legislative from state's executive branch, frequency and duration of sessions, compensation of members, regulating of special interest groups and lobbyists, control of conflicts of interest.

Representative—qualification, compensation, and voting requirements of legislators; size and complexity of each legislative body; diffusion and restraints on the leadership; relationship of members and constituents.

Overall Rank	State	Functional	Accountable	Informed	Independent	Representative
1	California	1	3	2	3	2
2	New York	4	13	1	8	1
3	Illinois	17	4	6	2	13
4	Florida	5	8	4	1	30
5	Wisconsin	7	21	3	4	10
6	Iowa	6	6	5	11	25
7	Hawaii	2	11	20	7	16
8	Michigan	15	22	9	12	3
9	Nebraska	35	1	16	30	18
10	Minnesota	27	7	13	23	12
11	New Mexico	3	16	28	39	4
12	Alaska	8	29	12	6	40
13	Nevada	13	10	19	14	32
14	Oklahoma	9	27	24	22	8
15	Utah	38	5	8	29	24
16	Ohio	18	24	7	40	9
17	South Dakota	23	12	15	16	37
18	Idaho	20	9	29	27	21
19	Washington	12	17	25	19	39
20	Maryland	16	31	10	15	45
21	Pennsylvania	37	23	23	5	36
22	North Dakota	22	18	17	37	31
23	Kansas	31	15	14	32	34
24	Connecticut	39	26	26	25	6
25	West Virginia	10	32	37	24	15
26	Tennessee	30	44	11	9	26
27	Oregon	28	14	35	35	19
28	Colorado	21	25	21	28	27
29	Massachusetts	32	35	22	21	23
30	Maine	29	34	32	18	22
31	Kentucky	49	2	48	44	7
32	New Jersey	14	42	18	31	35
33	Louisiana	47	39	33	13	14

TABLE 5-5 (Cont.)

Overall Rank	State	Functional	Accountable	Informed	Independent	Representative
34	Virginia	25	19	27	26	48
35	Missouri	36	30	40	49	5
36	Rhode Island	33	46	30	41	11
37	Vermont	19	20	34	42	47
38	Texas	45	36	43	45	17
39	New Hampshire	34	33	42	36	43
40	Indiana	44	38	41	43	20
41	Montana	26	28	31	46	49
42	Mississippi	46	43	45	20	28
43	Arizona	11	47	38	17	50
44	South Carolina	50	45	39	10	46
45	Georgia	40	49	36	33	38
46	Arkansas	41	40	46	34	33
47	North Carolina	24	37	44	47	44
48	Delaware	43	48	47	38	29
49	Wyoming	42	41	50	48	42
50	Alabama	48	50	49	50	41

SOURCE: Citizens Conference on State Legislatures.

structive opposition."[35] Leaders are also expected to administer the legislature and expedite business. This includes "promoting teamwork," "being accessible," "cracking the whip in the interest of time and smooth operation," starting the sessions on time, keeping them on schedule, and distributing the workload. It involves communication, coordination, and liaison with the governor, the administrative departments, and the other chambers.

Another set of legislative roles that are commonly encountered and which make important contributions to the legislative process are the "subject-matter experts." Unlike leadership roles, the roles of subject-matter experts are not embodied in formal offices. The committee system introduces specialization into the legislature, and the seniority system places at the head of the committee those persons longest exposed to the information about the committee's subject matter. Thus, subject-matter experts emerge among legislators in the fields of law, finance, education, agriculture, natural resources, local government, labor, transportation, and so on. There is some evidence to support the view that subject-matter experts exercise more influence over bills within their fields than nonexperts.[36]

Legislators might also be classified according to the way in which they see the legislative function—in other words, according to the expectations they place upon their own behavior. *The Legislative System* study found four types of self-conceptions among legislators—the rit-

[35]Quotations from state legislators interviewed by Wahlke et al., *The Legislative System*, pp. 170–90.
[36]William Buchanan et al., "The Legislator as Specialist," *Western Political Quarterly*, 13 (1960), 636–51.

pectations they place upon their own behavior. *The Legislative System* study found four types of self-conceptions among legislators—the ritualist, the tribune, the inventor, and the broker.[37] The ritualist sees his job in a technical fashion as one of "making laws." The ritualist is concerned with the mechanics of legislative operations, parliamentary rules and routine, and committee work. The technical perfection of a law seems almost as important to him as its policy implication. The tribune perceives his role as the discoverer of popular needs and the defender of popular interests. He sees his task as one of understanding his constituents' problems, making himself available to them, and keeping track of public opinion. Only a few legislators consider themselves inventors. The inventor sees himself as the initiator and creator of public policy. He wants to see the legislature take the lead in solving important problems in his state—welfare, education, highways, taxes, and so on. The fact that few legislators even claim to approach their task in a creative manner is further evidence that legislators themselves realize that policy initiation has shifted from the legislature to the governor, executive agencies, and interest groups. The true inventors of legislatures are probably frustrated men, since seldom does the legislature do anything but respond to the governor, civil servants, or active pressure groups. Finally, some legislators see their role as that of referee or broker in the struggle between interest groups, constituencies, and executive agencies. The broker's task is to balance, to compromise, to arbitrate between conflicting interests. It is interesting that legislative leaders are more likely to see themselves in this role than nonleaders.

Still another way of describing characteristic behaviors in a legislature is to discover the legislators' orientations toward the expectations of constituents and party. Legislators have been classified as "trustees" (those who are guided in legislative affairs solely by their personal conscience), "delegates" (those who are guided by instructions or wishes of their constituents), or "partisans" (those who look to the party leadership for guidance).[38] Despite the concern of many political scientists with the classic question of whether legislators should represent their party, their constituency, or their own conscience, few legislators actually exhibit in their behavior a firm commitment to any one of these. Most legislators when facing specific issues do not see any conflict between the wishes of their constituents, their party, or their own judgment. Even where such conflict is perceived, most legislators attempt to find a compromise between conflicting demands rather than choose one role or the other exclusively. One legislator even denied that such

[37]The discussion that follows relies upon Wahlke et al., *The Legislative System,* pp. 245–60.

[38]Sorauf, *Party and Representation,* pp. 121–46; and Wahlke et al., *The Legislative System,* pp. 281–86.

FIGURE 5–1   The Many Roles of a State Legislator

Source: The *Atlanta Journal and Constitution,* January 23, 1966. Reproduced by permission.

a question would ever arise: "A representative's judgment should arise from knowing the needs and wants of his district and state."[39] Of course, if legislators are asked how they make their decisions, they *claim* to be guided solely by their own conscience. But this is little more than a verbalism; it reflects a heroic image of the courageous defender of the public interest, who acts out of personal virtue and conviction regardless of the consequences.

The more politically experienced legislator is more likely to assume the role of a trustee. There is some evidence that legislators who come to the office with little prior experience as public officials, and those

[39]Sorauf, *Party and Representation,* p. 125.

with less service in the legislature, are more likely to respond in the manner of a "delegate" or politico, while their more experienced colleagues give "trustee" responses to interviewers.[40]

The future political ambitions of legislators also influence their legislative roles and behavior. Legislators who express the desire to remain in the legislature for several terms and those who express a desire to run for higher public office are more likely to see themselves as "trustees" who use their own judgment in reaching legislative decisions.[41] In contrast, legislators who express little desire to remain in public office are more likely to see themselves as "delegates" who represent their constituents' opinions. Furthermore, the more ambitious legislators are more likely to express a "state orientation" to legislative issues in contrast to a "district orientation." Apparently the politically ambitious legislator seeks to broaden his constituency in legislative affairs and assume a more state-oriented role.

CONFLICT IN STATE LEGISLATURES

Many decisions made by state legislatures do not involve conflict, and most bills are enacted into law without a single negative vote. This does not mean, however, that the legislative chambers are free from conflict; unanimous bills are generally local bills or minor bills involving decisions that are not deeply divisive. What are the principal types of conflict that affect legislative decision making? If we can rely on the perceptions of legislators themselves about the types of conflict that consume their energies, then Table 5–6 is a valuable indicator of what types of conflict prevail in different states. Note that only rural-urban conflicts are rated as important by over half the legislators in all four states.

What kinds of issues generate conflict in legislatures? Wayne L. Francis reports that a national sample of legislators rank as "important" issues those that fall into the following categories: taxation, apportionment, education, finance, labor, health, business, and civil rights.[42] If legislators are asked to indicate what kinds of issues generate various types of conflict—party, factional, regional, or interest group—the re-

[40]Charles G. Bell and Charles E. Price, "Pre-Legislative Sources of Representational Roles," *Midwest Journal of Political Science*, 13 (May 1969), 254–70.

[41]John W. Soule, "Future Political Ambitions and the Behavior of Incumbent State Legislators," *Midwest Journal of Political Science*, 13 (August 1969), 439–54. These findings are confirmed at the level of city councilmen by Kenneth Previtt and William Noulin, "Political Ambitions and the Behavior of Incumbent Politicians," *Western Political Quarterly*, 22 (June 1969), 298–308.

[42]Wayne L. Francis, *Legislative Issues in the Fifty States* (Chicago: Rand McNally & Co., 1967).

TABLE 5-6
Conflicts Perceived as Important by State Legislators
in Four States

Types of Conflict	Percent declared "important," House and Senate							
	California		New Jersey		Ohio		Tennessee	
	H	S	H	S	H	S	H	S
Rural-urban	65	74	53	50	79	65	91	63
Party	26	26	96	85	49	59	23	17
Governor-legislature	18	24	76	70	36	38	89	96
Liberal-conservative	58	74	22	25	52	59	29	37
Labor-management	65	62	18	15	61	55	54	67
Regional	69	44	18	40	17	10	13	20

SOURCE: John C. Wahlke et al., THE LEGISLATIVE SYSTEM (New York: John Wiley & Sons, Inc., 1962), p. 425.

sults turn out as shown in Table 5-7. Party conflicts occur in issues touching on elections, state administration, and apportionment, as well as on broader social issues of labor, land, finance, taxation, and welfare. Certain kinds of issues bring dissension *within* parties more frequently than *between* parties: liquor regulation, constitutional revision, agriculture, business regulation, and gambling. Regional conflicts occur most frequently on apportionment, powers of local governments, and constitutional revision. Interest group divisions are most frequently observed as labor legislation, liquor and business regulation, civil rights, gambling, natural resources, agriculture, and taxation. Of course, these rankings

TABLE 5-7
Legislative Issues Arranged by Types of Conflict

Ranking	Types of Conflict				
	Party	Factional	Regional	Interest Group	Issue "Importance"
1	Elections	Liquor	Apportionment	Labor	Taxation
2	Labor	Constitutional revision	Local government	Liquor	Apportionment
3	Land	Agriculture	Constitutional revision	Business	Education
4	Finance	Civil rights	Social welfare	Civil rights	Finance
5	Administration	Business	Civil rights	Gambling	Labor
6	Apportionment	Apportionment	Gambling	Natural resources	Health
7	Taxation	Gambling		Agriculture	Business
8	Social welfare	Taxation		Taxation	Civil rights

SOURCE: Derived from Wayne L. Francis, LEGISLATIVE ISSUES IN THE FIFTY STATES (Chicago: Rand McNally & Co., 1967).

are the product of a national sample (838) of state legislators from all fifty states; issues and conflicts will vary from state to state in importance.

PARTY POLITICS IN STATE
LEGISLATURES

There are ninety-six partisan legislative chambers in the United States; Nebraska and Minnesota legislatures are elected on a nonpartisan ballot. The influence of parties in legislative decision making in the fifty states is by no means uniform. First of all, it is obvious that parties in one-party states do not exercise tight party discipline over the voting of legislators. In terms of legislative behavior, one-party states are really no-party states. As a Tennessee legislator expressed it: "You never thought about the Democratic party unless the Republicans were trying something—for example reapportionment.[43]

The extent of partisanship in legislative decision making varies even among the more or less competitive states. One common measure of party influence on voting is the percentage of nonunanimous roll-call votes on which a majority of Democrats voted against the majority of Republicans. The compilations by the *Congressional Quarterly* show that the proportion of congressional roll calls in which the two parties have been in opposition has ranged from 35 to 50 percent. Table 5–8 suggests that party voting may be higher in the state legislatures of New York, Pennsylvania, Ohio, Delaware, Rhode Island, Massachusetts and Michigan than it is in Congress. Party voting is also common in Indiana, New Hampshire, New Jersey, Washington, and West Virginia. Parties appear less influential in Idaho, Kansas, Nevada, Utah, and California. Notice that Table 5–8 excludes unanimous or nearly unanimous votes in determining the influence of parties. Of course since most legislative decisions are unanimous, party votes would represent only a very small proportion of *all* roll-call votes. Yet this does not justify the conclusion that parties are insignificant in legislative decision making. The function of political parties is to offer alternatives where significant conflict exists, and a unanimous vote is evidence that no real demand existed for an alternative decision. Thus, the importance of parties is best observed on nonunanimous votes.

Party cohesion is the tendency of legislators to vote with their own party majority on roll calls in which a majority of one party voted in opposition to a majority of the other. The party cohesion of individual legislators is measured by the percentage of roll calls in which parties

[43]Wahlke et al., *The Legislative System*, p. 359.

TABLE 5-8
Party Voting in State Senates

State	Party Votes: Percentage of Nonunanimous Roll Calls with Party Majorities in Opposition*	Mean Index of Cohesion on Party Votes	
		Democrats	Republicans
California	17	48	57
Connecticut	50	90	67
Delaware	62	84	87
Idaho	30	58	62
Illinois	27	75	63
Indiana	51	65	68
Iowa	39	69	60
Kansas	35	49	82
Kentucky	39	51	59
Massachusetts	74	78	77
Michigan	58	81	75
Missouri	35	49	63
Montana	37	54	56
Nevada	28	70	43
New Hampshire	62	63	38
New Jersey	46	85	90
New York	70	76	88
Ohio	69	83	71
Oregon	29	55	64
Pennsylvania	82	82	90
Rhode Island	100	99	96
South Dakota	44	67	67
Utah	26	41	53
Vermont	40	63	41
Washington	50	60	78
West Virginia	54	85	73

*All roll calls in which at least 10 percent of those voting dissented from the majority position.

SOURCE: Derived from Hugh L. LeBlanc, "Voting in State Senates: Party and Constituency Influences," MIDWEST JOURNAL OF POLITICAL SCIENCE, 13 (February 1969), p. 36.

were in opposition and on which the legislator sided with his own party; the average party cohesion of Democratic or Republican legislators is simply their mean party cohesion scores. In a comprehensive analysis of roll-call voting in state legislatures, Hugh L. LeBlanc computed the mean party cohesion of Democrats and Republicans in twenty-six state senates in a single session. The results are presented in Table 5–9. Party cohesion is high in Connecticut, Delaware, Ohio, Massachusetts, Michigan, Pennsylvania, Rhode Island and West Virginia. It is low in Idaho, Kansas, Kentucky, Missouri, Utah, and California.

On what types of issues did the parties exercise great influence? Minor bills involving the licensing of water well drillers, beauticians, or barbers do not usually become the subject matter of party votes, and only infrequently will the parties divide over such matters as the designation of an official state bird. In the more urban and industrialized states, parties usually display the greatest cohesion on issues involving taxation and appropriations, welfare, and regulation of labor—in short, the major social and economic controversies that divide the national parties. (See Table 5–9.) Party influence in budgetary matters is particularly apparent, since the budget often involves issues of social welfare and class interest on which parties in urban states are split. In addition, the budget is clearly identified as the product of the governor and carries the label of the party of the governor. Appeals are made for legislators to support the budget of the governor of their party, while opposition legislators are stimulated to force changes in the budget in order to create issues for coming elections. Another type of bill that is often the subject of party voting is one involving the party as an interest group. Parties often exhibit an interest in bills proposing to transfer powers from an office controlled by one party to an office controlled by the other, or bills proposing to create or abolish non-civil service jobs. Parties display considerable interest in bills affecting the organiza-

TABLE 5-9

Party Cohesion on Roll-Call Votes by Issue Category in State Senates

	Mean Index of Cohesion	
	Democrats	Republicans
Election administration	78	66
Legislative organization	73	70
Labor	67	79
Taxation and revenue	63	68
Appropriations	70	69
State administration	68	63
Transportation	57	62
Local subdivisions	64	58
Judicial and legal	61	58
Education	65	57
Health and welfare	55	66
Regulation of business	58	57
Natural resources	55	59

SOURCE: Derived from Hugh L. LeBlanc, "Voting in State Senates: Party and Constituency Influences," MIDWEST JOURNAL OF POLITICAL SCIENCE, 13 (February 1969), p. 43.

tion of local government, state administration, the civil service, registration and election laws, and legislative procedure. On issues that directly affect the party organization and prestige, the parties react in a manner characteristic of interest groups.

What factors distinguish those states in which the party substantially influences legislative decision making from those states in which it does not? First of all, party cohesion is found in the competitive states rather than in the noncompetitive states. Since the noncompetitive states are the rural nonindustrial states, party voting appears related to urbanism and economic development if all fifty states are considered. Party voting is more frequent in the legislatures of urban industrial states. There are, however, some urban states in which party voting is not a frequent occurence; California is a notable example. Party cohesion is really strongest in those urban industrial states in which the parties represent separate socio-economic constituencies. Party voting occurs in those competitive states in which Democratic legislators represent central-city, low-income, ethnic, and racial constituencies, and Republican legislators represent middle-class, suburban, small-town, and rural constituencies. Party cohesion is weak in states where party alignments do not coincide with socioeconomic divisions of the constituencies.[44]

Party cohesion is not related to the majority or minority status of parties in the legislature. On the basis of his twenty-six state study, LeBlanc concludes that party cohesion was no greater among minority party legislators than among those of the majority party. Nor was the level of cohesion obtained by a party affected by whether or not it controlled the office of the governor.

What then is the basis of party cohesion in the states where it exists? Is party cohesion a product of effective party organization and discipline? Or is it really a result of similarities in the constituencies represented by each party? For example, is Democratic party cohesion in industrial states a result of party organization pressures? Or is it because Democrats are typically elected from metropolitan centers with strong labor groups, many Catholic voters, racial and ethnic minorities, and persons with few skills and poor education, and it is really constituency

---

[44]Perhaps the best systematic comparative study of party voting in state legislatures is Hugh L. LeBlanc, "Voting in State Senates: Party and Constituency Influences," *Midwest Journal of Political Science*, 13 (February 1969), 33–57; Malcolm Jewell also provides useful comparative data on party voting in state legislatures—see *The State Legislature*, p. 52, and "Party Voting in American State Legislatures," *American Political Science Review*, 49 (1955), 773–91. Jewell cites the following published studies as sources of data on roll-call votes: Duane Lockard, *New England State Politics* (Princeton: Princeton University Press, 1959); William J. Keefe, "Parties, Partisanship and Public Policy in the Pennsylvania Legislature," *American Political Science Review*, 48 (1954), 450–64; Thomas A. Flinn, "The Outline of Ohio Politics," *Western Political Quarterly*, 13 (1960), 702–21; and Dean R. Cresap, *Party Politics in the Golden State* (Los Angeles: The Haynes Foundation, 1954).

similarities that hold the Democratic legislators together? Can it be that Republican cohesion in these states occurs because Republicans typically represent middle-class suburbs, small towns, and rural areas, and these types of constituencies have similar ideas about public policy?

CONSTITUENCY INFLUENCE IN
LEGISLATIVE POLITICS

It is unlikely that party organization and discipline alone are the cause of party voting, for organization and discipline can only be effective under certain conditions. The weight of evidence seems to support the hypothesis that party influence is only effective where the parties represent separate and distinct socioeconomic coalitions. Where the constituencies of a state are divided along social and economic lines and where the party division coincides with these constituency divisions, only then will party program and discipline be effective in shaping policy legislative chambers.

After investigating the correlations between party cohesion and constituency characteristics in twenty-six state senates, LeBlanc found that (1) senators were more loyal to their party when their constituents voted heavily for their party in gubernatorial and presidential elections; (2) senators were more loyal to their party in partisan states where the Democratic party was heavily supported in constituencies of racial and ethnic minorities, low-income groups, and the poorly educated; (3) senators were less loyal to their party in states where a more ambiguous relationship existed between the Democratic party and socioeconomic constituencies. He observed:

> It is understood, of course, that constituency influences on legislative voting are sometimes difficult to disentangle from party influences and the dictates of the legislator's own conscience or convictions. Often the several influences reinforce one another. Thus an individual of liberal convictions is politically involved in the Democratic party for that reason and, as the Democratic party's candidate for senator, is victorious at the polls in a constituency conventionally associated with Democratic party success—perhaps a racially-mixed, low income, urban constituency, heavily populated with industrial workers. In voting to increase workmen's compensation payments, the senator could be said to vote his convictions, his party's program, and his constituency.[45]

Pennsylvania is an excellent example of a state in which Republican and Democratic legislative districts are clearly differentiated by socioeconomic variables. The parties are first divided along rural-urban lines,

[45]LeBlanc, "Voting in State Senates," p. 45.

and within urban areas they are further divided along indices of socio-economic status. Republicans dominate in rural areas and in the wealthier urban areas (upper-middle-class suburbs and several "silk-stocking" districts in Philadelphia and Pittsburgh). Democratic districts are predominantly found in the less wealthy urban areas of the state. A similar pattern emerges if occupational, religious, or racial character-istics are considered. Republican districts within urban areas prove to be the districts with greater concentrations of professional, managerial, sales, and clerical jobs. Republican candidates fare badly among black voters. The Democrats dominate the southern and eastern European, Irish, Catholic districts which are frequently the big-city, mining, or mill districts. The Republicans draw heavily in the Anglo-Saxon northern and western European, Protestant districts of the state. This same sort of party division of legislative districts has been documented in Massa-chusetts and Michigan. In short, the Democratic and Republican divi-sion of legislative constituencies in these states follows the socioeconomic divisions of national party politics.

It is this division of constituencies that is the basis of party cohesion and influence in the leigslature. Evidence to support this view is pro-vided if we examine the voting behavior of legislators elected from districts *atypical* of districts that usually elect members of their party. Since rural and high-income urban districts in Pennsylvania generally elect Republicans, and low-income urban districts generally elect Dem-ocrats, atypical districts are rural or wealthy urban districts that elect Democrats and low-income urban districts that elect Republicans. Studies in Pennsylvania, Massachusetts, and Michigan of the voting be-havior of representatives from these atypical districts show that they tend to cross party lines much more frequently than representatives elected from districts typical of their party.[46] The threat to Demo-cratic party cohesion in these states came from small bands of rural Democrats; insurgency within the Republican party originated from the urban Republican legislators. The fact that party cohesion breaks down among representatives elected by districts atypical of their party indicates that cohesion may really be a function of constituency similari-ties rather than party organization and discipline.

One of the more rigorous investigations into the causes of party voting in a state legislature is Thomas A. Flinn's study of party voting in Ohio.[47] Flinn expresses the constituency basis of party cohesion in

[46]MacRae, "Relation between Roll-Call Votes and Constituencies," pp. 1046–55; Dye, "Malapportionment and Public Policy," pp. 473–80; Sorauf, *Party and Representa-tion*, pp. 133–46; Becker et al., "Correlatives of Legislative Voting," pp. 384–96.

[47]Thomas A. Flinn, "Party Responsibility in the States: Some Causal Factors," *American Political Science Review*, 58 (1964), 60–71.

the following hypothesis: ". . . legislators from similar constituencies will vote together and in opposition to legislators from constituencies with contrasting characteristics. To the extent that parties find their support in contrasting constituencies, party responsibility is the consequence." Flinn argues that constituency factors alone do not fully explain party cohesion, since members of the same party representing dissimilar districts show greater cohesion than members of the rural and urban blocs. On the other hand, the experience in Ohio does indicate a relationship between constituency and party loyalty. Within each party, members from districts typical of their party in socioeconomic attributes support the party position more often than members from districts atypical of the party. Flinn concludes:

> Party responsibility is a consequence of party competition. . . . Various factors may intervene to inhibit or promote party responsibility, but the only important one located with substantial confidence . . . is constituency. Prospects for increased party responsibility depend, therefore, on the spread of party competition and upon a sorting out of legislative constituencies so that the districts represented by the respective parties are more homogeneous.[48]

The effect of constituency on voting behavior can be observed in still another manner. In the urban states, "close" legislative districts (where the margin of victory is less than two to one) are those with typically Democratic socioeconomic differences. In contrast, "safe" districts (where the margin of victory is two to one) are those with a socioeconomic imbalance favoring one or the other party. It turns out that legislators elected from "safe" districts generally show greater party loyalty on roll-call votes than legislators elected from "close" districts.[49] Legislators with relatively thin margins of victory reflect the socioeconomic balance of their districts in their voting and exhibit less party loyalty.

Constituency characteristics, then, help to explain not only the outcome of elections but the behavior of the elected. The constituency basis of party cohesion has been studied in Pennsylvania, Michigan, Massachusetts, Ohio, and Kansas and appears to be operative in New York, Illinois, and many other states.[50] In contrast, Washington presents an example of a state where party lines do not follow constituency differences, and, as a consequence, party unity is lower despite a high degree

48*Ibid.*, p. 71.

49MacRae, "Relation between Roll-Call Votes and Constituencies," pp. 1046–55; Dye, "Malapportionment and Public Policy," pp. 473–80.

50For an analysis of the constituency basis of party cohesion in Kansas, see John C. Grumm, "A Factor Analysis of Legislative Voting," *Midwest Journal of Political Science*, 7 (1963), 336–56.

of organization in the legislature.[51] The constituency of each party in Washington includes both rural and urban legislative districts in reasonable, balanced proportions. Democratic party cohesion is broken down by the existence of liberal and conservative wings which roughly follow rural-urban division. In California, too, the parties do not clearly follow rural-urban divisions within the state, and the result is a lack of party cohesion and influence in the legislature. The California system of apportionment, which grants one senate seat to each county regardless of population, strengthens the rural wing of the Democratic party in the senate. This contributes to a lower level of party voting in the senate than in the assembly. Of course the tradition of nonpartisanship in California has also tended to reduce the influence of party in the legislature. Phrases like "playing at parties" and "captive of your party" from interviewed legislators attest to the persistence of antiparty bias in California.[52] Party voting is also low in Missouri, and there, too, we do not find a clear urban-rural or metropolitan-outstate alignment of the parties.[53]

To say that constituencies make themselves felt in legislative decision making is not to swallow whole the image of a legislator as an errand boy, a delegate, or a "lackey." In fact, most legislators seem to side with Burke's classic argument that the representative should be guided not by "local purposes" or "local prejudices," but by "his unbiased opinion, his mature judgment, his enlightened conscience." Sixty-three percent of legislators in four states identified themselves with the Burkean position, rather than subscribe to the role of district delegate or even admit to balancing personal views with those of constituents.[54] It is not surprising that most legislators perceive themselves as unfettered decision makers drawing their wisdom chiefly, if not completely, from their own virtue, knowledge, and experience. Yet formal protestations of independence in an interview obscure more than they reveal the real influence of the constituencies. Aside from the social incentive to assert their independence, legislators themselves are seldom conscious of the many ways in which their constituency impinges upon their behavior. The classic choice posed by Burke between district demands and personal judgment is an artificial issue to most legislators. They are products of their constituency and they share its goals and values. Conflicts between their district's views and their own are rare. We have seen that

[51]Daniel M. Ogden, Jr., and Hugh A. Bone, *Washington Politics* (New York: New York University Press, 1960); also cited by Jewell, *The State Legislature,* p. 55.

[52]Wahlke et al., *The Legislative System,* pp. 351–59.

[53]Robert H. Salisbury, *Missouri Politics and State Political Systems* (Columbia: University of Missouri, Bureau of Governmental Research, 1959); also cited by Jewell, *The State Legislature,* p. 59.

[54]Wahlke et al., *The Legislative System,* pp. 267–86.

legislators have roots deep in their constituencies—many organizational memberships, lifetime residency, shared religious and ethnic affiliations, for example. The party with which the legislator identifies is also a creature of the constituency; it accedes to local interests, local political mores, local political style. The legislator is so much "of" his constituency that he needs little direct prompting or supervision. As one discerning legislator commented: "Basically you represent the thinking of the people who have gone through what you have gone through and who are what you are. You vote according to that. In other words, if you come from a suburb you reflect the thinking of people in the suburbs; if you are of depressed people, you reflect that. You represent the sum total of your background."[55]

INTEREST GROUPS IN STATE LEGISLATURES

The character and influence of organized groups in legislative decision making varies from state to state. Chapter 3 discussed interest groups in state politics and gave an analysis of their relative influence in the fifty states. One way to approach interest group activity in the legislative process is to ask legislators what groups, if any, they perceive as being powerful. This was the approach of the authors of *The Legislative System*. In the course of their interviews, California legislators referred to fifty-six specifically named organizations; New Jersey legislators named thirty-eight formal organizations; Ohio legislators mentioned sixty-eight organizations; and Tennessee lawmakers mentioned forty organizations.[56] Thus, there seems to be little doubt that most legislators are aware of considerable organized interest group activity. There is also considerable agreement among legislators about which types of in-interest groups were perceived as most powerful. Business interests were named as "most powerful groups" more often than any other interests in all four states. Educational interests ranked second in three states and tied for third in the other, and labor interests ranked third in all four states. Agricultural interests, government interests (associations of city, township, and county governments and government employee associations), ethnic and demographic interests, and religious, charitable, and civic interests were given some mention as powerful interests.

It is difficult to measure the effects of lobbying in the legislative process. We can ask legislators what they perceive to be the impact of lobbying activity. This was the approach of Harmon Zeigler and Michael

[55]*Ibid.*, p. 253.
[56]*Ibid.*, pp. 311–42.

Baer in their study of lobbying in four states.[57] They asked legislators to evaulate the worth of the information they received from lobbyists and the degree to which they depended upon this information, and they asked legislators how much they believed they had been influenced by lobbyists. The results are shown in Table 5–10. Note that there are considerable differences among legislators in different states in their estimate of the effects of lobbyists. Only about one-fifth of the legislators in Massachusetts and North Carolina admitted that lobbying activity "frequently" or "occasionally" changed their position on an issue, while closer to one-half of the legislators in Oregon and Utah made such an admission. Note also that the legislators in Massachusetts and North Carolina had less confidence in the information supplied by lobbyists than legislators in Oregon and Utah. Zeigler and Baer report that, generally, the greater the number of contacts between legislators and lobbyists, the greater the degree of influence enjoyed by the lobbyists. They also report that lobbyists and legislators tend to share similar socioeconomic backgrounds; many lobbyists, like legislators are lawyers and have held previous governmental positions.

Legislators disagree about the usefulness of interest groups in the legislative process. *The Legislative System*[58] study classifiied 36 percent

TABLE 5-10
Perceived Effect of Lobbying By Legislators in Four States

	Mass.	No Car.	Ore.	Utah
Persuasion				
Percentage of legislators believing they have been influenced to the extent of:				
Changing from one position to another	20%	18%	51%	42%
Leaving more to the news of lobbyist	31	20	42	38
Questioning a previously held opinion	34	22	45	32
Information				
Percentage of legislators indicating they:				
Depend upon information from lobbyists	50	41	83	80
Have confidence in information from lobbyists	55	56	88	70
Find information from lobbyists helpful	41	28	61	43

SOURCE: Derived from data supplied in Harmon Zeigler and Michael Baer, LOBBYING: INTERACTION AND INFLUENCE IN AMERICAN STATE LEGISLATURES (Belmont: Wadsworth Publishing Co., 1969).

[57]Zeigler and Baer, *Lobbying: Interaction and Influence in American State Legislatures.*
[58]Wahlke et al., *The Legislative System*, pp. 311–42.

of the legislators interviewed in four states as "facilitators" (those having knowledge of group activity and a friendly attitude toward it); 37 percent of the interviewees were classified as "resisters" (those having knowledge of group activity but a hostile attitude toward it); 27 percent were classified as "neutrals" (those having either little knowledge about group activity or no strong favorable or unfavorable attitudes toward it). Facilitators were more ready than neutrals or resisters to attribute importance to the views of interest groups and were more ready to use the aid of lobbyists in drafting bills and lining up support for their own bills. Resisters and neutrals were less likely to feel that the views of interest groups were important in shaping the opinions of legislators. Facilitators and resisters could not be differentiated with regard to income or occupational status or rural-urban residence or age. Better-educated legislators, however, tended more than others to be facilitators. This finding suggests that increased knowledge of the complexity of society is associated with greater realization and acceptance of group activity.

On what kinds of decisions are interest groups most likely to exercise influence? Party and constituency interests are most apparent on broad social and economic issues. On narrower issues parties are less likely to have either an interest or an opinion. The legislator is, therefore, freer to respond to the pleas of organized groups on highly specialized topics than he is on major issues of public interest. The absence of both party and constituency influences on certain types of issues contributes to the effectiveness of organized interests. Economic interests seeking to use the law to improve their competitive position are a major source of group pressure on these specialized topics. Particularly active in lobbying are the businesses subject to extensive government regulation. The truckers, railroads, insurance companies, and liquor interests are consistently found to be among the most highly organized and active lobbyists in state capitals. Organized pressure also comes from associations of governments and associations of government employees. State chapters of the National Education Association are persistent in presenting the demands of educational administrators and occasionally the demands of the dues-paying teachers as well. Lobbying is largely unregulated except for registration requirements established by about half of the states.

THE GOVERNOR IN THE LEGISLATURE

The responsibility for the initiation of major statewide legislative programs falls upon the governor, and he relies heavily upon his staff and executive personnel to fulfill this responsibility. There is not much incentive for a governor to shirk his responsibility. In the eyes of a large segment of the public the governor is responsible for everything that happens in the state during his term of office, whether he has the authority or capacity to do anything about it or not. The governor's programs are presented to the legislature in various governor's messages and in his budget. Through his power of policy initiation alone, the governor's impact on the legislature is considerable. The governor sets the agenda for public decision making; he largely determines what the business of the legislature will be in any session. Few major state undertakings ever get off the ground without gubernatorial initiation. And in setting the agenda of legislative business he frames the issues, determines their context, and decides their timing. Few would argue that these functions have little to do with the outcome of issues. As influential as a governor can be through policy initiation alone, however, few governors seem content with the role of "initiator" and most act to interject themselves into the role of "arbiter" as well.

A variety of formal and informal powers accrue to governors which enable them to directly involve themselves in legislative decisions.[59] Among the formal powers is the governor's right to call special sessions; by utilizing this power a governor can focus attention on an issue and intensify pressure on the legislature. Another formal power is the veto which every governor has, except in North Carolina; in thirty-five states it requires a two-thirds vote to override a veto rather than a simple majority. The governor has an item veto on appropriations measures in forty-one states. The closing days of any legislative session generally see a flurry of bills passed. A governor can exercise his veto on these measures after the legislature has adjourned and for all practical purposes foreclose the opportunity of being overriden. Overriding vetoes is a difficult process, since a governor is seldom so weak that he cannot count on at least one-third of the legislature to sustain his veto. The mere threat of a veto can also operate to change the course of legislative action. The state constitution may limit or strengthen the governor's influence in the legislature by determining his frequency of election and ability to succeed himself. All other things being equal, a governor with a four-year term and an opportunity to succeed himself should be in a stronger position than a governor who faces election every other year or one who cannot serve more than four years.

The governor's informal powers over legislatures center around his role in the state political system. The governor's office carries prestige

---

[59]For a discussion of the governor's legislative powers, see Jewell, *The State Legislature,* pp. 105–27; and Coleman B. Ransone, Jr., *The Office of Governor in the United States* (Tuscaloosa: University of Alabama Press, 1956).

in any state; no man becomes governor without considerable political resources of one kind or another. It is natural that a governor will attempt to use his prestige and resourcefulness to influence legislatures. The governor is the most visible state official. His comments are more newsworthy than those of legislators. He is much more sought after for television, radio, and public appearances. As a consequence, he is able to focus public attention on issues that he deems important. There is no assurance that he will always be able to influence public opinion, but there is little doubt that he has ample opportunity to be heard. Skillfully used, the power of publicity can be more influential than any formal power. Legislators must respect the governor's greater access to the communication media and hence to the minds of their constituents.

In addition to the influence inherent in the office of governor, a governor will also be an important figure in his party, perhaps even its dominant figure. In states with competitive two-party systems, the program of the governor is likely to be identified in the public's mind as the program of his party. Legislators know that they will carry that same party label into the next election. In some measure they will share with the governor the responsibility for the success or the failure of his program because of their common party label. It may be sufficient for a governor to tell his party leaders in the legislature that he feels that his prestige is at stake on a particular measure and that he expects the support of the party faithful. The governor can thus be instrumental in bringing to bear upon the legislature all the cohesive forces described earlier that are associated with party. In the urban industrial states, where party lines reflect socio-economic, religious, and ethnic affiliation, the governor can exercise great power over legislators in his party by making any issue a party issue, and thereby activating these underlying affiliations. Given the absence of divided government, gubernatorial influence in lawmaking appears strong in a competitive two-party state. Of course, when a governor in a competitive two-party state faces a legislature controlled by the opposition party, the fact that the governor's program is linked to the fortunes of his party operates to reduce his influence over the legislature rather than strengthen it. The more his program bears a party label, the more likely it is to activate the cohesive forces of the party in opposition to the governor.

In contrast to the situation in competitive two-party states, the governor of a one-party state cannot inspire either intense loyalty or intense opposition by virtue of party identification alone. Legislators run independently of the governor and have no political stake in the success of the governor's program.

In the one-party states where party appeals in themselves are insufficient, the astute use of patronage and pork is indispensable in securing support for the governor's program. Pork can include construction contracts, roads, parks, hospitals and other institutions, state insurance contracts, and innumerable other items. It is to one-party states, with their rural economies, lower family incomes, and poorly educated work forces, that state jobs look most attractive and local pork is most important. Frank Sorauf reports that patronage jobs in urban industrial economies are insecure and unattractive, at best "short term desperation job alternatives."[60] But in economically depressed states including large parts of the South, state jobs are more highly valued.[61]

It is apparent that the legislative influence of governors varies from state to state and varies over time within states. Ira Sharkansky has attempted to isolate the factors that influence the success of state executive agencies and governors in getting legislatures to fund their budgetary requests.[62] It is interesting to note some of the key findings about interaction between governors and legislatures: (1) The governor's support appears to be a critical ingredient in the success enjoyed by executive agencies in their budgetary requests to the legislature. Legislatures respond more to governors' recommendations than to agency requests. Agencies with the largest budget expansions enjoyed the greatest gubernatorial support. (2) The governors who enjoyed the greatest budgetary success in the legislature tended to be governors who could be reelected. Governors with high-tenure potential were better able to elicit legislative cooperation in funding requests than those who could not expect to remain in office because of constitutional limitations on their terms.

Another study of the success of governors in passing their legislative programs in a number of states produced the following interesting conclusions:[63] (1) Governors appear more successful in competitive two-party states where they hold a small majority in the legislature than in one-party states where their party holds an overwhelming majority in the legislature. We might think that the more seats the governor had to spare, the more successful he would be, but this is not the case. Apparently the governor is better able to rally support within his own party when he has only a modest majority; when his party has a large majority, he has a more difficult time holding the support of various factions within his party. (2) A governor is more successful when he wins a large popular vote in a general election. Moreover, his success in the

---

[60]Frank J. Sorauf, "The Silent Revolution in Patronage," *Public Administration Review*, 28 (1960), 30.

[61]Robert B. Highsaw, "The Southern Governor—Challenge to the Strong Executive Theme," *Public Administration Review*, 19 (1959), 7.

[62]Ira Sharkansky, "Agency Requests, Gubernatorial Support, and Budget Success in State Legislatures," *American Political Science Review*, 62 (December 1968), 1220–31.

[63]Sarah P. McCally, "The Governor and His Legislative Party," *American Political Science Review*, 60 (December 1966), 923–42.

legislature is also closely related to his showing in the primary election. Apparently strong opposition in the party's primary indicates factionalism within the party and the resulting inability of the governor to secure the support of party members in the legislature.

LEGISLATURES IN STATE POLITICS

At least three general propositions about state legislatures emerge from the discussions in this chapter. First of all, state legislatures reflect the socio-economic environment of their states. Levels of urbanization, income, and education in the fifty states help to explain many of the differences one encounters in state legislative politics: the level of legislative activity, the degree of interparty competition, the extent of party cohesion, the professionalism of the legislature, the nature of legislative conflict, the level of interest group activity and influence, the nature of legislative relations with the executive, and so on. Of course, there are some unique features of legislative politics in each of the fifty states based upon particular events, individuals, or historical experiences. But generally, the characteristics of a state's legislative system are closely linked to a state's environment.

Second, it seems safe to say that most state legislatures function as "arbiters" of public policy rather than as "initiators." Policy initiation is the function of the governor, the bureaucrat, and the interest group. It is principally these elements that develop policy proposals in the first instance; legislatures are placed in the role of responding to the stimulus provided by these groups. The structure of legislatures clearly reflects their deliberative function. Their rules and procedures and their leadership and committee systems do not lend themselves to policy initiation so much as they lend themselves to deliberation, discussion, and delay. The size and complexity of state government has reached a scale where expert knowledge rather than lay enlightenment is the critical ingredient in policy formation. The state budget, for example, perhaps the single most important policy-making document, is drawn up by bureaucrats subordinate to the governor and modified by the governor before submission to the legislature. Legislatures make further modifications but seldom do they undertake to rewrite an executive budget. Legislatures are still critical obstacles through which appropriation and revenue measures must pass; they are still the scenes of bloody battles over the ends for which public money is to be spent. Yet before legislative deliberation, the agenda for decision making has already been drawn up, the framework for conflict has already been established, and the issues have already been placed in particular bills. Sophisticated lawmakers are aware of their function as arbiters rather than as initiators of public policy. As one of them put it: "We're the policy-making body of the state government, and basically we should give leadership necessary to meet the problems the state faces. But in practice it comes from the executive branch."[64]

A third general proposition about legislatures is that they function to inject into public decision making a parochial influence. Legislatures function to represent locally organized interests, interests that are manifested in local rather than statewide constituencies. Legislators have deep roots in their local constituencies. They have the religious and ethnic affiliations of their constituents, they have lived among them for most of their lives, and they meet them frequently in their businesses and clubs. The process of recruiting legislators is carried on at the local level. State legislators clearly function to represent local interests in state politics. This localistic bias has often been attributed to malapportionment and rural overrepresentation in state legislatures, but actually it derives from the decentralized character of legislative and party systems in the American states. Precisely because the constituency of the legislature is territorially defined as many small segments of the state, the legislature will exhibit a parochial bias in decision making. Any representative body whose members are chosen by partial interests throughout a society represents that society in a manner different from a representative body chosen by the society at large. By representing small segments of a state, each legislator represents a more homogeneous constituency than the governor who is chosen by the state at large. The legislator's constituents share a local environment whether it be rich or poor, rural or urban, mining or manufacturing. As a result they are more likely to have roughly similar opinions on policy matters. The constituency influences on legislators are relatively clear, unmixed, and unambiguous. A governor, on the other hand, must please a wider, more heterogeneous constituency. No single local interest can dominate his judgment; he can balance one interest against another; he is free to represent widely shared interests throughout the state; and he is freer to direct himself to statewide problems and concerns.

[64]Quotation from Wahlke et al., *The Legislative System*, p. 255.

SIX

Governors
in
State Politics

THE MANY ROLES OF A GOVERNOR

The governor is the central political figure in American state politics. In the eyes of many Americans, the governor is responsible for everything that happens in his state during his term of office, whether or not he has the authority or the capacity to do anything about it. Governors are expected to bring industry into their states, discourage riots in universities, prevent floods, raise teachers' salaries, keep taxes low, reduce unemployment, see that the state gets its fair share of defense contracts from Washington, remove "chiselers" from the welfare roles, prevent violence in big cities, speed up highway construction, bring tourists into the state, and prevent the bussing of black and white school children. These public expectations far exceed the formal authority given to governors in state constitutions. In many ways the expectations placed upon the governor resemble those placed upon the president. But few governors have the powers in state political systems that the president has in the national government. Like the president, the governor is expected to be his state's chief administrator, chief legislator, leader of his party, ceremonial head of his government, chief ambassador to other governments, and leader of public opinion.

As chief executive, he must try to achieve coordination within the state's bureaucracy, oversee the preparation of the state's budget, and supervise major state programs. He must resolve conflicts within his administration and troubleshoot where difficulties arise. He must be concerned with public scandal and endeavor to prevent it from becoming public, or act decisively to eliminate it if it does. The public will hold him responsible for any scandal in his administration, whether he was a party to it or not. The public will hold him responsible for the financial structure of the state, whether it was he or his predecessors who were responsible for the state's debts.

Yet, as we shall see in this chapter, the formal administrative powers of a governor are severely restricted. Many of the governor's administrative agencies are headed by elected officials or independent boards or commissions, over which the governor has little or no control. His powers of appointment and removal are severely restricted by state constitutions. Despite a generation of recommendations by political scientists and public administrators that the governor's control over his administration should be strengthened, governors still do not have control over their administration that is commensurate with their responsibility for it.

As chief legislator, the governor is responsible for the major statewide legislative programs. There is a general public expectation that every governor will put forward some sort of legislative program, even a governor committed to a "caretaker" role. The governor largely determines what public issues will be considered by the legislature. By sending bills to the legislature, the governor is cast in the role of the "initiator" of public policy decisions. And if he wants to see his legislative proposals enacted into law, he must also persuade legislators to support them. In other words, he must also involve himself directly in legislative decisions and become an "arbiter" in public policy as well. Yet the governor has very few formal powers over legislation. He can call special sessions of the legislature, and he has the power to veto bills passed by the legislature (except in North Carolina where the governor has no veto power). In thirty-five states it requires a two-thirds vote to override a veto rather than a simple majority. Yet these formal powers do not by themselves make a governor a state's "chief legislator."

Governors also function as leaders of their party. The governor's office carries great prestige in any state, and no man becomes governor without considerable political resources of one kind or another. The program of the governor is likely to be identified in the public's mind as the program of its party. To some extent, everyone who runs for public office under the same party label as the governor has a stake in his success. Since all who run under the party's label share its common fortunes, and since its fortunes are often governed by the strength of its gubernatorial candidate, there will always be a tendency for loyal party members to support their governor. However, governors do not have the power to deny party nominations to recalcitrant legislators in their own party. Party nominations are determined at the local level in the American states. The governor has little formal authority over members of his own party.

Ceremonial duties occupy a great deal of a governor's time. Yet a governor is seldom able to mobilize the symbolic and ceremonial power of his office on behalf of state goals in the same way that the president can mobilize the power of his office on behalf of national goals. Emotional ties to state government are not at all comparable to those associated with the national government, not even in the South.

The governor is the chief negotiator with other governments in the American federal system, a variation on the diplomatic role of the president. Governors must negotiate with their local governments on the division of state and local responsibilities for public programs, and with other state governments over coordinating highway development, water pollution, resource conservation, and reciprocity in state laws. Increasingly, governors must undertake responsibility for negotiation with the national government as well. The governor shares responsibility with United States senators in seeing to it that his state receives a "fair share" of defense contracts, highway monies, educational monies, poverty funds, and so on.

Finally, the governor is a leader of public opinion in his state. He is the most visible of state officials. His comments on public affairs make news, and he is sought after for television, radio, and public appearances. He is able to focus public opinion on issues he deems important. He may not always be able to win public opinion to his side, but at least he will be heard.

If the governor has little formal authority to deal with the complex problems of his state, what political resources are available to him to make the most of his leadership? How can he provide the leadership required for the development of the major state programs for education, welfare, highways, taxation, and so on? How can he control his administration, get his bills passed, and negotiate effectively with the federal government? Why is the governor a leader instead of a figurehead? How does he make his influence felt in questions of public policy?

Much of the rest of this chapter is an attempt to come to grips with these questions. But it is clear at the outset that the governor's power rests largely upon his abilities of persuasion. His power depends upon his ability to persuade administrators over whom he has little authority, legislators who are jealous of their own powers, party leaders who are selected by local constituents, federal officials over whom the governor has little authority, and a public that thinks he has more authority than he really has. Professor Richard Neustadt has pointed out that even the president of the United States, whose authority over his subordinates is legally much greater than the authority of a governor over his subordinates, must depend upon the power of persuasion to get results.[1] Certainly what is true about the presidency is even more true about American state governors. Constituents expect more of him in relation to his formal powers than Americans expect of their president in relationship to his formal powers. Consequently, the role of a governor is, above all, that of a persuader—of his own administrators, state legislators, federal officials, party leaders, the press, and the public.

THE MAKING OF A GOVERNOR

As the central position in American state politics, the governorship is a much sought after office. The prestige of being called "governor" for the rest of one's life, and the opportunity to use the office as a stepping-stone to the United States Senate, or even the presidency or vice-presidency of the United States, is extremely attractive to men of ambition in American politics. The governor's office is the center of attention in state politics. It has gained in popularity and power in recent years, even though turnover in the office has been very high.

There are many types of governors, just as there are many different constituencies in the United States, The urbanity and concern for international affairs displayed by Governor Nelson Rockefeller is a totally different political style from the folksy,. provincial approach of Governor Lester Maddox of Georgia. Many governors are the sons of families of great wealth, who have chosen public service as an outlet for their energies—the Roosevelts, the Harrimans, the Rockefellers, the Scrantons. Some are men with successful business careers behind them, such as George Romney of Michigan, former president of American Motors. Others are men of the people, who have emphasized, or exaggerated, their humble beginnings—Huey Long of Louisiana, Al Smith of New York, Gene Talmadge of Georgia. Some promise to bring industry into their state as did Winthrop Rockefeller of Arkansas; others promise to develop the state's educational system as did Terry Sanford of North Carolina; others promise to improve the conditions of minority and labor groups as did Soapy Williams of Michigan; others promise to resist federally imposed "race mixing" as did George Wallace of Alabama, or to aid the farmer as did Orville Freeman of Minnesota, or to shift the burden of taxation to corporations as did Reubin Askew of Florida,

[1]Richard E. Neustadt, *Presidential Power* (New York: John Wiley & Sons, Inc., 1960).

and so on. Governors have been movie actors (Ronald Reagan of California), restaurant owners (Lester Maddox of Georgia), and even party bosses (David Lawrence of Pennsylvania). But the majority of governors have been lawyers by profession. (The predominance of lawyers in public office is explained in Chapter 5.) The advent of television has apparently increased the accent on youth and good looks among state governors. The median beginning age among governors has declined over the last few decades.

Historically, presidents were chosen from among the ranks of America's state governors, particularly the governors of the larger states. But recently the importance of international affairs in American politics has detracted somewhat from the popular image of the governorship as a training ground for the presidency. Governors tend to be associated with domestic rather than foreign policy questions. Men such as Nixon, McGovern, Humphrey, Kennedy, Goldwater, and Johnson found the United States Senate a good place to promote their campaigns for presidential nominations. Some scholars have attributed the decline in the number of governors selected as presidential candidates to a general decline in the popularity of governors. But a closer examination of the "vulnerability" of governors reveals that governors seeking reelection are just as successful today as in years past.[2] Approximately two-thirds of all incumbent governors who seek reelection are returned to office. This rate of success has remained roughly constant over the decades. So governors are no more "vulnerable" today than in the past, and we must conclude that recent senatorial accession to the presidency is the result of other factors, perhaps the increased role of Washington in domestic affairs and the increased attention given to war and international affairs in presidential politics.

Governors, unlike state legislators, usually come to their office with considerable experience in public affairs.[3] "Promotion" from a statewide elective office, particularly lieutenant governor or attorney general, is the most well worn path to the governorship. For example, of the fifty governors holding office in 1965, twenty-one had previously served in a statewide elective office, including attorney general, lieutenant governor, public service commissioner, comptroller, secretary of state, and state auditor.[4] Experience in the state legislature was also quite common among these fifty governors—twenty-one had served in their state legislatures at some time before becoming governor. Eight of the fifty

2J. Stephen Turrett, "The Vulnerability of American Governors, 1900–1969," *Midwest Journal of Political Science*, 15 (February 1971), 108–32.

3See Joseph A. Schlesinger, *How They Became Governor* (East Lansing: Michigan State University Press, 1957).

4*Book of the States 1965–66* (Lexington, Ky.: Council of State Governments, 1965).

TABLE 6-1

Democratic and Republican Margins in Elections for Governor

	1960	1962	1964	1966	1968	1970	1972
Alabama	—	D-96.3	—	D-63.4	—	D-74.5	—
Alaska	—	D-52.3	—	R-50.0	—	D-52.4	—
Arizona	R-59.3	R-54.8	D-53.2	R-53.8	R-57.8	R-50.9	—
Arkansas	D-69.2	D-73.3	D-57.0	R-54.3	R-52.4	D-61.7	D-75.8
California	—	D-51.9	—	R-57.6	—	R-52.8	—
Colorado	—	R-56.7	—	R-54.0	—	R-52.5	—
Connecticut	—	D-53.2	—	D-55.7	—	R-53.8	—
Delaware	D-51.7	—	D-51.4	—	R-51.5	—	D-51.3
Florida	D-59.8	—	D-56.1	R-55.1	—	D-56.9	—
Georgia	—	D-100.0	—	R-47.4 *	—	D-59.3	—
Hawaii	—	D-58.3	—	D-51.1	—	D-57.6	—
Idaho	—	R-54.6	—	R-41.4	—	D-52.2	—
Illinois	D-55.5	—	D-51.9	—	R-51.1	—	D-51.2
Indiana	D-50.4	—	D-56.2	—	R-52.8		R-57.2
Iowa	R-52.1	D-52.6	D-68.0	D-55.3	R-54.0	R-51.0	R-58.4
Kansas	R-56.0	R-53.4	R-50.9	D-54.8	D-52.2	D-54.3	D-62.7
Kentucky	D-60.6	—	D-50.7	—	R-51.2	—	D-50.6
Louisiana	D-80.5	—	D-60.7	—	D-100.0	—	D-57.2
Maine	R-52.7	R-50.1	—	D-53.1	—	D-50.1	—
Maryland	—	D-55.7	—	R-49.6	—	D-65.7	—
Massachusetts	R-52.9	D-49.9	R-50.3	R-62.6	—	R-56.7	—
Michigan	D-50.6	R-51.4	R-55.9	R-60.5	—	R-50.4	—
Minnesota	R-50.6	D-49.7	—	R-52.6	—	D-54.0	—
Mississippi	D-100.0	—	D-61.9	—	D-65.0	—	D-100.0
Missouri	D-58.0	—	D-62.1	—	D-61.1	—	R-55.2
Montana	R-55.1	—·	R-51.3	—	D-53.6	—	D-54.1
Nebraska	D-52.3	D-52.2	D-60.0	R-61.5	—	D-53.9	—
Nevada	—	D-66.8	—	R-52.2	—	D-48.1	—
New Hampshire	R-55.5	D-58.9	D-66.8	D-54.0	R-52.4	R-46.0	R-41.6
New Jersey	—	D-50.4	—	D-57.4	—	R-59.7	—
New Mexico	R-52.0	D-53.0	D-60.2	R-51.7	R-50.2	D-51.3	—
New York	—	R-53.1	—	R-54.6	—	R-52.4	—
North Carolina	D-54.4	—	D-56.6	—	D-52.7	—	R-51.1
North Dakota	D-49.4	D-50.4	D-55.7	—	D-54.8	—	D-51.0
Ohio	—	R-58.9	—	R-62.2	—	D-54.2	— .
Oklahoma	—	R-55.3	—	R-55.7	—	D-48.4	—
Oregon	—	R-54.2	—	R-55.3	—	R-55.6	—
Pennylvania	—	R-55.4	—	R-52.1	—	D-55.2	—
Rhode Island	D-56.9	R-50.1	R-61.1	R-63.3	D-51.7	D-50.1	D-52.9
South Carolina	—	D-100.0	—	D-58.2	—	D-51.7	—
South Dakota	R-50.7	R-56.1	R-51.7	R-57.7	R-57.6	D-54.8	D-60.0
Tennessee	—	D-50.8	—	D-81.2	—	R-52.0	—
Texas	D-72.8	D-54.0	D-73.8	D-72.8	D-56.5	D-53.6	D-48.1
Utah	R-52.7	—	D-57.0	—	D-68.6	—	D-69.1
Vermont	R-56.4	D-50.6	D-64.9	D-57.7	R-55.0	R-57.0	D-55.4
Virginia	—	D-63.8	D-47.9	D-47.9	—	R-52.5	—
Washington	D-51.3	—	R-55.8	—	R-53.2	—	R-53.2
West Virginia	D-54.0	—	D-54.9	—	R-50.9	—	R-54.7
Wisconsin	D-51.6	D-50.4	R-50.6	R-53.5	R-52.6	D-54.2	—
Wyoming	—	R-54.5	—	R-54.3	—	R-62.8	—

* Republican candidate Howard Calloway won the popular vote but failed to obtain the necessary majority; Democratic candidate Lester Maddox was elected by the state legislature.

governors had been both legislators and holders of statewide elective office. Four governors had served in the state judiciary before assuming office. Eleven governors had experience in local government. Five governors had experience in Congress, and seven had experience in the executive branch of the national government. In fact, only five of the fifty governors had no prior experience in public office.

In recent years more governors have been Democrats than Republicans. Only in 1966 and 1968 was this tide reversed, and the GOP held more governor's chairs than the Democratic Party (see Table 6–1).

EXECUTIVE POWER IN STATE GOVERNMENT

Frequently we speak of "strong" and "weak" governors. Yet it is difficult to compare the power of one governor with that of another. To do so, one must examine the constitutional position of the governor, his powers of appointment and removal over state officials, his ability or inability to succeed himself, his powers over the state budget, his legislative influence, his position in his own party and its position in state politics, and his influence over interest groups and public opinion in the state.

Let us examine first of all the governor's constitutional position in state government. In many ways the organization of American state government resembles political thinking of one hundred or two hundred years ago. This colonial experience emphasized "fear of the executive" and resulted in state constitutional restrictions on a governor's term of office, his ability to succeed himself, his control over appointments and removals, the proliferation of separate boards and commissions to govern particular state programs, and long overlapping terms for the members of these boards and commissions. The Jacksonian era of "popular democracy" brought with it the idea that the way to insure popular control of state government was to elect separately as many state officials as possible. The Reform movement of the late nineteenth and early twentieth centuries led to merit systems and civil service boards, which further curtailed the governor's power of appointment.[5] Not all of these trends were experienced uniformly by all fifty states, and there are considerable variations from state to state in the powers that governors have over the state executive branch. Figure 6–1 is an example of a "weak" executive type of state administrative organization. Many im-

[5] For a description of the Reform movement in state and local government see Chapter 9.

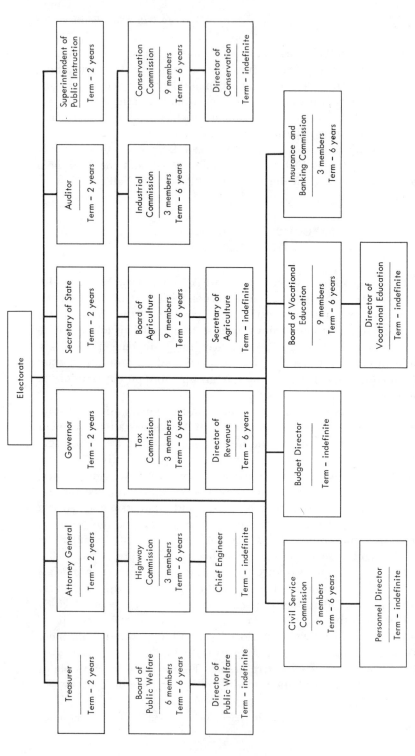

FIGURE 6-1 "Weak" Executive Type of State Administrative Organization

Source: Frederic A. Ogg and P. Orman Ray, *Introduction to American Government,* 13th ed. by William H. Young (New York: Appleton-Century-Crofts, 1966), pp. 772–73. Reproduced by permission of the publisher.

170

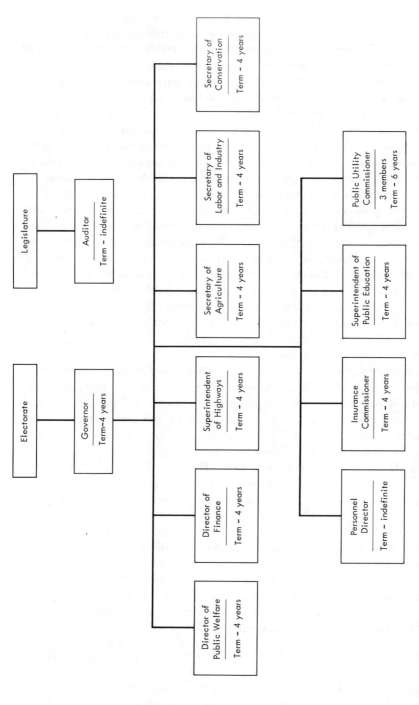

FIGURE 6–2 "Strong" Executive Type of State Administrative Organization

Source: Frederic A. Ogg and P. Orman Ray, *Introduction to American Government,* 13th ed. by William H. Young (New York: Appleton-Century-Crofts, 1966), pp. 772–73. Reproduced by permission of the publisher.

portant state offices are governed by boards or commissions whose members may be appointed by the governor with the consent of the state senate but for long overlapping terms, which reduces the governor's influence over members of these boards and commissions. Figure 6–2 is an example of a "strong" executive type of state government organization. Only the governor and lieutenant governor and legislature are elected directly by the people. The governor appoints the heads of all major state agencies for a term that is coterminous with his own.

Fortunately, the trend toward separately elected officials and independent boards and commissions appears to be on the wane. In recent years "administrative efficiency" has emerged as the central theme in state government reorganization proposals. Since World War II, reorganization proposals have generally emphasized a reduction in the number of departments, more functional integration of state programs, and more power in the governor's office. Yet even though the trend may be toward more streamlined state government organization, it is clear that separately elected officials and independent boards and officials will be around for a long time. Political parties and public officials develop a stake in the continued existence of separately elected public offices; separately elected offices provide more party nominations for the party faithful. Moreover, as we observed in Chapter 3, many interest groups prefer to be governed by boards and commissions that are independent of executive authority. They feel they have more influence over independent boards than those that come directly under a governor's authority. There is often the assumption that boards and commissions enable divergent interests to be represented in the governing of state agencies. Groups are thereby permitted to have a voice in state programs in which they are interested.

Another component of a governor's influence is his ability or inability to succeed himself in office. Turnover in governors' offices is quite high: ten states have a two-year term for the office of governor, and forty states have a four-year term. However, several of the states providing for a four-year term forbid the incumbent to succeed himself. Turnover figures suggest that minor elected state officials have longer tenures in office than governors. Apparently a typical secretary of state, state treasurer, or state auditor can expect to stay in office longer than the governor (lieutenant governor and attorney general are positions of high turnover like the governor), and this long tenure for minor elected officials further reduces the governor's control over them.

Joseph A. Schlesinger has ranked the states according to the power that a governor derives from his tenure in office.[6] Governors with the

---

[6]Joseph A. Schlesinger, "The Politics of the Executive," *Politics in the American States*, 2nd Ed., Herbert Jacob and Kenneth Vines, eds. (Boston: Little, Brown and Co., 1971).

highest "tenure power" are those who are elected for a four-year term and are permitted to succeed themselves indefinitely. Seventeen states fall into this category (see Table 6–2.) Governors with the lowest "tenure power" are those who have only two year terms and are permitted only one reelection (New Mexico and South Dakota). The Twenty Second Amendment to the U.S. Constitution suggests that most Americans believe in restricting executive tenure at the presidential level, and many states have similar restrictions on their governors. However, these constitutional restrictions can be circumvented by a very powerful governor. When Governor Wallace of Alabama was restricted by his state's constitution to a single four-year term, his wife ran in his place, with Wallace openly avowing that if she were elected he would run the state. Apparently the voters of Alabama were quite willing to accept this arrangement despite the obvious circumvention of the Alabama Constitution; Lurleen Wallace won an overwhelming victory at the polls. A similar circumvention of constitutional intent on the governor's tenure occurred

TABLE 6-2

Tenure Provisions for Governors

Four-Year Term, No Restrictions on Reelection		
California	Massachusetts	North Dakota
Colorado	Michigan	Utah
Connecticut	Minnesota	Washington
Hawaii	Montana	Wisconsin
Idaho	Nevada	Wyoming
Illinois	New York	
Four-Year Term, Restricted to Two Terms		
Alaska	Maryland	Ohio
Delaware	Missouri	Oklahoma
Louisiana	Nebraska	Oregon
Maine	New Jersey	Pennsylvania
Four-Year Term, consecutive Reelection Prohibited		
Alabama	Mississippi	Tennessee
Florida	North Carolina	Virginia
Georgia	South Carolina	West Virginia
Indiana		
Kentucky		
Two-Year Term, No Restrictions on Reelection		
Arizona	New Hampshire	
Arkansas	Rhode Island	
Iowa	Texas	
Kansas	Vermont	
Two-Year Term, Restricted to Two Terms		
New Mexico	South Dakota	

in the 1930s when "Ma" and "Pa" Ferguson alternately governed the state of Texas.

THE GOVERNOR'S MANAGERIAL POWERS

Perhaps the most important managerial power is the power to appoint subordinate officials. Personal appointment of subordinates does not guarantee their responsibility, but there is a greater likelihood that an official appointed by a governor will be someone whose values coincide with those of the governor. Of course a governor is subject to many different pressures in exercising his appointing power; often he must pay off political debts or win the support of a political faction by his selection. Salary limitations and the shortness of tenure make it exceedingly difficult to find capable men for positions of high responsibility in state government. But it is safe to infer that a governor who can name his major department heads is stronger than a governor who cannot. As we have already seen, many department heads in state government are popularly elected, and many departments are headed by elected or appointed boards or commissions over whom the governor has relatively little control.

Joseph M. Schlesinger has undertaken to compare the governors' appointive powers in all fifty states. Taking sixteen major governmental functions in every state, he scored each according to the relative influence, in formal terms, which the governor has over the appointment of the head of each agency handling these functions.[7] If the governor can appoint an agency head without the need for legislative confirmation, this gives him strong appointive power. The need for legislative confirmation by one or both houses reduces the governor's formal appointive power; and of course, if an agency head is appointed by a separate board rather than the governor, this further reduces his appointive power. Finally, if an agency head is separately elected by the people, the governor has no formal authority over his appointment. Schlesinger classified the fifty states according to the degree to which the governor had formal appointive powers within the executive branch of government (see Table 6–3). States that have had major constitutional revisions in recent years, such as New Jersey, New York, and Tennessee, rate high. This is a reflection of the extent of management reform in these states. The reason why Tennessee ranks so high is that its governor is the only elected officer (with the exception of three public utilities commissioners),

[7]These functions are finance, agriculture, attorney general, auditor, budget officer, conservation, comptroller, education, health, highways, insurance, labor, secretary of state, tax commissioner, treasurer, and welfare.

TABLE 6-3
Appointive Powers of Governors

Very Strong	Strong	Moderate
Tennessee	Arkansas	Alabama
New Jersey	California	Missouri
Pennsylvania	Connecticut	Washington
Maryland	Idaho	West Virginia
New York	Kentucky	Alaska
Hawaii	Michigan	Nebraska
Indiana	Minnesota	Rhode Island
Massachusetts	Ohio	Utah
Virginia	South Dakota	Iowa
Illinois	Vermont	Montana
	Delaware	

Weak	Very Weak
Maine	Florida
Oregon	Texas
Nevada	Colorado
Wisconsin	Georgia
Louisiana	Mississippi
New Hampshire	North Dakota
North Carolina	New Mexico
Kansas	South Carolina
Wyoming	Oklahoma
	Arizona

and most of the other major positions in state government are filled by him without the need for legislative approval. However, even in Tennessee, the secretary of state, treasurer, and comptroller are chosen by the legislature rather than the governor. At the other extreme, Colorado's governor has weak appointive powers not only because Colorado's secretary of state, attorney general, treasurer, and auditor are popularly elected but also because major departments, such as agriculture, labor, health, and so on, are headed by civil service appointees. North Dakota's governor has weak appointive powers because, in addition to the usual elective offices, the tax commissioner and the commissioner of agriculture, labor, and insurance are also elected positions.

Restrictions on a governor's power of appointment are further complicated by restrictions on his power of removal. A common statutory or constitutional provision dealing with the governor's removal power states that removal must be "for cause only"; that is, the governor must provide a clear-cut statement of charges and an opportunity for an open hearing to the employee he is trying to oust. This process is often unpleasant, and governors seek to avoid it unless they have strong evidence of incompetence, fraud, or mismanagement. When a governor's removal powers are limited "for cause only," it is next to impossible to remove a subordinate for policy differences. Of course a governor may request an officeholder to resign, even when the governor's removal power is limited, and such a request may be honored by the officeholder in preference to continued unhappy relationships with the governor's office or in fear of the governor's ability to mobilize public opinion against him. As a final resort, a determined governor with influence in the legislature can always oust an official by a legislative act, which abolishes the office or agency the official heads and replaces it with another; this device is sometimes called a "ripper bill."

Certain elected state officials, notably the lieutenant governor and the attorney general, often use their positions to advance their own candidacy for the governorship or the U.S. Senate, thus creating further problems for a governor, particularly when their ambitions are in competition with his own. Lieutenant governors, of course, have few substantive duties in state government, other than the ceremonial one of presiding over the state senate. But the attorney general has more influence—his legal opinions have great importance for a governor's program. Governors are often bound by statute to conform to the attorney general's legal opinion in interpreting state laws and constitutions.

The governor's control over patronage is another potential source of executive power in state government. A governor can win the support of party chairmen throughout the state by providing them with jobs to dispense to "deserving" party workers. This provides prestige and power to party chairmen within their communities, and they are expected to return the favor by supporting the governor. Patronage jobs are particularly important in depressed economies. In the one-party states of the South, for example, with their rural economies, lower family incomes, and poorly educated work forces, state jobs look most attractive. But patronage jobs in urban industrial economies are insecure and unattractive.[8] A large number of state jobs on highways and public works are lower paid, menial positions, which are not very attractive in a wealthy state. Other state jobs require specialized skills and training and do not lend themselves to patronage appointments. Patronage has declined in recent years in importance not only as a product of economic development but also as a result of the growth of civil service systems. A great expansion of state civil service systems occurred after 1936, as a result of the requirement of the federal Social Security Act of that year that states participating in national grants under that law must install civil service systems for employees in the federally aided public as-

[8]Frank J. Sorauf, "State Patronage in a Rural County," *American Political Science Review*, 50 (1956), 1046.

sistance, insurance, and health programs. Civil service coverage is now required in state agencies financed even in part by federal grants-in-aid. This national requirement inspired many states to extend civil service coverage to a large number of their own employees. Today more than half of all state employees are under civil service.

Civil service systems, particularly those administered by independent civil service commissions, significantly reduce executive control over program administration. There is a persistent tendency for civil service systems to be routine, mechanical, and unimaginative. Job classification schemes, to which recruitment, qualifications, and pay scales are closely tied, become so rigid with time that executives have little flexibility in recruiting really talented people to state government. Executives whose authority to promote, hire, and fire their employees is severely curtailed can hardly be expected to obtain maximum effort and cooperation from their employees. Even the public administration experts, who originally supported the civil service movement and the removal of state jobs from the governor's authority, are beginning to recommend that the power over personnel administration be returned to the governor.

THE GOVERNOR'S FISCAL POWERS

The state budget is the most important policy document in state government. The governor's control over the state budget is perhaps his most formidable power. While the legislature must enact the state budget into law, and no state monies may be spent without a legislative appropriation, in practice the greatest amount of control over state government rests with the governor and his budget staff. The governor has full responsibility for the preparation of the budget and its submission to the legislature in a majority of states, but in some states he shares this responsibility with a civil service appointee or an appointee of someone other than himself, and in other states he shares the power to prepare the budget with popularly elected officials or members of the legislature (see Table 6–4).

Budget-making involves bringing together the requests of all existing state agencies, calculating the costs of new state programs, estimating the probable income of the state, and evaluating these costs and income estimates in the light of program and policy objectives. The final budget document is submitted to the legislature for its adoption as an appropriations measure. No state monies can be spent without a legislative appropriation, and the legislature can make any alterations in the state budget that it sees fit. Potentially, then, a legislature can control any activity of the state government through its power over appropriations, but as a practical matter, the legislature seldom reviews every item of the governor's budget.

TABLE 6-4
Budget Powers of Governors

Full Responsibility		
Alabama	Maryland	Ohio
Alaska	Massachusetts	Oklahoma
Arizona	Michigan	Oregon
California	Minnesota	Pennsylvania
Delaware	Missouri	South Dakota
Georgia	Montana	Tennessee
Hawaii	Nevada	Utah
Idaho	New Hampshire	Vermont
Illinois	New Jersey	Virginia
Iowa	New Mexico	Washington
Kentucky	New York	Wisconsin
Maine	North Dakota	Wyoming
Responsibility Shared with Appointee		
Colorado	Louisiana	North Carolina
Connecticut	Nebraska	Rhode Island
Kansas		
Responsibility Shared with Independent Officials		
Arkansas	Mississippi	Texas
Florida	South Carolina	West Virginia
Indiana		

In practice, budgets tend to reflect the views of those responsible for their preparation, namely, the governor. Thomas Anton summarizes the role of state agencies, budget officers, governors, and legislatures in budget making as follows: "A peek into the decision making black box in most states, I submit, would probably reveal a system in which operating agency heads consistently request more funds, executive and/or legislative reviewers consistently reduce agency requests, governors consistently pursue balanced budgets at higher expenditure levels, and legislatures consistently approve higher appropriations while engaging in frequent disputes with the governor over revenues."[9]

The pressure for budget increases comes from the request of agency officials. Most agency officials feel compelled to ask for more money each year. According to Anton, requesting an increase in funds "affirms the significance and protects the status of agency employees, assures clientele groups that new and higher standards of service are being pursued aggressively,"[10] and gives the governor's office and the legislature something to cut that will not affect existing programs. The governor's budget staff gen-

[9]Thomas J. Anton, "Roles and Symbols in the Determination of State Expenditures," *Midwest Journal of Political Science*, 11 (February 1967), 36; see also Thomas J. Anton, *The Politics of State Expenditure in Illinois* (Urbana: University of Illinois Press, 1966).

[10]Anton, "Roles and Symbols," p. 29.

erally recognizes the built-in pressure to expand budgets. The budget staff see themselves as "cutters." As Allen Schick describes it: "The agencies, anticipating a cut, overestimate their needs and pad the budget, while the budget office, in the conviction that the budget is padded, make deep cuts in the agency's estimates."[11] Agencies press for budgetary expansion with better programs in mind, while the governor's budget staff tries to reduce expenditures with cost cutting in mind.

While most states have executive budget systems, and the governor is responsible for the activities of his budgetary staff, the governor's actual control over state spending is limited in many ways. First of all, it is quite common to "earmark" in state constitutions and laws certain funds for particular purposes, such as gasoline taxes for highways. The earmarking device provides certain agencies with an independent source of income, thus reducing the governor's control over operations. In addition, Anton writes: "The governor will probably come to his position without any direct experience in dealing with state finance. His own inexperience will thus provide a sharp contrast to the wisdom of the old hands who occupy administrative and legislative positions of influence, and who will probably regard the governor as an outsider—a "new boy" come to meddle in their affairs. Moreover, since the average length of service for most governors is less than five years, the old hands can constantly think of the "new boy" as someone who is likely to be gone from the scene far in advance of their own departure."[12] It is not easy for a governor to master the "constitutional limitations, marvelously incoherent divisions of financial accountability, incomprehensible budget documents, and, worst of all, an intricate maze of general funds, special funds, revolving funds, loan funds, trust funds, federal funds, all conspired to shroud the state's financial situation in mystery."[13]

Governors have little influence over many items of state spending. Over 50 percent of state finances come from special "earmarked" funds. What is left, "general fund expenditures," is also largely committed to existing state programs, particularly welfare and education. Governors typically campaign on platforms stressing both increased service and increased economy. Once in office, however, they typically find it impossible to accomplish both and very difficult to accomplish either one. Often new programs planned by a governor must be put aside, because money must be found to educate more students who are entitled to an education under existing programs; or money must be found to pay the welfare costs of additional clients who are entitled to care under existing programs; or

[11]Allen Schick, "Control Patterns in State Budget Execution," *Public Administration Review*, 24 (1964), 99.
[12]Anton, "Roles and Symbols," p. 32.
[13]*Ibid.*, p. 33.

money must be found to raise the salaries of state personnel who are administering existing programs. The result is that social and economic conditions really "determine" expenditures, and governors have little flexibility in budget making. Anton feels that governors must focus most of their attention on revenue, which typically must be increased just to keep pace with existing programs. "Governors may be be regarded as 'money providers' or as 'budget balancers'; only infrequently can they be viewed as 'decision makers' in the determination of state expenditures."[14] (See Chapter 18 for further discussion.)

THE GOVERNOR'S LEGISLATIVE POWERS

The responsibility for initiating major statewide legislative programs falls upon the governor. The governor's programs are presented to the legislature in various governor's messages and in his budget. Much of the governor's power over the legislature stems from this power as party leader of public opinion.[15] However, the governor's veto power is a source of formal authority over legislature and deserves special attention. Only in North Carolina does the governor have no veto power at all. In some states, the veto power is restricted by giving the governor only a short time to consider a bill after it has passed the legislature, by permitting a simple majority of legislative members to override the veto, or by requiring vetoed bills to reappear at the next legislative session. In other states governors have the added power of the item veto, they are given longer

TABLE 6-5

The Governors' Veto Powers

Very Strong		Strong	Medium	Weak
Alaska	Mississippi	Alabama	Connecticut	Indiana
Arizona	Missouri	Arkansas	Florida	Iowa
California	Nebraska	Kentucky	Idaho	Maine
Colorado	New Jersey	Tennessee	Massachusetts	Nevada
Delaware	New York		Montana	New Hampshire
Georgia	North Dakota		New Mexico	North Carolina
Hawaii	Ohio		Oregon	Rhode Island
Illinois	Oklahoma		South Carolina	Vermont
Kansas	Pennsylvania		South Dakota	West Virginia
Louisiana	Utah		Texas	
Maryland	Washington		Virginia	
Michigan	Wyoming			
Minnesota				

[14]*Ibid.*, p. 34.
[15]See Chapter 5, "The Governor in the Legislature," pp. 157–61.

periods of time to consider a bill, and a two-thirds vote of both houses of the legislature is required to override a veto rather than a simple majority. Thus, it is possible to rank states according to the strength of the governor's veto; this is done in Table 6–5.

Since we have already discussed the governor's power over the legislature in Chapter 5, let us turn to a consideration of the legislature's power

TABLE 6-6

Attitudes of American State Executives on
Political Relationships

	Percentages (N=933)
Who Exercises Greater Control over Your Agency's Affairs?	
Governor	32
Each About the Same	22
Legislature	44
Other and N.A.	2
	100
Who Has the Greater Tendency to Reduce Budget Requests?	
Governor	25
Legislature	60
Other and N.A.	15
	100
Who Is More Sympathetic to the Goals of Your Agency?	
Governor	55
Each About the Same	14
Legislature	20
Other and N.A.	11
	100
What Type of Control Do You Prefer?	
Governor	42
Independent Commission	28
Legislature	24
Other and N.A.	5
	100

NOTE: For the source of data and the survey instrument containing the precise wording of the questions, see Deil S. Wright and Richard L. McAnaw, "American State Administrators: Study Code and Marginal Tabulations for the State Administrative Officials Questionnaire" (Iowa City, Iowa: Department of Political Science and Institute of Public Affairs, January 1965), mimeographed, 40 pp. Tabled percentages may not add to 100 because of rounding.

SOURCE: Deil S. Wright, "Executive Leadership in State Administration," MIDWEST JOURNAL OF POLITICAL SCIENCE, 11 (February 1967), 4.

over executive departments. Professor Deil S. Wright asked 933 department and agency heads from all fifty states a series of questions about legislative versus gubernatorial influence in their departments.[16] One question asked the agency heads to judge whether the governor or the legislature exercised greater control over the affairs of this department. As Table 6–6 indicates, more agency heads felt that the legislature exercised greater control over their departments than the governor. Agency heads also felt that the legislature was more likely to reduce their budget requests than the governor, and that the governor was more sympathetic to the goals of their agency than the legislature. Agency heads generally preferred gubernatorial control to control by the legislature, but many agency heads seemed to prefer independence from either direct gubernatorial or direct legislative control.

THE POWERS OF GOVERNORS:
A COMPARATIVE VIEW

It is possible to combine several of the measures of the governors' formal powers into a combined index of governors' powers in all fifty states. In Table 6–7 Joseph A. Schlesinger has combined four measures of the governor's strength already presented: his tenure potential, his appointive powers, his budget powers, and his veto powers. These rankings of the formal powers of governors suggest that it is the urban industrial states that require strong executive government. The large urban industrial states—New York, Illinois, New Jersey, Michigan, Pennsylvania, and California—all rate near the top in formal gubernatorial powers. States at the bottom of the rankings tend to be small rural agricultural states. Apparently size, urbanization, and industrialization increase the complexity of state administration and need for formal gubernatorial powers.[17] This does not necessarily mean that within the context of their own states the governors of Mississippi and North Dakota do not have as much influence as the governors of New York and Illinois. It means only that the governors of New York and Illinois need more formal powers to control the large complex bureaucracies in those states. Within their own borders, the governors of Mississippi and North Dakota are still central figures in their states' political systems. We have already observed that minor jobs, contracts, and patronage provide governors of small rural agricultural states with more power than the governors of urban, indus-

---

[16]Deil S. Wright, "Executive Leadership in State Administration," *Midwest Journal of Political Science*, 11 (February 1967), 1–26.

[17]See Thomas R. Dye, "Executive Power and Public Policy in the States," *Western Political Quarterly*, 22 (December 1969), 926–39.

TABLE 6-7
A Combined Index of the Formal Powers of the Governors

	Tenure Potential	Appointive Powers	Budget Powers	Veto Powers	Total Index
New York	5	5	5	5	20
Illinois	5	5	5	5	20
Hawaii	5	5	5	5	20
California	5	4	5	5	19
Michigan	5	4	5	5	19
Minnesota	5	4	5	5	19
New Jersey	4	5	5	5	19
Pennsylvania	4	5	5	5	19
Maryland	4	5	5	5	19
Utah	5	3	5	5	18
Washington	5	3	5	5	18
Ohio	4	4	5	5	18
Massachusetts	5	5	5	3	18
Wyoming	5	2	5	5	17
Missouri	4	3	5	5	17
Alaska	4	3	5	5	17
Tennessee	3	5	5	5	17
Idaho	5	4	5	3	17
North Dakota	5	1	5	5	16
Kentucky	3	4	5	4	16
Virginia	3	5	5	3	16
Montana	5	3	5	3	16
Nebraska	4	3	4	5	16
Connecticut	5	4	4	3	16
Delaware	4	1	5	5	15
Oklahoma	4	1	5	5	15
Alabama	3	3	5	4	15
Wisconsin	5	2	5	3	15
Colorado	5	1	4	5	15
Louisiana	4	2	4	5	15
Georgia	3	1	5	5	14
Oregon	4	2	5	3	14
Nevada	5	2	5	2	14
Arizona	2	1	5	5	13
South Dakota	1	4	5	3	13
Maine	4	2	5	2	13
Vermont	2	4	5	2	13
Kansas	2	2	4	5	13
Arkansas	2	4	3	4	13
Iowa	2	3	5	2	12
New Hampshire	2	2	5	2	11
Rhode Island	2	3	4	2	11

TABLE 6-7 (cont.)

	Tenure Potential	Appointive Powers	Budget Powers	Veto Powers	Total Index
New Mexico	1	1	5	3	10
North Carolina	3	2	4	1	10
Mississippi	3	1	1	5	10
Indiana	3	5	1	1	10
Florida	3	2	1	3	9
South Carolina	3	1	1	3	8
West Virginia	3	3	1	1	8
Texas	2	1	1	3	7

SOURCE: Joseph A. Schlesinger, "The Politics of the Executive," in Herbert Jacob and Kenneth Vines (eds.), POLITICS IN THE AMERICAN STATES (Boston: Little, Brown and Co., 1971), p. 232.

trial states. These small favors are less important in urban industrial states where the governors require formal hierachical controls.

It is also interesting to observe that the governors' formal powers are greatest in the states with the highest party competition.

THE GOVERNOR AS POLITICAL LEADER

The governor is the most visible figure in state politics. He commands the attention of press, radio, and television. He has a greater opportunity than any other state official to exercise leadership by persuasion. An attractive governor who is skillful in public relations can command support from administrators, legislators, local officials, and party leaders through public appeals to their constituents. Politicians must respect the governor's greater access to the communications media and hence to the minds of their constituents. An effective governor not only understands the broad range of issues facing his state but also is able to speak clearly and persuasively about them. A governor's reputation as a leader, however, stems not only from what he says but also from what he does. His reputation must include a capacity to decide issues and to persist in his decision once it is made. A reputation for backing down, for avoiding situations that involve him in public conflict, or for wavering in the face of momentary pressures invites the governor's adversaries to ignore or oppose him. A sense of insecurity or weakness can damage a governor's power more than any constitutional limitation. A governor can also increase his influence by developing a reputation for punishing his adversaries and rewarding his supporters. Once his reputation as an effective leader is established, cooperation is often forthcoming in anticipation of the governor's reaction.

Governors are also the recognized leaders of their state parties. In a majority of states, it is the governor who picks the state party chairman and who is consulted on questions of party platform, campaign tactics, nominations for party office, and party finances. The amount of power that a governor derives from his position as party leader varies from state to state according to the strength, cohesion, and discipline of the state parties. A few governors have been able to build strong party organization in their states and have gained power through partisan appeal. In urban industrial states, where party lines reflect socioeconomic, religious, and ethnic divisions, the governor can exercise great power by an appeal to party loyalty. Of course in one-party states, particularly in the South and the Midwest, the party mechanism is not really an effective instrument of gubernatorial power. Governors in one-party states must rely upon personal organizations or factional support. As we observed earlier, one-party states are really no-party states. The governor must negotiate with individuals and factions in the legislature on an issue-by-issue basis to accomplish his program.

There are at least three limitations to the power that a governor derives from his role as party leader. First of all, a governor cannot deny party renomination to disloyal members. City and county leaders and state legislators hold their positions by their own efforts and owe the governor nothing. Party machinery is localized; it responds to constituency demands, not the voice of the governor. Second, the frequency of divided control, where the governor faces the legislature dominated by the opposition party, requires him to bargain with individuals and groups in the opposition party. If he has acquired a reputation for being too "partisan" in his approach to state programs, he will find it difficult to win over the necessary support of opposition party members. Finally, the use of patronage may make as many enemies as friends. An old political maxim states that "For every one patronage appointment, you make nine enemies and one ingrate."

BUREAUCRATIC, EXECUTIVE, LEGISLATIVE INTERACTION

One of the rare studies of the interaction between administrative agencies, governors, and legislatures, which focuses on the impact of this interaction on budgetary outcome, is political scientist Ira Sharkansky's analysis of the budgetary process in nineteen states. Professor Sharkansky examined the relationships between agency requests, governors' recommendations regarding these requests, and legislative appropriations vis-à-vis agency requests and governor's recommendations. First he measured the "acquisitiveness" of an executive agency by the agency's request for the coming budget period as a percentage of current expenditures. Then he measured the "governor's support" of the agency's request by the governor's recommendation for each agency as a percentage of its request. He measured the "governor's success" by legislative appropriations as a percentage of the governor's recommendation. Finally, he measured "budgetary short-term success" in the legislature by legislative appropriation as a percentage of agency requests, and "budgetary expansion" by legislative appropriations as a percentage of the agency's current expenditures. The results for nineteen states are shown in Table 6–8.

Several interesting ideas emerge from the analysis of these data: (1) The more-acquisitive agencies get their requests cut down more by governors and legislatures than the less-acquisitive agencies. The more-acquisitive agencies, however, end up with generally higher appropriations than the less-acquisitive agencies. (2) The governor's support appears to be a critical ingredient in the success enjoyed by executive agencies in their budgetary requests to the legislature. Legislatures respond more to governors' recommendations than to agency requests. (3) the governors who enjoyed the greatest budgetary success in the legislature tended to be governors who could be reelected. Governors with high-tenure potential were better able to elicit legislative cooperation in funding requests than those who could not expect to remain in office because of constitutional limitations on their terms.

OTHER EXECUTIVE OFFICES

The lieutenant governor's office in many states is looked upon as a campaign platform for the governorship. Lieutenant governors are said to have a two- or four-year head start for the top job. The lieutenant governor's formal duties are comparable to those of the vice-president of the United States; in other words, lieutenant governors have relatively little to do. The two basic functions of the office are to serve in direct line of succession to the governor and replace him in the event of a vacancy in that office, and to be the presiding officer of the state senate. Since lieutenant governors generally have political ambitions of their own, they seldom make good "assistant governors" who will submerge their own interests for the success of the governor's administration. Unlike the vice-president, lieutenant governors are separately elected and are sometimes members of the governor's opposition party. Some efforts have been made to reduce the boredom of the lieutenant governor's office by assigning him membership on various boards and commissions.

TABLE 6-8

Changes in the Budgetary Process by Stages for Selected States

State, with Year of Budget Analyzed	Agency Acquisitiveness: Agency Requests as % of Current Expenditures	Governor's Support: Governor's Recommendation as % of Agency Requests	Governor's Success: Appropriation as % of Governor's Recommendation	Budget Short-term Success: Appropriation as % of Agency Requests	Budget Expansion: Appropriation as % of Agency Current Expenditures
Florida (1965-67)	120%	90%	93%	84%	109%
Georgia (1965-67)	153	86	100	87	139
Idaho (1967-69)	119	93	92	86	109
Illinois (1963-65)	118	83	102	85	108
Indiana (1965-67)	123	83	103	86	112
Kentucky (1966-68)	120	90	93	84	109
Louisiana (1966-67)	121	90	101	91	110
Maine (1965-67)	114	85	108	92	109
Nebraska (1965-67)	122	87	119	104	124
North Carolina (1965-67)	120	84	105	87	112
North Dakota (1965-67)	124	74	111	82	111
South Carolina (1966-67)	117	96	104	99	116
South Dakota (1967-68)	136	82	98	80	109
Texas (1965-67)	128	82	104	86	117
Vermont (1965-67)	121	87	106	91	115
Virginia (1966-68)	120	97	100	91	114
West Virginia (1966-67)	125	88	97	81	101
Wisconsin (1965-67)	115	96	98	94	111
Wyoming (1967-69)	133	69	109	75	112

SOURCE: Derived from Ira Sharkansky, "Agency Requests, Gubernatorial Support and Budget Success in State Legislatures," AMERICAN POLITICAL SCIENCE REVIEW, 62 (December 1968), 1220-31.

Lieutenant governors are frequently members of pardon and parole boards, boards of education, and so on.

The office of attorney general has more real powers and responsibilities than that of lieutenant governor. Attorneys general are elected in forty-two states, appointed by the supreme court in Tennessee, by the legislature in Maine, and by the governor in Alaska, Hawaii, New Hampshire, New Jersey, Pennsylvania, and Wyoming. The attorney general is the chief legal counsel for the state. He represents the state in any suits to which it is a party. He acts as legal counsel for the governor and for other state officials. The legal business of state agencies is subject to his supervision. The source of the attorney general's power comes from his quasi-judicial duty of rendering formal written opinions in response to requests from the governor, state agencies, or other public officials regarding the legality and constitutionality of their acts. His opinions have the power of law in state affairs unless they are successfully challenged in court. The governor and other state officials are generally obliged to conform to the attorney general's legal opinion until a court specifies otherwise. He renders authoritative interpretations of state constitutions, laws, city ordinances, and administrative rulings.

The attorney general also has substantial law enforcement powers. Most states allow the attorney general to initiate criminal proceedings on his own motion, and nearly all states assign him responsibility for handling criminal cases on appeal to higher state courts or to federal courts. In some states the attorney general has supervisory powers over law enforcement throughout the state. The California Constitution, for example, gives the attorney general supervisory powers over all district attorneys and sheriffs in the state.

TABLE 6-9

Number of States with Elected Executive Officials

Governor	50	Labor Commission	6
Attorney General	42	University Regents	5
State Treasurer	40	Mining Commissioner	5
Secretary of State	39	Tax Commission	3
Lieutenant Governor	38	Highway Commissioner	1
State Auditor	29	Board of Equalization	1
Superintendent of Education	23	Printer	1
Public Utilities Commission	14	Railroad Commission	1
Agriculture Commission	12	Fish and Game Commission	1
Board of Education	11	Corporation Commission	1
Controller	10	Commissioner of Charities	1
Insurance Commission	9	Secretary of Internal Affairs	1
Land Commission	7	Adjutant and Inspector General	1

Most states have elected treasurers, and treasurers in other states are appointed by either the governor or the legislature. Treasurers are custodians of state funds: collecting taxes, acting as paymaster for the state, and administering the investment of state funds. The principal job of the treasurer is to make payments on departmental requisitions for payrolls and for checks to be issued to those who have furnished the state with goods or services. Generally, the department's requests for checks must be accompanied by a voucher showing the proper legislative authority for such payment. Generally, requests for payment must also be accompanied by a statement from the auditor's or the comptroller's office that legislative appropriations are available for such payment. Thus the treasurer's office works in close relation to another executive office of importance: that of auditor or comptroller. The principal duty of the office of state "auditor" is that of insuring the legislature that expenditures and investment of state funds have been made in accordance with the law. This function is known as a "postaudit" and occurs after state expenditures have been made. The primary duty of the office of the state "comptroller" is to insure that a prospective departmental expenditure is in accordance with the law and does not exceed the appropriations made by the legislature. This "preaudit" occurs before any expenditure is made by the treasurer. Public administration experts consider the comptroller's job of preaudit to be an executive function, and they urge that the comptroller be appointed by the governor. On the other hand, the job of postaudit is essentially a legislative check on the executive, and students of public administration generally feel that the auditor should be elected or appointed by the legislature. However, there is still some confusion in state organizations about the separate functions of auditors and comptrollers—some auditors do "preauditing" and some comptrollers do "postauditing."

Another interesting state office is that of secretary of state. Thirty-nine states elect secretaries of state and they are appoined by the governor in seven states and by the legislature in three. Only Hawaii does not have a secretary of state. Like the lieutenant governor, the secretary of state has very little to keep him busy. He is the chief custodian of state records and, in the case of several states, "keeper of the great seal of the commonwealth." He keeps many state documents filed in his office, including corporation papers. He also supervises the preparation of ballots and certifies election results for the state. The keeping of documents and the supervision of elections does not involve much discretionary power, since these activities are closely regulated by law.

SEVEN

Courts, Crime, and Correctional Policy

POLITICS AND THE JUDICIAL PROCESS

Courts are "political" institutions because they attempt to resolve conflicts among men. Like legislative and executive institutions, courts make public policy in the process of resolving conflict. Some of the nation's most important policy decisions have been made by courts rather than legislative or executive bodies. In recent years the federal courts have taken the lead in eliminating segregation in public life, insuring the separation of church and state, defining relationships between individuals and law enforcers, and guaranteeing individual voters an equal voice in government. These are just a few of the important policy decisions made by courts—policy decisions that are just as significant to all Americans as those made by Congress or the president. Courts, then, are deeply involved in policy making, and they are an important part of the political system in America. Sooner or later in American politics, most important policy questions reach the courts. Interests that are unsuccessful in the legislative and executive branches of government usually turn to the courts in a final effort to win their arguments. All manner of political controversy are brought to the courts—election disputes, rivalries between governmental agencies, disputes over the meaning of laws and constitutions, and so on.[1]

[1]For a discussion of courts as political institutions, see Herbert Jacob, *Justice in America* (Boston: Little, Brown and Company, 1965); and Henry J. Abraham, *The Judicial Process* (New York: Oxford University Press, Inc., 1962).

In resolving conflict and deciding about public policy, courts function very much like other government agencies. However, the *style* of judicial decision making differs significantly from legislative or executive decision making. First of all, courts rarely initiate policy decisions. Rather, they wait until a case involving a policy question they must decide is brought to them. However, the vast majority of cases brought before courts do not involve important policy issues. Much court activity involves the enforcement of existing public policy. Courts punish criminals, enforce contracts, and award damages to the victims of injuries. Most of these decisions are based upon established law. Only occasionally are important policy questions brought to the court. This "passive" character of the judicial process restricts the policy initiative of judges; neither legislators nor executives suffer from such restrictions. In defining the judicial process, Carl Brent Swisher observed that a court "determines the facts involved in particular controversies brought before it, relates the facts to the relevant law, settles the controversies in terms of the law, and more or less incidentally makes new law through the process of decision."[2]

Courts also differ from other government agencies in that *access* to them is governed by a special set of requirements. An interested individual or group must have an attorney and sufficient money to bear the expense of the court suit. Courts must accept "jurisdiction," which means that a dispute must meet judicial criteria of a "case" or the courts cannot settle it. A case must involve two disputing parties, one of which must have incurred some real damages as a result of the action or inaction of the other. For example, an individual who objects to the state welfare program cannot take his objections to a court unless he can show that the program inflicted some direct personal or property damage on him.

The *procedures* under which judges and other participants in the judicial process operate are also quite different from procedures in legislative or executive branches of government. Facts and arguments must be presented to the courts in the manner specified. Generally these communications are quite formal, and legal skills are generally required to provide written briefs or oral arguments that meet the technical specifications of the courts. While an interest group may hire a public relations firm to pressure a legislature, they must hire a law firm to put their arguments into a legal context. Decorum in courtrooms is rigorously enforced in order to convey a sense of dignity; seldom do legislatures or executive offices function with the same degree of decorum.

Courts must direct their decisions to *specific cases*. While higher courts sometimes depart from particular cases and announce general policy positions, most courts refrain from general policy statements and limit their

[2]Carl B. Swisher, "The Supreme Court and the Moment of Truth," *American Political Science Review*, 54 (December 1960), 879.

decisions to the particular circumstances of a case. Rarely do the courts announce a comprehensive policy in the way the legislature does when it enacts a law. Of course, the implication of a court's decision in a particular case is that future cases of the same nature will be decided the same way. This implication amounts to a policy statement; however, it is not as comprehensive as a legislative policy pronouncement, because future cases with only slightly different circumstances might be decided differently.

Perhaps the most important distinction between judicial decision making and decision making in other branches of government is that judges must not appear to permit political consideration to affect their decisions. Judges must not appear to base their decisions on partisan considerations, to bargain, or to compromise in decision making. Legislators and governors may base their decisions on party platforms or on their estimate of what will win in the next election, but such considerations are not supposed to influence judges. The *appearance of objectivity* in judicial decision making gives courts a measure of prestige that other governmental institutions lack. While it is true that judges have fewer direct ties with political organizations than legislators or governors, they are, of course, subject to social, economic, and political pressures just as other men are. Judges hold socioeconomic and political views just as everyone else, and they would be less than human if these views did not affect their decisions; but it is important that a large portion of the American public perceive judges as unaffected by personal considerations. Court decisions become more acceptable to the public if they believe that the courts have dispensed unbiased justice.

The distinctive features of the judicial process—its passive appearance special rules of access, specialized legal procedures, decorum, focus on particular cases, and appearance of objectivity in decision making—help to provide essential support for judicial decisions and thus enable the courts to play an influential role in the political system. These distinctive features help to "legitimize" the decisions reached by the courts; that is, they help to win popular acceptance of these decisions.

Legal traditions are influential in court decisions. English common law has vitally affected the law of all of our states except Louisiana, which was influenced by the Napoleonic Code. English common law developed in the thirteenth century through the decisions of judges who applied their notions of justice to specific cases. This body of judge-made law grew over the centuries and is still the foundation of our legal system today. Legislated statutes take precedence over common law, but the common law is applied by the courts where no statutory provisions are relevant. The degree to which statutory law has replaced common law varies among the states according to the comprehensiveness of state statutes and codes. Common law covers both criminal and civil law, although for the most part, the common law of crimes has been replaced by comprehensive criminal codes in the states.

THE STRUCTURE OF COURT SYSTEMS

State courts are generally organized into a hierarchy similar to that shown in Figure 7–1. The courts of a state constitute a single, integrated judicial system; even city courts, traffic courts, and justices of the peace are part of the state judicial system.

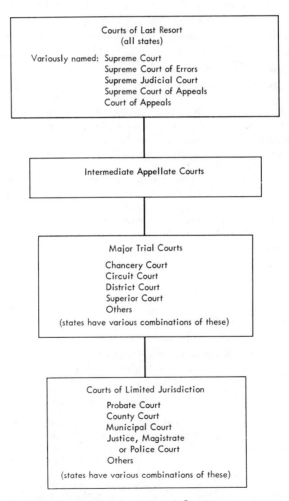

FIGURE 7–1 The Structure of State and Local Courts

At the lowest level are minor courts presided over by justices of the peace, magistrates, or police judges, who frequently have little formal training. These courts are concerned principally with traffic cases, small claims, and misdemeanors, although they may hold preliminary hearings to determine whether a person accused of a felony shall be held in jail or placed under bond. These grassroot courts have often bred distrust for the law because of their incompetence, their reliance upon the fee system, or their direct links with partisan politics.[3] Many justices of the peace have no training in the law.[4] There are frequent complaints about collusion between justices of the peace and local police in the maintenance of "speed traps" for collecting heavy fines from out-of-town motorists. Many "J.P.'s" are paid on a fee basis, which means that the J.P. is paid for the number of convictions he obtains; this has led to the cynical observation that "J.P." signifies "judgment for the plaintiff."

Kenneth N. Vines comments on the links between minor courts and party politics in the states:

> In many areas, particularly in those states with partisan elective methods of judicial selection, or where the judiciary is appointed by the governor, judicial office at the county and municipal level is one of the most important sources of patronage existent for the political parties. A careful study of the selection of judges in Chicago has shown how closely local judges are sometimes joined to the activities of political parties. Chicago judges recognized the need for taking time to maintain good party relations, for securing endorsement of party leaders to secure the judicial nomination, and on occasion were responding to political pressures that were brought to bear when important cases occur in which party influentials were interested. Often judges campaigned for judicial office and contributed to political campaign funds in order to hold their judgeships.[5]

Major trial courts of general jurisdiction—sometimes called district courts, circuit courts, superior courts, chancery courts, county courts, or common pleas courts—handle major civil and criminal cases arising out of statutes, common law, and state constitutions. The geographic jurisdiction of these courts is usually the county or city; there are about fifteen hundred major trial courts in the United States. Juries are used in these

---

[3]See Arthur T. Vanderbilt, *The Challenge of Law Reform* (Princeton: Princeton University Press, 1955).

[4]On the other hand, Henry J. Abraham quotes a Philadelphia chief magistrate as saying: "A law degree doesn't make a magistrate more qualified. Living with people is more essential than going to a law library to find out what it's all about . . . If you take Purdon's law books away from them (lawyers), they're out of business." Abraham, *The Judicial Process*, p. 130.

[5]Kenneth N. Vines, "Courts as Political and Governmental Agencies," in *Politics in the American States*, ed. Herbert Jacob and Kenneth Vines (Boston: Little, Brown and Company, 1965).

courts, and judges are generally qualified in the law. These courts handle criminal cases involving felonies and important civil suits. Almost all cases decided by state courts originate in these major trial courts; trial courts make the initial decision in cases carried to appellate and supreme courts and may also handle some appeals from minor courts. Although trial courts are courts of original jurisdiction rather than appeal courts, they are the only courts most individuals ever face.

Every state has a court of last resort, which is generally called the supreme court. These courts consist of three to nine judges, and most of their work is devoted to cases on appeal from major trial courts, although some states grant original jurisdiction to supreme courts in special types of cases. Since they consider questions of law rather than questions of fact, they sit without jury. State supreme courts are the most important and visible judicial bodies in the states. Their decisions are written, published, and distributed like the decisions of the U.S. Supreme Court. Judges can express their views in majority opinions, dissenting opinions, or concurring opinions. These courts get the most controversial cases and those with the most at stake, since these cases are most likely to be appealed all the way to the state's highest court. To relieve supreme courts of heavy case burdens, many of the more populous states maintain intermediate courts of appeal between trial courts and courts of last resort.

There is no appeal from the state supreme courts, except to the U.S. Supreme Court on federal constitutional grounds. This means that state supreme courts have the final word in the interpretation of state constitutions and laws. These courts seldom hesitate to exercise judicial review over state legislative acts.

Special courts can always be found in addition to those already mentioned, notably in large cities. These specialized courts handle domestic relations, juvenile delinquency, the probation of wills, small claims, and so on. It is interesting to note that many of the more populous urban states have created very complex court structures with many specialized types of courts.

THE MAKING OF A JUDGE

Political debate over methods of selecting judges in the states has been carried on for many years. In writing the federal Constitution, the Founding Fathers reflected conservative views in establishing an independent federal judiciary, whose members were appointed by the president for life terms and were not subject to direct popular control. Jacksonian views of popular election were strong in the states, however, and today a majority of state judges are directly elected by the people on partisan or non partisan ballots. Table 7–1 shows the several ways in which judges are selected. About half of the states elect their judges, some in partisan elections and some in nonpartisan elections in which candidates for the bench do not carry party labels. In five states, judges are chosen by their legislatures, and in seven states, they are appointed by the governor. Other states have adopted the "Missouri plan," in which governors appoint judges on the recommendations of a select committee, and after the judge has been in office for a year or more, the voters are given the opportunity to retain or oust the appointed judge.

The argument for selecting judges by appointment rests upon the value of judicial independence and isolation from direct political involvement. Critics of the elective method feel that it forces judges into political relationships and compromises their independence on the bench. This is particularly true if judicial elections are held on a partisan rather than a nonpartisan ballot, where judges must secure nomination with the support of party leaders. Moreover, it is argued that voters are not able to evaluate

TABLE 7-1
Methods of Judicial Selection in the States

Partisan Election	Election by Legislature	Nonpartisan Election	Appointment	Missouri Plan*
Alabama	Connecticut†	Alaska	Delaware	Arizona
Arkansas	Rhode Island	California	Hawaii	California
Florida	South Carolina	Colorado	Maine	Idaho
Georgia	Vermont	Illinois	Maryland	Michigan
Indiana	Virginia	Iowa	Massachusetts	Minnesota
Kentucky		Kansas	New Hampshire	Missouri
Louisiana		Missouri	New Jersey	Montana
Mississippi		Nebraska		Nevada
New Mexico		Oklahoma		North Dakota
New York		Utah		Ohio
North Carolina				Oregon
Pennsylvania				South Dakota
Texas				Tennessee
West Virginia				Washington
				Wisconsin
				Wyoming

* Several Missouri plan states select some judges according to the Missouri plan, other judges by election.

† Formally by legislature, actually by nomination of the governor.

SOURCE: STATE COURT SYSTEMS (Lexington, Ky.: Council of State Governments, 1970).

"legal" qualifications—knowledge of the law, judicial temperament, skill in the courtroom, and so on. Hence, judges should be appointed, rather than elected by voters. Attorneys, bar associations, and judges themselves prefer an appointive method in which they are given the opportunity to screen candidates and evaluate legal qualifications prior to appointment.

In contrast, supporters of an elective judiciary stress the importance of popular control over judges. If American voters are competent to select legislators and governors, why should they not select judges as well? William J. Keefe argues that elected, partisan judges better reflect society's values:

> The judgments of the courts reflect not only the established body of substantive law but also reflect in their opinions the changed economic conditions and social mores of our times. Therefore, it is to be hoped that a judge's political affiliation, which cannot help but have a substantial impact on his decisions, should be representative of the party which elects him. Any system which makes more remote the influence of the free electorate on those who hold high office should be discarded.[6]

Actually it is not possible to "take judges out of politics." Selection by appointment or by the Missouri plan removes the selection of judges from *party* politics, but simply places the selection in different political hands. Instead of party leaders, the governor or the bar association become the principal actors in judicial selection. Party leaders are assumed to be familiar with the wishes of attorneys. It is not clear which influence leads to "better" judges, or whether "better" judges are those more sensitive to community values or more trained in legal procedures. Interestingly, states with competitive two-party systems are not necessarily the same states that select their judges through partisan elections. Some of the competitive states appoint as well as elect their judges.

Although a majority of states elect their judges, in practice many judges come to the bench in elective states through the appointment procedure. The apparent paradox comes about because even in elective states, governors generally have the power to make interim judicial appointments when a judgeship is vacant because of the retirement or death of a judge between elections. An interim-appointed judge must seek election at the next regular election, but by that time he has acquired the prestige and status of a judge, and he is unlikely to be defeated by an outsider. Many members of the judiciary in elective states deliberately resign before the end of their term, if they are not seeking reelection, in order to give the governor the opportunity to fill the post by appointment. It is interest-

---

[6]William J. Keefe, "Judges and Politics: The Pennsylvania Plan of Judge Selection," *University of Pittsburgh Law Review* (May 1959), p. 628.

ing to note that over half of the supreme court judges in states that elect their judiciary come to the bench initially by means of appointment. In practice, then, the elective system of judicial selection is greatly compromised by the appointment of judges to fill unexpired terms.

Another feature of the elective system of judicial selection, which often escapes attention, is that few incumbent judges are ever defeated in running for reelection. The majority of judges seeking reelection are unopposed by anyone on the ballot, and fewer than 10 percent of the judges seeking reelection are ever defeated.[7] This suggests that even in states with elective systems of judicial selection, judges are still separated from the normal political recruitment process. Judges enjoy more stability and independence from popular control than do legislators or governors.

The Missouri plan is an interesting attempt to combine the elective and appointive systems of selection. The Missouri plan calls for a select committee of judges, attorneys, and laymen to make nominations for judicial vacancies. The governor appoints one of the committee's nominees to office. After the judge has served at least one year, his name is placed on a nonpartisan ballot without any other name in opposition. "Shall judge (the name of the judge is inserted) of the (the name of the court is inserted) be retained in office. Yes _____ No _____." If the voters vote yes, the judge is then entitled to a full term of office. If the voters vote no, the governor must select another name from those submitted by his nominating committee and repeat the whole process. In practice, a judge is hardly ever defeated under the Missouri plan, in part for the same reasons that make it difficult to defeat an incumbent judge (see preceding discussion). Moreover, since "you can't beat somebody with nobody," running under the referendum feature of the Missouri plan is the equivalent of being unopposed. One study reports that only one judge in 179 Missouri plan elections has been defeated—and that one under very extraordinary circumstances.[8] The effect is to place judicial selection in the hands of the judges or attorneys who compose the nominating committee and the governor, with only a semblance of voter participation. Reformers argue that the plan removes judges from politics and spares the electorate the problem of voting on judicial candidates when they know little about their professional qualifications. Actually, the Missouri plan has *not* resulted in the selection of better-qualified judges, although Missouri plan judges have had more experience as lower court judges than men selected by other methods.[9] The Missouri plan, however, is

[7]Jack Ladinsky and Alan Silver, "Popular Democracy and Judicial Independence," *Wisconsin Law Review* (1966), 132–33.

[8]Richard A. Watson and Rondal G. Downing, *The Politics of the Bench and Bar: Judicial Selection under the Missouri Nonpartisan Court Plan* (New York: John Wiley & Sons, Inc., 1969).

[9]*Ibid.*, Chapter 6.

very popular among reformers, and the list of Missouri plan states is growing rapidly.

Republicans have fared better in capturing judgeships than in winning legislative seats or governors' chairs. Stuart Nagel reports that Republicans outnumber Democrats almost two to one in judicial posts.[10] Of course, the one-party Democratic states have Democratic judges just as one-party Republican states have Republican judges; but Republicans do surprisingly well in winning judgeships in the competitive states, proportionately much better than Republican candidates for the legislature or governorship in these states. Most of the judges selected in nonpartisan elections refuse to identify themselves with a political party, as do nearly all the judges selected under the Missouri plan. Judges selected in partisan elections, of course, usually do not hesitate to identify themselves as Republicans or Democrats.

JUDICIAL DECISION MAKING

Conflict in state supreme courts, as measured by the number of divided opinions, is less frequent than in the U.S. Supreme Court. Dissenting votes are reported on more than half of all U.S. Supreme Court decisions, but state judges dissent in very few cases. The Council of State Governments reports that the rate of dissent in the state supreme courts is less than 10 percent in more than half of the states.[11] In only a few states is the rate of dissent regularly more than 20 percent—California, New York, Ohio, Michigan, and Pennsylvania. Public disagreement is somewhat more frequent in competitive party states where judges of both parties are represented on the court.

The infrequency of dissenting opinions may obscure a great deal of conflict in state courts. Supreme Court justices write dissenting opinions in order to keep alive a point of view that may serve as a basis for a majority decision by a later court. Well-written dissenting opinions on the U.S. Supreme Court attract the attention of scholars, judges, attorneys, and law students throughout the nation. They can have an important impact on legal thinking even though they represent a minority view on the Court. But seldom do state supreme courts attract enough attention to merit the writing of dissenting opinions. At the state level many judges feel that dissenting opinions are useless. Moreover, many judges feel that a lack of unanimity damages judicial prestige and may tend to destroy the myth of certainty within the law.

[10]Stuart Nagel, "Unequal Party Representation in State Supreme Courts," *Journal of the American Judicature Society*, 44 (1961), 62–65.

[11]*Workload of State Courts of Last Resort* (Chicago: Council of State Governments, 1962).

A great deal of judicial decision making involves economic interests. A large number of cases involving economic interests result from the important role of the states in the allocation of economic resources. All states regulate public utilities, including water, electrical companies, gas companies, and public transportation companies. The insurance industry is state regulated. Labor relations and workmen's compensation cases are frequently found in state courts. Litigation over natural resources, real estate, small-business regulations, gas, oil, lumber and mining, alcoholic beverage control, racing, and gambling all reflect the importance of state regulation in these fields.

Judges are also called upon to make decisions in political controversies—disputes over elections, appointments to government positions, and jurisdictional squabbles between governments. These cases may constitute 5 to 10 percent of the work load of the courts.

What is the impact of the party affiliation of the judges in court decision making? Party affiliation probably has little impact in decisions in lower trial courts, where much of the litigation has little to do with policy making. But at least two studies have shown party affiliation to be an important influence on state supreme court decision making.[12] Stuart Nagel found that Democratic judges differed from Republican judges by deciding more frequently:

1. For the defense in criminal cases;
2. For the administrative agency in business regulation cases;
3. For the claimant in unemployment compensation;
4. For finding a constitutional violation in criminal cases;
5. For the government in tax cases;
6. For the tenant in landlord-tenant cases;
7. For the consumer in sale-of-goods cases;
8. For the injured in motor vehicle cases;
9. For the employee in employee injury cases.

These decisions suggest that Democratic judges were more in sympathy with the consumer, the workingman, and the defendant in criminal cases, and less in sympathy with business and utilities seeking to avoid public regulation. These are the kinds of attitudes that we might expect Democrats to express, although there is no evidence that the party itself influences these judges. Rather it is likely that the judges' social, economic, and political views influence both their decisions on the court and their decision to affiliate with the Democratic or Republican party. Sidney

12Stuart Nagel, "Political Party Affiliation and Judges' Decisions," *American Political Science Association*, 55 (1961), 843–51; and Sidney Ulmer, "The Political Party Variable on the Michigan Supreme Court," *Journal of Public Law*, 11 (1962), 352–62.

Ulmer traced the influence of party affiliation on judges' decisions in the Michigan Supreme Court, particularly in workmen's compensation and contributory negligence cases involving attitudes toward labor. He found that Democratic judges are more likely to hold with the workingman in these cases, while Republican judges are more likely to decide in favor of the company.

What is the effect of social and ethnic group membership on judges' decisions? Judges, like other decision makers, generally belong to higher social and economic groups; white, Anglo-Saxon Protestants are disproportionately represented among state judges. Stuart Nagel found that judges who were members of ethnic minority groups in America were more likely to decide (1) for the defense in criminal cases, (2) for finding a violation in criminal constitutional cases, and (3) for the wife in divorce cases than were judges with white, Anglo-Saxon backgrounds.[13] He also found a difference in the decisions of Catholic and non-Catholic judges. Catholic judges tended to decide (1) for the defense in criminal cases, (2) for the administrative agency in business regulation cases, (3) for the wife in divorce settlement cases, (4) for the debtor in debtor-creditor cases, and (5) for the employee in employee injury cases. Nagel's studies suggest that party influence in judicial selection, with its tendency to grant representation to religious and ethnic groups in proportion to their electoral influence, may help to bring about decisions that reflect popular values.

Kenneth Vines has documented the influence of social and political views in race relations cases.[14] As one might expect, he found that southern state supreme courts were much less likely to find in favor of a black person's claims than federal courts handling the same claims. He also found that supreme courts in border states, those on the periphery of the Deep South, were more favorable toward blacks in race relations decisions than supreme courts in the Deep South. From 1954 to 1963, the average percentage of cases in which favorable decisions were rendered for blacks in Alabama, Arkansas, Georgia, Louisiana, Mississippi and South Carolina was 29 percent; the average for Florida, North Carolina, Tennessee, Texas, and Virginia during these same years was 37 percent. Georgia and Florida appear to be exceptions to the general proposition that the supreme courts reflect the prevailing social views in the state. Although racial attitudes in Florida are considered moderate by southern standards, the Florida Supreme Court compiled a very "anti-Negro" record, deciding for blacks in less than 10 percent of the cases, a record exceeded only by the Alabama Supreme Court. In contrast, in Georgia,

    13Stuart Nagel, "Ethnic Affiliation and Judicial Propensities," *Journal of Politics*, 24 (1962), 92–110.
    14Kenneth N. Vines, "Southern State Supreme Courts and Race Relations," *Western Political Quarterly*, 18 (1965), 5–18.

a Deep South state, the supreme court decided more than half of its race relations cases in favor of black claims. Southern supreme court judges are also prone to be more conservative than nonsouthern judges in areas outside of race relations.

On the whole, courts tend to be very conservative political bodies. Judicial activism on behalf of social reform in the U.S. Supreme Court is a relatively recent phenomenon. Historically, the Supreme Court was considered a bastion of conservatism, and state courts continue to be viewed as very conservative institutions. Doubtlessly, the heavy reliance that courts place on precedents in decision making is partly responsible for the conservatism of court decisions. The recent liberal posture of the U.S. Supreme Court has required it to overturn many earlier precedents; state courts feel more bound by earlier precedents than the U.S. Supreme Court and consequently are committed to a more conservative posture. Yet reliance upon precedents cannot be the whole explanation of judicial conservatism, because state judges appear to evidence conservative attitudes even when they are off the bench. Stuart Nagel reports that not only do the judges evidence a great deal of conservatism in their off-the-bench views, but also conservatism seems to make a difference in case decisions.[15] When Nagel compared judges having conservative off-the-bench attitudes with judges having liberal attitudes, the two groups differed significantly. Judges with higher liberal scores decided more frequently (1) for the defense in criminal cases, (2) for the administrative agency in business regulation cases, (3) for the injured party in motor vehicle accident cases, and (4) for the employee in employee injury cases. In other words, conservative judges were more likely to find for the state in criminal cases, against the state in business regulation cases, and in favor of insurance companies and employers in cases brought against them.

Judicial decision making is also influenced by judges' perceptions of their own role. The great debate of American jurisprudence centers about whether judges should make law in their decisions or whether they should limit themselves to interpreting the law. Great legalists have argued the merits of activism versus self-restraint in judicial decision making for more than a century.[16] Of course, popular debate about judicial activism is generally focused on the U.S. Supreme Court, but state court judges must also come to grips with this question. Henry Glick undertook to interview state supreme court judges in four states to ascertain their

---

[15]Stuart Nagel, "Off-the-Bench Judicial Attitudes," in *Judicial Decision-Making*, ed. Glendon Schubert (Glencoe: The Free Press, 1963).

[16]Jerome Frank, *Law and the Modern Mind* (New York: Coward-McCann, Inc., 1930); Benjamin N. Cardozo, *The Nature of the Judicial Process* (New Haven: Yale University Press, 1921); and Roscoe Pound, *Justice According to Law* (New Haven: Yale University Press, 1951).

views of their roles in decision making.[17] About half of the judges interviewed opted for the more restrained role of law interpreter:

> "We interpret the law. That is our function. We're not authorized to write the law. We can only act in one way: that is to be solely interpreters of the law. The moment he steps out of the role of interpreter, he violates the Constitution which separates the legislative from the judiciary."

Less than one-quarter saw themselves as "lawmaker":

> "Inevitably a judge makes law as does a legislative body. No matter how you decide a case you're making law. Whether you say yes or no in a case, you're making law. . . . Judges always make law and always will."

And some judges were characterized as "pragmatists":

> "When you're a judge, you're part legislator, executive, and judge. You're a creature of all three branches of government when you make a decision. All sorts of things come into consideration."

Some state courts as a whole are more active in policy making than others. For example, Glick found that the New Jersey court had a majority of activists who not only saw themselves as lawmakers in judicial decision making but also regularly made recommendations to the state legislature about laws they wanted passed. In contrast, the Louisiana Supreme Court was nearly unanimous in its strict constructionism.

In summary, judicial decision making is influenced by interest group activity, political party affiliation, social and ethnic ties, religious affiliations, and the liberal and conservative views of judges. This does not mean that "judicial impartiality" is nonexistent or that judges are as free as legislators or governors to write their social and political views into the law. Judges participate in the game of politics as players as well as umpires, but they are limited by the rules of the game, the decisions of legislatures and governors, and public expectations about the way judges ought to behave.

CRIME IN THE STATES

Crime rates are the subject of a great deal of popular discussion. Very often they are employed to express the degree of social disorganization or even the effectiveness of law enforcement agencies. Crime rates are

[17]Henry Glick, *Supreme Courts in State Politics* (New York: Basic Books, Inc., Publishers, 1971). The quotations are from state supreme court judges, pp. 39–42.

based upon the Federal Bureau of Investigation's *Uniform Crime Reports,*
but the FBI reports are based on figures supplied by state and local police
agencies. (See Table 7–2.) The FBI has succeeded in establishing a uniform classification of the number of serious crimes per 100,000 people
that are known to the police—murder and nonnegligent manslaughter,
forcible rape, robbery, aggravated assault, burglary, larceny, and theft,
including auto theft. But record keeping is still a problem, and one
should be cautious in interpreting official crime rates. They are really a
function of several factors: the diligence of police in detecting crime,
the adequacy of the reporting system tabulating crime, and the amount
of crime itself. Yet the evidence seems inescapable that crime in the
United States is increasing at a rapid pace. The greatest increase in
crime rates occurs in nonviolent crimes—burglary, larceny, theft—and
lesser increases are found in crimes involving violence against the person—murder and nonnegligent manslaughter and robbery.

Crime rates are related to urbanization and economic development in
the states.[18] The nation's highest crime rates are in California, New York,
and Nevada, and its lowest are in North Dakota and Mississippi. Generally, the urban industrial high-income states have higher crime rates
than the rural agricultural low-income states. Urbanization and economic

TABLE 7-2

Crime Rates in the United States
Offenses Known to the Police
(Rates per 100,000 Population)

	1960	1965	1970	Percent Increase 1960-1970
Murder and non-negligent manslaughter	5	5	8	56
Forcible rape	9	12	18	95
Robbery	52	61	172	186
Aggravated assault	82	107	162	92
Burglary	465	605	1,068	113
Larceny	271	393	859	204
Auto theft	179	251	454	150
Total crimes against person	148	185	360	126
Total crimes against property	916	1,260	2,381	147

SOURCE: FBI, UNIFORM CRIME REPORTS, 1966-1971.

[18]See Thomas R. Dye, *Politics, Economics, and the Public* (Chicago: Rand McNally
& Co., 1966), pp. 219–22.

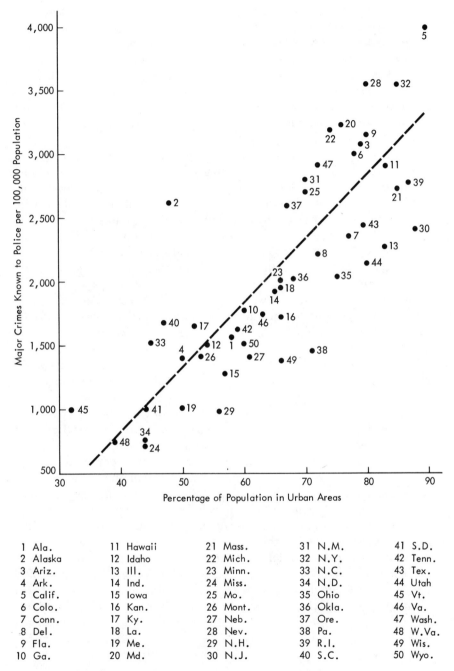

FIGURE 7–2   The Fifty States Arranged According to Urbanization and Crime Rates

1	Ala.	11	Hawaii	21	Mass.	31	N.M.	41	S.D.
2	Alaska	12	Idaho	22	Mich.	32	N.Y.	42	Tenn.
3	Ariz.	13	Ill.	23	Minn.	33	N.C.	43	Tex.
4	Ark.	14	Ind.	24	Miss.	34	N.D.	44	Utah
5	Calif.	15	Iowa	25	Mo.	35	Ohio	45	Vt.
6	Colo.	16	Kan.	26	Mont.	36	Okla.	46	Va.
7	Conn.	17	Ky.	27	Neb.	37	Ore.	47	Wash.
8	Del.	18	La.	28	Nev.	38	Pa.	48	W.Va.
9	Fla.	19	Me.	29	N.H.	39	R.I.	49	Wis.
10	Ga.	20	Md.	30	N.J.	40	S.C.	50	Wyo.

development involve certain social complications: a certain degree of unemployment seems inevitable; the transition from rural to urban life creates many social problems; social isolation and hostility are frequent by-products; traditional value systems and social control are undermined and not immediately replaced by other values and institutions. All these traditions are associated with crime. Figure 7–2 shows the relationship between urbanization and crime rates in the states. Nevada is the most deviant state; it has a much higher crime rate than its degree of urbanization would suggest.

Crime rates in Nevada suggest that crime is related to gambling. Nevada has the most permissive gambling laws of any state in the nation. About half of the states report revenue from gambling or pari-mutuel betting. The highest amount is, of course, reported in Nevada, which receives about a quarter of its state revenue from gambling taxes. Gambling and pari-mutuel betting are found more frequently in the urban industrial states than in the rural agricultural states. Since both gambling and crime rates are associated with urbanization and industrialization, it is difficult to say whether or not gambling itself brings about an increase in the crime rate, or whether the association between the two is merely a product of the fact that they both occur in urban, industrial states. Nevada's extraordinarily high crime rate, however, suggests that gambling does contribute to an increase in crime.

Police statistics vastly understate the real amount of crime. Citizens do not report many crimes to police. The National Opinion Research Center of the University of Chicago asked a national sample of individuals whether they or any member of their household had been a victim of crime during the past year. This survey revealed that the actual amount of crime is several times greater than that reported by the FBI. There are more than twice as many crimes committed as reported to the police. The number of forcible rapes was more than three and one-half times the number reported, burglaries three times, aggravated assaults and larcenies more than double, and robbery 50 percent greater than the reported rate. Only auto theft statistics were reasonably accurate, indicating that most people call the police when their cars are stolen.

Interviewees gave a variety of reasons for their failure to report crime to the police. The most common reason was the feeling that police could not be effective in dealing with the crime. This is a serious comment about police protection in America today. Other reasons included the feeling that the crime was "a private matter" or that the victim did not want to harm the offender. Fear of reprisal was mentioned much less frequently, usually in cases of assaults and family crimes.

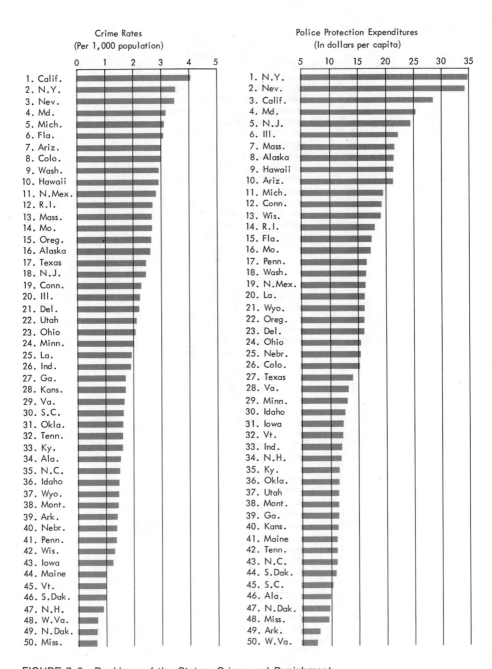

Crime Rates
(Per 1,000 population)

0   1   2   3   4   5

1. Calif.
2. N.Y.
3. Nev.
4. Md.
5. Mich.
6. Fla.
7. Ariz.
8. Colo.
9. Wash.
10. Hawaii
11. N.Mex.
12. R.I.
13. Mass.
14. Mo.
15. Oreg.
16. Alaska
17. Texas
18. N.J.
19. Conn.
20. Ill.
21. Del.
22. Utah
23. Ohio
24. Minn.
25. La.
26. Ind.
27. Ga.
28. Kans.
29. Va.
30. S.C.
31. Okla.
32. Tenn.
33. Ky.
34. Ala.
35. N.C.
36. Idaho
37. Wyo.
38. Mont.
39. Ark.
40. Nebr.
41. Penn.
42. Wis.
43. Iowa
44. Maine
45. Vt.
46. S.Dak.
47. N.H.
48. W.Va.
49. N.Dak.
50. Miss.

Police Protection Expenditures
(In dollars per capita)

5   10   15   20   25   30   35

1. N.Y.
2. Nev.
3. Calif.
4. Md.
5. N.J.
6. Ill.
7. Mass.
8. Alaska
9. Hawaii
10. Ariz.
11. Mich.
12. Conn.
13. Wis.
14. R.I.
15. Fla.
16. Mo.
17. Penn.
18. Wash.
19. N.Mex.
20. La.
21. Wyo.
22. Oreg.
23. Del.
24. Ohio
25. Nebr.
26. Colo.
27. Texas
28. Va.
29. Minn.
30. Idaho
31. Iowa
32. Vt.
33. Ind.
34. N.H.
35. Ky.
36. Okla.
37. Utah
38. Mont.
39. Ga.
40. Kans.
41. Maine
42. Tenn.
43. N.C.
44. S.Dak.
45. S.C.
46. Ala.
47. N.Dak.
48. Miss.
49. Ark.
50. W.Va.

FIGURE 7–3   Rankings of the States: Crime and Punishment

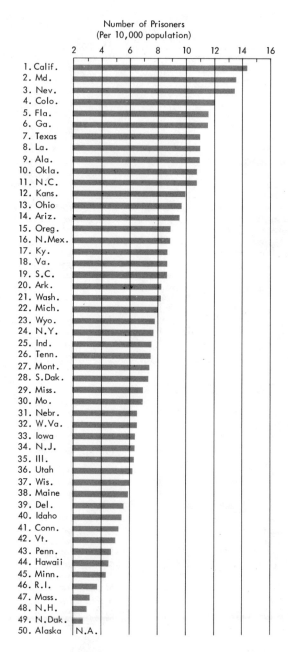

Number of Prisoners
(Per 10,000 population)

FIGURE 7–3   (cont.)

POLICE PROTECTION IN THE STATES

State, county, and municipal governments are all directly involved in law enforcement. Every state has a central law enforcement agency, sometimes called the state police, state troopers, state highway patrol and even Texas Rangers. At one time, state governors had only the National Guard at their disposal to back up local law enforcement efforts, but the coming of the automobile and intercity highway traffic led to the establishment in every state of a centralized police system. In addition to patrolling the state's highways, these centralized agencies now provide expert aid and service for local police officers and strengthen law enforcement in sparsely populated regions. Three-quarters of the states have given their central police agencies full law enforcement authority in addition to highway duties: they may quell riots, cooperate with local authorities in the apprehension of criminals, or even intervene when local authorities are unable or unwilling to enforce the law. The size and influence of these agencies vary from state to state. State police range in number from two dozen in Nevada and Alaska to over three thousand in California. On the whole, however, state police forces constitute a very small proportion of the total law enforcement effort in America. Law enforcement in the nation is principally a local responsibility.

Historically, the county sheriff has been the keystone of law enforcement in the United States. He and his deputies are still the principal enforcement and arresting officers in the rural counties and in the unincorporated fringe areas of many urban counties. In addition, the sheriff serves as an executive agent for county and state courts in both civil and criminal matters, and he maintains the county jail for the retention of persons whose trials or sentences are pending or who are serving short terms of punishment. The sheriff's office is a political one; in every state except Rhode Island he is an elected official. Very often the office of sheriff is a lucrative one. Antiquated fee systems exist in many states in which a sheriff collects a fee for every order, process, warrant, or arrest in which he is involved. Small fortunes can be made by "diligent" sheriffs in one term of office. Constables are elected in most states to perform many of the same functions of sheriffs for rural townships or other subdivisions of the county. Reliance upon the sheriff's office for law enforcement is a characteristic of rural states. Since municipal police forces usually assume the sheriff's law enforcement duties within the boundaries of municipalities, the sheriff's office has seriously atrophied in most urban states; often he is reduced to a process server for the courts.

Urban police departments are the most important instruments of law enforcement and public safety in the nation today. About two-thirds of the nation's population live in municipalities and depend upon municipal police for their protection. City policemen vastly outnumber all other state and county law enforcement officers combined. The urban police department does more than merely enforce the law; it engages in a wide range of activities for social control.

Urban industrial states employ more policemen than rural farm states.[19] We have already seen that urbanization brings about increases in crime rates, so it is not surprising that urbanization also requires an increase in police protection. Urbanization, crime rates, and police protection are all interrelated. But even if urbanization has stabilized, there is still a significant relationship between crime rates and police protection. An increase in the crime rate leads to an increase in police protection.

THE POLITICS OF PROSECUTION

Prosecution is part of the political process. Legislatures and governors enact policy, but its enforcement depends upon the decisions of prosecutors as well as judges. Political pressures are most obvious in the enforcement of controversial policies—gambling laws, Sunday closing laws, liquor rules, laws against prostitution, and other laws that are contrary to the interests of significant segments of the population. But prosecution also involves decision making about the allocation of law enforcement resources to different types of offenses—traffic violations, juvenile delinquency, auto theft, assault, burglary, larceny, and robbery. Decisions must be made about what sections of the city should be most vigorously protected and what segments of the population will be most closely watched. The public prosecutor, sometimes called the district attorney (D.A.) or state's attorney, is at the center of diverse pressures concerning law enforcement.

The political nature of the prosecutor's job is suggested by the frequency with which this job leads to higher political office. Prosecuting attorney is often a stepping-stone to state and federal judgeships, congressional seats, and even the governorship. An ambitious D.A., concerned with his political future, may seek to build a reputation as a crusader against crime and vice, while at the same time maintaining the support and friendship of important interests in the community. The political power of the prosecutor stems from his discretion in deciding (1) whether or not to prosecute in criminal cases, and (2) whether prosecution will be on more-serious or less-serious charges.

[19]Dye, *Politics, Economics, and the Public*, pp. 223–26.

Kenneth Vines describes some of the discretionary power of the prosecutor:

> The important points at which criminal procedures against persons may either be dropped or carried through by the prosecutor begin with actual arrest and the possibility of police discharge after arrest. Next, failure to issue an affidavit showing the cause of arrest may also result in dropping charges. A flexible weapon in the hands of the prosecutor is a device of "nolle prosequi" or "nol-pros." . . . a case is "nol-pros" whenever an arrest has been made and a charge issued but the prosecutor feels that adequate proof is lacking or for some other reason he feels that the case should not be pressed. . . . Even when a person is indicted for a crime, the consequences of conviction may be considerably mitigated by a decision of the prosecutor to allow a guilty plea, possibly with a lesser charge than the one originally contemplated, or on a promise of a lighter sentence. Even if an individual is convicted, the prosecutor may play a role in allowing him to seek bench parole with all of the attendant advantages that a respite for the conviction may bring.[20]

Herbert Jacob has documented the extent of discretion in the criminal prosecution in New Orleans.[21] Nearly half of all offenses were dismissed by the prosecutor. An additional 5 percent were permitted to plead guilty on reduced charges; 40 percent of the defendants apparently felt it was to their advantage to plead guilty on the original charge; only 10 percent pleaded innocent and went to trial. In short, the prosecutor is a central figure in the judicial process, and his power makes him an important political figure in the community.

CRIME AND THE COURTS

Chief Justice Warren E. Burger has argued persuasively that rising crime in America is partly due to inadequacies in our system of criminal justice. "The present system of criminal justice does not deter criminal conduct," he said in a special State of the Federal Judiciary message. "Whatever deterrent effect may have existed in the past has now virtually vanished."[22] He urged major reform in law enforcement, courts, prisons, probation, and parole.

A major stumbling block to effective law enforcement is the current plight of America's judicial machinery.

20Vines, "Courts as Political and Governmental Agencies," p. 251.
21Herbert Jacob, "Politics and Criminal Prosecution in New Orleans," in *Studies in Judicial Politics*, Tulane Studies in Political Science, Vol. VIII, ed. Kenneth Vines and Herbert Jacob (New Orleans: Tulane University, 1963).
22Chief Justice Warren E. Burger, address on the State of the Federal Judiciary to the American Bar Association, August 10, 1970.

Major congestion on court dockets which delays the hearing of cases months or even years. Moreover, actual trials now average twice as long as they did ten years ago.

Failure of courts to adopt modern management and administrative practices to speed and improve justice.

Increased litigation in the courts. Not only are more Americans aware of their rights, but more are using every avenue of appeal. Seldom do appeals concern the guilt or innocence of the defendant, but usually focus on procedural matters.

Excessive delays in trials. "Defendants, whether guilty or innocent, are human; they love freedom and hate punishment. With a lawyer provided to secure release without the need for a conventional bail bond, most defendants, except in capital cases, are released pending trial. We should not be surprised that a defendant on bail exerts a heavy pressure on his court-appointed lawyer to postpone the trial as long as possible so as to remain free. These postponements—and sometimes there are a dozen or more—consume the time of judges and court staffs as well as of lawyers. Cases are calendared and reset time after time while witnesses and jurors spend endless hours just waiting."[23]

Excessive delays in appeals. "We should not be surprised at delay when more and more defendants demand their undoubted constitutional right to trial by jury because we have provided them with lawyers and other needs at public expense; nor should we be surprised that most convicted persons seek a new trial when the appeal costs them nothing and when failure to take the appeal will cost them freedom. Being human a defendant plays out the line which society has cast him. Lawyers are competitive creatures and the adversary system encourages contention and often rewards delay; no lawyer wants to be called upon to defend the client's charge of incompetence for having failed to exploit all the procedural techniques which we have deliberately made available."[24]

Excessive variation in sentencing. Some judges let defendants off on probation for crimes that would draw five- or ten-year sentences by other judges. While flexibility in sentencing is essential in dealing justly with individuals, perceived inconsistencies damage the image of the courts in the public mind.

Excessive "plea bargaining" between the prosecution and the defendant's attorney in which the defendant agrees to plead guilty to a lesser offense if the prosecutor will drop more serious charges.

The current system of criminal justice is certainly no serious deterrent to crime. Most behavioral research suggests that it is not the severity of punishment that affects behavior, but the establishment of a sure linkage between the errant behavior and the punishment. In other words, crime is more likely to be deterred by making puishment sure, rather than severe. The best available estimates of the ratio between crime and

[23]*Ibid.*
[24]*Ibid.*

punishment, however, suggest that the likelihood of an individual's being jailed for a serious crime is less than one in a hundred. (See Figure 7–4.) Most crimes are not even reported by the victim. Police are successful in clearing only about one in five reported crimes by arresting the offender. The judicial system convicts only about one in four of the persons arrested and charged; others are not prosecuted, are handled as juveniles, are found not guilty, or are permitted to plead guilty to a lesser charge and released. Only about half of the convicted felons are given prison sentences.

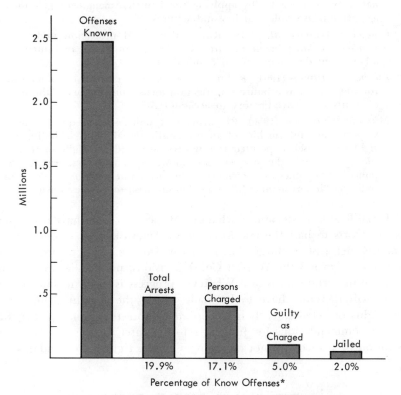

Percentage of Know Offenses*

*Actual crime is estimated to be two and one-half times the known offenses. If the base were actual crime, these percentages would be less than half of those appearing in the figure. Thus, the number of persons jailed as a percentage of actual crime is less than one percent.

FIGURE 7–4   Law Enforcement in Relation to Crime

Source: Statistical Abstract of the United States, 1970, p. 146.

RIGHTS OF DEFENDANTS

The Warren Court—the Supreme Court of the 1950s and 1960s, under the guidance of Chief Justice Earl Warren—greatly strengthened the rights of accused persons in criminal cases. Several key decisions were made by a split vote of the Court and drew heavy criticism from law enforcement officers and others as hamstringing police in their struggle with lawlessness. These decisions included:

> *Mapp* v. *Ohio* (1961). Barring the use of illegally seized evidence in criminal cases in the states by applying the Fourth Amendment guarantee against unreasonable searches and seizures.
>
> *Gideon* v. *Wainwright* (1963). Ruling that equal protection under the Fourteenth Amendment requires that legal counsel be appointed for all indigent defendants in all criminal cases.
>
> *Escobedo* v. *Illinois* (1964). Ruling that a suspect is entitled to confer with counsel as soon as a police investigation focuses on him once "the process shifts from investigatory to accusatory."
>
> *Miranda* v. *Arizona* (1966). Requiring that police—before questioning a suspect—must inform him of all his constitutional rights including the right to counsel, appointed free if necessary, and the right to remain silent. Although the suspect may knowingly waive these rights, the police cannot question anyone who at any point asks for a lawyer or indicates "in any manner" that he does not wish to be questioned.

It is difficult to ascertain to what extent these decisions have really hampered efforts to halt the rise in crime in America. The Supreme Court under Chief Justice Burger has not extended the rights of accused persons much beyond the Warren Court decisions, nor has it reversed any of these important decisions. Whatever progress is made in law enforcement will therefore have to be made within the current definition of the rights of defendants. It is important to note that Chief Justice Burger's recommendations for judicial reform center on the speedy administration of justice and not on changes in the rights of defendants.

THE MIRANDA CASE: TWO VIEWS

> The cases before us raise questions which go to the roots of our concepts of American criminal jurisprudence: the restraints society must observe consistent with the Federal Constitution in prosecuting individuals for crime.
>
> . . . These precious rights were fixed in our Constitution only after centuries of persecution and struggle. . . .

In the cases before us today, given this background, we concern ourselves primarily with this interrogation atmosphere and the evils it can bring. . . .

It is obvious that such an interrogation environment is created for no purpose other than to subjugate the individual to the will of his examiner. This atmosphere carries its own badge of intimidation. To be sure, this is not physical intimidation, but it is equally destructive of human dignity. The current practice of incommunicado interrogation is at odds with one of our nation's most cherished principles—that the individual may not be compelled to incriminate himself.

—Chief Justice Earl Warren in *Miranda* v. *Arizona* (1966).

There can be little doubt that the Court's new code would markedly decrease the number of confessions. . . .

How much harm this decision will inflict on law enforcement cannot fairly be predicted with accuracy. . . . We do know that some crimes cannot be solved without confessions, that ample expert testimony attests to their importance in crime control, and that the Court is taking a real risk with society's welfare in imposing its new regime on the country. The social costs of crime are too great to call the new rules anything but a hazardous experimentation.

. . . confessions, and the responsible course of police action they represent, are to be sacrificed to the Court's own finespun conception of fairness which I seriously doubt is shared by many thinking citizens in this country.

—Justice John H. Harlan, dissenting in *Miranda* v. *Arizona*.

POLICE AND LAW ENFORCEMENT

Police perform at least three important functions in urban society— law enforcement, keeping the peace, and furnishing services. Actually, law enforcement may take up only a small portion of a policeman's daily activity, perhaps only 10 percent.[25] The service function is far more common—attending accidents, directing traffic, escorting crowds, assisting stranded motorists, handling drunks, and so on. (See Table 7–3). The function of peace keeping is also very common—breaking up fights, quieting noisy parties, handling domestic or neighborhood quarrels, and the like. It is in this function that police exercise the greatest discretion in the application of the law. In most of these incidents blame is difficult to determine, participants are reluctant to file charges, and police must use personal discretion in handling each case.

Police are generally recruited from working-class families; only a hand-

[25]James Q. Wilson, *Varieties of Police Behavior* (Cambridge: Harvard University Press, 1968), p. 18; Arthur Niederhoffer, *Behind the Shield* (New York: Doubleday & Company, Inc., 1967), p. 71.

TABLE 7-3

Police Functions

Citizen Complaints Radioed to Police Vehicles,
Syracuse Police Department, June 3-9, 1966[a]

Calls [b]	Number in Sample	Percentage
Information Gathering		69	22.1
Book and check	2		
Get a report	67		
Service		117	37.5
Accidents, illnesses, ambulance calls	42		
Animals	8		
Assist a person	1		
Drunk person	8		
Escort vehicle	3		
Fire, power line or tree down	26		
Lost or found person or property	23		
Property damage	6		
Maintenance of Order		94	30.1
Gang disturbance	50		
Family trouble	23		
Assault, fight	9		
Investigation	8		
Neighbor trouble	4		
Law Enforcement		32	10.3
Burglary in progress	9		
Check a car	5		
Open door or window	8		
Prowler	6		
Make an arrest	4		
Totals		312	100.0

[a] Based upon a one-fifth sample of the week's calls.

[b] Not included are internal calls: those originating with other police officers or purely administrative calls.

SOURCE: James Q. Wilson, VARIETIES OF POLICE BEHAVIOR
(Cambridge: Harvard University Press, 1968), p. 18.

ful come from middle-class backgrounds, and only a few have more than
a high school education. Yet the tasks that they are assigned in society
would confound highly trained social scientists. Generally the segment
of the population from which police are recruited is more intolerant of
unpopular views and authoritarian in its ideas of family and social life.
Formal police training emphasizes self-control and caution in dealing with

the public, but on-the-job experiences probably reinforce predispositions toward intolerance and distrust of others. The element of danger in the policeman's job makes him naturally suspicious of others. Policemen see much of the "worst kind" of people, and they see even the "best kind" at their worst.

Policemen are engaged in rule enforcement as members of a semi-military organization. They are concerned with authority themselves, and they expect others to respect authority. It is often difficult for even the most well-meaning police officer to develop respect or sympathy for ghetto residents. One policeman described this problem as follows:

> The police have to associate with lower class people, slobs, drunks, criminals, riff-raff of the worst sort. Most of these . . . are Negroes. The police officers see these people through middle class or lower middle class eyeballs. But even if he saw them through highly sophisticated eye-balls he can't go in the street and take this night after night. When some Negro criminal says to you a few times, "you white mother-fucker, take that badge off and I'll shove it up your ass," well it's bound to affect you after a while. Pretty soon you decide they're all just niggers and they'll never be anything but niggers. It would take not just an average man to resist this feeling, it would take an extraordinary man to resist it, and there are very few ways by which the police department can attract extraordinary men to join them.[26]

Police themselves are not immune to social prejudice. The policeman's attitude toward ghetto residents is often affected by the high crime rates in ghetto areas. The policeman is suspicious of ghetto residents because crime rates tell him that his suspicions are often justified. Sociologists interviewing policemen in the cities that experienced riots in 1967 reported that 79 percent of the policemen did not think that blacks were treated unequally.[27] The policemen, however, accurately perceived the hostility directed at them in the ghettos. They believed that only a small minority of blacks, as compared with a substantial majority of whites, regarded them as friends. Moreover, the police viewed themselves much as blacks viewed them—as unwelcome aliens in the ghetto: they reported feeling isolated in a hostile atmosphere but could not understand why blacks resented them. Finally, antiblack attitudes among the policemen interviewed were fairly strong; for example, 49 percent did not approve of socializing between whites and blacks, and 56 percent were disturbed by the movement of blacks into white neighborhoods.

Policemen tend to view ghetto riots as acts of criminal irresponsibility rather than as social or political protest. A large majority of the

---

26Wilson, *Varieties of Police Behavior*, p. 43.

27*Supplemental Studies for the National Advisory Commission on Civil Disorders* (Washington, D.C.: Government Printing Office, 1968), p. 44.

policemen interviewed in 1967 believed that the riots "are caused by nationalists and militants" (77 percent) and that "criminal elements are involved in riots" (69 percent); fewer than one-third of the policemen (31 percent) believed that "unheard Negro complaints are involved in riots."[28] Policemen are not particularly sensitive to the underlying social and economic problems of the ghetto. They tend to regard a riot as primarily a problem in mob control and the suppression of criminal activity. High crime rates in the ghetto make the police naturally suspicious of ghetto residents, particularly young people. Policemen frequently view judges as too lenient in law enforcement. They often look upon civil rights groups as contributors to violence and upon social agencies as misguided social reform institutions that do not understand the legitimacy of force.

One commentator described the dilemma of police-ghetto relations as follows:

> First, the police department recruits from a population (the working class) whose numbers are more likely than the average population to hold anti-Negro attitudes; second, the recruits are given a basic classroom training program that is unlikely to change the anti-Negro sentiments; third, the recruit goes out on the street as a patrolman and is more likely than not to have his anti-Negro attitudes reinforced and hardened by the older officer; fourth, in the best departments, the most able officers are soon transferred to specialized administrative duties in training, recruitment, juvenile work, etc., or are promoted after three to five years to supervisory positions; fifth, after five years the patrolman on street duty significantly increases in levels of cynicism, authoritarianism, and generalized hostility to the nonpolice world. Finally, it is highly likely that the worst of the patrolmen will wind up patrolling the ghetto because that tends to be the least wanted assignment.

> If this is an accurate description of the urban police system (and my personal observations over the past five years tell me this is so), then the reason is clear why every poll of black citizens shows the same high level of distrust and hostility against policemen.[29]

THE GROWING FEDERAL ROLE
IN LAW ENFORCEMENT

Historically, state and local governments exercised principal responsibility for law enforcement in America. The Federal Bureau of Investigation and the Justice Department were charged with the responsibility

28*Ibid.*, p. 96.
29Burton Levy, "Cops in the Ghetto," in *Riots and Rebellion*, ed. Louis Masotti and Donald Bowen (New York: Sage Publications, 1968), p. 353.

of enforcing federal law. The federal government employs less than fifty thousand persons in all law enforcement activities, compared with over five hundred thousand state and local law enforcement personnel. Federal prisons contain twenty-five thousand inmates, compared with two hundred thousand in state prisons. Federal involvement in state and local law enforcement, however, is growing.

In the Crime Control and Safe Street Act of 1968, Congress created the Law Enforcement Assistance Administration within the Department of Justice to channel federal grants-in-aid to the states for use in upgrading state and local law enforcement programs. Most of these funds come to the states as "bloc grants" to be employed by the states as they see fit in improving state or local law enforcement. The money may be spent on court reform and correctional programs as well as on police protection. While it is too early to evaluate the effectiveness of this grant program, critics have charged that the states do not always channel this money into the cities where crime rates are highest.

Congress has the opportunity to lead the nation in fighting urban crime in the District of Columbia. Responsibility for the governance of the District of Columbia rests with Congress itself, and this area has one of the highest crime rates in the nation. In 1970 Congress enacted a series of proposals by the Nixon administration to reduce crime in the area and provide a model for urban law enforcement throughout the nation. Among other things, the District of Columbia Court Reorganization and Criminal Procedure Act of 1970:

1. Established a modern independent court system for the District of Columbia with an executive officer to manage court operations;
2. Lowered to fifteen the age at which a juvenile charged with a felony could be tried as an adult;
3. Authorized a life sentence for a third felony conviction and set a minimum five-year sentence for a second armed crime of violence;
4. Authorized "no-knock" search and arrest warrants if police have "probable cause to believe" that notice was likely to result in the destruction of evidence, danger to police, or escape;
5. Authorized pretrial detention of up to sixty days of a defendant so dangerous that no conditions of release (bail) would assure the community's safety.

It is still too early to judge the effectiveness of these provisions, but critics have challenged both their constitutionality and their effectiveness. Although many crimes are committed by persons out on bail, pretrial detention of "dangerous" suspects might be questioned as a violation of the Eighth Amendment guarantee against excessive bail; the "no-knock" provisions might violate the Fourth Amendment prohibition on "unreasonable" searches and seizures. Yet it is clear that states and communities are increasingly turning to Washington for guidance and assistance in the fight against crime.

STATE CORRECTIONAL POLICIES

Correctional policies vary enormously among the states. States differ in the number of persons committed to prison, correctional expenditures per capita, the care and treatment provided offenders, and the policies governing the parole of prisoners and in many other aspects of penology. Perhaps the explanation for the wide range of state policies in correction lies in the deep division among the American people concerning correctional philosophy. At least four separate theories of crime and punishment compete for preeminence in guiding correctional policies.[30] First, there is the ancient Judeo-Christian idea of holding the individual responsible for his guilty acts and compelling him to pay a debt to society. Another philosophy argues that punishment should be sure, speedy, and commensurate with the crime, and sufficiently conspicuous to deter others from committing crime. Still another consideration in correctional policy is that of protecting the public from lawbreakers or habitual criminals by segregating these people behind prison walls. Finally, there is the theory that criminals are partly or entirely victims of social circumstances beyond their control and that society owes them comprehensive treatment in form and rehabilitation.

Over two million Americans each year are prisoners in a jail, police station, or juvenile home or penitentiary. The vast majority are released within one year. There are, however, about a quarter of a million inmates in state and federal prisons in the United States. These prisoners are serving time for serious offenses: 90 percent had a record of crime before they committted the act that led to their current imprisonment.

If correctional systems could be made to work—that is, actually to rehabilitate men as useful law-abiding citizens—the benefits to the nation would be enormous. The Law Enforcement Assistance Administration estimates that 80 percent of all felonies are committed by repeaters—individuals who have had prior contact with the criminal justice system and were not corrected by it.[31] Penologists generally recommend more education and job training, more and better facilities, smaller prisons,

---

30See Daniel Glaser, *The Effectiveness of a Prison and Parole System* (Indianapolis and New York: The Bobbs-Merrill Co., Inc., 1964).

31See Congressional Quarterly, *Crime and the Law* (Washington: Congressional Quarterly Inc., 1971), p. 11.

halfway houses where offenders can adjust to civilian life before parole, more parole officers, and greater contact between prisoners and their families and friends. But as Daniel Glaser points out: "Unfortunately there is no convincing evidence that this investment reduces what criminologists call 'recidivism,' the offenders return to crime."[32] In short, there is no evidence that men *can* be "rehabilitated," no matter what is done! But prison policies now combine conflicting philosophies in a way that accomplishes none of society's goals. They do not effectively punish or deter individuals from crime. They do not succeed in rehabilitating the criminal. They do not even protect the public by keeping criminals off the streets; nineteen out of every twenty persons sent to prison will eventually return to society. Even the maintenance of order *within* prisons, and the protection of the lives of guards and inmates, have become a serious national problem. The deaths of forty-three prisoners and guards in Attica State Prison in New York in a bloody riot in 1971 directed public attention to the serious dilemmas of state correctional policy.

The prisoner populations of the states, even on a population basis, differ significantly. New Hampshire and North Dakota imprisoned about three persons per ten thousand population, while California imprisoned fourteen. In short, per capita prison populations vary a great deal among the states. Differences among the states in prisoner population may be partly explained by the difference in crime rates: there is a relationship between the two.[33] However, prisoner populations also represent differences in sentences and parole policies. The fact that the statistical probability of a person's landing in a state penitentiary is six times greater in some states than in others is more than a result of differences in crime rates. It also reflects differences among the states in correctional philosophy.

Over two-thirds of all prisoner releases come about by means of parole. Modern penology, with its concern for reform and rehabilitation, appears to favor parole releases rather than unconditional releases.[34] The function of parole and postrelease supervision is (1) to procure information on the parolees' postprison conduct, and (2) to facilitate and graduate the transition between the prison and complete freedom. These functions are presumably oriented toward protecting the public and rehabilitating the offender. But states differ substantially in their use of parole: in some states, 90 percent of all releases come about because of parole, while in other states, parole is granted to less than 30 percent of all prisoners. Gen-

---

[32]Glaser, *Effectiveness of a Prison and Parole System*, p. 4.
[33]Dye, *Politics, Economics, and the Public*, pp. 226–32.
[34]Glaser, *Effectiveness of a Prison and Parole System*, Chaps. 16, 17.

erally, urban industrial states with higher income and educational levels release a higher proportion of prisoners on parole than rural farm states with lower income and educational characteristics.

One of the more heated debates in correctional policy today concerns capital punishment. Opponents of the death penalty argue that it is "cruel and unusual punishment" in violation of the Eighth Amendment of the U.S. Constitution. They also contend that nations and states which have abolished the death penalty have not experienced higher homicide rates, and hence there is no concrete evidence that the death penalty discourages crime. They also argue that the death penalty is applied unequally. A large proportion of those executed have been poor, uneducated, and nonwhite. In contrast, there is a strong sense of justice among many Americans that demands retribution for heinous crimes—a life for a life. A mere jail sentence for a multiple murderer or a rapist murderer seems unjust compared with the damage inflicted upon society and the victims. In most cases, a life sentence means less than ten years in prison under the current parole and probation policies of many states. Convicted murderers have been set free, and some have killed again. Moreover, prison guards and other inmates are exposed to convicted murderers who have "a license to kill," because they are already serving life sentences and have nothing to lose by killing again. Public opinion polls continue to support the death penalty, although opponents have been gaining supporters over time.

Prior to 1972, the death penalty was officially sanctioned by thirty states; only fifteen states had abolished capital punishment.[35] Federal law also retained the dealth penalty. However, no one had actually suffered the death penalty since 1967, because of numerous legal tangles and direct challenges to the constitutionality of capital punishment.

In 1972, the Supreme Court ruled that capital punishment *as currently imposed* violates the Eighth and Fourteenth Amendment prohibitions against cruel and unusual punishment and due process of law. The decision was made by a narrow 5 to 4 vote of the justices, and the reasoning in the case is very complex. Only two justices—Brennon and Marshall—declared that capital punishment itself is cruel and unusual. The other three justices in the majority—Douglas, White and Stewart—felt that death sentences had been applied unfairly: a few individuals were receiving the death penalty for crimes for which many others were receiving much lighter sentences. These justices left open the possibility

---

[35]Alaska, Hawaii, Iowa, Maine, Michigan, Minnesota, New Hampshire, New Mexico, New York, North Dakota, Oregon, Rhode Island, Vermont, West Virginia, and Wisconsin (although in Michigan, New York, North Dakota, Rhode Island, and Vermont there were provisions for certain serious exceptions, for example, killing a prison guard).

that capital punishment would be constitutional if it was specified for certain kinds of crime and applied uniformly. All four Nixon appointees on the Court—Burger, Blackman, Powell, and Renquist—dissented, mainly on the ground that the abolition of the death penalty is a decision that should be left to the people and their elected representatives, and not a decision for the Supreme Court to impose upon the nation. Some states can be expected to rewrite their laws on capital punishment to try to insure fairness and uniformity in the application of this penalty; so even though the death penalty is currently in abeyance, the issue will continue to be debated in state capitals and federal courts.

EIGHT

Community
Political Systems

COMMUNITIES AS SETTINGS FOR POLITICS

American communities come in different shapes and sizes, and community politics come in a variety of styles. Generalizing about community politics is perhaps even more difficult than generalizing about American state politics. There are over eighteen thousand municipalities in America, seventeen thousand townships, three thousand counties, and a host of other school districts and special districts. Cities range in size from less than one hundred persons to New York's eight million. Two-thirds of the American people live in urban units of local government known as "municipalities," including "cities," "boroughs," "villages," or "towns." Other Americans are served by county or township governments. More-over, there were 233 metropolitan areas in the United States in 1970; these are clusterings of people and governments around a core city of fifty thousand or more persons. These metropolitan areas are as small as Meriden, Connecticut, with few local governments and only fifty-five thousand persons, or as large as the New York area with six hundred local governments and eleven million people. In short, one may conceive of community political systems as rural counties, country towns, villages, cities of all sizes, or even sprawling metropolitan areas.

Community political systems serve two principal functions. One is that of supplying goods and services—for example, police protection or sewage disposal—that are not supplied by private enterprise. This is the "service" function. The other function is the "political" one, that of managing conflict over public policy. Of course, the "political" and the "service" functions of local governments are often indistinguishable in practice. A mayor who intervenes in a dispute about the location of a park is managing a local government service, namely recreation, at the same time that he is managing political conflict about whose neighborhood should get the most benefit from the new park. In the day-to-day administration of the service functions of local government, officials must decide a variety of political questions. Where are the facilities to be located? Often the question is where *not* to locate facilities, since many neighborhoods avoid having public facilities for fear that they will displace families, attract "undesirables," or depress local property values. How are public services to be paid for? Which agency or official will be in charge of a particular service? What policies or practices will govern the provision of this service? What level of service will be provided? What will the budget for the service be?

Occasionally, students are led to believe that local governments should be less "political" than state or national governments. Many people feel that it would be best to eliminate "politics" from local government. Historically, this attitude arose in conjuction with the municipal reform movement of the Progressive Era.[1] The reform movement involved a preference for nonpartisan elections, city-manager government, and an "antiseptic," "no-party" style of local government, devoid of the stigma of "politics." A city without politics appealed to many idealists who were disenchanted with boss rule. Perhaps another incentive for banishing politics from communities has been the distaste that many people have for conflict. Conflict is psychologically discomforting and arouses strong, unpleasant emotions. Often associated with these feelings is a belief that there is always a "right" answer to public questions, that conflict is unnecessary, and that reasonable men can arrive at the right answer by thought and discussion. It is a belief that differences of opinion are not really legitimate, that the pursuit of special interests is immoral, and that all men should devote themselves to the public interest. Such beliefs force many politicians to *claim* that their decisions are based solely on efficiency, economy, or service considerations, even when the real grounds are to satisfy the political demands of individuals or groups.

The politician who responds to political considerations, in contrast to service considerations, is not necessarily sacrificing the welfare of his community. It is not necessarily true that the community is best served by

[1] See Richard Hofstadter, *The Age of Reform* (New York: Alfred A. Knopf, Inc., 1955); and Lorin Peterson, *The Day of the Mugwump* (New York: Random House, Inc., 1961).

treating the service function of government as if it were more important or more worthy of government attention than the political one. A politician who undertakes to arrange political compromises and balance competing interests in a community is performing a very important function. Helping people with different incomes, occupations, skin colors, religious beliefs, and styles of living to live together in a reasonably peaceful fashion is a vital task.

Edward C. Banfield and James Q. Wilson in their important study, *City Politics*, point out:

> Where there exists conflict that threatens the existence of the good health of the society, the political function should certainly take precedence over the service one. In some cities race and class conflict has this dangerous character. To govern New York, Chicago, or Los Angeles, by the canons of efficiency—of efficiency *simply*—might lead to an accumulation of restless tension that would eventually erupt in meaningless, individual acts of violence, in some irrational mass movement, or perhaps in the slow imperceptible weakening of the social bonds. Politics is, among other things, a way of converting the restless, hostile impulses of individuals into a fairly stable social product (albeit perhaps a revolution!) and in doing so, of giving these impulses moral significance.[2]

Government is only an imperfect instrument for managing conflict in society. Government tries to lay down certain "rules of the game" in political activity; it tries to make decisions among competing interests, and it tries to see that these decisions are carried out. Yet governments often fail in these tasks. The rules of the game are sometimes violated by those who have never accepted them in the first place or those who feel they have not won enough games to merit their continued adherence to the rules. Riots in Watts, Newark, Detroit, Harlem, Cleveland, Chicago, Buffalo, and almost every other major city in America provide ample evidence that the rules often break down, that conflict cannot always be resolved peacefully, that governments do not always succeed in getting their laws obeyed.

VARIETY IN COMMUNITY POLITICS

There is great variety in community political systems. The politics of some communities are dominated by individuals, families, or cliques, while the politics of other communities are dominated by large, formal organzations —the press, business firms, city bureaucracies, civic associations, black

---

[2]Edward C. Banfield and James Q. Wilson, *City Politics* (Cambridge: Harvard-M.I.T. Press, 1963), pp. 20–21.

or ethnic groups, or labor unions. Small-town politics are more likely to be characterized by individual or family friendships and associations rather than organized interest groups. There seems to be less conflict in small-town politics, at least on the surface. Meetings of the village council are dull and meaningless, decisions are usually unanimous, only occasionally do citizens drop by to make a request of the council. Perhaps the intimacy of small-town life makes harmony, or at least the appearance of it, almost indispensable. Where people have frequent face-to-face contacts and nearly everyone is related to everyone else, bitter controversies must be avoided if life is to be at all pleasant. Perhaps there is more homogeneity or like-mindedness among people in a small town: class cleavages may not be as deep, and there are few minority groups. Small towns may be agricultural towns or one-industry towns, where nearly everyone has a stake in the dominant economic enterprise. In contrast, large cities often have diverse and competing economic activities, antagonisms between labor and management, and large minority and ethnic populations. In the relatively small and homogeneous community, it is easier to develop shared ideas of the common good or "what is good for the community." There are fewer large organizations with rival interests, and therefore less need for the "balancing" of competing interests. Individuals can act as individuals in politics rather than as representatives of large organizations. On the other hand, in larger cities and metropolitan areas, participation of individuals in politics is probably less important, as large organizations overshadow the activities of individuals and preempt the political field for themselves.

The classic style of big-city organization politics is the "machine" model. These are tightly disciplined party organizations, held together and motivated by a desire for tangible benefits rather than by principle or ideology, and staffed by professional politicians. These urban party organizations have been dubbed "machines" and their leaders "bosses." Big-city machines won notoriety in the era of muckrakers and have remained the focus of attention ever since. Yet for a long time the machine has been the major instrument for regulating conflict and maintaining order in the nation's major cities. There can be no doubt that America's cities thrived, prospered, and grew under boss rule. The machine was like a large brokerage organization, obtaining votes from the poor and recent immigrants in return for social services, patronage, and petty favors. To get the money to pay for these votes, it traded city contracts, protection, and privileges to business interests, who paid for them in cash. The machine helped to centralize power; it could "get things done in city hall." It humanized and personalized assistance to the indigent. It was a source of upward social mobility for Irish, Italian, and other immigrants to whom upward mobility was denied in private enterprise.

In many ways the urban machine served the very rich and the very poor. The middle class was excluded, and much of the opposition to the machine has come from this group. The middle class was largely responsible for introducing another style of community politics—the reform or "good government" style. The good-government movement was concerned largely with efficiency, economy, and saving the tax dollars of the middle class; it offered very little to the low-income, low-status elements of the large metropolis. As the middle class grew in power in American cities, many aspects of machine politics began to go out of style. Today good government is more likely to be supported by the white middle-class voters than by blacks or the poor. The good-government movement included nonpartisan elections, municipal home rule, the short ballot, centralized municipal administration, and a professional city manager. It promoted the belief that government should be honest, impartial, efficient, and operated by professional administrators directly responsible to the citizens, and that the institutions of government should be structured to bring "good" people into control. It deplored boss rule, machines, and partisan politics.

While the good-government movement has been important in America's large cities, its real successes came in the suburbs of the nation's large metropolitan areas. The suburban style of politics is neither the folksy, individualistic, "friends and neighbors" style of small-town politics, nor the highly organized, conflict-ridden style of the big city. It is based on the conviction that good government comes in small packages and that the best government is the one closest to home. Suburban politics might be characterized as an incomplete attempt to recreate in the large metropolis an idea of small-town grass-roots democracy. Economically, the suburbanite retains his association with the city, but politically, he can enter the civic life of a small community, where a man is no longer a face in the crowd, but a citizen whose votes count and whose opinions make a difference. Suburban life provides an escape from the central city with its corrupt politics and complex diversity of interests. Yet the suburbanite is not altogeher willing to go back to rural living; for he demands high-quality schools, water supply, sewage and refuse disposal, and other modern, urban services.

Another way of characterizing community politics is to distinguish between the *pluralist* and the *elitist* models of community power. *Pluralist* communities are those in which there are many competing interests and structures of power. These competing interests tend to balance each other in policy making, and interests that exercise influence over certain kinds of policies do not necessarily have influence on other kinds of policies. In pluralist communities, there is no single interest or elite that dominates decision making in all policy areas—there is considerable competition

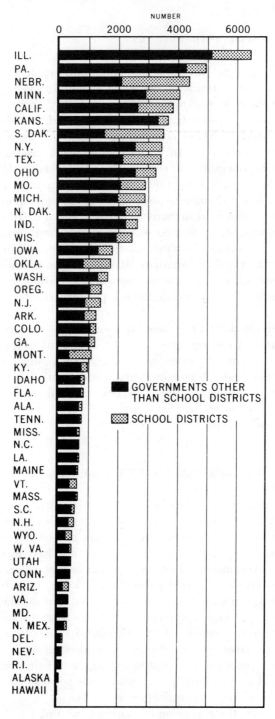

FIGURE 8–1 Local Governments in the States

Source: U.S. Department of Commerce, Bureau of the Census.

229

among interest groups, and influential community leaders are not united by any common interests and do not act in unison. In short, pluralist communities are those in which competition, fluidity, access, and equality characterize political activity. On the other hand, *elitist* communities are those in which power is concentrated in the hands of a very small portion of the population. In elitist communities, decision makers are *not* typical or representative of the people at large; rather they are usually people who have control over the economic resources of a community, which gives them a dominant position in community politics. Thus, a single "elite" is influential in many different kinds of decisions, and members of this elite share an interest in maintaining the *status quo*. Such an elite is not really subject to much control by the masses of people, who are largely uninformed and apathetic about community affairs. The elitist model of community politics stresses the concentration of power in the hands of business leaders, who influence political events in many subtle ways.

Finally, metropolitan areas provide another kind of setting for "community" politics. A metropolitan area is a community in the sense that its residents are economically interdependent, but the political system of metropolitan areas is highly fragmented, and conflict, rather than cooperation, ofter characterizes relations between city and suburban governments. (The following chapters will examine all types of community political systems in more detail.)

COMMUNITIES AS GOVERNMENTAL UNITS

Local government is not mentioned in the U.S. Constitution. Although we regard the American federal system as a mixture of federal, state, and *local* governments, from a constitutional point of view, local governments are really a part of state governments. Communities have no constitutional right to self-government: all of their governmental powers legally flow from state governments. Local governments—cities, townships, counties, special districts, and school districts—are creatures of the states, subject to the obligations, privileges, powers, and restrictions that state governments impose upon them. The state, either through its constitution or its laws, may create or destroy any or all units of local goverment. To the extent that local governments can collect taxes, regulate their citizens, and provide services, they are actually exercising *state* powers delegated to them by the state in either its constitution or its laws.

All states, with the exception of Connecticut and Rhode Island have organized *county* governments. Connecticut abolished its eight counties in 1960. In Louisiana, counties are called "parishes," and in Alaska

TABLE 8-1
Local Governments in the United States

	1967	1962	1957	1952
Counties	3,049	3,043	3,050	3,052
Municipalities	18,048	17,997	17,215	16,807
Townships	17,105	17,144	17,198	17,202
School districts	21,782	34,678	50,454	67,355
Special districts	21,264	18,323	14,424	12,340
Total (including States and National Government)	81,299	91,185	102,341	116,756

SOURCE: U.S. Bureau of the Census, CENSUS OF GOVERNMENTS, 1967.

they are called "boroughs." It is difficult to generalize about the powers of counties. The average population served by a county government is 52,135, but Hinsdale County, Colorado, had only 202 inhabitants in 1970, while Los Angeles County, California, had more than 6 million. The legal powers, organization, and officers of counties also vary a great deal.

Perhaps it would be best to begin a description of county government by distinguishing between rural and urban counties. Obviously there is a great deal of difference between Los Angeles County with 6 million people, Cook County, Chicago, with 5.1 million, and Wayne County, Detroit, with 2.7 million, and the more than eight hundred rural counties in the nation with populations of 10,000 or less. Traditionally, the rural county was the most important unit of local government: it handled such essential matters as law enforcement, courts, schools, roads, elections, poor relief, and the legal recording of property deeds, mortgages, wills, and marriages. Rural communities competed with each other for the location of the county seat, because the community named as county seat won social and political prestige, county jobs, a county fair, and preferential treatment in county roads and public buildings. Moreover, many rural dwellers identify themselves as "coming from" a particular county. The county seat attracted retail business: farm markets were generally located in county seats, where a farmer could transact both public and private business. Rural county government provided an arena for a folksy, provincial, individualistic, "friends and neighbors" type of politics. Rural county government was the province of laymen and amateurs rather than experts or professionals. Decision making was personalized and informal. Often rural counties resemble urban counties about as much as the old-fashioned country store resembles a modern supermarket.

Although county governments differ markedly in their organization, they generally have (1) a governing body variously called the "county commissioners," "county board," "board of supervisors," or even "judges," which is composed of anywhere from three to fifty elected members; (2) a number of separately elected officials with countywide jurisdictions, such as sheriff, county attorney, auditor, recorder, coroner, assessor, judge, treasurer, engineer, and so on; (3) a large number of special boards or commissions which have authority over various functions, such as the county welfare board, county tax equalization committtee, hospital board, library board, and civil service commission, whose members may be elected or appointed by the county commissioners or may even include the county commissioners in an ex officio capacity; and (4) an appointed county bureaucracy in roads, health, welfare, libraries, schools, and so on.

Typically, county officials have the following duties:

Sheriff: maintains jail; furnishes police protection in unincorporated areas; carries out orders of the county court.

Auditor: maintains financial records and tax rolls; authorizes payment of county obligations.

County attorney: serves as chief prosecuting attorney; conducts criminal investigations and prosecutes law violators.

Coroner: conducts medical investigations to determine cause of death; maintains county morgue.

Treasurer: collects, disburses, and maintains county funds; makes county fiscal reports.

Clerk: registers and records legal documents including deeds, mortgages, plats, marriages, divorces, births; certifies election returns.

Assessor: determines value of all taxable property in the county.

The many separately elected county officials and the surplus of independent boards and commissions in county government are generally considered an obstacle to the emergence of strong executive leadership at the county level. The ability of county governments to assume more important functions and responsibilities, particularly in urban areas, probably hinges upon a reorganization of county government to provide for stronger executive leadership.

County government in urban areas is acquiring many of the responsibilities of city governments, and urban counties are increasingly adopting more streamlined, manager types of government organization. Urban counties may provide recreation, flood control, water supply, sewage disposal, library services, airport facilities, countywide police and fire protection, and other urban services. Urban counties may provide these traditional "city services" to the unincorporated areas of the county, that is, to the areas not within the boundaries of cities, and occasionally to cities as well. (See Chapter 11 for further discussion of the future of county government in metropolitan areas.)

County governments can only exercise those powers delegated to them by state laws or constitutions. Even the organization of county government is determined by state law. Some states have enacted "home rule" laws under which counties might operate more independently and even provide more streamlined, manager-type governmental structures. Yet, to date, very few counties have undertaken to reorganize themselves. The large number of elected county officials, the "courthouse gangs," county employees, and party organizations, which use county jobs for patronage, all tend to obstruct the reorganization of county government. Only gradually have county managers been introduced into the structure of urban counties.

Another interesting unit of local government is the "township" or "town," which is found in about half of the states—the northern states from New England to the Midwest. Southern and western states have made little use of this unit of government. Townships are subdivisions of counties and perform many of the functions of county governments at a grass-roots level—schools, elections, road repair, tax administration, fire protection, and even law enforcement through local justices of the peace. Townships are unincorporated, which means they do not have charters from state governments guaranteeing their political independence or authorizing them to provide many municipal services. The jurisdiction of townships may extend over many square miles of sparsely populated rural territory. About 40 million people, or one-fifth of the U.S. population, live under township governments today.

Township governments vary considerably in their powers and organization. Perhaps it would be best to classify them as "towns," and "rural townships," and "urban townships." In the New England states, the "town" is a significant unit of local government, with long traditions and deep roots in the political philosophy of the people of the region. In fact, the New England "town meeting" is often cited by political philosophers as the ideal form of *direct* democracy as distinguished from *representative* democracy. For the town meeting was, and to some extent still is, the central institution of "town" government. The New England town included a village and all of its surrounding farms. The town meeting was open to all eligible voters; it was generally an important social as well as political event. The town meeting would levy taxes, make appropriations, determine policy, and elect officers for the year. Between town meetings, a board of selected men, "selectmen," would supervise the activities of the town—schools, health, roads, care of the poor, and so on. Other officers included town clerk, tax assessors and collectors, justices of the peace, constables, road commissioners, and school board members. Although the ideal of direct democracy is still alive in many smaller New England towns, in the large towns, the pure democracy of the town meeting has given away to a representative system, in which town meeting members are elected prior to the town meeting. Moreover, much of the determination of the towns' financial affairs, previously decided at town meetings, has now been given over to the "selectmen," and many towns have appointed town managers to supervise the day-to-day administration of town services.

Rural townships outside of New England have lost much of their vitality in recent years. The school district consolidation movement (see Chapter 14) has centralized the control of public schools at the county level or in school districts, which span villages and townships. Population decline in America's rural areas has made it difficult for many rural *counties* to operate effectively, let alone smaller rural *townships*. Township government seldom has the financial resources to provide the level of public services that even rural dwellers now insist upon. As communities grow, they incorporate themselves into cities and remove valuable property from the tax roll of the township. Cities, unlike townships, are usually authorized by state governments to choose among various forms of government organization, levy higher taxes, spend more money, and provide a higher level of public service.

Some urban townships appear to have a brighter future as units of government than rural townships. This is particularly true in certain suburban areas of larger cities where metropolitan growth has enveloped township governments. Some states, Pennsylvania for example, have authorized urban townships to exercise many of the powers and provide many of the services previously reserved to city governments. While these urban townships are not incorporated, they often function very much as if they were cities. Of course by not incorporating, they risk the possibility of being annexed by nearby cities, since ordinarily only a municipal charter can guarantee political independence.

CITIES AS "MUNICIPAL CORPORATIONS"

Nearly 70 percent of the American people live in cities. Legally speaking, cities are "municipal corporations," which have received charters from state governments setting forth their boundaries, governmental powers and functions, structure and organization, methods of finance, and powers to elect and appoint officers and employees. The municipal *charter* is intended to grant the powers of local self-government to a community. Of course, the powers of self-government granted by a municipal charter are not unlimited. A state can change a charter or take it away altogether, as it sees fit. Cities, like other local governments, have only the powers that state laws and constitutions grant them. They are still subdivisions of the state. And, of course, state laws operate within the boundaries of cities. In fact, municipal corporations are generally responsible for the enforcement of state law within their boundaries. But they also have the additional power to make local laws, "ordinances," which operate only within their boundaries. But perhaps the most serious limitation on the powers of cities is the fact that American courts have insisted upon interpreting the powers granted in charters very narrowly. The classic statement of this principle of restrictive interpretation of municipal powers was made by John F. Dillon over sixty years ago and is now well known as "Dillon's rule":

> It is a general and undisputed proposition of law that a municipal corporation possesses and can exercise the following powers, and no others: first, those granted in express words; second, those necessarily or fairly implied in or incident to the powers expressly granted; third, those essential to the accomplishment of the declared objects and purposes of the corporation—not simply convenient, but indispensable. Any fair, reasonable, substantial doubt concerning the existence of power is resolved by the courts against a corporation, and the power is denied.[3]

As Banfield and Wilson point out, "This means that a city cannot operate a peanut stand at the city zoo without first getting the state legislature to pass an enabling law, unless, per chance, the city's charter or some previously enacted law unmistakably covers the sale of peanuts."[4]

The restrictive interpretation of the powers of cities leads to rather lengthy city charters, since nearly everything a city does must have specific legal authorization in the city charter. The city charter of New York, for example, is several hundred pages long. City charters must cover in detail such matters as boundaries, structure of government, ordinance-making powers, finances, contracts, purchasing, bonds, courts, municipal elections, property assessments, zoning laws and building codes, licenses, franchises, law enforcement, education, health, streets, parks, public utilities, and on and on. Since any proposed change in the powers, organization, or responsibilities of cities requires an act of a state legislature amending the city's charter, state legislatures are intimately involved in local legislation. This practice of narrowly interpreting city charters may appear awkward, but its effect is to increase the power of courts and state legislators in city affairs. Courts acquire power from their ability to interpret complex city charters; and state legislators with city constituencies acquire power through the practice of granting a local legislator the courtesy of accepting his views on local legislation that affects only his constituency.

[3] John F. Dillon, *Commentaries on the Laws of Municipal Corporations*, 5th ed., (Boston: 1911), p. 448.
[4] Banfield and Wilson, *City Politics*, p. 65.

State legislative control over cities is most firmly entrenched in *special act* charters. These charters are specially drawn for the cities named in them. Cities under special act charters remain directly under legislative control, and specific legislative approval for that city and that city alone must be obtained for any change in its government or service activities. Such charters give rise to local acts dealing with small details of city government in a specially named city, for example, "that Fall River be authorized to appropriate money for the purchase of uniforms for the park police and watershed guards of said city."[5] Under special act charters, laws that apply to one city do not necessarily apply to others.

Municipal reformers, with the political support of city officials, have long argued that *special act* charters place the city at the mercy of political forces outside the city, particularly rural-dominated legislatures; lead to legislative logrolling among the delegations from several cities in a state; and consume a large amount of state legislatures' time, which ought to be concerned with statewide rather than local legislation. Agitation against special act charters has led many states to outlaw them by constitutional amendment. In their place, *general act* charters usually classify cities according to their size and then apply municipal laws to all cities in each size classification. Thus, a state's municipal law may apply to all cities of less than 10,000 people, another law to all cities with populations of 10,000–25,000, another to cities with 25,000–50,000 people, and so on. These general act charters make it difficult to interfere in the activities of a particular city without affecting the activities of all cities of a similar size category. Yet in practice there are often exceptions and modifications to general act legislation. For example, since legislators know the populations of their cities, they can select size categories for municipal law that apply to only one city. The Pennsylvania legislature can pass laws for cities of over 1 million, aware that only Philadelphia falls into this category, and for cities of 500,000 to 1 million, aware that only Pittsburgh falls into this category.

Optional charter laws provide cities with some choice in the structure and organization of their governments. Such laws generally offer a choice of governmental forms: strong mayor and weak council, weak mayor and strong council, commission, city manager, or some modification of these.

Home rule charters are designed to give cities the power to adopt governmental forms and provide municipal services, as they see fit, without state legislative interference. Home rule charters may be given to cities by state constitutions or by legislative enactments; legislative home rule is considered less secure, since a legislature could retract the grant if it

[5]*Ibid.*, p. 66.

wished to do so. Beginning with Missouri in 1875, more than half the states have included in their constitutions provisions for the issuance of home rule charters. About two-thirds of the nation's cities with populations over 200,000 have some form of home rule.

The intended effect of home rule is to reverse "Dillon's rule" and enable cities to "exercise all legislative powers not prohibited by law or by charter." In other words, instead of preventing a city from doing anything not specifically authorized, home rule permits the city to do anything not specifically prohibited. The theory of home rule grants sweeping powers to cities; however, in practice, home rule has not brought self-government to cities. Home rule provisions in state constitutions range from those that grant considerable power and discretion over local affairs, to provisions that are so useless that no city has ever made use of them. First of all, these constitutional provisions may be too cumbersome or vague for effective implementation. In some states, cities feel that it is easier to use the general law charters, particularly if they provide for optional forms of government, than to use the cumbersome procedures for obtaining home rule. Another important limitation on home rule is the distinction between "self-enforcing" and "non-self-enforcing," or "permissive," home rule provisions in state constitutions. Non-self-enforcing home rule provisions merely permit the state legislature to grant home rule to its cities; cities cannot acquire home rule without legislative action. Only about a dozen states have "self-enforcing" home rule provisions, which enable cities to bypass the state legislature and adopt home rule for themselves. (Missouri's original constitutional home rule amendment was a self-enforcing type.) Finally, home rule may be limited by court interpretations of the language of the constitutional provisions granting power to home rule in cities. Constitutional provisions may grant to home rule cities the power to make "all laws and ordinances relating to municipal concerns" (Michigan), or the "powers of local self-government" (Ohio), or all powers "in respect to municipal affairs" (California).[6] Of course, ordinances passed under home rule authority cannot be in conflict with state law. Courts must distinguish between municipal and statewide concerns. In cases where doubt exists, legal traditions of municipal law require that courts resolve the doubt in favor of the state and against local powers of home rule. State legislatures can intervene in local affairs in home rule cities by simply deciding that a particular matter is of statewide concern.

The politics of home rule often pits reform groups, city mayors, and administrators against state legislators and large municipal taxpayers.

[6]See Duane Lockard, *The Politics of State and Local Government* (New York: The Macmillan Company, 1963), p. 124.

State legislators are generally wary of giving up their authority over cities. Rural legislators have little reason to support city home rule, and even city legislators seldom welcome proposals to give up their authority over local bills. Sometimes city employees with good access to the legislature will oppose giving a mayor or a city manager too much control over their employment. Taxpayer groups may fear that home rule will give the city the ability to increase taxes. Local bills may be pictured as a distraction to legislators by reformers, but many legislators enjoy the power that it brings them in local affairs and welcome the opportunity to perform legislative services for their constituents. And so, even with reapportionment adding to the number of urban legislators, the League of Women Voters, good-government groups, and mayors may still be frustrated in their attempts to achieve genuine home rule for American cities.

Courts figure prominently in municipal politics. This is because of the subordinate position of the municipal corporation in the hierarchy of governments, and legal traditions, such as Dillon's rule, which narrowly interpret the power of local governments. The power of courts over municipal affairs grants leverage to defenders of the *status quo* in any political battle at the local level. Proponents of a new municipal law or municipal service not only must win the battle over whether a city *ought* to pass the new law or provide the new service but also must win the legal battle over whether the city *can* pass the law or provide the service. Limitations and uncertainties abound about the validity of local enactments. Legal challenges to the authority of the city to pass new regulations or provide new services are frequent. The city attorney becomes a key official because he must advise the city about what it can or cannot do. Not only must the city obey the federal constitution, but it is also subject to the restraints of the state constitution, state laws, its municipal charter, and, of course, Dillon's rule. The result is to greatly strengthen courts, attorneys, and defenders of the *status quo*.

FORMS OF CITY GOVERNMENT

American city government comes in three structural packages. There are some adaptations and variations from city to city, but generally one can classify the form of city government as mayor-council, commission, or council-manager. Approximately 51 percent of American cities have the mayor-council form of government; 6 percent have the commission form; and 43 percent have the council-manager form.

The nation's largest cities tend to function under the *mayor-council* plan. Figure 8–2 shows the structure of the mayor-council government.

This is the oldest form of American city government and is designed in the American tradition of separation of powers between legislature and executive. One may also establish subcategories of "strong" or "weak" mayor forms of mayor-council government. A strong mayor is one who is the undisputed master of the executive agencies of city government and who has substantial legislative powers in the form of budget making, vetoes, and opportunity to propose legislation. Only a few cities make the mayor the sole elected official among city executive officers; it is common for the mayor to share budgetary and administrative powers with other elected officials. In New York, an eight-member board of estimate (mayor, council president, comptroller, and five borough presidents) draw up the city's budget. In Chicago a council committee prepares the budget. Minneapolis is perhaps the prime example of a weak mayor system: voters elect a library board, the parks board, a board of estimate and taxation, thirteen aldermen, a treasurer, and a comptroller; the council, not the mayor, appoints the city attorney, city engineer, city assessor, and city clerk; the mayor makes only one major appointment—the city chief of police. Yet many mayors, by virtue of their prestige, persuasive abilities, or role as party leader, have been able to overcome most of the weaknesses of their formal office. Mayor Daley of Chicago must deal with a fifty-member city council, a wide variety of independent boards and agencies like the park district, board of education, and housing authority, a large legislative delegation, and various lesser elected officials. Yet Mayor Daley is the undisputed center of political influence in Chicago.

In recent years, large cities have been adding to the formal powers of their chief executives. Cities have augmented the mayor's role by providing him with direction over budgeting, purchasing, and personnel controls, and independent boards and commissions and individual councilmen have relinquished administrative control over city departments in many cities. Moreover, many cities have strengthened the mayor's position by providing him with a chief administrative officer, "CAO," to handle important staff and administrative duties of supervising city departments and providing central management services.

The *commission* form of city government gives both legislative and executive powers to a small body, usually consisting of five members (see Figure 8–3). The commission form originated at the beginning of the century as a reform movement designed to end a system of divided responsibility between mayor and council. One of the commission members is nominally the mayor, but he has no more formal powers than his fellow commissioners. The board of commissioners is directly responsible for the operation of city departments and agencies. In practice, one commission member will become responsible for the management of a specific department, such as finance, public works, or public safety. As long as the coun-

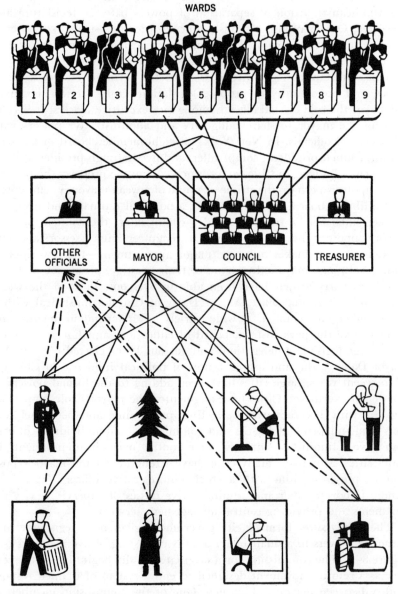

WARDS

FIGURE 8–2 Mayor-Council Form

Source: National Municipal League. Reproduced by permission.

FIGURE 8–3 Commission Form

Source: National Municipal League. Reproduced by permission.

cilmen are in agreement over policy, there are few problems; but when commissioners differ among themselves and develop separate spheres of influence in city government, city government becomes a multiheaded monster, totally lacking in coordination. The results of a commission form of government were generally so disastrous that the reform movement abandoned its early support of this form of government in favor of the council-manager plan. Memphis, Portland, St. Paul, and Tulsa, are principal cities that still operate under this plan. Even Galveston, the birthplace of the commission plan in 1901, abandoned it in 1960 in favor of the council-manager plan.

The *council-manager* form of government revived the distinction between legislative "policy making" and executive "administration" in city government. Policy-making responsibility is vested in an elected council, and administration is assigned to an appointed professional administrator known as a manager (see Figure 8-4). The council chooses the manager and he is responsible to them. All departments of the city government operate under the direction of the manager, who has the power to hire and fire personnel within the limits set by the merit system. The council's role in administration is limited to selecting and dismissing the city manager. The plan is based on the idea that policy making and administration are separate functions, and that the principal task of city government is to provide the highest level of services at the lowest possible cost—utilities, streets, fire and police protection, health, welfare, recreation, and so on. Hence, a professionally trained, career-oriented administrator is given direct control over city departments.

URBAN ENVIRONMENT AND
THE STRUCTURE OF CITY GOVERNMENT

We shall return to the political roles of mayors, managers, and councils in Chapter 10, but let us examine for a moment the social, economic, and political forces shaping the structure of city government: that is, the conditions associated with the selection of one of the principal forms of government.

First of all, city-manager government is closely associated with the *size* of cities. Large cities show a distinct preference for the more "political" form of mayor-council government in contrast to the more "efficient" form of council-manager government. (See Table 8–2.) All cities over one million have the mayor-council form of government. Only five of the nation's twenty-six cities with more than 500,000 people have council-manager government: Dallas, San Antonio, Kansas City, San Diego, and Phoenix. The council-manager and commission forms of government

FIGURE 8–4   Council-Manager Form

Source: National Municipal League. Reproduced by permission.

TABLE 8-2
Urban Environments and Form of Government

	Number of Cities	Percentage of Cities		
		Manager	Commission	Mayor-Council
All Cities	(2784)	43	6	51
Size of City				
Over 1,000,000	(6)	0	0	100
500,000 to 1,000,000	(20)	25	0	70
250,000 to 500,000	(27)	48	11	41
100,000 to 250,000	(93)	54	11	35
50,000 to 100,000	(215)	54	7	39
25,000 to 50,000	(439)	54	9	37
10,000 to 25,000	(1072)	46	8	46
5,000 to 10,000	(1112)	34	4	62
Growth Rate				
Large Increase: 15% or more	(359)	59	10	31
Small Increase: 0 to 15%	(152)	39	17	44
Small Decline: 0 to 6%	(77)	30	21	49
Large Decline: 6% or more	(50)	26	36	38
Mobility[1]				
Low: under 12%	(192)	23	22	55
Medium: 12 to 20%	(250)	47	14	39
High: over 20%	(194)	73	9	18
Region				
East	(161)	21	24	55
Midwest	(179)	37	10	53
South	(185)	61	19	20
West	(115)	81	5	14
Educational Level				
High: over 50% High School	(190)	67	10	33
Medium: 40 to 50% High School	(203)	49	12	39
Low: under 40% High School	(247)	33	21	46
White Collar Occupation[2]				
Low: under 35%	(232)	32	20	48
Medium: 35 to 42%	(201)	51	12	37
High: over 42%	(193)	62	13	25
Ethnicity[3]				
Low: under 10%	(213)	54	20	26
Medium: 10 to 20%	(204)	59	11	30
High: over 20%	(223)	32	14	54

[1] Mobility is measured by the percentage of residents who lived in a different county in the previous five years.

[2] White collar occupation is measured by the percentage of persons employed in professional, technical, managerial, clerical, and sales occupations.

[3] Ethnicity is measured by the percentage of persons with foreign-born parents.

SOURCES: Data derived from MUNICIPAL YEARBOOK, 1968 (Chicago: National Municipal League, 1968); Robert R. Alford and Harry M. Scoble, "Political and Socio-economic Characteristics of American Cities," MUNICIPAL YEARBOOK, 1965 (Chicago: National Municipal League, 1965), pp. 82-97.

are most popular in the middle-sized cities—cities with populations of 25,000–250,000 people. Probably, cities with less than 10,000 persons do not have sufficient resources to justify hiring a trained professional city manager, nor in all probability, do they have the administrative problems requiring his expertise. Thus, small cities, like large cities, tend to rely upon mayor-council government, although probably for different reasons.

If the lack of resources and the absence of complex administrative problems in small cities explain the absence of council-manager government in these cities, what explains its absence in larger cities? A common explanation is that the political environment of large cities is so complex, with many competing interests, that these cities require strong political leadership, which can arbitrate struggles for power, arrange compromises, and be directly responsible to the people for policy decisions. A large city requires a "political" form of government that can arbitrate the conflicting claims of diverse interests. This implies that in smaller cities there are fewer competing interests, more acceptance of a common public interest, and less division over community policy. A professional city manager would have less difficulty in accepting cues about correct behavior in a small city than in a large city with a complex and political structure. There is a greater degree of consensus on policy direction in a smaller city; therefore, such a city requires a professional administrator rather than a political negotiator. The question is whether or not political skill or administrative expertise is more important in a city, and there is reason to believe that larger cities require political skills more than professional administration.

Growing cities face more administrative and technical problems than cities whose population is stable. There is a strong relationship between population *growth* and council-manager government. (see Table 8–2.) A rapidly growing city faces many administrative problems in providing streets, sewers, and the many other services required by an expanding population. This creates a demand for a professional administrator. Population mobility is closely related to manager government. In contrast, the mayor-council form of government is associated with cities having relatively stable populations, in which administrative and technical problems are not quite so pressing, and political conflict is more likely to be well defined and persistent. Council-manager government is more popular in the rapidly growing cities of the West and the South. Table 8-2 reveals that mayor-council government is preferred in Eastern and Midwestern cities, while manager government prevails in the South and especially the West.

Council-manager cities tend to be *middle-class* cities. Cities with large proportions of working-class residents, low-income families, and ethnic minorities are not likely to adopt council-manager government. Schnore and Alford have presented conclusive evidence, for three hundred suburbs in twenty-five large metropolitan areas, that communities with council-manager government have a smaller proportion of foreign born and persons over sixty-five years of age, a larger proportion of white-collar workers, with a high school education or better, and tend to grow more rapidly in population than communities with mayor-council or commission forms of government.[7] In a study of the Chicago area, a ranking of seventy-four suburban cities, according to the median value of homes, shows that eighteen of the twenty cities with the highest home values had council-manager government, whereas none of the thirty-one cities with the lowest home values had it.[8] Table 8–2 shows a decrease in manager government associated with an increase in foreign-born population of a city. Table 8–2 also shows that white-collar employees in personnel services, retail stores, and financial establishments, as well as professional people and public administrators, appear to prefer manager government more than blue-collar workers in wholesale trade, transportation, diversified industry, and manufacturing. Blue-collar workers appear to prefer a mayor-council system which provides political channels for the expression of their interests.

Why is it that middle-class communities prefer the manager form of government while working-class communities prefer a mayor-council government? Middle-class citizens, those in white-collar jobs with good educations and reasonably high incomes, are more likely to want government conducted in a businesslike fashion, with a council serving as a board of directors and a city manager as the president of a "municipal corporation." They are primarily concerned with efficiency, honesty, and saving their tax dollars. These values are not necessarily shared by labor, low-status, low-income, ethnic and minority groups, which may prefer a government that grants small favors, dispenses patronage jobs, awards representation and "recognition" to minority groups, and can be held directly responsible by the voters at election time. In a campaign for city-manager government, one usually finds business leaders, newspapers, and civic associations supporting the plan, and labor unions and minority group organizations far less enthusiastic. Party organizations and professional politicians can usually be expected to oppose this plan. Its support generally comes from white-collar, high-income, well-educated, white

[7]Leo Schnore and Robert R. Alford, "Forms of Government and Socioeconomic Characteristics of Suburbs," *Administrative Science Quarterly* (June 1963), pp. 1–17. See also, John H. Kessel, "Governmental Structure and Political Environment," *American Political Science Review*, (September 1962), 612–21.

[8]Edgar L. Sherbenov, "Class, Participation, and the Council-Manager Plan," *Public Administration Review* (Summer 1961), pp. 131–35.

neighborhoods, and its opposition from low-income, blue-collar, black and ethnic neighborhoods.

Communities with well-organized *competitive party systems* are less likely to have council-manager government than one-party communities or communities in which the formal party organization is weak. States with the highest percentages of medium-sized cities with manager plans are Virginia, North Carolina, California, Texas, and Florida; in contrast, states with the highest percentages of mayor-council plans are Indiana, Connecticut, and Ohio. The former states are either one-party states or, in the case of California, states with relatively weak party organization. The states with mayor-council cities are competitive two-party states. It is sometimes argued that the introduction of the manager plan decreases party activity in communities, but it is also true that the presence of strong party organizations may be a significant factor in the defeat of manager plans. Thus, manager government may depress party activity, or strong parties may kill off manager government, or both; but whatever the case, manager government appears incompatible with strong partisan politics in a community. Thus, social, economic, and political forces influence the structure of city government.

NINE

Styles
of
Community Politics

MACHINES AND BOSSES

Machine politics may be going out of style, but something resembling machine politics still exists in many large cities. Party organizations in cities tend to be better organized, more cohesive, and better disciplined than state or national party organizations. Tightly disciplined party organizations, held together and motivated by a desire for tangible benefits rather than by principle or ideology, and staffed by professional politicians, emerged in the nation's large cities early in the nineteenth century. The "machine" style of city politics has historical importance: between the Civil War and the New Deal, every big city had a machine at one time or another, and it is sometimes easier to understand the character of city politics today by knowing what went on in years past. But a more important reason for examining the machine style of politics is to understand the style of political organization and activity that employs personal and material inducements to control behavior. These kinds of inducements will always be important in politics, and the big-city machine serves the prototype of a style of politics, in which ideologies and issues are secondary and personal friendships, favors, jobs, and material rewards are primary.

The political machine was essentially a large brokerage organization. It was a business organization, devoid of ideologies and issues, whose business it was to get votes and control elections by trading off social services, patronage, and petty favors to the urban masses, particularly the poor and the recent immigrants. To get the money to pay for these social services and favors, it traded off city contracts, protection, and privileges to business interests, which paid off in cash. Like other brokerage organizations, a great many middlemen came between the cash paid for a franchise for a trolley line or a construction contract and a Christmas turkey sent by the ward chairman to the Widow O'Leary. But the machine worked. It performed many important and social functions for the city.[1]

First of all, it personalized government. With keen social intuition, the machine recognized the voter as a man, generally living in a neighborhood, who had specific personal problems and wants. The machine politician avoided abstract and remote public issues or ideologies, and he concentrated instead on the personal problems and needs of his constituents. Lincoln Steffens once quoted a Boston ward leader:

> I think that there's got to be in every ward somebody that any bloke can come to—no matter what he's done—and get help. Help, you understand; none of your law and justice, but help.[2]

The machine provided individual attention and recognition. As Tammany Hall boss George Washington Plunkitt, the philosopher king of old-style machine politics, explained:

> I know every man, woman, and child in the 15th district, except them that's been born this summer—and I know some of them, too. I know what they like and what they don't like, what they are strong at and what they are weak in, and I reach them by approachin' at the right side. For instance, here's how I gather in the young men. I hear of a young feller that's proud of his voice, thinks that he can sing fine. I ask him to come around to Washington Hall and join our Glee Club. Then there's the feller that likes rowin' on the river, the young feller that makes a name as a waltzer on his block, the young feller that's handy with his dukes—I rope them all in by givin' them opportunities to show themselves off. I don't trouble them with political arguments. I just study human nature and act accordin'.[3]

The machine also performed functions of a welfare agency:

> What tells in holdin' your grip on your district is to go right down among the poor families and help them in the different ways they need help.

[1]See Robert K. Merton, *Social Theory and Social Structure* (Glencoe: The Free Press, 1957), pp. 71–81.

[2]Lincoln Steffens, *Autobiography* (New York: Harcourt, Brace & World, Inc., 1931), p. 618; also cited by Merton, *Social Theory*, p. 74.

[3]William L. Riordan, *Plunkitt of Tammany Hall* (New York: McClure, Phillips & Co., 1905), p. 46.

I've got a regular system for this. If there's a fire in Ninth, Tenth, or Eleventh Avenue, for example, any hour of the day or night, I'm usually there with some of my election district captains as soon as the fire engines. If a family is burned out I don't ask whether they are Republicans or Democrats, and I don't refer them to the Charity Organization Society, which would investigate their case in a month or two and decide they were worthy of help about the time they are dead from starvation. I just get quarters for them, buy clothes for them if their clothes were burned up, and fix them up till they get things runnin' again. It's philanthropy, but it's politics, too—mighty good politics. Who can tell how many votes one of these fires bring me? The poor are the most grateful people in the world, and let me tell you, they have more friends in their neighborhoods than the rich have in theirs.[4]

The machine also functioned as an employment agency. In the absence of government unemployment insurance or a federal employment service, patronage was an effective political tool, particularly in hard times. Not only were city jobs at the disposal of the machine, but the machine also had its business contacts:

Another thing, I can always get a job for a deservin' man. I make it a point to keep on the track of jobs, and it seldom happens that I don't have a few up my sleeve ready for use. I know every big employer in the district and in the whole city, for that matter, and they ain't in the habit of sayin' no to me when I ask them for a job.[5]

Banfield and Wilson argue effectively that it was not so much the petty favors and patronage that won votes among urban dwellers, as it was the sense of friendship and humanity that characterized the "machine" and its "boss."[6] The free turkeys and bushels of coal were really only tokens of this friendship. As Jane Addams, the famous settlement house worker, explained: "On the whole, the gifts and favors were taken quite simply as evidence of genuine loving kindness. The alderman is really elected because he is a good friend and neighbor. He is corrupt, of course, but he is not elected because he is corrupt, but rather in spite of it. His standard suits his constituents. He exemplifies and exaggerates the popular type of a good man. He has attained what his constituents secretly long for."[7]

The machine also played an important role in educating recent immi-

[4]*Ibid.*, p. 52.
[5]*Ibid.*, p. 53.
[6]Edward C. Banfield and James Q. Wilson, *City Politics* (Cambridge: Harvard-M.I.T. Press, 1963), Chap. 9.
[7]Jane Addams, *Democracy and Social Ethics* (New York: 1902), p. 254; also cited by Banfield and Wilson, *City Politics*, p. 118.

grants and assimilating them into American life.[8] Machine politics provided a means of upward social mobility for ethnic group members, which was not open to them in businesses or professions. City machines sometimes met immigrants at dockside and led them in groups through naturalization and voter registration procedures. Machines did not keep out people with "funny" sounding names, but instead went out of the way to put these names on ballots. Politics became a way "up" for the bright sons of Irish and Italian immigrants.

Finally, for the businessman, and particularly for public utilities and construction companies with government contracts, the machine provided the necessary franchises, rights of way, contracts, and privileges. As Lincoln Steffens wrote: "You cannot build or operate a railroad, or a street railway, gas, water, or power company, develop and operate a mine, or cut forests or timber on a large scale, or run any privileged business, without corrupting or joining in the corruption of government."[9] The machine also provided the essential protection from police interference, which is required by illicit businesses, particularly gambling. In short, the machine helped to centralize power in large cities. It could "get things done at city hall."

Political analysts frequently remark that the day of the political machine has passed and that big-city political organizations have radically altered their style of operation. Federal and state welfare agencies now provide the basic welfare services that the bosses used to provide. Large-scale immigration has stopped, and there are fewer people requiring the kinds of services once provided by the machine. Patronage jobs do not look as attractive in an affluent economy, and today civil service examinations cover most governmental jobs anyhow. The middle class was excluded from machine politics, and much of the opposition to the machine came from the middle class. As the middle class grew in American society (today white-collar workers outnumber blue-collar workers), opposition to the machine has grown in every city. Middle-class voters supported reform movements and good-government crusades, which often succeeded in replacing the machine with professional city managers, civil service, reorganized city government, and city administrations pledged to eliminate corruption and exercise economy and efficiency in government.

Big-city party organizations continue to thrive, although in a somewhat modified form, because they continue to perform important political and social functions in their communities. In a system of "fragmented" government in the nation's large cities, these party organizations continue to play an important part in organizing power: that is to say, in "getting

---

[8]See Elmer E. Cornwell, Jr., "Bosses, Machines, and Ethnic Groups," *Annals of the American Academy of Political and Social Science* (May 1964), pp. 27–39.
[9]Steffens, *Autobiography*, p. 168.

things done at city hall." A centralized, well-disciplined party organization helps to overcome the dispersion of power one finds in a normal structure of a big-city government, with its maze of authorities, boards, commissions, agencies, and separately elected officials.

Machine politics will remain with us as long as there is an unmet need to personalize the operations of government, and as long as individuals need services that the formal machinery of government cannot provide. Machine politics will remain as long as people place little or no value on their vote, or more precisely, as long as they place a lower value on their vote than they do on the things a machine can offer them in exchange for it. Voters who are indifferent to issues and candidates, and there are still many of these, and who put little value on their vote, can be easily induced to trade it for the small favors that the party organization can offer. And urban party organizations continue to perform important welfare duties, employment services, and petty favors. A survey of precinct politicians in a New Jersey county revealed the following list of services.

1. Help poor people to get work;
2. Help deserving people to get jobs on a highway crew, police force, or fire department or in state positions;
3. Show people how to get their social security benefits, welfare, and unemployment compensation;
4. Help citizens with problems like rent gouging, unfair labor practices, zoning, or unfair assessments;
5. Help one's precinct to get a needed traffic light, more parking space, or more policemen;
6. Run clambakes or other get togethers for interested people even though no political campaign is involved;
7. Help people who are in difficulty with the law;
8. Help newcomers to this county to get adjusted and get places to live and work;
9. Work with some of the other party's people to reduce the friction and keep the campaign from getting too rough;
10. Help boys with military service problems with advice on the best way to serve.[10]

It is unlikely that these kinds of services will ever go out of style completely. A certain amount of machine politics will be found in every city.

---

[10]Richard T. Frost, "Stability and Change in Local Politics," *Public Opinion Quarterly*, 25 (Summer 1961), 231–32.

THE BOSS: RICHARD J. DALEY
OF CHICAGO

Mayor Richard J. Daley of Chicago governs the city in the style of traditional politics. (When Mayor Daley himself was asked about his "machine," he replied, "Organization, not machine. Get that. Organization, not machine.") In Chicago, few others understand so well the labyrinths of formal and informal power, the complex structure of federal, state, and local government and public opinion, as the mayor. Daley has won election to five four-year terms as mayor of Chicago beginning in 1955. He won his fifth election by an astounding 74 percent of the votes cast. He remains the captain of his old Eleventh Ward Democratic committee, and he is chairman of the Cook County Democratic committeee. He picks candidates' slates, runs the patronage machinery, and works his will on nearly all the fifty aldermen who comprise Chicago's city council. Illinois Democratic governors must be responsive to his wishes, and Chicago's nine-member delegation to the U.S. House of Representatives also acts promptly on Daley's recommendations. The Cook County Democratic delegation to the Illinois legislature is firmly in his hands. No presidential candidate can ignore Daley's political clout, either in the Democratic National Convention or in the general election. Daley may be the most successful mayor in America, not only for his political acumen but also for his ability to manage a great metropolis.

Chicago has had bosses before. There was "Big Bill" Thompson 1915–23, 1927–31), a Republican who left a safe deposit box stuffed with $1.5 million in cash when he died. There was Democratic Ed Kelley (1933–47), who used his power mostly to throw public projects to his personal and political pal, contractor Pat Nash. Chicago has also had reform mayors; one of these was Democrat Martin Kennelley (1947-55), whose good intentions were frustrated by a lack of political judgment and who was unseated by Daley in 1955.

Daley, a Roman Catholic, was born in the impoverished Bridgeport district of Chicago near the stockyards.[11] He sold newspapers on the street as a boy and worked in the stockyards. He worked his way to clerk in the stockyards office and then went at night to the law school at DePaul University. He was appointed secretary to the city council at the age of twenty-five and has remained on the public payroll ever since. He still lives with his large family in his old city neighborhood. In 1936, when

[11]For an excellent description of the functions of Mayor Daley's political organization in Chicago, see Edward C. Banfield, *Political Influence* (Glencoe: The Free Press, 1961). For a hostile account of Mayor Daley by a liberal reformer, see Mike Royko, *Boss: Richard J. Daley of Chicago* (New York: E. P. Dutton & Co., Inc., 1971).

a state legislator from Daley's district died, Democratic boss Ed Kelley and ward leader Jake Arvey gave the job to Daley, who gradually worked his way up in the Kelley-Arvey machine. When Adlai Stevenson became governor of Illinois in 1949, he rewarded the Chicago machine by making Daley the state revenue director. But more important to Daley's political power, he was also made county clerk for Cook County, which placed him in charge of all the voting machinery in the county and many patronage jobs. Daley's old teacher, Boss Jake Arvey, always felt that a boss should be a "behind-the-scenes operator" and should not run for public office himself, but Daley broke with his old boss Arvey to run for mayor against a Republican reform candidate, who charged scandal and corruption in Chicago in the Democratic government. Daley replied: "If I am elected I will embrace mercy, love, charity, and walk humbly with my God." When he was elected, one commentator observed: "Chicago ain't ready for reform!" From his base in Chicago, Daley quickly made himself the unchallenged leader of Illinois Democrats. Adlai Stevenson was not a "machine" Illinois Democrat, and Daley always remained somewhat cool toward Stevenson but was a staunch supporter of Senator John F. Kennedy. Daley was a key supporter and consultant in Kennedy's race for the presidential nomination. On election day, 1960, Daley's machine in Chicago gave Kennedy a margin of 450,000 votes, giving the crucial state of Illinois to Kennedy, who lost the rest of the state so badly that his statewide edge was only 9,000 votes.

In an era when successful politicians increasingly reflect the slick "Madison Avenue" image—tall, handsome, glamorous, articulate, at ease with television and press—Mayor Daley is a throwback to an earlier era of municipal politics. Daley looks like an old-time city boss—short and paunchy, with heavy jowls and deep-set eyes. He speaks with "deses" and "dems," but he is smart enough to limit his public appearances to ceremonial occasions. He is not likely to be found exchanging urbane witticisms with Johnny Carson on late-night television. His malapropisms have become legendary: "We will reach greater and greater platitudes of achievement"; "They have vilified me, they have crucified me, yes, they have even criticized me." But these characteristics only seem to endear him to his constituents.

Like other city mayors, Daley's biggest problem today is race relations. Chicago's blacks compose nearly a third of the city's population and half of the public school pupils. Daley remains close to many older black leaders whose support he has always courted, but he is not very close to younger, more militant black leaders like black comedian Dick Gregory of Chicago. Many younger blacks refer to Daley's urban renewal and slum clearance programs as "Negro removal." Many white residents of Chicago have become upset by what they consider Daley's "concessions" to blacks. Yet Daley is in the classic style of the political broker, who continues to try to arrange compromises and win support from both blacks and whites.

Unlike older bosses, Daley maintained a progressive image. He has not tolerated much corruption in office, and he has kept a tight reign on gambling, prostitution, and organized crime. He brought in the nation's leading criminologist, University of California Professor Orlando W. Wilson, to clean up and revitalize the city police force, which he did, although he was later criticized by black leaders because of his strict enforcement policies. Daley also inaugurated many reforms, including an executive budget for the city, an extended merit system, a new zoning and housing code, and many other organizational improvements. Although a big-city Democrat. Daley earnestly solicited the support of prominent businessmen for city projects, and downtown business and commercial investment has flourished. He has sought and won newspaper support and has even appealed with success to civic leaders and good-government associations.

Even a liberal critic of Mayor Daley is forced to admit:

> Daley's municipal ambition is backed up, to use the Chicago expression, with political clout. When he wants something done, it gets done. He knows every minuscule aspect of the city, both municipally and politically, knows the balance and has the political power to handle the people who don't measure up. . . . He has managed to keep the machine viable, to bring cost accounting to the city government, to keep up with many reforms in the New Deal tradition, and in the words of one political scientist, "to make the machine a limited instrument for social progress." He has bound together this unnatural consensus at a particularly difficult time, and part of the reason comes from the consensus itself; each member of it is aware of the others and of the counterpressure on the Mayor. This acts as a restraint; they will not push too far for fear of rocking the boat. Part of the reason, too, is that Daley simply works harder than his opponents. He is at early Mass when his enemies are still sleeping, and he is still working on city problems at night when they've all gone to bed or are out drinking. He pays enormous attention to detail; he goes over every job application, to a ridiculously low level. Finally he knows more about the petty details of Chicago than almost any of his critics. They, as Dr. Martin Luther King did, criticize the broad outlines of life in Chicago; he comes armed with details of its daily life, what he is doing and what he would like to do but can't.[12]

As a political broker, Daley is seldom the initiator of public policy. His approach to policy questions is more like that of an arbitrator between competing interests. When political controversies develop, Daley

[12]David Halberstam, "Daley of Chicago, *Harper's Magazine*, August 1968. Copyright © 1968 by Harper's Magazine, Inc. Reprinted by permission of the author and publisher.

often waits on the sidelines without committing himself, in the hope that public opinion will soon "crystallize" behind a particular course of action. Once the community is behind a project—and this determination Daley makes himself after lengthy consultations with his political advisers—he then awards his stamp of approval. This suggests that in policy matters many political "bosses" are not so much bosses as referees among interested individuals and groups. The boss is really "apolitical" when it comes to policy matters. He is really more concerned with resolving conflict and maintaining his position and organization than he is with the outcome of public policy decisions.

REFORMERS AND DO-GOODERS

A reform style of politics appeared in the United States shortly after the Civil War to battle the "bosses." Beginning in 1869, scathing editorials in the *New York Times* and cartoons by Thomas Nast in *Harper's Weekly* attacked the "Tammany Society" in New York City, a political organization that controlled the local Democratic organization. William M. Tweed was president of the board of supervisors of New York County, and undisputed boss of "Tammany Hall," as the New York County Democratic committee was called, after its old meeting place on Fourteenth Street. This early reform movement achieved temporary success under the brilliant leadership of Samuel J. Tilden, who succeeded in driving the "Tweed Ring" out of office and went on in 1876 to be the only presidential candidate ever to win a majority of popular votes and then be denied the presidency through the operation of the electoral college. George William Curtis, editor of *Harper's Weekly*, E. L. Godkin, editor of the *Nation,* and Senator Carl Schurz of Missouri laid the foundations for a style of reform politics that continues to have great influence in American cities.[13]

Early municipal reform is closely linked to the Progressive movement in American politics. Leaders such as Robert M. La Follette of Wisconsin, Hiram Johnson of California, Gifford Pinchot of Pennsylvania, and Charles Evans Hughes of New York backed municipal reform at the local level as well as the direct primary and direct election of senators and women's suffrage at the national level. In 1912 social worker Jane Addams, who labored in the slums and settlement houses in New York, sang "Onward Christian Soldiers" at the Progressive party convention in 1912, which nominated Teddy Roosevelt for president. Lincoln Steffens

[13]See Richard J. Hofstadter, *The Age of Reform* (New York: Alfred A. Knopf, Inc., 1955); and Lorin Peterson, *The Day of the Mugwump* (New York: Random House, Inc., 1961).

wrote in *The Shame of the Cities* ". . . St. Louis exemplified boodle; Minneapolis, police graft; Pittsburgh, a political industrial machine; and Philadelphia (the worst city in the country), general civic corruption."[14] The National Municipal League was formed in 1900 by representatives of reform citizens' associations throughout the country.

From its beginning, reform politics was strongly supported by the native upper-class, Anglo-Saxon, Protestant, longtime residents of cities whose political ethos was very different from that which the new immigrants brought with them. The immigrant, the machine that relied upon his vote, and the businessman who relied upon the machine for street railway and other utility franchises had formed an alliance in the nineteenth century, which had displaced the native, old family, Yankee elite that had traditionally dominated northern cities. This upper-class elite fought to recapture control of local government through the municipal reform movement.

Richard Hofstadter described the social, ideological, and political clash between the new immigrants and the Anglo-Saxon, Protestant, upper class in the *Age of Reform:*

> Out of the clash between the needs of the immigrants and the sentiments of the natives, there emerged two thoroughly different systems of political ethics . . . one, founded upon the indigenous yankee-Protestant political traditions, and upon middle class life, assumed and demanded the constant, disinterested activity of the citizen in public affairs, argued that political life ought to be run to a greater degree than it was in accordance to general principles, abstract laws, apart from and superior to personal needs, and expressed a common feeling that government should be in good part an effort to moralize the lives of individuals, while economic life should be intimately related to the stimulation and development of individual character. The other system, founded upon the European background of the immigrants, upon their unfamiliarity with independent political action, their familiarity with hierarchy and authority, and upon the urgent needs that so often grew out of their migration, took for granted that the political life of the individual would arise out of family needs, interpreted political and civic relations, chiefly in terms of personal obligations, and placed strong personal loyalties above allegiance to abstract codes of law or morals.[15]

This conflict can still be observed today in American politics. Machine politicians cater to ethnic groups, organized labor, blue-collar workers ("hardhats"), and other white working-class elements of the city. The reform politician appeals to the upper- and middle-class affluent American who is well educated and public service minded. Reform is popular among liberals, television and newspaper reporters, college professors, and others

14Lincoln Steffens, *The Shame of the Cities* (Sagamore Press, 1957), p. 10.
15Hofstadter, *The Age of Reform.*

who consider themselves "intellectuals." It is no coincidence that Mayor Daley of Chicago was born of Irish immigrant parents, while reform Mayor John Lindsay of New York is a wealthy WASP and a scion of one of the city's oldest families. In an interesting study entitled *"The La-Guardia Years: Machine and Reform Politics in New York City,* Charles Garrett notes that "the good government advocates of this period came mainly from the professional and business classes. They tended to be native Americans of the older sort, Protestant, well-to-do, and well educated."[16]

Reform politics includes a belief that there is a "public interest" that should prevail over competing, partial interests in a city. The idea of balancing competing interests or compromising public policy is not part of the reformers' view of political life. Rather, the reform ethos includes a belief that there is a "right" and "moral" answer to public questions. Conflict and indeed even "politics" is viewed as distasteful. Since reasonable men can agree upon the public interest, municipal government is really a technical and administrative problem rather than a political one. City government should be placed in the hands of those who are best qualified, by training, ability and devotion to public service, to manage public business. These best-qualified men can decide on policy and then leave a separate activity of administration to professional experts. Any interference by special interests in the policies or administration of the best-qualified people would be viewed as corruption.

The objectives of the early reform movement were:

1. The elimination of corruption in public office, and the recruitment of "good men" (educated, upper-income men who were successful in private business or professions) to replace "politicians" (men who were no more successful than their constituents in private life and who were dependent upon public office for their principal source of income).

2. The provision of means by which party machinery could be bypassed in nominations and elections. This meant nomination by petition, and the initiative, recall, and referendum. (Reformers were not really sure about the necessity of this item; it was left to local option in the model city charter.)

3. The reorganization of local government to eliminate many separately elected offices (the "short ballot" movement) in order to simplify the voter's task and focus responsibility for the conduct of public affairs on a small number of top elected officials.

4. The strengthening of executive leadership in city government—longer terms for mayors, subordination of departments and commissions to a chief executive, and an executive budget combined with modern financial practices.

[16]Charles Garrett, *The LaGuardia Years: Machine and Reform Politics in New York City* (New Brunswick, N.J.: Rutgers University Press, 1961), pp. 20–21.

5. The establishment of "at-large" city-wide constituencies in municipal elections in lieu of "ward" constituencies in order to insure that an elected official would consider the welfare of the entire city in public decision making and not merely his own neighborhood or "ward."

6. The replacement of patronage appointments with the merit system of civil service.

7. The separation of local politics from state and national politics by home rule charters and the holding of local elections at times when there were no state and national elections.

8. The elimination of parties from local politics by nonpartisan elections. (The effect of nonpartisanship is described below in more detail.)

9. The establishment of the council-manager form of government, and the separation of "politics" from the "business" of municipal government.

All these objectives are interrelated. Ideally, a "reformed city" would be one with a council-manager form of government, nonpartisan election for mayor and council, a home rule charter, a short ballot, at-large constituencies, a modern budgeting and financial system, a civil service personnel system, initiative, recall and referendum system, and "good men" at the helm. Later, the reform movement added comprehensive city planning to its list of objectives—official planning agencies with professional planners authorized to prepare a master plan of future development for the city. The National Municipal League incorporated its program of reform into a *Model City Charter*, which continues to be the standard manual of municipal reform.[17] There is reason to believe that the early reformers also opposed immigration (which was very logical, of course, since the immigrant was the backbone of machine politics). Many persons active in municipal reform at the time also supported the passage of the Immigration Act of 1921, reducing immigration to a trickle and establishing quotas heavily weighted in favor of Anglo-Saxon Protestant immigrants and against southern and eastern European Catholic immigrants. One of the most effective of the early municipal reformers was Richard S. Childs, an advertising executive who took up municipal reform as a hobby. He started a National Short Ballot organization and is often credited with inventing the council-manager form of government. He used his advertising skills to sell city-manager government with the popular symbols of big business—"economy and efficiency, businesslike government, municipal corporation, professional management, just like a corporation with its board of directors."[18]

[17]National Municipal League, *Model City Charter* (Chicago: National Municipal League, 1961).

[18]Andrew D. White, first president of Cornell University, summarized early reform thinking when he wrote in 1890:

What is this evil theory? It is simply that the city is a political body; that its interior affairs have to do with national political parties and issues. My fundamental

Today reform movements assume a variety of forms.[19] There is, first of all, the "enlightened businessmen's association," which operates outside formal governmental or party structures as a voluntary association, often with paid staffs and researchers. Members of these associations scrutinize local government structure, programs, and expenditures and recommend changes and reforms. Ordinarily, they do not endorse candidates, participate in election campaigns, or take sides in controversial policy questions. The Pennsylvania Economy League, the Chicago Civic Confederation, New York's Citizens Budget Commission, the Greater Philadelphia Movement, and the Detroit Citizens' League are examples of extraparty, policy-orented, citizens' committees that are active in reform efforts. At the state and national level, the Committee for Economic Development (CED) plays a somewhat similar role. These business and citizens' associations claim to provide "objective" information about taxes, expenditures, services, and administration. This information generally stresses the need for economy and efficiency, lower taxes, or streamlined administration. "Enlightened businessmen" are generally moderate on urban social issues—more liberal than white working-class voters, but more conservative than other reform groups.

A second type of reform movement is the voter education association, which also operates outside the political parties and reviews or evaluates candidates for public office. The League of Women Voters is probably the largest organization of this kind. These organizations are probably more effective in nonpartisan cities or cities in which party organizations are weak than in cities with strong two-party systems. These associations also avoid direct political endorsements, but they are moderately liberal on most policy questions and strongly supportive of a variety of "reforms."

---

contention is that a city is a corporation; that as a city it has nothing whatever to do with general political interests; that party political names and duties are utterly out of place there. The questions in a city are not political questions. They have reference to the laying out of streets; to the erection of buildings; to sanitary arrangements, sewerage, water supply, gas supply, electrical supply; to the control of franchises and the like; and to provisions for the public health and comfort in parks, boulevards, libraries, and museums. The work of a city being the creation and control of the city property, it should logically be managed as a piece of property by those who have created it, or a real substantial part in it, and who can therefore feel strongly their duty to it. Under our theory that a city is a political body, a crowd of illiterate peasants, freshly raked in from Irish bogs, or Bohemian mines, or Italian robber nests, may exercise virtual control.

Andrew D. White, "The Government of American Cities," in *Forum* (1890); reprinted in Edward C. Banfield, *Urban Government: A Reader in Administration and Politics* (Glencoe: The Free Press, 1961).

[19]James Q. Wilson, "Politics and Reform in American Cities" in *American Government Annual 1962–63* (New York: Holt, Rinehart, & Winston, Inc., 1962); see also James Q. Wilson, *The Amateur Democrat* (Chicago: University of Chicago Press, 1963).

Occasionally, reform movements assume the form of an independent local party. Reform parties, however, usually do not last very long. Since they are committed to "reform," they are prevented by their principles from offering jobs or other material enticements to maintain the continued disciplined support of their party workers. They must rely upon social and ideological rewards, and their supporters often grow tired of these intangible satisfactions. The Liberal party of New York provides an interesting contrast. The Liberal party has had considerable success at the polls and has operated successfully over many years. It has the strong support of the International Ladies' Garment Workers union, and it is liberal on most national policy issues.

Most reform movements are factions operating within existing party organizations, particularly the Democratic party. A reform faction may coalesce around a "blue-ribbon" candidate, usually a man of high social class, high professional achievement, and devotion to public service. He may come from a distinguished old family or be a wealthy and successful businessman with a record of statesmanlike participation in public affairs, and although a loyal party member, he may have no personal identification with local machines or professional politicians. Politics permits him to indulge his fancy for public service and do-goodism.

The prevailing philosophy of the modern reformer is liberal and public regarding. It is a philosophy of *noblesse oblige*—the righteous man's responsibility for the welfare of the poor and downtrodden, particularly the blacks. It is not the broad mass of increasingly affluent white working-class Americans that elicits the reformer's sympathies, but only the most deprived segments of society—the poor, the blacks, the slum dwellers, the sick, the criminal defendants, and so forth. The reformer defies simplistic Marxian interpretations of American politics. Wealth, education, sophistication, and upper-class culture values do *not* foster attitudes of exploitation, but rather attitudes of public service and do-goodism. Reformers are frequently paternalistic toward segments of the masses they define as "underprivileged," "culturally deprived," "disadvantaged," and so forth, but they are not hostile toward them. Indeed, hostility toward such groups as blacks, welfare recipients, and criminal defendants is more characteristic of white working-class masses than it is of upper-class reformers.

Political divisions in American cities do not always take the form of upper classes versus lower classes. Increasingly in urban politics, one finds upper-class liberal reformers allied with certain minority segments of the lower classes, notably blacks, in opposition to white middle-class and working-class masses. Democratic reformers in municipal politics are generally liberal Democrats in national politics, while Republican reformers are frequently supporters of the progressive wing of that party.

Reformers are generally amateurs in politics, in contrast to the professional politicians who constitute the regular party organizations. The "amateur" is more motivated by the ideological and psychological rewards of mixing in government and public affairs; in contrast, the "professional" is interested in tangible rewards—jobs, contracts, public offices. Amateurs are concerned with the great issues facing the nation—war, racism, pollution, poverty. They do not deal with the personal problems confronting individuals, but rather with the broad social problems confronting groups or classes. Reformers view government as an instrument for achieving broad social reforms, and not merely as a source of jobs, buildings and civic improvements, or upward social mobility for gifted individuals from the lower classes. The politics of reform is frequently more ideological than pragmatic. Appeals are made to lofty principle rather than material welfare. All of this, of course, is in direct contrast to the machine style of politics.

Today's reformers differ from earlier reformers in several respects. First of all, they place greater emphasis on the reform of party machinery at all levels of government, rather than the elimination of parties from municipal government. Second, most reformers no longer want to separate national elections from local or state elections; instead, they want local and state politics to become more issue oriented. Finally, concern for the conditions of blacks in America has led many reformers to reassess their traditional views on government organization and the political participation of the lower classes. Whereas early reformers wanted to discourage lower-class political participation (when white, ethnic, recent immigrants constituted the bulk of the urban lower class), today liberal reformers are attempting to build a coalition with urban blacks. To do so they must encourage black political participation, and this involves structural changes that promote voter turnout and facilitate black access to public office. Reformers are now rethinking their support for "at-large" elections, which frequently dilute black representation on city councils, and reconsidering their insistence on merit systems of appointment, which frequently restrict black access to public employment. Thus reformers, as well as bosses, change over time.

THE REFORMER: JOHN LINDSAY
OF NEW YORK

Mayor John Lindsay's administration in New York City is typical of the style of municipal reform in America. Lindsay himself is "silk-stocking" New York: liberal, upper class, wealthy, Episcopalian, St. Paul's Academy, Yale University, Yale Law School, Council on Foreign Relations, Yale trustee. He began his political career as president of the New York Young Republican Club and was rewarded for his work on behalf of Eisenhower in the 1952 presidential campaign by appointment as assistant to the attorney general. Lindsay ran for Congress in Manhattan's Park Avenue district in 1958 and served in Congress as a liberal Republican.

Lindsay returned to New York politics in 1965 to mount the most expensive campaign for mayor in the history of American city elections. Lindsay's principal opponent was a lackluster former city controller, Abraham Beame, who was heir to the crumbling Democratic party organization headed by retiring Mayor Robert Wagner. The third candidate in the race was the well-known conservative intellectual and editor of the *National Review,* William Buckley. It was clear that Buckley had little chance of winning, but he seemed to enjoy the race and it provided him the opportunity to attack both the liberalism of Lindsay and the Democratic machine supporting Beame. Typical of reform campaigns, Lindsay avoided his Republican party identification. His campaign was expensive ($1.5 million), and it was a model of professional, "Madison Avenue," advertising. He relied on his good looks, personality, and television image. He gave few specifics about what he intended to do about New York's many ills; his campaign theme was simply "He's fresh while everyone else is tired." He saturated the mass media and campaigned heavily in black wards of the city. Lindsay received 46 percent of the vote to Beame's 41 percent and Buckley's 13 percent.

Lindsay is one of society's "beautiful people"—tall, handsome, photogenic, witty, urbane, comfortable in the glare of camera lights. He communicates directly with his constituents by letting himself be seen—on television, in the streets, in the press. He promotes New York as "Fun City" and conveys a mood of concern for the poor and the black of his city. He is a frequent guest on late-night television talk shows. His actual accomplishments as mayor are few. It is not clear that Lindsay knows much about the intricacies of the city's vast municipal bureaucracy or the complex technical aspects of its many problems. By implication, Lindsay seems to acknowledge that New York City is "ungovernable." He concentrates most of his energies on trying to convince state and national governments that they must come to the financial aid of American cities. He has become a leader among America's mayors in pressuring Congress for increased attention to urban problems. New York City during his administration has been plagued by an incredible number of municipal mishaps: a giant power blackout; innumerable strikes by subway workers, dock workers, and others; a bridge tenders' strike which caused massive traffic snarls; a sanitation workers' strike which piled mountains of garbage in the city's streets; evidence of widespread corruption in the police force; and a city-wide teachers' strike which seriously impaired public education for more than a year. All of this on top of New York's perennial ills—crime, drugs, delinquency, poverty, poor housing, spiraling welfare rolls, traffic congestion, pollution, and financial crisis.

Lindsay has had some success in avoiding ghetto riots. During tense summer evenings, he walked through ghetto streets in an effort to calm the crowds and show interest and concern for their problems. A sample of responses to Lindsay's walks: "It's important. It shows he cares about us." "He wants to do the right thing." "I got to take my hat off to that dude." In recognition of his closeness to the problem of urban violence, President Johnson appointed him vice-chairman of the Commission on Civil Disorder. (See Chapter 13.)

As a modern reformer, Lindsay worked to build a coalition of upper- and middle-class liberal whites and ghetto blacks among the city's voters. The effort paid off in his campaign for reelection in 1969. Lindsay lost the Republican primary to a little-known New York assemblyman, John Marchi, who convinced Republican New Yorkers that Lindsay was soft on "law and order." But Lindsay remained in the race as a liberal independent. The Democratic candidate was a longtime party regular, Mario Procaccino, who also attacked Lindsay for "crime in the streets." White working-class New Yorkers had little good to say about Lindsay. When he attempted one of his famous walks around the Italian section of the Lower East Side, he heard, "That's Lindsay? You're kidding. There ain't no niggers here." But Lindsay's reform coalition gave him enough votes to win a three-man election in which white, ethnic, working-class votes were split. Lindsay won 42 percent of the vote (less than his earlier victory) to Democrat Procaccino's 35 percent and Republican Marchi's 23 percent.

It is seldom that a mayor is catapulted directly into presidential politics. Generally the springboard to the White House is the U.S. Senate or a governorship. But in 1972 Lindsay left the Republican party, which had denied him its mayoralty nomination, and carried his message of urban reform into the Democratic party's presidential race. Lindsay's presidential bid was a complete failure; the Democrats already had a host of liberal reform candidates of their own. But it is likely that the municipal reform movement will continue to be a source of state and national leadership.

THE FUTURE STYLE OF CITY POLITICS

Boss Plunkitt once observed that "reform administrations never succeed themselves." Plunkitt realized that the emotional fervor of reform could arouse the public to "throw the rascals out" in moments of righteous reform, but he was confident that, in the long run, organization politics, with its reliance upon personal and material rewards, could outlast the emotional appeal of reform. Reform administrations, he felt, would come and go, but the machine would remain to govern the city with only occasional interruptions. Yet these interruptions occurred with increased frequency in the twentieth century. The machine style of politics still exists, but it has declined noticeably in recent years. City government is vastly more honest, efficient, and democratic than it was a generation ago.

Several factors are generally cited as contributing to the decline of machine politics:

1. The *decline in immigration* and the gradual assimilation of white ethnic groups—Irish, Italians, Germans, Poles, Slavs;
2. Federal *social welfare programs,* which undercut the machine's role in welfare work—unemployment insurance, workmen's compensation, social security, and public assistance have ended the party's monopoly of welfare services;
3. Rising *levels of prosperity* and higher educational levels, which make the traditional rewards of the machine less attractive;
4. The *spread of middle-class values* about honesty, efficiency, and good government, which inhibit party organizations in purchases, contracts, and vote buying, and other cruder forms of municipal corruption. The more successful machines today, like Daley's in Chicago, have had to reform themselves to maintain a good public image;
5. *Structural reforms* such as nonpartisanship, better voting procedures, city-manager government, and—most important of all—civil service which have weakened the party's role in municipal elections and administration.

Edwin O'Connor, in an interesting novel *The Last Hurrah,* based upon the life of Mayor Curley of Boston, describes the defeat of Boss Skeffington in his bid for reelection as Mayor:

Well, of course, the old boss was strong simply because he held all the cards. If anybody wanted anything—jobs, favors, cash, he could only go to the boss, the local leader. What Roosevelt did was to take the handouts out of the local hands. A few little things like social security, unemployment insurance, and the like—that's what shifted the gears, Sport. No need now to depend on the boss for everything; the federal government is getting into the act . . . the old timers would still string along with the boss, of course, because that's the way they always did things. But what about the kids coming along? Did you ever stop to think, Sport, about the *age* of the people around (Boss Skeffington)? I wouldn't mind betting that it didn't exactly look like a youth movement . . . and what about the kids? To begin with, they were one step further away from the old country; he didn't have the old emotional appeal for them. You know, the racial spokesman kind of thing. For another, a lot of them have been educated away from home. They didn't know much about Skeffington, and they didn't much care.[20]

Patronage was once very useful in maintaining a party organization, attracting voters, financing the party, insuring favorable government actions for party requests, and maintaining discipline within the party's ranks, yet Frank Sorauf has commented on the declining usefulness of patronage in an era of economic prosperity and high levels of employment: "While low pay and chronic job insecurity plague the patronage job holder, private employment has become progressively more attractive with rising wage levels, union protections and securities, unemployment compensation, pension plans, and fringe benefits. Viewed by most Americans as a short term desperation job alternative, the patronage position has lost considerable value as a political incentive.[21] Sorauf also notes that patronage runs contrary to the prevailing values of the growing middle class in America: "Patronage is also losing its respectability. Its ethic—the naked political quid pro quo—no longer seems to many a natural and reasonable ingredient in politics . . . the mores of the middle class and image of civic virtue instilled by public education extolled the unfettered, independent voter, rather than the patronage seeking party liner . . . briefly, patronage has fallen into public disfavor for appearing to approach an outright political payoff, with the result that its usefulness to the parties has diminished."[22]

NONPARTISANSHIP

The nonpartisan ballot was the most widely adopted reform ever put forward to curb the machines and insure an "antiseptic," "no party" style of politics. Nearly two-thirds of America's cities use the nonpartisan ballot to elect local officials. Reformers felt that nonpartisanship would take the "politics" out of local government and raise the caliber of candidates for elected offices. They believed that nonpartisanship would restrict local campaigning to local issues and thereby rule out extraneous state issues from local elections. They also believed that by eliminating party labels, local campaigns would emphasize the qualifications of the individual candidates rather than their party affiliations.

Nonpartisanship is found in large as well as small cities. Party labels

[20]Edwin O'Connor, *The Last Hurrah* (Boston: Little, Brown and Company, 1956), pp. 374–75.
[21]Frank J. Sorauf, "State Patronage in a Rural County," *American Political Science Review*, 50 (1956), 1046–56.
[22]*Ibid.*, p. 1055.

have been removed from local elections in Detroit, Los Angeles, Denver, Dallas, Houston, Boston, Cincinnati, Cleveland, Milwaukee, San Francisco, Seattle, San Antonio, and San Diego. Nonpartisanship is even more widespread than council-manager government. However, there is a tendency for these two forms to be related: 82 percent of all council-manager cities have nonpartisan ballots, while only 49 percent of all mayor-council cities are nonpartisan (see Table 9–1).

Party politics is still the prevailing style of local elections in Eastern cities: 76 percent of Eastern cities have partisan elections and only 24 percent have nonpartisan elections. But elsewhere in the nation nonpartisanship prevails: 74 percent of Central cities, 78 percent of Southern cities, and 94 percent of Western cities are nonpartisan. While nonpartisan cities are found in both one-party and two-party states, there is some tendency for competitive two-party states to have a smaller percentage of nonpartisan cities than one-party Democratic or Republican states. Table 9–2, by Phillips Cutright, shows that 56 percent of the cities in competitive states have nonpartisan ballots, compared with 74 percent of the cities in Democratic states and 86 percent of the cities in Repub-

TABLE 9-1

Nonpartisanship in American Cities

	Number of Cities Reporting	Percent Partisan	Percent Nonpartisan
All Cities	2,880	35	65
Form of Government			
Mayor-council	1,387	51	49
Commission	174	30	70
Council-manager	1,229	18	82
Population			
Over 500,000	26	42	58
250,000-500,000	25	24	76
100,000-250,000	90	41	59
50,000-100,000	208	32	68
25,000- 50,000	427	33	67
10,000- 25,000	1,057	34	66
5,000- 10,000	1,049	37	63
Region			
East	767	76	24
Central	901	26	74
South	768	22	78
West	444	6	94

SOURCE: MUNICIPAL YEAR BOOK, 1968, p. 58.

TABLE 9-2

State Party Systems, Community Cleavage, and Nonpartisanship

State party system	Percent nonpartisan	Number of cities[2]
Competitive states[1]	56	280
Democratic states	74	115
Republican states	86	85
Total	65	480
Religious composition[3]		
High Catholic	56	225
Low Catholic	73	255
Manufacturing levels		
High manufacturing employment	56	218
Low manufacturing employment	73	262

[1] Competitive States: California, Colorado, Connecticut, Delaware, Illinois, Indiana, Kentucky, Massachusetts, Idaho, Michigan, Maryland, Montana, Missouri, New Mexico, New York, Nevada, Ohio, Pennsylvania, Vermont, Washington, West Virginia, Wyoming.

[2] All incorporated cities with 25,000 inhabitants in 1950.

[3] From U.S. Department of Commerce, RELIGIOUS BODIES, 1936 (Washington, D.C.: Government Printing Office, 1941); I.

SOURCE: Adapted from figures presented in Phillips Cutright, "Nonpartisan Electoral Systems in American Cities," COMPARATIVE STUDIES IN SOCIETY AND HISTORY (January 1963).

lican states. The nonpartisan ballot is also more likely to be adopted in homogeneous middle-class cities, where there is less social cleavage and smaller proportions of working-class and ethnic group members. Cutright reports that there is a tendency for cities with large Catholic populations to retain the partisan ballot; there is also a tendency for cities with heavy factory employment to prefer partisan over nonpartisan elections.[23] However, Cutright's findings are subject to many exceptions: Cleveland, Detroit, and Boston are located in competitive party states and have large working class populations, large Catholic populations, and deep social cleavages—yet they are officially nonpartisan cities.

To what extent has nonpartisanship succeeded in removing "politics" from local government? Of course, if "politics" is defined as conflict over public policy, then "politics" has certainly not disappeared with the elimination of party labels. There is no evidence that eliminating party ballots can reduce the level of community conflict. If we define "politics" to mean

[23]Phillips Cutright, "Nonpartisan Electoral Systems in American Cities," *Comparative Studies in Society and History* (January 1963), pp. 212–26.

"partisanship," that is, *party* politics, then nonpartisanship may have removed some party influences from local government, although the evidence is by no means clear on this point.

Apparently several types of political systems can be found in nonpartisan cities.[24] First of all, in some nonpartisan cities, parties continue to operate effectively behind the scenes in local affairs. Denver, Seattle, Cincinnati, and Kansas City have been cited as nonpartisan cities in which the parties continue to play a vital role in local elections.

Another type of nonpartisan political system is one in which the major parties are inactive, but other formal organizations function very much like parties. Freqently these organizations are civic organizations led by newspapers or business firms. Occasionally, liberal or labor groups arise to challenge middle-class civic associations. These organizations may "slate" candidates, manage their campaigns, and even exercise some influence over them while they are in office. These organizations are not usually as permanent as parties, but they may operate as clearly indentifiable political entities over a number of years. Cities with these "local parties" include San Francisco, Detroit, Dallas, Fort Worth, and Cambridge, Massachusetts. Many of these local party systems are indirectly related to the national parties. In a Massachusetts city, J. Lieper Freeman found that the "progressives" and the "nonpartisans," who opposed each other consistently in local elections, were largely Democrats and Republicans in disguise.[25] Williams and Adrian studied four nonpartisan Michigan cities and found identifiable blocs of candidates and a high correlation between party identification and voting for a particular local slate.[26] Salisbury and Black testify that after the adoption of nonpartisanship in Des Moines, party organizations ceased to play an active role in campaigns, but there continued to be significant relationships between party identification and voting for particular slates of candidates in local nonpartisan elections.[27]

A third type of nonpartisan political system is one in which the Democratic and Republican parties play no role at all and in which there are no local parties or slate-making associations. This is the most common type of nonpartisanship in small cities. Individual candidates select themselves, collect their own money, and create their own temporary campaign or-

[24]The following discussion relies upon Charles Adrian, "A Typology of Non-Partisan Elections," *Western Political Quarterly*, 12 (June 1959), 449–58; see also Banfield and Wilson, *City Politics*, Chap. 12.

[25]J. Lieper Freeman, "Local Party Systems: Theoretical Considerations and a Case Analysis," *American Journal of Sociology*, Vol. 64 (1958).

[26]Oliver P. Williams and Charles R. Adrian, "The Insulation of Local Politics under the Non-Partisan Ballot," *American Political Science Review*, 53 (1959), 1052–63.

[27]Robert Salisbury and Gordon Black, "Class and Party in Partisan and Non-Partisan Elections," *American Political Science Review*, 57 (September 1963), 587–97.

ganizations. Voting does not correlate highly with party identification, but instead tends to follow a "friends and neighbors" pattern, rather than socioeconomic or partisan lines.

Does nonpartisanship increase Republican influence in city government? It is sometimes argued that the removal of party designations from local elections hurts Democrats by disengaging their traditional support from urban voters—the low-income, labor, ethnic, and black groups that traditionally vote the Democratic ticket. Moreover, the well-educated, high-income groups and interests that are normally Republican have a natural edge in organization, communication, and prestige in the absence of parties. Republicans also have better turnout records in nonpartisan elections.[28] All of this may help to explain why many cities that are heavily Democratic in state and national elections elect mayors and councilmen who are somewhat more conservative. Eugene Lee found that the decline in voter turnout in local (nonpartisan) elections, in contrast to national (partisan) elections, is greatest in Democratic precincts and least in Republican precincts.[29] In other words, Democratic voters are less likely than Republican voters to cast ballots when the familiar party labels do not appear on the ballot and when a local Democratic organization does not prod them to the polls. Williams and Adrian conclude: "A nonpartisan election leads to an increased voice in local affairs for persons who normally vote Republican."[30]

It seems safe to conclude that a minority party member has a better chance of winning against a majority party member in a nonpartisan election than in a partisan election. And since the Democratic party is the majority party in most of the nation's large and middle-sized cities, nonpartisan elections probably make it easier for the Republicans to win municipal office.

Does nonpartisanship result in "better-qualified" candidates winning public office? Of course the answer to this question depends upon one's definition of better qualified. Nonpartisanship may result in more high-income, "respectable," white, Anglo-Saxon Protestants, with prestige jobs, running for public office. Working-class candidates are disadvantaged by nonpartisanship, for several reasons. First of all, as we have already observed, nonpartisanship reduces the turnout of labor, low-income, ethnic, Democratic voters and, consequently, increases the influence of well-educated, high-income, white, Anglo-Saxon Protestant Republican voters, who continue to come to the polls in nonpartisan elections. In addition,

---

[28]See Charles E. Gilbert, "Some Aspects of Nonpartisan Elections in Large Cities," *Midwest Journal of Political Science*, 6 (November 1962), 346–54.

[29]Eugene C. Lee, *Nonpartisan Politics* (Berkeley: University of California Press, 1960).

[30]Williams and Adrian, "The Insulation of Local Politics," p. 1063.

nonpartisanship means the recruitment of candidates will be left to civic associations, or ad hoc groups of one kind or another, rather than Democratic or Republican party organizations. This difference in recruitment and endorsement practices tends to give an advantage to middle-class candidates. Candidates from the lower classes are rarely put forward and endorsed by newspapers and influential civic associations. They seldom receive the kind of public attention in private life that would make their names well known enough to place on a ballot, nor do they have the organizational ties or memberships that would bring them to the attention of civic associations that are recruiting in nonpartisan elections. In contrast, in partisan big-city politics, being a member of a working class, ethnic, or minority group may be a positive advantage. Parties traditionally try to "balance the ticket" with candidates who represent various groups, in rough proportion to their voting strength. This practice of having a balanced party ticket with Irish, Italian, Polish, Jewish, and black names on the ballot is thought to add strength to the entire party ticket, since voters will be asked to vote for the party ticket rather than for the individual candidates. Eugene C. Lee reports that the "typical" nonpartisan councilman is a registered Republican, forty-five to fifty years old, who has a professional, managerial, or sales occupation and lives in the "better part of town."[31] He is likely to be a Protestant, a Mason, a member of the chamber of commerce, and a member of a veterans' group, and to have lived in the city for a long time, and to have made his mark in the Community Chest, the Red Cross, or some other civic or welfare association. Of course, there are exceptions to this generalization about nonpartisan candidates. Certainly, in nonpartisan Boston, one is more likely to encounter Irish or Italian Democrats on the city council than Yankee Republicans.

Banfield and Wilson observed that the influence of newspapers in city politics is strengthened by nonpartisan elections. Newspapers are particularly important to the election of candidates in nonpartisan cities, where voters do not have party organizations to keep them informed about candidates. "You can't tell the players without a scorecard," a newspaperman remarked happily, "and we sell the scorecards."

Nonpartisanship contributes to the reelection of incumbent councilmen particularly when nonpartisanship is combined with at-large elections. Incumbents are more likely to have a name that is known to the voters. Gilbert and Clague found that in Chicago and Pittsburgh, with their machine style of politics, incumbent councilmen were easily reelected.[32] However, incumbent councilmen in all other partisan cities were not reelected

---

[31]Lee, *Nonpartisan Politics,* p. 170.

[32]Charles E. Gilbert and Christopher Clague, "Electoral Participation and Electoral Systems in Large Cities," *Journal of Politics,* 24 (1962), 323–30.

as often as incumbents in nonpartisan cities. Moreover, incumbent councilmen running at-large in the city were more likely to be reelected than incumbent councilmen running from districts. This suggests that it is difficult to hold public officials accountable in a nonpartisan election. The
voter does not have the opportunity to hear organized criticisms of incumbent officeholders from an opposition party. When the only challenge
to an incumbent officeholder is an unknown name on the ballot, he is
more likely to be reelected than if he is challenged by a candidate backed
by an opposition party. The higher rates of reelection in nonpartisan
systems suggest that accountability is harder to achieve where party labels
are absent.

POLICY STYLES IN LOCAL GOVERNMENT

Community political systems have been classified according to their governmental structure and political style, but we can also classify them according to the types of policies their citizens and officials expect of them.
Oliver P. Williams has suggested a typology of four different policy roles
for local government: (1) promoting economic growth; (2) providing or
securing life's amenities; (3) maintaining traditional public services, that
is, a caretaker role; and (4) arbitrating among conflicting interests.[33]

A community whose major policy concern is the promotion of economic
growth is interested in population expansion, industrial development,
commercial activities, total wealth, and the like. This type of community
is prepared to enact zoning regulations, reduce tax assessments, develop industrial parks, install utilities, and do whatever else may be required to
attract business and industry and promote production. These policies
may be most vigorously endorsed by business and commercial interests
that have a stake in the community's growth, but the appeal of these policies is much broader. A growing, thriving community infects its residents
with a certain pride that gives them a feeling of being a part of community progress. Of course it is the merchant, the chamber of commerce,
the banker, the newspaper editor, and the city official who see each new
resident as a potential customer, taxpayer, or contributor to the growth
of their business enterprise. To aid in economic growth, a city should
have a good reputation. This means politics should be conducted in a
low key, the image of stability and regularity in city finances should be
assured, and friendliness toward business should be the prevailing attitude of city officials.

[33]The following discussion relies upon Oliver P. Williams, "A Typology for Comparative Local Government," *Midwest Journal of Political Science*, 5 (May 1961),
150–64.

The major policy concern of other communities is providing and securing life's amenities; that is, preserving a certain "way of life" that is
highly valued by the residents and safeguarding and improving the advantages of the city as a place to live. "Amenity" communities are less
concerned with economic growth and more concerned with providing
the comforts of life for their citizens. Policies accent the home environment rather than the working environment—the citizen as consumer
rather than producer. Laws stress safety, slowness, quiet, beauty, convenience and restfulness. The rights of pedestrians and children take
precedence over the claims of commerce. Neighborhoods are defended
by rigid zoning laws and building codes, open space is guarded, traffic
is routed around the city, and noise and smoke are curtailed. Population
growth is not particularly welcome. Heavy industry may be excluded.
Since the costs of such policies are quite high, and these policies discourage business and industrial tax bases, amenity communities must
have residential populations with above-average incomes. Middle- and
upper-income residential suburbs in large metropolitan areas are likely
to be amenity communities. Amenities may also become the major concern of the traditional small town that is threatened by engulfment from
a nearby major urban complex. Such a small town may not have the
middle-class homogeneity of the exclusive suburb, but its amenities may
not require the costly expenditures required in a suburb. Because the
growth of the town was slow, necessary capital investments for amenities
were amortized over a very long time. A sudden population influx
threatens the way of life of the community and the cost of maintaining
that way of life.

A caretaker government, on the other hand, is expected to provide
minimum public services in the community, and nothing more. Caretaker
government is limited to government, where extreme conservative views
toward the role of government can be effectively realized. "Freedom" and
"self-reliance of the individual" are preferred over government programs
of any kind. The overriding policy consideration is keeping the costs of
government low. Tax increases are hardly ever justified. Nothing new is
ever tried. Pressing public problems are passed onto higher levels of government (the county, state, or federal government) or given to private
groups or charities (the chamber of commerce, the churches, or the Salva-
tion Army), or they are ignored. Caretaker policies are often preferred
by farmers, small merchants, and homeowners who can barely afford
the home they are buying and do not want to pay taxes for amenities
of any kind.

A fourth type of local government role suggested by Williams is that of
arbitrator between conflicting interests. Strictly speaking, this is not a
policy role because emphasis is placed upon the process of decision mak-

ing rather than the substance of governmental action. An arbiter government is primarily concerned with managing conflict among competing interests and finding workable compromises that can be enacted into public policy. An arbiter government is more likely to be found in a large, heterogeneous community, where social and economic cleavages create demands for different policies, rather than in a homogeneous community, where there is substantial agreement on the proper policies for government to follow. Arbiter governments frequently exist in larger cities, and they are generally preferred by minority groups. As we have already observed, ethnic-based, patronage-oriented political machines usually provide arbiter government. But such organizations are not confined to large cities. In an arbiter government, individual group access to decision making is more important than any substantive policy orientation.

REFORMISM AND PUBLIC POLICY

What are the policy consequences of reform government? Other things being equal, do reformed cities pursue significantly different policies than unreformed cities?

There is some evidence that urban renewal policies may be effected by manager versus mayor government. Political scientist George S. Duggar reports that mayor cities were quicker to respond to the lure of federal money than manager cities and got a faster start on their urban renewal programs.[34] This finding would testify to the political awareness of mayors. On the other hand, Duggar reports that once urban renewal programs were begun, manager cities experienced slightly greater program achievement than mayor cities. Duggar admits that population size is a more influential variable in urban renewal achievement than governmental structure: greater achievement is associated with greater size. He concludes, however, that governmental structure does have some independent effect on urban renewal policies.

The structure of city governments has been found to be related to outcomes in water fluoridation battles. In comparative studies of several hundred cities, sociologists Robert L. Crain and Donald B. Rosenthal found that fluoridation has a better chance of consideration and adoption in cities having a strong executive (a manager or a strong partisan mayor) and a relatively low level of direct citizen participa-

[34]George S. Duggar, "The Relation of Local Government Structure to Urban Renewal," *Law and Contemporary Problems* (Winter 1961), 55–65.

tion. [35] Broad popular participation, particularly in the absence of strong executive leadership, frequently spelled defeat for fluoridation. Moreover, a mayor's public endorsement is closely correlated with fluoridation adoption, even when a referendum is held. Another structural variable—partisanship—is also related to fluoridation outcomes. In both mayor and manager cities, partisan electoral systems are marked by the largest proportion of adoptions of fluoridation laws by city councils.

Perhaps the most important systematic study of the policy consequences of reformism is a comprehensive analysis of taxing and spending policies in two hundred American cities with populations of fifty thousand or more by political scientists Robert L. Lineberry and Edmund P. Fowler. They found that reformed cities tended to tax and spend *less* than unreformed cities.[36] Cities with manager governments and at-large council constituencies were *less* willing to spend money for public purposes than cities with mayor-council governments and ward constituencies. (Cities with partisan elections, however, did not actually spend any more than cities with nonpartisan elections.) In short, reformism *does* save tax money.

Lineberry and Fowler also found that environmental variables had an important impact on tax and spending policies. For example, they concluded that

1. The more middle class the city, measured by income, education, and occupation, the lower the general tax and spending levels.
2. The greater the home ownership in a city, the lower the tax and spending levels.
3. The larger the percentage of religious and ethnic minorities in the population, the higher the city's taxes and expenditures.

What turned out to be an even more important finding in the Lineberry and Fowler study was the difference in *responsiveness* of the two kinds of city governments—reformed and unreformed—to the socioeconomic composition of their populations. Reformed cities (cities with manager governments, at-large constituencies, and nonpartisan elections) appeared to be unresponsive in their tax and spending policies to differences in income and educational, occupational, religious, and ethnic characteristics of their populations. In contrast, unreformed cities (cities with mayor-council governments, ward constituencies, and partisan elec-

[35]Robert L. Crain and Donald B. Rosenthal, "Structure and Values in Local Political Systems: The Case of Fluoridation Decisions," *Journal of Politics*, 28 (February 1966), 169–95.

[36]Robert L. Lineberry and Edmund P. Fowler, "Reformism and Public Policy in American Cities," *American Political Science Review*, 61 (September 1967), 701–16.

TABLE 9-3

Environmental Characteristics and Tax and Spending Policy in Reformed and Unreformed Cities

Relationship between	Correlation between Environmental Characteristics and Taxing and Spending	
	Reformed Cities	Unreformed Cities
TAXES and		
Ethnicity	.62	.34
Private school attendance	.40	.25
Home ownership	-.70	-.44
Education	-.55	-.13
EXPENDITURES and		
Ethnicity	.51	.05
Private school attendance	.46	.08
Home ownership	-.67	-.38
Education	-.49	-.37

SOURCE: Adapted from figures in Robert L. Lineberry and Edmund P. Fowler, "Reformism and Public Policy in American Cities," AMERICAN POLITICAL SCIENCE REVIEW, 61 (September 1967), 701-16.

tions) reflected class, racial, and religious composition in their taxing and spending decisions. As Table 9–3 shows, the strength of the correlation between environment and taxing and spending, by categories of reform, decreases regularly with an increase in reform government.

Reformism tends to reduce the importance of class, home ownership, ethnicity, and religion in city politics. It tends to minimize the role that social conflicts play in public decision making. In contrast, mayor-council governments, ward constituencies, and partisan elections permit social cleavages to be reflected in city politics and public policy to be responsive to socioeconomic factors. These findings suggest that reformed cities have gone a long way toward accomplishing the reformist goal— that is, "to immunize city governments from 'artificial' social cleavages— race, religion, ethnicity, and so on." Thus, political institutions seem to play an important role in policy formation.

> . . . a role substantially independent of a city's demography. . . . Non-partisan elections, at-large constituencies, and manager governments are associated with a lessened responsiveness of cities to the enduring conflicts of political life.[37]

[37]*Ibid.*, p. 715.

TEN

Participation
in
Community Politics

VOTERS IN MUNICIPAL ELECTIONS

The influence of the voter is felt not only on election day, but on every day that elected officials act to win his support or avoid his displeasure. The successful political leader is always concerned with what the voter will think.

Voter turnout in local elections is substantially lower than in state or national elections. While two-thirds of the nation's eligible voters can be expected to cast ballots in a presidential election, voter turnouts of 30–50 percent are all that can be expected in local elections, even in the nation's largest cities.

Nonpartisanship depresses voter turnout quite substantially. The *Municipality Yearbook* reports that the median voter turnout for partisan cities was 50 percent, while the median voter turnout for nonpartisan cities was only 30 percent (see Table 10–1). Partisan campaigns heighten voter turnout, in part because of the greater interest they generate and in part because of the role of party workers in getting out the vote. The difference in voter turnout in partisan and nonpartisan local elections is an important comment on the role of parties in stimulating political participation.

Voter participation in local government can be further reduced by holding municipal elections at odd times of the year when no other state

TABLE 10-1

Governmental Structure and Voter Turnout
in Municipal Elections

	All City Elections	Elections Held Concurrently with State or National Elections	Elections Held Independently of Other Elections
	MEAN PERCENTAGE OF ADULTS VOTING		
Form of election			
Partisan	50	51	41
Nonpartisan	30	43	27
Form of government			
Mayor-council	50	51	44
Commission	38	33	38
Council-manager	27	43	23
Population			
Over 500,000	39	57	20
250,000 to 500,000	37	56	34
100,000 to 250,000	32	50	29
50,000 to 100,000	33	51	29
25,000 to 50,000	33	47	29
All cities over 25,000	33	50	29

SOURCE: MUNICIPAL YEARBOOK, 1963, p. 83.

or national elections are being held. A common rationale for holding municipal elections at times other than state or national elections is to separate local issues from state or national questions, but the real effect of scheduling local elections independently is to reduce further voter turnout and to increase the influence of middle-class groups, which vote regularly.

Voter turnout in municipal elections is greater in large than in small cities. Voter turnout in cities with a mayor-council form of government is much higher than in cities with a council-manager plan. In summary, nonpartisanship, council-manager government, and separate municipal elections—all part of the municipal "reform" movement—operate to reduce voter turnout and probably strengthen the influence of middle-class voters at the polls.

Voter turnout in municipal elections is also affected by the social character of cities. We know that *individuals* who are less well educated, less wealthy, more ethnic, and more mobile, vote less often than *individuals* who are educated, wealthy, upper- or middle-class longtime residents of

TABLE 10-2

Socioeconomic Characteristics of Cities
and Voter Turnout in Municipal Elections

MEAN PERCENTAGE OF REGISTRANTS VOTING

(Cities with Noncurrent Municipal Elections)

	All Cities	East	Midwest	South	West
Ethnicity					
High	51	64	48	53	40
Low	44	—	49	42	43
Education					
High	44	56	45	41	41
Low	52	69	53	45	39
Mobility					
High	42	52	41	43	41
Low	54	67	53	43	41
Age of city					
Old	51	66	52	42	48
Young	43	60	43	43	39
All cities	47	64	48	43	41

SOURCE: Figures reported by Robert R. Alford and Eugene C. Lee,
"Voting Turnout in American Cities," AMERICAN POLITICAL
SCIENCE REVIEW, 62 (September 1968), 796-813.

cities. An important study by Alford and Lee, however, reveals that *cities* with larger proportions of poorly educated, ethnic, and mobile populations have *higher* voter turnouts than *cities* with well-educated, middle-class, stable populations. (See Table 10–2). This apparent paradox is explained as follows:

> Voting turnout is higher, not lower, in cities with less well educated populations, perhaps because in those cities political cleavages based on economic interests are more explicit and visible than in middle-class suburbs or other communities likely to have high proportions of college-educated persons. Cities with more stable populations also have higher levels of voting turnout, possibly because of the greater likelihood of integration of the different elements of social and political structure.[1]

In summary, voter turnout in municipal elections can be described as follows:

[1]Robert R. Alford and Eugene C. Lee, "Voting Turnout in American Cities," *American Political Science Review*, 62 (September 1968), 810.

Low voter turnout is expected with:	*High voter turnout is expected with:*
Nonpartisan electoral systems	Partisan elections with competitive parties
Council-manager form of government	
City elections held separately from state or national elections	Strong mayor form of government
Small or middle-sized cities	City elections held concurrently with state and national elections
Middle-class, homogeneous cities	Large cities
Midwestern, western, and southern cities	Ethnic, heterogeneous cities
	Eastern cities

EMERGING COALITIONS: HARDHATS VERSUS LIBERALS AND BLACKS

As we know from Chapter 3, *party voting* is closely related to income, occupation, education, religion, race, and ethnic origin. Sample surveys and election studies at the state and national level demonstrate repeatedly that the Republican party draws its voter strength from high-income, well-educated, white-collar, Anglo-Saxon, Protestant, and suburban and small-town residents; and in contrast, the Democratic party draws its strength from low-income, poorly educated, blue-collar, black, Catholic, Jewish, and ethnic populations living in larger cities. There is reason to believe that these socioeconomic divisions are influential in partisan elections at the local level as well. Of course, the "class" theory of voting in American politics is subject to many important exceptions. At the national level, there are large numbers of voters, whose socioeconomic backgrounds would indicate a tendency to the Democratic party, who regularly vote Republican; and vice versa. For this reason, we can only state that lower socioeconomic groups "tend to" vote Democratic, that "by and large" they support Democratic candidates, and that "on the whole" they prefer the Democratic ticket. (See Table 10–3.)

The nation's large, central cities tend to be Democratic, while their suburbs are normally Republican. Only one of the nation's ten largest cities has elected a Republican mayor in the last decade: Mayor Lindsay's startling victory in New York City in 1965 attracted nationwide attention and suggested that normally Democratic city voters can become disenchanted with "politics as usual" at city hall. Lindsay's later defection from the Republican to the Democratic party reconfirmed the heavily Democratic bias of big-city politics. The growing racial problem in the nation's central cities poses a challenge to the Democratic party's winning urban coalition. Working-class whites in large cities may increasingly resent the liberal posture of the national Democratic leadership on such issues as bussing, ghetto violence, and street crime. These issues,

TABLE 10-3

Democratic Presidential Percentages in Ten Major Cities

	1936	1940	1944	1948	1952	1956	1960	1964	1968
Baltimore	68.3	64.0	59.2	53.3	51.7	44.2	63.9	76.0	61.6
Boston	69.9	63.3	62.3	69.2	59.6	53.8	74.7	86.4	75.3
Chicago	66.9	58.5	61.4	58.6	54.4	49.0	63.6	63.2	60.8
Cleveland	76.5	69.9	67.9	61.8	59.9	54.6	70.9	82.8	67.4
Detroit	68.9	63.0	65.0	59.6	60.5	61.8	71.0	80.0	71.2
Milwaukee	82.1	64.1	61.7	59.4	51.5	47.3	61.8	70.0	55.4
New York	75.4	61.2	61.6	51.1*	55.4	51.0	62.8	73.2	60.5
Philadelphia	62.1	60.0	58.9	49.2*	58.4	57.1	68.1	73.7	61.8
Pittsburgh	70.7	61.6	60.8	60.1	56.1	52.3	67.0	74.7	62.2
St. Louis	67.0	58.1	60.4	64.3	62.0	61.0	66.6	77.7	64.7

* The Progressive party of Henry Wallace polled 13.5% in New York City and 2.4% in Philadelphia.

SOURCE: Adapted from Richard M. Scammon, ed., AMERICAN VOTES, A HANDBOOK OF CONTEMPORARY AMERICAN ELECTION STATISTICS, Vol. 8 (Washington, D.C.: Government Affairs Institute, 1970).

however, are more likely to cause splits *within* the Democratic party, and it is doubtful that the GOP can make any permanent inroads into Democratic control of the nation's large cities.

Studies of voting behavior in Philadelphia and its surrounding suburbs in the early 1960s supports the view that socioeconomic divisions that are important in national politics also operate in local partisan elections.[2] Within the city of Philadelphia, Democratic and Republican party voting for mayor, district attorney, and other local offices was closely correlated with income, education, occupation, and race. Likewise, outside of Philadelphia, in suburban Delaware County, Republican and Democratic party strength was correlated with income, occupation, and educational levels among suburban communities. In short, class cleavages could be observed in voting patterns in both the city and the suburbs. While Democrats dominated city politics and Republicans suburban politics, in both city and suburb, party voting correlated with socio-economic divisions.

The relationships between class and party voting, however, seem to vary according to the size of the city. Masters and Wright report that laborers in small Michigan cities were less likely to vote Democratic than were laborers in large cities.[3] V. O. Key, in *Public Opinion and American*

[2]See Oliver P. Williams, Harold Herman, Charles S. Liebman, and Thomas R. Dye, *Suburban Differences and Metropolitan Policies* (Philadelphia: University of Pennsylvania Press, 1964).

[3]Nicholas A. Masters and Deil S. Wright, "Trends and Variations in the Two-Party Vote: The Case of Michigan," *American Political Science Review*, 53 (December 1958), 1078–90.

Democracy, reports that blue-collar and white-collar workers differ more over policy questions in large metropolitan areas than in smaller cities.[4] In smaller cities, the blue-collar workers tended to adopt attitudes similar to those of the white-collar workers, which suggests that class cleavages are not as important in smaller cities as in large metropolitan areas, and hence Democratic and Republican voting is less likely to correlate with socio-economic class position.[5]

Emerging coalitions between upper-class liberal whites allied with ghetto blacks, in opposition to working-class home-owning whites, can be observed in elections and referenda voting in many large cities. *Referenda voting* is an important aspect of local politics—an aspect not found at the national level. City charters frequently require that referenda be held on all proposals to increase indebtedness or to increase property taxation. These referenda votes provide us with an excellent opportunity to examine the factors influencing voter attitudes toward local government and to test some theories about voting behavior on local issues.

One theory is that a voter in local referenda will try to maximize his family income by weighing the benefits that will come to him from a bond issue against the amount of the tax that will fall on him as a result of the expenditure.[6] This theory assumes that voters act rationally in pursuit of their own narrowly conceived self-interest: if the estimated benefit from a bond issue is more than the estimated cost, they vote for the expenditure, but if it is less, they vote against it. One problem connected with this theory is that voters seldom know whether a public expenditure proposal will benefit them or not. Usually ballots in municipal referenda do not specify precisely *which* streets are to be paved or *where* a bridge is to be built. Even if a facility is to serve a whole city (for example, a zoo, civic center, or county hospital), it is difficult for the voter to judge what benefits he will derive from the expenditure or to estimate the amount of the tax that will result from the expenditure. Yet the theory that voters will try to maximize their economic self-interest deserves examination.

One would certainly expect voters who would have no tax levied upon them from passage of an expenditure proposal to vote affirmatively, even if they will derive only trivial benefits. Non-property owners, having nothing to lose by the expenditure and something to gain, however small, can

---

[4]V. O. Key, Jr., *Public Opinion and American Democracy* (New York: Alfred A. Knopf, Inc., 1961), pp. 116–18.

[5]See also Edward C. Banfield and James Q. Wilson, *City Politics* (Cambridge: Harvard-M.I.T. Press, 1963), Chap. 16.

[6]The following discussion of voter behavior on referenda relies heavily upon James Q. Wilson and Edward C. Banfield, "Public Regardingness as a Value Premise in Voting Behavior," *American Political Science Review*, 58 (December 1964), 876–87; see also Raymond E. Wolfinger and John Field, "Political Ethos and the Structure of City Government," *American Political Science Review*, 60 (June 1966), 306–26.

be expected to favor the passage of bond and expenditure referenda. (Renters seldom realize that landlords will pass the tax increase on to them in high rent.) Property owners should be far less willing to favor municipal expenditure proposals. Wilson and Banfield examined returns on thirty-five expenditure proposals, voted in twenty separate elections in seven cities, and their findings give strong support to the theory that property owners and non-property owners differ consistently over municipal expenditure proposals. The voters in non-home-owning districts almost invariably supported all expenditure proposals (see Table 10–4). Home-owners show a greater distaste for public expenditures that are financed from property taxes than nonhomeowners.

Up to this point, the Wilson and Banfield findings tend to support the theory that voters in municipal referenda act rationally in pursuit of their own economic self-interest. However, Wilson and Banfield came up with some very interesting, contrasting findings when they examined the voting behavior of large and small property owners. One might suppose that the

TABLE 10-4
Referenda Voting Behavior of Four Major Economic
Groups, Cook County, Illinois

| | PERCENT "YES" VOTE | |
Group	County hospital	Welfare building
High income homeowners		
Winnetka	64	76
Wilmette	55	70
Lincolnwood	47	64
Middle income homeowners		
Lansing	30	54
Bellwood	21	55
Brookfield	22	51
Middle income renters		
Chicago ward 44	65	71
Chicago ward 48	61	72
Chicago ward 49	64	74
Low income renters		
Chicago ward 2	88	73
Chicago ward 3	87	76
Chicago ward 27	87	78

SOURCE: James Q. Wilson and Edward C. Banfield, "Public Regardingness as a Value Premise in Voting Behavior," AMERICAN POLITICAL SCIENCE REVIEW, 58 (December 1964), 878.

more property a voter has, the less likely he is to favor public expenditures that increase his tax rate, since the more property he owns, the higher his tax bill. The owner of a $50,000 home, for example, probably gets no more benefit from a new city zoo than does the owner of a $10,000 one, yet his share of the tax increase is five times as much. Moreover, since many municipal health and welfare facilities will probably never be used by high-income families, these families have added reason to oppose such facilities if they are acting solely on behalf of their own economic self-interest. However, these expectations are *not* borne out by the voting returns. Wilson and Banfield found that the *higher* the family income and value of their property, the *greater* the support for public expenditures in municipal referenda: that is, higher-income groups and the owners of more valuable property can usually be counted upon to support rather than oppose public expenditures—in contrast to lower-income families and owners of less valuable property.

Banfield and Wilson offer an explanation: support for public expenditures is a function of a liberal, "public-regarding" ethic, which is rooted in upper- and middle-class values. Banfield and Wilson argue effectively that "public-regardingness," in contrast to "private-regardingness," is part of the middle-class, white, Anglo-Saxon, Protestant subculture in America. The public-regarding voter has a conception of the public interest, which inspires him to support measures that benefit the whole community, whether or not they produce specific rewards for himself. In contrast, private-regarding voters—lower-income, working-class, Irish, Italian, Polish and other eastern European, white voters—tend to vote against public expenditures that do not directly benefit them. Blacks are much more likely to support public expenditures than low-income whites; both black renters and homeowners are more favorable to all proposals than white ethnic voters, although black homeowners are somewhat less enthusiastic than black renters. Jews tend to support public expenditures as much as upper-income Anglo-Saxon homeowners. The middle-class conception of "the public interest" caused upper-income, white, Anglo-Saxon homeowners to vote *against* veterans' bonuses and other proposals they regard as serving special interests rather than the entire community. Wilson and Banfield summarize their public-regardingness theory as follows:

> Each subcultural group, we think, has a more or less distinctive notion of how much a citizen ought to sacrifice for the sake of the community, as well as of what the welfare of the community has constituted; in a word, each has its own idea of what justice requires and of the importance of acting justly. According to this hypothesis, the voter is presumed to act rationally; the ends he seeks are not always verily self interested ones,

however. On the contrary, depending upon his income and ethnic status they are more or less public-regarded.[7]

Whether one accepts Banfield and Wilson's explanation or not,[8] their findings are important: (1) nonhomeowners give greater support to proposals for public spending than homeowners; (2) among homeowners, wealthy families support public expenditures more than middle- or low-income families; (3) white Anglo-Saxon Protestants, blacks, and Jews tend to support public expenditures more than Irish, Italian, Polish, or other eastern European ethnic voters.

The emerging coalition between affluent, educated, upper-class whites and ghetto blacks may turn out to be an important force in urban politics in the coming decade. Working-class ethnic whites see themselves increasingly threatened by both blacks and white liberals on the issues of bussing, welfare, crime, and violence. We shall return to this important topic in Chapter 13.

MANAGERS IN MUNICIPAL POLITICS

When council-manager government was first introduced as part of the municipal reform movement, managers were expressly forbidden to participate in community "politics." Early supporters of manager government believed in the separation of "politics" from "administration."[9] "Politics," not only partisanship but policy making as well, should be the exclusive domain of the elected city council. The manager was to be hired by the council to carry out its policy directives, and the manager could be removed by the council by majority vote at any time. This belief in the separation of policy making from administration was intended to produce the "nonpolitical," efficient, and economical government, which middle-class supporters of the reform movement valued so highly. Popular control of government was to be guaranteed by making the manager's tenure completely dependent upon the will of the elected council.

The idea that policy making could be separated from administration was slow to die. Managers themselves, in meetings and publications of the International City Managers Association, discussed their role in policy making for many years. The first code of ethics of the ICMA stated flatly

[7]Wilson and Banfield, "Public Regardingness," p. 885.
[8]The explanation is disputed by Wolfinger and Field, "Political Ethos and the Structure of City Government," pp. 326–34.
[9]Leonard D. White, *The City Manager* (Chicago: University of Chicago Press, 1927), portions of which are reprinted in Edward C. Banfield, *Urban Government: A Reader in Administration and Politics* (New York: Free Press, 1961).

that "no manager should take an active part in politics."[10] Managers agreed that they should stay out of partisan politics and election campaigns, but there was a great deal of debate about the role of managers in community policy making. Not until 1938 did the managers revise their code of ethics to recognize their role in policy leadership: ". . . [the city manager] encourages positive decisions on policy by the council instead of passive acceptance of his recommendations."[11]

By 1940 even political scientists who believed that policy making and administration *ought* to be separate had come to the conclusion that in practice it was not. In one of the first comprehensive studies of city-manager government, Stone, Price, and Stone noted that:

> it is generally impossible for a city manager to escape being a leader in matters of policy, for it is an essential part of his administrative job to make recommendations. The most important municipal policy is embodied in the budget, and the city manager, of course, must prepare and propose the budget. The city manager's recommendation on an important policy, even if he makes it in an executive session of the council, is usually a matter of common knowledge.[12]

While it is recognized that managers participate in policy making, their style of participation differs from that of elected political leaders. Generally, a city manager does not wish to *appear* to be a policy maker even when he is. He seeks to have others present his policy proposals to the community, and he avoids the brasher methods of policy promotion. Like any successful politician, he tries to avoid taking public stands on the more controversial issues facing the community. His dependence upon the council for his job prevents him from being too extreme in policy promotion. Managers can push their councils but can seldom fight them with any success. Open disputes between the manager and his council are usually resolved by the dismissal of the manager. Managers who assume strong policy leadership roles have shorter tenures than those who do not.

Nonetheless, the manager is the most important policy initiator in most council-manager cities. Most managers determine the agenda for city council meetings.[13] This permits them to determine the kinds of issues to be raised and the policy options to be considered. The council may not

[10]See Harold A. Stone, Don K. Price, and Kathryn H. Stone, *City Manager Government in the United States* (Chicago: Public Administration Service, 1940).

[11]See Charles R. Adrian, "Leadership and Decision-Making in Manager Cities," *Public Administration Review*, 18 (Summer 1958), 208–13.

[12]Stone, Price, and Stone, *City Manager Government*.

[13]Deil S. Wright, "The City Manager as a Development Administrator," in *Comparative Urban Research*, ed. Robert T. Daland (Beverly Hills: Sage, 1969), p. 219.

accept everything recommended by the manager, but the manager's recommendations will be given serious consideration.

In his study of council-manager politics in three Michigan communities, Charles Adrian observed that managers often assumed leadership of policy proposals that originated in city departments (for example, the police department on parking policies, advisory groups (for example, the planning commission's urban renewal plans), citizens' groups (for example, citizens seeking to prevent the breakdown of public transportation), or private enterprise (for example, downtown merchants interested in off-street parking). As Adrian explained:

> There appeared to be a psychological advantage to the manager if he could place himself in the position of defending a policy developed by these individuals or groups. He would take a strong stand, but would use protective coloration of saying, "Professional planners tell me . . ." He would, in other words, take a public position of *leadership* in policy matters, but preferred to attribute policy *innovation* to technical experts or citizens groups.[14]

Yet even though managers were providing leadership for their communities, they went to great pains to avoid the public appearance of being the tail that wags the dog—that is, the appearance of making policy for the city council rather than merely executing it.

Thus managers really have two important roles in community politics: administration and policy making. The administrative role involves the supervision of the municipal bureaucracy; this role requires administrative skills and technical expertise. Managers themselves report that they obtain more personal satisfaction from this role than from any other.[15] The manager directs his personal staff, develops and controls the city budget, and appoints and removes department heads. In most council-manager cities, managers try to guard these powers from direct council interference; these powers are the managers' most important formal resources.

Today most city managers are professionals who have been trained in university graduate programs in public administration. They are familiar with budgeting and fiscal administration, public personnel management, municipal law, and planning. They tend to move from city to city as they advance in their professional careers. They may begin their careers as staff assistant to a city official and then move to assistant city manager, then manager of a small town, and later perhaps of a larger city. About three-quarters of all city manager appointments are made from outside the city, and only about one-quarter are local residents, which indicates

14Adrian, "Leadership and Decision-Making," p. 210.
15Wright, "The City Manager as a Development Administrator," p. 236.

the professionalism of city management. The turnover rate among the nation's city managers is about 7.5 percent per year. The average tenure of managers who resigned or were removed from office has been about five years.[16]

Undoubtedly, managers are much more happy and secure in their jobs in communities where there is little or no conflict and few controversial issues—usually small communities with homogeneous, middle-class populations. This why manager government itself is found more frequently in such communities than in larger communities with deeper socioeconomic cleavages. The tenure of managers, and indeed the tenure of the council-manager system itself, is more secure in communities devoted to economic growth and communities concerned with providing a high level of public services. In a city concerned with "managing" conflicting political interests, there is often too much instability for a manager to survive for long. In a strictly "caretaker" community, a trained professional manager may be an unnecessary luxury. Occasionally, caretaker communities will appoint a local resident or "amateur," perhaps a former city clerk or city engineer, to the position of city manager.

COUNCILMEN AND COMMISSIONERS

The typical councilman or county commissioner is a local businessman who is respected in his community and active in civic organizations. He is more likely to be a small businessman with many contacts among his constituents—retail merchants, real estate brokers, insurance agents, and so on; seldom do executives of large corporations concern themselves with local affairs, although they may encourage lower management personnel to do so. In other words, councilmen are recruited from lower-middle-class groups in a community and not from the community's leading men in industry or finance. Councilmen serve because of the prestige it gives them or because of the free advertising and public contacts for their businesses. With the exception of a few very large cities, the pay of councilmen is very nominal. The councilman's job is a part-time one; it is a "community service," which he undertakes in addition to his occupation or business. The low rate of pay is a deliberate attempt to discourage candidates who are interested in the salary alone. This is supposed to get "better men" into the office; but it also restricts opportunities for working men and lower-income groups, who cannot afford to spend their time in jobs without pay.

City councils in larger cities may be quite different from councils in smaller cities. First of all, they are likely to have more members; more-

[16]*Municipal Yearbook, 1963*, p. 519.

over, members are more likely to be elected by wards rather than at-large. Since the pay is higher and the opportunity for political advancement is greater in a large city council, one is more likely to find lawyers and professional politicians on these councils than on the councils of smaller cities. Since there is more conflict in larger communities, there is more likelihood of open disputes and divided votes at council meetings. In contrast, council meetings in smaller communities are likely to be very dull affairs, with most decisions being made unanimously. Any disagreement or factionalism is not likely to be expressed openly at council meetings but is resolved prior to an official meeting, through consultation and discussion.

A majority of American cities elect their councilmen in nonpartisan elections in "at-large" (city wide) districts. This reflects the success of the reform movement (described in Chapter 9) and the widespread acceptance of the idea of nonpartisanship in muncipal government (described in this chapter). Most city councilmen are elected for four-year terms. Specifically, 50 percent of all cities elect their councilmen for four-year terms; 10 percent for three-year terms; and 38 percent for two-year terms. The terms of councilmen overlap in 66 percent of American cities; in these cities only a portion of the council seats are filled in any particular election. Presumably, overlapping terms insure continuity in the deliberations of the council.

At-large districts are designed to promote a city-wide approach to municipal problems among councilmen. Table 10–5 reveals that 59 percent of American cities elect their councilmen at-large, 25 percent by wards, and 14 percent by a combination of at-large and ward constituencies. Reformers believe that ward constituencies encourage parochial views, neighborhood interests, "log-rolling," and other characteristics of "ward politics." These "undesirable" characteristics occur because councilmen are responsible to local majorities in the particular sections or wards from whch they are elected. In contrast, councilmen elected at-large are responsible to city-wide majorities; this should encourage impartial, cosmopolitan, and community-wide attitudes. Moreover, in council-manager cities, it is argued that the manager can be more effective in serving the "general good" of the whole community if he is responsible to councilmen elected at-large rather than by wards. (Seventy percent of manager cities elect councilmen at-large, compared to only 44 percent of mayor-council cities.) Occasionally, it is even argued that at-large elections result in the selection of "better men" for the council, although recent research suggests that there are no significant differences in the social status, occupations, or experience of councilmen elected at-large and by wards.[17]

17John Rehfus, "Are At-Large Elections Best for Council-Manager Cities?" *National Civic Review* (May 1972), pp. 236–41.

TABLE 10-5

At-Large and Ward Elections for City Council

PERCENTAGE OF COUNCIL ELECTIONS

	Number of Cities	At-Large	Wards	Combination	Other
All Cities	2,823	59	25	14	3
Form of Government					
Mayor-Council	1,378	44	32	21	3
Commission	165	85	12	0	3
Council-Manager	1,207	70	20	8	2
Population					
Over 500,000	26	35	31	31	3
250,000 to 500,000	26	58	19	23	0
100,000 to 250,000	89	53	28	17	2
50,000 to 100,000	211	50	26	22	2
25,000 to 50,000	402	60	24	13	3
10,000 to 25,000	1,031	60	26	11	3
5,000 to 10,000	1,038	83	10	6	1

SOURCE: MUNICIPAL YEARBOOK, 1968, p. 59.

Blacks and other minorities are seriously disadvantaged by at-large elections. Commenting on reformed cities, Banfield and Wilson observe: "In a city with a nonpartisan, at-large system the nature of Negro politics is radically affected by the fact that the candidate must face the whole (predominantly white) electorate and must do so without benefit of a party label."[18]

Banfield and Wilson go on to note the dilemma faced by Negro councilmen facing reelection in an at-large system:

Without a strong Negro vote he cannot hope to be re-elected, and to get a strong Negro vote he must . . . be aggressive on at least some racial issues. But he must also have the support of the press and the civic associations in order to be re-elected, and he will not have this unless he is "reasonable" from the standpoint of conservative, middle-class whites.[19]

On the basis of this analysis, it appears that minority groups, especially blacks, are generally better represented in a partisan ward system of elections. Given the prevalence of residential segregation, this system seems to assure genuine black representation. Ward elections in the nation's largest cities have guaranteed blacks representation on city coun-

[18]Edward C. Banfield and James Q. Wilson, *City Politics* (Cambridge, Mass.: Harvard University Press and MIT Press, 1963), p. 307.
[19]*Ibid.*, p. 308.

cils in approximate proportion to their percentage of the population. But black representation in cities with at-large and combination at-large and ward elections is very uneven. Sociologist Lee Sloan writes that "if black Americans today were to seek governmental reform in local politics, they could perhaps do worse than ask for a repeal of certain institutional arrangements established and defended in the name of good government."[20]

The composition of a council will generally reflect the composition of the community itself. In communities with well-educated, affluent residents, councilmen may come from upper-middle-class backgrounds; whereas in predominantly working-class communities, councilmen may be independent contractors or store owners or even blue-collar workers.[21] Typically, councilmen are attorneys, realtors, engineers, insurance brokers, sales managers, professors or high school teachers, salesmen, and proprietors of local businesses.

According to orthodox theory about city government, the city council is supposed to "make policy" for the city. But, of course, the actual policy-making role of councilmen varys a great deal from city to city. Councilmen have more formal power in commission or weak mayor form of government, where the council itself sometimes appoints officials, prepares the budget, supervises departments, and performs other administrative tasks. But in other cities—particularly strong mayor or manager cities—the council merely oversees city affairs. In these cities, the function of the council may be principally the representation of the interests of local constituents—forwarding complaints, making inquiries, pushing for new sidewalks or streetlights, and so forth. This may be particularly true in a ward system.[22]

Contrary to orthodox theory, Adrian found that councilmen do not serve as either general policy innovators or general policy leaders. When councilmen do take a stand on public issues, they are more likely to oppose a proposal than to support one. Adrian describes a typical response of the council to a community problem, as follows:

> When the bus companies came to the councils from time to time asking for fare increases, each councilman would deplore the trend toward higher

[20]Lee F. Sloan, "Good Government and the Politics of Race," *Social Problems*, 17 (Fall 1969), 161–75.

[21]See Bryan T. Downes, "Municipal Social Rank and the Characteristics of Local Political Leaders," *Midwest Journal of Political Science*, 12 (November 1968), 514–37.

[22]Williams and Adrian report one ward councilman's speech at a Michigan city council meeting as follows: "You bastard, you had three more blocks of blacktopping in your ward last year than I had, you'll not get another vote from me until I get three extra blocks." Oliver P. Williams and Charles Adrian, *Four Cities* (Philadelphia: University of Pennsylvania Press, 1963), p. 264.

fares and poorer service, but since the only discernible alternative to refusing the rate increase was a discontinuance of service, almost all councilmen voted in favor of the request. In each of the cities, study committees of lay citizens were appointed to seek solutions to the bus
problem. . . . In each case, the council gratefully, and with little discussion, accepted the proposed solutions.[23]

Adrian concludes that the role of the council is one of a largely passive
body, granting or withholding its approval in the name of the community,
when presented with proposals from a leadership outside of itself. The
outside leadership consists of a manager, city departments, the planning
commission, citizens groups, or private enterprise.[24]

Adrian concludes:

It might be noted that the important policy and leadership role of the
manager, of his administration, and of leaders of nonofficial groups differs from the patterns intended in the original theory of the council-
manager plan. That theory assumed that able, respected leaders of the
community would be willing to serve on councils and would take responsibility for policy decisions in government as they did in their businesses. While the typical councilman in the three city study gave the
impression of being a sufficiently competent person, it seemed clear
enough that he was not willing to assume a leadership role under circumstances where he might thereby be planted in controversy. The politician
in the council manager's city, though he may be an amateur, thus follows
the traditional practice of American politicians and seeks to avoid taking
sides in closely matched battles.[25]

Many councilmen have little interest in a political career and serve
out of a sense of public service (frequently at considerable personal expense in time and energy). "Volunteerism" is widespread in American
cities;[26] it is probably most prevalent in suburban middle-class communities. Volunteers see their service as a sacrifice, and they are relatively immune from direct constituency pressure. Threats to oust them
at the next election have little meaning. Only insofar as they tend to
have the attitudes and characteristics of their constituents can they be
said to be "representative." Constituents cannot really hold volunteers
accountable by threatening them with defeat at the next election. "I

---

[23]Adrian, "Leadership and Decision-Making," p. 212.

[24]Of course, councilmen themselves are not likely to agree that their role is a passive one. They like to think of themselves as policy innovators—men of vision and
leadership—who follow their own convictions in public affairs regardless of what
others want them to do. See Downes, "Municipal Social Rank."

[25]Adrian, "Leadership and Decision-Making," p. 212.

[26]See Kenneth Prewitt, "Political Ambitions, Volunteerism, and Electoral Accountability," *American Political Science Review*, 64 (March 1970), 5–17.

don't really give a damn whether I am reelected or not" is a common response.[27]

The problem of political accountability in local politics is further aggravated by several factors:

1. The frequency of appointment to elected office. It is probable that as many as one-quarter of the nation's councilmen initially came into office by appointment rather than election.[28] They are appointed, usually by the mayor, to fill unexpired terms.
2. The effective constituency is very small. Given the low turnout in municipal elections, and the small constituencies served by a councilman, only a very few votes are required to elect a man to office. (One estimate is that only 810 votes are required to elect an average councilman in a city of 13,000.) A councilman's personal friends, immediate neighbors, business associates, fellow church members, and acquaintances at the Rotary Club may be enough to get him elected.
3. The infrequency of electoral defeat. Incumbents running for reelection are hardly ever defeated. (Incumbent councilmen are only slightly easier to beat than incumbent congressmen, 90 percent of whom are reelected.) Councilmen are not likely to be preoccupied with voter preferences.
4. The frequency of voluntary retirement from elected office. (The vast majority of councilmen voluntarily retire from office, over half of them after two terms.) Officeholders simply conclude that the obligations of office exceed the rewards.

All these factors, together with low participation votes in local politics, tend to remove municipal government from direct citizen control.

MAYORS

Today, more than ever before, the nation's cities need forceful, imaginative leadership. The nation's major domestic problems—race relations, poverty, slum housing, violence, transportation, poor schools, urban blight—are concentrated in cities. Mayors are in the "hot seat" of American politics; they must deal directly with these pressing issues. No other elected official in the American federal system must deal face-to-face, eyeball-to-eyeball, with these problems in quite the same fashion as mayors. Next to the presidency, the office of mayor in a big city may be the most challenging job in American politics. In one of his more harried moments, President Lyndon B. Johnson is reported to have said, "Things could be worse, I could be a mayor."[29]

[27]*Ibid.*, p. 7.
[28]*Ibid.*, p. 8.
[29]*Newsweek*, March 13, 1967, p. 38.

TABLE 10-6

Term of Office of Mayors in Cities Over 5,000

| Form of Government | Percent of Reporting Cities | | | |
	One Year	Two Years	Three Years	Four Years
Mayor-council	2.9	54.2	1.0	41.7
Commission	3.9	19.3	6.4	67.0
Council-manager	21.3	54.6	2.3	24.0
All cities	10.3	51.4	2.0	35.9[1]

[1] An additional 3 percent of reporting cities have five or six year terms for mayors.

SOURCE: MUNICIPAL YEAR BOOK, 1966, p.92.

The challenges facing big-city mayors are enormous; however, their powers to deal with these challenges are restricted on every side. Executive power in major cities is often fragmented among a variety of elected officials—city treasurer, city clerk, city comptroller, district attorney, and so on. The mayor may also be required to share power over municipal affairs with county officials. Many city agencies and functions are outside the mayor's formal authority: independent boards and commissions often govern important city departments—for example, the board of education, board of health, zoning appeals board, planning commission, civil service board, library board, park commission, sewage and water board, and so on. Even if the mayor is permitted to appoint the members of the boards and commissions, they are often appointed for a fixed term, and the mayor cannot remove them. The mayor's power over the affairs of the city may also be affected by the many public authorities and special district governments operating within the city, including the public housing authority, urban renewal authority, community action agency (poverty program), sewage and water authority, a mass transit authority, port authority, and so on. Traditionally, school districts have been outside the authority of the mayor or city government. The mayor's powers over city finances may even be restricted—he may share budget-making powers with a board of estimate, and powers over expenditures with an elected comptroller or treasurer. Civil service regulations and independent civil service boards can greatly hamper the mayor's control over his own bureaucrats. The activities of federal and state agencies in his city are largely beyond his control.[30]

Of course the method of selecting the mayor also influences his powers over city affairs. Nearly a quarter of the nation's mayors are not directly elected by the people of their cities (see Table 10–6). These mayors are

[30]Few people realize how hamstrung a mayor may be in dealing with urban problems. For a close-up account of a mayor's problems by the mayor of Milwaukee, see Henry W. Maier, *Challenge to the Cities* (Random House, Inc., 1966).

selected by their city councils or commissions and generally have little more power than other councilmen or commissioners. Their job is generally ceremonial: they crown beauty queens, dedicate parks, lay cornerstones, and lead parades. Mayors may be elected for anything from one to six years, but the two-year and four-year terms are most common in American cities.

The mayor's legislative powers also vary widely. Of course in all cities he has the right to submit messages to the council and to recommend policy. These recommendations will carry whatever prestige the mayor possesses in the community. In cities where the mayor is chosen by the council, he almost always has voting power equal to that of other council members, and more than one-quarter of the mayors who are elected directly have the power to cast a vote on all issues coming before the council. Most mayors preside over meetings of the city council, and this gives them an opportunity to cast votes in case of a tie. Less than one-fifth of the nation's mayors have no voting powers at all on city councils. The veto power over municipal ordinances is another source of legislative strength for the mayor. However, over one-half of the directly elected mayors have no veto power; one-fifth may veto only selected items (usually appropriations). Only one-fifth of the nation's mayors have full veto powers over their councils. Mayors in mayor-council governments are more likely to have veto powers than mayors in commission or council-manager cities (see Table 10–7).

The formal distinction between "strong mayors" and "weak mayors" is made on the basis of their powers of administration. The weak mayor has very limited appointing powers and even more limited removing powers. He has little control over separately elected boards and commissions or separately elected offices, such as clerk, treasurer, tax assessor, comptroller, and attorney. The council rather than the mayor often appoints

TABLE 10-7
Method of Selection and Voting Powers of Mayors
in Cities Over 5,000

Form of Government	PERCENT OF REPORTING CITIES			PERCENT OF DIRECTLY ELECTED MAYOR VOTING		
	Directly elected	Selected by council	Councilman with highest vote	On all issues	In case of tie	No voting power
Mayor-council	96.6	3.4	0	16.3	58.7	25.0
Commission	77.5	21.2	0.7	92.0	7.0	1.0
Council-manager	50.1	49.1	1.3	54.1	41.3	4.6
All cities	74.5	24.9	0.6	31.7	50.7	17.6

SOURCE: MUNICIPAL YEAR BOOK, 1968, p. 55.

TABLE 10-8
Veto Powers of Mayors in Cities Over 5,000

| Form of government | PERCENT OF REPORTING CITIES WHERE MAYOR MAY | | |
	Veto all measures	Veto selected items	No veto
Mayor-council	35.1	33.9	31.0
Commission	11.3	3.5	85.2
Council-manager	6.7	9.4	83.9
All cities	20.8	21.1	58.1

SOURCE: MUNICIPAL YEAR BOOK, 1968, p. 57.

the key administrative officers. No single individual has the complete responsibility for law enforcement or coordinating city administraton.

One summary of the mayor's difficulties with "good government," civil service, fragmented authority, state interference, and suburban opposition was presented in *The Exploding Metropolis:*

One of the biggest threats to his leadership, indeed, is too much "good government." The big problem at the city hall is no longer honesty, or even simple efficiency. The fight for these virtues is a continuous one, of course, and Lucifer is always lurking in the hall, but most big city governments have become reasonably honest and efficient. Today the big problem is not good housekeeping: it is whether the mayor can provide the aggressive leadership and the positive programs without which no big city has a prayer. . . .

The mayor is hemmed in. As he strives to exercise policy leadership. his power is challenged on all sides. In his own house the staff experts and the civil service bureaucrats threaten to nibble him to death in their efforts to increase their own authority. Then there are the public "authorities." Some are single purpose authorities—like the city housing authorities, and the sewer districts; some, like the Port of New York Authority, handle a whole range of functions. They are eminently useful institutions, but however efficient they may be, they are virtually laws unto themselves and they have severely limited the mayor's ability to rule in his own house and, more important, his ability to plan for long range development.

The power struggle also goes on between the mayor and state legislature, which has a controlling voice in the city's fiscal affairs, but whose membership is apportioned in favor of the rural areas. It is the rare mayor who need not make frequent trips to the state capitol for additional funds, and the legislature is usually unsympathetic. . . .

There is the continuing struggle between the mayor and the suburbs, whose people, the big city firmly believes, are welching on their obligations to the city. The mayor must win the cooperation of his suburban counterparts if he is to do anything at all about the city's most pressing problems—e.g., the traffic mess—and the going is grim.[31]

Only occasionally will mayors create issues themselves or initiate pet projects. Several mayors have taken the initiative on urban renewal—rebuilding a city is a very dramatic way of illustrating one's achievements in office. Typically, new programs or new issues are first raised by large public or private organizations in the community.[32] The planning commission, for example, may propose that the city embark upon a program for mass transit. City departments may notify the mayor that it is time to build a new sewage disposal plant, or that new policemen must be hired, or that water rates must be increased. Citizens groups, like the chamber of commerce, may propose that the city build a new civic auditorium. Downtown merchants may suggest that the city build new parking facilities. Newspapers play a very important role in initiating new programs and in creating public issues. Editors believe, rightly or wrongly, that public crusades help to sell newspapers, and they bring many issues to the attention of mayors and decision makers as well as their readers.

The role of mayors is to watch the maneuvers of the prime-moving organizations with critical attention. As Banfield and Wilson explain:

> They [mayors] know well enough what is going on behind the scenes and they know approximately how many—if any—votes the organizations may be able to swing. Usually they wait as long as possible before making a decision. They know that as long as they do nothing they are probably safe, and anyway, they want to allow time for public opinion to form. When a magazine writer suggested to Mayor Richard Daley of Chicago that the mayor had never in his whole life committed himself to anything whatsoever until he absolutely had to, the mayor laughed. "That's a pretty good way to be, don't you think? Pretty good way to run any business."[33]

What happens when a mayor is unable to overcome the fragmentation of authority in a city? What happens when there is no party organization that can "get things done at city hall," and there is no strong charismatic leader who possesses the charm or salesmanship to "put things across" to the community? Banfield and Wilson provide an excellent summary as to how this decentralization of authority is overcome:

1. To a large extent it is *not* overcome; many things are not done because it is impossible to secure the collaboration of all those whose collaboration is needed.

[31]Seymour Freedgood, "New Strength in City Hall," *The Exploding Metropolis* (New York: Doubleday & Co., 1958) , pp. 66–67. Courtesy of *Fortune Magazine*.
[32]See Banfield and Wilson, *City Politics*, Chap. 2.
[33]*Ibid.*, p. 30.

2. When overcome at all, it is overcome on an ad hoc basis; the mayor, for example, must consider anew with each issue how to get the eight votes he needs in council.

3. Widespread indifference and apathy among the voters mitigates the effect of decentralization of authority to them.

4. The mass communications media are fairly effective in overcoming by salesmanship such decentralization of authority to the voters as remains; causes with strong newspaper support and with big budgets for TV advertising are usually approved at the polls.

5. The devices of salesmanship are extensively used. It was in Los Angeles that the mayor scolded Khrushchev to his face in public while Khrushchev was the city's guest (a stunt like this would not have been resorted to by Mayor Daley of Chicago, whose machine makes salesmanship unnecessary).

6. Measures are frequently compromised so as to "give something to everybody" in order to get them accepted.[34]

In summary, most mayors do not have the formal authority sufficient to deal with the many challenges facing city government. The successful mayor must rely chiefly upon his own personal qualities of leadership: his powers to persuade, to organize, to promote, to sell, to publicize, to compromise, to bargain, and to "get things done." The mayor's role is not usually to initiate proposals for new programs or to create public issues. Nor is his primary concern the administration of existing programs, although he must always seek to avoid scandal and gross mismanagement, which would give his administration a bad public "image." He must rely upon other public agencies, planners, citizens groups, and private enterprise to propose new programs, and he can usually rely upon his department heads and other key subordinates to supervise the day-to-day administration of city government. The mayor is primarily a promoter of public policy: his role is to promote, publicize, organize, and finance the projects that others suggest.

PLANNERS

Professional planners are playing an increasingly important role in community decision making. The modern city planning movement was given its impetus in the 1920s, when Secretary of Commerce Herbert Hoover approved a Standard City Planning Enabling Act by Edward Bassett, Alfred Bettman, and several other founders of the planning movement. Within a few years this act had been adopted by most of the states, and cities throughout the nation began establishing official planning commis-

[34]*Ibid.*, p. 111.

sions. Today over 90 percent of the cities with populations of ten thousand or more have official planning agencies, although only about one-third of these cities employed a full-time professional planner. Nearly all cities with populations over one hundred thousand employ full-time professional planners.[35]

Early city planners were concerned primarily with the physical development of the city and the use of land.[36] They concentrated on writing zoning laws, preparing "subdivision regulations" governing the division of large plots of land into smaller ones, laying out public streets, and choosing the location of parks, public building sites, public utilities, and other public facilities.

Early city planning dealt almost exclusively with topics that could be shown on a map. Planners were trained primarily as engineers or landscape architects. Planners were expected to prepare a *master plan* or overall blueprint, for the physical development of the community. The master plan is a set of maps, information, and policy statements intended to serve as guides for both public and private decision makers. The master plan shows recommendations for

> the most desirable use of land within the municipality for residential, recreational, commercial, industrial, and other purposes; for the most desirable density of population in several parts of the municipality; for a system of thoroughfares, parks, bridges, streets, and other public ways; for airports, parks, playgrounds, and other public grounds; for general location, relocation, and extent of public utilities and terminals, whether publicly or privately owned, for water, sewage, light, power, transit, and other purposes; and for the extent and location of public housing projects.[37]

In recent years the definition of planning has been broadened to include more than physical and land use planning. Today, planners stress the interrelatedness of urban life and argue that planning is a continuing activity, which attempts to anticipate human needs and goals, to prepare for them and guide them into desirable patterns, and to influence and shape public policy to serve the community's needs and goals most effectively.[38] In addition to land use and physical development considerations, planners now direct their attention to population projections, economic conditions, social patterns, life-styles, cultural developments,

[35]*Municipal Yearbook, 1963*, p. 324.

[36]For an introduction to city planning, see Donald H. Webster, *Urban Planning and Municipal Public Policy* (New York: Harper & Row, Publishers, 1955).

[37]General Statutes of Connecticut (1949 revision), Title 8, Chapter 45; cited by John C. Bollens and Henry J. Schmandt, *The Metropolis* (New York: Harper & Row, Publishers, 1965), p. 279.

[38]See Bollens and Schmandt, *The Metropolis*, Chap. 10.

education, transportation, and beautification. The phrase *comprehensive planning* has largely replaced the earlier term *master plan*, in recognition of the new emphasis on planning as a continuing activity. Obviously this extended definition of planning plunges the planner deep into the political life of the community.

What formal powers do planners have to influence community policy? The master plan itself is not legally binding on anyone. Planners are legally powerless to effectuate their plan themselves—they must rely on its appeal to policy makers. Mayors and councils can simply file the master plan away and forget it. However, cities that choose to implement comprehensive planning and guide physical development by law have a variety of legal tools available to them: zoning ordinances, subdivision regulations, an official map, building and construction codes, locational decisions on public facilities and buildings, and a captal improvement program. Planning agencies often have an important role in all these activities, even though the principal responsibility for these tools of implementation rests with the mayor and council.

Planning commissions usually prepare the *zoning ordinance* for the approval of the council. The zoning ordinance divides the community into districts for the purpose of regulating the use and development of land and buildings. Zoning originated as an attempt to separate residential areas from commercial and industrial activity, thereby protecting residential property values. The zoning ordinance divides the community into residential, commercial, and industrial zones, and perhaps subdivisions within each zone, such as "light industrial" and "heavy industrial," or "single-family residential" and "multifamily residential." Owners of land in each zone must use their land in conformity with the zoning ordinance; however, exceptions are made for persons who have used the land in a certain way before the adoption of the zoning ordinance. An ordinance cannot prevent a person from using the land as he has done in the past; thus zoning laws can only influence land use if they are passed prior to the development of a community. Many rapidly expanding suburban communities pass zoning ordinances too late—after commercial and industrial establishments are strung out along highways, ideal industrial land is covered with houses, good park and recreational land has been sold for other purposes, and so on. Zoning ordinances also contain regulations on the size and height of buildings, setback lines, and the like. Once adopted, the zoning ordinance is enforced by the building commissioner or another public official, not the planning agency.

Since the planning commission prepares the zoning ordinance as well as the master plan, the ordinance is expected to conform with the plan. In many communities, the role of the planning commission is strengthened by the requirement that a city council must submit all proposed changes in the zoning ordinance to the planning commission for their recommendation before any council action. The council may ignore the recommendations of the planning commission and rezone areas as they see fit; nevertheless, the requirement that the planning commission review requests for zoning changes doubtlessly contributes to their influence in community development.

Another means of implementing the master plan is *subdivision regulations*, which govern the way in which land is divided into smaller lots and made ready for improvements. Subdivision regulations, together with the zoning ordinance, may specify the minimum size of lots, the standards to be followed by real estate developers in laying out new streets, and the improvements developers must provide, such as sewers, water mains, and sidewalks. Often planning commissions are given direct responsibility for the enforcement of subdivision regulations. Builders and developers must submit their proposed "plats" for subdividing land and for improvements to the planning commission for approval before deeds can be recorded.

The planning commission also prepares the *official map* of the city for enactment by the council. The official map shows proposed, as well as existing, streets, water mains, public utilities, and the like. Presumably no one is permitted to build any structures on land that appears as a street or other public facility on the official map. Many cities require the council to submit to the planning commission for their recommendation any proposed action that affects the plan of streets or the subdivision plan and any proposed acquisition or sale of city real estate. Here again the recommendation of the planning commission may be ignored by the council, but at least the planners must be listened to.

Finally, comprehensive planning can be implemented through a *capital improvement program*. This program is simply the planned schedule of public projects by the city—new public buildings, parks, streets, and so on. Many larger cities instruct their planning commissions to prepare a long-range capital improvement program for a five- or ten-year period. Of course, the council may choose to ignore the planning commission's long-range capital improvement program in their decisions about capital expenditures, but at least the planning commission will have expressed its opinions about major capital investments.

The federal government has strengthened the position of planning commissions by requiring *planning as a prerequisite to receiving federal money* for public housing, urban renewal, airports, sewage systems, highways, recreation and open space facilities, and even hospitals. The Housing Act of 1949 required cities to undertake extensive planning in housing and urban renewal projects, and the federal government agreed to pay much of the cost of this planning. The Housing Act of 1954 went even further and required cities to adopt a "workable program" and a "comprehensive plan" as a prerequisite to federal housing and urban renewal grants. A "workable program" was defined to include adequate zoning and subdivision control ordinances, building and construction codes, and other land use policies, which would help prevent the spread of urban blight to new areas and rehabilitate and conserve those areas that could still be restored. A requirement for "comprehensive planning" included the preparation of a long-range plan and a capital improvement program. At the same time, federal grants were offered to communities for participation in city-wide or regional planning programs. Presumably the federal government's interest in community planning stems from its desire to see that its grant money is not wasted. Local planning makes it easier for federal agencies to evaluate the impact of their own grants on total community development. These federal requirements for planning greatly strengthened the influence of planners at the local level: without planning, a community would be deprived of federal money in a wide variety of grant-in-aid programs, and much of the cost of planning is paid for by federal planning grants anyhow. The result is that very few communities today are without planning agencies.

The formal role of planners is advisory, but they can have a substantial influence on community policy. In smaller cities, planners may be preoccupied with the day-to-day administration of the zoning and subdivision control ordinances. They may have insufficient time or staff resources to engage in genuine long-range comprehensive planning. In large cities, the planning staff may be the only agency that has a really comprehensive view of community development. Although they may not have the power to "decide" about public policy, they can "initiate" policy discussion through their plans, proposals, and recommendations. The planners can project the image of the city of the future and thereby establish the agenda of community decision making. Their plans can initiate public discussion over the goals and values to be implemented in the community. The master plan can be a tool for mobilizing public interest in community developemnt.

There are, of course, serious limitations on the influence of planners. First of all, most of the important decisions in community development are made by private enterprise rather than by government. Real estate interests, developers, builders, and property owners make most of the key decisions shaping the development of the community. The most important influence on their decisions is not the actions of government, but the economics of the marketplace. There is very little evidence that *any* governmental tools—planning, zoning, subdivision control, or capital programming, and so on—can overcome market forces. Property owners will find a way to make the most profitable use of their land, the ideals of the planners notwithstanding. Second, the planners can only advise policy makers, they are just one voice among many attempting to influence public decisions about land use and physical development. As Norton Long explains:

> This work of art, the master plan, once adopted becomes holy writ to be defended by an amateur lay board of hopefully high civic prestige, spurred on and kept to the mark by a professional staff of planners. The battle is fought along lines of piecemeal engagements as the facts of power, the pressure of economics, and the haste of the populace force a patchwork desecration of the architect's pretty rendering of green and white lines and dots. Like the WCTU, the proponents of planning find it is one thing to achieve the noble experiment in law, another in the drinking habits of sinful men. In both cases bootlegging represents the recrudescence of rugged individualism. People want their prohibition and their liquor, too. The same is true of planning.[39]

Historically, planning was part of the municipal reform movement. Planners generally showed the antipolitical bias of the reform movement and were deeply suspicious and distrustful of political leaders. Their maps and charts were drawn with little regard to political realities; "If one were to insist that it was as much the planner's business to face the facts of political feasibility as to face the facts of economics or topography, he would be regarded as an agent of the devil if not the tempter himself."[40] Yet today many planners are coming to realize that plans are policies and policies spell politics. There is no doubt that planning will reflect politics; the only question is whose politics it will reflect. What values and whose values will become part of the comprehensive plan?

Like reformers, planners tend to be "public regarding"—they are concerned with the welfare of the community as a whole, particularly its most deprived minorities. They are hostile to what they regard as narrow, private-regarding interests, particularly businessmen and developers. They share with reformers a distaste for "politics." David C. Ranney notes that "planners have traditionally distrusted local government, viewing it as a pawn of special interest groups. This distrust is at least partly the result of the relationship between the planning movement and the municipal reform movement."[41]

Planners can play a variety of roles in the policy-making process.[42] One role is that of the pure "technician"—who develops plans strictly

[39]Norton Long, "Planning and Politics in Urban Development," *Journal of the American Institute of Planners*, 25 (November 1959), 167.

[40]*Ibid.*

[41]David C. Ranney, *Planning and Politics in the Metropolis* (Columbus, Ohio: Charles E. Merrill Books, Inc., 1969), p. 28.

[42]See Francine Rabinowitz, *City Politics and Planning* (New York: Atherton, 1969).

on the basis of professional planning theory, avoiding political entangle-
ments and remaining aloof from struggles over the acceptance or implementation of plans. The technician-planner emphasizes his neutral
expertise. Another role is that of the "broker"—who acts as confidential
adviser to policy makers and consider the political "marketability" of
his plans and recommendations. Another role is that of the "mobilizer"—
who actively seeks community support for his plans and enlists the backing of civic, business, professional, and service clubs. An even more political role for planners has been proposed in recent years under the
label "advocacy planning."[43] The advocate planner recognizes that plans
must always embody someone's values at the expense of someone else's,
and he expects that various groups in a community will develop and
support alternative plans. The advocate planner is overtly political, particularly on behalf of the poor and the black, and he frequently stresses
social rather than physical planning. Most planners view themselves
primarily as "technicians," although from time to time they will act
as "brokers" and "mobilizers."

Recognition of the political nature of planning has brought about a
gradual shift in the organization of city planning agencies. Historically,
planning agencies were semi-independent commissions, whose members
were appointed from outside the government for long terms. Ordinarily
the mayor could not remove the commissioner. Sometimes their recommendations regarding changes in the zoning and subdivision ordinances
or the capital budget could not be overriden by council, except by a
two-thirds or three-quarters vote. This semi-independent status for planning commissions reflected the reform movement's desire to remove planning from "politics."

Recently the trend has been to organize planning agencies as part of
the city government, directly responsible to the mayor or council. Organizing planners as staff to the mayor and council is expected to make
them more sensitive to community values as they are expressed in the
political process. Norton Lang has commented: "This change will both
compel political realism and enrich the end systems of the planners by
forcing them to understand the politician's prospectives and incentives,
and it will jeopardize the planner's capacity to take the long and de-
tached view. Realism will not be an unmixed blessing, though it is essential to get a sufficient range of values into the planner's thinking."[44]

There is some evidence to suggest that the best plans are often jeopard-

[43]Paul Davidoff, "Advocacy and Pluralism in Planning," *Journal of the American
Institute of Planners*, 31 (December 1965), 331–38; and Lisa Peattie, "Reflections of an
Advocate Planner," *Journal of the American Institute of Planners*, 34 (March 1968),
80–89.

[44]Long, "Planning and Politics," p. 169.

ized when they reach the political arena. In a study of capital programming in Philadelphia, Professors Brown and Gilbert compared the capital expenditures *proposed* in the city's planning commission's capital program with the *actual* capital expenditures authorized by the city council.[45] The *actual* capital expenditures bore no resemblance whatsoever to the capital expenditures proposed by the planning commission and envisioned in the master plan. The deviations between the planning commission's capital program and the council's capital budget ranged up to 3,000 percent! The authors point out that some of this deviation resulted from unexpected availability of land and other economic factors, which the planners could not have predicted. They acknowledge, however, that political considerations had a very dramatic effect upon the capital budget. These vast differences between the planners' capital program and the city's actual capital budget suggest that planners do not yet control life in the metropolis.

INTEREST GROUPS

Interest group activity may be more influential in community politics than in state or national political affairs. Since the arena of local politics is smaller, the activities of organized interest groups may be more obvious at the local level. As one local councilman was once quoted:

> Pressure groups are probably more important in local government than they are nationally or in the state, because they are right here. You see them and they see you, and what you do affects them. It's not like in Washington, where half the time a businessman doesn't really know what the result will be for him.[46]

A study of interest group activity in city councils in California discovered that only 16 percent of the 115 councilmen interviewed did not perceive any groups or organizations as "influential" in their city.[47] Twenty-three percent named one organization as "influential," and 61 percent named two or more groups as influential in their community. Fourteen percent were able to name as many as five influential groups. The median number of groups seen as influential by these councilmen was 2.4. By comparison, the median number of active groups perceived by state legislators in a four-state legislative system study were as follows:

[45]W. H. Brown, Jr., and C. E. Gilbert, *Planning Municipal Investment* (Philadelphia: University of Pennsylvania Press, 1961).
[46]Betty Zisk, Heinz Eulau, and Kenneth Prewitt, "City Councilmen and the Group Struggle," *Journal of Politics*, 27 (August 1965), 633.
[47]*Ibid.*, pp. 618–46.

California—1.15, New Jersey—1.28, Ohio—.90, and Tennessee—.89.[48]
In other words, local councilmen in California perceived more group
activity at the local level than legislators in four states perceived at the
state level!

At the local level, interest groups frequently assume the form of "civic
associations." Few communities are too small to have at least one or two
associations devoted to civic well-being, and larger cities may have hundreds of these organizations. In the California study of local councilmen, 94 percent of the councilmen who perceived group activity at the
local level named civic associations (service clubs, citizens commissions,
improvement associations) as the most influential groups or organizations, which were active and appeared before the council.[49] Only 28 percent of these councilmen named economic groups (merchants, realtors,
unions, and so on), and 21 percent named taxpayer associations and reform groups. Actually these results do not mean that economic interests
or taxpayer associations are less active than civic associations, but probably that civic associations are the predominant style of organized interest
group activity at the local level, and that businessmen, reform groups, taxpayer associations, merchants, service clubs, developers, and so on, all
organize themselves into civic associations for action at the local level.
Civic associations generally make their appeals in terms of "the welfare
of the community," "the public interest," "civic responsibility," "making
Janesville a better place to live." In other words, civic associations claim
to be community serving rather than self-serving. Many local civic associations can be classified as "good government" groups who seek to implement the program of the municipal reform movement—council-
manager government, civil service, home rule, nonpartisan elections,
and efficiency and economy in government. (The reform movement is
described in greater detail in Chapter 9). Good-government civic associations are not seeking specific material inducements for their members;
they are really seeking to promote a middle-class ethic of government.
Members belong to these groups as a hobby, because of the sense of
prestige and civic participation they derive from membership. Occasionally, of course, participation in civic assocations can be a stepping-stone
to local office. The League of Women Voters can be classified as a good-
government group, although its principal interest is participation per
se, rather than any particular program of civic action. The league is
nonpartisan, and its traditional activity is to prepare a set of questions
on current issues, which it submits to candidates whose responses are

48John C. Wahlke *et al.*, *The Legislative System* (New York: John Wiley & Sons,
Inc., 1962), pp. 311–42.
49Zisk *et al.*, "City Councilmen," p. 632.

then circulated throughout the community. When the league does endorse policies, their aims are usually similar to those of reform groups.

Another form of civic association is a neighborhood improvement association, generally composed of businessmen or residents who are interested in safeguarding the value of their property. They may be interested in zoning laws because they do not want unsightly trailer parks located nearby; they may insist on stop signs to make the streets safer for their children; or they want potholes repaired immediately; or they want an extra policeman to patrol their neighborhood. They are also concerned with keeping tax rates low and with keeping a close watch on property assessments. Often, improvement associations lead the fight to keep "undesirables" out of the neighborhood, whose presence, they fear, will reduce property value. This type of endeavor is usually directed against blacks, but depending on the "purity" of the neighborhood may also be directed at other ethnic groups or simply "the kinds of people who build cheaper homes on smaller lots." Since there is little empirical evidence that property values are really affected by the presence of blacks or other ethnic group members, it is probably safe to say that the real objective of neighborhood improvement associations in these sorts of campaigns is to maintain the social and economic homogeneity of the neighborhood.

Organized taxpayer groups generally stand for lower taxes and fewer governmental activities and services. Their most enthusiastic support comes from the community's larger taxpayers, generally the businessmen with large investments in commercial or industrial property in the community.

Business interests may be the most influential of all group interests in community politics. (See Chapter 12 for a detailed discussion of the role of businessmen and economic interests.) Many businessmen or "economic notables" occupy an important role in the structure of community decision making or "the power structure." Business interests are also represented in local politics by organized groups: the chamber of commerce and the junior chamber of commerce, or "jaycees," are found in nearly every community, representing the general views of men in business. The program of the chamber of commerce is likely to be more general than interests of particular sectors of the business community—banks, utilities, contractors, real estate developers, downtown merchants, or bar and club owners. The chamber or the jaycees can be expected to support lower taxes and more economy and efficiency in government operations. They are also active "promoters" of community growth and business activity. They can be expected to back civic improvements, so long as it does not raise the tax rate too much. "Service to the community" creates a "favorable image," which the chamber and businessmen are anxious to cultivate.

Generally, the active members of the chamber of commerce or the jaycees are younger businessmen in the community who are still on their way "up" in business. Owners of larger businesses, banks, utilities—the "big men" in the community—are more likely to function informally in the community's power structure than to take an overt role in organized interest group activity. Because chamber and jaycee leaders are likely to come from a wide variety of business concerns, from banks to insurance companies to real estate agencies, it is easier for them to agree on a program of "boosterism" and a variety of civic happenings than it is for them to pursue specific policy objectives that might divide the business community.

The so-called service clubs—the Lions, Kiwanis, Rotarians, and others—are basically for businessmen. Their interests are likely to be more social than political, but their service projects often involve them in political activity and their meetings provide an excellent opportunity for speechmaking by political candidates.

The businesses most active in community affairs are those most directly affected by policies of local government, such as department stores, banks, utilities, contractors, real estate operators, bar and club owners, and television and newspaper interests.

Banks often own, or hold the mortgages on, downtown business property. They have an interest in maintaining business, commercial, and industrial property values. Banks are also interested in the growth and prosperity of the city as a whole, particularly large business enterprises who are their primary customers. Bankers are influential because they decide who is able to borrow money in a community and under what conditions. Banks are directly involved in local governments in financing municipal bond issues for public works, school buildings, and so on, and in pledging financial backing for urban renewal projects. Banks are also influential in land development, for they must provide the financial backing for real estate developers, contractors, businesses, and home buyers; hence they are interested in business regulation, taxation, zoning, and housing.

Public utility companies may be primarily concerned with *state* agencies that determine rates and services, but they are also active in community politics. They must work closely with streets and public works departments. They generally favor policies that would increase the city's population and income. They are generally advocates of city planning and land use control because they benefit from steady and predictable urban growth. They are particularly interested in community policies to attract large industries that would be heavy users of electricity, gas, water, and other utility services. Finally, utilities must guard against proposals to place utilities under public ownership.

Contractors are vitally interested in city government because the city has the power of inspection over all kinds of construction. Local governments enforce building, plumbing, electric, and other codes, which are of great interest to contractors. Some contractors, particularly road-grading and surfacing companies, depend on public contracts, and they are vitally concerned with both city policy and the personnel who administer this policy. While municipal contracts are generally required by law to be given to the "low bidder" among "responsible" contractors, definitions about what is or is not a "low bid," and who is or who is not a "responsible" contractor, make it important for contractors to maintain close and friendly relationships with municipal officials.

Real estate developers are particularly interested in planning, zoning, and subdivision control regulations and urban renewal programs. (Urban renewal programs are discussed at length in Chapter 17.) The success of urban renewal depends upon participation of private developers and re-developers. When land is cleared, that portion of it not used for public housing or civic improvements is placed on the open market. At this point the ideas of city planners about beautiful, clean, low-cost housing, scenic open spaces, and artistic and cultural amenities must face the economic realities of the marketplace. The land must be sold for as high a price as possible in order to reduce the city's local dollar contribution to the project. It must be sold quickly in order to get the land back on the city's tax rolls. Successful renewal projects generally secure the support of the city's developers before they are even begun. This means that big-city mayors, whether they be Democrats or Republicans, must be on speaking terms with developers and real estate interests. Private developers generally show greater enthusiasm for renewal projects that result in high-rent apartments, office buildings, stores, or new industrial plants. They are usually cool to low- or moderate-priced housing.[50]

Newspapers are an important force in community politics.[51] The influence of the press would be relatively minor if its opinions were limited to its editorial pages. The influence of the press arises from its power to decide what is "news," thereby focusing public attention on the events and issues that are of interest to the press. Newspapermen must first decide what proportion of space in the paper will be devoted to local news in contrast to state, national, and international news. A big-city paper may

[50]For a critical view of urban renewal, see Martin Anderson, *The Federal Bulldozer* (Cambridge: Harvard University Press, 1964); and William G. Grigsby, "Housing and Urban Renewal: Elusive Goals," *Annals of the American Academy of Political and Social Science*, 352 (March 1964), 107–18.

[51]See Banfield and Wilson, *City Politics*, Chap. 21; and Morris Janowitz, *The Community Press in an Urban Setting* (Glencoe: The Free Press, 1954).

give local news about the same amount of space that it gives to national or foreign news. Suburban or small-town papers, which operate within the circulation area of a large metropolitan daily, may give a greater proportion of the news space to local events than to national and international affairs. Crime and corruption in government are favorite targets for the press. Editors believe that civic crusades, and the exposure of crime and corruption, help sell newspapers. Moreover, many editors and newspapermen believe they have a civic responsiblity to use the power of the press to protect the public. In the absence of crime or corruption, newspapers may turn to crusades on behalf of civic improvements—a city auditorium, a cultural center, and the like.

The politics of newspapers can be understood in part by some insight into the economics of the newspaper business. While it is true that, on occasion, some newspapers make financial sacrifices in order to defend the public interest as they see it, in the long run, newspapers are businesses and they must consider profit and loss statements like any other business. Only occasionaly can a wealthy newspaper owner ignore business considerations and run his paper at a loss. Newspapers get two-thirds of their revenue from advertising. The daily circulation of newspapers is at an all-time high, but in recent years the newspapers' percentage of all advertising dollars has declined in the face of stiff competition from television. At the same time the cost of newsprint and labor has risen steadily. Many big-city newspapers have either merged or gone out of business in recent years because of a lack of sufficient advertising revenue to offset increasing costs; it was not a lack of readers that brought about their collapse. Moreover, it is important to know that downtown department stores provide the largest source of advertising revenue. Big-city newspapers have been hurt by the flight of the middle class to the suburbs and the declining role of downtown department stores in retail sales in the metropolitan area. In metropolitan affairs, one can expect big-city newspapers to support the position of downtown interests. This means support for urban renewal, mass transit, downtown parking, and other pro-central-city policies in metropolitan affairs. On the other hand, suburban daily and weekly newspapers are supported by the advertising from suburban shopping centers, and they can be expected to take a pro-suburban position on metropolitan issues.

Newspapers are more influential among middle-class populations than among working-class, ethnic, or black populations. This is a product of differences in reading habits and educational levels between these groups. Newspapers are more influential in the absence of strong party organizations, which would compete with newspapers as channels of communication to the voters. Nonpartisanship, lengthy ballots, numerous referenda, all contribute to the influence of newspapers. Any situation that tends to obscure candidates or issues to the voter contributes to the power of newspapers, since the voter is obliged to rely upon them for information. Newspapers doubtlessly have more influence in local than in state or national politics because of (1) the relative importance in local politics of middle-class groups who read newspapers, (2) the relative obscurity of local politics to the voter in his reliance upon newspapers for information about local affairs, and (3) the relative weakening of party affiliations in local politics.

On the whole, labor unions are much less active or influential at the local level than at the state or national level. It is at the state and national level that the economic and regulatory issues that vitally affect labor are resolved. Economic prosperity, social security, minimum wages, fair labor standards, and protection of the rights to organize and bargain collectively are all issues determined primarily at the state or national level. Occasionally unions will become interested in police involvement in strikes and picketing at the local level, or they will become aroused by a local judge who enjoins them from striking or picketing. Labor unions in America are principally concerned with "bread-and-butter" matters—better wages, hours, benefits, and job tenure. They are also concerned with protecting the right to organize, to bargain collectively, and to strike, for these are the tools that labor unions require in order to achieve their economic objectives.

No one has a greater personal stake in municipal government than municipal employees—policemen, firemen, street crews, transit employees, welfare workers, sanitation workers, clerks, secretaries. Their rate of voter turnout in municipal elections is very high, and they are politically influential in small towns and suburbs whether they are organized into unions or not. Municipal employee unions are more influential in large cities where fragmentation of authority and public acceptance of union activity encourage unions to assert their employees' interests. In New York City, for example, associations of teachers, policemen, firemen, transit workers, social workers, sanitation workers, and so on, have great political significance. Employee work stoppages and other forms of protest occur frequently, even though state law prohibits strikes of municipal employees. The American Federation of State, County, and Municipal Employees, the International Association of Fire Fighters, and the American Federation of Teachers, all AFL–CIO unions, are directly concerned with organization and collective bargaining in public employment. In addition, certain other unions, such as the Transport Workers Union, were organized to bargain on behalf of both public and private employees. In the absence of union representation, public employees may form "professional associations," such as the Fraternal Order of Police and, of course, the National Education Association, which do not engage in collective bargaining in the strictest sense but do attempt to represent their members.

Finally, any listing of influential interest groups in local politics should include the community's churches and church-related organizations. Ministers, priests, rabbis, and leaders of religious lay groups are frequent participants in community decision making. The Catholic Church and its many lay organizations, are vitally concerned with the operations of parochial schools. Protestant ministerial associations in large cities may be concerned with public health, welfare, housing, and other social problems. Ministers and church congregations in small towns may be concerned with the enforcement of blue laws, limitations on liquor sales, prohibitions on horse racing and gambling, and other public policies relative to "vice" and public morality. In recent years Catholic groups have also led the opposition to the distribution of birth control information and devices at city hospitals and public health clinics.

Robert H. Salisbury summarizes interest group policies in St. Louis as follows:

> St. Louis . . . displays two broad configurations of interest. On one side are the locally oriented labor unions, Negroes, neighborhood businessmen, and lower income people generally. This grouping focuses its attention primarily on the specific bread and butter issues of jobs, stop signs, spot zoning, and the like, and exhibits a sharp antipathy toward any suggestion of increase of tax rates. Downtown business interests and the middle and upper middle income residents, on the other hand, are primarily interested in broader policy questions—economic growth, urban renewal—and their approach to problems of fiscal solvency is more sympathetic to the needs for more tax revenue.[52]

[52]Robert H. Salisbury, "St. Louis Politics: Relationships among Interests, Parties and Government Structure," *Western Political Quarterly*, 13 (June 1960), 498–507.

ELEVEN

Metropolitics:
Cities and Suburbs

THE ANATOMY OF A METROPOLIS

Two out of every three Americans live in population clusters called metropolitan areas. The rapid growth of these population clusters in recent years is perhaps the most striking and significant social change taking place in America. Most of the nation's population increase is occurring in these metropolitan areas—the increase in metropolitan area population from 1960 to 1970 was 24.4 million, in contrast to a 1.3 million decline in the rest of the United States. (See Table 11–1.) Moreover, most of this increase in metropolitan population is occurring outside the core cities in the nation's booming suburbs. The suburban population of the United States, persons living in metropolitan areas but outside the core city, grew by an amazing 36.0 percent in a single decade, while the core cities grew only 8.4 percent. Today American *suburbanites* outnumber either city or rural residents.

What is a metropolitan area? Briefly, a metropolitan areas consists of a large central city of fifty thousand or more persons together with the surrounding suburbs, which are socially and economically tied to the central city. The Census Bureau calls a metropolitan area a "Standard Metropolitan Statistical Area" (SMSA) and defines it as a city of fifty thousand or more persons together with adjacent counties which have predominantly urban industrial populations with close ties to the central city. (See Figure 11–1.)

TABLE 11-1
Population Growth in Cities and Suburbs
of Metropolitan Areas in the United States

| | Total U.S. Population | Metropolitan Areas | | | Outside Metropolitan Areas |
		Total	Central Cities	Suburbs	
1960					
Population (thousands)	179,993	111,886	57,360	54,526	68,107
Percent of U.S. total	100.0	62.2	31.9	30.3	37.8
1970					
Population (thousands)	203,185	136,330	62,193	74,137	66,855
Percent of U.S. total	100.0	67.1	30.6	36.5	32.9
Percentage increase	12.9	21.8	8.4	36.0	−1.9

SOURCE: U.S. Bureau of the Census, 1970 CENSUS OF POPULATION, PC (P3)-3 (Washington, D.C.: Government Printing Office, 1971).

Urban sociologists tell us that the very definition of metropolitan life involves *large numbers* of *different* types of people living *close together* who are socially and economically *dependent* upon one another.[1] *Numbers, density, heterogeneity,* and *interdependence* are said to be distinguishing characteristics of metropolitan life. It is not difficult to envision a metropolitan area as a large number of people living together; we can see these characteristics in metropolitan life from a map or an airplane window. But it is more difficult to understand the heterogeneity and interdependence of people living in metropolitan areas.

The modern economic system of the metropolis is based upon a highly specialized and complex division of labor. We are told that in the simple farm community, a dozen occupations exhausted the job opportunities available to men. An agricultural economy meant homogeneous employment opportunities; that is to say, nearly everyone was a farmer or was closely connected to and depended upon farming. But in the modern metropolis there are tens of thousands of different kinds of jobs. An industrial economy means highly specialized jobs and accounts for much of the heterogeneity in urban populations. There are wide differences between occupational worlds. It is on the basis of his job that the individual receives an income and his share of the goods and services available in life. Different jobs produce different levels of income, dress, and styles of living. The individual's job shapes the way he looks at the world and his evaluations of social and political events. In acquiring his job, he attains a certain level and type of education that also distinguishes him from those in other jobs with different educational requirements. Dif-

[1]See especially Scott Greer, *Governing the Metropolis* (New York: John Wiley & Sons, Inc., 1962).

FIGURE 11-1 Standard Metropolitan Statistical Areas

Source: U.S. Bureau of the Census.

ferences in educational level in turn produce a wide variety of differences and opinions, attitudes, and styles of living. Metropolitan living concentrates people with all these different economic and occupational characteristics in a very few square miles. This is what is meant by heterogeneity in metropolitan life.

Ethnic and racial diversity are also present. A few decades ago opportunities for human betterment in the cities attracted immigrants from Ireland, Germany, Italy, Poland, and Russia; today, the city attracts blacks, Puerto Ricans, and rural families. These newcomers to the metropolis bring with them different needs, attitudes, and ways of life. The "melting pot" tends to reduce some of this diversity over time, but the pot does not "melt" people immediately, and there always seem to be new arrivals.

People always differ in where they live and how they live. There is a certain uniformity to rural life; day-to-day family life on the farm is remarkably similar from one county to the next. But urban dwellers may live in apartments in the central city or in single-family homes in the suburbs. Some urban dwellers choose a familistic style of life—raising two or more children in their own single-family house, with the wife functioning as a homemaker. Others are less familistic—raising no children or a single child in a rented apartment with the wife holding down a job outside the home.

The list of social, economic, and life-style differences among the people in a metropolitan area is almost endless. Scott Greer writes, "The city is a maze, a social zoo, a mass of heterogeneous social types."[2] Moreover, urban sociologists tell us that people with different social, economic, and life-style characteristics generally live in different parts of a metropolitan area. Physical separation of residences generally accompanies social and economic separation, and so there are "ghettos," "silk-stocking districts," "little Italys," middle-class suburbs, and so on. This physical separation tends to emphasize and reinforce differences among people in a metropolitan area.

But another fundamental characteristic is interdependence. Rural living involves very little interdependence. While the traditional farm family was not wholly self-sufficient, its members were much less dependent upon the larger community for employment, goods, and services than is the modern metropolitan dweller.

In contrast, urban dwellers are highly dependent upon one another in their daily economic and social activities. Suburbanites, for example, rely upon the central city for food, clothing, newspapers, entertainment, hospitalization, and a host of other modern household needs. More importantly, they rely upon the central city for employment opportu-

2*Ibid.*, p. 5.

nities. Conversely, the central city relies upon the suburbs to supply its labor and management forces. Downtown merchants look to the entire metropolitan area for consumers. This interdependence involves an intricate web of economic and social relationships, a high degree of communication, and a great deal of daily physical interchange among residents, groups, and firms in a metropolitan area. Just as specialization produces diversity among men, it also produces interdependence and the need for coordinated human activity.

Suburbs account for most of the growth of America's metropolitan areas. In the last decade, nearly 20 million Americans moved to the suburbs. Rows upon rows of "ranches," and "split-levels," and "cape cods" now encircle our major cities as if to lay siege to them. No other sector of American life has grown so rapidly. Very few large *central cities* are growing in size; metropolitan areas are growing because their *suburbs* are growing (see Table 11-1). This suburbanization is due to technological advances in transportation—the automobile and the expressway. In the nineteenth century an industrial worker had to live within walking distance of his place of employment. This meant that the nineteenth-century American city crowded large masses of people into relatively small central areas, often in tenement houses and other high-density neighborhoods. But new modes of transportation—first the streetcar, then the private automobile, and now the expressway—eliminated the necessity of workers living close to their jobs. Now a man can spend his working hours in a central business district office or industrial plant and spend his evenings in a residential suburb many miles away. The same technology that led to the suburbanization of residences has also influenced commercial and industrial location. Originally industry was tied to waterways or railroads for access to supplies and markets. This dependence has been reduced by the development of motor truck transportation, the highway system, and the greater mobility of the labor force. Now many industries can locate in the suburbs, particularly light industries, which do not require extremely heavy bulk shipment that can only be handled by rail or water. When industry and people move to the suburbs, commerce follows. Giant suburban shopping centers have sprung up to compete with downtown stores. Thus, metropolitan areas are becoming decentralized over time as people, business, and industry spread themselves over the suburban landscape. As Lewis Mumford puts it: "The city has burst open and scattered its complex organs and organizations over the entire landscape."[3]

How far will the trend toward suburbanization go? There is good reason to believe that suburbanization will continue until America be-

[3]Lewis Mumford, *The City in History* (New York: Harcourt, Brace, & World, Inc., 1961), p. 34.

FIGURE 11–2   The Megalopolis

Source: U.S. Bureau of the Census.

comes one vast sprawling suburban development.[4] Jean Gottmann, a French geographer, has described a vast urban complex that stretches from New Hampshire to Virginia, where the suburbs of one metropolitan area blend with the suburbs of another metropolitan area all along the northeastern coast of the United States.[5] (See Figure 11 2.)

Another characteristic of metropolitan areas is "fragmented" govern-

[4]Oscar Handlin and John Burchard, eds., *The Historian and the City* (Cambridge: Harvard-M.I.T. Press, 1963), p. 1.

[5]Jean Gottmann, *Megalopolis: The Urbanized Northeastern Seaboard of the United States* (New York: Twentieth Century Fund, 1961).

TABLE 11-2

Local Governments in Metropolitan Areas

	Number of local governments
Total in 227 SMSAs[*]	20,703
Municipalities	4,977
Townships	3,255
Counties	404
Special districts	7,049
School districts	5,018
Total in selected SMSAs	
Chicago, Illinois	1,113
Philadelphia, Pennsylvania	876
Pittsburgh, Pennsylvania	704
New York, New York	551
St. Louis, Missouri	474
San Francisco-Oakland, Calif.	312
Portland, Oregon	385
Denver, Colorado	269
Seattle, Washington	268
Indianapolis, Indiana	282
Kansas City, Missouri	272

[*] Standard Metropolitan Statistical Areas

SOURCE: U.S. Bureau of the Census, CENSUS OF
GOVERNMENTS, 1972, V, 3.

ment. This is another result of suburbanization. Suburban development, spreading out from central cities, generally ignored governmental boundaries and engulfed counties, townships, towns, and smaller cities. Twenty-six metropolitan areas even spread across state lines, and four metropolitan areas of the United States—Detroit, San Diego, El Paso, and Laredo adjoin urban territory in Canada and Mexico. This suburbanization has meant that hundreds of governments may be operating in a single metropolitan area. Thus, while metropolitan areas are characterized by social and economic interdependence, and consequently require coordinating mechanisms, metropolitan government is generally "fragmented" into many smaller jurisdictions, none of which is capable of governing the entire metropolitan area in a unified fashion.

Governmental fragmentation in metropolitan areas is a function of the size: the larger the metropolitan area, the more fragmented the governmental structure.[6] Fragmentation is also related to the age of settlement and to income levels in the metropolis, although these factors are less in-

[6]See Brett W. Hawkins and Thomas B. Dye, "Metropolitan Fragmentation," *Midwest Review of Public Administration*, 4 (February 1970), 17–24.

fluential than size. Apparently the older a metropolitan area, the more complex its governmental structure becomes; and the more affluent its citizens are, the more complexity in the form of separate, relatively small units of government can be afforded.

THE BATTLE BETWEEN CITIES
AND SUBURBS

Since a metropolitan area consists of *large numbers* of *different kinds* of people *living closely together,* the problem of regulating conflict and maintaining order in a heterogenous metropolitan community assumes tremendous proportions. Persons with different occupations, income, and education levels are known to have different views on a wide variety of public issues. Persons well equipped to compete for jobs and income in a free market sometimes have different views about governmental housing and welfare programs than those not so well equipped. People at the bottom of the social ladder have a different view toward police, and government authority in general, than those on higher rungs. Persons who own their own home view taxation in a different light from those who do not. Families with children have different ideas about school systems than those without children. And so it goes. Differences among men and the way they make their living, in their income and education levels, and the color of their skin, and the way they worship, and their style of living, and so on, are at the roots of political life in the metropolis.

Social, economic, and racial conflict can be observed at all levels of government, but at the metropolitan level, it is most obvious in the conflict that occurs between central cities and their suburbs. At the heart of city-suburban conflict are the differences in the kinds of people who live in cities and suburbs. And city-suburban conflict is at the heart of "the metropolitan problem"; that is, the failure to achieve metropolitan-wide consensus on public policy questions affecting the entire metropolitan area and the failure to develop metropolitan government institutions. It is very difficult to arrive at metropolitan-wide consensus about questions involving desegregation and the bussing of students out of their neighborhood to achieve it, mass transit and highway construction, the sharing of welfare costs, the distribution of tax burdens, water supply and sewage disposal problems, planning and zoning, housing policy (including the concentration of blacks in central cities), and a host of other problems. We shall refer to the social, economic, and racial differences between city and suburb as "social distance." This social distance accounts for much conflict between cities and suburbs and constitutes the chief obstacle to the development of metropolitan-wide policies and government institutions.

Of course, generalizing about cities and suburbs is a dangerous thing. While we will talk about some common characteristics of cities and suburbs, students are cautioned that individual suburbs may be quite different from one another, just as there are wide differences between social and economic groups living in central cities. Nonetheless, a clear perception of the social distance between cities and suburbs is important in understanding metropolitan politics.

Cities and suburbs can be differentiated, first of all, on the basis of *occupation, income,* and *educational levels* of their populations. The cultured class of an earlier era established "country" living as a symbol of affluence; widespread prosperity has made possible mass imitation of the aristocracy by an upwardly mobile middle-class population. The occupational, education, and income characteristics of persons living in the suburbs of our nation's large metropolitan areas can be clearly differentiated from those of central city dwellers. The suburbs house greater proportions of white collar employees, of college graduates, and of affluent families than any other sector in American life. Table 11–3 contrasts several common measures of social status for American central cities and suburbs.

TABLE 11-3
Social, Economic, and Life Style Differences
Between Cities and Suburbs

	Average for United States	Average for SMSAs	
		Central cities	Suburbs
White-collar occupation, male (percent of work force)	48.2	51.7	56.8
Median family income	$9,590	$9,519	$11,771
Population under poverty level (percent of population)	12.2	13.4	6.3
Families over $25,000 (percent of all families)	4.6	4.6	7.4
Median school year completed	12.1	12.0	12.3
High school graduates (percent)	52.3	50.9	61.9
Nonwhite percentage	11.1	20.6	4.7
Mobility (percent living in different county 5 years ago)	17.1	14.1	18.9
Fertility rate (children ever born per 1,000 females 25-34)	1,986	1,943	2,035
Families with children under 6 (percent of families)	26.1	25.3	27.1
Females in labor force (percent of all females over 16)	41.4	44.5	42.5

State differentials in favor of suburbs are more pronounced in larger metropolitan areas; Leo Schnore reports that status differentials in smaller metropolitan areas are not as great as in larger areas, and sometimes even favor the city rather than the suburbs.[7] However, on the whole, suburban living reflects middle-class values.[8] And, social differences between city and suburb are increasing rather than decreasing, as middle-class Americans continue to flee from the central city to the suburbs, and low-income, occupational, and educational groups are concentrated in central cities.

Cities and suburbs can also be differentiated on the basis of *"familism,"* or life-style. Perhaps the most frequently mentioned reason for a move to the suburbs is "the kids." Family after family lists consideration of their young as the primary cause for their move to suburbia. The city is hardly the place for most child-centered amenities. A familistic or child-centered life-style can be identified in certain social statistics. One measure is the "fertility ratio," or the number of children born per thousand women from fifteen to forty-four years of age. Another measure is the percentage of women aged fourteen or over who are in the work force. A large number of children per thousand married females of childbearing age, together with a small proportion of women who work, suggest a family-centered environment. In addition, the single-family, free-standing home is the *sine qua non* of familistic living in an affluent society. Cumulatively, these three life-style measures are said to identify a familistic or child-centered way of life. Table 11–3 shows that (1) there are proportionately more children in the suburbs than in the central cities; (2) a larger proportion of suburban mothers stay at home to take care of these children; and (3) a larger proportion of suburban families are housed in single-family units. The nonfamilistic life-style is characteristic of the central city where there are proportionately fewer children, more apartment living, and greater numbers of employed mothers. A familistic style of life in suburbia suggests the importance of the most fundamental of all child amenities—the school.

Again, it should be pointed out that the suburbs of smaller metropolitan areas are less differentiated from their central cities in terms of life-style than the suburbs of larger metropolitan areas. Smaller cities seem to be able to support a familistic life-style almost as well as their suburbs.

Perhaps the most important difference between cities and suburbs is their contrasting *racial composition.* Black populations in most large cities are growing at a very rapid rate, partly from natural increases and partly from migration from the rural South. New arrivals go into slums,

[7]Leo Schnore, "The Socio-economic Status of Cities and Suburbs," *American Sociological Review*, 28 (February 1963), 76–85.

[8]See Robert C. Wood, *Suburbia: Its People and Their Politics* (New York: Houghton Mifflin Company, 1958).

which almost everywhere are located in the oldest part of the central city. The increases in nonwhite populations in large central cities in recent years have been truly astounding. (Table 13-4 shows the increase in nonwhite population percentages of the largest cities in the United States, from 1960 to 1970.) The nonwhite population of most of these cities has doubled and redoubled over the past twenty years. At the same time the white populations of these central cities have been fleeing to the suburbs. Very few large cities gained in white population. The result has been striking changes in the racial composition of central cities.

Many whites have fled to the suburbs to get away from heavy concentrations of blacks in central cities. One reason why many suburbanites may want to remain politically separate from the central cities is that it might make it easier for them to resist "invasion" by blacks. As blacks gain majorities in central cities, they, too, may resist metropolitan governmental consolidation in order to avoid dilution of their political power through merger with white suburbs. The restriction of suburban home sales to whites only and the generally higher costs of suburban homes and property have made it difficult or impossible for blacks to follow whites to the suburbs in any significant number. The nonwhite percentage of all United States suburbs was 4.7 percent in 1970 in contrast to a nonwhite percentage for all central cities of 21.0 percent.

American life is becoming more, not less, segregated over time. These population statistics clearly show that America is building racial "ghettos" in its large central cities and surrounding them with white middle-class suburbs. As the population exodus to the suburbs continues, cities are becoming increasingly bereft of their middle-class, white, high-income, tax-paying populations. Increasingly, nonwhite, low-income, low-education, unskilled, nonfamilistic populations are being concentrated in the central cities. This means we have also concentrated the problems of these people in downtown areas—racial imbalance, crime, violence, inadequate education, poverty, slum housing, and so on. By moving to the suburbs, white middle-class families not only separate themselves from blacks and poor people but also place physical distance between themselves and the major social problems that confront metropolitan areas. This permits them, for the time being, to avoid problems of slum housing, poor schools, expanding welfare rolls, crime and juvenile delinquency, and rioting in the central cities.

POLITICAL DIFFERENCES
BETWEEN CITIES AND SUBURBS

City and suburban social differences are reflected in divergent political patterns in cities and suburbs. Table 11-4 shows that, in general, large

TABLE 11-4
Democratic and Republican Party Vote in Cities
and Suburbs in Presidential Elections

	1956		1960		1964		1968	
	Dem.	Rep.	Dem.	Rep.	Dem.	Rep.	Dem.	Rep.
New York City	51.0	49.0	62.8	37.2	73.2	26.8	60.5	33.9
Suburban counties								
Rockland	29.0	71.0	45.0	55.0	63.7	36.3	44.3	49.1
Westchester	27.8	72.2	43.2	56.8	62.0	38.0	43.4	50.3
Nassau	30.9	69.1	44.8	55.2	60.5	39.5	43.3	51.2
Suffolk	22.3	77.7	40.6	59.4	55.5	44.5	32.7	58.2
Chicago	49.0	51.0	63.6	36.4	71.0	29.0	63.1	36.3
Cook Co. outside of Chicago	27.7	72.3	40.9	59.1	52.1	47.9	34.2	58.5
Philadelphia	57.1	42.9	68.1	31.9	73.7	26.3	61.8	29.9
Suburban counties								
Bucks	39.1	60.9	45.7	54.3	60.6	39.4	40.2	48.6
Chester	29.7	70.3	36.2	63.8	54.1	45.9	33.3	57.2
Delaware	38.0	62.0	47.8	52.2	56.8	43.2	40.0	50.2
Montgomery	30.7	69.3	39.2	60.8	56.7	43.3	39.3	54.3
Detroit	61.8	38.2	71.0	29.0	80.0	20.0	71.2	20.0
Wayne Co. outside of Detroit	49.6	50.4	57.7	42.3	30.3	69.7	52.3	39.2
Pittsburgh	52.3	47.7	67.0	33.0	74.7	25.3	62.2	25.8
Allegheny Co. outside of Pittsburgh	40.3	59.7	51.5	48.5	61.7	38.3	46.1	42.2
St. Louis	61.0	39.0	66.6	33.4	77.7	22.3	64.1	26.4
St. Louis Co.	46.9	44.1	51.3	48.7	61.3	38.7	48.6	51.4
San Francisco	48.0	52.0	57.8	42.8	71.2	28.8	59.2	33.7
Suburban counties								
Marin	33.8	65.2	42.5	57.5	61.7	38.3	43.8	50.1
San Mateo	38.8	61.2	48.0	52.0	64.3	35.7	47.2	43.7
Cleveland	54.6	45.4	70.9	29.1	82.8	17.2	67.4	20.5
Cuyahoga Co. outside of Cleveland	37.4	62.6	49.9	50.1	62.6	37.4	45.3	43.0
Minneapolis	48.3	51.7	52.3	47.7	65.6	34.4	59.1	36.1
Hennepin Co. outside of Minneapolis	38.6	61.4	44.5	55.5	55.1	44.9	49.5	42.0
Buffalo	42.3	57.7	64.9	35.1	79.7	20.3	65.7	26.6
Erie Co. outside of Buffalo	29.5	70.5	48.6	51.4	67.5	32.5	48.0	49.1
Milwaukee	47.3	52.7	61.8	38.2	70.0	30.0	35.4	34.9
Milwaukee Co. outside of Milwaukee	34.6	65.4	49.1	50.9	56.7	43.3	43.8	48.3
Cincinnati	37.5	62.5	50.4	49.6	62.0	38.0	45.7	43.2
Hamilton Co. outside of Cincinnati	28.3	71.7	39.4	60.6	57.7	42.3	29.2	56.5

SOURCE: R. M. Scammon, AMERICA VOTES (Washington: Government Affairs Institute, 1966).

cities are much more Democratic than their suburban rings, which are generally Republican. While temporary shifts may occur from one election to another, this general pattern of Democratic cities and Republican suburbs is likely to prevail for the near future. As long as the national Democratic party represents central-city, low-income, ethnic, labor, and racial constituencies, and the Republican party represents middle-class, educated, managerial, white, Anglo-Saxon, Protestant constituencies, the political coloration of cities and suburbs is likely to be different. Persons who are leaving cities for the suburbs include a disproportionate number of Republicans. Their places in the cities are being taken by blacks, Puerto Ricans, and poor whites, most of whom are normally Democratic in their politics.

A possible challenge to the Democratic cities–Republican suburbs pattern is the increasing affluence of ethnic, working-class populations in America, which permits many of them to buy suburban homes, and leave their central-city neighborhoods. If these new suburbanites retain their ethnic and labor affiliations and traditions of Democratic party voting, they could make serious inroads into Republican party strength in the suburbs. However, while some low-income industrial suburbs regularly support the Democratic ticket, on the whole, the Republican suburban vote percentages have suffered very little from the vast increase in suburban population. In fact, suburban population explosion has saved the Republican party the slow death that it would have experienced if its appeal had been limited to the diminishing ranks of small-town and rural voters.[9]

These party differences pose an obstacle to the consolidation of metropolitan governments. Metropolitan consolidation schemes would place Democratic control of central cities in jeopardy just as they might threaten Republican control of suburban counties. Political leaders, both Democratic and Republican, are not likely to view with favor any proposal that would substitute political insecurity for "a good thing." Republican party leaders outside central cities are just as well satisfied with a local one-party system as are the Democrats of the central cities.

In commenting on city-suburban political differences, Edward C. Banfield also pointed out the following political problems raised by metropolitan government:

> It would be a mistake to suppose that the conflict lies altogether or even mainly between the two party organizations or among the professional politicians who have a stake in them. The party differences are important in themselves, but they reflect deeper but still more important differences. Metropolitan government would mean the transfer of power over the central cities from the largely lower class Negro and Catholic elements who live in them to the largely middle-class, white, and Protestant elements who live in the suburbs . . .

[9]On suburban voting behavior, see Herbert Hirsch, "Suburban Voting and National Trends," *Western Political Quarterly*, 21 (September 1968), 508–14; and Frederick M. Wirt, "The Political Sociology of American Suburbia," *Journal of Politics*, 27 (August 1965), 647–66.

The few Republicans of the central cities, and in general, the good government forces—in short, all those who want to weaken the Democratic
machines—will favor adding the suburban vote to the central city vote
wherever the suburbs are predominantly middle or upper class . . .

As the Negro tide rises in the central cities, many white Democrats begin
to think of annexation and consolidation as ways to maintain a white (but
alas, a Republican!) majority. Unless there is consolidation, some cities
will probably have Negro mayors within the next 20 years. Negroes can
be expected to oppose annexation and consolidation under these circumstances, of course.[10]

In other words, metropolitan government threatens the political *status
quo* where both Democrats and Republicans share political power. It
threatens to replace this happy arrangement with a "winner take all" political system, which threatens both Democratic and Republican party interests in metropolitan areas.

POLICY DIFFERENCES
BETWEEN CITIES AND SUBURBS

City and suburban social differences are also reflected in the divergent
public policies of city and suburban governments. First of all, there is
some evidence that the child-centered character of suburban living produces higher educational expenditures in suburbs than in cities. Suburban
parents with high hopes and plans for their children's occupational success tend to focus more concern upon the school system, and spend more
money on it per pupil, than city residents (see Table 11–5). (Of course,
in smaller metropolitan areas, where social and life-style differences between city and suburb are slight, differences between city and suburb
in educational expenditures are very slight and occasionally run opposite from the expected direction.)

Large central cities show substantially higher operating expenditures
per capita than their suburbs. The maintenance of a large physical plant
for the entire metropolitan area requires city residents to make higher
per capita operating expenditures than those required for suburbanites.
In addition, many living costs in suburban communities are shifted from
public to private spending (private septic tanks instead of public sewers,
private instead of public recreation, and so on). Differences in the public
services provided by city and suburban governments are greatest in the
area of police protection, recreation, and health. This reflects a concen-

---

[10]Edward C. Banfield, "The Politics of Metropolitan Area Organizations," *Midwest
Journal of Political Science*, 1 (May 1957), 77–91.

TABLE 11-5

Differential in Tax and Expenditures Policies of City and
Suburban Governments in Wisconsin by Urbanized Area, 1960

	Total oper- ating school expen- ditures $ per pupil	Total oper- ating munic- ipal expen- ditures $ per capita	Full value property tax rate (in mills)				Indebtedness	
			Total	Munic- ipal	School	County	$ per capita	$ per $1,000 full value
Milwaukee area								
City	438	87	31.0	11.3	12.4	8.9	163	32
18 suburbs	590	67	26.7	4.0	13.2	9.1	189	28
Madison area								
City	441	75	25.9	9.9	11.7	4.4	223	40
7 suburbs	467	31	25.2	2.8	17.3	4.8	79	22
Green Bay area								
City	455	69	22.5	6.6	10.3	5.3	178	32
6 suburbs	405	34	20.0	4.4	9.8	5.8	55	11
Racine area								
City	401	62	24.9	7.5	13.4	3.8	204	40
5 suburbs	394	24	18.0	1.4	15.0	3.9	4	1
Kenosha area								
City	435	62	26.5	5.7	15.0	5.6	201	40
2 suburbs	365	12	22.2	.9	14.8	6.0	0	0

SOURCE: Thomas R. Dye, "City-Suburban Social Distance and Public Policy," SOCIAL
FORCES, 44 (September 1965), 100-106.

tration in the city of people who are likely to require these public services, in contrast to the suburbs.

The tax bill in suburbs may be slightly lower than in central cities.
Taxes had much to do with the migration of the "pioneer" suburbanites,
those who moved to the suburbs in the 1930s and 1940s. At that time,
suburban living offered a significant savings in property taxation over
what were thought to be heavy city taxes. But the tax advantage of the
suburbs turned out partly to be a "self-denying prophecy": the more people who fled to the suburbs to avoid heavy taxes, the greater the demand
for public services in these new suburban communities, and the higher
suburban taxes became to meet these new demands. Yet, the tax bill
in most suburbs remains lower than in central cities. The difference in
tax burden between city and suburb would be even greater if suburbanites did not choose to spend more per pupil in education than city resi-

dents, which produces higher school taxes in the suburbs. The suburbs also manage to limit their indebtedness more than cities, and most of the indebtedness incurred by the suburbs is for school, rather than municipal, purposes.

Finally, it should be noted that policy differences between city and suburb in smaller metropolitan areas do not appear to be as great as policy differences in cities and suburbs in larger metropolitan areas. This corresponds to our earlier point that social and economic differences between city and suburb in smaller metropolitan areas are not as great as in larger metropolitan areas. Of course, it should also be remembered that all these generalizations about cities and suburbs are, indeed, generalizations. Individual cities and suburbs can be found that do not conform to these national patterns.

THE CASE FOR METROPOLITAN CONSOLIDATION

The term *metropolitan problem* has been given to any situation requiring cooperation between city and suburban governments. And there is hardly any governmental activity that has not been identified as a metropolitan problem. Too often civic reformers have tended to limit the discussion of metropolitan problems to the technical problems of providing public services in a metropolis, such as water supply, sewage disposal, transportation, and fire and police protection. But metropolitan problems include all the major social and economic problems confronting American society. Poverty, racial imbalance, slum housing, crime and juvenile delinquency, financial crisis—these problems may be "national" in scope, but they occur principally in the metropolis.[11] In short, the major social problems facing American society are also "metropolitan problems." Nor is it possible to argue convincingly that these major social, economic problems are problems of central cities rather than of the entire metropolitan area. John C. Bollens and Henry J. Schmandt in *The Metropolis* addressed themselves to this point very effectively:

> Some myopic defenders of suburbia go so far as to say that the major socio-economic problems of urban society are problems of the central city, not those of the total metropolitan community. Where but within the boundaries of the core city, they ask, does one find an abundance of racial strife, crime, blight of housing, and welfare recipients? Superficially, their logic may seem sound, since they are in general correct about the prev-

[11]Mitchel Gordon, *Sick Cities: The Psychology and Pathology of American Urban Life* (New York: The Macmillan Company, 1963), pp. 339–40.

alent spatial location of these maladies. Although crime and other social problems exist in suburbia, their magnitude and extent are substantially less than in the central city. But why in an interdependent metropolitan community should the responsibility of suburbanites be any less than that of the central city dwellers? Certainly no one would think of contending that residents of higher income neighborhoods within the corporate limits of the city should be exempt from responsibility for its less fortunate districts. What logic then is there in believing that neighborhoods on the other side of a legal line can wash their hands of social disorders in these sections?

. . . No large community can hope to reap the benefits of industrialization and urbanization and yet escape their less desirable byproducts. The suburbanite and the central city resident share the responsibility for the total community and its problems. Neither can run fast enough to escape involvement sooner or later.[12]

Many scholars over the years have insisted that "the metropolitan problem" was essentially the problem of "fragmented" government—that is, the proliferation of governments in metropolitan areas and the lack of coordination of public programs.[13] The objective of the metropolitan reform movement of the last thirty years was to reorganize, consolidate, and enlarge government jurisdictions. The goal was to rid metropolitan areas of "ineffective multiple local jurisdictions" and "governments that do not coincide with the boundaries of the metropolis."

Many advantages were claimed for metropolitan governmental reorganization. First of all, the reorganization and consolidation of metropolitan governments was expected to bring about *improved public services* as a result of centralization. Consolidation of governments was expected to achieve many economies of large-scale operations and enable government to provide specialized public services, which "fragmented" units of government could not provide. For example, larger water treatment plant facilities can deliver water at lower per gallon costs, and larger sewage disposal plants can handle sewage at a lower per gallon cost of disposal. Additional specialized public services that could be provided on a metropolitan-wide level are police crime laboratories, central record systems, and central communications systems, which cannot be provided by small suburban police forces. Robert Wood described the technical and administrative arguments for the metropolitan government consolidation as follows:

Technical specialist after technical specialist moves from one city to an-

---

[12]John C. Bollens and Henry J. Schmandt, *The Metropolis* (New York: Harper & Row, Publishers, 1965), pp. 249–50.
[13]See Luther Gulick, *The Metropolitan Problem and American Ideas* (New York: Alfred A. Knopf, Inc., 1962).

other, engaging in painstaking operations of conditions in his own proficiency, and solemnly proclaiming that no public health department would work properly without a clientele of at least 50,000 people; or that no zoning regulation made sense without reference to a master plan for the whole region; or that no police force could support a qualified laboratory until x number of precinct stations were in being to refer to sufficient quantity of cases to keep scientific technicians analyzing at optimum speed.[14]

Second, it was argued that metropolitan consolidation would provide the necessary *coordination of public services* for the metropolis. Study after study reported that disease, crime, fire, traffic congestion, air pollution, water pollution, and so on, do not respect municipal boundary lines. The transportation problem is the most common example of a coordination problem. Traffic experts have pleaded for the development of a balanced transportation system in which mass transit carries many of the passengers currently traveling in private automobiles. Experience indicates that new expressways are congested during peak hours on the day that they are opened. Yet mass transit requires decisive public action by the entire metropolitan area. Metropolitan reformers have contended that the absence of metropolitan government has also contributed to the inability to solve traffic problems. Certainly, the city government is in a poor position to provide mass transit by itself without the support of the surburbanites who will be riding on it. And of course small suburban governments are totally inadequate to this task. The demonstrated inability of local government to deal with the transportation problem has shifted attention to Washington. Action in many metropolitan areas on mass transit has come to a near standstill, awaiting the helping hand of the federal government. It is argued by some that this sad state of affairs may not have come about if strong, metropolitan-wide governments had been in existence that could have acted effectively to solve the mass transit problem at the local level.

The third major argument for metropolitan consolidation stresses the need to eliminate *inequalities in financial burdens* throughout the metropolitan area. Suburbanites who escaped many city taxes continue to add to the cities' traffic and parking problems, use city streets and parks, find employment in the cities, use city hospitals and cultural facilities, and so on. By concentrating the poor, uneducated, unskilled minorities in central cities, we also saddle central cities with costly problems of public health and welfare, crime control, fire protection, slum clearance, and the like, all the social problems that are associated with poverty and discrimination. We concentrate these costly problems in cities at the same time that

[14]Robert C. Wood, "A Division of Powers in Metropolitan Areas," in *Area and Power*, ed. Arthur Maass (Glencoe: The Free Press, 1959), p. 59.

middle-class, tax-paying individuals, tax-paying commercial enterprises, and tax-paying industries are moving into the suburbs. Thus, metropolitan government fragmentation often succeeds in segregating financial needs from resources.[15]

The financial crisis facing the central cities has resulted in their turning to Washington for financial support. Direct federal grants to cities began with the Housing Act of 1937, when the federal government initiated its financial support for public housing and urban renewal. There is now a truly staggering array of federal grant-in-aid programs for cities—for community facilities, sewage and water plants, urban planning, mass transit, urban beautification, air pollution control, schools and hospitals, ports, airports, and so on. It might be argued that metropolitan government, by eliminating financial inequalities between cities and suburbs, may reduce the dependence of city governments on federal handouts and enable the metropolitan areas to solve at least some of their financial problems themselves.

It is also argued that metropolitan government would *clearly establish responsibility for metropolitan-wide policy*. One of the consequences of "fragmented" government is the scattering of public authority and the decentralization of policy making in the metropolis.[16] This proliferation in the number of autonomous governmental units reduces the probability of developing a consensus on metropolitan policy. Each autonomous unit exercises a veto power over metropolitan policy within its jurisdiction; it is often impossible to secure the unanimity required to achieve metropolitan consensus on any metropolitan-wide problem. An opponent of any particular solution need only find, among the countless independent governmental bodies whose consent is required, one that can be induced to withhold its consent in order to obstruct action.

Fragmented government divides political power into many small units with limited jurisdiction. As a result, decisions on matters of general concern, such as improving mass transit or water pollution, may be binding on only a portion of the metropolitan area. The dispersion of power among a large number of governmental units makes it possible for each of them to reach decisions without concern for the possible spillover effects, which may be harmful to other governments or residents of the metropolis.

Metropolitan leadership has no institutional means of implementing metropolitan-wide policy proposals. There is no metropolitan-wide government, with the legal authority or political relationship with a metropolitan constituency, capable of resolving metropolitan conflict, develop-

---

[15]See Lyle C. Fitch, "Metropolitan Financial Problems," *Annals of the American Academy of Social and Political Science* (November 1957), pp. 66–73.

[16]See Robert C. Wood, *1400 Governments* (Cambridge: Harvard University Press, 1961).

ing consensus in metropolitan policy, or implementing metropolitan projects. As a result, metropolitan leadership, what there is of it, must be content to transmit its proposals for metropolitan-wide policy to a large number of separate governmental units, where its reception depends upon voluntary acceptance. Moreover, the decision of these independent units to accept a proposal is usually based on the *local* effect of the proposal rather than its impact upon the total metropolitan community. The proliferation of metropolitan governments, with a scattering of public authority and the overlapping of governmental jurisdictions, makes it extremely difficult even for the most conscientious citizen to hold public officials accountable for their decisions. Conscientious citizens have enough difficulty remaining reasonably knowledgeable about local, state and national affairs without sorting through the maze of city, county, township, school district, authority, and special district governments that operate in metropolitan areas. Metropolitan government, it is argued, could simplify and streamline government organization in the metropolis and make it easier for citizens to hold public officials accountable and responsible for the decisions.

THE CASE FOR "FRAGMENTED" GOVERNMENT

So long as we view local government exclusively as a mechanism for providing municipal services, the "fragmented" character of metropolitan government will appear to be obsolete and in need of reform.

But, the suburbanite does not look upon the efficient provision of public service as the *only* function of local government. Nor does he look upon "the optimum development of the metropolitan region" as a particularly compelling goal. Rather, there are a variety of social, political, and psychological values at stake in maintaining the existing "fragmented" system of local government.[17] First of all, the existence of separate and independent local governments for suburbs plays a vital role in *developing and maintaining a sense of community identity*. The suburbanite identifies his residential community by reference to the local political unit. He does not think of himself as a resident of the "New York metropolitan region," but rather as a resident of Scarsdale or Mineola. Even the existence of community problems, the existence of a governmental forum for their resolution, and the necessity to elect local of-

---

[17]Oliver P. Williams, Harold Herman, Charles S. Liebman, and Thomas R. Dye, *Suburban Differences and Metropolitan Policies* (Philadelphia: University of Pennsylvania Press, 1965), Chap. 8.

ficials heighten community involvement and identity. The suburban community, with a government small in scale and close to home, represents a partial escape from the anonymity of mass urban culture. The institutional apparatus of government helps the suburban community to differentiate itself from "the urban mass," by legislating differences in the size and design of buildings, neighborhood and subdivision plans, school policies, types and quality of public services, and tax expenditure levels.

The political advantages of a fragmented suburbia cannot easily be dismissed. The existence of many local governments *provides additional forums for the airing of public grievances.* People feel better when they can publicly voice their complaints against governments, regardless of the eventual outcome of their grievance. The additional points of access, pressure, and control provided by a decentralized system of local government give added insurance that political demands will be heard and perhaps even acted upon. Opportunities for individual participation in the making of public policy are expanded in a decentralized governmental system.

Maintaining the suburb as an independent political community *provides the individual with a sense of personal effectiveness* in public affairs. The individual can feel a greater sense of manageability over the affairs of a small community. A smaller community helps relieve feelings of frustration and apathy, which people often feel in their relations with larger bureaucracies. The suburbanite feels that his vote, his opinion, and his political activity count for more in a small community. He clings to the idea of grass-roots democracy in an organizational society.

Fragmented government clearly *offers a larger number of groups the opportunity to exercise influence* over government policy. Groups that would be minorities in the metropolitan area as a whole can avail themselves of government position and enact diverse public policies. This applies to blacks in the central city as well as white Anglo-Saxon Protestants in the suburbs. Fragmented government creates within the metropolitan area a wide range of government policies. Communities that prefer, for example, higher standards in their school system at higher costs have the opportunity to implement this preference. Communities that prefer higher levels of public service or one set of services over another or stricter enforcement of particular standards can achieve their goals under a decentralized governmental system. Communities that wish to get along with reduced public services in order to maximize funds available for private spending may do so.

Political independence also *allows the suburbanite to insulate himself* from those whose standards and way of life he does not share. Persons who have strived to place physical distance between themselves and those with different cultures and life-styles are unlikely to look with favor on attempts to remove or weaken identifiable boundaries between their communities and communities that are socially dissimilar. It is not necessarily the color of the black doctor who first moves into an all-white suburb that "frightens" the suburbanite. It is the belief that he will be followed by other blacks with "lower" cultural and economic standards. The cultural homogeneity that the suburbanite seeks for himself and his children is better protected when he can make use of the legal machinery of an independent government to maintain this homogeneity by excluding those who might change it. Of course, a suburban government cannot directly discriminate, but it can establish and enforce, through building, zoning, subdivision, and tax ordinances, specific standards that are high enough to make it economically unlikely that a "disrupting" element could enter the community. These formal controls, together with informal pressures on builders, real estate firms, and others, can operate to preserve effectively the cultural uniformity valued so highly in the suburban community.

Racial imbalance and the plight of central-city schools are important forces in maintaining the political autonomy of suburban school systems in the nation's large metropolitan areas. Many suburbanites left the central city to find "a better place to raise the kids," and this means, among other things, better schools. As we have already observed, suburbs generally spend more on the education of each child than central cities. Moreover, the increasing concentration of blacks in central cities has resulted in racial imbalance in center-city schools. Conditions in ghetto schools have long been recognized as a national scandal.[18] Efforts to end de facto segregation within the cities frequently involves bussing school children into and out of ghetto schools in order to achieve racial balance. In Chapter 13 we will discuss de facto segregation and ghetto schools in greater detail. But it is important to note here that independent suburban school districts are viewed by many suburbanites as protection against the possibility that their children might be bussed to ghetto schools. Autonomous suburban school districts lie outside the jurisdiction of city officials. While it is possible that federal courts may someday order suburban school districts to cooperate with cities in achieving racial balance in schools (a federal judge in Detroit issued such an order in 1971), nonetheless, the political independence of suburban schools helps to assure that suburban school children will not be used to achieve racial balance in city schools.

---

[18]Bel Kaufman, *Up the Down Staircase* (Englewood Cliffs, N.J.: Prentice-Hall, Inc., 1964).

"SOLUTIONS" TO THE METROPOLITAN
PROBLEM

Let us examine various strategies for metropolitan governmental consolidation in the light of the preceding discussion of the values involved in suburban independence and the need for coordinating governmental activity in metropolitan areas.

The most obvious method of achieving governmental consolidation in the metropolitan area would be for the central city to annex suburban areas. *Annexation* continues to be the most popular integrative device in the nation's metropolitan areas.[19] Approximately three-fourths of the nation's central cities have succeeded in annexing some territory and people over the last ten years. Not all cities, however, have been equally successful in annexation efforts. Opposition to central-city annexation is generally more intense in the larger metropolitan areas. The bigger the metropolis, the more one can expect that suburbanites will defend themselves against being "swallowed up" or "submerged" by the central city. Table 11–6 suggests that central cities in smaller urbanized areas experience slightly more success in annexing people than cities in large urbanized areas. Yet size does not appear to be the most influential factor affecting annexation success. Actually, the "age" of a city appears more influential than size in determining the success of annexation efforts. City boundary lines in "older" metropolitan areas are relatively more fixed than in "newer" areas. Perhaps the immobility of boundaries is a product of sheer age. Over time, persons and organizations adjust themselves to circumstances as they find them. The longer these adjustments have been in existence, the greater the discomfort, expense, and fear of unanticipated consequences associated with change.

Central cities with higher proportions of well-educated, white-collar, middle-income, white persons are more successful in annexing their suburbs than cities with smaller proportions of these "middle-class" attributes. Table 11–6 shows that annexation success is correlated with the education level of the central-city population, and similar correlations can be obtained between annexation success and income, occupation, and racial composition. In general, cities with higher status populations, and fewer minority groups, are able to annex more suburbanites than cities with lower status populations and larger minority groups. Actually,

---

[19]The following discussion of annexation activity relies upon Thomas R. Dye, "Urban Political Integration: Conditions Associated with Annexation in American Cities," *Midwest Journal of Political Science*, 8 (November 1964), 430–46.

TABLE 11-6

Conditions Associated with Annexation Success in American Cities
(figures are mean annexation success scores for cities in each category)*

Size of Urbanized Area		
Under 150,000	150,000-500,000	Over 500,000
13.5	11.5	11.1

Age: Number of Decades since City Surpassed 50,000 Population			
0	1-5	5-7	Over 7
22.3	13.6	7.8	4.2

Education Level of Central-City Population: Median School Year Completed			
Less than 10	10-11	11-12	more than 12
4.4	12.2	16.2	20.1

City-Surburban Social Distance on Education: Difference between City and Suburbs in Median School Year Completed	
Favors City	Favors Suburbs
14.5	5.9

* Annexation success scores are the percentage of the 1960 central-city
population which was annexed to it between 1950 and 1960.

SOURCE: Thomas R. Dye, "Urban Political Integration," MIDWEST
JOURNAL OF POLITICAL SCIENCE, 8 (November 1964), 430-46.

the important variable in annexation success, and probably other efforts
at metropolitan consolidation, seems to be the *differential* in status between the central city and its surrounding suburbs. Social class distance
favoring the suburbs appears to be a distinct barrier to successful annexation efforts by central cities. Cities are more likely to be successful in annexing persons where there is little social differential between city and
suburb.

Three-quarters of the nation's metropolitan areas lie entirely within
single counties. From the standpoint of administration there is much to
be said for *city-county consolidation.* It would make sense administra-
tively to endow county governments with the powers of cities and to organize them to exercise these powers effectively. Yet, important political
problems—problems in the allocation of influence over public decision
making—remain formidable barriers to strong county government.
Central-city interests can be expected to demand representation on
county boards on the basis of population, "one man, one vote," yet sub-

urbanites are likely to fear that consolidation will give city residents a dominant voice in county affairs. Suburbanites may also fear that city-county consolidation may force them to pay higher taxes to help support the higher municipal costs of running the city. Suburbanites may not welcome uniform, countywide policies in taxation or zoning or any number of other policy areas. Suburbanites who have paid for their own wells and septic tanks will hardly welcome the opportunity to help pay for city water or sewer services. Suburbanites with well-established, high-quality public school systems may be unenthusiastic about integrating their schools with city schools in a countywide system, and so on. A variety of policy differences may exist between city and suburb, which will reflect themselves in any attempt to achieve city-county consolidation. Unless these political issues can be resolved in a responsible manner by political leaders who are willing to bargain and compromise, the prospect for city-county consolidation will not be great.

Another serious obstacle to city-county consolidation is that the typical county government organization is still unsuited to administering urban functions. Often the county has limited powers under state law (even more limited than cities); it may have numerous elected officials and a cumbersome and antiquated organization, and it may be unaccustomed to effective and efficient performance of the heavy responsibilities of metropolitan government. Before counties can be granted authority to provide urban services, they will probably have to be reorganized. Perhaps in the long run we may see a slow transfer of functions from the city to the county in those metropolitan areas lying entirely within the single county. Functional consolidation involves the transfer of an activity, such as public health, sewage disposal, or water supply, previously performed by two or more municipal units, to the county level with no change in the general structure of relationships between cities and the county.

One of the more popular approaches to metropolitan integration is the creation of *special districts or authorities* charged with administering a particular function or service on a metropolitan-wide or at least an inter-municipal level, such as a park, sewage, water, parking, airport, planning, other district or authority. Because the special district or authority leaves the social and governmental *status quo* relatively undisturbed, important integrative demands are met with a minimum of resistance with this device. The autonomy of suburban communities is not really threatened, loyalties are not disturbed, political jobs are not lost, and the existing tax structure is left relatively intact. Special districts or authorities may be preferred by suburban political leaders when they believe it will lessen the pressure for annexation by the central city. Special districts or authorities may also be able to incur additional debt after existing units of government have already reached their tax and debt limits. Thus, special districts or authorities may be able to operate in an area wider than that of existing units of governments and at the same time enable governments to evade tax or debt limits in financing a desired public service.

Yet, experience in cities that have relied heavily upon special districts or authorities has suggested that these devices may create as many problems as they solve. Many special districts and authorities are governed by a quasi-independent board or commission, which, once established, becomes largely immune from popular pressures for change. These agencies may be quite independent of other governmental jurisdictions in the metropolis; their concerns might be water, air or water pollution control, city planning, and so on. Remoteness from popular control or close political responsibility often results in the professional administrators of these authorities exercising great power over their particular function. While authorities and special districts are supposed to be non-profit governmental agencies, they often act very much like private enterprises, concentrating their resources on those activities that produce revenue and ignoring equally important non-revenue-producing responsibilities.[20] Independent authorities often borrow money, collect tolls and services charges, and otherwise control their own finances in a manner very much like a private business. While a local government has a clearly defined constituency in a position of ultimately sanctioning the actions of officials, the constituencies of special districts are usually other governmental bureaucracies. The determination of program, budget, and finance for authorities and special districts often follows a complicated and unseen route through executive and legislative branches of a variety of state and local government agencies. The structure of these districts and authorities usually confuse the voters and make it difficult for the average citizen to hold officials of these agencies responsible for their decisions. Moreover, since these special districts and authorities are usually created for a single purpose, they often come to define the public interest in terms of the promotion of their own particular function—recreation, mass transit, water, parks, and so on—without regard for other metropolitan concerns. This "single-mindedness" can lead to competition and conflict between authorities and other governmental agencies in the region. Sooner or later, the problem of coordinating the activities of these independent authorities of special districts arises. Thus, even from the point of view of administrative efficiency, it is not clear whether the special district or authority, with its maze of divided responsibility, in the long run reduces or compounds the problem of governmental coordination in the metropolis.

Perhaps the Port Authority of New York and New Jersey is the largest

20See Wood, *1400 Governments*, Chap. 4.

and best known metropolitan authority in the nation. Established by interstate compact in 1921, the Port Authority is controlled by a twelve-man board, appointed for long overlapping terms by the governors of New Jersey and New York. While the governors have a veto on the actions of the authority and the legislatures of the two states must authorize new undertakings, the authority, nevertheless, has considerable independence. Governors rarely reverse a decision of the authority and legislatures have proved unable to alter substantially policy decisions made by the authority. The Port Authority of New York and New Jersey is a billion-dollar business, which is financially independent and self-sustaining; it operates airports, bridges, piers, tunnels, bus and freight terminals, and a heliport.

Robert C. Wood has characterized the Port Authority as a "metropolitan giant," which is deeply involved with the politics of the New York region but operates more as a private business than as a government responsible to a local constituency:

> Where the institution takes the form of a public corporation, its creation is formally designed to remove the program "from politics," yet political pressures do arise in the informal relations that are established between the corporation's executives and other public officials, influential groups and private individuals. In this instance, the officeholders are not seeking "votes" in the usual sense. More likely they are cultivating "public opinion" in such forms as favorable editorial comment, the assistance of a strategically placed bureaucrat, or the support of an influential civic leader. . . .
>
> As for the public corporations and authorities, their process of collecting revenues closely resembles that of a private corporation. The Port of New York Authority and the Tri-Borough Bridge and Tunnel Authority rely on user charges, fees paid by the individual consumer for their services. The consumer's payment is not always a completely free choice, given the nature of the facilities involved, but neither is it as completely mandatory as the charges imposed by the local special districts concerned with streetlighting, water distribution, public schools and refuse collection. Whatever the consumer's position, his patronage frees the corporations of having to depend upon general tax revenues. Because their activities are self-supporting, their objectives, programs, and operations are likely to be self-determined. Hence, in their behavior they are more closely akin to private enterprise than to other government agencies. . . .[21]

"METRO" GOVERNMENT

The American experience with federalism at the national level has prompted consideration of federated governmental structures for metro-

[21]Wood, *1400 Governments*, pp. 120–22.

politan areas. A "metro" government with authority to make metropolitan-wide policy in selected fields might be combined with local control over functions that are "local" in character. Metropolitan federation, in one form or another and at one time or another, has been proposed for many major metropolitan regions in the nation. Yet, with the exception of Toronto, Miami, and Nashville, proposals for metropolitan federation have been consistently rejected by both voters and political leaders throughout the nation. While metropolitan federation promises many of the advantages of governmental consolidation listed earlier—administrative efficiency, economy of large-scale operation, elimination of financial inequalities, and public accountability for metropolitan-wide policy—it seriously threatens many of the social, political, and psychological values in the existing "fragmented" system of local government in the metropolis. Metropolitan federation also poses a problem discussed earlier, that of deciding what is a "metropolitan" problem. In order to allocate functions to a "metro" government in a federation arrangement, one must first determine what is a metropolitan problem in which all the citizens of the area have a responsibility. Let us examine the metro governments of Toronto, Miami, and Nashville in more detail and then identify sources of political opposition.

It is interesting to note that Toronto's metropolitan federation was *not* adopted by popular referendum in the area, but rather was imposed upon the area by the Province of Ontario.[22] The Municipality of Metropolitan Toronto was created in 1954 by the provincial government, after many years of fruitless negotiations over metropolitan federation between Toronto and its suburbs. The Municipality of Metropolitan Toronto, the new metro government, was given authority over water supply, sewage services, major roads, police, school buildings, metropolitan planning, and mass transit. The Metropolitan government is financed by proportional assessments on the tax of the local governments; these local governments retain their tax-collecting duties. They also retain authority over fire protection, street maintenance, garbage collection, and more importantly, public schools. Metropolitan Toronto is governed by a Metropolitan Council. Representation on the council is not accorded on the basis of population but rather on the basis of equality between cities and suburbs.

Miami's metropolitan experiment, the first in the United States, was approved by popular referendum in the area, but only by a bare majority of 26 percent of Dade County registered voters who voted on May 21,

---

[22]This discussion relies upon Bollens and Schmandt, *The Metropolis*, pp. 477–88; see also Frank Smallwood, *Metro Toronto: A Decade Later* (Toronto: Bureau of Municipal Research, 1963).

1957.[23] They approved a Dade County home rule charter, under which the county government became in effect a metro government. The county government assumed a number of functions performed by the local governments in the metropolitan area, including sewage, water supply, transportation, traffic, central planning, and "those municipal functions which are susceptible to area-wide control." All other municipal powers are reserved to the cities, although the county may set minimum performance standards. Vagueness in the charter over precisely what is an area-wide problem has resulted in a great deal of court litigation over the powers of the metro government. The Miami metro plan included council-manager government for the county, to replace the traditional commission form of county government. The Dade County Commission consisted of five members elected at large; five by districts, and one from each city. Since its beginning, the commission has been badly divided; the first county manager was forced to resign, and controversy and court cases have surrounded the activities of the county. Miami Beach even attempted to secede from the metropolitan federation. Amendments to the charter that would have crippled the powers of the metro government were defeated at the polls by very slim margins. Opponents of metro included the Dade County League of Municipalities, municipal employees, labor unions, several mayors and elected officials, and local chambers of commerce. Metro supporters have been concentrated among Miami's business and political leadership, including the Miami Chamber of Commerce, *The Miami Herald, The Miami News*, the League of Women Voters, and the Dade County legislators.

Edward Sofen explained the narrow victory of the "metro" idea in Miami in the following way:

> Greater Miami is unique in a number of ways; it is warm when almost every other place in the nation is cold—a fact which has attracted a constant influx of migrants from all over the nation ... Miami is almost wholly devoid of strongly organized political factions and strongly organized labor or minority groups. It is generally lacking in organized and consistent community leadership.

> Is there, perhaps, a high correlation between these "negative" or passive factors in the successful emergence of metropolitan government in Miami? The reply to this question must be in the affirmative. This seems certain for the following reasons. Miami with its "every man for himself" type of politics in effect has a no party system and, consequently, was spared the kind of struggle that might have occurred if the fate of political parties

23This discussion relies upon Edward Sofen, *The Miami Metropolitan Experiment* (Bloomington: University of Indiana Press, 1963); and Edward Sofen, "The Politics of Metropolitan Leadership: The Miami Experience," *Midwest Journal of Political Science*, 5 (February 1961), 18–38.

had turned on the outcome of the move to create a metropolitan government. By contrast, certain other metropolitan areas, such as Cuyahoga
County in the Cleveland area, with its more formal party structure, have
reflected sharp divisions between the parties, as well as within the parties
on the issue of metropolitanization. Metropolitan government has been
rejected there.[24]

In short, Sofen seems to believe that the newspapers and the good-
government forces were able to prevail in Miami because of the heavy
influx of "newcomers" and the absence of strongly entrenched parties
or powerful interest groups.

In 1962 the voters of Nashville and Davidson County, Tennessee, approved a metro charter which consolidated the city and the county.[25] Following the defeat of a 1958 consolidation proposal, in which city residents voted three to two in favor of consolidation and suburban residents
voted three to two against it, the city of Nashville undertook a very aggressive annexation program in which suburban residents and industries were
incorporated into the city without a referendum and probably against
their will. Voter approval of the Nashville metro charter is a product
of unique and interesting political circumstances in that area. Nashville
politics was dominated by Mayor Ben West, an ardent champion of
urban causes including reapportionment, urban renewal, and federal
and state aid in cities. He headed a strong political organization which
was reputedly maintained by the use of patronage. Like many city bosses,
West was disliked and distrusted by newspapers, businessmen, and suburbanites. The *Nashville Tennesseean,* long a political foe of Mayor
West, portrayed the annexation as an assault on county residents and
began a campaign to convince them that metro government would protect them from the evils of the West administration in the city. Unlike
1958 when West supported metro government and it was presented to
suburbanites as a city program, in 1962 it was presented as a means to
abolish the city and eliminate Mayor Ben West! The city also passed
an ordinance levying a ten-dollar tax on all automobiles using the streets
of Nashville for thirty days or more. This "green sticker law" raised a
storm of protest among suburbanites as "taxation without representation," a storm that reached hurricane proportions when Mayor West
ordered the police to arrest and jail suburbanites whose cars were found
on the streets of Nashville without green stickers. Thus, prometro forces
were able to present metropolitan government to suburbanites as an
anticity proposal, which would cripple the city political machine and pro-

[24]Sofen, "Problems of Metropolitan Leadership," p. 20.
[25]This discussion relies upon Brett W. Hawkins, *Nashville Metro* (Nashville: University of Vanderbilt Press, 1966); and Brett W. Hawkins, "Public Opinion and
Metropolitan Reorganization in Nashville," *Journal of Politics,* 28 (May 1966), 408–18.

tect the suburbs from the green sticker tax and the threat of annexation.

While opposition to the 1958 proposal had come from the suburban and quasi-rural areas of Davidson County, opposition in 1962 was led by Mayor West, city councilmen, and city employees. Metro's proponents relied on a newspaper campaign to stigmatize the governmental *status quo* and to personalize the issue by attacking Mayor West. Metro's opponents hoped to use the well-oiled West political organization to obtain an overwhelming *no* vote in the city. They counted on a heavy *no* vote from the city's blacks, who feared a dilution of their influence in a metropolitanwide government. Lining up behind metro were the city's businessmen, the chamber of commerce, the League of Women Voters, the *Nashville Tennesseean*, the Tennessee Taxpayers Association, the Citizens Committee for Better Government, and many suburban jaycee and civic clubs. In addition to the mayor, city employees, particularly firemen and policemen, and the Davidson County Democratic party, opposition to metro was expressed by many labor and black leaders in the city. The metro charter passed by a vote of 57 percent in the suburbs and 56 percent in the cities.

Professor Brett W. Hawkins in an interesting study, *Nashville Metro*, has analyzed the politics of successful metropolitan consolidation. He concludes that the political circumstances surrounding the adoption of Nashville metro were unlike those in other areas:

> Certainly the annexation of 85,000 county residents helped metro's proponents to put the issue on a personal, barely relevant, nonrational basis —namely for or against Mayor West. The insertion of a "devil," moreover, simplified the task of selling a highly complicated government organization. It is certainly true, in any case, that the circumstances which pertained to Nashville from 1958–1962 have not been common to proposals for governmental reorganization in metropolitan areas. This in turn lends some support to Robert C. Wood's proposition that "program expansion of urban governments" not initiated from without the system, nor by highly mobilized elite groups is random—"the result of accident, not design."[26]

The voting returns in the Nashville metro referendum clearly suggest that the aggressive, if not hostile, behavior of the city toward its suburbs, contributed significantly, if not decisively, to the victory of metropolitan government. Voters who had been recently annexed to the city, that is, voters who had been most recently the victims of city "aggression," were most heavily in favor of reorganization. The second highest vote for reorganization came from voters in the unincorporated suburban areas, those who may have felt the greatest threat of further annexations. Incorporated

[26]Hawkins, "Public Opinion and Metropolitan Reorganization," p. 418.

suburbs and rural areas voted against reorganization, even though it was presented as an anticity proposal. No doubt the voters in these areas are just as "anticity" as other suburbanites, but apparently they did not feel any immediate threat from the city. In the old city, it appears that entrenched political organizations carried the day with an assist from black voters in turning out a substantial *no* vote on reorganization. The Hawkins research also indicated that voters who anticipate higher taxes with reorganization are more likely to oppose it than those who do not, that voters who are dissatisfied with public services are more likely to support reorganization than those who are not, that less-knowledgeable voters are more likely to oppose reorganization than more-knowledgeable voters.

The important lesson in the success of the Nashville metro is that it succeeded *not* because of an absence of city-suburban conflict, but because many suburbanites and others who were hostile to the city administration perceived metro government as a means of attacking the city. A metro proposal, which failed when it was presented as a reform, economy, and efficiency proposal, was later successful when it was presented as a political proposal.

BARGAINING AND METROPOLITAN DECISION MAKING

Since conflict, rather than coordination, characterizes many of the relations between city and suburb, it seems reasonable to use a decision-making technique—bargaining—which is especially designed for conflict situations. Bargaining is made possible by the fact that conflict between city and suburbs, or even among suburbs, is necessarily of the "non-zero sum" type; that is, a gain for the city is not necessarily a loss for the suburbs, and vice versa.

Bargaining can be used in many different types of cooperative efforts in metropolitan governments. Cooperation may take the form of *informal*, verbal understandings, or 'gentlemen's agreements," which might involve for example, the exchange of information on cases between welfare departments or cooperation among police departments in the apprehension of a lawbreaker, or an agreement among local fire departments to come to the assistance of each other in the event of a major fire. Cooperation may result in *formal*, interjurisdictional agreements among governments, perhaps to build and operate a major facility, such as a garbage incinerator or a sewage treatment plant. Interjurisdictional agreements may provide for (1) one government performing a service or providing a facility for one or more other governments on a contractual basis; (2)

two or more governments performing a function jointly or operating a facility on a joint basis; or (3) two or more local governments agreeing to assist and supply mutual aid to each other in emergency situations.

One of the attractions of interjurisdictional agreements is that they provides a means for dealing with metropolitan problems on a voluntary basis while retaining local determination and control. Interjurisdictional agreements do not threaten the existence of communities or governments. They do not threaten the jobs of incumbent public officials. Yet at the same time they enable governments to achieve the economies and provide the specialized services that only a larger jurisdiction can make possible.

Apparently, most metropolitan areas have developed a complex network of interjurisdictional relationships.[27] Cooperative arrangements embrace a broad sweep of local services and facilities, including airports, jails and other public buildings, fire protection, public health, law enforcement, library services, recreation, planning, refuse disposal, road maintenance, sewage disposal, tax assessment and collection, welfare activities, and water supply. Many suburban communities have been able to reach agreement on the creation of joint school districts. Often central cities, which are locked in bitter combat with their suburbs over annexation, are still able to negotiate agreements with these same suburbs for water supply, sewage disposal, or fire protection. County governments have often negotiated agreements with one or more of their municipalities, in which the county government provides the tax-collecting and assessment services, ambulance services, fire protection, street maintenance, and so on, all on a contractual basis. Of course, interjurisdictional agreements may be ended or renegotiated by the participating governments from time to time. These agreements are not necessarily permanent, and they depend upon the voluntary participation of the governments involved; this is both a weakness and a strength of the interjurisdictional agreement.

Interjurisdictional agreements are not a "cure-all" for the problems in the metropolis. Often communities are unable to reach agreement with each other on common problems because of social, partisan, or policy differences. An interesting study of the pattern of interjurisdictional agreements in the Philadelphia metropolitan area revealed that agreements were influenced by social and economic differences between communities.[28] Adjacent communities similar to each other in social composition, party affiliation, and wealth were much more likely to negotiate

[27]See Bollens and Schmandt, *The Metropolis*, pp. 379–80.
[28]Thomas R. Dye, Oliver P. Williams, Harold Herman, and Charles Liebman, "Differentiation and Cooperation in a Metropolitan Area," *Midwest Journal of Political Science*, 7 (May 1963), 145–55.

interjurisdictional agreements than dissimilar adjacent communities. Social, economic, and partisan differences between adjacent communities
were particularly influential factors in the decision to create a joint
school district. Socially dissimilar communities are not likely to reach
agreement on a joint school district, but social differences were not quite
so important in the negotiation of police radio agreements.

Metropolitan councils of governments are another form of cooperation in metropolitan areas. Metropolitan councils are voluntary associations of governments or government officials that provide an opportunity
for study, discussion, and recommendations regarding common metropolitan problems. These metropolitan councils are not governments
themselves; they have no power to implement decisions but must rely
instead upon voluntary compliance by member governments. Metropolitan councils provide an arena where elected heads of metropolitan governments can come together regularly, discuss problems, make recommendations, and hopefully coordinate their actvities. Metropolitan
councils are in operation in Detroit (Supervisors Inter-County Committee),
Washington, D.C., (Metropolitan Washington Council of Governments),
New York (Metropolitan Regional Council), Philadelphia (Regional Conference of Elected Officials), Seattle (Puget Sound Government Conference),
Salem, Oregon (Mid-Willamette Valley Council of Governments), and
San Francisco (Association of Bay Area Governments). Generally, metropolitan councils strive for unity in their decisions and recommendations, because their recommendations must be acted upon by member
governments, who are unlikely to implement proposals they oppose.
The result, for the most part, is that studies and recommendations of
metropolitan councils are likely to be rather bland in character. It is
very difficult for these councils to deal with the really divisive issues
in the metropolis. Since councils have no authority to act upon metropolitan problems, they may be, in the words of Bollens and Schmandt, a
"toothless tiger or—even worse—a protector of the inadequate status
quo."[29]

[29]*Ibid.*, p. 392. See Thomas M. Scott, "Metropolitan Governmental Reorganization
Proposals," *Western Political Quarterly*, 21 (June 1968), 252–61; and Advisory Commission on Intergovernmental Relations, *Factors Affecting Voter Reactions to Governmental Reorganization* (Washington, D.C.: Government Printing Office, 1962).

TWELVE

Community
Power Structures

MODELS OF COMMUNITY POWER

Who runs this town? Do the elected public officials actually make the important decisions? Or is there a "power structure" in this community that really runs things? If so, who is in the power structure? Are public officials "errand boys" who carry out the orders of powerful men who operate "behind the scenes"? Or are community affairs decided by democratically elected officials acting openly in response to the wishes of many different individuals and groups? Is city government of the people, by the people, and for the people? Or is it a government run by a small "elite," with the "masses" of people largely apathetic and uninfluential in public affairs? Do people who make the important decisions in business and finance also make the important decisions in urban renewal, public works, education, taxation, public charity, land development, and so on? Or are there different groups of people making decisions in each of these areas, with little or no overlap except for elected officials?

Social scientists have differed over the answers to these questions. Some social scientists, whom we shall refer to as "elitists," believe that power in American communities is concentrated in the hands of relatively few people, usually top business and financial leaders. They believe that this "elite" is subject to relatively little influence from the "masses" of people. Other social scientists, whom we shall refer to as "pluralists," believe that power is widely shared in American communities among many leadership groups, who represent segments of the community and who are held responsible by the people through elections and group participation. Interestingly, both elitists and pluralists seem to agree that decisions are made by small minorities in the community. The idea of direct, individual citizen participation in decision making has suffered with the coming of organizational society and high levels of urbanization and industrialization. Elitists describe a more monolithic structure of power, with a single leadership group making decisions on a variety of issues, while pluralists describe a polycentric structure of power, with different elite groups active in different issues and a great deal of competition, bargaining, and sharing of power among elites.

Let us summarize the points of conflict between elitist and pluralist models of community power. These points have been distilled from a large body of rapidly expanding literature on community power,[1] and they can provide us with a framework for further discussion.

Elitist thinking about community power includes the following ideas.

1. Power stems from roles within the social system of the community. Political power is inextricably bound together with social and economic power. Men of wealth and social position in the community will also be men of power.

2. Power is "structured"—that is, power relationships tend to persist over time. Issues and elections may come and go, but the same men will continue to exercise power in the community.

3. There is a reasonably clear and persistent distinction over time between those who exercise power (elite) and those who do not (mass).

4. This distinction is based primarily upon the unequal distribution of control over economic resources in the community. Business and financial leaders will compose the major part of the "elite." Elected public officials are largely "errand boys" who knowingly or unknowingly respond to the wishes of the dominant economic elite.

5. The elite constitutes a very small proportion of the people in the

---

[1]This literature is becoming so voluminous that it seems appropriate to cite only some of the major summary pieces: Thomas J. Anton, "Power, Pluralism, and Local Politics," *Administrative Science Quarterly*, 7 (March 1963), 425–57; Lawrence Herson, "In the Footsteps of Community Power," *American Political Science Review*, 55 (December 1961), 817–31; Peter Bachrach and Morton S. Baratz, "Two Faces of Power," *American Political Science Review*, 56 (December 1962), 947–53; Herbert Kaufman and Victor Jones, "The Mystery of Power," *Public Administration Review*, 14 (Summer 1954), 205–12; Nelson Polsby, *Community Power and Political Theory*, (New Haven: Yale University Press, 1963); Robert Presthus, *Men at the Top* (New York: Oxford University Press, Inc., 1964); Robert Dahl, *Who Governs?* (New Haven: Yale University Press, 1961); Floyd Hunter, *Community Power Structure* (Chapel Hill: The University of North Carolina Press, 1953); Robert Agger, Daniel Goldrich, and Burt Swanson, *The Rulers and the Ruled* (New York: John Wiley & Sons, Inc., 1965); other citations are given in footnotes below.

community. They are not typical or representative of the people of the community in income, education, occupation, or ethnic background. They have higher incomes, better educations, and more prestigious occupations than the "masses" and they come from the culturally dominant ethnic group in America—the white Anglo-Saxon Protestants.

6.　There is considerable convergence of power at the "top" of the political system. A diagram of community power would take the shape of a pyramid.

7.　Persons in the elite may disagree from time to time, but they share a certain commonality of interests, particularly in support of the basic values that underlie the social system itself.

8.　The elite is subject to relatively little influence from the masses, even through elections or any other form of political activity. The masses are largely misinformed and apathetic, if not completely alienated, from the community's political system. Of course, the elite is usually benevolent and does not oppress the masses because of a sense of "high-mindedness" and "civic responsibility" and the need to avoid violence and revolution.

In contrast, pluralist thinking involves the following notions.

1.　Power is an attribute of individuals in their relationship with other individuals in the process of decision making. An individual has power to the extent that he can get another individual to do something he would not otherwise do, regardless of social positions.

2.　Power relationships do not necessarily persist over time. They are formed for a particular decision, and after this decision is made, they disappear, to be replaced by a different set of power relationships when the next decision is made.

3.　There is no permanent distinction between "elites" and "masses." Individuals who participate in decisions at one pont in time are not necessarily the same individuals who participate at some other time. Many individuals have the *opportunity* to exercise power, whether they choose to do so or not.

4.　The distinction between those who participate in a decision and those who do not is based primarily upon the level of interest people have in that particular decision. Individuals can move in and out of the ranks of decision making, simply by becoming active or inactive in politics. Men of wealth and social position are often defeated on community issues by active, skillful leaders who win popular support.

5.　Leadership is fluid and mobile. Access to decision making is based primarily upon acquiring the skills of leadership—information about issues, knowledge about democratic processes, skill, organization, and public relations, and so on. Wealth is an asset in politics, but it is only one of many kinds of assets.

6.　There are multiple centers and bases of power within a community. Persons who exercise power in some kinds of decisions do not necessarily exercise power in other kinds of decisions. No single elite dominates decision making in all issue areas.

7. There is considerable competition among leaders. Community leaders are not united by any common interest. They seek many divergent policies. Community policy also represents bargains or compromises reached between competing leadership groups.

8. Individuals can participate and make their views felt, through their membership in organizations of many kinds. Elections are also important instruments of mass participation in political decisions. Leaders are constantly concerned with public opinion and often refer to it in decision making. Nonparticipation in elections or community affairs may be a product of popular satisfaction with the conduct of leaders.

While these statements describe "ideal" models of elite and pluralist communities, most "real" world communities will probably fall somewhere in between—that is, along a continuum from the monolithic elite model of power to a diffused and polycentric pluralist model. Many social scientists are neither confirmed "elitists" nor "pluralists," but they are aware that different structures and power may exist in different communities. Yet these ideal models of community power may be helpful in understanding the different ways in which community power can be structured. Later we shall suggest some social, economic, and political conditions that may be associated with elite or pluralist power configurations in American communities.

THE ELITE MODEL OF COMMUNITY POWER

European social theory has long been at odds with democratic political writers about the existence and necessity of elites. Gaetano Mosca, in his book *The Ruling Class,* wrote, "In all societies . . . two classes of people appear—a class that rules and a class that is ruled."[2] For Mosca, elitism is explained by the nature of social organization. Organization inevitably results in the concentration of political power in the hands of a few. Organized power cannot be resisted by an unorganized majority in which each individual ". . . stands alone before the totality of the organized minority. A hundred men acting uniformly in concert, with a common understanding, will triumph over a thousand men who are not in accord and can therefore be dealt with one by one."[3] Since organized power will prevail over individual effort in politics, sooner or later, organizations

[2]Gaetano Mosca, *The Ruling Class* (New York: McGraw-Hill Book Company, 1939), p. 50.
[3]*Ibid.,* p. 51.

will come to be the more important actors in political life. And organizations cannot function without leaders. In Robert Michels's words, "He who says organization, says oligarchy."[4] The masses are permanently incapable of running or controlling political organizations. They must cede that power to active, expert, and interested leadership groups. The idea that economic elites will tend to dominate in politics is also found in a great deal of social theory. Mosca wrote that the ruling class will possess ". . . some attribute real or apparent which is highly esteemed or very influential in the society in which they live." Needless to say, in a capitalist society, control over business and financial resources generally makes one "highly esteemed and very influential."

One of the earliest studies of American communities, the classic study of Middletown, conducted by Robert and Helen Lynd in the mid-1920s and again in the mid-1930s, tended to confirm a great deal of elitist thinking about community powers.[5] The Lynds found in Muncie, Indiana, a monolithic power structure dominated by the owners of the town's largest industry. Community power was firmly entrenched in the hands of the business class, centering on, but not limited to, the X family. The power of this group was based upon its control over the economic life in the city, particularly its ability to control the extension of credit. The city was run by a "small top group" of "wealthy local manufacturers, bankers, the local head managers of . . . national corporations with units in Middletown, and . . . one or two outstanding lawyers." Democratic procedures and governmental institutions were so much window dressing for business control. The Lynds described the typical city official as a "man of meager calibre" and as "a man whom the inner business control group ignore economically and socially and use politically." Perhaps the most famous quotation from the Lynds' study was a comment by a Middletown man made in 1935:

> "If I'm out of work, I go to the X plant; if I need money I go to the X bank, and if they don't like me I don't get it; my children go to the X college; when I get sick I go to the X hospital; I buy a building lot or house in the X subdivision; my wife goes downtown to buy X milk: I drink X beer, vote for X political parties, and get help from X charities; my boy goes to the X YMCA and my girl to their YWCA; I listen to the word of God in X subsidized churches; if I'm a Mason, I go to the X Masonic temple; I read the news from the X morning paper; and, if I'm rich enough, I travel via the X airport."[6]

[4]Robert Michels, *Political Parties* (Glencoe: The Free Press, 1949).
[5]Robert S. Lynd and Helen M. Lynd, *Middletown* (New York: Harcourt Brace & World, Inc., 1929); and *Middletown in Transition* (New York: Harcourt Brace & World, Inc., 1937).
[6]*Middletown in Transition*, p. 74.

W. Lloyd Warner, a noted sociologist, studied Morris, Illinois, in the 1940s, and he describes a somewhat similar power structure to that encountered by the Lynds in Muncie.[7] About one-third of all the city's workers had jobs in "the mill," which Warner says dominated the town:

> The economic and social force of the mill affects every part of the life of the community. Everyone recognizes its power. Politicians, hat in hand, wait upon Mr. Waddell, manager of The Mill, to find out what he thinks on such important questions as "Shall the tax rate be increased to improve the education our young people are getting?"—"Shall the new minister be Mr. Jones or Mr. Smith?"—"Should the city support various civic and world enterprises?"—"Should new industries enter the town and possibly compete with The Mill for the town's available labor supply?" They want to know what Mr. Waddell thinks. Mr. Waddell usually lets them know.[8]

Sociologist August B. Hollingshead studied the same town (sociologists seem to prefer to disguise the names of towns they are studying: Warner called the town Jonesville while Hollingshead called it Elmtown), and his findings substantially confirmed those of Warner.[9]

One of the most influential studies of community politics was sociologist Floyd Hunter's *Community Power Structure*, a study of Atlanta, Georgia.[10] According to Hunter, no one man or family or business dominated "Regional City" (a synonym for Atlanta), as might be true in a smaller town. Instead, Hunter described several tiers of influentials, with the most important community decisions reserved for a top layer of the business community. Admission to the innermost circle was based primarily on one's position in the business world. These top decision makers were not formally organized but conferred informally and passed down decisions to government leaders, professional personnel, civic organizations, and other "front men." Hunter explained that the top power structure only concerned itself with major policy decisions; there were other substructures—economic, governmental, religious, educational, professional, civic, and cultural—which communicated and implemented the policies at the top levels. These substructures:

> . . . are subordinate, however, to the interests of the policy makers who operate in the economic sphere of community life in Regional City. The institutions of the family, church, state, education, and the like draw

[7]W. Lloyd Warner *et al., Democracy in Jonesville* (New York: Harper & Row, Publishers, 1949).

[8]*Ibid.,* p. 101.

[9]August B. Hollingshead, *Elmtown's Youth* (New York: John Wiley & Sons, Inc., 1949).

[10]Floyd Hunter, *Community Power Structure* (Chapel Hill: University of North Carolina Press, 1953).

sustenance from economic institutional sources and are thereby subordinate to this particular institution more than any other. . . . Within the policy forming groups the economic interests are dominant.[11]

Top power holders seldom operated openly. "Most of the top personnel in the power group are rarely seen in the meetings attended by the associational understructure personnel in Regional City."[12]

Hunter describes the process of community action as follows:

> If a project of major proportions were before the community for consideration—let us say a project aimed at building a new municipal auditorium—a policy committee would be formed. . . . Such a policy committee would more than likely grow out of a series of informal meetings, and it might be related to a project that has been on the discussion agenda of many associations for months or even years. But the time has arrived for action. Money must be raised through private subscription or taxation, a site selected, and contracts let. The time for a policy committee is propitious. The selection of the policy committee will fall largely to the men of power in the community. They will likely be businessmen in one or more of the large business establishments. Mutual choices will be agreed upon for committee membership. In the early stages of policy formulation there will be few men who make basic decisions. . . . Top ranking organizational and institutional personnel will then be selected by the original members to augment their numbers, i.e., the committee will be expanded. Civic associations and the formalized institutions will next be drawn into certain phases of planning and initiation of the projects on a communitywide basis. The newspapers will finally carry stories, the ministers will preach sermons, the associations will hear speeches regarding plans. This rather simply is the process, familiar to many, that goes on in getting any community project underway.[13]

Note that in Hunter's description of community decision making, decisions tend to flow *down* from top policy makers, composed primarily of business and financial leaders, to civic, professional, and cultural association leaders, religious and education leaders, and government officials, who implemented the program; and the masses of people have little direct or indirect participation in the whole process. Policy does not go *up* from associational groupings or from the people themselves. "The top group of the power hierarchy has been isolated and defined as being comprised of policy makers. These men are drawn largely from the businessmen's class in Regional City. They form cliques or 'crowds,' as the term is more often used in the community, which formulate policy. Committees for the formulation of policy are commonplace, and on communitywide issues policy is channeled by a 'fluid committee structure'

[11]*Ibid.*, p. 94.
[12]*Ibid.*, p. 90.
[13]*Ibid.*, pp. 92–93.

down to institutional, associational groupings through a lower level bureaucracy which executes policy."[14] According to Hunter, elected public officials are clearly part of the power-level institutional substructure, which "executes" policy rather than formulates it. Finally Hunter found that this whole power structure is held together by "common interests, mutual obligations, money, habit, delegated responsibilities, and in some cases, by coercion and force.[15]

BUSINESSMEN IN POLITICS—
AN ALTERNATIVE VIEW

While Hunter describes the role of Atlanta's business elite as one of top policy making, a study of businessmen in big-city politics by Peter B. Clark suggests that businessmen are used as prestigious "front men" for policies initiated by civic associations and governmental agencies.[16] Clark argues that big businessmen themselves almost never think up or suggest proposals. Rather, ideas for community action generally come from the professional staffs of various community organizations, for example, a professional hospital director, a civic association staff worker, the newspaper's city editor, or the heads of governmental agencies. Once an idea has been generated at the professional staff level, the next stage is to seek out top businessmen to lend their prestige to the project. As one enthusiastic staff man put it:

> "I've got a project now. One of the greatest things we can do for the central area. . . . I am not doing it alone. . . . I am sitting with it until I can present it to the proper man to handle it as *his* idea. I think so much of it that I've got to find the right guy to take credit for it. . . . The man I'm going to pick has to be president of his club . . . head of his business. That's 50, 70 percent of the success of the project."[17]

A proposal's presentation to the public and submission to city government for ratification is the third stage in policy making. If the proposal has been well thought out in advance by the professional staff, and has the support and public backing of prominent businessmen, this final stage may be a mere formality. Only if organized opposition has developed in some influential segment of the community, and this opposition

14*Ibid.*, p. 113.
15*Ibid.*
16Peter B. Clark, "Civic Leadership: The Symbols of Legitimacy," paper delivered at the 1960 Annual Meeting of the American Political Science Association, New York, September 1960; see also Peter B. Clark, *The Businessman as a Civic Leader* (Glencoe: The Free Press, 1964).
17Clark, "Civic Leadership," p. 4.

also has the support of some businessmen, will the mayor and council be faced with an important decision.

Business support for community projects is thought to be essential for several reasons. First of all, business support bestows great prestige on a proposal. The low prestige of municipal officials helps to explain why businessmen are needed to help put across any major community project. Moreover, middle-class people, whose vote is relatively more important in local than in state or national politics, tend to respect the views of businessmen more than the views of city officials. Peter Clark supplies a quotation from a Chicago attorney who had long been involved in civic affairs:

> "By and large, those with strong business backgrounds command greater respect . . . than those with the same skills who don't have that background. And the same is true of a lawyer versus the president of General Motors. They both could say the same thing . . . but the president would be listened to more. They transfer part of their business achievement into their public life."[18]

The views of businessmen are respected in part because the community's economic growth and continued prosperity are linked to business firms and the men who head them. Any suggestion from these men that a particular proposal might "hurt business" or "slow down the economy" must be taken seriously by a community that depends upon these businessmen for employment. Only occasionally will a business firm be required to issue a direct threat to the community that it will close down and move elsewhere in order to get its way in policy matters. While direct public threats like this are not infrequent, businessmen prefer to rely more on subtle hints that a particular policy might hurt the growth of business and employment. Business support is also sought to lend a "conservative" image to community proposals. Businessmen are expected to be sound guardians of the *status quo*. They are expected to oppose "radical," sweeping changes in governmental structure, tax programs, public services, and so on. Thus, the endorsement by these conservatives of any new program helps to assure the community that it does not represent any radical break with the past. For this reason, too, the support of businessmen from older established firms is often more valued than the support of businessmen from newer firms in the community.

In addition to considerations of respect and prestige, business support is also sought because so many community projects require financial investment—public works, urban renewal, schools, streets, auditoriums, hospitals, and so on—and banks and investment firms must be called in to

[18]*Ibid.*, p. 6.

underwrite the bond issues. Businessmen also have technical information which local governments, normally operating without much professional staff, cannot themselves provide. Finally, business support is often sought to disarm potentially influential businessmen who might provide opposition to a proposal if they were not consulted about it in its earliest stages.

In short, Clark's argument is that businessmen do not initiate policy proposals, but business support is essential to their success. This means that big businessmen have a potential or actual veto over policy proposals. According to Clark, a businessman's power comes from his ability to grant or withhold the approval that others seek: "It is his capacity to withhold his approval and participation—even if participation means only his name on a letterhead—that constitutes the most significant basis of the big businessman's potential veto."[19]

Business support is especially vital on proposals involving great change in the community—programs like metropolitan area government, urban renewal, public housing, freeway construction, and other massive public works involving bond issues, condemnation of properties, increased tax burdens, and so on. The highest-ranking businessmen in the community are needed for these kinds of undertakings. More routine governmental decisions—school, water, and park systems, for example—usually require less business support. The businessmen associated with these activities may come from smaller firms or the vice-presidential level of larger firms.

The influence of businessmen can be felt even in matters in which they are not directly involved. Many government officials and civic organization workers admit that they anticipate the views of big businessmen in policy decisions even when businessmen are not directly consulted. Clark quotes a civic staff man who explained why a particular community project failed: "This thing wasn't done right. It was just announced. The power structure and the newspaper people weren't checked out. All hell broke loose."[20] Another staff man revealed both his style and his motives when he said: "My method of operation is to touch base early before I raise a question. I do my homework thoroughly to get the controversy out of it. Either revise it or throw it out. I have never proposed anything that hasn't been accepted. I don't want to propose anything that would fail."[21]

Big businessmen are not equally powerful in all cities. Nor are they equally powerful in all issues. Endorsement by big businessmen does not always guarantee success. It is not quite clear whether businessmen are "using" public officials to achieve the goals of business, or whether public

19 *Ibid.*, p. 10.
20 *Ibid.*, p. 11.
21 *Ibid.*

officials are "using" business leaders to achieve their political goals. Mayor David Lawrence of Pittsburgh seldom undertook a major city project without the support of Richard K. Mellon, president of the Mellon Bank and chairman of the Allegheny Conference on Community Development, a small group of top business leaders concerned with Pittsburgh's economy. Pittsburgh's dramatic "renaissance" of the 1950s was engineered and financed by the "Mellon Group," so much so that some commentators referred to Pittsburgh as "Mellon town." The Mellon Group "used" the Lawrence administration to accomplish Pittsburgh's redevelopment. On the other hand, it could be said that Mayor Lawrence "used" the Mellon Group to help make his administration the most successful in the city's history. Lawrence was elected to four consecutive four-year terms as mayor, an unprecedented accomplishment itself, and then was elected governor of Pennsylvania; these political successes could largely be attributed to the dramatic renaissance of the city, for which Lawrence took much of the credit.

Several studies have suggested interesting variations on the power elite model. Robert O. Schultze's study of Cibola (Ypsilanti, Michigan) describes shifts in the power structure in that community, resulting from the town's integration into a "national" economy and the appearance of absentee ownership and a new managerial class in the power structure.[22] Schultze contends that in an earlier era of the town's history, locally owned industries dominated the political and economic life of the community. But as local industrialists were replaced by the managers of large national absentee-owned corporations, the power structure became less concentrated. The managers of Cibola's plants had great potential for power within the community, but they were preoccupied with their relationships to their national firms and tended to neglect community affairs. The result was that political power came to rest in the hands of a group of middle-class, local professionals and small businessmen. Delbert C. Miller described the power structure of Pacific City (Seattle, Washington) and compared it with an English city of comparable size.[23] His thesis is that power is related to whatever is highly valued by the community. Where the American power structure is largely business dominated and employs government merely to ratify its decisions, the English power structure showed less business domination and greater deference

[22]Robert O. Schultze, "The Role of Economic Dominants in Community Power Structure," *American Sociological Review*, 23 (February 1958), 3–9; see also Robert O. Schultze, "The Bifurcation of Power in a Satellite Community," *Community Political Systems*, ed. Morris Janowitz (Glencoe: The Free Press, 1961).

[23]Delbert C. Miller, "Industry and Community Power Structure," *American Sociological Review*, 23 (February 1958), 9–15; and "Decision-Making Cliques in Community Power Structures," *American Journal of Sociology*, 64 (November 1958), 299–310.

to intellectuals and public officials, who have more prestige in the English community. Miller's model of community power includes a layering of influential persons, distinguishing between "potential influentials" and "key influentials." The key influentials actually took part in community decision making, while potential influentials could have done so but did not.

Belief in the elite model of community power is widespread. In an opinion poll about community power in the Philadelphia metropolitan area, approximately three-fourths of the respondents perceived community decision making in an essentially elitist fashion.[24] In response to the question, "In your judgment, do you feel that the big community decisions tend to be made by the same small crowd of people or do these people change according to the issue confronting the community?" residents overwhelmingly responded that the "same small crowd" made all the decisions. In response to the question, "Are important issues usually quietly solved without the public knowing what they are or are they usually brought out into the open?" a majority of respondents believed that most issues were resolved privately. Respondents were more or less equally divided over whether or not community decision makers acted in a socially responsible manner. The question was, "Do you feel that the people involved in making decisions have a broad sense of community responsibility or are they more concerned with protecting or furthering their own interest?" Interestingly, when elected public officials were asked the same questions, they responded in a completely different fashion from their constituents. Elected public officials did not feel that "the same small crowd" decided things but instead adopted the pluralist view that decision makers changed according to the issues confronting the community. They strongly asserted that decisions were made openly and that decision makers were motivated by a broad sense of community responsibility. There is also evidence to suggest that elitist and pluralist images of community power are related to socioeconomic status. Well-educated, prestigiously employed, high-income respondents tend to view community power in a pluralist fashion and have much more favorable attitudes toward decision makers. In contrast, poorly educated, low-income respondents are much more likely to see "a small clique" running things and to have unfavorable attitudes toward decision makers.[25]

[24]Thomas R. Dye, "Popular Images of Decision-Making," *Sociology and Social Research*, 47 (October 1962), 75–83.

[25]See also John Haer, "Social Stratification in Relation to Attitudes toward Sources of Power," *Social Forces*, 35 (December 1956), 137–42.

THE PLURALIST MODEL
OF COMMUNITY POWER

Political science had largely ignored the study of community power prior to the publication of Floyd Hunter's *Community Power Structure*. While sociologists had been developing an important body of literature on community power even before the Lynds' safari to darkest Indiana in the 1920s, community politics remained a "lost world" for political scientists.[26] Political science had been preoccupied with the municipal reform movement, the structure of local government, and the administrative problems of economy and efficiency; they had largely ignored informal structures of power and decision making. Hunter's findings were very discomforting. They suggested that in reality American communities were not governed very democratically. Hunter's research challenged the notion of popular participation in "grass-roots" democracy and raised doubts as to whether or not the cherished values of Jeffersonian democracy were being realized in community life. While admitting that "none of us [political scientists] has moved in with such a structure in dynamics of power in a metropolitan community," political scientists Herbert Kaufman and Victor Jones were willing to assert on the basis of their own "administrative experience" that Hunter's study was "at best . . . incomplete; at worst . . . invalid."[27] These political scientists believed that much more competition, access, equality, and popular participation occurred in community politics than the work of the Lynds, Warner, Hollingshead, Hunter, and others implied.

Modern pluralism does not mean a commitment to "pure democracy," where all citizens participate directly in decision making. The underlying value of individual dignity continues to motivate contemporary pluralist thought, but it is generally recognized that the town-meeting type of pure democracy is not really possible in an urban industrial society. The modern pluralist is aware of the rise of giant industrial and financial organizations and the threat they pose to individual liberty. (Historically, liberals perceived the threat to individual liberty to be the concentration of government power; but after the Industrial Revolution, liberals became more concerned with business power and often turned to the government to protect individual rights.) But it is the hope of modern

---

[26]See Lawrence J. R. Herson, "The Lost World of Municipal Government," *American Political Science Review*, 51 (June 1957), 330–45.
[27]Kaufman and Jones, "The Mystery of Power," pp. 205–12.

pluralists that "countervailing" centers of power can help to offset corporate power and protect the interests of the individual. Hopefully competition between big business, big labor, and big government will keep each interest from abusing its power. Pluralism accepts strong government as protection against economic dominance. Likewise pluralism accepts the growing importance of organized group activity in politics, since it is recognized that the unorganized individual is no match for industrial bureaucracies. A central value in liberal political thought has always been individual participation in decision making. Historically, this meant voting, interest and activity in public affairs, information about public issues, and knowledge about democratic procedures, on the part of individuals. But to modern pluralists, individual participation has come to mean membership in organized groups. In an age of organization, meaningful participation and decision making are said to take place through the individual's membership in groups that make their influence felt in decision making. Interest groups become the means by which individuals gain access to the political system. Government is held responsible not directly by individuals, but by organized interest groups and political parties. Pluralists believe that competition between parties and organized groups, representing the interests of their citizen members, can protect the dignity of the individual and offer a viable alternative to individual participation in decision making.

The pluralist model of community power stresses the fragmentation of authority, the influence of elected public officials, the importance of organized group activity, and the role of public opinion and elections in determining public policy. Who rules in the pluralist community? "Different small groups of interested and active citizens in different issue areas with some overlap, if any, by public officials, and occasional intervention by a large number of people at the polls."[28] Citizen influence is felt not only through organized group activity but also through leaders anticipating the reactions of citizens and endeavoring to satisfy their demands. In addition, to the elected public officials, leadership in community affairs is exercised by interested individuals and groups, who confine their participation to one or two issue areas. What are leaders? "Leaders are activists. More precisely they are the most active activists."[29] The pluralist model sees interest and activity rather than economic resources as the key to leadership. Competition, fluidity, access, and equality characterize community politics.

Perhaps the most influential of the pluralist community studies was Robert A. Dahl's *Who Governs?*, a detailed analysis of decision making

[28]Aaron Wildavsky, *Leadership in a Small Town* (Totowa, N.J.: Bedminster Press, 1964), p. 8.
[29]*Ibid.*, p. 282.

in New Haven, Connecticut. Dahl chose to examine sixteen major decisions on redevelopment and public education in New Haven and on nominations for mayor in both political parties for seven elections. Dahl found a polycentric and dispersed system of community power in New Haven, in contrast to Hunter's highly monolithic and centralized power structure. Influence was exercised from time to time by many individuals, each exercising power over some issue but not over others. When the issue was one of urban renewal, one set of individuals was influential; in public education, a different group of leaders were involved. Business elites, who were said by Hunter to control Atlanta, were only one of many different influential groups in New Haven. According to Dahl, "The Economic notables far from being a ruling group, are simply one of many groups out of which individuals sporadically emerge to influence the politics and acts of city officials. Almost anything one might say about the influence of the economic notables could be said with equal justice about a half dozen other groups in the New Haven community."[30] The mayor of New Haven was the only decision maker who was influential in most of the issue areas studied, and his degree of influence varied from issue to issue. "The mayor was not at the peak of a pyramid but at the center of intersecting circles. He rarely commanded. He negotiated, cajoled, exhorted, beguiled, charmed, pressed, appealed, reasoned, promised, insisted, demanded, even threatened; but he most needed support and acquiescence from other leaders who simply could not be commanded. Because he could not command them, he had to bargain."[31]

Aaron Wildavsky's study of Oberlin, Ohio, revealed, if anything, an even more pluralist structure of decision making than Dahl found in New Haven.[32] Wildavsky's study of Oberlin was a reaffirmation of small-town democracy, for in Oberlin, "The roads to influence . . . are more than one; elites and non-elites can travel them, and the toll can be paid with energy and initiative as well as wealth."[33] Wildavsky studied eleven community decisions in Oberlin, including such diverse issues and events as the determination of municipal water rates, the passage of the fair-housing ordinance, the division of United Appeal funds, and a municipal election. Wildavsky set out to resolve once and for all the dispute between elitists and pluralists:

> If (after examining these issues) we find that the same participants exercise leadership in nearly all significant areas of decision, that they agree, and that they are not responsible to the electorate, we conclude that a

[30]Dahl, *Who Governs?* p. 72.
[31]*Ibid.*, p. 204.
[32]Wildavsky, *Leadership in a Small Town.*
[33]*Ibid.*, p. 214.

power elite rules in Oberlin. . . . If we find that the leaders vary from one issue to another with such overlap as there is between issue areas concentrated largely in the hands of public officials, we must conclude that there is a pluralist system of rule in Oberlin.[34]

Wildavsky found "that a number of citizens and outside participants who exercise leadership in most cases is an infinitesimal part of the community," but no person or group exerted leadership in *all* issue areas. To the extent that overlap among leaders in issue areas existed, this overlap involved public officials—the city manager, the mayor, and the city councilmen—who owed their positions directly or indirectly "to expressions of the democratic process through a free ballot with universal suffrage." In addition to public officials, leadership was exercised by individual "specialists," who confined their participation to one or two issue areas. Leaders very often competed among themselves and did not appear united by any common interest. Persons exercising leadership were of somewhat higher social status than the rest of the community, but it was not status or wealth that distinguished leaders from nonleaders, rather it was their degree of interest and activity in public affairs.

A team of Syracuse University social scientists provided additional support for the pluralist interpretation of community power.[35] They compiled a long list of community decisions in Syracuse and identified individuals who participated formally or informally in these decisions. Not one leadership group, but many, were revealed, each one dealing with issues in a separate field, such as health or education. In summing up the results of this massive study, Frank Munger writes:

> Only three overall conclusions seem warranted by the materials examined. First, the myth that significant decisions in Syracuse emanate from one source does not stand up under close scrutiny. Second, there tend to be as many decision centers as there are important decision areas, which means that the decision making power is fragmented among institutions, agencies, and individuals, which cluster about these areas. Third, in reality, there appear to be many kinds of community power, with one differing from another in so many fundamental ways as to make virtually impossible a meaningful comparison.[36]

In many ways New York City is in a class by itself, not only with regard to size but also in the complexity of its government. New York is simply too big, too diverse, to be dominated by a single family, a single industry,

[34]*Ibid.*, p. 253.

[35]Frank J. Munger, *Decisions in Syracuse* (Bloomington: Indiana University Press, 1961); see also Linton C. Freeman *et al.*, *Metropolitan Decision-Making* (Syracuse: Syracuse University Press, 1962).

[36]*Ibid.*

or even a small group of business and financial leaders. It came as no surprise when Wallace Sayre and Herbert Kaufman in their monumental *Governing New York City* concluded:

> No single ruling elite dominates the political and governmental system of New York City. . . . Most individual decisions are shaped by a small percentage of the city's population—indeed by a small percentage of those who engage actively in politics—because only the participants concerned have the time, energy, skill, and motivation to do much about them. The city government is most accurately visualized as a series of semi-autonomous little worlds, each of which brings forth programs and policies through the interactions of its own inhabitants. . . . New York's huge and diverse system of government and politics is a loose-knit and multicentered network in which decisions are reached by ceaseless bargaining and fluctuating alliances among the major categories of participants in each center, and in which the centers are partially but strikingly isolated from one another.[37]

Edward Banfield's excellent description of decision making in Chicago also fails to reveal a "ruling elite," although the structure of influence is much more centralized than in New York City.[38] But Banfield finds that Mayor Daley's political organization is at the center of Chicago's influence structure, rather than a business or financial elite. According to Banfield: "Civic controversies in Chicago are not generated by the efforts of politicians to win votes, by differences about ideology or group interest, or by the behind-the-scenes efforts of a power elite. They arise, instead, out of the maintenance and enhancement needs of large formal organizations. The heads of an organization see some advantage to be gained by changing the situation. They propose changes. Other large organizations are threatened. They oppose, and a civic controversy takes place."[39] It is not usually business organizations that propose changes but "in most of the cases described here the effective organizations are public ones, and their chief executives are career civil servants." While Banfield acknowledged that business and financial leaders played an important role in Chicago politics, they did not really amount to a ruling elite. After studying seven major decisions in Chicago, Banfield concluded that political heads, such as Mayor Daley, and public agencies and civic associations employed top business leaders to lend prestige and legitimacy to policy proposals. The "top leaders" of Chicago—the Fields, McCormicks, Ryersons, Swifts, and Armours—and the large corporations—Inland Steel, Sears-Roebuck, Field's Department Store, and the

[37]Wallace Sayre and Herbert Kaufman, *Governing New York City*, paperback edition (New York: W. W. Norton & Company, Inc., 1965), pp. 710, 715–16.
[38]Edward Banfield, *Political Influence* (Glencoe: The Free Press, 1961).
[39]*Ibid.*, p. 263.

Chicago Title and Trust Company—were criticized less for interfering in public affairs than for "failing to assume their civic responsiblities." Few of these top leaders participated directly in the decisions studied by Banfield. Banfield admits that this is not proof that the top business leadership did not exercise a great deal of influence behind the scenes. And Banfield acknowledges that the belief in the existence of a ruling elite is widespread in Chicago; he quotes the head of a black civic association as saying: "There are a dozen men in this town who could go into City Hall and order an end to racial violence just like you or I could go into a grocery store and order a loaf of bread. All they would have to do is say what they wanted and they would get it."[40] And Banfield states that top business leaders in Chicago have great "potential for power": "Indeed, if influence is defined as the *ability* to modify behavior in accordance with one's intentions, there could be little doubt that there exist 'top leaders' with aggregate influence sufficient to run the city."[41] However, Banfield maintains that these top leaders do not in fact run the city, for several reasons. First of all, there were many fundamental conflicts of interest and opinion among business leaders. Business leaders do not have sufficient unity of purpose in community politics to decide controversial questions. Second, top business leaders have no effective communication system among themselves which would enable them to act in concert. Third, the top business leaders in Chicago did not have the necessary organization to carry out their plans even if they could agree on what should be done. Banfield concludes: "The notion that 'top leaders' run the city is certainly not supported by the facts of the controversies described in this book. On the contrary, in these cases the richest men of Chicago are conspicuous by their absence. Lesser business figures appear, but they do not act concertedly: some of them are on every side of every issue."[42]

HOW TO STUDY COMMUNITY POWER

Social scientists have used different methods to study community power. To some extent the differences explain the different findings of elitists and pluralists. Sociologists, including the elitists, insist upon studying the entire social structure of the community, and they view power as a by-product of social and economic position. Persons in a position to control the social and economic life of the community are said to have political power whether they exercise it or not. In contrast, pluralists define power

[40]*Ibid.*, p. 289.
[41]*Ibid.*, p. 290.
[42]*Ibid.*, p. 288.

as participation in decision making. Persons are said to have power only when they participate directly in a particular community decision. Pluralists object to the presupposition that people with control over the local and economic resources are necessarily in positions of power:

> . . . nothing categorical can be assumed about power in any community. . . . If anything, there seems to be an unspoken notion among pluralist researchers that at bottom nobody dominates in a town, so that their first question is not likely to be, "Who runs this community?," but rather, "Does anyone at all run this community?" The first query is somewhat like, "Have you stopped beating your wife?," in that virtually any response short of total unwillingness to answer will supply the researchers with a "power elite" along the lines presupposed by the stratification theory.[43]

The pluralists also object to the presupposition that power relations persist:

> Pluralists hold that power may be tied to issues, and issues can be fleeting or persistent, provoking coalitions among interested groups and citizens, ranging in their duration from momentary to semi-permanent. . . . To presume that the set of coalitions which exists in the community at any given time is a timelessly stable aspect of social structure is to introduce systematic inaccuracies into one's description of social reality.[44]

The pluralist also attacks the use of certain sociological methods in community research. According to the pluralists, the interview technique, which was at the heart of Hunter's work, inquired about the *reputation* of power rather than about the *reality* of power.[45] By asking people what they thought about power distributions in the community, Hunter was at best only conducting a public-opinion poll about power. Hunter was asking about beliefs and reputations; he paid little attention to actual behavior, preferring instead to rely on the ranking of knowledgeable people about how much power other people possessed.

Moreover, Hunter's concern for social structure, the persistence through time of power relations, led him to phrase his questions about influence and leadership in general terms rather than to tie them to particular issues or decisions. For example, both Hunter and Schultze asked the following question:

[43]Nelson Polsby, "How to Study Community Power: The Pluralist Alternative," *Journal of Politics*, 21 (1960), 476.
[44]*Ibid.*, 478–79.
[45]Raymond E. Wolfinger, "Reputation and Reality in the Study of Community Power," *American Sociological Review*, 25 (1960), 636–44.

Suppose a major project were before the community, one that required decision by a group of leaders whom nearly everyone would accept. Which persons would you choose to make up this group—regardless of whether or not you know them personally?

Hunter asked very bluntly: "Who is the biggest man in town," But pluralists argued that general power rankings can be misleading:

> Most of the reputational researchers, by their failure to specify scopes in soliciting reputations for influence, assume that the power of their leader-nominees is equal for all issues. . . . This is an exceedingly dubious assumption. It is improbable, for instance, that the same people who decide which houses of prostitution are to be protected . . . also plan the public school curriculum.[46]

Pluralists argued that the "reputational technique" results in confusing *status* with *power*. Respondents may offer names of persons who have high status and are well known in the community even though such persons may not actually wield power. A related problem confuses potential for power with the exercise of power. Respondents may nominate persons who occupy high formal positions in industry or government and could conceivably exercise a great deal of power but who, as a matter of practice, do not. Pluralists believe that the potential for power is not power itself, unless it is actually exercised over specific community decisions. Further, respondents may not have an accurate perception of the distribution of power in a community. The images people have of the decision-making process are more likely to be a product of their personal attitudes toward power than any real conditions prevailing in their communities.

Finally, the pluralists argue that Hunter's research did not adequately inquire about the existence of unity among the "elite." The problem of how much unity among decision makers must exist before we conclude that an elitist structure exists is a very confusing one. Early in the debate Dahl erected a straw man when he said that the test for a ruling elite was that *no* competition existed among leaders.[47] It is doubtful, of course, that a society ever existed in which *no* competition prevailed among influentials. It is unreasonable to expect sociologists to prove that members of the elite *always* agree on everything and that they *always* impose their ideas on unwilling masses. On the other hand, to constitute a "ruling elite" a number of persons should have some common attitudes and interests that are distinguishable from the attitudes and interests of non-elites. The question remains however, *how much* unity among leaders is

---

[46]*Ibid.*, p. 638.

[47]Robert Dahl, "Critique of the Ruling Elite Model," *American Political Science Review*, 52 (1958), 463–69.

required in order to verify the existence of an elite? The fault in Hunter's methodology is that he never attempted to test for any commonality of attitudes or interests among his elite members. Instead, he inferred unity of interest from similarity in the class or status background of his elite members. Yet ample evidence is available that business and financial leaders disagree on many things.

Pluralist methods of research, however, are not above criticism either. To the pluralists power means participation in decision making; it means the activities of individuals in relation to other individuals. In Dahl's words: *A* has power over *B* to the extent that he can get *B* to do something that *B* would not otherwise do.''[48] Dahl conceives of power primarily in terms of the behavior of individuals at a specific point in time. His unit of analysis is the individual actor and not the social system. This is a very critical difference in conceptual starting places, and this difference leads directly to contrasting methodologies.

Because the pluralist defines power as decision making activity, it follows that pluralist research into power involves the "decisional technique," that is, a careful examination of a series of concrete public decisions. To study community power, the pluralist first selects a number of "key public decisions" that have received widespread publicity in the community. He then identifies the people who took an active part in making these decisions and obtains a full account of their actual behavior while these decisions were being made. The methodology involves reportorial techniques that have characterized case studies in political science for many years.

But, like that of the elitists, the pluralists' definition of power and their methods of study help to determine their findings and conclusions.[49] First, the case study approach, to which the pluralists are committed, predisposes the researcher to regard each decision as, in part, unique. By examining power in relation to a particular decision, one's findings about power are likely to be tied to particular decisional situations. It is not surprising that the pluralist researcher, after compiling a series of separate case studies, concludes that the exercise of power is situational, that different people exercise power over different decisions, and that generalizations about the exercise of power in different issue areas are unwarranted. The case study method predisposes the researcher to see power in situational terms.

Dahl himself is very pessimistic about the comparability of power studies and the likelihood of developing generalizations about power in communities: "We are not likely to produce—certainly not for some considerable time to come—anything like a single consistent coherent

---

[48]Robert Dahl, "The Concept of Power," *Behavioral Science*, 2 (1957), 202.
[49]Anton, "Power, Pluralism, and Local Politics," pp. 425–57; Bachrach and Baratz, "Two Faces of Power," pp. 947–53.

'Theory of Power.' "[50] Dahl's concept of power includes reference to (a) the source, domain, or base of an actor's power; (b) the means or instruments used by the actor; (c) the amount of the actor's power; and (d) the range or scope of the actor's power. The task of the research, as Dahl sees it, is to describe (or preferably to measure) (a) the amount of change in the position of B in response to the behavior of A; (b) the subjective psychological costs of B's compliance; (c) the difference in the probability of B's compliance with and without the behavior of A; (d) the range of activities in which A has power over B; and (e) the number of respondents over which A has power. Having identified all these different aspects of power in interpersonal situations, it is unlikely that the pluralist researcher will ever find any two cases in which power was exercised in precisely the same fashion. In short, the pluralist concept of power and the case study method assume the noncomparability of power relations even before the research has begun.

The pluralist approach also implies that political power is completely reflected in open public decisions. No doubt power is exercised in resolving the well-publicized public issues, but is this the whole story of community power? Bachrach and Baratz argue effectively that power is also exercised when social or political values or institutions limit public consideration to only those issues that are relatively unimportant to the power holders.[51] A is exercising power over B when A succeeds in suppressing issues which might in their resolution be seriously detrimental to A's preferences. In other words, elites exercise power when they prevent issues from becoming public controversies. As Schattschneider explains:

> All forms of political organization have a bias in favor of the exploitation of some kinds of conflict and the suppression of others, because organization is the mobilization of bias. Some issues are organized into politics while others are organized out.[52]

Bachrach and Baratz refer to this phenomenon as the "*non*decision-making." The pluralist researcher who concentrates his attention on open "concrete decisions" may overlook the possibility that public decision making has been deliberately limited to relatively noncontroversial matters, notwithstanding the fact that there are serious latent conflicts in a community. Pluralists have pooh-poohed the problem of "nondecision," referring to it as "spook-like."[53]

---

[50]Dahl, "The Concept of Power."

[51]Bachrach and Baratz, "Two Faces of Power," pp. 947–53.

[52]E. E. Schattschneider, *The Semi-Sovereign People* (New York: Holt, Rinehart & Winston, 1961).

[53]Polsby, "How to Study Community Power," p. 481.

Another problem in pluralist research is in the selection of "key" public decisions. The pluralist proposes to study public decisions "which are generally agreed to be significant." But what decisions are generally agreed to be significant? The pluralist must accept as significant those decisions that are reputed to be significant. Decisions that are reputed to be significant are probably those that appear in the newspapers and those that come before formal governmental bodies. Pluralist methodology not only overlooks nondecisions but also overlooks decisions that are not highly visible. To put it conversely, pluralist methodology assumes that the significant community decisions are made publicly; yet there is ample evidence that many of the most important decisions in a community are private decisions. Land use and development decisions, industrial location and employment decisions, housing decisions, and many other important economic decisions which profoundly affect every aspect of community life are largely private decisions made with little public visibility. How can the pluralist legitimately exclude these kinds of decisions from his analyses? He cannot claim that such decisions are not made. His only recourse is to distinguish between public and private decisions and to claim that his interest is in public decisions, that is, visible decisions. In other words, his only recourse is to narrow the scope of political science to public decision making. By arbitrarily limiting his subject matter he can escape the responsibility for dealing with private decisions—that is, decisions that are not highly visible.

Dahl and others acknowledge that the total number of people who are involved in concrete public decisions is a very small minority of the community. For example, Dahl writes: "It is not too much to say that urban redevelopment has been the direct product of a small handful of leaders. . . . The bulk of the voters had virtually no direct influence on the process of nomination. . . . The number of citizens who participate directly in important decisions bearing on the public schools is small.[54] Moreover, all pluralist researchers recognize that persons exercising leadership in each issue area are of higher social status than the rest of the community. These middle- and upper-class people possess more of the skills and qualities required of leaders in a democratic system.

In short, neither the elitist nor the pluralist model of community power is the equivalent of the American ideal of grass-roots democracy— a government of, by, and for the people, in which individuals decide their own future and all have an equal voice in the affairs of their communities.

[54]Dahl, *Who Governs?;* see also Presthus, *Men at the Top*, p. 40; and Wildavsky, *Leadership in a Small Town*, p. 265.

COMPARATIVE STUDY OF
COMMUNITY POWER

Only by comparing structures of power and decision-making processses in a wide variety of communities can social scientists learn the actual extent of elitism or pluralism in American community life. Some communities may have concentrated, pyramidal structures of power, while others have diffused, multicentered power arrangements. For example, it is very likely that decision making in Atlanta is much more centralized than in Chicago, and that decision making in Chicago is more centralized than in New York City or New Haven, Connecticut. Community power structures probably range from monolithic to very dispersed pluralistic patterns.

The key to understanding community power lies in identifying different types of community power structures and then relating these to social, economic, and political conditions in communities. For example, we may find that large communities with a great deal of social and economic diversity, a competitive party system, and a variety of well-organized competing interest groups tend to have pluralist decision-making systems. On the other hand, small communities with a homogeneous population, a single dominant industry, nonpartisan elections, and few competing organizations may have power structures resembling the elite model.

One of the most important comparative studies of community power is *The Rulers and the Ruled* by Professors Robert Agger, Daniel Goldrich, and Bert Swanson, an intensive study of "power and impotence" in four American communities over a fifteen-year period.[55] These scholars

Distributions of Political Power Among Citizens

		Broad	Narrow
Political Leadership	Convergent	Consensual Mass	Consensual Elite
	Divergent	Competitive Mass	Competitive Elite

FIGURE 12–1 Types of Power Structures

Source: Robert Agger, Daniel Goldrich, and Bert Swanson, *The Rulers and the Ruled* (New York: John Wiley & Sons, Inc., 1946), p. 73. Reproduced by permission.

[55]Agger, Goldrich, and Swanson, *The Rulers and the Ruled* (New York: John Wiley & Sons, Inc., 1964).

identified four types of power structure, based upon the degree of citizen participation and influence and the degree of competition and conflict among political leaders. (See Figure 12–1). If many citizens shared political influence and there were two or more competing leadership groups, the community was said to have a "competitive mass" power structure. If many citizens shared political influence and there was little disagreement or conflict among leaders, the community's power structure was termed "consensual mass." If few citizens shared political influence and there was little disagreement among leaders, the power structure was said to be "consensual elite." If few citizens shared political influence, but leaders divided into competing groups, it was said to be "competitive elite" structure.

The "consensual elite" structure in *The Rulers and the Ruled* most closely resembles the elite model described earlier, since citizen influence is limited and leaders share a single ideology. The "competitive mass" structure most closely resembles our pluralist model, since many citizens share power and there are competing leadership groups. Of course the "ideal" community is probably the "consensual mass" type, where influence is widely shared among the citizens and there is little conflict among leaders. The municipal reform movement envisions such a community, where democracy prevails and "reasonable men" agree to govern in "the public interest."

The authors also proposed a typology of community "regimes" based upon the recognized "rules of the game" in community politics and the degree to which people believed they could be politically effective. See Figure 12–2.) If the rules of the game were adhered to by political leaders, and citizens believed they could influence policy, the regime was labeled a "developed democracy." If the rules of the game were adhered to by political leaders, but citizens felt politically ineffective, the regime was an "underdeveloped democracy." If leaders frequently resorted to illegitimate means to curtail political participation or free ex-

FIGURE 12–2 Types of Regimes

Source: Robert Agger, Daniel Goldrich, and Bert Swanson, *The Rulers and the Ruled* (New York: John Wiley & Sons, Inc., 1964), p. 73. Reproduced by permission.

pression—including loss of employment, discrimination, or severe social ostracism—a regime was labeled either a "guided democracy," if public confidence remained high, or an "oligarchy," if people no longer felt they could affect policy.

The Rulers and the Ruled studies produced many interesting findings about community power. First of all, a "competitive mass" type of power structure (pluralist) is related to a "developed democracy" regime. A sense of political effectiveness among citizens and adherence to the rules of the game by leaders is essential for the development of broad citizen participation in community affairs and the emergence of competitive leadership groups. A lack of political confidence among residents, and a widespread belief that political activity is useless, often result in a monopoloy of political leadership and a "consensual elite" (elitist) power structure.

If leadership changes from competitive to consensual over time, the distribution of power tends to change from mass to elite. In other words, with the disappearance of competition among leadership factions, citizen participation declines, fewer issues are submitted to popular referendum, and the power distribution becomes more elitist. Conversely, when the distribution of power changes from elite to mass, that is, when an increasing number of people begin to "crack" the power structure, political competition is likely to increase.

A competitive mass (pluralist) type of power structure will be more stable over time if the competing leadership groups represent high and low socioeconomic classes than if the competitors represent the same socioeconomic class. Pluralism depends in part upon socioeconomic cleavages in the community being represented by separate leadership groups. When competitive leaders represent the same socioeconomic class, competition can easily disappear over time and the power structure becomes "consensual" rather than "competitive."

The authors found that developed democracy regimes and competitive mass power structures were less likely to occur in communities where the major industries were home owned. Economic leaders of home-owned industries tended to be members of a single group of political leaders in the respective communities, which discouraged political competition. The prominence of these people influenced some groups in their communities to refrain from political activity because they feared illegitimate political sanctions, even though the actual use of these sanctions was relatively infrequent.

POWER AND COMMUNITY: A SUMMARY

What factors are likely to affect the structure of power and pattern of decision making in American communities? Let us conclude with a series of hypotheses that have some support in the available literature but require additional systematic investigation.

1. Homogeneous communities, lacking deep socioeconomic, ethnic, or racial cleavages, have more concentrated power structures than heterogeneous communities. Social cleavages and community conflict are associated with pluralism.[56]

2. An increase in industrialization of economic diversity increases pluralism. Elite structures will be found in communities with single dominant industries more often than in communities with several leading industries.[57]

3. Decision making for metropolitan areas follows pluralist patterns. Elite structures are likely to be found in independent cities that are not part of a metropolitan area. The politics of central cities in metropolitan areas is likely to be pluralistic, while power structures of independent suburbs will usually be more concentrated.[58]

4. As the size of a city increases, decision making becomes more specialized and a multicentered power structure develops. The larger the city, the more likely that elected officials will be able to challenge business and financial leaders as independent sources of power.[59]

5. Older communities are more likely to have elitist power structures than newer, growing communities. Rapid growth and a large influx of "newcomers" reduce the influence of established leadership groups and create competition for leadership.[60]

6. The power structures of southern cities of the United States are usually more elitist than those in other regions of the nation. The tradition of white solidarity on behalf of segregation, the slow development of an industrial economy, and the absence of white ethnic minorities to challenge Anglo-Saxon Protestant dominants has impeded the development of pluralism in southern communities.[61]

7. Nonpartisan elections, council-manager governments, and professional civil services are associated with monolithic power structures. Strong political party organizations and a mayor-council form of government are associated with multicenter, pluralistic power structures.

8. Community power becomes less concentrated through time owing

[56]Miller, "Industry and Community Power Structure," pp. 9–15; and "Decision-Making Cliques in Community Power Structures," pp. 299–310.

[57]Delbert C. Miller and William H. Form, *Industry, Labor and Community* (New York: Harper & Row, Publishers, 1960).

[58]Charles Gilbert, *Governing the Suburbs* (Bloomington: Indiana University Press, 1967).

[59]Schultze, "The Role of Economic Dominants in Community Power Structure," pp. 3–9; and "The Bifurcation of Power in a Satellite Community."

[60]Ernest H. T. Barth, "Community Influence Systems: Structure and Change," *Social Forces*, 40 (October 1961), 58–63; and Gilbert, *Governing the Suburbs*.

[61]Agger, Goldrich, and Swanson, *The Rulers and the Ruled*; and Hunter, *Community Power Structure*.

to a greater integration of American communities into the national economy. An increase in absentee ownership of industry and increasing urbanization multiplies the number of separate organized interests participating in community politics. Moreover, rising educational levels in the population and the spread of middle-class values stressing popular participation in government reduce the opportunities for a single leadership group to control community politics.[62]

[62]David A. Booth and Charles R. Adrian, "Power Structure and Community Change," *Midwest Journal of Political Science*, 6 (1962), 277–96; Roland J. Pellegrin and Charles H. Coates, "Absentee-Owned Corporations and Community Power Structure," *American Journal of Sociology*, 61 (March 1956), 413–19; and Schultze, "The Role of Economic Dominants in Community Power Structure," pp. 3–9.

THIRTEEN

Black Politics, Civil Rights, and Public Order

THE STATES
AND SCHOOL DESEGREGATION

The Fourteenth Amendment declares:

> All persons born or naturalized in the United States, and subject to the jurisdiction thereof, are citizens of the United States and of the State wherein they reside. No State shall make or enforce any law which shall abridge the privileges or immunities of citizens of the United States; nor shall any State deprive any person of life, liberty, or property, without due process of law; nor deny to any person within its jurisdiction the equal protection of the laws.

The language of the Fourteenth Amendment and its historical context leave little doubt that its original purpose was to achieve the full measure of citizenship and equality for the American Negro. Some Radical Republicans were prepared in 1867 to carry out the revolution in southern society that this amendment implied. But by 1877 it was clear that Reconstruction had failed and that the national government was not prepared to carry out the long, difficult, and disagreeable task of really reconstructing society in the eleven states of the former Confederacy.[1] In

---

[1] C. Vann Woodward, *Reunion and Reaction: The Compromise of 1877 and the End of Reconstruction* (Boston: Little, Brown and Company, 1951).

what has been described as the compromise of 1877, the national government agreed to end military occupation of the South, give up its efforts to rearrange southern society, and lend tacit approval to white supremacy in that region. In return, the southern states pledged their support of the Union, accepted national supremacy, and, of course, agreed to permit the Republican candidate to assume the presidency after the disputed election of 1876.

The Supreme Court adhered to the terms of the compromise. The result was an inversion of the meaning of the Fourteenth Amendment so that by 1896 it had become a bulwark of segregation. State laws segregating the races were upheld so long as persons in each of the separated races were treated equally. The constitutional argument on behalf of segregation under the Fourteenth Amendment was that the phrase "equal protection of the laws" did not prevent state-enforced *separation* of the races. Schools and other public facilities that were "separate but equal" won constitutional approval. This separate but equal doctrine became the Supreme Court's interpretation of the Equal Protection Clause of the Fourteenth Amendment in *Plessy* v. *Ferguson*:

> The object of the [Fourteenth] Amendment was undoubtedly to enforce the absolute equality of the two races before the law, but in the nature of things it could not have been intended to abolish distinctions based upon color, or to enforce social, as distinguished from political, equality, or a commingling of the two races upon terms unsatisfactory to either. Laws permitting, and even requiring, their separation in places where they are liable to be brought into contact do not necessarily imply the inferiority of either race to the other, and have been generally, if not universally, recognized as within the competency of the state legislatures in the exercise of their police power. The most common instance of this is connected with the establishment of separate schools for white and colored children, which has been held to be a valid exercise of the legislative power . . .[2]

As a matter of fact, of course, segregated facilities, including public schools, were seldom if ever equal, even with respect to physical conditions. In practice, the doctrine of segregation was "separate and *un*equal." The Supreme Court began to take notice of this after World War II. While it declined to overrule the segregationist interpretation of the Fourteenth Amendment, it began to order the admission of individual blacks to white public universities, where evidence indicated that separate black institutions were inferior or nonexistent.[3]

Leaders of the newly emerging civil rights movement in the 1940s and 1950s were not satisfied with court decisions that examined the circum-

[2]163 U.S. 537 (1896).
[3]Sweatt v. Painter, 339 U.S. 629 (1950); McLaurin v. Oklahoma State Regents, 339 U.S. 637 (1950).

stances in each case to determine if separate school facilities were really equal. Led by Roy Wilkins, executive director of the National Association for the Advancement of Colored People, and Thurgood Marshall, chief counsel for the NAACP, the civil rights movement pressed for a court decision that segregation itself meant inequality within the meaning of the Fourteenth Amendment, whether or not facilities were equal in all tangible respects. In short, they wanted a complete reversal of the "separate but equal" interpretation of the Fourteenth Amendment, and a holding that laws *separating* the races were unconstitutional.

The civil rights groups chose to bring suit for desegregation in Topeka, Kansas, where segregated black and white schools were equal with respect to buildings, curricula, qualifications, and salaries of teachers, and other tangible factors. The object was to prevent the Court from ordering the admission of a black because *tangible* facilities were not equal, and to force the Court to review the doctrine of segregation itself.

On May 17, 1954, the Court rendered its decision in *Brown* v. *Board of Education* of Topeka, Kansas:

> Segregation of white and colored children in public has a detrimental effect upon the colored children. The impact is greater when it has the sanction of law, for the policy of separating the races is usually interpreted as denoting the inferiority of the Negro group. A sense of inferiority affects the motivation of a child to learn. Segregation with the sanction of law, therefore, has a tendency to retard the educational and mental development of Negro children and to deprive them of some of the benefits they would receive in a racially integrated school system.
>
> Whatever may have been the extent of psychological knowledge at the time of Plessy *v.* Ferguson, this finding is amply supported by modern authority. Any language in Plessy *v.* Ferguson contrary to this finding is rejected.[4]

The symbolic importance of the original *Brown* v. *Topeka* decision cannot be overestimated. While it would be many years before any significant number of black children would attend formerly segregated white schools, the decision by the nation's highest Court undoubtedly stimulated black hopes and expectations. Sociologist Kenneth Clark writes:

> This [civil rights] movement would probably not have existed at all were it not for the 1954 Supreme Court school desegregation decision which provided a tremendous boost to the morale of Negroes by its *clear* affirmation that color is irrelevant to the rights of American citizens. Until this time the Southern Negro generally had accommodated to the separatism of the black from the white society.[5]

[4]Brown v. Board of Education of Topeka, 347 U.S. 483 (1954).
[5]Kenneth B. Clark, *Dark Ghetto* (New York: Harper and Row, 1965), pp. 77–78.

STATE RESISTANCE

The Supreme Court had spoken forcefully in the *Brown* case in 1954 in declaring segregation unconstitutional. From a constitutional viewpoint, any state-supported segregation of the races after 1954 was prohibited. Article VI of the Constitution declares that the words of that document are "the supreme law of the land. . . . anything in the constitution or laws of any state to the contrary notwithstanding."

From a political viewpoint, however, the battle over segregation was just beginning. Segregation would remain a part of American life, regardless of its constitutionality, until effective political power was brought to bear to end it. The Supreme Court, by virtue of the American system of federalism and separation of powers, has little formal power at its disposal. Congress, the president, the state governors and legislatures, and the people have more power at their disposal than the federal judiciary. The Supreme Court must rely largely on the other branches of the federal government, on the states, and on private individuals and organizations to effectuate the law of the land.

Yet in 1954 the practice of segregation was widespread and deeply ingrained in American life. Seventeen states required the segregation of the races in public schools. These seventeen states were:

Alabama	North Carolina	Delaware
Arkansas	South Carolina	Kentucky
Florida	Tennessee	Maryland
Georgia	Texas	Missouri
Louisiana	Virginia	Oklahoma
Mississippi		West Virginia

The Congress of the United States required the segregation of the races in the public schools of the District of Columbia.[6] Four additional states—Arizona, Kansas, New Mexico, and Wyoming—authorized segregation upon the option of local school boards. (See Figure 13–1.)

Thus, in deciding *Brown v Topeka*, the Supreme Court struck down the laws of twenty-one states and the District of Columbia in a single opinion. Such a far-reaching decision was bound to meet with difficulties in implementation. In an opinion delivered the following year regarding the question of relief for Brown and others similarly situated, the Supreme Court said:

---

[6]The Supreme Court also ruled that Congress was bound to respect the equal protection doctrine imposed upon the states by the Fourteenth Amendment as part of the "due process" clause of the Fifth Amendment. Bolling v. Sharpe, 347 U.S. 497 (1954).

FIGURE 13-1 Segregation Laws in the United States in 1954

Segregation Required
Local Option on Segregation
No Legislation
Segregation Prohibited

Full implementation of these constitutional principles may require solution of varied local school problems. School authorities have the primary responsibility for elucidating, assessing, and solving these problems; courts will have to consider whether the action of school authorities constitutes good faith implementation of the governing constitutional principles.[7]

Thus, the Supreme Court did not order immediate nationwide desegregation, but instead turned over the responsibility for desegregation to state and local authorities under the supervision of federal district courts. The way was open for extensive litigation, obstruction, and delay by states that chose to resist desegregation.

The six border states with segregated school systems—Delaware, Kentucky, Maryland, Missouri, Oklahoma, and West Virginia—together with

[7]Brown v. Board of Education of Topeka, 349 U.S. 294 (1955).

TABLE 13-1
Public School Desegregation, Southern and Border States, 1964–70

| | Blacks in School with Whites, As a Percentage of Total Black Enrollment | | |
	1964	1967	1970*
Alabama	0.03	4.4	61.1
Arkansas	0.8	15.1	84.5
Florida	2.6	22.3	78.1
Georgia	0.4	8.8	69.2
Louisiana	1.1	3.4	62.9
Mississippi	0.02	2.5	70.1
North Carolina	1.4	15.4	87.8
South Carolina	0.1	5.6	82.8
Tennessee	5.3	28.6	49.1
Texas	7.3	44.9	58.1
Virginia	5.1	25.3	79.1
Southern States	2.1	15.9	70.8
Delaware	57.8	100.0	81.3
Kentucky	62.5	90.1	75.5
Maryland	51.7	63.3	54.3
Missouri	44.1	77.7	40.9
Oklahoma	31.7	50.8	61.7
West Virginia	88.1	93.4	99.2
Border States	59.2	75.7	70.0

* Percentages for 1970 are based upon blacks attending schools that are not 95-100 percent minority schools, whereas percentages in earlier years are based upon blacks who are not attending all-black schools.

SOURCE: Data from U.S. Office of Education.

the school districts in Kansas, Arizona, and New Mexico which had operated segregated schools, chose not to resist desegregation formally. The District of Columbia also desegregated its public schools the year following the Supreme Court's decision. Progress in desegregation in the border states is shown in Table 13–1; by 1964 over half the black children in these states were attending integrated schools.

Resistance to school integration was the policy of the eleven states of the Old Confederacy. Refusal of a school district to desegregate until it is faced with a federal court injunction is the most common form of delay. Segregationists pressed for state laws that would create an endless chain of litigation in each of the nearly three thousand school districts in the South, in the hope that integration efforts would drown in a sea of protracted court controversy.

Other schemes have included state payment of private school tuition in lieu of providing public schools, amending compulsory attendance laws to provide that no child shall be required to attend an integrated school, requiring schools faced with desegregation orders to cease operation, and the use of pupil placement laws to avoid or minimize the extent of integration.[8] State officials have also attempted to prevent desegregation on the grounds that it would endanger public safety. State officials themselves precipitated and encouraged violent resistance through attempts to "interpose" and "nullify" federal authority within their states.[9]

On the whole, those states that chose to resist desegregation were quite successful in doing so during the ten-year period from 1954 to 1964. Table 13–1 indicates that in 1964 only about 2 percent of the black school children in the eleven southern states were attending integrated schools. Only 604 of the South's 2,220 school districts which encompassed black students were officially desegregated; and most of these 604 districts experienced only token desegregation. The effectiveness of state policy up to 1964 in resisting the policy of the federal court is an important, although regrettable, comment on the powers of the states in our federal system.

[8]State laws that were obviously designed to evade constitutional responsibilities to end segregation were struck down in federal courts. See Aaron v. Cooper, 261 F.2d 97 (1958); Harrison v. Day, 106 S.E.2d 636 (1959). However, federal courts have upheld pupil assignment laws, including the so-called freedom of choice plan, which permit parents to request school assignments and school authorities to assign pupils on an individual basis according to nonracial criteria—space available, etc. Pupil assignment laws were not held to be invalid on their face, although they give school authorities great discretion and it is difficult to prove that race did not influence pupil assignment. See Shuttlesworth v. Birmingham Board of Education, 358 U.S. 101 (1958); Bush v. Orleans Parish School Board, 308 F.2d 491 (1962).

[9]The Supreme Court declared that the threat of violence was not sufficient reason to deny constitutional rights to Negro children and again dismissed the ancient interposition arguments. Cooper v. Aaron, 358 U.S. 1 (1958).

The decision of eleven southern states to resist desegregation was, of course, a product of the total cultural history of the region. The roots of racial attitudes in the South are too deep to examine here. However, progress in desegregation is not uniform throughout the southern states, and it is therefore possible to contrast the characteristics of those states that have made some progress toward integration with those that have not. For example, desegregation has been slow and painful in Mississippi, Alabama, and South Carolina, while changes have been somewhat easier in Texas, Tennessee, Virginia, and Florida. How do these states differ? What accounts for differences among southern states in their degree of resistance to desegregation?

Does a large proportion of blacks in a state's population strengthen the integration movement or does it strengthen the resolve of segregationists to resist integration? The evidence is very strong that a large black population strengthens the position of segregationists. States with large black populations made slower progress toward desegregation than states with smaller proportions of black residents. While large black populations appear to stimulate resistance to desegregation, wealth and urbanization appear to have the opposite effect. These variables are not as influential as black population percentages in explaining progress toward desegregation. However, the wealth and urbanism of Texas, Florida, and North Carolina helped to explain their somewhat more progressive posture toward desegregation. The ruralism and poverty in Mississippi, Alabama, and South Carolina helped to explain their slower progress.

In the Civil Rights Act of 1964, Congress finally entered the civil rights field in support of court efforts to achieve desegregation. Among other things, the Civil Rights Act of 1964 provided that every federal department and agency must take action to end segregation in all programs or activities receiving federal financial assistance. It was specified that this action was to include termination of financial assistance if states and communities receiving federal funds refused to comply with federal desegregation orders. Thus, in addition to court orders requiring desegregation, states and communities faced administrative orders, or "guidelines," from federal executive agencies, particularly the U.S. Office of Education, threatening loss of federal funds for noncompliance. Acting under the authority of Title VI, the U.S. Office of Education required all school districts in the seventeen formerly segregated states to submit desegregation plans as a condition of federal assistance. "Guidelines" governing the acceptability of these plans were frequently unclear, often conflicting, and always changing, yet progress toward desegregation was speeded up.

The last vestige of legal justification for delay in implementing school desegregation collapsed in 1969 when the Supreme Court rejected a request by Mississippi school officials for a delay in implementing school desegregation plans in that state. School officials, with the support of the Nixon administration, contended that immediate desegregation in several southern Mississippi counties would encounter "administrative and legislative difficulties." The Supreme Court stated that no delay could be granted because "continued operation of segregated schools under a standard of allowing 'all deliberate speed' for desegregation is no longer constitutionally permissible."[10] The Court declared that every school district was obligated to end dual school systems "at once" and "now and hereafter" to operate only unitary schools. The effect of the decision—fifteen years after the original *Brown* case—was to eliminate any further legal justification for the continuation of segregation in public schools.

By 1970 southern school desegregation had proceeded to the point where more black pupils were attending integrated schools in the South than in the North. The Department of Health, Education, and Welfare reported that the percentage of black pupils in the North attending schools which were predominately black (95 to 100 percent black) was greater than the percentage of black pupils in the South attending such schools. This is an important comparison between the diminishing impact of *segregation law* in the South and the continuing impact of *de facto segregation* in the North. If the issue is posed as one of "racial isolation," it turns out that by 1970 the efforts of the federal courts and executive agencies in eliminating the last vestiges of segregation by law had reduced racial isolation in the South to the point where it was less than racial isolation in the North.

Thus, the pattern of national enforcement and local resistance in school desegregation suggested that (1) national policy could not be implemented until Congress and the executive branch threatened financial sanctions: (2) state and local resistance could be surprisingly effective in frustrating national policy over a prolonged period of time; (3) state and local resistance is *greater* where black populations are greater; (4) well-educated, affluent, urban populations are less likely to oppose black demands for equality than undereducated, poor, rural populations.

BUSSING AND NEIGHBORHOOD SCHOOLS
IN THE SOUTH

As we have noted, southern school officials face both federal court orders and U.S. Office of Education guidelines to end segregated schools and establish unitary school systems. On the surface, this mandate seems

10Alexander v. Holmes County Board of Education, 396 U.S. 19 (1969).

clear enough, but is it really? Are southern school districts permitted to operate predominantly black schools in black neighborhoods and predominantly white schools in white neighborhoods? In other words, in establishing unitary school districts, can southern school officials draw school boundaries along neighborhood lines similar to the practice in northern school districts, if the resulting neighbhorhood schools are racially imbalanced? Or are southern school officials required to bus black and white children out of their neighborhoods in order to achieve a racial balance in each school equivalent to the racial composition of the district at large?

It has been argued that because of past legal segregation southern school officials have a special constitutional obligation to eliminate the last vestiges of segregation. This means eliminating *all* predominantly black schools even in black neighborhoods where extensive bussing would be required to do so. It is contended that southern school districts come under a special constitutional duty to racially balance their schools because of past segregation.

In contrast, many southern school officials have argued that the elimination of segregation and the establishment of unitary school districts should not mean "forced bussing" where neighborhood residential patterns result in some predominantly black and some predominantly white schools. Southern congressmen and governors argue that southern school districts should be given "equal" treatment with northern school districts and not be required to bus students out of their neighborhoods to achieve racial balancing.

In the important case of *Swann* v. *Charlotte-Mecklenburg Board of Education,* the Supreme Court held that southern school districts have a special affirmative duty to eliminate all vestiges of dual school systems, and this responsibility may entail "bussing" and the breakup of neighborhood schools.[11] Where evidence indicates that school districts previously segregated students by law, these districts have a special constitutional mandate under the Equal Protection Clause of the Fourteenth Amendment to take whatever steps are necessary, including bussing, to end manifestations of dual schools. Moreover, the Court held that the racial composition of a school, in a district that previously segregated by law, could be used as prima facie evidence of violation of constitutional rights, and that bussing to achieve racial balance could be imposed as a means of ending all traces of dualism in the schools. The Court was careful in saying, however, that racial imbalance in a school was not in itself grounds for ordering bussing, unless it is shown that some government action contributed to that imbalance. Thus, the im-

---

[11]Swann v. Charlotte-Mecklenburg Board of Education, 39 L.W. 4437 (1971).

pact of the *Swann* decision falls largely on southern schools. (We will return to this topic later in this chapter in dealing with "de facto" segregation and "bussing" in northern cities.)

CIVIL RIGHTS AND THE NEW MILITANCY

The initial objective of the civil rights movement in America has been to prevent discrimination and segregation as practiced by or supported by *governments,* particularly states, municipalities, and school districts. But even while important victories for the civil rights movement were being recorded in the prevention of discrimination by governments, particularly in the *Brown* case, the movement began to broaden its objectives to include the elimination of discrimination in all segments of American life, private as well as public. Civil rights was redefined to mean not merely a legal, but an actual, possibility of developing human capacities and sharing in the goods a society has produced and the way of life it has built. This was a more positive concept of civil rights. It involved not merely restrictions on government but a positive obligation of government to act forcefully to end discrimination in public accommodations, employment, housing, and all other sectors of private life.

As long as the civil rights movement in America was combating *government* discrimination, it could employ the Constitution as a weapon in its struggle for liberty, for the Constitution by definition governs the activities of *governments.* Since the Supreme Court and federal judiciary is charged with the responsibility of interpreting the Constitution, the civil rights movement could concentrate on Court action to serve their objective of preventing government discrimination. But the Constitution does not govern the activities of private individuals. It is the laws of Congress and the states that govern the conduct of private individuals. When the civil rights movement turned to combating private discrimination, it had to carry its fight into the legislative branch of government. The federal courts could help restrict discrimination by state and local governments and school authorities, but only Congress, state legislatures, and city councils could restrict discrimination practiced by private owners of restaurants, hotels and motels, private employers, and other individuals who were not government officials.

Prior to 1964, Congress had been content to let the president and the courts struggle with the problem of civil rights. In 1957 and 1960, Congress passed weak civil rights bills which made it illegal for any person to interfere with the exercise of rights under a federal court order or to use interstate commerce for the purpose of burning or bombing any building. So strong was the reluctance of Congress to enter the field of civil rights that even those bills were extensively debated and compromised before final passage. Yet by 1964 the demand for strong civil rights legislation was so great that Congress could no longer ignore the nation's most pressing domestic issue.

A new militancy, expressed in Martin Luther King's call for nonviolent direct action, appeared in the civil rights movement in the mid-1950s. Between 1941 and 1954, black protests were primarily in the form of legal cases brought by the NAACP to federal courts; negotiation and bargaining with white businessmen and government officials, often by the National Urban League; and local lobbying on behalf of black constituents by black political leaders in northern communities. But in 1955 the black community of Montgomery, Alabama, began a yearlong boycott with frequent demonstrations against the Montgomery city buses over segregated seating practices. The dramatic appeal and the eventual success of the boycott in Montgomery brought nationwide attention to a local black minister, Martin Luther King, and led to the creation in 1956 of the Southern Christian Leadership Conference. In 1960 black students from the North Carolina Agricultural and Technical College began a "sit-in" demonstration at the segregated Woolworth lunch counter in Greensboro, North Carolina. Soon, "sit-ins" in restaurants, "read-ins" in libraries, "pray-ins" in white churches spread throughout the South, generally under the leadership of the Southern Christian Leadership Conference, which followed "nonviolent" techniques. The Congress of Racial Equality (CORE), which at this time was also committed to the philosophy of nonviolence, initiated a series of "freedom rides" into the South, in which groups of white and black bus travelers attempted to desegregate travel and terminal facilities. Years before, the Supreme Court had held that segregation of interstate travel facilities was unconstitutional, but throughout the South, travel facilities remained segregated. The freedom riders underwent arrest and mob violence in many southern communities. In 1961 President Kennedy was obliged to send four hundred federal marshals to Montgomery, Alabama, to protect the freedom riders.

Perhaps the most dramatic confrontation between the civil rights movement and southern segregationists occurred in Birmingham, Alabama, in the spring of 1963. In support of a request for desegregation of downtown eating places and the formation of a biracial committee to work out the integration of public schools, Martin Luther King led several thousand Birmingham blacks in a series of orderly street marches. The demonstrators were met with strong police action, including fire hoses, police dogs, and electric cattle prods. Newspaper pictures of blacks being attacked by police and bitten by dogs were flashed all over the world. More than twenty-five thousand demonstrators, including Dr. King, were jailed.

The year 1963 was probably the most important for nonviolent direct action. The Birmingham action set off demonstrations in many parts of the country; the theme remained one of nonviolence, and it was usually whites rather than blacks who resorted to violence in these demonstrations. Responsible black leadership remained in control of the movement and won widespread support from the white community. The culmination of the nonviolent philosophy was a giant, yet orderly march on Washington, held on August 28, 1963. More than two hundred thousand blacks and whites participated in the march, which was endorsed by many labor leaders, religious groups, and political figures. It was in response to this march that President Kennedy sent a strong civil rights bill to Congress, which was later to be passed after his death as the famous Civil Rights Act of 1964.

Again, in 1965, Martin Luther King led a successful nonviolent voting rights march from Selma to Montgomery, Alabama. This march was a protest against a refusal of local southern registrars to register black voters. The hostility of southern segregationists and the failure of state and local authorities to protect the marchers led President Johnson to federalize the national guard and order them to protect the demonstrators. After the march, President Johnson sent another historic civil rights measure to the Congress—the Voting Rights Act of 1965.

The Civil Rights Act of 1964 passed both houses of Congress by better than a two-thirds favorable vote; it won the overwhelming support of both Republican and Democratic congressmen. It was signed into law on July 4, 1964. It ranks with the Emancipation Proclamation, the Fourteenth Amendment, and *Brown* v. *Topeka* as one of the most important steps toward full equality for the black in America.

The Civil Rights Act of 1964 provides:

I. That it is unlawful to apply unequal standards in voter registration procedures, or to deny registration for irrelevant errors or omissions on records or applications.

II. That it is unlawful to discriminate or segregate persons on the grounds of race, color, religion, or national origin in any place of public accommodation, including hotels, motels, restaurants, movies, theatres, sports areas, entertainment houses, and other places which offer to serve the public. This prohibition extends to all establishments whose operations affect interstate commerce or whose discriminatory practices are supported by state action.

III. That the Attorney General shall undertake civil action on behalf of any person denied equal access to a public accommodation, to obtain a federal district court order to secure compliance with the act. If the owner or manager of a public accommodation continued to discriminate, he would be in contempt of court and subject to peremptory fines and imprisonment without trial by jury. This mode of

POLITICS IN STATES AND COMMUNITIES

enforcement gave establishments a chance to mend their ways without punishment, and it also avoided the possibility that southern
juries would refuse to convict persons for violations of the act.

IV. That the Attorney General shall undertake civil actions on behalf
of persons attempting orderly desegregation of public schools.

V. That the Commission on Civil Rights, first established in the Civil
Rights Act of 1957, shall be empowered to investigate deprivations
of the right to vote, study and collect information regarding discrimination in America, and make reports to the President and
Congress.

VI. That each federal department and agency shall take action to end
discrimination in all programs or activities receiving federal financial assistance in any form. This action shall include termination of
financial assistance.

VII. That it shall be unlawful for any employer or labor union with 25
or more persons after 1965 to discriminate against any individual in
any fashion in employment, because of his race, color, religion, sex,
or national origins, and that an Equal Employment Opportunity
Commission shall be established to enforce this provision by investigation, conference, conciliation, persuasion, and, if need be, civil
action in federal court.

Opponents of the Civil Rights Act of 1964 argued that Congress unconstitutionally exceeded its delegated powers when it prohibited discrimination and segregation practiced by *privately owned* public accommodations
and *private* employers. Nowhere among the delegated powers of Congress
in Article I of the Constitution, or even in the Fourteenth or Fifteenth
Amendments is Congress specifically given the power to prohibit discrimination practiced by *private* individuals. In reply, supporters of the
act argued that Congress has the power to regulate interstate commerce.
Instead of relying upon the Fourteenth Amendment, which prohibits
only *state-supported* discrimination, Congress was relying on its powers
over interstate commerce. In unanimous opinions in *Heart of Atlanta
Motel* v. *United States* and *Katzenbach* v. *McClung*[12] in December 1964,
the Supreme Court upheld the constitutionality of the Civil Rights Act.
The Court held that Congress could, by virtue of its power over interstate commerce, prohibit discrimination in any establishment that serves
or offers to serve interstate travelers or that sells food or goods previously
moved in interstate commerce. This power over commerce included not
only major establishments, like the Heart of Atlanta Motel, but also the
family-owned Ollie's Barbecue serving a local clientele.

[12]Heart of Atlanta Motel v. United States, 379 U.S. 241 (1964); Katzenbach v.
McClung, 379 U.S. 294 (1964).

PROTEST AND CIVIL DISOBEDIENCE

The civil rights movement invented new political techniques for minorities in American politics. In 1963 a group of Alabama clergymen petitioned Martin Luther King, Jr., to call off mass demonstrations in Birmingham. King, who had been arrested in the demonstrations, replied in his famous "Letter from Birmingham City Jail":

> You may well ask, "Why direct action? Why sit-ins, marches, etc.? Isn't negotiation a better path?" You are exactly right in your call for negotiation. Indeed, this is the purpose of direct action. Nonviolent direct action seeks to create such a crisis and establish such creative tension that a community that has constantly refused to negotiate is forced to confront the issue. It seeks to so dramatize the issue that it can no longer be ignored. . . .
>
> In no sense do I advocate evading or defying the law as the rabid segregationist would do. This would lead to anarchy. One who breaks an unjust law must do it openly, lovingly (not hatefully as the white mothers did in New Orleans when they were seen on television screaming "nigger, nigger") and with a willingness to accept the penalty. I submit that an individual who breaks a law that conscience tells him is unjust, and willingly accepts the penalty by staying in jail to arouse the conscience of the community over its injustice, is in reality expressing the very highest respect for law. . . .[13]

Mass demonstrations, sit-ins, and other militant tactics often involve violations of state and local laws. For example, remaining at a segregated lunch counter after the owner orders one to leave may violate trespass laws. Marching in the street may involve the obstruction of traffic, "disorderly conduct," or "parading without a permit." Demonstrations may involve "disturbing the peace" or refusing to obey the orders of a police officer. Even though these tactics are nonviolent, they involve disobedience of civil law. Needless to say, violence, rioting, stoning, looting, and burning also violate the law, regardless of the causes of such activity.

Civil disobedience is not new. It has played an important role in American history, from the Boston Tea Party to the abolitionists who hid runaway slaves, to the suffragettes who paraded and demonstrated for women's rights, to the labor organizers who picketed to form the nation's major industrial unions, to the civil rights marchers of recent years. Civil

[13]From "Letter from Birmingham City Jail—April 16, 1963," in *Why We Can't Wait* by Martin Luther King Jr. Copyright © 1963 by Martin Luther King Jr. By permission of Harper & Row and Joan Daves.

disobedience is a political tactic of minorities. Since majorities can more easily change laws, they seldom have to disobey them. It is also a tactic for groups who wish to change the social *status quo* in some way.

The political purpose of disobedience is to call attention, or "bear witness," to the existence of injustice.[14] Punishment is actively sought, rather than avoided, since punishment will help to emphasize the injustice of the law. The object is to stir the consciences of an apathetic majority. Punishment inflicted for violation of an unjust law can shame a majority and make it ask itself how far it is willing to go to protect the *status quo*.

Clearly, the participation of the mass news media, particularly television, contributes measurably to the success of civil disobedience. Breaking the law makes news; the news calls the attention of the public to the existence of unjust laws or practices. The public's sympathy is won when injustices are spotlighted, the willingness of the disobedients to accept punishment is evidence of their sincerity, and the whole drama lays the groundwork for changing unjust laws or practice. Cruelty or violence directed against civil disobedients by policemen, or other defenders of the *status quo,* plays into the hands of the civil disobedients by further emphasizing the injustices they are experiencing.

Is it ever right to break a law? It would be difficult to argue that civil disobedience is *never* justified.[15] To do so would be so say that those who carried out Hitler's orders to murder millions of people were acting justly in following his orders. The Nuremburg trials held that individuals had a legal and moral duty to refuse to perform criminal acts even when ordered by government authorities to do so. When people are denied the right to participate in lawmaking, through free elections and representative governments, it is difficult to argue that they are morally bound to obey laws that they had no share in making.

But how does one justify breaking laws in a democratic society which provides its members with legal means for the redress of their grievances—courts, legislatures, elections, political activity, and peaceful persuasion? In defense of civil disobedience in democratic countries, it can be argued that it is often necessary to convince an apathetic majority of the need to correct an evil suffered by a minority. There is also the argument that democratic processes work slowly; often decades are re-

14For a thorough discussion of protest politics, see Michael Lipsky, "Protest as a Political Resource," *American Political Science Review,* 62 (December 1968), 1144–58; James Q. Wilson, "The Strategy of Protest: Problems of Negro Civil Action," *Journal of Conflict Resolution,* 5 (September 1961), 292–99; and Jack L. Walker, "Protest and Negotiation: A Case Study of Negro Leadership in Atlanta," *Midwest Journal of Political Science,* 7 (May 1963), 99–124.

15See Charles Frankel, "Is It Ever Right to Break the Law?" *New York Times Magazine* (January 12, 1964); reprinted in Thomas R. Dye and Brett W. Hawkins, *Politics in the Metropolis* (Columbus, Ohio: Charles E. Merrill Books, Inc., 1967).

quired to achieve even modest progress. If the suffering of a minority is particularly serious, long waits may be quite painful and a cry may go up for "Freedom Now," with the emphasis on "Now." Civil disobedience can jolt democratic processes into motion.

Yet civil disobedience cannot be lightly undertaken. It can arouse extreme passions on either side, excite and provoke thoughtless masses, and make disrespect for law a commonplace and popular attitude. Leaders of the civil rights movement may talk of nonviolence, yet the risk of violence is very great. Mass followers may not always understand the distinction between nonviolent demonstrations directed against injustice, and rioting, looting, and vandalism directed against society itself.

FAIR HOUSING

Housing in America is becoming more, not less, segregated. Not only do population figures show that blacks are being concentrated in central cities while whites are fleeing to the suburbs, but even *within* central cities black housing is highly segregated. This separation of racial groups between cities and suburbs, and within cities, is aided by the practices of the private housing industry—builders, mortgage lenders, landlords, and real estate brokers. While the housing industry contends that it is merely reflecting the preferences and financial resources of its customers, the Commission on Race and Housing concluded that "it is the real estate brokers, builders, and mortgage finance institutions which translate prejudice into discriminatory action.[16] The typical housing development concentrates homes in a single price bracket, so that most homeowners live on a street in which the prices of homes do not vary by more than $2,000 or $3,000. Real estate developers contend that the alternative pattern of building high- and low-income houses in the same neighborhood does not appeal to their customers. The result of this practice of building neighborhoods with uniformly priced homes is the creation of social class homogeneity within neighborhoods. This homogeneity even means that whites at different income levels live in different neighborhoods, and, of course, it also means that less-affluent blacks are concentrated in areas where low-priced housing is concentrated. Thus, social class segregation of neighborhoods leads to de facto segregation of blacks in residential housing.

But in addition to economically imposed de facto housing segregation, blacks also face a great deal of direct discrimination in the sale and rental of housing. Until recently a large proportion of private housing in Amer-

---

[16]U.S. Commission on Race and Housing, *Where Shall We Live?* (Washington, D.C.: Government Printing Office, 1958), p. 27.

ica carried racially restrictive covenants in deeds: "No part of the land hereby conveyed shall ever be used, or be occupied by or sold, demised, transferred, conveyed unto, or in trust for, leased, or rented or given to Negroes, or any other person or persons of Negro blood or extraction, or to any person of the semitic race, blood, or origin, which racial description shall be deemed to include Armenians, Jews, Hebrews, Persians, and Syrians."[17] Not until 1948 was the judicial enforcement of such covenants held unconstitutional, and not until 1953 was enforcement by way of money damages held unlawful.[18] Although racially restrictive covenants are no longer judicially enforceable, the pattern they helped to create still exists.

Government policies have also contributed to housing segregation in America. Under Federal Housing Administration and Veterans Administration housing practices until the late 1950s, some $150 billion in mortgage loans, representing more than 15 million housing units, were insured or guaranteed under the "homogeneous neighborhood" policies then in effect.[19] These FHA and VA housing programs were partly responsible for the flight of the white middle class to the suburbs by making home ownership easily available to the middle class. But in addition to the de facto segregation resulting from suburban growth, the FHA and the VA also did nothing prior to 1964 to prevent direct discrimination in the sale of homes. The result was the creation of many all-white suburbs around major urban centers.

Low-rent public housing has been an important source of housing for blacks, but public housing has been confined almost entirely to central cities. The effect of the public housing program, therefore, has been to intensify the concentrations of the poor and nonwhite in the central city. Moreover, even within central cities, local public housing authorities, instead of locating projects on small sites scattered throughout the city, concentrated public housing projects in large blocks located in particular areas of the city, and most frequently in areas of already existing black concentrations.

For many years "fair housing" had been considered the most sensitive area of civil rights legislation. Discrimination in the sale and rental of housing was the last major civil rights problem on which Congress took action. Discrimination in housing had not been mentioned in any previous legislation; even the comprehensive Civil Rights Act of 1964 made no reference to housing. Prohibiting discrimination in the sale or

---

[17]*Hearings before the U.S. Commission on Civil Rights on Housing in Washington, D.C.* (1958), p. 58; also cited U.S. Commission on Civil Rights, *Racial Isolation in the Public Schools*, I, 21.

[18]Shelley v. Kraemer, 334 U.S. (1948); Barrows v. Jackson, 346 U.S. 249 (1953).

[19]U.S. Commission on Civil Rights, *Racial Isolation in the Public Schools*, I., 22–44.

rental of housing affected the constituencies of northern members of Congress more than any of the earlier, southern-oriented, legislation. The real estate industry in America was strongly opposed to restricting the "rights" of property owners "to determine the acceptability and desirability of any prospective buyer or tenant of his property.[20] Moreover, there was reason to believe that a majority of white Americans opposed laws prohibiting discrimination in sale or rental housing. When the California legislature passed a fair housing law, the state's voters replied by overwhelmingly supporting a state constitutional amendment, know as Proposition 14, which prohibited the legislature from abridging the rights of citizens to sell, lease, or rent to the person of their choice. The effect of this constitutional amendment was to nullify the state's fair housing law, and it won a statewide referendum in California by a two to one margin of voters! Later the California Supreme Court held Proposition 14 to be a violation of the Fourteenth Amendment of the United States Constitution and in effect threw out the results of the referendum; but nonetheless the vote itself was clear evidence of widespread popular opposition to fair housing.

Thus, the prospects for a fair housing law were not very good at the beginning of 1968. When Martin Luther King, Jr., was assassinated on April 4, however, the mood of the nation and of Congress changed dramatically, and many felt that Congress should pass a fair housing law as a tribute to the slain civil rights leader. Moreover, the final version of the Civil Rights Bill of 1968 included amendments which made it a crime for persons to travel in interstate commerce with intent to incite or take part in a riot or to manufacture or transport firearms and explosives for use in a civil disorder. These "antiriot" amendments won crucial support for the bill.

The Civil Rights Act of 1968 prohibited the following forms of discrimination:

> Refusal to sell or rent a dwelling to any person because of his race, color, religion or national origin.
>
> Discrimination against a person in the terms, conditions or privileges of the sale or rental of a dwelling.
>
> Advertising the sale or rental of a dwelling indicating a preference or discrimination based on race, color, religion or national origin.
>
> Inducing persons to sell or rent a dwelling by referring to the entry into the neighborhood of persons of a particular race, religion or national origin (the "blockbusting" technique of real estate selling).

[20]National Association of Real Estate Boards, "Property Owners' Bill of Rights," June 4, 1963.

The act applied to all apartments and houses, rented or sold, by either real estate developers or by private individuals who used the services of real estate agents. It exempted private individuals who sold their own home without the services of a real estate agent, provided they did not indicate any preference or discrimination in advertising in the sale or rental of a house. It also exempted apartments with four or less units where the owner maintained his own residence. The enforcement provisions allowed a person who believed he had been discriminated against to file a complaint with the secretary of Housing and Urban Development, who would then investigate and attempt to conciliate the matter; if conciliation failed the individual could sue in a federal court for injunctive relief. But where state and local remedies were available, the individual must seek these local remedies first before federal court action. Thus, the enforcement procedure was quite cumbersome upon the individuals discriminated against.

STATE AND LOCAL
ANTIDISCRIMINATION LAWS

States and communities in America were active in antidiscrimination legislation long before the federal government got around to its Civil Rights Act of 1964.[21] In 1945 New York passed the first state antidiscrimination law dealing with private employment; this law was similar to Title VII of the federal Civil Rights Act passed nineteen years later. Connecticut and New Jersey passed laws preventing discrimination in public accommodations in 1949; these laws were similar to Title II of the Civil Rights Act. By 1966 a total of thirty-three states had fair employment practice laws; twenty-eight of these states strengthen their laws with commissions whose responsibility is to secure employment. Thirty-five states had public accommodation laws. Even more noteworthy is the fact that in 1966, twenty-two states had legislation outlawing discrimination in the sale or rental of housing. Thus, the record of states and communities in fighting discrimination in America is not wholly a negative one.

The typical state fair employment law operates as follows: after a complaint has been filed by an individual, an investigator from the commission tries to determine whether there is probable cause to believe that there is some "unfair" or "unlawful" practice relating to discrimination or segregation in employment; if probable cause is found, in-

[21]See Duane Lockard, *Toward Equal Opportunity* (New York: The Macmillan Company, 1968).

formal conciliation is attempted between the commission and the employer; if conciliation is unsuccessful, a formal complaint is issued and a hearing is held, at the conclusion of which the employer may be issued an order requiring him to cease the practice in question; if he refuses to comply, the commission may ask for a court order requiring compliance; if a court order is issued, of course, continued failure to comply would result in contempt of court proceedings with resultant fines or jail sentences. The problem with this approach is that it requires individuals to make complaints before action is taken, and the commission must proceed with one case at a time. Employers are given many opportunities at various stages of the proceedings to cease discrimination in the particular case in question and thereby avoid penalty. The case-by-case approach does not necessarily result in the opening of whole fields of employment to blacks. There are instances in which a single black has been aided in getting employment by a commission order, but few other blacks were subsequently hired. And occasionally, employers may be threatened into hiring less-than-qualified blacks out of fear that refusal to do so would result in costly, time-consuming, and embarrassing legal proceedings.

In 1957 the city of New York adopted a fair housing law that became a model for subsequent laws in a number of states and cities. Fair housing laws are enforced in much the same manner as fair employment laws: each proceeds on complaint, investigation, conciliation, formal notice and hearing, commission orders, and ultimately court sanctions to force compliance. However, most fair housing laws exclude certain housing from their coverage, for example, the rental of rooms within a residence or owner-occupied building (the "Mrs. Murphy" clause) or an even more significant exclusion—sales or rental of single-family homes. Procedural delays are a particularly difficult problem in the enforcement of fair housing laws, since often the home in question is already sold to someone else and taken off the market before a complaint can be processed.

There is reasonable doubt as to whether fair housing laws—federal, state, or local—would ever succeed in breaking up America's ghettos. A crucial problem is the enforcement of fair housing laws. These laws may eliminate overt discrimination, but it is very difficult to detect discrimination when a seller or his agent chooses to mask his prejudice. But perhaps the most important obstacle to the success of fair housing legislation is the economic inability of many blacks to take advantage of it and purchase homes in affluent neighborhoods. Until the income levels of blacks are raised sufficiently to enable them to buy suburban homes, fair housing legislation will remain largely a paper commitment.

There is, yet, no evidence that cities with fair housing laws are any less segregated than those without such laws. This suggests that the economic constraints upon blacks may be more effective in creating ghettos than any direct discrimination that can be eliminated through legislation. Finally, it should be pointed out that established residential patterns are very difficult to reverse. Many blacks and whites become accustomed to prevailing residential patterns. Even if the housing market were open, so that housing choice could be freely exercised, there is some question as to whether there would be immediate significant changes in racial patterns of residence.

"DE FACTO" SEGREGATION
AND "BUSSING" IN NORTHERN CITIES

In *Brown* v. *Board of Education* of Topeka, Kansas, the Supreme Court stated that segregation had "a tendency to retard the educational and mental development of Negro children and to deprive them of some of the benefits they would receive in a racially integrated school system." The U.S. Civil Rights Commission reported that even when the segregation was *de facto,* that is, a product of segregated housing patterns and neighborhood schools rather than direct discrimination, the adverse effects on black students were still significant.[22] In northern urban school districts the commission reported that predominantly black schools were less likely to have good libraries or advanced courses in sciences and languages than predominantly white schools and more likely to have overcrowded classrooms, poorly trained teachers, and teachers who were dissatisfied with their school assignments. Black students attending predominantly black schools had lower achievement scores and lower aspiration levels than blacks from similar economic backgrounds attending predominantly white schools. When a group of black students in class with a majority of advantaged whites was compared with a control group of blacks attending school with a majority of disadvantaged blacks, the difference in achievement amounted to more than two grade levels. On the other hand, the commission contended that the achievement of white students in classes that were roughly half white was no different from that of a control group of white students in all-white schools. Therein lies the essential argument for ending de facto segregation in northern urban school systems.

However, ending de facto segregation would require drastic changes in the existing concept of "neighborhood schools." Schools would no longer be part of the neighborhood or local community but part of a larger city-wide or metropolitan-wide school system. Students would have to be bussed

---

[22]United States Commission on Civil Rights, *Racial Isolation in the Public Schools,* 2 vols. (Washington, D.C.: Government Printing Office, 1967).

on a large scale into and out of the ghettos. In several large cities where blacks comprise the overwhelming majority of public school students, desegregation would require city students to be bussed to the suburbs and suburban students to be bussed to the core city. Many suburbanites moved out of the central city in order to get their children out of city schools, and they are not likely to look with favor upon proposals to bus them back to the ghettos. Finally, the ending of de facto segregation would require school districts to classify students on the basis of race and use racial categories as a basis for school placement. Although this is supposedly a benign form of racial discrimination, it represents a return to government-sponsored racial classification and the differential application of laws to the separate races.

Racial isolation in the fifty states is described in Table 13–2 for 1968 and 1970. The Department of Health, Education, and Welfare reports a dramatic decrease in the percentage of black pupils attending predominantly black schools during that period. Nationwide, HEW reports that 38.2 percent of all black pupils were attending predominantly black schools in 1970, compared with 61.0 percent in 1968. But most of this decrease in racial separation occurred in the *southern* states. Southern states which in 1968 ranked at the bottom of state rankings on racial integration no longer do so. De facto segregation in northern cities is now the principal source of racial isolation.

The extent of de facto segregation in the public elementary schools of the nation's twenty largest cities is shown in Table 13–3. It is easier to achieve desegregation when the black percentage of school enrollment is low; obviously desegregation is difficult if not impossible when there are few white students in public schools with whom to integrate black children. Thus Washington, D.C., is virtually unable to achieve desegregation. Desegregation in Philadelphia, Chicago, Detroit, Baltimore, Cleveland, St. Louis, and New Orleans is also made difficult by the fact that a majority of the students in the cities are black. With the exception of Washington, D.C., however, no city as yet has so few white pupils that it is physically unable to bring an end to segregation, if we define segregation as schools with more than 90 percent black pupils, if the white pupils were spread around. (If a segregated school is defined as one with a *majority* of black students, there are about a dozen large cities which would be unable to desegregate, owing to a lack of white pupils.) Of course it is true that the greater the black proportion of the school population, the more extensive the policy change required to accomplish desegregation. But it is not impossible. The U.S. Civil Rights Commission has suggested several policy options for school districts wishing to desegregate: the "pairing" or merging of attendance areas of two or more schools; the establishment of central "educational parks" integrating stu-

TABLE 13-2
Racial Isolation in Northern and Southern States, 1968 and 1970

Rank	State	Pct. Negro (1968)	Pct. Seg. (1968)	Rank	State	Pct. Negro (1970)	Pct. Seg.[1] (1970)
	U.S. Average	14.5	61.0		U.S. Average	14.9	38.2
1	Alaska	3.0	0.0	1	Alaska	2.7	0.0
	Idaho	0.2	0.0		Idaho	0.2	0.0
	Maine	0.6	0.0		Iowa	1.6	0.0
	Montana	0.1	0.0		Maine	0.3	0.0
	New Hampshire	0.4	0.0		Montana	0.3	0.0
	North Dakota	0.4	0.0		New Hampshire	0.4	0.0
	Oregon	1.6	0.0		North Dakota	0.5	0.0
	Rhode Island	4.7	0.0		Oregon	1.7	0.0
	Utah	0.5	0.0		Rhode Island	4.2	0.0
	Vermont	0.1	0.0		South Dakota	0.3	0.0
	Washington	2.4	0.0		Utah	0.5	0.0
	Wyoming	0.8	0.0		Vermont	0.1	0.0
13	South Dakota	0.3	3.1		Wyoming	1.1	0.0
14	Iowa	1.5	3.6	14	West Virginia	4.7	0.9
15	Minnesota	1.1	4.0	15	Washington	2.6	1.6
16	West Virginia	5.0	5.7	16	Minnesota	1.1	3.4
17	New Mexico	2.1	15.9	17	New Mexico	2.2	9.9
18	Connecticut	8.3	18.3	18	North Carolina	29.4	12.2
	Massachusetts	4.3	18.3	19	Arkansas	24.7	15.5
20	Delaware	19.4	21.6	20	South Carolina	40.9	17.2
21	Kentucky	9.2	26.6	21	Delaware	20.6	18.7
22	Arizona	4.3	27.6	22	Virginia	24.1	20.9
23	Kansas	5.9	31.8	23	Connecticut	9.0	21.3
24	New Jersey	14.9	32.8	24	Massachusetts	4.5	21.7

25	Nebraska	4.6	35.0	25	Florida	23.1	21.9
26	New York	14.1	35.8	26	Arizona	3.9	22.2
27	Nevada	7.7	39.5	27	Kansas	6.5	22.6
28	Wisconsin	4.0	39.6	28	Nebraska	4.7	23.8
29	Ohio	12.0	42.8	29	Kentucky	9.2	24.5
30	Indiana	8.8	43.5	30	Nevada	8.2	27.3
31	Pennsylvania	11.7	44.1	31	Colorado	3.5	28.0
32	Colorado	3.4	45.0	32	Mississippi	50.8	29.9
33	Michigan	13.3	46.4	33	Georgia	33.2	30.8
34	California	8.7	47.8	34	New Jersey	15.4	36.3
35	Oklahoma	9.0	48.3	35	Louisiana	40.4	37.1
36	Maryland	23.4	52.6	36	Wisconsin	4.2	37.7
37	Texas	15.1	63.1	37	Oklahoma	9.5	38.3
38	North Carolina	29.4	65.1	38	Alabama	34.3	38.9
39	Missouri	14.5	66.0	39	Nebraska	15.4	39.3
40	Virginia	23.5	68.2	40	Indiana	8.9	41.3
41	Tennessee	20.8	71.6	41	Texas	15.3	41.9
42	Florida	23.2	72.1	42	Ohio	12.1	42.8
43	Illinois	18.0	72.4	43	Pennsylvania	11.8	44.3
44	Arkansas	25.6	74.1	44	Maryland	24.2	45.7
45	Georgia	31.5	83.4	45	California	9.2	46.7
46	Louisiana	38.8	88.1	46	Michigan	13.4	49.8
47	South Carolina	39.4	89.1	47	Tennessee	21.2	50.1
48	Alabama	34.9	90.9	48	Missouri	14.6	59.1
49	Mississippi	49.0	92.7	49	Illinois	18.2	71.2
N/A	Hawaii	*	*	N/A	Hawaii	*	*

N/A — Not Available; * — data not available; Southern States are underscored.

1 Negroes attending 95-100 percent minority schools.

SOURCE: Department of Health, Education, and Welfare, HEW News Release, June 18, 1971.

TABLE 13-3

Racial Isolation in Public Elementary Schools of Large Cities
in 1965-66

	Negro Students as a Percent of Total Students	Percentage of Negro Students in Schools 90-100 Percent Negro	Percentage of Negro Students in Schools 90-100 Percent White
New York	31.0	20.7	56.8
Chicago	52.8	89.2	88.8
Los Angeles	19.2	39.5	94.7
Philadelphia	58.6	72.0	57.7
Detroit	55.3	72.3	65.0
Baltimore	64.3	84.2	67.0
Houston	33.9	93.0	97.3
Cleveland	53.9	82.3	80.2
Washington	90.9	90.4	34.3
St. Louis	63.3	90.9	66.0
Milwaukee	26.4	72.4	86.3
San Francisco	28.8	21.1	65.1
Boston	28.9	35.4	76.5
Dallas	27.5	82.6	90.1
New Orleans	65.5	95.9	83.8
Pittsburgh	39.4	49.5	62.3
San Antonio	14.3	65.9	89.4
San Diego	11.6	13.9	88.7
Seattle	10.5	9.9	89.8
Buffalo	34.6	77.0	81.1

SOURCE: U.S. Commission on Civil Rights, RACIAL ISOLATION IN THE PUBLIC SCHOOLS (Washington, D.C.: Government Printing Office, 1967), I, 4.

dents from throughout the school district; and the closing of predominantly black schools and the dispersal of their students among other schools in the community.[23] The only technological innovation these policies call for is the school bus, and since most public school children in the nation already ride buses, the feasibility of the bus seems beyond question.

The political problems of "bussing" far exceed its physical dislocations in creating obstacles to school desegregation. Yet several states have made more or less official policy pronouncements against de facto segregation. Massachusetts has taken the strongest policy stand of any state in its Racial Imbalance Act of 1965. This provides that a school district, upon notification by the state board that one of its schools is racially imbal-

[23] United States Commission on Civil Rights, *Racial Isolation*, 140–84.

anced (50 percent or more black pupils), must prepare and file with the board a plan to eliminate the imbalance. If the school district fails to show progress within a reasonable time in eliminating racial imbalances, the commissioner of education must refuse to certify all state school aid for that school district. In New York, New Jersey, and Illinois, there are general laws guaranteeing equal educational opportunity, which have been construed by state boards and commissioners as mandating the elimination of racial imbalance in the selection of school sites and the drawing of attendance lines.

Political opposition to bussing children for the purpose of achieving racial balance in the schools comes from white parents who fear their children will be transported into the violent crime-ridden culture of the ghetto. They fear that their children will be exposed to what black children have long had to cope with—rape, robbery, extortion, mugging, dope addiction—which have made ghetto schools blackboard jungles where surviving is more important than learning. Many white parents moved to the suburbs at great cost to themselves to obtain a better education for their children, and they do not appreciate the prospect of federal judges ordering their children back into ghetto schools. Generally, white parents are less fearful of black pupils being transported to white schools (as long as blacks remain a minority) than they are of white pupils being transported to predominantly black schools. Thus, limited one-way bussing over relatively short distances is politically feasible. But the specter of large-scale two-way bussing, transporting white children ten to thirty miles from the suburbs to the ghetto, is another matter.

To date the Supreme Court has not issued any sweeping order to end de facto segregation in Northern cities. It is true that the Supreme Court approved of a bussing order in the Swann case involving a Southern city, but the Court's order was based on that city's history of direct segregation by law. Southern cities have a special obligation to correct long-standing racial imbalances stemming from state action. In contrast, it is difficult to prove that racial imbalance in Northern city schools is a product of any state or local government actions. Nonetheless, some federal district courts have issued orders to Northern cities to begin bussing to achieve racial balance in their schools. (In Detroit, a federal district judge ordered the city and separate surrounding suburban school districts to begin mass bussing of children to and from the suburbs and the ghetto; he also ordered the state to create a new metropolitan-wide school district and to purchase the necessary new busses.)

Doubtlessly the Supreme Court will soon be called upon to formulate a national policy on bussing and racial imbalance in schools. Does the Fourteenth Amendment require state and local school officials to racially balance public schools where racial imbalance is not a direct product of state action? This question has already generated a great deal of political controversy. President Richard M. Nixon recommended that Congress legislate a moratorium on court-ordered bussing until after the Supreme Court considered the issue and came to a clear and binding decision. Some Congressional critics of court-ordered bussing have proposed a constitutional amendment prohibiting federal courts from ordering racial balancing in public schools. Public opinion polls consistently show heavy public opposition to bussing and racial balancing. But supporters of bussing argue that black children have a constitutional right to equal educational opportunity and that bussing is a necessary tool in achieving this constitutional right.

BLACK POPULATION TRENDS

While blacks constitute only 11 percent of the total population of the United States, they are rapidly approaching a numerical majority in many of the nation's largest cities. Blacks already constitute a majority of the population of Washington, Atlanta, and Newark, and make up more than 40 percent of the population of Detroit, Baltimore, St. Louis, New Orleans, Oakland, Birmingham, and Gary. (See Table 13–4.) They will make up nearly a third of the population of Chicago, Philadelphia, Cleveland, Memphis and Norfolk. These population trends are bound to have an impact on politics and public policy in these cities.

The two outstanding trends in black population migration in recent decades has been the tendency of blacks to leave the South and to move from rural to urban areas. Census figures show, for example, that while 87 percent of the nation's blacks lived in the South in 1900, only 56 percent did so in 1960. While only 27 percent of the nation's blacks lived in urban areas in 1910, 73 percent did so in 1960, and 81 percent did so in 1970. Moreover, in leaving rural areas, blacks tended to concentrate heavily in the central cities of metropolitan areas, rather than in small towns or in metropolitan suburbs. This concentration of blacks in large central cities is a product of the availability of low-priced rental units in older run-down sections of central cities and of discriminatory housing practices of private owners and developers. Of course, underlying the concentration of blacks in run-down sectors of central cities is often a lack of sufficient income to purchase housing in suburbs or in better city neighborhoods. This poverty and unemployment that contributes to the concentration of blacks in "ghettos" is in turn a product of inadequate training and education, low aspiration levels, and often a lack of motivation. And problems in education and motivation are themselves related to a breakdown in family life, delinquency, and crime. Thus, urban blacks face a whole series of interrelated problems in addi-

TABLE 13-4

Nonwhite Population as a Percent of Total Population, 1960 and 1970, and Percent Change in White and Nonwhite Population, 1960–70, 40 Largest Cities in Continental United States

City	Percent Nonwhite			Percent Change 1960-1970	
	1950	1960	1970	White	Nonwhite
New York	9.8	14.7	23.4	−9.2	61.6
Chicago	14.1	23.6	34.4	−18.6	38.4
Los Angeles	10.7	16.8	22.8	5.4	54.0
Philadelphia	18.3	26.7	34.4	−12.9	25.2
Detroit	16.4	29.2	44.5	−29.1	38.1
Houston	21.1	26.0	26.6	25.6	50.6
Baltimore	23.8	35.0	47.0	−21.4	29.7
Cleveland	16.3	28.9	39.0	−26.5	15.7
Washington, D.C.	35.4	54.8	72.3	−39.4	30.7
Milwaukee	3.6	10.5	15.6	−10.4	69.9
Dallas	13.2	18.7	25.8	14.2	66.3
San Francisco	10.5	18.4	28.6	−15.4	50.5
St. Louis	18.0	28.8	41.3	−31.6	19.1
Boston	5.3	9.8	18.1	−16.5	69.9
New Orleans	32.0	37.4	45.5	−17.6	14.9
San Antonio	7.2	7.9	8.6	9.7	30.6
San Diego	5.5	8.5	11.1	17.2	72.8
Pittsburgh	12.3	16.8	20.7	−18.0	6.0
Seattle	5.8	9.8	12.6	−9.1	43.9
Memphis	37.2	42.7	39.2	21.2	32.3
Buffalo	6.5	13.8	21.3	−20.7	34.1
Phoenix	6.2	8.4	6.7	31.2	52.2
Atlanta	36.6	46.6	51.6	−20.0	37.3
Denver	4.4	7.7	11.0	−.09	60.2
Columbus, Ohio	12.5	19.0	19.0	11.3	30.8
Indianapolis	15.0	23.0	18.4	61.0	38.5
Kansas City, Mo.	12.3	19.3	22.8	.04	37.3
Cincinnati	15.6	22.0	28.0	−17.2	15.9
Minneapolis	1.6	3.2	6.4	−32.5	79.5
Newark, N.J.	17.2	34.4	55.9	−36.7	53.6
Fort Worth	13.1	17.3	20.6	4.4	42.2
Louisville	15.7	21.4	24.0	−14.3	23.4
Long Beach	2.6	5.1	8.2	−.09	100.7
Portland, Ore.	3.5	5.7	7.8	.24	43.3
Oklahoma City	9.3	13.8	16.0	9.1	39.0
Oakland, Calif.	14.5	26.4	40.9	−21.1	52.6
Birmingham	39.9	41.1	42.2	−15.4	−6.5
Norfolk, Va.	27.9	32.6	30.4	−4.5	15.2
Miami, Fla.	16.3	22.6	23.4	13.5	19.3
Omaha	6.7	10.0	10.6	12.8	39.8

SOURCE: U.S. Bureau of the Census, 1970 CENSUS OF POPULATION, Series PC (S1) 2 (Washington, D.C.: Government Printing Office, 1971).

tion to discrimination: poverty, slum housing, undereducation, lack of job skills, family problems, lack of motivation, delinquency, and crime. It is difficult to talk about any one of these problems without reference to them all.

The migration of blacks into cities, particularly in the North, has been accompanied by a heavy out-migration of whites fleeing to the suburbs for a variety of reasons. The total populations of many large central cities have remained stagnant in recent years or even declined slightly; black population percentages have increased because black in-migration has countered the white out-migration. Black birthrates in urban areas have also tended to be slightly higher than those of whites.

Politically, these population trends mean that there will be an increase in organized black participation in urban politics and increasing black importance and power in city administrations. The election of black mayors in Cleveland, Gary, and Newark provides evidence that there will be a rise in the number of black officeholders. Black city councilmen, state legislators, and congressmen are likely to become commonplace in the next few years and evoke little comment from the news media. The number of blacks in the U.S. House of Representatives will also increase. The election of a black, Edward W. Brooke, to the U.S. Senate from Massachusetts, suggests that blacks may also win important statewide elections. This increase in black office holding can be attributed in a large measure to the concentration of black voters in large cities.

However, increasing black percentages in central cities are not likely to lead to black "takeovers," in the sense that black officeholders can afford to ignore or override the interests of white city dwellers. In the first place, whites are going to continue to constitute a majority of the population in most central cities. Second, black candidates are likely to find that there is more political mileage in appealing to white votes by pledging impartiality and promising to be "mayor of *all* of the people." There is little incentive in a strict racist appeal by black candidates, as long as whites remain a substantial proportion of the city voting population.

STYLES OF BLACK POLITICS

Styles of black politics have been changing rapidly in recent years. In part these changes reflect the massive migration of blacks from the rural South into northern metropolitan slums, but they reflect equally the differing perspectives of successive generations of blacks.

The political style that we have labeled " 'Uncle Tom' politics" has been well described by Dwaine Marvick:

Traditionally, Negro civic leaders occupying symbolic positions of respect were "tapped" by leaders in the white community as contact points. The influence of such "anointed" figures often depended more on their near monopoly over liaison channels to the all important white communities' decision-makers than on any spontaneous following within the Negro community which they might have generated. Undertakers, insurance men, bankers, teachers, a few professional men—above all, ministers of Negro churches; these were the men who traditionally were treated as spokesmen for their local Negro communities. Accommodationist, conservative, dignified, personally successful men: they have been for more than half a century the prime models for Negro children asking to be shown local "men of influence."[24]

This style of black political leadership was quite common in southern communities until very recently. It is important to note that this traditional black leadership was almost exclusively middle class in character. Since most blacks found themselves in lower-class circumstances, this middle-class leadership could hardly be genuinely representative of the black community. Often these middle-class leaders were completely out of touch with the black masses, since their acceptability to the white community, not their popularity among the black masses, was the crucial criterion for selection.

The traditional black leadership did not make "demands," but simply "requests," of the white community. Black leaders were dependent upon white leaders: only by appealing to the latter's interests and beliefs could blacks gain their objectives. The ability of blacks to make "demands" was severely limited. Black leaders had to manipulate and to persuade whites. They had to "behave themselves." Compliance with white-imposed behavioral norms was necessary to make any headway, even when fellow blacks called it "Tomming."

The massive infusion of blacks from the rural South to the urban centers of key northern industrial states—New York, Pennsylvania, New Jersey, Ohio, Michigan, Illinois, and California—provided American blacks with an important measure of political leverage, especially in presidential elections. This leverage derives from the pivotal nature of these states in presidential politics: they are characterized by strong two-party competition and they possess a large bloc of electoral votes. Black votes in the North provided crucial support for black protests in the South and for the passage of federal legislation protecting the rights of southern blacks.

The increase in black voting populations in northern cities in the

[24]Dwaine Marvick, "The Political Socialization of the American Negro," *Annals of the American Academy of Political and Social Science*, 361 (September 1965), 123.

1920s and 1930s and the increase in black voter registration in the South in the 1940s and 1950s brought about a gradual modification of the "Uncle Tom" style of black politics. The mobilization of black electoral strength in both North and South gradually improved the bargaining position of black leaders. They were no longer required to depend exclusively upon white goodwill; an expanded black electorate provided a new political instrument and gave rise to an "organizational style" of black politics.

Disadvantaged black masses provide a pool of support for a machine style of politics that relies upon personal and material rewards. Black political machines have emerged in large cities where the prevailing style of white politics was the machine model. In these cities the black machine was tied closely to the existence of the white machine. The organizational style of black politics does not stress "racial" issues but instead concentrates its attention on material rewards. For example, the organization is not likely to oppose the location of a new public hospital in a black residential area merely because the hospital would contribute to segregation; the machine would rather have the jobs and material rewards of the hospital, even if it were segregated, than the ideological victory of building an integrated hospital in a white neighborhood.

For many years the most powerful black organization leader in the nation has been Congressman William L. Dawson of Chicago. Dawson exercises predominant influence over five all-black wards in that city and therefore controls a large contingent of local officials and state representatives as well as his own safe seat in Congress. The Dawson organization is part of the larger political organization controlled by Mayor Richard J. Daley. Dawson depends upon Daley for support and vice versa. Dawson delivers a heavy black vote to the Daley machine, and in return Daley provides the jobs, favors, protection, and material rewards that enable Dawson to hold his organization together. Edward C. Banfield and James Q. Wilson write of the Dawson style:

> Dawson maintains his machine in the usual way, by exchanging jobs, favors, and protection for votes. Almost every weekend he flies to Chicago to sit in a shabby ward office in the midst of the slums and to listen to all who come to him. Where the direct, material interests of his constituents are at stake, he and his organization are ready to help; they will get a sick man into the county hospital, find out why an old lady's welfare check has not arrived, defend a beleaguered homeowner against the urban renewal authority, and go to the police commissioner, and if necessary the mayor, to see to it that a case of alleged police brutality is properly investigated. Matters involving Negro rights in the abstract do not interest them, however. These concern the militants, but they are not the base upon which the machine builds.[25]

25Edward C. Banfield and James Q. Wilson, *City Politics* (Cambridge, Mass.: Harvard-M.I.T. Press, 1963), pp. 304–5.

Black organizational politics is most likely to be found in cities where the prevailing style of white politics is organizational. In other words, the style of black politics depends largely upon the style of white politics. Organizational politics is strengthened by the concentration of blacks in one or a few all-black geographical areas in the city, and it is further strengthened when the political system is based on a large number of relatively small wards or other geographic subdivisions. Of course organizational politics is closely tied to the existence of strong party organizations. In summary, organizational politics is strengthened by residential segregation, ward organization, and strong partisan politics. In contrast, it is weakened by residential integration, at-large elections, and non-partisan politics.

In contrast to organizational styles of black politics, the "racial style" emphasizes ideological values rather than material rewards. Appeals are made to principle, to lofty moral and racial goals, to the aspirations and fears of black masses, but not necessarily to their material welfare. The political style depends upon the existence of an "enemy"–discrimination, "racism," injustice against blacks. Black status and black power are the goals of the racial leader; the improvement of the material welfare of the black is of secondary importance. The racial leader derives his support from his appeal to principle, and therefore it is difficult for him to engage in bargaining with white leaders.

Black militants have frequently attacked black organizational leaders. For example, William L. Dawson has been the object of the following uncomplimentary report:

> Chicago provides an excellent example of how Negroes can be co-opted into inactivity. . . . Dawson surrendered far more than he has obtained for the Negro community. What Dawson obtained were the traditional benefits of the big-city political machine: low-paying jobs for a lot of followers; political intervention with the police and with bail bondsmen, social workers, housing officials, and other bureaucrats whose decisions can affect a poor constituent's life; and a slice of the "melon" in the form of public housing projects, welfare payments, and the like.

> What Dawson surrendered was the pride and dignity of his community; he threw away the opportunity to force Chicago's political and civic leaders to identify and deal with the fundamental problems of segregation and oppression.[26]

James Q. Wilson describes the late Congressman Adam Clayton Powell, Jr., of Harlem as the prime example of a racial politician.[27] Wilson draws

[26]Charles E. Silberman, *Crisis in Black and White* (New York: Random House, Inc., 1964), pp. 204 and 206; quoted with approval by Stokeley Carmichael and Charles V. Hamilton, *Black Power: The Politics of Liberation in America* (New York: Random House, Inc., 1967), pp. 11–12.

[27]James Q. Wilson, "Two Negro Politicians: An Interpretation," *Midwest Journal of Political Science*, 4 (November 1960), 346–69; see also James Q. Wilson, *Negro Politics* (New York: The Free Press, 1960).

an interesting contrast between the organizational style of politics of Dawson and the more flamboyant racial politics of Powell:

> The one is an orator, the other an organizer; one is flamboyant, the other is conservative; one is militant on the race question, the other is moderate. One seeks publicity and speaks almost always "on the record"; the other shuns publicity and speaks to interviewers only off the record. One is considered by most of his House colleagues to be demagogic and unreliable; the other has the confidence and respect of many influential Congressmen. . . . One raises the race issue on every occasion; the other goes out of his way to avoid discussing race or race questions. One is light-skinned, handsome, boyish, gregarious, fun-loving; the other is brown-skinned, aged, reserved, quiet. One spends his free time (of which he has a great deal) in world travel, entertaining, and night life; the other rarely travels, devotes himself completely to politics, and leads a home life carefully screened by privacy and silence. The two most prominent Negro politicians are radically dissimilar, avoid each other's company, speak disparagingly of one another, and elicit the violent attitudes of love and hate from their friends and enemies.[28]

It is possible to make a further distinction between militant and organizational styles of racial politics. The militant is likely to cast racial issues into simplistic terms such as a fight between good and evil and to see white racism as the sole difficulty facing blacks. The moderate is more likely to see racial issues in the broader context of complex social problems and to recognize that the black faces other problems besides white racism. The militant is more likely to assume the posture of protest and agitation, regardless of whether any tangible results might accrue from such activity. The moderate is proud of past accomplishments. The militant wants massive legislative action to resolve race problems. The moderate is more likely to accept informal agreements or bargains with white leaders. The militant is willing to agitate for sweeping reform, while the moderate concentrates on more specific or limited goals. The militant wants immediate change, while the moderate is more willing to wait a longer period of time for progress. The militant emphasizes how bad the conditions are at the present time, while the moderate is more likely to look backward and to compare present conditions with the even worse conditions of the past.

CARL B. STOKES OF CLEVELAND

Blacks do not occupy public office in America in proportion to their percentage of the nation's population. However, in recent years black candidates have been more successful at the polls than at any time since

---

[28]Wilson, "Two Negro Politicians," p. 347.

Reconstruction. But the black population migration to northern cities, the concentration of black people in ghettos, the increase in black registration, and finally the legislative reapportionment of the 1960s prompted by *Baker* v. *Carr,* have all combined to promote black office holding.

Observing the political styles of the national black officeholders is an instructive exercise. Most successful black candidates to date have avoided racial militancy, pledging instead to represent "all of the people." Most have avoided positions that would be threatening to whites. They have been generally willing to form electoral and political alliances with white groups.

Race was certainly the key issue in the election of Carl B. Stokes as mayor of Cleveland in 1967. Blacks comprised an estimated 36 percent of Cleveland's population in that year. Thus, even though race was an issue in the election, Stokes clearly had substantial white support.

The political circumstances surrounding Stokes's victory suggest that black candidates can win high office if they can secure the near-unanimous support of the black community while at the same time appealing to a substantial number (though not necessarily a majority) of white voters. Stokes defeated the incumbent mayor Ralph S. Locher in the Democratic primary, despite Locher's endorsement by party leaders. At the time, Locher's administration as mayor was generally considered to have been uninspiring; the Cleveland *Plain Dealer,* the largest daily newspaper in Ohio, endorsed Stokes over Locher. Stokes mounted a massive voter registration drive in black wards, but at the same time he campaigned in white wards, speaking in churches, clubs, and homes.

Stokes won the Democratic primary with 52.5 percent of the vote. An analysis of returns leaves little doubt that race was the principal determinant in the voting. Recognized black wards gave Stokes 96.2 percent of their vote while recognized white wards gave him only 15.2 percent; predictably, mixed black and white wards divided their votes, giving Stokes a combined total of 54.4 percent. Stokes's victory was the product of three factors: (1) an unprecedented number (73.4 percent) of registered blacks turned out at the polls to vote for him; (2) many whites were unenthusiastic about Locher, and only 58.4 percent turned out to vote; and (3) Stokes was able to win about 20 percent of the white vote.

In the general election when Stokes as a Democratic candidate faced his Republican opponent Seth Taft, race again became the principal issue—despite the fact that Taft did not exploit the issue. Normally, Taft as a Republican would have had little chance in a Democratic city. The *Plain Dealer* again endorsed Stokes, as did organized labor. Taft attempted to project the image of the new breed of liberal Republican *à la* John Lindsay and Charles Percy, pointing proudly to his own record on civil rights (he was one of the authors of the Ohio Fair Housing

Law). His attacks on Stokes were all legitimate: he accused him of absenteeism in the state legislature and charged that Stokes himself was a slumlord who owned dilapidated rental projects in the ghetto.

Again Stokes's problem in the campaign was to hold on to his high turnout of black voters while at the same time winning over some whites. Stokes opened his campaign with an overt racial appeal: "The personal analysis of Seth Taft . . . is that Seth Taft may win the November 7 election, but for only one reason. Taft's reason is that his skin happens to be white." When whites reacted negatively to this approach, Stokes quickly changed his strategy and played down the racial issue. But even though both Taft and Stokes said little about race during the campaign, it turned out to be the most important issue in the campaign.

Stokes won the general election by holding on to his near-unanimous high-turnout black vote while at the same time winning about 20 percent of the white vote. With large numbers of white Democrats voting for a Republican mayor for the first time in their lives, Stokes barely squeaked by with only 50.5 percent of the total vote. He received 95 percent of the vote in black wards while Taft received 80 percent of the vote in white wards; again the mixed wards were divided, with Stokes receiving 54 percent of the vote in these wards.

Thus Stokes's victory in Cleveland was not a great victory for racial tolerance. Four out of five whites voted against the black candidate, and blacks were nearly unanimous in their opposition to the white candidate. In his term of office Stokes was faced with problems similar to those he faced in the election. He tried to demonstrate to blacks that his presence in city hall did make a difference, but his programs could not seem so preferential toward blacks as to run the risk of unifying white opposition.

LIFE IN THE GHETTOS

It is not easy for white middle-class Americans to understand what ghetto life is all about. As Roger Kahn, a white journalist who has tried to understand life in the ghettos, reports:

> Harlem is strange and dark and frightening, and if your skin is white, you are a marked alien. It doesn't matter whether you are a Quaker full of compassion, or a Jew, full of sympathy, or a Baptist, full of guilt, or a Roman Catholic, full of missionary zeal. "Man," they say in Harlem, "long as you white, you ain't one of us, and what you doin' roun' here anyway, white man? Get on back downtown where you belong."[29]

[29]Roger Kahn, "White Man, Walk Easy," *Saturday Evening Post*, June 13, 1964; also reprinted in Dye and Hawkins, *Politics in the Metropolis*.

Poll takers and interviewers have a difficult time: "Man, you know why I run first time I see you come? I thought you was fuzz, man, and I was a hustlin' to stash my .45."[30] It is unlikely that many whites, liberal or conservative, understand the full extent of frustration, bitterness, and hatred in America's black ghettos. White conservatives may be shocked to learn that many middle-class values about thrift, hard work, and the sanctity of property are not universally shared with ghetto residents. White liberals may be shocked to learn that racial prejudice is not the monopoly of the white man.

Daniel P. Moynihan has argued effectively that one of the worst effects of slavery and segregation has been its impact on black family life.[31] It was the black male who was most humiliated by segregation. The submissiveness which segregation implies is surely more destructive to the male than to the female personality. Keeping the black "in his place" usually means keeping the black *male* in his place; the female is not a threat to anyone. The female-headed black family emerges as one of the striking features of life in the ghetto. Over 25 percent of all black families are headed by women. For the male offspring of a matriarchal ghetto family, the future is often depressing, with defeat and frustration repeating itself throughout his life. He may drop out of school in the ninth grade as a protest to his lack of success. If he fails his armed forces qualification test (and a majority of young men from the ghetto do so), he may never again have an opportunity for further education or job training. Lacking parental supervision, and with little to do, he may get into trouble with the police. A police record will further hurt his chances of getting a job. The ghetto male with limited job skills enters the job market seriously handicapped. His pay is usually not enough to support a family and he has little hope of moving up. He may tie up much of his income in installment debts for a car, television set, or other conveniences, which he sees in widespread use among middle-class Americans. Because of his low credit rating, he will be forced to pay excessive interest rates, and sooner or later his creditors will garnish his salary. If he marries, he is likely to have at least five children, and he and his family will live in overcrowded, substandard housing. As pressures and frustrations mount, he may decide to leave his family, either because he has found his inability to support his wife and children humiliating, or because only in this way will his wife and children be eligible for welfare payments. Welfare policy again strengthens the role of the female in

[30]*Ibid.*
[31]See Daniel P. Moynihan, *The Negro Family: The Case for National Action* (Washington, D.C.: Government Printing Office, 1965); portions of the Moynihan report are reprinted in Dye and Hawkins, *Politics in the Metropolis.*

the black family, because she can get the family on welfare (particularly aid to families with dependent children) while the male cannot. In fact, his remaining with the family is an obstacle to receiving welfare payments.

The civil rights movement opened new opportunities for black Americans. But equality of *opportunity* is not the same as *absolute* equality. In a significant speech to the graduating class of Howard University in 1965, President Lyndon B. Johnson identified the fundamental problem of equality in America today:

> You do not take a person who for years has been hobbled by chains and liberate him, bring him up to the starting line of a race, and say, "you are free to compete with all the others," and still justly believe that you have been completely fair.
>
> Thus it is not enough to open the gates to opportunity. All our citizens must have the ability to walk through those gates.
>
> This is the next and most profound stage of the battle for civil rights . . . the task is to give twenty million Negroes the same choice as every other American to learn to work and share in society to develop their abilities—physical, mental, and spiritual—and to pursue their individual happiness.[32]

But the complexity of this task is enormous. The problems are manifold—how to overcome the interlocking effects of deprivation in education, job training, health, housing, employment, crime and delinquency, and human motivation. Can deprivation resulting from unequal treatment of blacks in the past be eliminated without preferential treatment for present-day victims? And if preferential programs are begun, how will we know when blacks have been brought to the starting line? What about blacks who do succeed in joining the affluent American middle-class—will they suffer from feelings of guilt in leaving most of their black brothers behind in the ghetto? Will integration of middle-class blacks result in a "skimming off of the cream" of potential leadership of black masses?

Another problem: "Integration" assumes that individual blacks will acquire the skills, education, jobs, and income requisite for a secure position in affluent middle-class America, and it assumes that the values and institutions of this America are looked upon as legitimate and desirable by most blacks. In the past, blacks have not had much of a share in shaping these institutions or determining these values; the most they can expect is a greater share in their joint determination in the future.

[32]President Lyndon B. Johnson in a speech at Howard University, June 4, 1965.

Given these conditions, can we assume that blacks will voluntarily choose to join affluent white America? Once the right to choose has been established, will blacks choose to be "integrated," or will they choose separation?

It is not our intention here to review all the proposed or existing public programs that may contribute to a reduction of inequality in American society. In Chapter 16 we will examine the Economic Opportunity Act of 1964, the core of the widely heralded "war on poverty," which constituted the national government's most direct attempt to cope with the complex problems of poverty and inequality. The experience of the Economic Opportunity program is an instructive example of the political issues involved in public efforts aimed at equalizing "life chances." The war on poverty illustrates the difficulties and complexities of dealing effectively with the problem of equality. There is no guarantee that equality can be achieved *even if* the government embarks upon a multibillion-dollar effort to do so.

Occasionally, the rhetoric of politics suggests that the conditions of blacks in America are worsening, that America is hopelessly "racist," and that there is no possibility of real progress. This is not true. Blacks have made great progress over the last decade in income, jobs, education, housing, and other conditions of life—not only in absolute terms but also in narrowing the gap between themselves and whites. Black leaders can be expected to concentrate on what still must be done to achieve equality in America. But it is important that we do not mistake failure to progress fast enough with failure to progress at all. American society has moved toward equality very rapidly over the last decade. Of course whites have made progress too, and in every measure of "life chances" blacks remain below average white levels. Doubtlessly the progress made by blacks in recent years has been long overdue, and no rate of progress can be considered fast *enough*. But recent progress has been very impressive.

Median black family income was only slightly more than half of the median white family income in the 1950s, but by 1970 black family income had increased to 64 percent of white family income. (See Table 13–5.) In a single decade the proportion of blacks living below the recognized poverty line had fallen from 56 percent of all blacks to 31 percent. Blacks increased their percentage of professional, managerial, sales, clerical, and other white-collar jobs and reduced their percentage of laborers, service workers, and farmers. The proportion of blacks living in substandard housing fell from nearly one-half to less than one-quarter. Blacks also narrowed the gap in education: the proportion of young black males who completed high school rose from 37 percent to over 59 percent in a single decade.

TABLE 13-5
Change in Black-White Life Chances

Median Income of Families

	1947	1960	1968	1970
White	$4,916	$6,857	$8,937	$10,236
Negro	$2,514	$3,794	$5,590	$ 6,516

Median Income of Families of Negro and Other Races as a Percent of White Family Income

Year	Percent	Year	Percent
1950	54	1964	56
1955	55	1966	60
1959	52	1968	63
1960	55	1970	64

Persons Below Poverty Level

	Millions		Percent of Total	
	Negro	White	Negro	White
1959	11.0	28.5	56	18
1965	10.7	22.5	47	13
1969	7.6	16.7	31	10

Occupation: Negro and Other Races as a Percent of All Workers in Selected Occupations

Total	1960	1969
Professional	4	6
Medical	4	8
Teachers	7	10
Managers	2	3
Clerical	5	8
Sales	3	4
Craftsmen	5	7
Operatives	12	14
Nonfarm laborers	27	24
Private household	46	44
Other service	20	19
Farm	16	11

Percent of Persons 25 to 29 Years Old Who Completed 4 Years of High School or More

	Male		Female	
	Negro	White	Negro	White
1960	37	64	42	66
1968	55	78	58	77
1971	59	21	63	80

SOURCE: Bureau of the Census, "The Social and Economic Status of Negroes in the United States," Current Population Reports Series No. 29, p. 23. Updated.

VIOLENCE IN AMERICAN CITIES

The civil rights legislation of the 1960s had relatively little impact on the black masses in urban ghettos. The breakthroughs that the civil rights movement made in open public accommodations, fair employment, fair housing, and voting rights may have opened new opportunities for the educated black middle class, but the undereducated black poor living in the ghetto environment could not really take advantage of these new opportunities. The victories of the civil rights movement were primarily *symbolic* victories; the *actual* conditions of ghetto blacks in income, education, health, employment, housing, and other conditions of life were left unchanged. It was inevitable that the resentment, bitterness, and frustration of the ghetto masses would find expression in some fashion.

Civil disorder and violence are not new on the American scene. On the night of December 16, 1773, a group of "agitators" in Boston, Massachusetts, illegally destroyed 342 chests of tea. And violence as a form of political protest has continued intermittently in America to the present day. The nation itself was founded in armed revolution. Yet even though domestic violence has played a prominent role in America's history, the ghetto riots of the 1960s shocked the nation with the most massive and widespread civil disorders ever to face the nation. All these riots involved black attacks on established authority—policemen, firemen, National Guardsmen, whites, in general, and property owned by whites. Three of these riots—Watts, California, in 1965 and Newark and Detroit in 1967—amounted to major civil disorders.

The Watts riot in August 1965 was described in the McCone Commission's report:

> In the ugliest interval . . . perhaps as many as 10,000 Negroes took to the streets in neurotic bands. They looted stores, set fires, beat up white passers-by whom they had hauled from stopped cars, many of which were turned upside-down and burned, exchanged shots with law enforcement officers, and stoned and shot at firemen. The rioters seemed to have been caught up in an insensate rage of destruction. By Friday, disorder spread to adjoining areas, and ultimately, an area covering 46.5 square miles had to be controlled with the aid of military authority before public order was restored. . . .
>
> Of the 34 killed, one was a fireman, one was a deputy sheriff, and one a Long Beach policeman [the remainder were Negroes].
>
> More than 600 buildings were damaged by burning and looting. Out of this number, more than 200 were completely destroyed by fire. The rioters concentrated primarily on food markets, liquor stores, furniture stores, clothing stores, department stores, and pawn shops.

. . . We note with interest that no residences were deliberately burned, that damage to schools, libraries, churches and public buildings, was minimal, and that certain types of business establishments, notably service stations and automobile dealers, were for the most part unharmed.[33]

In the summer of 1967, New Jersey's governor proclaimed Newark a city "in open rebellion," declared a state of emergency, and called out the National Guard. For four consecutive days and nights snipers fired at police and firemen, looters made off with the inventories of scores of stores, and arsonists set fire to large portions of commercial property in the black section of that city. More than 4 thousand city policemen, state troopers, and National Guardsmen were required to restore order. Before the riot was over, twenty-three persons had been killed, and property damage was widespread. Of the dead, only two were white—a policeman and a fireman. Of the black dead, two were children and six were women.

But it was Detroit that became the scene of the bloodiest racial violence of the twentieth century. A week of rioting in Detroit, July 23–28, 1967, left forty-three dead and more than 1 thousand injured. Whole sections of the city were reduced to charred ruins and smoke. Over 13 hundred buildings were totally demolished and 27 hundred businesses sacked. Detroit's upheaval began when police raided an after-hours club and arrested the bartender and several customers for selling and consuming alcoholic beverages after authorized closing hours. A force of 15 thousand city and state police, National Guardsmen, and finally federal troops fought to quell the violence. Most of the looted retail businesses were liquor stores, grocery stores, and furniture stores. Many black merchants scrawled "Soul Brother" on their windows in an attempt to escape the wrath of the black mobs. Eventually, homes and shops covering a total area of fourteen square miles were gutted by fire. Firemen who tried to fight fires were stoned and occasionally shot by ghetto residents. Of the forty-three persons who were killed during the riot, thirty-nine were black and ten were white. Among the dead were one National Guardsman, one fireman, one policeman, and one black private guard. Both the violence and the pathos of the ghetto riots were reflected in the following report from Detroit:

. . . a spirit of carefree nihilism was taking hold. To riot and destroy appeared more and more to become ends in themselves. Late Sunday afternoon it appeared to one observer that the young people were "dancing amidst the flames."

[33]Governor's Commission on the Los Angeles Riots, John A. McCone, Chairman, *Violence in the City—An End or a Beginning* (Sacramento: Office of the Governor of California, 1965), pp. 3–5.

A Negro plainclothes officer was standing in an intersection when a man threw a Molotov cocktail into a business establishment on the corner. In the heat of the afternoon, fanned by the 20–25 mile per hour winds of both Sunday and Monday, the fire reached the home next door within minutes. As its residents uselessly sprayed the flames with garden hoses, the fire jumped from roof to roof of adjacent two- and three-story buildings. Within the hour the entire block was in flames. The ninth house in the burning row belonged to the arsonist who had thrown the Molotov cocktail. . . .

. . . employed as a private guard, fifty-five year old Julius L. Dorsey, a Negro, was standing in front of a market, when accosted by two Negro men and a woman. They demanded he permit them to loot the market. He ignored their demands. They began to berate him. He asked a neighbor to call the police. As the argument grew more heated, Dorsey fired three shots from his pistol in the air.

The police radio reported: "Looters, they have rifles." A patrolcar driven by a police officer and carrying three National Guardsmen arrived. As the looters fled, the law enforcement personnel opened fire. When the firing ceased, one person lay dead. He was Julius L. Dorsey. . . .[34]

The National Advisory Commission on Civil Disorders concluded:

1. No civil disorder was "typical" in all respects . . .
2. While civil disorders of 1967 were racial in character, they were not *inter*-racial. The 1967 disorders, as well as earlier disorders of the recent period, involved action within Negro neighborhoods against symbols of white American society—authority and property—rather than against white persons.
3. Despite extremist rhetoric there was no attempt to subvert the social order of the United States. Instead, most of those who attacked white authority and property seemed to be demanding fuller participation in the social order and the material benefits enjoyed by the vast majority of American citizens.
4. Disorder did not typically erupt without preexisting causes, as a result of a single "triggering" or "precipitating" incident. Instead, it developed out of an increasingly social atmosphere, in which typically a series of tension-heightening incidents over a period of weeks or months became linked in the minds of many in the Negro community with a shared network of underlying grievances.
5. There was, typically, a complex relationship between the series of incidents, and the underlying grievances. For example, grievances about allegedly abusive police practices, . . . were often aggravated in the minds of many Negroes by incidents involving the police, or the inaction of municipal authorities on Negro complaints about police action.
6. Many grievances in the Negro community resulted from discrimination, prejudice, and powerlessness which Negroes often experience. . . .

[34]National Advisory Commission on Civil Disorders, *Report* (Washington, D.C.: Government Printing Office, 1968), p. 4.

7. Characteristically the typical rioter was not a hoodlum, habitual criminal, or riff-raff. . . . Instead, he was a teenager or young adult, a lifelong resident of the city in which he rioted, a high school drop-out—but somewhat better than his Negro neighbor—and almost invariably underemployed or employed in a menial job. He was proud of his race, extremely hostile to both whites and middle class Negroes and, though informed about politics, highly distrustful of the political system and of political leaders.

8. Numerous Negro counter-rioters walked the street, urging the rioters to "cool it." . . .

9. Negotiation between Negro and white officials occurred during virtually all of this disorder. . . .

10. . . . Some rioters may have shared neither the conditions nor the grievance of their Negro neighbors; some may have coolly and deliberately exploited the chaos created by others; some may have been drawn into the melee merely because they identified with, or wished to emulate, others.

11. The background of disorder in the riot cities was typically characterized by severely disadvantaged conditions for Negroes, especially as compared with those of whites. . . .

12. In the immediate aftermath of disorder, the status quo of daily life before the disorder generally was quickly restored. Yet despite some notable public and private efforts, little basic change took place in the conditions underlying the disorder. In some cases, the result was increased dislike between blacks and whites, diminished inter-racial communication, and the growth of Negro and white extremist groups.[35]

ASSESSING THE CAUSES OF RIOTS

One explanation of urban violence is that it is a product of the relative deprivation of ghetto residents.[36] *Relative deprivation* is the discrepancy between people's expectations about the goods and conditions of life to which they are justifiably entitled and what they perceive to be their chances for getting and keeping what they feel they deserve. Relative deprivation is not merely a complicated way of saying that people are deprived and therefore angry because they have less than what they want; it is more complex than that. Relative deprivation focuses on (1) what people think they *deserve*, not just what they want in an ideal sense,

[35]*Ibid.*, pp. 110–12.

[36]For a full discussion of the *relative deprivation* explanation as well as alternative explanations, see Dan R. Bowen and Louis H. Masotti, "Civil Violence: A Theoretical Overview," in *Riots and Rebellion*, ed. Masotti and Bowen (Beverly Hills: Sage Publications, 1968). See also James C. Davies, "Toward a Theory of Revolution," *American Sociological Review*, 27 (February 1962), 6; and Ted Gur, *Why Men Rebel* (Princeton: Princeton University Press, 1970).

and (2) what they think they have a *chance* of getting, not just what they have.

Relative deprivation differs considerably from the *absolute deprivation* hypothesis. The absolute deprivation idea suggests that individuals who are the most deprived are those who are most likely to rise up. Of course, it is true that conditions in America's ghettos provide the necessary environment for violence. Racial imbalance, de facto segregation, slum housing, discrimination, unemployment, poor schools, and poverty all provide excellent kindling for the flames of violence. But these underlying conditions for violence existed for decades in America, and the nation never experienced simultaneous violent uprisings in nearly all its major cities before the 1960s. This suggests that the deprivation itself is not a sufficient condition for violence. Some new ingredients were added to the incendiary conditions in American cities whch touched off the violence of the 1960s.

Relative deprivation focuses on the distance between current status and expectation level. According to this hypothesis, it is neither the wholly downtrodden—who have no aspirations—nor the very well off—who can satisfy theirs—who represent a threat to civil order. The threat is posed by those whose expectations about what they deserve outdistance the capacity of the political system to satisfy them. Often, rapid increases in expectations are a product of minor symbolic or token improvements in conditions. This leads to the apparent paradox of violence and disorder occurring at the very time that improvements in the conditions of blacks are being made. It is hope, not despair, that generates civil violence and disorder. Masotti and Bowen remark: "The reason why black Americans riot is because there has been just enough improvement in their condition to generate hopes, expectations, or aspirations beyond the capacities of the system to meet them."[37]

The civil rights movement made many blacks acutely aware of discrimination in American society and reduced their tolerance for injustice. The civil rights movement increased the aspiration level of the black masses and inspired impatience and hostility toward the "white establishment." The civil rights movement had to awaken blacks to their plight in American society before progress could be made in eliminating discrimination, but the price of this awakening was a major increase in aspiration levels and the risk of frustration and bitterness when aspirations were unfulfilled. The breakthroughs that the established civil rights movement made in public accommodations, employment, voting, and office-holding in the 1960s may have opened new opportunities for the educated middle class. But the undereducated black poor, living in the

[37]Masotti and Bowen, *Riots and Rebellion*, pp. 24–25.

ghetto environment, could not really take advantage of many of these opportunities. The movement increased their expectation level, but it failed to significantly alter their condition in life. Thus, it is no coincidence that the urban disorders followed on the heels of some of the most significant legislative gains in the civil rights struggle.

Once racial violence has broken out anywhere in the nation, the mass media play an important role in disseminating images of violence as well as the symbols and rationalizations of the rioters. Television offers the rioter a mass audience. It was not unknown for rioters to leave the scene temporarily to hurry to their television sets to see themselves. Moreover, television images may reinforce predispositions to participate and even to legitimatize participation. Television enables blacks in one ghetto to see what blacks in another ghetto are doing, and it explains simultaneous rioting in ghettos across the nation.

THE NATIONAL ADVISORY COMMISSION
ON CIVIL DISORDERS

In July 1967, in the midst of widespread urban disorder, President Lyndon B. Johnson appointed a National Advisory Commission on Civil Disorders to study the riots and to make necessary recommendations. In its official report the commission enumerated "three of the most bitter fruits of white racial attitudes":

Pervasive discrimination and segregation. The first is surely the continuing exclusion of great numbers of Negroes from the benefits of economic progress through discrimination in employment and education, and their enforced confinement in segregated housing and schools. The corrosive and degrading effects of this condition and the attitudes that underlie it are the source of the deepest bitterness and at the center of the problem of racial disorder.

Black migration and white exodus. The second is the massive and growing concentration of impoverished Negroes in our major cities resulting from Negro migration from the rural South, rapid population growth and the continuing movement of the white middle-class to the suburbs. The consequence is a greatly increased burden on the already depleted resources of cities, creating a growing crisis of deteriorating facilities and services and unmet human needs.

Black ghettos. Third, in the teeming racial ghettos, segregation and poverty have intersected to destroy opportunity and hope and to enforce failure. The ghettos too often mean men and women without jobs, families without men, and schools where children are processed instead of educated, until they return to the street—to crime, to narcotics, to dependency on welfare, and to bitterness and resentment against society in general and white society in particular.[38]

The commission admitted, however, that "these facts alone—fundamental as they are—cannot be said to have caused the disorders." The commission identified three "powerful ingredients" that had "begun to catalyze the mixture":

Frustrated hopes. The expectations aroused by the great judicial and legislative victories of the civil rights movement have led to frustration, hostility and cynicism in the fact of the persistent gap between promise and fulfillment. The dramatic struggle for equal rights in the South has sensitized Northern Negroes to the economic inequalities reflected in the deprivations of ghetto life.

Legitimation of violence. A climate that tends toward the approval and encouragement of violence as a form of protest has been created by white terrorism directed against nonviolent protest, including instances of abuse and even murder of some civil rights workers in the South; by the open defiance of law and federal authority by state and local officials resisting desegregation; and by some protest groups engaging in civil disobedience who turn their backs on nonviolence, go beyond the Constitutionally protected rights of petition and free assembly, and resort to violence to attempt to compel alteration of laws and policies with which they disagree. This condition has been reinforced by a general erosion of respect for authority in American society and reduced effectiveness of social standards and community restraints on violence and crime. This in turn has largely resulted from rapid urbanization and the dramatic reduction in the average age of the total population.

Powerlessness. Finally, many Negroes have come to believe that they are being exploited politically and economically by the white "power structure." Negroes, like people in poverty everywhere, in fact lack the channels of communication, influence and appeal that traditionally have been available to ethnic minorities within the city and which enabled them—unburdened by color—to scale the walls of the white ghettos in an earlier era. The frustrations of powerlessness have led some to the conviction that there is no effective alternative to violence as a means of expression and redress, as a way of "moving the system." More generally, the result is alienation and hostility toward the institutions of law and government and the white society which controls them. This is reflected in the reach toward racial consciousness and solidarity reflected in the slogan "Black Power."[39]

The commission warned that "our nation is moving toward two societies, one black one white—separate and unequal." The principal "blame" for the riots was placed upon whites rather than blacks: "What

[38]National Advisory Commission on Civil Disorders, *Report*, pp. 203–4.
[39]*Ibid.*, pp. 204–5.

white Americans have never fully understood—but what the Negro can never forget—is that white society is deeply implicated in the ghetto. White institutions created it, white institutions maintain it, and white society condones it."[40] The commission recommended massive federal aid programs in employment, education, welfare, and housing, but it suggested no new departures from traditional programs in these areas. The commission called for the creation of 2 million new jobs in the ghettos, the elimination of de facto segregation, the construction of 6 million new units of public housing, and more liberal welfare benefits. In the commission's words: "These programs will require unprecedented levels of funding and performance, but they neither probe deeper nor demand more than the problems which called them forth. There can be no higher priority for national action and no higher claim on the nation's conscience."

[40]*Ibid.*, p. 2.

FOURTEEN

The
Politics
of
Education

DIRECTIONS IN EDUCATIONAL POLICY

Next to national defense, education is the nation's largest public under-taking. The primary responsibility for public education rests with the fifty state governments and their subdivisions. It is the largest and most costly of state functions.

It was in 1647 that the Massachusetts colonial legislature first required towns to provide for the education of children out of public funds. The rugged individualists of earlier eras thought it outrageous that one man should be taxed to pay for the education of another man's child. They were joined in their opposition to public education by those aristocrats who were opposed to arming the common man with the power that knowledge gives. But the logic of democracy led inevitably to public ed-ucation. The earliest democrats believed that the safest repository of the ultimate powers of society was the people themselves. If the people make mistakes, the remedy was not to remove power from their hands, but to help them in forming their judgment through education. Con-gress passed the Northwest Ordinance in 1787 offering land grants for public schools in the new territories and giving succeeding generations words to be forever etched on grammar school cornerstones: "Religion, morality, and knowledge being necessary to good government and the happiness of mankind, schools and the means for education shall ever be encouraged." When American democracy adopted universal manhood suffrage, it affected every aspect of American life, and particularly education. If the common man was to be granted the right of suffrage, he must be educated to his task. This meant that public education had to be universal, free, and compulsory. Compulsory education began in Massachusetts in 1852 and was eventually adopted by Mississippi in 1918.[1]

If there ever was a time when schools were only expected to combat ignorance and illiteracy, that time is far behind us. Today schools are expected to do many things: resolve racial conflict and build an integrated society; inspire patriotism and good citizenship; provide values, aspirations, and a sense of identity to disadvantaged children; offer various forms of recreation and mass entertainment (football games, bands, choruses, majorettes, and the like); reduce conflict in society by teaching children to get along well with others and adjust to group living; reduce the highway accident toll by teaching students to be good drivers; fight disease and ill health through physical education, health training, and even medical treatment; eliminate unemployment and poverty by teaching job skills; end malnutrition and hunger through school lunch and milk programs; produce scientists and other technicians to continue America's progress in science and technology; fight drug abuse and educate children about sex; and act as custodians for teen-agers who have no interest in education but who are not permitted to work or roam the streets unsupervised. In other words, nearly all the nation's problems are reflected in demands placed on the nation's schools. And, of course, these demands are frequently conflicting.

THE FEDERAL ROLE IN EDUCATION

The primary responsibility for administration and finance of public schools rests with the fifty *state* governments and their subdivisions. In the 1970s Americans will spend over $50 billion per year on their public schools. Currently, the federal government pays only about 10 percent of that cost; 90 percent of the cost of public schools is borne by state and local governments (see Figure 14–1).

The federal government's role in education, however, is a longstanding one. As already mentioned in the famous Northwest Ordinance of 1787, Congress offered land grants for public schools in the new territories. Then in 1862 the Morrill Land Grant Act provided grants of federal land to each state for the establishment of colleges specializing in agricultural and mechanical arts. These became known as "land-grant colleges." In 1867 Congress established a U.S. Office of Education, which is now a part of the

[1]See Thomas R. Dye, *Politics, Economics, and the Public* (Chicago: Rand McNally & Co., 1966), Chap. 4.

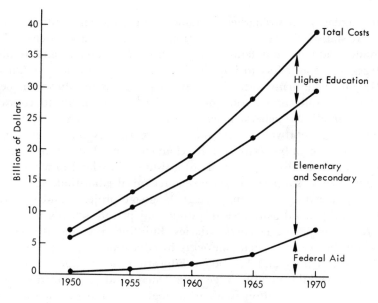

FIGURE 14-1   The Growing Costs of Education

Department of Health, Education, and Welfare. The Smith-Hughes Act of 1917 set up the first program of federal grants-in- aid to promote vocational education and enabled schools to provide training in agriculture, home economics, trades, and industries. In the National School Lunch and Milk programs, begun in 1946, federal grants and commodity donations are made for nonprofit lunches and milk served in public and private schools. In the Federal Impacted Areas Aid Program, begun in 1950, federal aid is authorized for "federally impacted" areas of the nation. These are areas where federal activities create a substantial increase in school enrollments or a reduction in taxable resources because of federally owned property. Federal funds can be used for construction, operation, and maintenance of schools in these public school districts. This program is an outgrowth of the defense impacted area aid legislation in World War II.

In response to the Soviet Union's success in launching the first satellite into space, Congress became concerned that the American educational system might not be keeping abreast of advances being made in other nations, particulary in science and technology. The Russian space shot created an intensive debate over education in America and prompted Congress to reexamine the responsibilities of the national government in public education. "Sputnik" made everyone realize that education was closely related to national defense. In the National Defense Education Act of 1958, Congress provided financial aid to states and public school districts to improve instruction in science, mathematics, and foreign languages; to strengthen guidance counseling and testing; and to improve statistical services—in addition to establishing a system of loans to undergraduates and fellowships to graduate students and funds to colleges, all in an effort to improve the training of teachers in America.

Despite these many individual federal programs in education, before 1965 the overall contribution of the federal government to education was very small. No general federal-aid-to-education bill was able to win congressional approval, for reasons that we will explore later. Federal programs were only peripheral in character and limited in impact—some aid to federally impacted areas; assistance in school lunch and milk programs; some support for vocational-technical education; some grants for science, mathematics, and foreign language projects, and so forth—but no real general assistance to public and private schools in building classrooms or paying teachers' salaries. Building costs and teachers' salaries are the really burdensome costs in education.

The Elementary and Secondary Education Act of 1965 marked the first real breakthrough in large-scale federal aid to education. ESEA doubled federal education funds in a single year and is now the largest federal-aid-to-education program. Yet even ESEA cannot be termed a *general* aid-to-education program—one that would assist all public and private schools in school construction and teachers' salaries. The main thrust of ESEA is in "poverty-impacted" schools, instructional materials, and educational research and training.

The Elementary and Secondary Education Act provided for the following:

Title   I   Financial assistance to "local educational agencies serving areas with concentrations of children from low-income families" for programs "which contribute particularly to meeting the special needs of educationally deprived children." Grants would be made on application to the Office of Education on the basis of the number of children from poverty-stricken families.

Title   II   Grants to "public and private elementary and secondary schools" for the acquisition of school library resources, textbooks, and other instructional materials.

Title III   Grants to public and private schools for "supplementary educational centers and services" including remedial programs, counseling, adult education, specialized instruction and equipment, etc.

Title IV   Grants to universities, colleges, or other nonprofit organizations for research or demonstration projects in education.

Title   V   Grants to stimulate and strengthen state educational agencies.

Note that the act does include private, church-related schools in some of its benefits, so long as the federal aid money is used for nonreligious purposes within such schools. The greatest amounts of money distributed under ESEA, however, have been to public schools in poverty-impacted areas.

ORGANIZING AND FINANCING
PUBLIC SCHOOLS

The fifty state governments, by means of enabling legislation, establish local school districts and endow them with the authority to operate public schools. These laws create local school boards and provide a means for choosing their members, usually, but not always, by popular election. State laws authorize boards to lay and collect taxes, to borrow money, to engage in school construction, to hire instructional personnel, and to make certain determinations about local school policy. Yet, in every state, the authority of local school districts is severely circumscribed by state legislation. State law determines the types and rates of taxes to be levied, the maximum debt that can be incurred, the number of days schools shall remain open, the number of years of compulsory school attendance, the minimum salaries to be paid to teachers, the types of schools to be operated by the local boards, the number of grades to be taught, the qualifications of teachers, and the general content of curricula. In addition, many states choose the textbooks, establish course outlines, fix styles of penmanship, recommend teaching methods, establish statewide examinations, fix minimum teacher-pupil ratios, and stipulate course content in great detail. In short, the responsibility for public education is firmly in the hands of our state governments.

State responsibility for public education is no mere paper arrangement. At one time there was no effective way that state governments could insure that local school districts conformed to state policies; there were no enforcement agencies or devices to guarantee that state regulations were enforced. But in recent years, two devices have been utilized effectively by the states to help insure that local districts do not deviate from state standards. The first device is the statewide administrative agency sometimes called the state board of education, the state department of education, or the superintendent of public instruction. The central task of these state administrative agencies is to oversee local school districts and insure that state policies are being implemented. While there are some variations among the states in the power vested in these agencies, one trend is common to all the states: state educational agencies are centralizing state control over education.

The operating head of these state agencies, generally called commissioner or superintendent of education, may exercise the most forceful

TABLE 14-1
Federal Aid to Education: Major Legislation

1. Elementary and Secondary Education Act, 1965: Cash grants for construction, operation, and maintenance of schools in poverty-impacted public school districts on the basis of the number of children enrolled from poverty-stricken families, and grants to public and private schools for the support of specialized educational facilities.

2. National Defense Education Act, 1958: Financial assistance to states and public school districts to improve instruction in science, mathematics, and foreign languages, to strengthen guidance counseling and testing, and to improve statistical services. Amended in 1963 to include assistance in history, English, civics, geography, remedial reading, and library sciences. (Also included loans to undergraduates, fellowships to graduate students, and funds to colleges to improve training of teachers.)

3. Federally Impacted Areas Aid Program, 1950: Where federal activities create a substantial increase in school enrollments or reduction in taxable resources because of federally owned property, federal funds can be used for construction, operation, and maintenance of schools in public school districts. This program is an outgrowth of defense impacted area aid legislation in World War II.

4. National School Lunch and Milk Programs, 1946: Federal grants and commodity donations for nonprofit lunches and milk served in public and private schools.

5. Smith-Hughes Vocational Education Act, 1917: Federal grants for vocational education to help states and public school districts provide training in agriculture, home economics, trades, and industries.

6. Federal Aid to Colleges and Universities: Although not direct aids to elementary and secondary schools, federal aid to colleges and universities indirectly helps elementary and secondary education by improving the educational climate of the nation. Major sources of federal aid include:
    a. "The GI Bill," providing federal grants for tuition and subsistence for veterans attending institutions of higher education.
    b. Morrill Land Grant Act of 1862, providing states with federal land, the proceeds from which were used to establish land-grant colleges and universities.
    c. Higher Education Act of 1965, providing federal funds for construction of college facilities and to upgrade college libraries.
    d. Medical and Dental Education Program, providing federal funds for construction of facilities and loans to medical and dental students.

influence over educational policy in the state. In a majority of states these chief school officers are appointed; in other states they are directly elected. The department that this officer oversees provides specialized technical services and information to local school officials; more importantly, it establishes and enforces statewide minimum standards in curriculum, teacher certification, school construction, and many other aspects of school policy and administration.

A second device for insuring the implementation of state educational policies is state grants of money to local school districts. Every state provides grants in one form or another to local school districts to supplement locally derived school revenue. This places the superior taxing powers of the state in the service of public schools operated at the local level. In every state, an equalization formula in the distribution of state grants to local districts operates to help equalize educational opportunities in all parts of the state. Equalization formulas differ from state to state as do the amounts of state grants involved, but in every state, poorer school districts receive larger shares of state funds than wealthier districts. This enables the state to guarantee a minimum "foundation" program in education throughout the state. In addition, since state grants to local school districts are administered through state departments of education, state school officials are given an effective tool for implementing state policies, namely, withholding or threatening to withhold state funds from school districts that do not conform to state standards. The growth of state responsibility for school policy was accomplished largely by the use of money—state grants to local schools.

Increasing state participation in school finance, then, is an indication of increasing centralization of education in the states. In 1900 the state proportion of total public school expenditures in the nation was only 17 percent. In the 1970s, however, state governments will contribute over 40 percent of total funds for the public schools.

One of the most dramatic reorganization and centralization movements in American government in this century has been the successful drive to reduce, through consolidation, the number of local school districts in the United States. By 1970 this number had been reduced to 20 thousand. In a thirty-year period, two out of every three school districts had been eliminated through consolidation. Support for school district consolidation has come from state school officials in every state. Opposition to consolidation has been local in character.

The extent of state participation in financing public schools and the

TABLE 14-2
Federal, State, and Local Contributions to Public
Elementary and Secondary Education

	Percent of Revenue Received from		
	Federal Sources	State Sources	Local Sources
1970	7.3	40.7	52.0
1967	7.9	39.1	53.0
1963	4.4	39.3	56.4
1960	4.4	39.1	56.5
1957	4.0	39.4	56.6

success of the school district consolidation movement are both important indices of educational centralization in the states. While it is clear from national trends in both of these indices that the states on the whole are centralizing education, nonetheless, these trends are by no means uniform throughout the states. In some states, the state government still provides only about 10 percent of school revenues, while in other states, the state pays over 70 percent of the cost of public schools. There is also considerable variation among the states in the success of the school district consolidation movement. Hawaii has a single, unified, statewide school system, but there are over 1 thousand independent school districts oprating in several states. These two indices of centralization—the percentage of total school revenue from state sources and the average size of school districts in pupils—are related. States that pay the largest proportion of the public school bill have been the most successful in consolidating local school districts.

State centralization in school finance was given added impetus in 1972 with a decision of the California Supreme Court that reliance upon local property taxation in school finance denied children in poorer communities of equal educational opportunity. The court argued that inequality in the availability of taxable property in local school districts resulted in inequality in educational opportunity and violated the equal protection clauses of both the California and U.S. constitutions. Some other state courts have followed with similar decisions, although the U.S. Supreme Court has not yet spoken on this issue. The effect of such decisions is to require states to shoulder a heavier burden of school financing themselves and to distribute school funds equally within their state. Local property taxation as a means of school finance is now under heavy fire. One way to continue reliance on property taxation and still insure equality among communities is to have the *state* collect property tax revenues state-wide and then redistribute these revenues to local school districts in an equal fashion. The effect would be to take funds from wealthier school districts to give them to poorer districts.

THE COST OF TEACHING JOHNNY
TO READ

Public elementary and secondary schools enroll over 50 million students. Public expenditures for education now amount to more than 5 percent of the nation's total personal income. Over $1,000 per year is spent on the public education of each child. Teachers' salaries have risen dramatically, and although the average teacher's salary is still lower than that of most other professions, it is more than the average industrial worker earns and a vast improvement over the salaries of even a few years ago. Teacher-pupil ratios have been lowered on the average to one teacher for every twenty-two pupils. State governments have undertaken a greater direct share of the responsiblity for public education than ever before.

This impressive record of progress in public education is a tribute to the capabilities of our fifty states. Yet national averages can obscure as much as they reveal about the record of the states in public education. Our federal system provides for the decentralization of educational policy making. Fifty state school systems establish policy for the nation, and this decentralization results in variations from state to state in educational policy. Only by examining public policy in all fifty states can the full dimension of American education be understood.

In 1971 public school expenditures for each pupil ranged from Mississippi's $521 to New York's $1,370. The nationwide figure for per pupil expenditures was $858.[2] Why is it that some states spend more than twice as much on the education of each child as other states? Economic resources are an important determinant of a state's willingness and ability to provide educational services. Urbanization, education, and, especially, income correlate significantly with variations among the states in per pupil expenditures for public education. The results are the same even if the southern states are excluded from analysis. Clearly, wealth is the principal determinant of the amount of money to be spent on the education of each child. (See Figure 14-2.)

Expenditures per pupil measure both the willingness and the ability of a state to spend money for education. The next problem is to separate "willingness to spend" from "ability to spend," in order to roughly determine the sacrifice a state is making for education. The desire for education can be expressed in terms of school expenditures relative to some measure of a state's ability to spend money. In this way, states that spend more or less relative to their ability can be identified. Public school expenditures, as a percentage of total personal income, really hold constant for ability to spend and more directly measure a state's willingness to sacrifice personal income for public education. This is referred to as a state's "educational effort."

It is interesting to note that increased industrialization, urbanization, and income actually result in a reduction in education *effort*. This is in striking contrast to the effect of these economic resources on per pupil expenditures: while per pupil expenditures increase with increasing in-

[2]U.S. Bureau of the Census, *Statistical Abstract of the United States, 1971* (Washington, D.C.: Government Printing Office, 1971), p. 121.

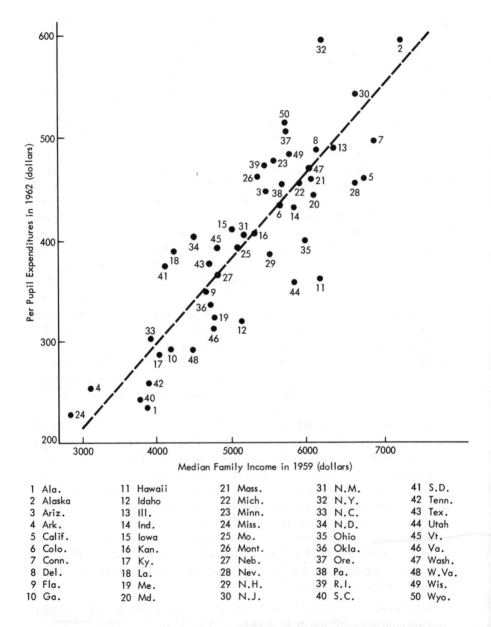

FIGURE 14-2 The Fifty States According to Median Family Income and Per Pupil Expenditures

Source: Thomas R. Dye, *Politics, Economics, and the Public* (Chicago: Rand McNally & Co., 1966), p. 83. Reproduced by permission.

come levels, school expenditures, as a percentage of personal income, decline. This means that the poorer, less industrialized, rural states are actually putting forth a *greater effort* in the educational field relative to their resources than the wealthy, urban, industrial states. But so great are the inequalities among the states in wealth that the poorer states, despite their greater effort, are unable to approach the wealthier states in per pupil expenditures. In short, wealthier states can provide better educations for their children with less of an economic sacrifice than that required of poorer states to provide an inferior education for their children.

The National Education Association has been cognizant of this situation for some time and has used these conditions to support appeals for federal aid to education. It is argued that federal aid will help to equalize educational opportunities throughout the nation:

> The operation of a national industrial economy appears to insure that average per capita incomes will be unequal among the states. The poorest states, if left to their own resources, have no reasonable prospect of raising the funds to provide adequate education. Some form of equalization is needed, because it is vital to the nation that the children in the poorest states also be well educated. Therefore, Federal participation in the financing of their schools is essential.[3]

THE QUALITY OF PUBLIC EDUCATION

Given conflicts over the objectives of public education, it is difficult to make any overall evaluation of educational output in the states. Is the goal of public education college preparation, vocational skill, emotional happiness, psychological adjustment, academic excellence, the reduction of automobile accidents, the inculcation of spiritual values, the ending of racial tension, the cultivation of patriotism, the production of engineers and scientists, the training of competent homemakers, or winning the Olympics? How can we tell whether the failure to achieve any one of these objectives is a product of our educational policies or an outgrowth of other national problems?

Two measures seemingly reflective of public education, which are available on a state-by-state basis, are the proportion of high school students who drop out of school before graduation and the proportion of selective service registrants who fail the mental examination prior to induction.

[3]Educational Policies Commission, *National Policy and the Financing of Public Schools* (Washington, D.C.: National Education Association, 1962), p. 23.

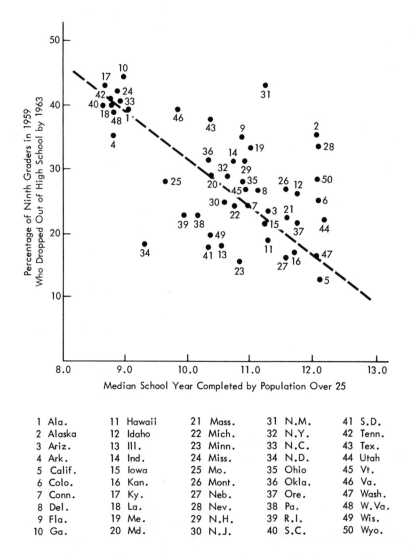

1 Ala.	11 Hawaii	21 Mass.	31 N.M.	41 S.D.
2 Alaska	12 Idaho	22 Mich.	32 N.Y.	42 Tenn.
3 Ariz.	13 Ill.	23 Minn.	33 N.C.	43 Tex.
4 Ark.	14 Ind.	24 Miss.	34 N.D.	44 Utah
5 Calif.	15 Iowa	25 Mo.	35 Ohio	45 Vt.
6 Colo.	16 Kan.	26 Mont.	36 Okla.	46 Va.
7 Conn.	17 Ky.	27 Neb.	37 Ore.	47 Wash.
8 Del.	18 La.	28 Nev.	38 Pa.	48 W.Va.
9 Fla.	19 Me.	29 N.H.	39 R.I.	49 Wis.
10 Ga.	20 Md.	30 N.J.	40 S.C.	50 Wyo.

FIGURE 14–3   The Fifty States Arranged According to Adult Education Levels and High School Dropout Rates

Source: Thomas R. Dye, *Politics, Economics, and the Public* (Chicago: Rand McNally & Co., 1966), p. 99. Reproduced by permission.

Certainly the child who does not complete at least twelve years of education in a highly technological society represents a national liability, and so does the young man so feebly equipped with mental faculties that he is of no use to the armed services of the nation.

TABLE 14-3

The Relationships Between Education and Environmental
Resources in the Fifty States

| | Simple Correlation Coefficients | | | Total Percent Explained |
	Income	Education	Urbanization	
Per pupil expenditure	.83	.59	.51	70
Educational effort	−.30	−.05	−.31	25
Average teachers salaries	.88	.57	.69	81
Teacher-pupil ratio	−.43	−.50	−.13	50
Per capita education expenditures	.61	.75	.20	61
Drop out rate	−.54	−.60	−.40	67
Mental failures	−.46	−.70	−.05	64

Among the fifty states, wealth and adult education levels are directly related to dropout rates and mental failures. (See Figure 14–3.) Wealthy states with well-educated adult populations are the same states that spend more per pupil on their public schools, pay higher teachers' salaries, attract more male teachers, and have better teacher-pupil ratios; and these same states tend to experience fewer high school dropouts and selective service mental failures. In contrast, the less-wealthy states with poorly educated adult populations spend less per pupil on their public schools, pay lower teachers' salaries, attract fewer male teachers, and have poor teach-pupil ratios; and these same states experience more dropouts and mental failures.

The average teacher's salary in the nation in 1971 was $9,265 per year.[4] School teachers in Alaska, Michigan, California, and New York were the best-paid teachers in the nation in 1971, with average annual salaries in excess of $10,000 per year. School teachers in Arkansas, South Dakota, and Mississippi were the lowest paid in the nation, with average annual salaries in that year below $7,000. Economic development is an important determinant in teachers' salaries. Income differences among the states explain most of the variation among the states in average teachers' salaries.

One final measure in instructional quality available for all fifty states is the pupil-teacher ratio, or the number of pupils enrolled per member of instructional staff. Two indices of economic development, family income and adult educational level, correlated significantly with teacher-pupil ratio in all states. (See Figure 14–4.)

[4] National Education Association, *Rankings of the States, 1971.*

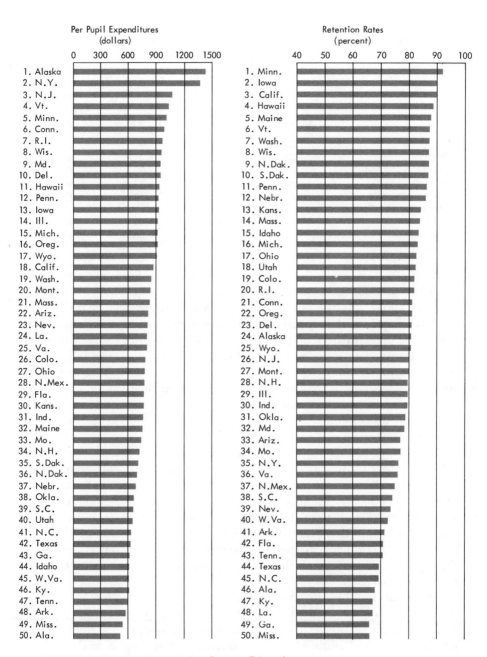

Per Pupil Expenditures
(dollars)

Retention Rates
(percent)

FIGURE 14-4   Rankings of the States: Education

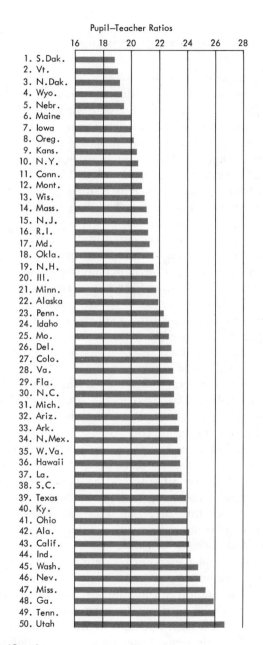

Pupil—Teacher Ratios

1. S.Dak.
2. Vt.
3. N.Dak.
4. Wyo.
5. Nebr.
6. Maine
7. Iowa
8. Oreg.
9. Kans.
10. N.Y.
11. Conn.
12. Mont.
13. Wis.
14. Mass.
15. N.J.
16. R.I.
17. Md.
18. Okla.
19. N.H.
20. Ill.
21. Minn.
22. Alaska
23. Penn.
24. Idaho
25. Mo.
26. Del.
27. Colo.
28. Va.
29. Fla.
30. N.C.
31. Mich.
32. Ariz.
33. Ark.
34. N.Mex.
35. W.Va.
36. Hawaii
37. La.
38. S.C.
39. Texas
40. Ky.
41. Ohio
42. Ala.
43. Calif.
44. Ind.
45. Wash.
46. Nev.
47. Miss.
48. Ga.
49. Tenn.
50. Utah

FIGURE 14–4   (Cont.)

SCHOOLS AND COMMUNITIES

Local control over public schools has been an article of faith for most Americans for many years. Responsibility for many basic decisions in public education lies with the twenty thousand separate school districts in America. In theory, these school districts are under local control. The people of the local school district are supposed to exercise that control through an elected school board, and the board appoints a superintendent to act as the chief executive of the community schools. There is some variation to that pattern—in approximately a quarter of the nation's school districts, the boards are appointed rather than elected, usually by city councils, county commissions, mayors, or even judges. In theory, these school boards exercise control over curriculum (that is, what should be taught in the schools), buildings and facilities, personnel, including both administrators and teachers, and perhaps most important of all, financing. These school districts are separate from city or county government. Education is independent of other local governmental responsibilities. In theory, separation of education from municipal government was meant to eliminate "politics" from education.

The formal structure of local school districts often obscures the realities of educational politics in communities. First of all, we have already seen that the concept of local control over education is circumscribed by both state and federal acts. Second, the concept of popular control over the schools through elected boards of laymen is challenged by the increasing professionalization of education. Finally, the idea that politics could be separated from education was never a reality. School districts are governmental units, and there has always been conflict between individuals and groups over what should be done in the public schools. School board members, school superintendents, and teachers are engaged in political activity whether they like it or not. School administrators may call this activity "community relations," but in any other profession outside of education it would be called "politics."

School politics will differ from one community to another, but it is possible to identify a number of political actors who appear on the scene in school politics in almost every community.[5] There is, first of all, that small band of voters who turn out for school elections. It is estimated that, on the average, less than one-third of the eligible voters bother to cast ballots in school elections. Voter turnout at school bond and tax

[5]See Thomas H. Eliot, "Toward an Understanding of Public School Politics," *American Political Science Review*, 52 (December 1959), 1032–50.

elections shows no ground swell of public interest in school affairs. Perhaps even more interesting is the finding that the larger the voter turnout in a school bond referendum, the more likely the defeat of pro-educational proposals.[6] In general, the best way to defeat a school bond referendum is to have a large turnout. Proponents of educational expenditures are better advised to work not so much for a large turnout as for a better-informed and more educationally oriented electorate.

School board members constitute another important group of actors in school politics. School board members are generally better educated than their constituents. However, school board members are selected largely from among business owners, proprietors, and managers. There is some evidence that people who are interested in education and have some knowledge of what the schools are doing tend to support education more than do the less informed citizens. Yet the occupational background of school board members suggests that they are sensitive to tax burdens placed upon businessmen and property owners.

Many professional educators are distrustful of the laymen who compose the school board; they often feel that educational policy should be in the hands of professional educators. They may feel that important decisions about curriculum, facilities, personnel, and finances should be the special province of persons trained in education. They view the school board's role as one of defending the schools against public criticism and persuading the community to open its pocketbook. Professional educators often support the idea that "politics" should be kept out of education; to them, this means that laymen should not interfere with decisions that professional educators wish to make for themselves. For example, on the critical question of what should be taught in the public schools, the American Association of School Administrators says: "Curriculum planning and development is a highly technical task which requires special training . . . Board members do not have and cannot be expected to have the technical competence to pass on the work of expert teachers in this field."[7] School boards and voters (those who supply the money for the public schools and therefore feel that it is their legitimate right to control them) believe that citizen control of education is a vital safeguard of democracy. But professional educators sometimes feel that school board members are often uninformed about school problems or either unwilling or unable to support the needs of education. For example, school board members throughout the nation were much less likely to support federal aid to education that professional educators;

---

[6]See Patricia Sexton, "City Schools," *Annals of the American Academy of Social and Political Science*, 352 (March 1964), 95–106.

[7]Eliot, "Toward an Understanding of Public School Politics," p. 1036.

many school board members felt that the federal government would strip them of their local power over the schools. Professional educators, on the other hand, were less fearful of dictation from Washington.

The professional educators can be divided into at least three distinct groups. Numerically the largest group, yet politically the least significant, are the school teachers. The most powerful group are the professional school administrators, particularly the superintendents of schools. A third group are the faculties of teachers colleges and departments of education at universities, who often have contacts with state departments of education and who influence requirements for teacher certification within the states. State and local chapters of the National Education Association (NEA) represent both teachers and administrators, but they are often dominated by professional administrators. The participation of administrators in the National Education Association is one of the major criticisms of that organization made by the American Federation of Teachers (AFT). The AFT has emerged as an important voice of teachers in the nation's largest cities. The American Federation of Teachers is a labor union representing classroom teachers, and it employs all the recognized techniques of labor organizations to achieve its goals. The AFT advocates collective bargaining for teachers and, whenever necessary, the strike. In the past, the much larger NEA viewed these techniques as unprofessional, and it criticized the AFT for its connection with labor unions through the AFL-CIO. However, the growing membership of the AFT in large cities has brought about a greater degree of militancy by the NEA and its local and state chapters.

HIGHER EDUCATION

The costs of higher education have grown even faster than the costs of elementary and secondary education. Not only has the number of young people of college age dramatically increased in the past decade, but so has the *proportion* of college-age persons entering college. In the 1970s 55 percent of all college-age persons are expected to enroll in college. (See Table 14–4.)

Federal aid to colleges and universities comes in a variety of forms. Historically, the Morrill Act of 1862 provided the groundwork for federal assistance in higher education. In 1890 Congress activated several federal grants to support the operations of the land-grant colleges, and this aid, although very modest, continues to the present. The GI Bills following World War II and the Korean War (enacted in 1944 and 1952 respectively) were not, strictly speaking, aid-to-education bills, but rather a form of assistance to veterans to help them adjust to civilian life. Nevertheless these bills had a great impact on higher education in terms of

TABLE 14-4
Growth of Higher Education Enrollment

	College Age Population (millions)	Higher Education Enrollment (millions)	Percentage Enrolled
1955	8.3	2.7	32
1960	9.7	3.6	37
1965	12.3	5.5	45
1970	14.5	7.3	50
1975	16.3	9.0	55

SOURCE: U.S. Department of Health, Education, and Welfare, Office of Education, PROJECTIONS OF EDUCATIONAL STATISTICS TO 1975-76 (Washington, D.C.: Government Printing Office, 1966).

the millions of veterans who were able to enroll in college. In 1966 Congress finally acted to make veterans' education benefits a permanent program for "all those who risk their lives in our armed forces." The National Defense Education Act of 1958 also affected higher education by assisting superior students through loans and grants to continue undergraduate and graduate education, and by directly assisting institutions in which they enroll. Preference was given to undergraduate students intending to teach in elementary or secondary schools, particularly in science, mathematics, and modern foreign languages, and graduate students preparing to teach in college.

Federal support for scientific research has also had an important impact on higher education. In 1950 Congress established the National Science Foundation to promote scientific research and education. NSF has provided fellowships for graduate education in the sciences, supported the development of science institutes and centers at universities, funded training institutes for science teachers at all levels, supported many specific scientific research projects, and supported other miscellaneous scientific enterprises. In addition to NSF, many other federal agencies—the Department of Defense, Atomic Energy Commission, Office of Education, Public Health Service, and so forth—have granted research contracts to universities for specific projects. Thus, research has become a very big item in university life.

The federal government directly assists institutions of higher education through the Higher Education Facilities Act of 1963 and the Higher Education Act of 1965. The first of these general support measures authorizes federal grants and loans for construction and improvement of both public and private higher education facilities; generally, matching grants are required from the institution. The 1965 act was much broader in scope, providing for federally insured student loans and scholarships, a National Teacher Corps, funds for library materials and specialized equipment, grants to expand university extension programs, and grants to strengthen colleges that "are struggling for survival and are isolated from the main currents of academic life."

States have been involved in public higher education since the colonial era. State governments in the Northeast frequently made contributions to support private colleges in their states, a practice that continues today. The first state university to be chartered by a state legislature was the University of Georgia in 1794. Before the Civil War, northeastern states relied exclusively on private colleges, and the southern states assumed the leadership in public higher education. The antebellum curricula at southern state universities, however, resembled the rigid classical studies of the early private colleges—Greek and Latin, history, philosophy, literature, and so forth.

It was not until the Morrill Land Grant Act of 1862 that public higher education began to make major strides in the American states. Interestingly, the eastern states were slow to respond to the opportunity afforded by the Morrill Act to develop public universities; eastern states continued to rely primarily on their private colleges and universities. The southern states were economically depressed in the post-Civil War period, and leadership in public higher education passed to the midwestern states. The philosophy of the Morrill Act emphasized agricultural and mechanical studies, rather than the classical curricula of eastern colleges, and the movement for "A and M" education spread rapidly in the agricultural states. The early groups of midwestern state universities were closely tied to agricultural education, including agricultural extension services. State universities also took over the responsibility for the training of public school teachers in colleges of education. The state universities introduced a broad range of modern subjects in the university curricula—business administration, agriculture, home economics, education, engineering. It was not until the 1960s that the eastern states began to develop public higher education.

Today public higher education enrolls three-quarters of the nation's college and university students. Perhaps more importantly, the nation's leading state universities can challenge the best private institutions in academic excellence. The University of California at Berkeley, the University of Michigan, and the University of Wisconsin are deservedly ranked with Harvard, Yale, Princeton, and Columbia.

The organization and governance of public higher education varies a great deal from state to state. In every state, however, public higher education is separated to some degree from elementary and secondary education. Most states have established boards of trustees (or "regents") with authority to govern the state universities. One of the purposes of the boards is to insulate higher education from the vicissitudes of politics. Prominent citizens who are appointed to these boards are expected to champion higher education with the public and the legislature, as well as set overall policy guidelines for colleges and universities. In the past, there were separate boards for each institution and separate consideration by the governor's office and the legislature of each institution's budgetary request. But the resulting competition has caused state after state to create unified "university system" boards to coordinate higher education. These university system boards consolidate the budget requests of each institution, determine system-wide priorities, and present a single budget for higher education to the governor and the legislature. The stronger and more independent the university system board, the less likely that universities and colleges throughout the state will be distributed to cities and regions in a pork barrel fashion by legislators seeking to enhance their local constituencies.

But the key factor in university politics is the university president. He is the chief spokesman for higher education, and he must convince the public, the regents, the governor, and the legislature of the value of state universities. The president's crucial role is one of maintaining support for higher education in the state; he frequently delegates administrative responsibilities for the internal operation of the university to the vice-presidents and deans. Support for higher education among the public and its representatives can be affected by a broad spectrum of university activities, some of which are not directly related to the pursuit of knowledge. A winning football team can stimulate legislative enthusiasm and win appropriations for a new classroom building. University service-oriented research—developing new crops or feeds, assessing the state's mineral resources, advising state and local government agencies on administrative problems, analyzing the state economy, advising local school authorities, and so forth—may help to convince the public of the practical benefits of knowledge. University faculty may be interested in advanced research and the education of future Ph.D.s, but legislators and their constituents are more interested in the quality and effectiveness of undergraduate teaching. And, of course, campus radicalism and disorder have had a very significant negative effect on support for higher education.

READING, WRITING, AND RELIGION

The First Amendment to the Constitution of the United States contains two important guarantees of religious freedom: (1) "Congress shall make no law respecting an establishment of religion . . . ," and (2) "Or prohibiting the free exercise thereof." The Due Process Clause of the Fourteenth Amendment made these guarantees of religious liberty applicable to the states and their subdivisions as well as to Congress. Most of the debate over religion in the public schools centers around the "no establishment" clause of the First Amendment rather than the "free exercise" clause. However, it was respect for the "free exercise" clause that caused the Supreme Court in 1925 to declare unconstitutional an attempt on the part of a state to prohibit private and parochial schools and to force all children to attend public schools. In the words of the Supreme Court: "The fundamental theory of liberty upon which all governments in this Union repose excludes any general power of the state and to standardize its children by forcing them to accept instruction from public teachers only. The child is not the mere creature of the state."[8] It is this decision that protects the entire structure of parochial schools in this nation.

A great deal of religious conflict in America has centered around the meaning of the "no establishment" clause, and the public schools have been the principal scene of this conflict. One interpretation of the clause holds that it does not prevent government from aiding religious schools or encouraging religious beliefs in the public schools, so long as it does not discriminate against any particular religion. Another interpretation of the no establishment clause is that it creates a "wall of separation" between church and state in America, which prevents government from directly aiding religious schools or encouraging religious beliefs in any way.

The Catholic Church in America enrolls over 6 million students from kindergarten through the twelfth grade (over half of all private school students in the nation), and the Catholic Church has led the fight for an interpretation of the no establishment clause that would permit government to aid religious schools. As Catholic spokesmen see it, Catholic parents have a right to send their children to Catholic schools, and since they are taxpayers, they also expect that some share of tax monies should go to the aid of church schools; to do otherwise, they argue, would discriminate against parents who choose a "God-centered" education for their children. Those who favor government aid to parochial schools frequently refer to the language found in several cases decided by the Supreme Court, which appears to support the idea that government can *in a limited fashion* support the activities of church-related schools. In the case of *Pierce* v. *The Society of Sisters* (1925), the Court stated that the right to send one's children to parochial schools was a fundamental lib-

---

[8]Pierce v. The Society of Sisters, 268 U.S. 510 (1925).

erty guaranteed to all. In *Cochran* v. *Board of Education* (1930), the Court upheld a state law providing free textbooks for children attending both public and parochial schools on the grounds that this aid benefited the *children* rather than the Catholic Church and hence did not constitute an "establishment" of religion within the meaning of the First Amendment.[9] In *Everson* v. *Board of Education* (1947), the Supreme Court upheld the provision of school bus service to parochial school children at public expense on the grounds that the "wall of separation between church and state" does not prohibit the state from adopting a general program which helps *all* children, regardless of religion, to proceed safely to and from schools.[10] In *McCollum* v. *Board of Education* (1948), the Court declared *un*constitutional religious instruction in the public schools given during school hours by representatives of Protestant, Catholic, and Jewish faiths.[11] However, in *Zorach* v. *Clauson* (1952), the Court upheld a religious "released time program," where the schools released children during school hours for religious instruction conducted *outside* the public schools.[12] In this case the Court stated, "We are a religious people whose institutions presuppose a supreme being." These cases suggest that the Supreme Court is willing to permit some forms of aid to parochial school *children* that indirectly aids religion, so long as this is not directly used for the teaching of religion.

Religious controversy was instrumental in the defeat of federal-aid-to-education bills prior to 1965. For many years supporters of federal aid to education outnumbered opponents, but supporters were badly divided over the question of whether or not federal aid should go to parochial schools. Bills that failed to provide aid to parochial schools lost the crucial support of Catholics in Congress, and bills that provided aid for parochial schools lost the necessary support of Protestants, who favored a strict separation of church and state. For example, in 1961, President Kennedy's federal-aid-to-education bill was strongly opposed by a Catholic hierarchy when he stated: "In accordance with the clear prohibition of the Constitution, no elementary or secondary school funds are allocated for constructing church schools or paying church school teachers' salaries, and thus nonpublic school children are rightfully not counted in determining the funds each state will receive for its public schools."[13]

As a result of these sharp religious divisions, federal aid to education

[9]Cochran v. Board of Education, 281 U.S. 370 (1930).
[10]Everson v. Board of Education, 330 U.S. 1 (1947).
[11]McCollum v. Board of Education, 333 U.S. 203 (1948).
[12]Zorach v. Clauson, 343 U.S. 306 (1952).
[13]See Hugh D. Price, "Race, Religion and the Rules Committee," in *The Uses of Power*, ed. Alan F. Westin (New York: Harcourt, Brace & World, Inc., 1962).

floundered in Congress until 1965. In the Elementary and Secondary Education Act of that year, President Johnson compromised the religious issue. The largest share of federal money distributed under this act goes to poverty-impacted *public* school districts, but the act also includes federal grants for the purchase of specialized educational services and facilities, such as laboratories, textbooks, and instructional materials. Federal funds for these specialized educational facilities and services may go to both public and private schools. Presumably federal aid to a church school for the purchase of a specialized educational facility would not violate the constitutional prohibition against the "establishment" of a religion so long as the federal aid was not directly used for the teaching of religion.

While the Supreme Court has consented to government programs aiding the child in parochial school, it has also voiced the opinion that the no establishment clause of the First Amendment should constitute a wall of separation between church and state. In the words of the Court:

> Neither a state nor the federal government can set up a church. Neither can pass laws which aid one religion, aid all religions, or prefer one religion over another. Neither can force nor influence a person to go to or to remain away from church against his will, or force him to profess a belief or disbelief in any religion. No person can be punished for entertaining or professing religious beliefs or disbeliefs, for church attendance or nonattendance. No tax in any amount, large or small, can be levied to support any religious activities or institutions, whatever they may be called, or whatever form they may adopt to teach or practice religion. Neither a state nor the federal government can, openly or secretly, participate in the affairs of any religious organizations or groups, and vice versa.[14]

One of the most important Supreme Court decisions in the history of church-state relations in America came in 1971 in the case of *Lemon v. Kurtzman*.[15] The Supreme Court held that it was unconstitutional for a state to pay the costs of teachers' salaries or instructional materials in parochial schools. The Court acknowledged that it had previously approved the provision of state textbooks and bus transportation directly to parochial school children. But the Court held that state payments to parochial schools involved "excessive entanglement between government and religion" and violated both the establishment and free exercise clauses of the First Amendment. State payments to religious schools, the Court said, would require excessive government controls and surveillance to insure that funds were used only for secular instruc-

[14]Hugo Black, Majority Opinion in Everson v. Board of Education, 330 U.S. 1
[15]Lemon v. Kurtzman, 403 U.S. 602 (1971).

tion. Moreover, the Court expressed the fear that state aid to parochial schools would create "political divisions along religious lines . . . one of the principal evils against which the First Amendment was intended to protect."

Religious conflict in public schools also centers around the question of prayer and Bible-reading ceremonies conducted by public schools. The practice of opening the school day with prayer and Bible-reading ceremonies is widespread in American public schools. Usually the prayer is a Protestant rendition of the Lord's Prayer, and Bible reading is from the King James version. To avoid the denominational aspects of these ceremonies, the New York State Board of Regents substituted a nondenominational prayer, which it required to be said aloud in each class in the presence of a teacher at the beginning of each school day:

> Almighty God, we acknowledge our dependence upon Thee, and we beg
> Thy blessings upon us, our parents, our teachers, and our country.

New York argued that this prayer ceremony did not violate the no establishment clause, because the prayer was denominationally neutral and because student participation in the prayer was voluntary. However, in *Engle* v. *Vitale* (1962), the Supreme Court stated that "The constitutional prohibition against laws respecting an establishment of a religion must at least mean in this country it is no part of the business of government to compose official prayers for any group of the American people to recite as part of a religious program carried on by government.[16] The Court pointed out making prayer voluntary did not free it from the prohibitions of the no establishment clause; that clause prevented the establishment of a religious ceremony by a government agency, regardless of whether the ceremony was voluntary or not:

> Neither the fact that the prayer may be denominationally neutral, nor the
> fact that its observance on the part of the students is voluntary can serve
> to free it from the limitations of the establishment clause, as it might
> from the free exercise clause, of the First Amendment, both of which
> are operative against the states by virtue of the 14th Amendment. . . . The
> establishment clause, unlike the free exercise clause, does not depend on
> any showing of direct governmental compulsion and is violated by the
> enactment of laws which establish an official religion whether those laws
> operate directly to coerce nonobserving individuals or not.[17]

One year later in the case of *Abbington Township* v. *Schempp,* the Court considered the constitutionality of Bible-reading ceremonies in the

[16]Engle v. Vitale, 370 U.S. 421 (1962).
[17]*Ibid.*

public schools.[18] Here again, even though the children were not required to participate, the Court found that Bible reading as an opening exercise in the schools was a religious ceremony. The Court went to some trouble in its opinion to point out that they were not "throwing the Bible out of the school," for they specifically stated that the study of the Bible or of religion, when presented objectively as part of a secular program of education, did not violate the First Amendment, but religious *ceremonies* involving Bible reading or prayer, established by a state or school, did so.

EDUCATION IN THE GHETTO

The plight of the ghetto schools has become popular knowledge through the writings of Bel Kaufman (*Up the Down Staircase*) and Jonathan Kozol (*Death at any Early Age: The Destruction of the Hearts and Minds of Negro Children in the Boston Public Schools*). Disadvantaged black pupils are behind whites in standard achievement tests in the primary grades, and they fall further behind as they move through school. By the twelfth grade, the average black student is more than two years behind the average white on standardized tests of achievement, the black dropout rate is more than double the white rate, and black self-esteem is lower. The validity of achievement and intelligence tests can be disputed, but there is little doubt that many ghetto blacks are educationally ill prepared for either college or post-high school training or the job market. The question of "equality of educational opportunity" is a serious one for urban schools and indeed for the entire nation. (See Figure 14–5.)

Government efforts at coping with ghetto educational deficiencies can be classified into three broad policy directions: (1) ending de facto school segregation by racial balancing in the assignment of pupils to public schools and bussing pupils wherever necessary to achieve racial balance (this policy was discussed in Chapter 13); (2) compensatory educational programs in ghetto schools to overcome learning difficulties of disadvantaged children; and (3) community control of ghetto schools in an effort to redesign public education to fit ghetto conditions.

To date the emphasis in public policy relative to equality of educational opportunity has been on compensatory programs for disadvantaged children. Compensatory educational programs generally assume that environmental problems create learning difficulties for the disadvantaged pupil—verbal retardation, lack of motivation, experiential and sensory

[18]Abbington Township v. Schempp, 374 U.S. 203 (1963).

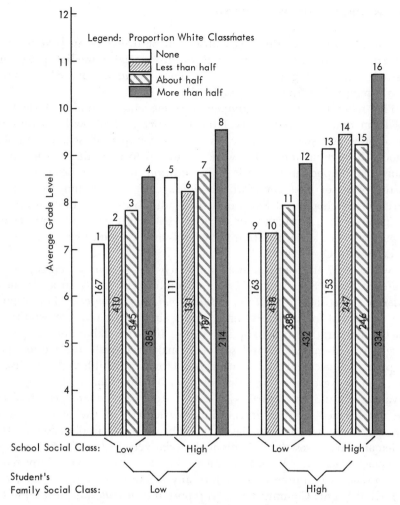

FIGURE 14–5   Average Grade Level Performance of Twelfth-Grade Negro Students by Individual Social Class Origin, Social Class Level of School and Proportion White Classmates Last Year; Metropolitan Northeast

Note: The numbers in the bars represent the number of cases.

Data from the Coleman Report is used by the U.S. Commission on Civil Rights to support the view that black pupils perform better academically in integrated schools. Note that performance of black children improves with the proportion of white classmates regardless of whether the black child's family social class is low or high, or whether the social class composition of the school is low or high. Note also that black children from higher family social class perform better academically than black children from lower family social class. Note also that black children from lower family social class perform better in schools with classmates of higher social class.

Source: U.S. Commission on Civil Rights, *Racial Isolation in the Public Schools* (Washington, D.C.: Government Printing Office, 1967), I, 90.

deprivation—and that these difficulties can be overcome in part by special educational programs. In addition to special remedial programs grafted onto the regular school experience, compensatory efforts have been attempted at the preschool level.

The major thrust of the compensatory movement came in Title I of the Elementary and Secondary Education Act of 1965 with its billion-dollar-plus per year assistance for "poverty-impacted schools. Public schools throughout the nation were stimulated to upgrade remedial programs for the poor under Title I. In addition, under the Economic Opportunity Act of 1964, community action agencies throughout the nation initiated preschool remedial programs for disadvantaged children under the popular Project Head Start. Project Head Start was later transferred to public school administration with funds and assistance from the Office of Economic Opportunity.

But in 1967 the compensatory approach was seriously challenged by Professor James S. Coleman of Johns Hopkins University in an influential report entitled *Equality of Educational Opportunity*.[19] This report concluded that formal educational inputs, such as per pupil expenditure, teacher preparation, teacher-pupil ratios, libraries, laboratories, special programs and materials, and so forth, make relatively *little* difference in pupil achievement and motivation. However, children from disadvantaged backgrounds (regardless of race) benefit from integration with advantaged children (regardless of race). Moreover, advantaged children are not harmed by such integration, particularly if the disadvantaged are not a majority in the classroom. The startling implication of the Coleman report was that schools make relatively little difference except as a place where kids learn from each other, and money spent improving ghetto schools is unlikely to produce any meaningful results. Later, the U.S. Civil Rights Commission in its report *Racial Isolation in the Public Schools* used the Coleman data as ammunition to support its contention that integration, and not compensatory education, was the key to the problem of equal educational opportunity.[20]

Decentralization of big-city school systems and "community control" of local schools as an approach to equality in urban education has produced a great deal of controversy recently.[21] Proponents of community control have suggested that ghetto residents should be given control over ghetto schools in order to (1) shift from professional and administrative "dom-

19James S. Coleman, *Equality of Educational Opportunity* (Washington, D.C.: Government Printing Office, 1966).

20U.S. Commission on Civil Rights, *Racial Isolation in the Public Schools*, 2 vols. (Washington, D.C.: Government Printing Office, 1967).

21See Marilyn Gittell and Alan G. Hevesi, eds. *The Politics of Urban Education* (New York: Frederick A. Praeger, Inc., 1969).

inance" of the schools to "a meaningful parental and community role in the education process; (2) deemphasize the acquisition of achievement skills (reading, writing, and arithmetic) in favor of "a humanistically-oriented curriculum modifying the skill-performance standard by which educational quality is primarily measured"; and (3) bring personnel into the schools who have "broader talents than the conventionally prepared career educator." Support for the community control concept is found among black power advocates and black racial separatists, as well as educational reformers. Black militants have attacked desegregation because it implies that black pupils can learn well only by sitting next to white pupils. They want educational programs that emphasize black identity and self-awareness, and they reject programs designed to make black pupils "like white pupils." More importantly, they want black political control of educational resources in the ghetto. Professor Marilyn Gittell explains:

> Community control implies a redistribution of power within the educational subsystem. It is directed toward achieving a modern mechanism for participatory democracy. It attempts to answer the political failure in education systems, and, as regards the educational failure, community control is intended to create an environment in which more meaningful educational policies can be developed and a wide variety of alternative solutions and techniques can be tested. It seems plausible to assume that a school system devoted to community needs and serving as an agent of community interests will provide an environment more conducive to learning.[22]

New York's unhappy experience with community control illustrates some of the problems involved in this concept.[23] In 1967 the Ford Foundation sponsored demonstration projects in community control in New York City, including a project in a ghetto area known as Ocean Hill-Brownsville. At the same time Mayor John V. Lindsay created an Advisory Panel on Decentralization of New York City Schools, headed by Ford Foundation President McGeorge Bundy, which reamended a city-wide program of school decentralization (the Bundy Plan).[24] An Ocean Hill-Brownsville Local Governing Board was established, which proceeded to act with considerable autonomy from the New York City Board of Education. When school opened in September 1967, the Ocean Hill-Brownsville Board appointed five principals who were not

[22]*Ibid.*, pp. 365–66.
[23]*Ibid.*, Sec. V, pp. 305–77.
[24]Mayor's Advisory Panel on Decentralization of the New York City Schools, *Reconnection for Learning: A Community Control System for New York City* (New York: Office of the Mayor, 1967); reprinted in Gittell and Heuesi, *Politics of Urban Education.*

on the civil service list and thereby incurred the opposition of the Council of Supervisory Associations representing school administrators. During a city-wide school strike over pay increases and smaller classes Ocean Hill-Brownsville schools stayed open, thereby incurring the opposition of the United Federation of Teachers representing the city's teachers. Throughout the 1967–68 school year there was growing hostility and an exaltation of rhetoric between white teachers and administrators on the one hand and the Ocean Hill-Brownsville Governing Board on the other. The board charged that certain white teachers were uncooperative and failed to understand ghetto problems. The teachers charged the board with black racism and even anti-Semitism (many New York teachers and administrators are Jewish). In May 1968 the board dismissed nineteen white teachers without notice or hearing seven weeks before the end of the term, apparently because they were "out of tune with the political atmosphere in the community." The United Federation of Teachers called a city-wide strike protesting the dismissals as violations of civil service regulations and due process of law. The strike seriously curtailed education in New York City during the 1968–69 school year. The issues of the strike were eventually mediated, but not without a tragic increase in distrust and suspicion between the races in the school system and the city at large.

Opponents of community control—particularly white teachers, teacher unions, and administrators—argue that decentralization creates administrative duplication, inefficiencies, and increased overhead costs. They contend that it results in wasted educational dollars, the destruction of the merit system, and the introduction of political and racial considerations in educational policies. Finally, they contend that it promotes racial separatism and black militancy. Decentralization suffered some setback in New York City as a product of the Ocean Hill-Brownsville experience (the state legislature rejected the Bundy Plan), but it may be put forward again in that city and elsewhere as an approach to ghetto education.

FIFTEEN

The
Politics
of
Transportation

PUBLIC HIGHWAY POLICY

Few inventions have had such a far-reaching effect on the life of the American people as the automobile. Henry Ford built one of the first gasoline-driven carriages in America in 1893, and by 1900 there were 8 thousand automobiles registered in the U.S. The Model T was introduced in the autumn of 1908. By concentrating on a single unlovely but enduring model, and by introducing the assembly line processes, the Ford Motor Company began producing automobiles for the masses. By 1921 there were over 20 million cars in existence, and the auto industry was established in the United States. Today there are over 110 million registered motor vehicles in the nation, one for every two persons living in the country; and the automobile population is increasing faster than the human population. The automobile and trucking industry ranks as the largest and wealthiest in the United States. It represents 10 percent of the gross national product, and it employs nearly 12 million persons, buys 22 percent of the steel output, 61 percent of the rubber, and 44 percent of all the radios produced in the nation. Automobiles and superhighways have radically changed the life-style of Americans. They have helped to create the nation's mushrooming suburbs, which have drained white middle-class Americans from the central cities. Automobiles threaten both to suffocate cities with polluted air and to strangle them with massive traffic jams. Automobiles and superhighways have made Americans more mobile, more travel conscious, more able to move about the country in search of opportunity. Freeways have reduced travel time and brought the farm closer to the city, and they have also contributed to the economic stagnation and decline of small towns and rural areas in the nation.

In addition to the economic and sociological significance, the invention of the automobile has had an important impact on politics and government. The provision of public highways is the second most costly function of state and local governments. Highway politics are of interest not only to the automotive industry and the driving public but also to the oil industry, the American Road Builders Association, the cement industry, the railroads, the trucking industry, the farmers, the outdoor advertising industry, and the county commissioners, taxpayer associations, ecologists and conservationists, and neighborhood improvement associations. These political interests are concerned with the allocation of money for highway purposes, the sources of funds for highway revenue, the extent of gasoline and motor vehicle taxation, the regulation of traffic on the highways, the location of highways, the determination of construction policies, the division of responsibility between federal and state and local governments for highway financing and administration, the division of highway funds between rural and urban areas, and many other important outcomes in highway politics.

Governments spent very little for public roads at the beginning of the century. The only hard-surface roads to be found then were provided by city governments. But the automobile brought an insatiable demand for bigger and better highways. The automobile owner provided the broad base of political support for highway construction, but the leadership has come from the automotive and oil industries, the construction industry, the cement and equipment manufacturers, the organized farm interests seeking farm-to-market roads, and the trucking industry, The railroad industry has provided the only substantial opposition to highway building, but all the battles have been won by the supporters of highway transportation. Today there are over 3 million miles of surfaced roads in America, and state and local expenditures for highways total over $16 billion annually. Highway expenditures account for about 12 percent of all state and local expenditures, making highways second only to education in costs to states and communities.[1]

At the beginning of the century, most expenditures were made by local governments, particularly cities. Cities had very early created hard-

[1]For a complete description of highway policy in the United States, see Phillip H. Burch, *Highway Revenue and Expenditure Policy in the United States* (New Brunswick, N.J.: Rutgers University Press, 1962).

surfaced street networks, which proved capable of servicing motor vehicles reasonably well. But rural areas were, to say the least, unprepared for the advent of the automobile. State after state established state highway departments charged with the task of constructing highways in rural areas. State highway systems came into being, and state governments assumed direct responsibility for the construction and maintenance of a large proportion of the public roads. States also began to distribute aid to local governments for highway purposes. Many state highway departments tried to distinguish between a "primary" state highway system, which was to connect cities and towns, and a "secondary" highway system, which would connect primary highways with local service routes and streets that provided direct access to farms and homes. Such a classification provided a logical division of responsibilities between state and local governments. But since the states generally financed the primary system, communities often pressured state highway departments to classify more roads as "primary" state highways, in order to shift the burden of finance onto the state. As a result, the proportion of roads designated as primary state highways gradually increased. The assumption of direct state responsibility for a "primary highway system" heavily favored rural areas; the goal of many state primary highway systems was to connect every county seat. The rural bias of state highway departments lingers even today.

FEDERAL HIGHWAY POLICY

It was in the Federal Aid Road Act of 1916 that the federal government, through its Bureau of Public Roads, first provided regular funds for highway construction under terms that gave the bureau considerable influence over state policy. For example, if states wanted to get federal money, they were required to have a highway department, and to have their plans for highway construction approved by the Bureau of Public Roads. In 1921, federal aid was limited to a connected system of principal state highways, now called the "federal aid primary highway system." Uniform standards were prescribed and even a uniform numbering system was added, such as "US 1," or "US 30." Federal aid was limited to a maximum of 7 percent of the total mileage of the state and was only to connect major cities. The emphasis of the program was clearly rural. The federal aid formula appropriated funds, one-third on the basis of population, one-third on the basis of area, one-third on the basis of total mileage of postal routes in the states. States were required to match federal monies dollar for dollar.

The Federal Highway Act of 1944 designated a federal aid "secondary" system of farm-to-market roads and provided for "urban extensions" of primary roads, in addition to the federal aid for the primary highway system. Federal funds for primary and secondary and urban extension roads, commonly called "ABC funds," are determined by three separate formulas, but all take into account area, population, postal routes, and mileage. These federal ABC funds are matched fifty-fifty by the states. In the use of their federal funds, states make the surveys and plans, let the contracts, and supervise the construction, but only with the approval of the U.S. Bureau of Public Roads. All ABC funds remain under the administrative control of the states, who are responsible for their operation and maintenance. All payments to contractors for work done on any federal project are made by the states; the Bureau of Public Roads makes very few direct payments.

The Federal Highway Act of 1944 also authorized the national system of interstate and defense highways ("I" highways)—now the most important feature of the federal highway policy. However, prior to 1956, only modest funds were provided by Congress for the I highway system, and these were provided on a fifty-fifty matching basis. It was not until the Federal Highway Act of 1956, under the Eisenhower administration, that Congress became serious about the I highway system. At that time, Congress provided for its completion by 1972, and changed the matching basis to 90 percent federal and 10 percent state. The Federal Highway

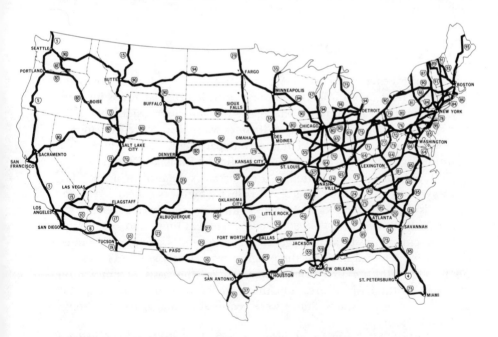

FIGURE 15–1   The National System of Interstate and Defense Highways

Source: U.S. Department of Transportation, Federal Highway Administration.

Act of 1956, as amended, authorizes 42,500 miles of highway, designed to connect principal metropolitan areas and industrial centers, and thereby shifts the emphasis of federal highway activity from rural to urban needs. Figure 15–1 shows the I highway system as it will look upon its completion. Although the system will constitute less than 2 percent of the total surface in the nation, it is expected to carry over 20 percent of all highway traffic. The Bureau of Public Roads has been given strong supervisory powers, including the selection of routes (it can even transfer interstate mileage and funds out of a noncooperative state), but administration and execution are still left to state highway departments. Federal monies are paid to the states, not to the contractors, as the work progresses. The Federal Highway Trust Fund in the Bureau of Public Roads is responsible for the orderly scheduling of federal aid and the phasing out of reimbursement requests for the states. A state can proceed at a more rapid rate in building its I highways if it chooses to do so without federal reimbursement for a period of time; in practice, however, this does not happen. The bureau makes the real determination of who gets what, when, and how in the interstate highway program. The 1956 act has established uniformity in construction and engineering specifications and the maximum size and weight limits for I highway users. It is also agreed to reduce by 0.5 percent the state's share of the cost of I highways if a state prohibits advertising on I highways. Delays and postponements have pushed back the expected completion date of the I highway system to the late 1970s.

Controversy has already developed about what to do with federal highway funds after the completion of the I highway system. The federal gasoline tax of four cents per gallon is a good revenue producer—nearly $6 billion per year in the early 1970s. These funds are currently deposited in the Federal Highway Trust Fund for disbursement as federal aid to the states for highway construction. Automotive and highway interests want to keep it that way. They want to use federal gasoline taxes exclusively for maintenance and repair and for the construction of additional links and connectors in the I highway system. But others have argued that the federal government should direct its attention and resources to mass transportation projects. Urban interests, including mayors and planners, combined with railroad interests, have urged greater federal investment in urban mass transit—trains, subways, buses—and high-speed rail connections between major metropolitan areas, particularly on the eastern seaboard.

The creation of the federal Department of Transportation (DOT) in 1966 was a small victory for mass transit forces. It placed the Federal Highway Administration in the larger cabinet-level department and awarded equal organizational status with the Federal Railroad Administration, Urban Mass Transportation Administration, U.S. Coast Guard,

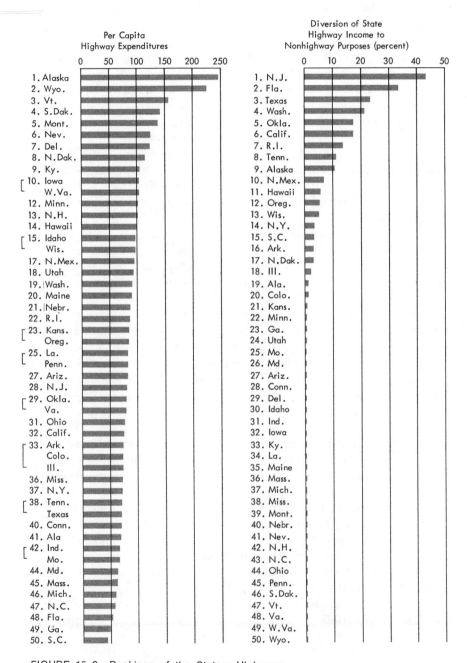

Per Capita
Highway Expenditures

Diversion of State
Highway Income to
Nonhighway Purposes (percent)

FIGURE 15–2   Rankings of the States: Highways

and Federal Aviation Administration. Many states are following the federal example and creating their own departments of transportation with jurisdiction over highways, motor vehicle registration, mass transit, bridges and harbors, turnpikes, airports, and so forth.

STATE HIGHWAY
ORGANIZATION AND FINANCE

The political importance of highway construction and the millions of dollars spent on highway building contracts each year have resulted in a tendency in some states to set highway departments and highway funds apart from the other functions of state government. Interests favorable to highway construction (road builders, oil and gas companies, automobile associations, and so on) have generally argued for the organization of independent highway departments or commissions, free from direct control by the governor. They have also supported a system of earmarking certain state revenues, generally gasoline taxes, motor vehicle registration fees, and other highway user revenues, for use on highways only. Of course, not all states have been willing to remove highways from the regular channels of public control, and the pattern of highway organization and finance varies from state to state.

Robert S. Friedman has classified fifty states according to their degree of organizational independence from the governor in highway policy.[2] He has defined a "dependent" highway department as one in which the governor is free to name, without restrictions, his own highway department head, who would serve at the pleasure of the governor. In contrast, an "independent" department is governed by a multimember board or commission, which chooses the department head. The board may be chosen by the governor under certain restrictions: their terms of office would not coincide with that of the governor, and board members could not easily be removed from office. Very often these board members or commissioners are chosen to represent geographic areas of the state, in formal recognition of the pork barrel character of much highway work. This localism is opposed by proponents of coordinated planning for state highways. States with independent boards or commissions spend slightly more per capita on highways than states with dependent highway departments. However, many of the states with gubernatorial control are the most urban, industrial states in the nation. It may be that

2Robert S. Friedman, "State Politics and Highways," in *Politics in the American State*, 2nd ed., eds. Herbert Jacob and Kenneth Vines (Boston: Little, Brown and Company, 1971).

ruralism produces both increased highway spending per capita and independent highway boards.[3]

The principal source of highway finance is highway user revenue. Federal highway aid constitutes about 30 percent of all highway funds, but most of the remaining 70 percent comes from taxes and fees levied upon highway users. In only a few states are general revenues used for highway purposes. The state gasoline tax alone accounts for approximately half of all highway receipts. All states levy gasoline taxes of six to nine and one-half cents per gallon. (The federal government now collects four cents per gallon.) The second most important highway revenue source is the motor vehicle registration fee. In some states, particularly in the South, this fee is primarily a regulatory device, with yearly charges running from only five dollars. In other states, fees for passenger cars are fifteen dollars or more, with higher fees for heavier vehicles, particularly trucks and buses. Toll road receipts constitute another major highway revenue source in some states. Tolls exact revenue from *through* traffic, which has originated in another state and is destined for still another state. New York, New Jersey, and Pennsylvania collect about half of all the toll receipts in the nation.

The segregation of highway user revenues from general state revenues is an article of faith among highway interests. Prior to the rise of the automobile, highway expenditures came out of general revenue. But automobile travel has made it possible to place heavy reliance on highway user revenues as a source of highway funds. The theory is that such taxes insure that the cost of highways is paid by the user. As highway revenues have grown, highway interests have pressed for legal and even constitutional principles preventing the use of these revenues for anything except highway purposes. Today, more than half the states have constitutional provisions restricting the diversion of highway user revenue to nonhighway purposes, and many other states restrict diversion by statute or administrative practice. This policy guarantees a continued flow of road-building funds and, in effect, gives highways preferential treatment over other public programs.

Urban industrial states are far more likely to divert highway receipts to nonhighway purposes than the rural agricultural states. If success in preventing the diversion of highway receipts to other public programs is a valid measure of the strength of the highway interest groups, these interest groups have been significantly more successful in rural than in urban areas.

[3]"Independent" highway departments are found in Arizona, Arkansas, Colorado, Delaware, Florida, Georgia, Idaho, Indiana, Iowa, Maine, Massachusetts, Michigan, Mississippi, Missouri, Montana, New Hampshire, New Mexico, North Carolina, South Carolina, Texas, Utah, Washington, and Wyoming. In other states the highway department is partially or totally "dependent" upon the governor. *Ibid.*, p. 488.

A COMPARATIVE VIEW OF
STATE HIGHWAY POLITICS

Interstate comparisons in highway policy are complicated by differences in area, geography, soil, and terrain among the states. Large but thinly populated states must maintain more miles of highway in relation to their populations than smaller, heavily populated states. It is relatively cheap to put highways in deserts, but expensive to do so in mountains. Highways built in climates that are subject to freezes, snowfalls, and rainfalls require more maintenance and repair than highways located in less rigorous climates. In short, natural factors, as well as economic and political factors, contribute to variations in highway policy among the states.

Highway expenditures do not guarantee a good highway system, but they do provide a rough index of the extent to which supporters of highways have succeeded in obtaining public funds for their objectives. Per capita highway expenditures in the states are significantly related to urbanization: increases in urbanization result in a *decrease* in per capita highway expenditures.[4] In other words, rural agricultural states spend more per capita on highways than urban industrial states. Not only do rural farm states spend more per capita on highways, but they also spend more in relation to their personal income. The federal government relieves some of the burden of highway financing in rural states by giving them proportionately more funds than it gives to urban states. But federal monies notwithstanding, rural states still expend more effort for highways than urban states. Whether one prefers to measure highway efforts in per capita expenditures or in relative terms, the tendency for rural agricultural states to emphasize highways is unmistakable.

Quite clearly, rural politics are much more highway oriented than urban politics. Part of the reason for this may be the problems of rural politics a few years ago. Rural roads disturb relatively few individuals, while metropolitan highways involve uprooting thousands of outraged residents and irate businessmen. Freeways are a good idea when they run through somebody else's backyard. Mileage is much cheaper and faster to build in rural areas; urban highways require more years and more money per mile. As Phillip H. Burch points out, "Urban highways are poor politics for a governor when his successor will be cutting all the tapes.[5] Finally, it may be that urban dwellers have come to accept traffic jams as facts of life. They have never known anything better, so

4See Thomas R. Dye, *Politics, Economics, and the Public* (Chicago: Rand McNally & Co., 1966), pp. 157–61.
5Burch, *Highway Revenue*, p. 173.

they fail to fight for highways with the same zest as their country cousins.

Not only do rural states spend relatively more for highways than urban states, but the distribution of highway funds within states generally favors rural areas. Burch argues effectively that "the American city is being woefully shortchanged in the allocation of state highway department money."[6] It is difficult to measure the extent to which rural and urban areas are not receiving a fair share of state highway expenditures. But Burch notes that U.S. Federal Highway Administration data show that about 44 percent of all traffic occurs in urban areas, while state highway departments spend only about 25 percent of their highway funds in urban areas. The most flagrant discrimination in the allocation of state funds occurs in rural states, and the fairest ratios occur in urban states.

All but two states offer some form of grants-in-aid to local governments for highway purposes. The justification for state grants-in-aid to localities centers on the need for minimum road conditions throughout the state, the inadequacy of local revenue sources, and the desire to equalize financial burdens throughout the state. Here again, the evidence seems quite conclusive that across the nation, urban areas are heavily discriminated against in state highway grants-in-aid to local communities. The U.S. Federal Highway Administration reports that most state grants to localities go to county and township roads and only a small percentage go to municipal streets.

It is important to note, however, that in recent years discrimination against urban areas in highway expenditures has been somewhat modified. In recent years urban areas in most states have made significant gains in the percentages of state highway funds they receive. The federal interstate highway program has also improved the relative position of urban areas in highway fund allocations.

In short, there is no real evidence that a "rural" conspiracy is involved in the allocation of highway funds. Highway construction and right-of-way acquisition in urban areas is very expensive. Urban dwellers do not always welcome highways the way rural dwellers generally do. Highway construction in urban areas means a dislocation of people, businesses, and neighborhoods, as well as the removal of property from tax rolls.

THE METROPOLITAN TRANSPORTATION MESS

To date, expressways have failed miserably in alleviating the transportation problems in large cities. Multimillion-dollar freeways designed to un-snarl traffic become snarled themselves at rush hours almost as soon as

[6]*Ibid.*, p. 165.

they are completed. Automobiles funneled into downtown areas slow city traffic to a crawl, create giant parking problems, pollute the air, and slowly bring about economic strangulation of the central city. The result is to speed the exodus to the suburbs of residents, businesses, and industries, which tends to threaten the very survival of the nation's central cities.

City planners, transportation specialists, and nearly all who have studied the modern city's traffic picture readily agree that the only way to relieve traffic congestion and preserve central cities is to get people out of private automobiles and into public transit, that is, "to move people, not vehicles."[7] Technological and economic evidence points to rail transit as the only reasonable way to move persons in and out of the central city at rush hours. Automobiles on expressways can move about 2 thousand people per lane per hour, buses can move between 6 thousand and 9 thousand, but rail systems can carry up to 60 thousand persons per hour. In other words, one rail line is estimated to be equal to that of twenty or thirty expressway lanes of automobiles in terms of its ability to move people.

Of course, as most commuters know all too well, privately owned commuter railroads are in generally deplorable operating condition and even worse financial condition. The average citizen has a tremendous investment in his automobile; the automobile has become a status symbol and even a way of life for the nation's suburbanites. Few Americans want to see their heavy financial investment sit in a garage all day. Americans clearly prefer private automobile transportation and costly expressways to mass transit, regardless of the arguments of transportation experts. The result is that existing private mass transit facilities have been steadily losing customers over the last two decades. As their operating costs increase and their patronage declines, many private bus and rail carriers resort to raising fares, reducing service, and putting off maintenance— all of which simply turns away more customers and accelerates the downward spiral. Very often service is poor and equipment is dirty and uncomfortable. Spokesmen for commuter railroads insist that the fault is not theirs—that they must compete with automobiles operating on publicly subsidized, multimillion-dollar expressways. The individual American cannot be lured away from his beloved automobile and the privacy and status he thinks it gives him.

It is virtually impossible for the nation's major cities to continue to rely upon automobile transportation over expressways to handle projected increases in transportation needs. Most of our cities are already

[7]See Francis Bello, "The City and the Car," *The Exploding Metropolis* (New York: Fortune Magazine, 1957).

experiencing expressway traffic jams at rush hours and a resulting increase in time and cost to the average automobile commuter. Needless to say, the cost of mass transit facilities on a per capita basis is infinitesimal compared with the cost of expressway building. Some pilot projects in New York, Philadelphia, San Francisco, and Boston found that it was necessary to provide public subsidies to commuter rail companies or to have city governments acquire these facilities at a loss if commuter service was to be restored. The cost of such public subsidies is very small in comparison with the cost of building and maintaining expressways. Thus, mass transit is a considerable saving to most cities, even if fares do not meet operating expenses. Moreover, these pilot projects indicated that new, speedier, more comfortable, air-conditioned, high-capacity trains with fewer stops and more frequent time schedules, together with an expensive advertising campaign, could lure many riders back to public transportation.

Mass transit facilities, while cheaper than expressways, are still quite costly, particularly for cities that do not already have commuter rail service. Requests for federal financial assistance for cities resulted in congressional enactment of the Urban Mass Transportation Act of 1964. The act provided for federal grants for mass transportation facilities and equipment, for expanded research and demonstration programs, for the relocation of businesses and families displaced by mass transit projects, and for the planning of urban mass transportation facilities. Thus far, federal spending for mass transit under this act has been very limited—a few hundred million dollars compared with over 5 billion per year for highways. Political support for this bill came from the nation's mayors, together with some assistance from railroad and transit car manufacturers. Political opposition to federal spending for urban mass transportation came, predictably, from the nation's rural areas. Suburban interests have played an ambiguous role in the urban mass transit debate: presumably, mass transit will make it easier for suburbanites to get in and out of the central city, but suburban commercial and industrial enterprises and real estate developers are not wholly in favor of strengthening the economic role of central cities.

Proponents of federally assisted mass transit argue that cities and states do not have sufficient resources to build mass transit facilities. They argue that mass transit is cheaper than expressway construction and that expressways can never handle predicted traffic increases anyhow. They emphasize the costs of traffic jams in time and wages lost and their economic impact on central cities. They point out that privately owned mass transportation facilities fail to show profits and that, therefore, these companies are not in a position to make improvements in equipment, facilities, and services at fare levels that would attract riders. Rural opposition stresses the increased centralization at the federal level that would be involved in federally aided mass transit. They object to the idea that the entire nation, including rural areas, should be asked to contribute to solving transportation problems of the nation's cities. Although the federal government contributes heavily to the expressway construction, they believe that states and communities should bear the cost of mass transit by themselves. Moreover, they are doubtful about the feasibility of convincing Americans that they should give up the convenience of their automobiles for mass transit.

To date, federal activity under the Urban Mass Transportation Act has largely been limited to financing urban mass transportation planning. For the most part, pleasant, rapid, convenient, and efficient mass transit continues to be a planner's dream, and federal, state and local policy continues to emphasize automobile transportation and expressway construction.

SIXTEEN

The
Politics
of
Poverty and Welfare

POVERTY IN AMERICA

Political conflict over poverty begins with disagreement about its definition. Proponents of programs for the poor frequently make high estimates
of the number of poor; they view the problem of poverty as a persistent
one, even in an affluent society; they contend that many millions of poor
people suffer from hunger, exposure, and remediable illness and that
some of them even starve to death. Their definition of the problem almost mandates immediate and massive public programs. Others minimize
the number of poor in America; they see poverty diminishing over time
without major public programs; they view the poor in America as considerably better off than the middle class of fifty years ago and even
wealthy by the standards of most other societies in the world; and they
deny that individuals need to suffer from hunger, exposure, remediable
illness, or starvation if they make use of the services and facilities available to them. This definition of the problem minimizes the need for
massive public programs to fight poverty.

According to the U.S. Social Security Administration there are about
25 million poor people in the United States, approximately 13 percent
of the population. These are the number of Americans falling *below* the
annual cash income level required to maintain a decent standard of liv-

ing. This definition of poverty was derived by careful calculation of costs of food, housing, clothing, and other items for rural and urban families of different sizes. The dollar amounts are flexible to take into account the effect of inflation; these amounts can be expected to rise each year with the rate of inflation. In the early 1970s the poverty line for an urban family of four was approximately four thousand dollars per year.

There are several problems in this definition of poverty. First of all, it does not account for regional differences in the costs of living, or climate, or accepted style of living. Second, it does not account for family assets—for example, a family that owns its own home does not usually devote as much income to housing as a family that rents. Third, there are many families and individuals whose particular circumstances may place them officially among the poor but who do not think of themselves as "poor people"—students, for example. Doubtless there are others whose income is above the poverty line but who have special problems—sickness, for example—which leave them impoverished. Finally, the official definition of poverty does not recognize the problems of those who spend their incomes unwisely. If money goes for liquor or dope or expensive cars, or if money is siphoned off by loan sharks, impoverished relatives and friends, or high prices charged by ghetto store owners, then even a reasonably high income family can live in poverty. Yet despite these problems, the Social Security Administration definition has provided the best available estimate of poverty in America.

How poor is "poor"? There is reason to believe that the 25 million Americans living in official poverty do not all suffer hardship and privation.[1] About 45 percent own cars, 42 percent own their own homes, and more than 50 percent have some savings. Nearly 80 percent of the poor have television sets, and 75 percent have refrigerators or freezers. Over 75 percent have hot water, access to a telephone for receiving calls, a kitchen with cooking equipment, a flush toilet and a bath. Yet the diets of the poor are nutritionally bad, whether from ignorance or poverty. The poor do not seek medical attention except in emergencies. The result is a great deal of preventable illness and malnutrition.

Who are the poor? Poverty occurs in many different kinds of families and in all environmental settings. The incidence of poverty varies sharply among groups living under different circumstances, however, and several groups experience poverty in greater proportions than the national average.[2] (See Table 16–1.) First of all, the likelihood of *blacks* experiencing poverty is three times greater than that of whites; the percentage of

---

[1]Herman P. Miller, "The Dimensions of Poverty," in *Poverty as a Public Issue*, ed. Ben B. Seligman (New York: The Free Press, 1965).

[2]U.S. Bureau of the Census, "Poverty in the United States," *Current Population Reports*, Series P–60 (1969).

TABLE 16-1

Percentage of Population Below Poverty Level

Total	12.2
White	9.5
Black	31.1
Central cities	13.4
Suburbs	6.3
Rural	17.1
Under 25	14.1
25-65	7.7
Over 65	25.3
Families with male head	8.0
Families with female head	38.3
Less than 8 yrs. school	25.2
8 years school	11.2
High school graduate	5.4
College graduate	2.0

SOURCE: U.S. Bureau of the Census, Current Population Reports, Series P-60, "24 Million Americans, Poverty in the United States" (Washington: Government Printing Office, 1970).

the black population of the United States falling under the poverty line is 31.1, compared with 9.5 percent for the white population. Second, *female-headed families* experience poverty far more frequently than male-headed families; 38.3 percent of all female-headed families live below the poverty line. Third, the *aged* experience more poverty than persons of working age; 25.3 percent of the population over sixty-five live below the poverty line. While we think of poverty as a characteristic of persons living in large, central-city ghettos, actually *rural* families experience more poverty more frequently than central-city families. On the other hand, central cities have more poverty than their surrounding suburbs.

Are the poor disappearing? In 1937 Franklin D. Roosevelt, in his Second Inaugural Address, said, "I see one-third of a nation ill-housed, ill-clad, ill-nourished." Since that time the American political and economic system has succeeded in reducing the proportion of poor to less than 13 percent. If current rates in the reduction of poverty in America continue in the future, there will be virtually no poverty remaining in twenty-five to fifty years.

Table 16–2 provides a closer look at the change in the number and percentage of poor over the last decade.[3] All these figures account for

[3]*Ibid.*

TABLE 16-2

Changes in the Number of Poor

	1959	1963		1967		1969	
	Millions	Millions	Change from 1959	Millions	Change from 1963	Millions	Change from 1967
Total	39.5	36.4	−2.0	27.8	−6.5	24.3	−3.5
White	28.5	25.2	−3.0	19.0	−6.8	16.7	−2.3
Nonwhite	11.0	11.2	0.4	8.8	−5.9	7.6	−1.2
Percent of total population	22.4%	19.5%	−3.4%	14.2%	−5.3%	12.2%	−2.0%

SOURCE: U.S. Bureau of the Census, Current Population Reports, Series P-60, "24 Million Americans, Poverty in the United States," (Washington: Government Printing Office, 1970).

the effect of inflation, so there is no question that the number and percentage of the population living in poverty is declining, despite increases in the population. Both white and black poverty is declining, although the rate of decline among blacks has not been as great as the rate of decline among whites.

POVERTY AS RELATIVE DEPRIVATION

It is also possible to define poverty as "a state of mind"—some people think they have less income or fewer material possessions than most Americans, and they believe they are entitled to more. Their sense of deprivation is not tied to any *absolute* level of income. Instead, their sense of deprivation is *relative* to what most Americans have and what they, therefore, believe they are entitled to. Even fairly substantial incomes may result in a sense of relative deprivation in a very affluent society; commercial advertising and the mass media portray the life of the "average American" as one of high levels of consumption and material well-being.

Today the poor are not any more deprived relative to the nonpoor than in the past. However, they *feel* more deprived—they perceive the gap to be wider and they no longer accept the gap as legitimate. Blacks are overrepresented among the poor; the civil rights movement made blacks acutely aware of their position in American society relative to whites. Thus, the black revolution contributed to a new awareness of the problem of poverty in terms of relative differences in income and conditions of life.

Defining poverty as relative deprivation really defines it as *inequality* in society. As Victor Fuchs explains:

By the standards that have prevailed over most of history, and still prevail over large areas of the world, there are very few poor in the United
States today. Nevertheless, there are millions of American families who,
both in their own eyes and in those of others, are poor. As our nation
prospers, our judgment as to what constitutes poverty will inevitably
change. When we talk about poverty in America, we are talking about
families and individuals who have much less income than most of us.
When we talk about reducing or eliminating poverty, we are really talking
about changing the distribution of income.[4]

Thus, eliminating poverty defined as relative deprivation would mean
achieving absolute equality of incomes and material possessions in
America.

Let us try to systematically examine poverty as relative deprivation.
Economists have already provided us with a way of measuring income
distributions within political systems.[5] Income inequality can be measured by a Gini coefficient or a Gini index, which ranges from a plus 1.00
(theoretically perfect inequality) to 0.00 (theoretically perfect equality).
Income inequality is greatest in Mississippi and least in Utah. In general, income inequality is greater in the Southern, rural, and poorer
states. Income distributions are more equalized in the wealthy, urban, industrialized states.

A major component of income inequality in America is the differential between black and white family incomes. Thus, another measure
of inequality is the ratio of black to white family incomes; this is a
measure of *racial* inequality in income, rather than a general measure
of income inequality like the Gini index. Figure 16–1 shows the ratio
of black to white median family incomes (expressed as one minus the
black percentage of white median family income). Racial inequality is
greatest in Mississippi (where black median family income is only 36 percent of white median family income), and the least in Hawaii (where
black and white incomes are equal).

Inequality in America is decreasing over time. However, the rate of
decrease is not very rapid. Certainly poverty as relative deprivation is
not disappearing at the same rate as absolute poverty. Table 16–3 divides all American families into five groups—from the lowest one-fifth
of personal income to the highest one-fifth—and shows the percentage
of total family personal income received by each of these groups over
the years, (If perfect income equality existed, each fifth of American
families would receive 20 percent of all family personal income, and it
would not be possible to rank fifths from highest to lowest). The poor-

---

[4]Victor R. Fuchs, "Redefining Poverty and Redistributing Income," *The Public
Interest* (Summer, 1967), p. 91.

[5]James Morgan, "The Anatomy of Income Distributions," *The Review of Economies and Statistics*, 44 (August 1962), 270–80.

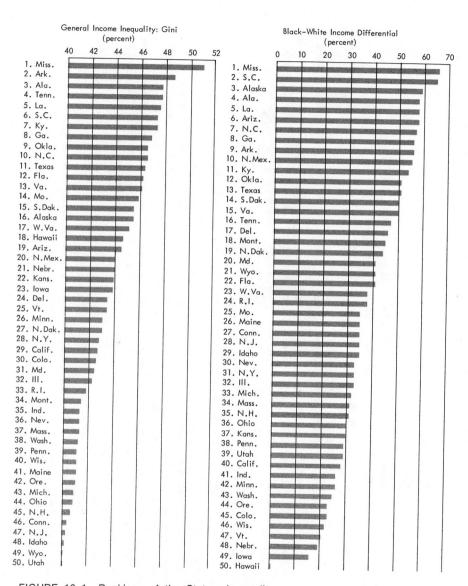

General Income Inequality: Gini
(percent)

| | 40 | 42 | 44 | 46 | 48 | 50 | 52 |

1. Miss.
2. Ark.
3. Ala.
4. Tenn.
5. La.
6. S.C.
7. Ky.
8. Ga.
9. Okla.
10. N.C.
11. Texas
12. Fla.
13. Va.
14. Mo.
15. S.Dak.
16. Alaska
17. W.Va.
18. Hawaii
19. Ariz.
20. N.Mex.
21. Nebr.
22. Kans.
23. Iowa
24. Del.
25. Vt.
26. Minn.
27. N.Dak.
28. N.Y.
29. Calif.
30. Colo.
31. Md.
32. Ill.
33. R.I.
34. Mont.
35. Ind.
36. Nev.
37. Mass.
38. Wash.
39. Penn.
40. Wis.
41. Maine
42. Ore.
43. Mich.
44. Ohio
45. N.H.
46. Conn.
47. N.J.
48. Idaho
49. Wyo.
50. Utah

Black-White Income Differential
(percent)

| 0 | 10 | 20 | 30 | 40 | 50 | 60 | 70 |

1. Miss.
2. S.C.
3. Alaska
4. Ala.
5. La.
6. Ariz.
7. N.C.
8. Ga.
9. Ark.
10. N.Mex.
11. Ky.
12. Okla.
13. Texas
14. S.Dak.
15. Va.
16. Tenn.
17. Del.
18. Mont.
19. N.Dak.
20. Md.
21. Wyo.
22. Fla.
23. W.Va.
24. R.I.
25. Mo.
26. Maine
27. Conn.
28. N.J.
29. Idaho
30. Nev.
31. N.Y.
32. Ill.
33. Mich.
34. Mass.
35. N.H.
36. Ohio
37. Kans.
38. Penn.
39. Utah
40. Calif.
41. Ind.
42. Minn.
43. Wash.
44. Ore.
45. Colo.
46. Wis.
47. Vt.
48. Nebr.
49. Iowa
50. Hawaii

FIGURE 16-1   Rankings of the States: Inequality

471

TABLE 16-3

Percent Distribution of Family Personal Income[1] by Quintiles and
Top 5 Percent of Consumer Units,[2] Selected Years, 1929-62

Quintiles	1929	1935-1936	1941	1944	1947	1950	1951	1954	1956	1959	1962
Lowest	3.5	4.1	4.1	4.9	5.0	4.8	5.0	4.8	4.8	4.6	4.6
Second	9.0	9.2	9.5	10.9	11.0	10.9	11.3	11.1	11.3	10.9	10.9
Third	13.8	14.1	15.3	16.2	16.0	16.1	16.5	16.4	16.3	16.3	16.3
Fourth	19.3	20.9	22.3	22.2	22.0	22.1	22.3	22.5	22.3	22.6	22.7
Highest	54.4	51.7	48.8	45.8	46.0	46.1	44.9	45.2	45.3	45.6	45.5
Total	100	100	100	100	100	100	100	100	100	100	100
Top 5 percent	30.0	26.5	24.0	20.7	20.9	21.4	20.7	20.3	20.2	20.2	19.6
Gini concentration ratio	.49	.47	.44	.39	.40	.40		.39	.39		.40

1 Family personal income includes wage and salary receipts (net of social insurance contributions), other labor income, proprietors' and rental income, dividends, personal interest income, and transfer payments. In addition to monetary income flows, it includes certain nonmonetary or imputed income such as wages in kind, the value of food and fuel produced and consumed on farms, net imputed rental value of owner-occupied homes, and imputed interest. Personal income differs from national income in that it excludes corporate profits taxes, corporate saving (inclusive of inventory valuation adjustment), and social security contributions of employers and employees, and includes transfer payments (mostly governmental) and interest on consumer and government debt.

2 Consumer units include farm operator and nonfarm families and unattached individuals. A family is defined as a group of two or more persons related by blood, marriage, or adoption, and residing together.

SOURCE: INEQUALITY AND POVERTY, edited and with introduction by Edward C. Budd. Copyright© 1967 by W. W. Norton & Company, Inc. Reprinted by permission of W. W. Norton & Company, Inc.

est one-fifth received 3.5 percent of all family personal income in 1929; in 1962, however, this group had increased its percentage of all family personal income to 4.6. (Most of this increase occurred during World War II.) The highest one-fifth received 54.4 percent of all family personal income in 1929; in 1962, however, this percentage had declined to 45.5. This was the only income group to lose in relation to other income groups. The middle classes improved their relative income position even more than the poor. Another measure of income equalization over time is the decline in the percentage of income received by the top 5 percent in America. The top 5 percent received 30.0 percent of all family personal income in 1929, but only 19.6 percent in 1962. The Gini coefficient of income inequality declined from .49 to .40 in that same time period. There is no doubt that income differences in America are decreasing over time.

It is unlikely, however, that income differences will ever disappear completely—at least not in a society that rewards skill, talent, risk, and ingenuity. If the problem of poverty is defined as relative deprivation— that is, *inequality*— then the problem is not really capable of solution. Regardless of how well off the poor may be in absolute terms, there will always be a lowest one-fifth of the population that receives something less than 20 percent of all income. Income differences may decline over time, but *some* differences will remain, and even minor differences can acquire great importance and hence pose a "problem."

In describing federal antipoverty programs, we will be dealing with policies that were primarily designed to raise the poor above the poverty line. Policies dealing with income redistributon are discussed in Chapter 18.

DEVELOPMENT OF HEALTH AND WELFARE POLICY

Concern for public health and welfare has been a recognized responsibility of government in English-speaking countries for almost 400 years. In the Poor Relief Act of 1601, the English parliament established principles of public welfare, which were to influence governments in England and the United States for centuries. This early "Elizabethan" welfare policy tended to view poverty as the product of moral or character deficiencies in individuals. Care of destitute persons was supposed to be minimal, to discourage all but the most desperate of the poor from seeking aid. Primary reliance was placed upon institutional care—county workhouses, poorhouses, or almshouses. The "able-bodied poor," those we call the unemployed, were sent to county workhouses;

while the "worthy poor," widows, aged, orphans, and handicapped, were sent to poorhouses. Indigent persons who were mentally or physically ill were often kept in the same institutions. Destitute children were kept in county orphanages or sent to foster homes. Thus, public welfare was limited almost exclusively to institutional care; the distribution of food or clothing or other aid to homes of the poor was left to private charities. Whatever relief was provided by the public could never exceed the value of the income of the lowest paid person in the community who was not on relief. Poor rolls were made public, and relief was forthcoming only if there were no living relatives who could be legally required to support a destitute member of their family.

Under Elizabethan law, the care of the poor was the responsibility of the local governments rather than the state and local governments. The parish in England, and the township and county in the United States, had to care for their poor out of their general tax funds. Since local governments wished to make certain that they were not caring for the poor of other communities, residence requirements were established for welfare care, and communities generally limited their support to those who had been born in the area or who had lived there for some time. By the late nineteenth century, state governments began to build and operate institutions for the insane, the deaf, the blind, and the orphaned. The federal government provided only for needy veterans, Indians, and merchant seamen; most people felt that the federal government had no legitimate interest in public health and welfare.

The Great Depression brought about significant changes in attitudes toward public welfare and in the policies and administration of welfare programs. Millions who had previously considered welfare recipients to be unworthy of public concern now joined in the breadlines themselves. One out of four Americans was unemployed, and one out of six was receiving some sort of welfare care. This widespread experience with poverty changed public attitudes toward welfare and led to a change away from Elizabethan policy.

The Great Depression quickly drained local governments of financial resources to aid the poor. The states rapidly increased their welfare activities, and a majority of states distributed money to local relief agencies. But state governments themselves were also running out of money. Frantic appeals for help from the national government were made by states and communities. Even Herbert Hoover was forced into approving limited federal relief programs. The Roosevelt administration plunged into several large-scale emergency relief public works programs. After a while, these emergency programs were abandoned by the New Deal, but the precedent of federal responsiblity for public welfare had been established.

In the Social Security Act of 1935, the federal government undertook to establish the basic framework for welfare policies for all levels of government. State and local welfare activities are greatly influenced by federal policies begun in the Social Security Act of 1935.

SOCIAL INSURANCE
AND UNEMPLOYMENT COMPENSATION

The Social Security Act placed great reliance on *social insurance* to supplement and, it was hoped, eventually to replace *public assistance.* The distinction between a *social insurance program* and a *public assistance* program is an important one, which has on occasion been a major political issue. If the beneficiaries of a government program are required to have made contributions to it before claiming any of its benefits, and if they are entitled to the benefits regardless of their personal wealth, then the program is said to be financed on the *social insurance* principle. On the other hand, if a program is financed out of general tax revenues, and if the recipients are required to show they are poor before claiming its benefits, then the program is said to be financed on the *public assistance* principle.

One of the key features of the Social Security Act is the Old-Age, Survivors, and Disability Insurance (OASDI) program; this is a compulsory social insurance program financed by regular deductions from earnings, which gives individuals a legal right to benefits in the event of certain occurrences that cause a reduction of their income: old age, death of the head of the household, or permanent disability.[6] OASDI is based on the same principle as private insurance—the sharing of a risk of the loss of income—except that it is a government program that is compulsory for all workers. OASDI is not public *charity,* but a way of compelling people to provide *insurance* against a loss of income. OASDI now covers about nine out of every ten workers in the United States. Both employees and employers must pay equal amounts toward the employees' OASDI insurance. Upon retirement, an insured worker is entitled to monthly benefit payments based upon his age at retirement and the amount he earned during his working years. However, average monthly payments are really quite modest: in the early 1970s the average monthly amount for a retired worker with a wife age sixty-five was less than $200. So OASDI has not eliminated poverty from the ranks of the retired in America.

---

[6]The original act did not include disability insurance; this was added by amendment in 1950.

OASDI also insures benefit payments to survivors of an insured worker, including his widow if she has dependent children. But if she has no dependent children, her benefits will not begin until she herself reaches retirement age. Finally, OASDI insures benefit payments to persons who suffer permanent and total disabilities that prevent them from working more than one year. However, on the whole, payments to survivors and disabled workers are just as modest as those provided retired workers.

OASDI is a completely federal program, administered by the Social Security Administration in the Department of Health, Education, and Welfare. But OASDI has an important indirect effect on state and local welfare programs, by removing people in whole or in part from welfare roles. By compelling people to insure themselves against the possibility of their own poverty, social security has doubtlessly reduced the welfare problems which state and local governments would otherwise face.

The second feature of the Social Security Act was that it induced states to enact unemployment compensation programs through the imposition of the payroll tax on all employers. A federal unemployment tax is levied on the payroll of employers of four or more workers, but employees paying into state insurance programs that meet federal standards may use these state payments to offset most of their federal unemployment tax. In other words, the federal government threatens to undertake an unemployment compensation program and tax, if the states do not do so themselves. This federal program succeeded in inducing all fifty states to establish unemployment compensation programs. However, the federal standards are flexible and the states have considerable freedom in shaping their own unemployment programs. In all cases, unemployed workers must report in person and show that they are willing and able to work in order to receive unemployment compensation benefits, and states cannot deny workers benefits for refusing to work as strikebreakers or refusing to work for rates lower than prevailing rates. But basic decisions concerning the amount of benefits, eligibility, and the length of time that benefits can be drawn are largely left to the states.

PUBLIC ASSISTANCE

A third major feature of the Social Security Act was its public assistance provisions. The OASDI and unemployment compensation programs were based upon the insurance principle, but the federal government also undertook to provide matching funds to the states, to provide public assistance to the aged, blind, disabled, and dependent children. Federal contributions are in the form of grants-in-aid to the states. The federal share is determined by a formula that attempts to equalize welfare efforts among the states by having the federal government pay a larger share to states with higher needs and less wealth.

Within broad outlines of the federal policy, states retain considerable discretion in their welfare programs in terms of the amounts of money appropriated, benefits to be paid to recipients, rules of eligibility, and rules of the programs. Each state may choose to grant assistance beyond the amounts supported by the national government, or it may choose to have no welfare programs at all. Each state establishes its own standards to determine "need." In 1969, however, the Supreme Court ruled out state residency requirements for welfare eligibility on the grounds that they violated the equal protection clause of the Fourteenth Amendment. Later we shall examine variations in average benefit payments in these categorical assistance programs.

It is important to note that the federal government aids only four categories of welfare recipients. Only persons who are aged, blind, disabled, or dependent children fall within the categories of recipients eligible for federal support. Aid to persons who do not fall in any of these categories but who, for one reason or another, are "needy" is referred to as *general assistance*. General assistance programs are entirely state financed and state administered. Without federal participation, these programs differ from state to state in terms of the persons aided, the criteria for eligibility, the amount and nature of benefits, and financing and administration. Many of these programs continue to resemble Elizabethan welfare policy. The average general assistance payment is lower than comparable payments in federally supported programs.

States also continue to maintain institutions to care for those individuals who are so destitute, alone, or ill that money payments cannot meet their needs. These institutions include state orphanages, homes for the aged, and homes for the ill. They are, for the most part, state financed as well as state administered. Persons living in these tax-supported institutions are not normally eligible for federal assistance, although they may receive old-age payments for medical care received in a nursing home. This feature of federal welfare policy has provided incentive for the states to turn their indigent institutions into nursing homes. The quality of these homes and of the people employed to care for their residents varies enormously from state to state.

Federal standards for state public assistance programs, which are established as a prerequisite to receiving federal aid, allow considerable flexibility in state programs. Federal law requires the states to make financial contributions to their public assistance programs and to supervise these programs either directly or through local agencies. Whatever standards a state adopts must be applicable throughout the state, and there must be no discrimination in these welfare programs. The Social

Security Administration demands periodic reporting from the states, insists that states administer federally supported programs under a merit personnel system, and prevents the states from imposing unreasonable residence requirements on recipients. But in important questions of administration, standards of eligibility, residence, types of assistance, and amounts of payments, the states are free to determine their own welfare programs. In some states, public assistance is administered directly by a state agency; in other states, by local agencies under state supervision; but in most states, by local agencies operating under city, county, or township governmental control.

PUBLIC HEALTH, MEDICARE, AND MEDICAID

Public health and sanitation are among the oldest functions of local government. Keeping clean is still one of the major tasks of cities today, a task that involves many different local governmental agencies in street cleaning, sewage disposal, garbage collection, and the provision of clean water supply. Very often these services are taken for granted in the United States, but in underdeveloped countries of the world, health and sanitation are still major tasks. Local public health departments are directly concerned with the *prevention* of disease. They engage in a compulsory vaccination, immunization, and quarantine, as well as regulatory activity in the processing of milk and the safeguarding of water supplies. In more recent years, these agencies have become concerned with the difficult problems of air and water pollution. In addition to the preventive activities of the public health departments, state and local governments also provide extensive, tax-supported hospital care. State and local governments provide both general and specialized hospitals, health centers, and nursing homes, and very often subsidize private hospitals and medical facilities as well. New York City operates twenty-two hospitals, twenty-seven health centers, employing over 40 thousand people with a budget of over $300 million per year. This is the nation's largest city hospital system, but almost every community subsidizes hospital facilities in some way. City and county hospitals and heavily subsidized private hospitals are expected to provide at least emergency care to indigent patients.

Health and hospital care are also supported by state governments. State health departments generally supervise local health departments, distribute state grants to local health departments, and provide health services in areas where there are no local health facilities. Generally, local health departments need state monies in order to operate effectively. But perhaps the states' greatest impact on public health is the provision of specialized state hospitals for tuberculosis, mental illness, and so on. These spe-cialized hospitals are managed directly by the states and are supposed to supplement local hospital care by providing facilities that local gov-ernments could not afford.

In nearly every community, decision making in health and hospital matters is firmly lodged in the hands of leaders of the local medical associations. These local physicians, men of prestige and influence in com-munity leadership structures, believe that questions of public policy should be determined predominantly by the doctors as a group, through their local medical society. Often professional social workers and health workers have chafed under the reins of the physicians; they sometimes contend that the doctors insist on a private practice approach where public measures are critically needed.

America's problems in health and medicine are severe and national. Although the United States is the richest nation in the world, it ranks well down on the list of nations in medical care provided the average citizen, number of physicians available, infant death rates, average life-span, and other indicators of national health and medical care. One particularly difficult problem is the small number of physicians gradu-ated by the nation's medical schools. Moreover, as professional speciali-zation becomes of more interest to doctors, the result is shortages in the ranks of general practitioners. It is ironic that the United States, the richest nation in the world, must turn to graduates of foreign medical schools for more than one-fourth of its hospital residents and interns. In state institutions, this ratio is even higher.

The federal government is also deeply involved in public health. The U.S. Public Health Service, now part of the Department of Health, Edu-cation, and Welfare, is one of the oldest agencies of the federal govern-ment, having been created in 1798 to provide medical and hospital care for merchant seamen. Today, the service provides medical care and hospital facilities to many categories of federally aided patients; en-forces quarantine regulations; licenses biological products for manu-facture and sale; engages in and sponsors medical research; and, most important of all, administers federal grant-in-aid programs to states and communities for the improvement of health and hospital services. Fed-eral grants-in-aid are available to promote the construction of hospitals, nursing homes, diagnostic centers, rehabilitation centers, medical schools, and other medical centers. Federal grants for hospital construction began in earnest with the passage of the Hill-Burton Act in 1946; these funds are usually made available on a matching basis of approximately two-to-one, with local communities carrying the heavier burden. The federal government's Veterans Administration also provides extensive medical and hospital care.

Direct federal involvement in hospital and medical care did not come until the passage of Medicare and Medicaid in 1965. Persons concerned with the state of the nation's health, and particularly the medical care problems of the poor and the aged, had urged the federal government for many years to undertake a broad national health care program. Proponents of the national health program generally shunned the English system of government-owned and government-operated hospitals and government-employed doctors, in favor of a compulsory medical *insurance* program closely linked to the Social Security Act. They envisioned a program in which all Americans would be required to insure themselves against the possibility of their medical indigency; the program would resemble private medical and hospital insurance, except that it would be compulsory. Individuals would continue to choose their own doctors, but their bills would be paid in whole or in part through their government medical insurance policy. Opponents of a national health program, led by the prestigious American Medical Association representing the nation's physicians, strongly opposed a national health program linked to social security. They deemed it "socialized medicine" and argued that it would interfere with the "sacred doctor-patient relationship." They argued that a large proportion of the population was already covered by voluntary private medical insurance plans and that charity hospitals and charitable services of doctors were readily available to the poor. Many physicians worried that if the Social Security Administration paid insured persons' doctors' bills, the Social Security Administration would begin to set maximum prices for physicians' services; the AMA feared that this would lead to the subservience of physicians to a government agency. Proponents of national health care waged a war of statistics, arguing that the poor and the aged were not receiving adequate medical care and that private insurance companies did not enroll these segments of the population.

In 1965, after more than 30 years of unsuccessful efforts, Congress finally enacted a historic comprehensive medical care act for persons over sixty-five, which became known as "Medicare." Passed over the opposition of the American Medical Association, Medicare provided for prepaid hospital insurance for the aged under Social Security, and low-cost voluntary medical insurance for the aged under federal administration. Medicare includes (1) a compulsory basic health insurance plan covering hospital costs for the aged, which is financed through payroll taxes collected under the social security system; and (2) a voluntary but supplemental medical program that will pay doctors' bills and additional medical expenses, financed in part by contributions from the aged and in part by the general tax revenues. It is not yet clear what the impact of this act will be at the local level, in terms of reducing state and local burdens of providing for charitable hospital and medical care. Social Security never eliminated the need for welfare rolls, and it is doubtful that Medicare will ever eliminate the need for tax-supported hospitals and health care. So far only aged persons are covered by Medicare provisions.

In 1965, Congress also passed a Medical Assistance Program (Medicaid) which provided federal funds to enable states to guarantee medical services to all public assistance recipients. Each state operates its own Medicaid program. Unlike Medicare, Medicaid is a welfare program designed for needy persons; no prior contributions are required, and recipients of Medicaid services are generally welfare recipients. States can extend coverage to other medically needy persons if they choose to do so. The cost of this program has far exceeded all original estimates, which suggests that the poor in America require much more medical attention than they have received in the past.

A COMPARATIVE VIEW OF STATE HEALTH AND WELFARE POLICIES

While the federal government plays a major role in shaping the state health and welfare programs, states continue to exercise major responsibilities in determination of health and welfare policy. States retain the right to determine whether they will participate in federal programs. Within broad federal regulations, the states determine the benefits to be allocated to recipients, the eligibility requirements, the extent of state financing, and the ways in which the programs are to be administered. For example, in 1971, the average weekly benefits per recipient of unemployment compensation ranged from a low of $33 in West Virginia to a high of $60 in Connecticut. Aid-to-dependent-children payments ranged from a high of $292 in New York to a low of $46 in Mississippi. Similar variations and benefits are reported for other welfare programs. (See Figure 16–2.) Wide variations among the states in per capita health and welfare expenditures can also be observed. In addition, states have different eligibility requirements and different standards of determining need; as a result, states will vary considerably in the number of welfare recipients per ten thousand population. States also vary with respect to the medical and hospital facilities available. Finally, states differ in the extent to which welfare services are state, rather than locally, financed and administered.

What accounts for differences among the states in health and welfare policy? All available evidence indicates that economic development is sig-

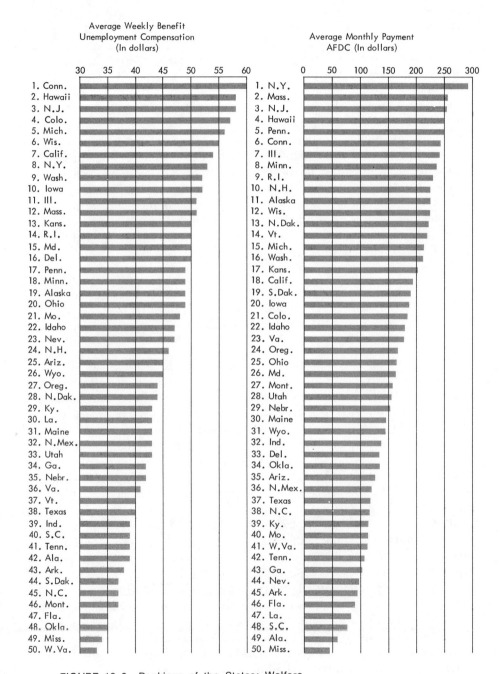

Average Weekly Benefit
Unemployment Compensation
(In dollars)

Average Monthly Payment
AFDC (In dollars)

1. Conn.	1. N.Y.
2. Hawaii	2. Mass.
3. N.J.	3. N.J.
4. Colo.	4. Hawaii
5. Mich.	5. Penn.
6. Wis.	6. Conn.
7. Calif.	7. Ill.
8. N.Y.	8. Minn.
9. Wash.	9. R.I.
10. Iowa	10. N.H.
11. Ill.	11. Alaska
12. Mass.	12. Wis.
13. Kans.	13. N.Dak.
14. R.I.	14. Vt.
15. Md.	15. Mich.
16. Del.	16. Wash.
17. Penn.	17. Kans.
18. Minn.	18. Calif.
19. Alaska	19. S.Dak.
20. Ohio	20. Iowa
21. Mo.	21. Colo.
22. Idaho	22. Idaho
23. Nev.	23. Va.
24. N.H.	24. Oreg.
25. Ariz.	25. Ohio
26. Wyo.	26. Md.
27. Oreg.	27. Mont.
28. N.Dak.	28. Utah
29. Ky.	29. Nebr.
30. La.	30. Maine
31. Maine	31. Wyo.
32. N.Mex.	32. Ind.
33. Utah	33. Del.
34. Ga.	34. Okla.
35. Nebr.	35. Ariz.
36. Va.	36. N.Mex.
37. Vt.	37. Texas
38. Texas	38. N.C.
39. Ind.	39. Ky.
40. S.C.	40. Mo.
41. Tenn.	41. W.Va.
42. Ala.	42. Tenn.
43. Ark.	43. Ga.
44. S.Dak.	44. Nev.
45. N.C.	45. Ark.
46. Mont.	46. Fla.
47. Fla.	47. La.
48. Okla.	48. S.C.
49. Miss.	49. Ala.
50. W.Va.	50. Miss.

FIGURE 16–2   Rankings of the States: Welfare

482

nificantly related to health and welfare policy in the states.[7] A state's income is the single most important variable determining the level of welfare benefits. In terms of welfare payments, it is far better to be poor in a wealthy state than in a poor one. (See Figure 16–3.)

Poorer states have larger proportions of their populations on public assistance rolls, and poorer states have lower welfare benefit payments. This means they pay smaller amounts of money to larger numbers of people. It is not surprising that economic development levels are closely related to benefits paid to recipients of *general assistance*, since relief in this area is paid for exclusively from state and local fiscal sources. But it is surprising that economic development in the states has such a great impact on benefit programs in which the federal government bears part of the cost. We would expect federal participation to reduce inequalities among the states. Actually the federal government does make larger health and welfare grants to the poorer states and therefore helps offset disparities among the states based upon levels of wealth. However, the reason federal participation does not equalize welfare payments among the states is to be found in the formula that allocates federal money to the states for public assistance. The federal government, under its public assistance formula, pays a larger share of minimum benefits and a lesser share of additional benefits up to a certain maximum benefit level, after which the federal government pays nothing. The object of this formula is to help poorer states provide a minimum level of welfare service. However, since the formula results in a higher proportion of federal support to states with lower welfare benefits, the federal government actually rewards states for low payments per recipient. Poorer states can get the most federal aid by paying smaller amounts of money to large numbers of people.

Even though the federal formula does not offset disparities among the states in welfare payment levels, it does offset disparities among states in the burden of welfare costs. The federal government pays a larger share of public assistance costs in poorer states, while requiring richer states to share a greater portion of their public assistance costs. Federal percentages of the total public assistance expenditures *decline* with increases in state income levels. (See Figure 16–4.)

What effect does pluralism—party competition and voter participation—have on welfare policies in the states? The traditional assumption in the political science literature was that pluralism in a political system increased the benefits to the masses, particularly the poor. It was assumed that competition and participation would make governments more responsive to the interests and needs of the have-nots. And, in-

[7]Thomas R. Dye, *Politics, Economics and the Public* (Chicago: Rand McNally & Co., 1966), pp. 115–48.

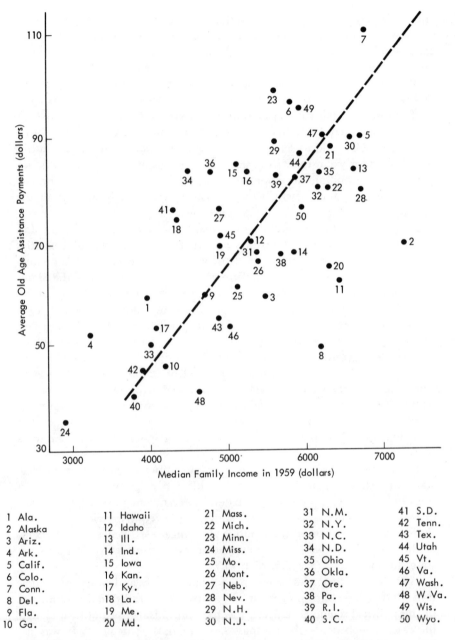

FIGURE 16–3 The Fifty States Arranged According to Median Family Income and Average Old-Age Assistance Payments

Source: Thomas R. Dye, *Politics, Economics, and the Public* (Chicago: Rand McNally & Co., 1966), p. 126. Reproduced by permission.

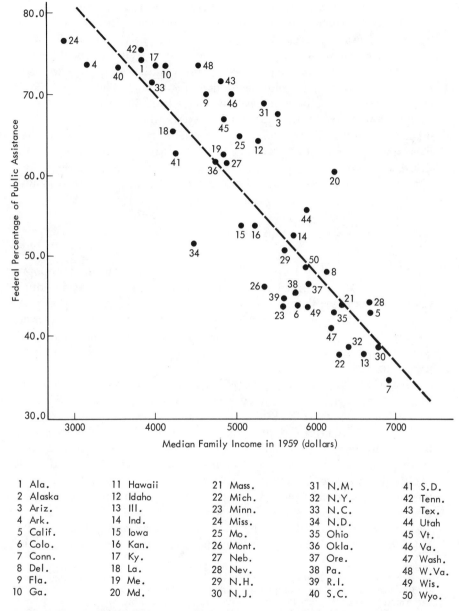

FIGURE 16–4 The Fifty States Arranged According to Median Family Income and the Federal Percentage of Public Assistance Funds

Source: Thomas R. Dye, *Politics, Economics, and the Public* (Chicago: Rand McNally & Co., 1966), p. 137. Reproduced by permission.

deed, it is true that welfare benefits are higher in those states with greater party competition and higher voter turnouts. But these states are also the more economically developed states with higher income, urbanization, and education levels. It is difficult to sort out the effect of pluralism from the effect of economic development on welfare benefits. However, several scholars have employed complex statistical analysis to assess the *independent* effect of pluralism on public policy.[8] The evidence supports the view that economic development is *more* influential *than* party competition or voter participation in determining welfare policies. In other words, states devote more money to helping have-nots because they have more economic resources to do so, and not necessarily because of political competition or participation. Competition and participation, however, do have *some* independent effect liberalizing welfare benefits.[9]

THE WELFARE MESS

Public assistance turned out to be politically one of the most unpopular programs ever adopted by Congress. It is disliked by the national, state, and local legislators who must vote the skyrocketing appropriations for it; it is resented by the taxpayers who must bear the ever-increasing burdens of it; it is denounced by the officials and caseworkers who must administer it; and it is accepted with bitterness by those who were intended to benefit from it.

First of all, dependence upon public assistance in America is increasing at a very rapid rate. (See Figure 16–5.) Whether or not it is the public assistance program itself that encourages dependency, one thing is certain: more Americans depend upon public assistance today than ever before, despite a healthy national economy. Certainly our public assistance programs have not succeeded in reducing dependency. In the last decade the number of welfare recipients has doubled, and public assistance costs have quadrupled. At present rates of expansion, we can expect soon 15 million welfare recipients, at a cost of nearly $20 billion per year. Interestingly, it is *not* the programs for the aged, blind, or disabled or even the general assistance programs that have incurred the

[8]See Dye, *Politics, Economics, and the Public*; and Richard E. Dawson and James A. Robinson, "Inter-Party Competition, Economic Variables and Welfare Policies in the American States," *Journal of Politics*, 25 (May 1963), 265–89.

[9]See Charles Cnudde and Donald J. McCrone, "Party Competition and Welfare Policies in the American States," *American Political Science Review*, 58 (September 1969), 858–66. For a full discussion of the problems of assessing the relative effects of political and economic forces on public policy, see Thomas R. Dye, *Understanding Public Policy* (Englewood Cliffs, N.J.: Prentice-Hall, Inc., 1972), Chap. 11.

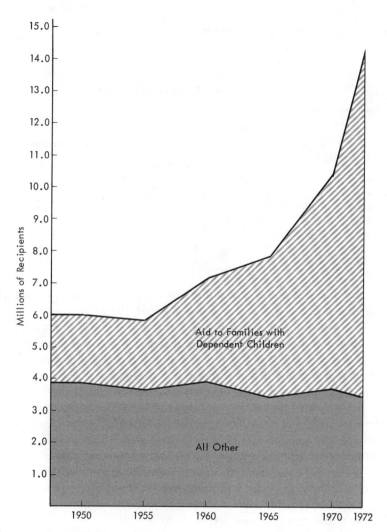

FIGURE 16–5 The Welfare Explosion

greatest burdens. It is the Aid to Families with Dependent Children (AFDC) program, which is the largest, most expensive, and most rapidly growing of all welfare programs, and the most controversial. Today approximately 5 percent of all children under eighteen years of age are under AFDC coverage. If the present trends continue, soon one out of every ten children will be under AFDC.

This growth in welfare rolls has occurred during a period of high employment; it cannot be attributed to economic depression. The acceleration has occurred because more people are applying for public assistance. They have been aided by the activities of civil rights and welfare rights organizations, Office of Economic Opportunity-supported

TABLE 16-4
Growth of Public Assistance Programs

	Total	AFDC	Aged	Disabled	Blind	General Assistance
			(Millions of Recipients)			
1950	6.0	2.2	2.8	.1	.1	.9
1955	5.8	2.2	2.5	.2	.1	.7
1960	7.0	3.1	2.3	.4	.1	1.2
1965	7.8	4.4	2.1	.6	.1	.7
1970	10.4	6.7	2.0	.87	.1	.8
1971	13.5	9.5	2.0	1.0	.1	.9
1972	15.0	10.8	2.1	1.0	.1	1.0

community action groups, and comparable groups, which have informed eligible persons of the law and encouraged them to apply for assistance. Increases in assistance levels, relaxation of eligibility requirements, and a more sympathetic attitude on the part of welfare administrators have also contributed to the increase in welfare rolls. So also has the movement of persons from southern and rural areas, where welfare administration is tighter, to northern urban areas, where access to welfare rolls is less restricted.

Despite increased dependency upon welfare and the growing burden of welfare costs, a majority of the nation's poor do *not* receive public assistance. Depending on one's definition of poverty, there were between 25 million and 40 million poor people in America in 1970, yet only 14 million were on welfare rolls. Most of the nation's poor are *working poor* who are ineligible for welfare assistance because they hold jobs, even though these jobs pay very little.

Not only does welfare fail to assist most of the nation's poor, it does not provide enough in the way of assistance to recipients to raise them out of poverty. While welfare benefits differ from state to state, in every state the level of benefits falls well below the recognized poverty line.

Operating policies and administration of welfare have produced a whole series of problems, including disincentives to family life and work. Until recently, most states denied AFDC benefits if a man was living with his family, even though he had no work. This denial was based on the assumption that an employable man in the household meant that children were no longer "dependent" upon the state. Thus, if a man lived with his family, he could watch them go hungry; if he abandoned them, public assistance would enable them to eat. Moreover, an unmarried mother could get on welfare rolls more easily than a married mother, who had to prove she was not receiving support from her husband. Occasionally, enforcement of the "man in the house" rule led to sensational reports of welfare caseworkers making surprise nighttime calls to discover whether a woman had a partner in her bed. These rules have been relaxed in recent years, but it is still more difficult for whole families to get on public assistance than fatherless families.

In most states, if a recipient of assistance takes a full-time job, assistance checks are reduced or stopped. If the recipient is then laid off, it may take some time to get back on the welfare roll. In other words, employment is uncertain, while assistance is not. More importantly, the jobs available to most recipients are very low-paying jobs which do not produce much more income than assistance, particularly when transportation, child care, and other costs of working are considered. All these facts discourage work.

Welfare administration is made difficult by the heavy load assigned to caseworkers, many of whom are recent college graduates. They spend much of their time determining eligibility, computing payments, and filling out an avalanche of proper forms. With case loads averaging up to 100 families or 200 families, their contacts with recipients must be hurried, infrequent, and impersonal. Caseworkers are unable to develop any close bonds of friendship or rapport with persons in need of help. Recipients often come to view caseworkers with distrust, or worse. The strain on caseworkers is very great; big-city welfare departments report 50 percent turnover among caseworkers each year.

While these problems are serious, it is important to note that some of the charges leveled against public assistance are unfounded. For example, there are very few individuals for whom welfare has become "a permanent way of life." The median length of time on AFDC is less than three years; only one-tenth of the persons aided have been receiving assistance for more than ten years. The number of "welfare chislers"—able-bodied employable adults who prefer public-assisted idleness to work—is probably quite small. The bulk of recipients are aged or blind or disabled or women or children; few employable men are on welfare rolls. The work alternative for the large numbers of AFDC mothers is fraught with problems—child care, lack of skills, no work experience, and so forth. It might be more costly to society to prepare these women for work than to support them.

In 1970 President Richard M. Nixon proposed a new "family assistance plan," which paralleled the so-called guaranteed annual income proposals that had been discussed for years in liberal circles.

> I propose that we abolish the present welfare system and adopt in its place a new family assistance system. Initially, this new system would cost more than welfare. But unlike welfare, it is designed to correct the condition it deals with and thus to lessen the long-range burden.

Under this plan, the so-called "adult categories" of aid—aid to the aged, the blind and disabled—would be continued and a national minimum standard for benefits would be set, with the Federal Government contributing to its cost and also sharing the cost of additional state payments above that amount.

But the program now called "Aid to Families with Dependent Children"— the program we normally think of when we think of "welfare"—would be done away with completely. . . .

Its benefits would go to the working poor as well as the nonworking; to families with dependent children headed by a father as well as to those headed by a mother, and a basic federal minimum would be provided, the same in every state.

I propose that the Federal Government build a foundation under the income of every American family with dependent children that cannot care for itself—wherever in America that family may live.

For a family of four now on welfare, with no outside income the basic federal payment would be $1,600 a year. [The proposed figure has now been raised to $2,400.] States could add to that amount, and most would do so. In no case would anyone's present level of benefits be lowered. At the same time, this foundation would be one on which the family itself could build. Outside earnings would be encouraged, not discouraged. The new worker could keep the first $60 a month of outside earnings with no reduction in his benefits, and beyond that his benefits would be reduced by only 50 cents for each dollar earned.

By the same token, a family head already employed at low wages could get a family assistance supplement, those who work would no longer be discriminated against. A family of five in which the father earns $2,000 a year—which is the hard fact of life for many families—would get family assistance payments of $1,260 for a total income of $3,260. A family of seven earning $3,000 a year would have its income raised to $4,360.

Thus, for the first time, the government would recognize that it has no less of an obligation to the working poor than to the nonworking poor, and for the first time, benefits would be scaled in such a way that it would always pay to work.

With such incentive, most recipients who can work will want to work. This is part of the American character.

But what of the others—those who can work but choose not to?

The answer is very simple.

Under this proposal, everyone who accepts benefits must also accept work or training provided suitable jobs are available, either locally or at some distance if transportation is provided. The only exceptions would be those unable to work and mothers of preschool children. Even mothers of preschool children, however, would have the opportunity to work— because I am also proposing along with this a major expansion of day-care centers to make it possible for mothers to take jobs by which they can support themselves and their children.[10]

Clearly, reform of the current welfare system is high on the agenda of both the president and Congress. Doubtlessly some form of "guaranteed annual income" along the lines suggested by President Nixon will be adopted soon. Reform will also increase federal responsibilities for welfare (perhaps making welfare an exclusively federal responsibility) and reduce the burdens on states and communities. It will probably assist working as well as nonworking poor and equalize welfare benefits throughout the nation. But difficulties will remain. The costs of a "guaranteed annual income" or "family assistance plan" may turn out to be three or four times greater than the costs of the current welfare system. Congress will be under great political pressure to raise the minimum guarantee each year. Moreover, it is not certain whether this expansion of welfare will increase social dependency in America and further undermine incentives to work. Work or training requirements in welfare programs have always proved difficult to administer. It is conceivable that such an expansion in welfare assistance would encourage dependency by making the acceptance of such assistance a common family practice, extending well up into the middle class.

THE WAR ON POVERTY

In attempting to identify the causes of poverty in America, John Kenneth Galbraith has distinguished between "case poverty" and "area poverty."[11] Case poverty its largely a product of the personal characteristics of affected persons. Some persons have been unable to participate in the nation's prosperity because of old age, illiteracy, inadequate education, lack of job skills, poor health, inadequate motivation, or racial discrimination. Area poverty is a product of economic deficiencies relating to a particular sector of the nation, such as West Virginia or much of the rest of Appalachia, and large parts of rural America. Urbanization, industrialization, and technological development appear to have passed up many of these areas, creating high rates of unemployment and large numbers of low-income families. The decline in employment

[10]President Richard M. Nixon, speech on national television networks, Aug. 12, 1970.
[11]John Kenneth Galbraith, *The Affluent Society* (Boston: Houghton Mifflin Company, 1958); another influential book in the development of antipoverty policy in the Kennedy-Johnson years is Michael Harrington, *The Other America* (New York: The Macmillan Company, 1963).

in the coal industry, the exhaustion of iron-ore mines, the squeezing out of the small farmer from the agricultural market, and other such economic factors create "pockets of poverty" or "depressed areas" throughout the nation. People in these areas suffer many of the problems of case poverty, because the two types of poverty are not mutually exclusive. But both case poverty and area poverty differ from the "mass poverty" of the 1930s or the mass poverty predicted for capitalist societies by Marxian doctrine. Today's poverty afflicts only a minority of Americans, but it does not disappear even when the economy expands and the nation is prosperous.

The federal government launched its campaign against area poverty with the Area Redevelopment Act of 1961.[12] This was a four-year program of assistance for "depressed areas," in which the Area Redevelopment Administration in the Department of Commerce provided long-term loans at low interest to attract businesses to these areas, loans and grants to local governments for public facilities needed to attract businesses, and support for other community economic development and worker retraining programs. President Johnson requested Congress to replace ARA with an expanded and broadened program for depressed areas under the Economic Development Act of 1965. It authorizes grants and loans for public works, development facilities, technical assistance, and other activities to help economically depressed areas and to stimulate planning for economic development. In this act, the responsibility is placed upon local and state governments to apply for economic development assistance from the Economic Development Administration and to create multicounty and multistate development areas and districts for the purposes of planning economic development.

The Appalachian Regional Redevelopment Act of 1965 is another federal approach to the problem of area poverty. The name *Appalachia* denotes an eleven-state region centering around the Appalachian mountains from southern New York to middle Alabama. It is generally conceded to be the largest economically depressed area in the nation, although it does contain "pockets of prosperity." The focus of the Appalachia Act is upon highway construction, which is believed necessary to open up the region to economic development, although it may make it even easier for the residents to leave. Programs under the Appalachia Act are carried out by existing national and state agencies, such as the U.S. Bureau of Public Roads and the state highway departments. However, the entire program is coordinated by the Appalachian Regional Commission, comprised of the governor of each state in the region or

---

[12]For an excellent summary of public policies in the war on poverty, see James E. Anderson, "Poverty, Unemployment, and Economic Development: The Search for a National Anti-Poverty Policy," *Journal of Politics*, 29 (February 1967), 70–93.

his representative, and a federal representative chosen by the president.

As an approach to case poverty, the federal government passed the Manpower Training and Development Act of 1962, which authorizes federal grants to state employment agencies and private enterprise for on-the-job training programs to help workers in depressed areas, or elsewhere, acquire new job skills. Originally the act called for matching funds on a fifty-fifty basis by state governments after the first two years of the program; but when it appeared certain that states would drop the program altogether rather than share its costs, the federal government amended the act to authorize 100 percent federal financing. It seems safe to conclude that state and local governments would not undertake manpower training programs for unskilled workers without full federal financial support.

The most important legislation in the "war on poverty" is the Economic Opportunity Act of 1964.[13] This Act establishes the Office of Economic Opportunity (OEO) directly under the president with authority to support varied and highly experimental techniques for combating poverty at the community level. The focus is upon case poverty, and the objective is to help the poor and unemployed become self-supporting and capable of earning adequate incomes, by bringing about changes in the individuals themselves or in their environment. The strategy is one of "rehabilitation, not relief." OEO has no authority to make direct grants to the poor as relief or public assistance. All its programs are aimed, whether accurately or inaccurately, at curing the causes of poverty rather than alleviating its symptoms.

The Economic Opportunity Act established several programs oriented toward young people. The strategy appeared to be aimed at breaking the cycle of poverty at an early age. The Job Corps is designed to provide education, vocational training, and work experience in rural conservation camps for unemployable youths between the ages of sixteen and twenty-one. Another program for teen-age youths is the Neighborhood Youth Corps. It is designed to provide some work, counseling, and on-the-job training for youths who are living at home. Participating youths may be in school or out of school. The Neighborhood Youth Corps is intended for youths who were somewhat more employable than those who were expected to enter Job Corps. A Work-Study Program helps students from low-income families remain in school by giving them federally paid part-time employment with cooperating public or private agencies. Many universities and colleges are participants in this program; they benefit from the federally paid labor, and students benefit from the part-time jobs created. The Volunteers in Service to America

---

[13]For a description of the programs under the Economic Opportunity Act, see Joseph A. Kershaw, *Government against Poverty* (Chicago: Markham, 1970).

(VISTA) was modeled after the popular Peace Corps idea, but volunteers were to work in domestic poverty-impacted areas rather than in foreign countries. Volunteers normally give one year service—frequently in migrant labor camps, Indian reservations, neighborhood service centers, and so on.

The core of the Economic Opportunity Act was a grass-roots Community Action Program to be carried on at the local level with federal financial assistance, by public or private nonprofit agencies. Communities were urged to form a "community action agency," composed of representatives of government, private organizations, and, most importantly, the poor themselves. It was originally intended that OEO would *support antipoverty programs* devised by the local community action agency. Projects might include (but were not limited to) literacy training, health services, homemaker services, legal aid for the poor, neighborhood service centers, manpower vocational training, and childhood development activities. The act also envisioned that a community action agency would help *organize the poor* so that they could become participating members of the community and avail themselves of the many public programs designed to serve the poor. Finally, the act attempted to *coordinate federal and state programs for the poor* in each community.

Community action was to be "developed, conducted, and administered with the maximum feasible participation of the residents of the areas and members of the groups served." This was one of the more controversial phrases in the act itself. Militants within the OEO administration frequently cited this phrase as authority to "mobilize" the poor "to have immediate and irreversible impact on the communities." This language implied that the poor were to be organized as a political force, by federal antipoverty warriors using federal funds. Needless to say, neither Congress nor the Democratic administration of President Lyndon Johnson intended to create rival political organizations in communities that would compete for power with local governments. But some OEO administrators thought that the language of the act gave them this authority.

Community action agencies were expected to devise specific antipoverty projects for submission to Washington offices of OEO for funding. The most popular of these projects was Operation Head Start—usually a cooperative program between the community action agency and the local school district. Preschool children from poor families were given six to eight weeks of special summer preparation before entering kindergarten or first grade. Another type of antipoverty project is the Legal Services Program. Many community action agencies established free legal services to the poor to assist them in rent disputes, contracts, welfare rules, minor police actions, housing regulations, and so on. Other kinds of antipoverty projects funded by OEO include family-planning programs—the provision of advice and devices to facilitate family planning by the poor; homemaker services—advice to poor families on how to stretch low family budgets; manpower training—special outreach efforts to bring hard-core unemployed into more established manpower programs; "Follow Through"—to remedy the recognized failures of Head Start and continue special educational experiences for poor children after they enter school; "Upward Bound"—educational counseling for poor children; and so forth.

The Office of Economic Opportunity was always the scene of great confusion. New and untried programs were organized at breakneck speed. There was a high turnover in personnel. There was delay and confusion in releasing funds to local community action agencies. There was scandal and corruption, particularly at the local level. Community action agencies with young and inexperienced personnel frequently offended experienced governmental administrators as well as local political figures. Congressional action was uncertain, the project's life was extended for a year at a time, and appropriations were often delayed. But most damaging of all, even though programs were put in operation, there was little concrete evidence that these programs were successful in their objectives, that is, in eliminating the causes of poverty.

Daniel P. Moynihan summarized the community action experiences as follows:

> Over and again the attempts by official and quasi-official agencies (such as the Ford Foundation) to organize poor communities led first to the radicalization of the middle-class persons who began the effort; next to a certain amount of stirring among the poor, but accompanied by heightened radical antagonism *on the part of the poor* if they happened to be black; next to retaliation from the larger white community; whereupon it would emerge that the community action agency, which had talked so much, been so much in the headlines, promised so much in the way of change in the fundamentals of things, was powerless. A creature of a Washington bureaucracy, subject to discontinuation without notice. Finally, much bitterness all around.[14]

Unhappy community experiences with the War on Poverty were bound to reverberate in Washington. The Democratic administration under President Johnson had never intended to finance a conflict between poor blacks and Democratic big-city mayors and party organization. The Democratic administration did not wish to stir up antagonisms in cities between blacks and low-income white labor and ethnic groups which

---

[14]Daniel P. Moynihan, *Maximum Feasible Misunderstanding: Community Action in the War on Poverty* (New York: The Free Press, 1969).

had made up the winning Democratic party coalition since the days of FDR. Local power structures are not without influence in Washington; they could strike at the financial roots of the program in Washington without risking direct confrontation at the local level. Even before Johnson left office, the war on poverty had been substantially downgraded in policy priorities. The Nixon administration began a gradual dismantling of OEO. The final verdict on the war on poverty is not yet in. But the interim report is very negative.

What are the political bases for the support and opposition to the war on poverty? Certainly the poor themselves are, in the words of Michael Harrington in *The Other America,* "politically invisible." "The people of the other America do not, by far and large, belong to unions, to fraternal organizations, or to political parties. They are without lobbies of their own; they put forward no legislative program. As a group, they are atomized. They have no face; they have no voice."[15] How then does one account for antipoverty legislation?

No doubt Presidents Kennedy and Johnson were motivated at least partly by the desire to be recognized as great presidents, which of course requires important accomplishments. Writers such as Galbraith and Harrington helped to focus attention on poverty. Third, the growing political power of the blacks and the success of the civil rights movement have contributed. Poverty is much higher among blacks than among whites, so as black political strength grows, it tends to focus attention on the poor.

At the local level, community action agencies were supported by, and sometimes even organized by, reform, civic, and charitable organizations, United Fund agencies, Catholic charities, civil rights groups, labor organizations, agricultural extension workers, school officials anxious to share in Head Start funds, and to some extent the poor themselves. Opposition was weakened by the fact that one who opposes an antipoverty program appears to be in favor of poverty. Critics usually attack some peripheral aspect of the program rather than the program itself, such as the high salaries for the administrative officials, waste and extravagance, or immorality and delinquency, which occur at any of the program sites. But the poverty program has also had some difficulties with its friends as well as its enemies. Welfare departments sometimes feel that the community action agency is usurping its functions with the poor. State employment service and vocational rehabilitation agencies object that the OEO programs duplicate their own services. School administrators have insisted that preschool development programs, such as Operation Head Start, must be administered by the schools and not by community action agencies; this has led to separation of Head Start

15Harrington, *The Other America,* p. 13.

programs from community action agencies and their administration being placed in the hands of local school districts. Local political figures often object to community action agencies organizing the poor, for they see this as an attempt to give the poor political power. Once organized, the poor have often made uncomfortable demands upon local governments for adequate street cleaning, garbage disposal, housing code enforcement, courteous police treatment, and so on, in slum areas. In short, organizing the poor threatens to upset established power relations in communities. City officials have often objected that community action agencies do not come directly under the control of city governments but instead are usually nonprofit, private corporations, in which government officials must share power with representatives of private organizations and of the poor. Finally, the poverty program is beset with all the difficulties associated with the problem of race. Since blacks constitute such a large proportion of the poor in most communities, the poverty program is seen by many as a program for blacks.

SEVENTEEN

The
Politics of Housing
and
Urban Development

Urban life has come under severe criticism in recent years. A profusion of books with ominous titles—*Sick Cities: The Psychology And Pathology of American Urban Life; The Death And Life Of Great American Cities; Cities In A Race with Time; Cities in Trouble*[1]—have decried the horrors of life in American cities. Politicians, commentators, scholars, and writers, all talk of the urban "crisis." A newspaperman describes the dangers of modern urban living:

> An observer of the sprawling urban scene today might be compelled to concede that the superficial monotony of physical similarity must be the least important of all the ailments of the squatting modern metropolitan region, whose air grows fouler and more dangerous by the day, whose water is threatened increasingly by pollution, whose mobility is undermined by accumulations of vehicles and withering transit, whose educational systems reel under a growing variety of economic, social, and national emergencies, and whose entire pattern is assuming an ominous shape and sociological form, with well-to-do whites in their suburban cities ringing poverty-ridden minority groups widening at the core.[2]

[1]Mitchell Gordon, *Sick Cities: The Psychology and Pathology of American Urban Life* (Baltimore: Penguin, 1963); Jane Jacobs, *The Death and Life of Great American Cities* (New York: Random House, 1961); Jeanne Lowe, *Cities in a Race with Time* (New York: Random House, 1967); Nathan Glazer, *Cities in Trouble* (Chicago: Quadrangle, 1970).
[2]Mitchell Gordon, *Sick Cities*, p. 3.

A health expert warns:

> In candid truth the city is not a healthful place to live. Its inhabitants do not live as long or as happily as dwellers elsewhere. More of them go insane. They are sick more often. Finally, and perhaps more disastrously, they fail to reproduce themselves.[3]

Even the President has bemoaned:

> Our chronic inability to provide sufficient low and moderate income housing, of adequate quality, at reasonable price.
>
> The special problem of the poor and the Negro, unable to move freely from their ghettos, exploited in the quest for the necessities of life.
>
> Increasing pressures on municipal budgets, with large city per capita expenditures. . . .
>
> The high human costs: crime, delinquency, welfare loads, disease, and health hazards. This is man's fate in those broken neighborhoods where he can "feel the enclosure of the flaking walls and see through the window the blackened reflection of the tenement across the street that blocks out the world beyond."
>
> The tragic waste, and, indeed, the chaos that threatens where children are born into the stifling air of overcrowded rooms, and destined for a poor diet, inadequate schools, streets of fear and sordid temptation, joblessness, and the gray anxiety of the ill prepared.
>
> And the flight to the suburbs of more fortunate men and women who might have provided the leadership and the means for reversing this human decline.[4]

If things are really this bad, why do many millions of Americans insist on living in metropolitan areas and many more move there every year? The American metropolis is today's land of economic opportunity. People are attracted to cities because they provide greater numbers of jobs as well as greater freedom of occupational choice. Metropolitan living means higher incomes and higher standards of living. In addition to more material things, they offer greater opportunities for the "good life." Metropolitan dwellers are better educated on the average than nonmetropolitan residents. Metropolitan areas have more and better schools at all educational levels, better housing, better hospitals and health care, a greater variety of entertainment, far more institutions of fine arts—libraries, museums, art cinemas, symphonies, and ballet.

John C. Bollens and Henry J. Schmandt, two of America's leading

---

[3] Jonathan Foremann, "Biological Truth and Public Health," in Elmer T. Peterson (ed.), *Cities are Abnormal* (Norman, Okla.: University of Oklahoma Press, 1956), p. 117.

[4] President Lyndon B. Johnson, Message to Congress on the Model Cities Program, January 26, 1966.

urban scholars, speak optimistically about urban life in their recent comprehensive book, *The Metropolis:*

> The metropolis represents an accumulation of the human and material resources that make possible the accomplishment of goals undreamed of in a simpler and smaller-scale society. By bringing together a variety of personal skills and capital, it fosters specialization and a wide diversity of economic and social activities. It serves as the producer of goods and services and as a marketplace not alone for its own population but for a larger hinterland. It performs a less tangible but still important function as a symbol of an area's culture, its industrial and commercial might, and its distinctive position in the broader national and international scene. The metropolitan community of today is a way of life, one might even say a civilization.[5]

HUD—FEDERAL HOUSING
AND URBAN DEVELOPMENT PROGRAMS

The Department of Housing and Urban Development (HUD) is the federal agency concerned primarily with public housing, mortgage insurance, urban renewal, community facilities, mass transit, and related programs, whose objective is better houses and improved communities. HUD was established in 1965 as a successor to the earlier independent agency, the Housing and Home Financial Administration. HUD administers federal programs in housing and urban affairs, which were begun in the 1930s. The organization of HUD reflects the structure of these major federal programs:

Federal Housing Administration
FHA programs of mortgage insurance
Federal National Mortgage Association
FNMA ("Fannie Mae") secondary mortgage market operations for federally insured mortgages
Housing Assistance Administration
Low-rent public housing programs for low-income families
Urban Renewal Administration
Federal programs for slum clearance, urban renewal, and planning assistance
Community Facilities Administration
Federal grants and loans to municipalities for sewer, water, mass transit, and other public works

[5]John C. Bollens and Henry J. Schmandt, *The Metropolis: Its People, Politics, and Economic Life,* 2nd ed. (New York: Harper & Row, 1970), p. 26.

Each of these agencies reports to the Secretary of Housing and Urban Development.

The Federal Housing Administration was created in 1934 to guarantee private mortgages against default by the individual home buyer, thereby enabling banks, savings and loan associations, and other lending agencies to provide long-term, low-interest, low down-payment mortgages for Americans wishing to buy their own homes. After checking the credit rating of the prospective home buyer, the FHA insures the private mortgage lender—bank, savings and loan company, insurance company, and so forth—of repayment of the loan in case the home buyer defaults. This reduces the risk and encourages mortgage lenders to make more loans at lower interest rates, lower down payments, and longer repayment periods. While these advantages in borrowing assist middle-class home buyers, note that the *direct* beneficiaries of the FHA program are the banks and mortgage-lending companies who are insured against losses. The FHA also establishes minimum building standards for homes it insures and thereby has raised the general quality of middle-class housing. The FHA adds a small charge to each mortgage to finance a revolving fund to repay defaulted mortgages. However, the record of Americans in mortgage repayment is so good that FHA has consistently returned premium payments to the U.S. Treasury.

The FHA has been extremely successful in promoting home ownership among millions of middle-class Americans. Millions of families have financed their homes through FHA-insured mortgages, and millions more have financed their homes through mortgages insured by the Veterans Administration. A great many of these mortgages financed *suburban* homes. In fact, the success of FHA and VA programs may have contributed to the deterioration of the nation's central cities, by enabling so many middle-class white families to acquire their cherished home in the suburbs and leave the city behind. The FHA is an entirely federally administered program, but its impact on city and suburban governments should not be underestimated.

The Federal National Mortgage Association, FNMA, or "Fannie Mae," was created in the 1930s to further assist the mortgage market. FNMA can buy mortgages on the open market, particularly FHA- and VA-insured mortgages, when private mortgage money dries up. When mortgage money becomes more plentiful, it sells its mortgages. These market operations help to stabilize the mortgage market and insure a steady flow of money for home buying.

The Housing Act of 1937 established a federal public housing agency, later named the Housing Assistance Administration, to provide low-rent public housing for the poor who could not afford decent housing on the private market. The public housing program was designed for persons

without jobs or incomes sufficient to enable them to afford home ownership even with the help of the FHA. The Housing Assistance Administration does not build, own, or operate its own housing projects; rather
it provides the necessary financial support to enable local communities
to provide public housing for their poor if the communities choose to
do so. The Housing Assistance Administration makes loans and grants
to *local* housing authorities established by local governments to build,
own, and operate low-cost public housing. Local housing authorities
must keep rents low in relation to their tenants' ability to pay. This
means that local housing authorities operate at a loss, and the federal
government reimburses them for this loss. No community is required to
have a Public Housing Authority; it must apply to the Public Housing
Administration and meet federal standards in order to receive federal
financial support.

The Community Facilities Administration was created in 1954 to provide technical and financial assistance to local governments in building
community facilities—water and sewer systems, airports, mass transit,
and other public works.

POLITICS OF PUBLIC HOUSING

Public housing has always been involved in more political controversy
than the FHA. Real estate and building interests, which support the
FHA because it expands their number of customers, have opposed public housing on the grounds that it is socialistic and wasteful. While in
theory public housing serves individuals who cannot afford private
housing, private real estate interests contend that public housing hurts
the market for older homes and apartments. In addition, owners of slum
dwellings seldom welcome competition from federally supported housing authorities. Political difficulties have also been encountered in the
location of public housing units. Many Americans will support public
housing for low-income persons, so long as it is not located in their
neighborhood. A majority of public housing occupants are black, and
this automatically involves public housing in the politics of race.[6]

In recent years many of the earlier supporters of public housing, including minority groups, labor, social workers, charitable organizations,
and big-city political organizations, have expressed doubts about the effects of public housing. Public housing, while providing improved living conditions, failed to eliminate poverty, ignorance, family disruption,

[6]For an analysis of public housing projects, see Leonard Freedman, *Public Housing*
(New York: Holt, Rinehart & Winston, 1969).

juvenile delinquency, crime, and other characteristic troubles of the slums. Very often, the concentration of large numbers of poor persons with a great variety of social problems into a single, mass housing project compounded their problems. The cost of central-city land required many big cities to build high-rise housing buildings of ten to twenty stories. These huge buildings frequently became unlivable—crime in the hallways, elevators that seldom worked, drugs and human filth in halls and stairways, families locking themselves in and alienating themselves from community life. Huge housing projects were impersonal and bureaucratic, and they often failed to provide many of the stabilizing neighborhood influences of the old slums. Children could be raised in public housing projects and never see a regularly employed male head of a household going to and from work. The behavior and value patterns of problem families were reinforced.

Moreover, removing thousands of people from neighborhood environments and placing them in the institutionlike setting of large public housing developments very often increased their alienation or separation from society and removed what few social controls existed in the slum neighborhood. A family living in public housing and successful in finding employment and raising its income level faced eviction to make room for more "deserving" families. Finally, black groups often complained that public housing was a new form of racial segregation, and, indeed, the concentration of blacks among public housing dwellers does lead to a great deal of de facto segregation in housing projects.

Requests by communities for federal aid for public housing have far exceeded the amount of money appropriated by Congress. The result in most communities is a long list of those persons who are eligible for public housing for whom no space is available. An estimated 2 million people live in public housing in America, but 10 million people are probably eligible for public housing under current standards.

To alleviate the shortage of public housing and to correct some of the problems involved in large-site housing projects, Congress authorized three new approaches to supplement public housing—a rent subsidy program, a dispersed public housing site program, and a "turn key" program of acquiring new public housing. The rent subsidy program authorizes federal grants to local housing authorities to provide cash grants to families living in substandard housing, thus enabling them to rent decent private housing facilities. The dispersed public housing site program will provide federal grants to local housing authorities to enable them to purchase single homes or apartment buildings throughout the community for operation as public housing units. The "turn key" program enables local housing authorities to purchase completed housing projects from private builders. The purpose of these programs is to speed up the availability of public housing units and, perhaps more importantly, to eliminate dependence upon large, institutionlike public housing facilities and achieve more dispersal of public housing residents throughout the community. Opponents of these programs argue that the federal government is subsidizing "block-busting" tactics in its attempt to disperse public housing dwellers, mostly blacks, throughout the community. It is, they argue, a subtle form of open housing legislation aimed at de facto housing segregation.

URBAN RENAISSANCEMANSHIP

In the Housing Act of 1937, the idea of urban renewal was closely tied to public housing. Slum residences were to be torn down as public housing sites were constructed. But in the Housing Act of 1949, the urban renewal program was separated from public housing, and the federal government undertook to support a broad program of urban redevelopment to help cities fight a loss in population and to reclaim the economic importance of the core cities. After World War II, the suburban exodus had progressed to the point where central cities faced slow decay and death if large public efforts were not undertaken. Urban renewal could not be undertaken by private enterprise because it was not profitable; suburban property was usually cheaper than downtown property, and it did not require large-scale clearance of obsolete buildings. Moreover, private enterprise did not possess the power of eminent domain, which enabled the city to purchase the many separately owned tracts of land to insure an economically feasible new investment. [7]

To save the nation's central cities, the Urban Renewal Administration was authorized to match local monies to acquire blighted land, clear off or modernize obsolete or dilapidated structures, and make downtown sites available for new uses. The federal government does not engage in these activities directly, but makes available financial assistance to local urban renewal authorities for renewal projects. When the sites are physically cleared of the old structures by the local urban renewal authority, they can be resold to private developers for residential, commercial, or industrial use, and two-thirds of the difference between the costs of acquisition and clearance and the income from the private sale to the developers is paid for by the federal government. In other words, local urban renewal authorities sustain a loss in their renewal activities and two-thirds of this loss is made up by federal grants; the rest must

[7] For a general discussion of urban renewal by a number of experts, see James Q. Wilson, ed., *Urban Renewal* (Cambridge: M.I.T. Press, 1966).

come from local sources. However, the local share may include noncash contributions in the form of land donations, schools, streets, or parks.

No city is required to engage in urban renewal, but if cities wish federal financial backing, they must show in their applications that they have developed a "workable program" for redevelopment and the prevention of future blight. They must demonstrate that they have adequate building and health codes, good zoning and subdivision control regulations, proper administrative structures for renewal and other government services, sufficient local financing and public support, and a comprehensive plan of development with provisions for relocating displaced persons.

Urban renewal is best understood from an economic standpoint. For example, an urban renewal activity may undertake a project as follows:

Project Costs

Land acquisition	$8 million
Demolition, relocation	1 million
Provision of new public facilities	1 million
Total	$10 million
Proceeds from sale of land to private developer	4 million
Net project cost (loss)	6 million

Contributions

Federal grant for ⅔ of net cost	4 million
Local contributions in cash or services	2 million
Total	$6 million

The key to success is to encourage private developers to purchase the land and make a heavy investment—in middle- or high-income housing or in commercial or industrial use. In fact, before undertaking a project, urban renewal authorities frequently "find a developer first, and then see what interests him." The city cannot afford to purchase land, thereby taking it off the tax rolls, invest in its clearance, and then be stuck without a buyer. Moreover, the private developer must be encouraged to invest in the property and thus enhance the value of the central city. For example, on the project mentioned above, if a private developer can be persuaded to invest an additional $20 million beyond his purchase price in the construction of housing or business or industry, the value of the land would rise to $24 million. A ten-mill city tax on $24 million returns $240,000 per year, instead of the $80,000 that the city received on a ten-mill tax on the original value of $8 million. So over time a city can more than pay off its own investment in urban renewal by increased tax returns from renewed property and hence make a "profit." Thus, many people can come out of a project feeling successful—the city increases its tax base and annual revenues, the private developer makes a profit (in part because he acquired land at only 40 percent of its cost), and mayors can point to the physical improvements in the city that occurred during their administration.

Moreover, there are many favorable "spillover effects" of a successful urban renewal project:

1. Each project stimulates jobs, not only during demolition and construction but also later in servicing the new housing, business, or industry.
2. The city increases its ability to attract and maintain middle-class residents as well as business and industry.
3. Universities, hospitals, cultural centers, etc., can be built or expanded when all or part of an urban renewal project is turned over to public purposes.
4. Downtown areas can be revitalized and attract private development in areas adjacent to urban renewal projects.

However, there are also drawbacks to urban renewal. The concern for "profit" frequently leads to fiscal conservatism on the part of urban renewal authorities. They do not undertake to renew the very worst slum areas because of the excessive costs involved and because private developers may not wish to go into these areas even after renewal. More importantly, the financial considerations often dictate the choice of profitable middle- or upper-income housing or commercial or industrial use of renewed land, rather than low-cost private or public housing development. Developers make more profit on the former types of investments, and the city gets better tax returns. The effect of urban renewal is frequently to redistribute land from lower-income to higher-income purposes.

Relocation is the most sensitive problem in urban renewal. The vast majority of people relocated by urban renewal are poor and black. They have no interest in moving simply to make room for middle- or higher-income housing, or business or industry, or universities, hospitals, and other public facilities. Even though relocated families are frequently given priority for public housing, there is not nearly enough space in public housing to contain them all. They are simply moved from one slum to another. The slum landowner is paid a just price for his land, but the renter receives only a small moving allowance, averaging about one hundred dollars. Urban renewal officials assist relocated families in finding new housing and generally claim success in moving families to better housing. But frequently the result is higher rents,[8] and urban renewal may actually help to create new slums in other sections of the city. Small businessmen are especially vulnerable to relocation. They often depend on a small, well-known neighborhood clientele, and they cannot compete successfully when forced to move to other sections of the city.

Political support for urban renewal has come from mayors who wish to make their reputation as rigorous proponents by engaging in large-scale renewal activities that produce impressive "before" and "after" pictures of the city. Businessmen wishing to preserve downtown investments and developers wishing to acquire land in urban centers have provided a solid base of support for downtown renewal. Mayors, planners, the press, and the good-government forces have made urban renewal politically much more popular than public housing.

Originally, liberal reform groups and representatives of urban minorities supported urban renewal as an attack on the slum problem. Recently, however, they have become disenchanted with urban renewal, complaining that urban renewal has not considered the plight of the slum dweller. Too often, slum areas have been cleared and replaced with high-income residential developments or commercial or industrial developments that do not directly help the plight of the slum dwellers. Urban renewal authorities are required to pay landowners a just price for their land, but slum dwellers who rent their apartments are shoved about the city with only a minimal amount of support from the "relocation" division of urban renewal authority. Downtown areas have been improved in appearance, but usually at the price of considerable human dislocation. Thus, the slum dwellers and the landlords who exploit them often join forces to oppose urban renewal.[9] When dislocated persons are poor and black, and the completed project is used for middle- or high-income white residences, the charge is leveled that urban renewal is simply "Negro removal."

A CRITIQUE OF FEDERAL
URBAN POLICY—MODEL CITIES

The critical deficiency in federal urban policy is that there are no concrete goals or clear priorities in the hundreds of separate programs affecting cities. James Q. Wilson writes about urban policy: *"We do not*

---

[8]See Chester Hartman, "The Housing of Relocated Families," *Journal of the American Institute of Planners*, 30 (November 1964), 266–86.

[9]For a scathing attack on urban renewal, see Jane Jacobs, *The Death and Life of Great American Cities* (New York: Random House, Inc., 1961).

know what we are trying to accomplish . . . . Do we seek to raise standards of living, maximize housing choices, revitalize the commercial centers of our cities, and suburban sprawl, eliminate discrimination, reduce traffic congestion, improve the quality of urban design, check crime and deliquency, strengthen the effectiveness of local planning, increase citizen participation in local government? All these objectives sound attractive—in part, because they are rather vague—but unfortunately they are many cases incompatible."[10]

The institutional arrangements of American government have proved remarkably well suited for pursuing different policies toward contradictory goals simultaneously. Government can maintain the support of competing groups in society by allowing different federal agencies to pursue incompatable goals and by permitting local communities to follow competing policies with federal money.

For example, the two federal program areas that account for the greatest expenditure of dollars for the physical improvement of cities are (1) the federal highway and transportation programs and (2) the federal housing and urban renewal programs. The first are operated by the Department of Transportation (DOT), and the second by the Department of Housing and Urban Development (HUD). The urban portion of the interstate highway system is costing billions of federal dollars; the effect of these dollars is to enable people to drive in and out of the central city speedily, safely, and conveniently and to open up suburban areas to business and residential expansion. Of course, these expressways also encourage middle-class (mostly white) families to move out of the central city and enable commercial establishments to follow them. This leads to further racial segregation within the metropolitan region in housing and schools and reduces the number of service jobs available to the poor living in the city. The encouragement of longer automobile trips from suburban residences to downtown offices adds to pollution and congestion. While federal investment in mass transit facilities (subways, railways, buses) might reduce pollution and congestion, such investment would still encourage suburbanization, "white flight," and de facto segregation.

At the same time, the Federal Housing Administration (in HUD) and the Veterans Administration are encouraging home ownership by insuring mortgages that are written on easy terms for millions of middle-class (mostly white) Americans. Most of these mortgages are for *new* homes because it is cheaper to build on vacant land and because so many prospective homeowners want to move to the suburbs. So it turns out that these programs actually facilitate the movement of middle-class people out of the central city.

[10]James Q. Wilson, "The War on Cities," *The Public Interest*, (1966).

In the meantime—the Urban Renewal Administration (in HUD) is helping cities to tear down slum dwellings, often displacing, at considerable hardship, the poor who live there in order to make way for office buildings, hotels, civic centers, industrial parks, and middle-class luxury apartments. In part, this effort is intended to lure suburbanites back to the central city. While urban renewal reduces the overall supply of housing to the poor in cities, the Housing Assistance Administration (in HUD) is assisting cities in building low-rent public housing units to add to the supply of housing for the poor.

Despite the emphasis in federal urban programs on the *physical* characteristics of cities, most observers now acknowledge that "the urban crisis" is not primarily, or even significantly, a physical problem. It is not really housing or highways or urban rebuilding that lies at the heart of urban discontent. Instead, when one thinks of the challenges confronting cities, one thinks of racial tension, crime, poverty, poor schools, residential segregation, rising welfare rolls, fiscal crisis—in short, all the major domestic problems facing the nation. In an urban society, *all* domestic problems become urban problems.

The federal government has never set any significant priority among its hundreds of grant programs. The result is that too few dollars chase too many goals. The maze of federal grant-in-aid programs for cities (nearly five hundred separate programs with separate purposes and guidelines) is uncoordinated and bureaucratic. Mayors and other municipal officials spend a great deal of time in "grantmanship"—learning where to find federal funds, how to apply, and how to write applications in such a way as to appear to meet the purposes and guidelines of the program. Cities are sometimes pressured to apply for funds for projects they do not really need, simply because federal funds are available, while they may receive little or no federal assistance for more vital programs. The reason for many of these administrative and organizational problems is not merely incompetency on the part of government planners. Frequently, conflicting policies, incompatible goals, and competing government programs reflect underlying conflicts about public policy. Government institutions often accommodate conflict about public policy by enacting conflicting policies and establishing separate agencies to implement these policies.

The Model Cities Program, enacted in 1966, was an attempt to cope with some of the organizational and administrative problems in federal urban programs. (The terminology was changed by Washington planners from "Demonstration Cities" in the original act, to "Model Cities" to avoid the implication that the act rewarded "demonstrations" or riots.) Model Cities is not a new program or new approach to urban problems, but rather an effort to reorganize old programs and approaches. The emphasis in Model Cities is upon "coordination" and "integrated planning" of federal programs in each participating city. The idea is to coordinate programs and grants in housing, urban renewal, and community facilities with programs and grants in transportation, job training, education, economic opportunity, crime control, and related programs. A federal coordinator is appointed for each participating city, and a community development agency is established to prepare a five-year community development plan. Supplemental federal funds, in addition to existing federal grant programs, are made available to participating cities as incentives for participation. Mayors and councils are directly involved in Model Cities planning; there is no bypassing of city hall as in the Community Action Program. Approximately 150 cities have been designated as model cities.

So far there is little evidence that the Model Cities Program has succeeded in bringing about better planning or coordination in federal or local urban programs. On the contrary, in some Model Cities the new community development agency came into conflict with established city planning agencies, OEO community action agencies, mayors and councils, city housing and urban renewal activities, and neighborhood resident groups. In other cities, the Model Cities agency simply rubber-stamped existing plans of other departments and agencies, and coordination was more apparent than real. It is doubtful whether this reorganization and imposition of another layer of poverty, racial conflict, crime and delinquency, poor housing, inadequate sources will succeed in reducing existing organizational chaos, let alone solve any significant urban problems.

THE URBAN "CRISIS" RECONSIDERED

For many years now, statesmen, scholars, and commentators have bemoaned the nation's urban "crisis." The cities are portrayed as centers of poverty, racial conflict, crime and deliquency, poor housing, inadequate education, ill health, white flight, pollution and congestion, and so forth. As Edward C. Banfield notes, "we are told on all sides that the cities are uninhabitable, that they must be torn down and rebuilt, or new ones must be built from the ground up, that something drastic must be done—and soon—or else."[11] But despite the real and persistent problems of urban life, the urban "crisis" is more a product of our rising standards and expectations about life in America than it is a product of any actual deterioration of city life. As Banfield observes:

[11]Edward C. Banfield, *The Unheavenly City* (Boston: Little, Brown and Company 1970), p. 3.

The plain fact is that the overwhelming majority of city dwellers live more comfortably and conveniently than ever before. They have more and better housing, more and better schools, more and better transportation, and so on. By any conceivable measure of material welfare the present generation of urban Americans is, on the whole, better off than any other large group of people has ever been anywhere. What is more, there is every reason to expect that the general level of comfort and convenience will continue to rise at an even more rapid rate through the foreseeable future.[12]

People come to cities precisely *because* they are congested. If they were not congested, they would not be cities and they would not be worth coming to. It is well within our technological know-how to drastically lower pollution levels. Yet we have not done so because the problem is not sufficiently serious to stimulate us into action. If there were a real "crisis"—people dying on the streets from asphyxiation—then we would certainly act on the pollution problem. The rush-hour traffic problem—so frequently referred to in terms of "crisis," "strangulation," and so forth—could be solved *if* people would trade the luxury of their own private cars for mass transit. (An even easier solution would be the staggering of business hours of downtown offices and businesses.)

Poverty and racial discrimination are more widespread outside central cities than inside them. Of course, unlike people living in rural areas and small towns, the poor and the black in cities live closely together and develop a collective consciousness and sense of identity. Their rhetoric, behavior, and politics call attention to the poverty and racial discrimination that still exists in urban life, and to the extent that this activity stimulates additional action on the part of governments and citizens, it is perhaps desirable. But it is also true that this activity makes us more *aware* of existing poverty and racial discrimination. And our expectation today is that any level of poverty or discrimination must be eliminated.

Police brutality was once defined as cops beating prisoners with nightsticks. Today it is defined as unexplained questioning and searching or the use of disrespectful language by police. A generation ago a majority of students dropped out of high school before graduation. But it was not until the 1960s when three-quarters of all students graduated that the "dropout" problem was cited as a problem, and each year the proportion of high school graduates is rising.

The number of people living in poverty is rapidly declining. Over the last decade alone the poor have declined from 22 to 13 percent of the total population. Moreover, the poor in America today live better than the middle class of fifty years ago, and certainly better than the over-

[12]*Ibid.*, pp. 3–4.

whelming majority of the world's inhabitants. Yet the widely publicized "war on poverty" was not begun until after the number of poor had dipped below 15 percent of the population. Poverty is greater in rural areas than in central cities.

Blacks have been moving to cities *because* of the greater opportunities, increased incomes, better schools, better health care, and better living conditions than they found in rural life. It is *because* of the greater hopes and expectations of urban blacks and their living close to each other that the ghettos are tinder for violent confrontation. When blacks were truly subjugated and oppressed and separated from each other in rural southern life, there was little likelihood of mass disorder. The progress of blacks over the last decade is truly dramatic; it is unlikely that any other ethnic group progressed so fast in a single decade. The overwhelming majority of blacks believe that "things are getting better," and there is solid statistical evidence to support their view. It is true that this progress was long overdue, that blacks still have far to go to achieve equality, and that any discrimination is to be deplored. But there are dangers in overemphasizing "racism" and in ignoring the tremendous strides that have already been made by blacks and that can be made by blacks in the future. It would be unfortunate indeed if blacks adopted the attitude that everything was futile and hopeless, that they had nothing to lose by violence and destruction, that the cities might as well be burned to the ground.

Edward C. Banfield writes: "To a large extent . . . our urban problems are like the mechanical rabbit at the racetrack which is set up to keep just ahead of the dogs no matter how fast they may run. Our performance is better and better, but because we set our standards and expectations to keep ahead of performance, the problems are never any nearer to solution. .. "[13] Perhaps it is a good thing that we set ever-higher standards for ourselves, because we are constantly spurred to improve the quality of life in America. However, there are dangers in this—we may mistake failure to progress as fast as we would like for failure to progress at all. The first danger in such a misinterpretation is that we will rush into a series of ill-considered and wasteful public programs that make matters worse rather than better. These programs may be presented in such a way as to lead people to believe that all their daily problems of life will soon be solved for them by the government. When it turns out that these programs fail to do so, disillusionment and bitterness set in. It is not so much the wasted public funds that constitute a loss as it is the dashed hopes and the loss of confidence that result.

Perhaps a more important danger is that society will be blamed for

13*Ibid.*, pp. 21–22.

all the problems that beset individuals, and individuals will be excused from all effort to improve their own lives. Available energies will be devoted to finding governmental programs to solve individual and family problems, and all forms of social dependency will increase. Individuals will come to assume *less* responsibility for their own lives, whereas the traditional democratic value was to encourage individuals to shape their own lives.

Finally, there is danger that people will take the rhetoric of "crisis," "racism," and so on, seriously and will overlook the tremendous progress that society has made. They may conclude that society is "not worth saving" and that they no longer have confidence or trust in their government or nation.

EIGHTEEN

The
Politics
of
Budgeting and Taxation

STATE-LOCAL TAX AND
REVENUE POLICIES

Federal, state, and local governments in the United States take about 40 percent of the nation's income in taxes and revenues. The largest share of this total tax bite, about two-thirds, goes to the federal government. But states and communities collect over one-third of all government revenues, and revenue raising presents states and communities with important political choices. Decisions must be made about how much revenue is to be raised, how it will be raised, from whom it will be raised, and how great a financial burden will be imposed. These decisions often embroil states and communities in their most important political battles.

The U.S. Constitution places very few restrictions on the power of the states to tax; it prohibits states, without the consent of Congress, from levying taxes on imports and exports; and by implication it prohibits states from using the taxing power to deny to citizens equal protection of the law or due process of the law. State constitutions, however, frequently restrict state taxing powers. These state constitutional restrictions often include maximum rates, prohibitions on incomes or sales taxes, prohibitions on progressive rates, and prohibitions on classification schemes. These restrictions, of course, are generally the product of politi-

TABLE 18-1
Total Government Revenues, 1902-1966

	Amount in Billions	Federal Percentage	State-Local Percentage	Percentage of National Income
1902	1.7	38.5	61.5	8.2
1913	3.0	32.3	67.7	8.6
1922	9.3	45.7	54.3	14.7
1932	10.3	21.6	78.4	24.2
1940	17.8	39.3	60.7	21.8
1950	66.7	80.3	19.7	27.6
1960	153.1	65.2	34.8	36.7
1965	202.9	62.0	38.0	39.4
1970	342.6	63.9	36.1	40.6

SOURCE: U.S. Bureau of the Census, STATISTICAL ABSTRACT.

cal victories by taxpayers who have succeeded in writing their views on taxes into state constitutions. In addition to taxes, states and communities also derive revenue from compulsory insurance payments, income from public businesses, fines, rents, and charges, and more importantly, grants-in-aid from the federal government. As we shall see, these non-tax revenues are an important part of state and local government finance.

Important changes have occurred in tax and revenue policies in America in the last few decades. In 1902 total government revenues amounted to only $1.7 billion. States and communities collected more revenue than the national government: 61.5 percent of all government revenues were raised in the states, while the federal government accounted for only 38.5 percent of all revenues. And total government revenues amounted to only 8 percent of the nation's income. Seven decades later, public revenue collections in the United States had risen to over $342 billion. Perhaps more important than dollar increases is the fact that governments now take about 40 percent of the national income. This means that the burden of government finance has grown much faster than the nation's income. Another important change is the change in the relative position of federal versus state-local revenue collections. Wars, depressions, and threats of war have resulted in the shifting of financial emphasis from the states and communities to the national government. The national government in 1970 collected about 64 percent of all revenues, while states and communities collected the remaining 36 percent.

There have also been some important changes in the sources of state and local revenues over the past few decades. In 1902, local revenues far surpassed the state revenues and the federal government provided very little help to states or communities. Today, state governments have assumed direct responsibility for many public programs, previously left to local communities, that were not undertaken at all. This trend toward centralized state government has meant that the states collect an increasing share of the total state and local revenue. States and communities now share total state-local revenues on an approximately equal basis.

A major share of state-local revenue now comes from the federal government. Federal grants constitute 14.5 percent of the revenue of state and local governments. And local governments receive over 25 percent of their revenue from state grants-in-aid. This dependence of local governments upon state governments for revenue arose during the depression years. Today, intergovernmental payments are a vital source of revenue for both state and local governments.

In recent years, both state and local governments have also received substantial incomes from various public enterprises and insurance programs. Today, many municipalities provide electric power, gas, recreational facilities, and transit and transportation facilities, as well as water supply, on a commercial basis. Liquor store revenues have become a major source of state revenues. Today, payments into state unemployment compensation funds, workmen's compensation funds, and employee retirement funds are another important source of state government revenue, even though these payments are made to special funds. These insurance premiums, utility receipts, and liquor store receipts amount to over 17 percent of all state-local revenue. Charges and miscellaneous general revenue have remained a relatively constant percentage of total state-local revenues over the years. These include everything from children's school lunch fees and textbook charges to interests from public investments, highway tolls, sewerage charges, and public hospital service fees.

Important changes have also occurred in the last fifty years in the types of taxes relied upon by state and local governments. At the turn of the century, general property tax reigned as the only really important source of state and local revenue. In theory, at least, all property within a community was assessed at market value and a single uniform rate of tax was applied. In practice, however, property assessments fell far below true market value, and they were not uniform from one county or municipality to the next; assessments varied from as high as 75 percent of fair market value to as low as 10 percent. Some property was specifically exempted from property taxation—for example, the property of government agencies and religious institutions. Some property, especially personal property such as furniture and automobiles and intangible property such as stocks and bonds, was simply hidden from the assessors. The property tax on real estate provided most state and local revenue.

TABLE 18-2
State and Local Tax Revenues, 1902-70

STATE GOVERNMENT REVENUE BY SOURCE

	Amount in Billions of Dollars	From Federal Govt.	Income Taxes	General Sales Taxes	Motor Fuel Taxes	Alcohol, Tobacco Taxes	Other Taxes Including Property	Charges	Insurance, Utilities & Stores
1902	0.2	1.6%	–	–	–	–	71.3%	13.0%	1.0%
1913	0.4	1.6	–	–	–	0.5%	79.5	15.7	0.0
1922	1.4	7.3	7.4%	–	1.0%	–	61.3	13.3	7.8
1932	2.5	8.7	6.0	0.3%	20.7	0.7	46.6	10.5	4.6
1940	5.7	11.6	8.0	8.7	14.6	5.1	21.3	6.0	23.6
1950	13.7	16.4	8.4	12.0	11.1	6.0	18.5	6.5	19.0
1960	32.8	19.9	10.3	13.1	10.2	4.8	16.6	7.9	16.7
1965	53.8	20.3	11.5	20.7	8.8	2.7	11.3	9.2	16.2
1970	88.9	22.7	14.4	16.0	7.1	4.2	11.8	10.7	12.5

LOCAL GOVERNMENT REVENUE BY SOURCE

	Amount in Billions of Dollars	From Federal & State Govt.	Income Taxes	Excise & Sales Taxes	Property Taxes	Other Taxes	Charges	Insurance, Utilities, & Stores
1902	0.9	6.1%	–	–	68.3%	8.8%	10.3%	6.5%
1913	1.8	5.5	–	0.2%	67.9	6.4	13.2	6.8
1922	4.1	7.7	–	0.5	71.7	1.8	11.5	6.8
1932	6.2	13.1	–	0.4	67.2	1.4	9.8	8.1
1940	7.7	25.0	0.2%	1.7	54.0	2.3	6.6	10.2
1950	16.1	27.4	0.4	3.0	43.7	2.4	9.9	13.2
1960	37.2	26.8	0.7	3.6	42.5	1.9	13.0	11.6
1965	53.8	28.6	0.8	3.9	41.3	1.5	13.3	10.5
1970	89.0	33.1	1.8	3.4	37.1	1.3	14.2	9.2

SOURCE: U.S. Bureau of the Census, HISTORICAL STATISTICS OF THE UNITED STATES (Washington, D.C.: Government Printing Office, 1960), pp. 727, 729. Updated.

Reliance upon property taxation involves many inequities. Some communities have expensive property and few public needs, while other communities have many needs but little taxable property. In other words, needs and resources are inequally distributed among communities. This is particularly troublesome for local school districts which must rely heavily on property taxes for revenue. Indeed, in 1972 the California Supreme Court held that reliance upon local property taxation in school district finance denied children in poorer communities of equality of educational opportunty guaranteed by the Calfornia and U.S. constitutions.

The awkwardness of the property tax, with its many inequalities and opportunities for evasion, eventually led to its disuse as an important source of *state* revenue; however, this tax continues to be the major source of revenue for *local* governments. Intangible property, such as stocks and bonds and personal property, has gradually been dropped from the local tax property rolls, either legally or illegally, but real estate is relatively easy to find and it cannot be easily moved about. A local sales tax can result in merchants moving beyond city boundaries, and a city income tax can speed the population exodus to suburbia. Because of the dependence of local governments on property taxation, the role of this tax in the total state-local revenue system in America remains significant. States that turn over government functions to communities will have a total tax structure that is heavily dependent on property taxation. States that assume more direct responsibility for public services will depend somewhat less on property taxation.

When prohibition ended, alcohol, and later tobacco, became important sources of revenue. It was relatively easy to win political support for taxes that penalized a recognized vice. The advent of the automobile and the heavy demand for public road construction made gasoline a natural object of taxation: the gasoline tax first adopted in 1919 spread to all states within ten years. This tax still supplies about 10 percent of all state revenue. Under political pressure from the automotive and trucking industries, revenues from this tax are usually segregated from other revenues for use on highways only.

While the property tax is the most important source of revenue for local communities, the general sales tax is now the most important source of tax revenue for state governments. Consumers are a notoriously weak pressure group, and opposition by retailers can usually be squelched by state kickbacks of a certain percentage of a tax for the retailers' efforts in collecting it. It is difficult for taxpayers to count pennies dribbled away two or three at a time; the tax does not involve obvious payroll deductions, as in income taxation, or year-end tax bills, as in property taxation. The burden of the sales tax is not as visible as the income or property taxes even when large items are purchased, and the purchaser usually considers the tax as part of the item's cost. By 1970 all but five states had imposed a general sales tax (See Table 18–3.)

Perhaps the popularity of the sales tax with state legislators is due to the fact that the federal government has "preempted" income taxation and communities have "preempted" property taxation. There seems to be nothing left for the states to tax except consumption. It seems natural that the three levels of government should have three separate sources of revenue. Of course, the notion of "preemption" involves a value judgment—that property taxes should go no higher and that the federal government is now taking as much income as should be spared for public purposes.

TABLE 18-3
States Without Sales and Income Taxes in 1970

States without General Sales or Gross Receipts Taxes	States without Individual Income Taxes	States without Corporate Income Taxes
Alaska	Connecticut*	Nevada
Delaware	Florida	New Hampshire
Montana	Nevada	Ohio
New Hampshire	New Hampshire*	Texas
Oregon	New Jersey	Washington
	Ohio	Wyoming
	Rhode Island*	
	South Dakota	
	Tennessee*	
	Texas	
	Washington	
	Wyoming	

* These states tax income from interest, dividends, or capital gains, but not wage income.

In 1911 Wisconsin passed the first modern, enforceable, state income tax. Many states fell in line after the national government began taxing income in 1913. Like the general sales tax, the income tax can produce a great deal of revenue. Most of the states (thirty-eight) have an individual income tax. A few of these are flat rates of 2 or 4 percent of taxable income, but most are graduated and progressive like the federal individual income tax. Rates of progressive state income taxes may run from a modest 1 to 4 percent (Missouri) to a steep 2 to 14 percent (New York). A few states (four) do not tax all income, but only income from interest, dividends, and capital gains. The corporate income tax is even more popular than the individual income tax; all except six states taxed corporate income in 1970. (See Table 18–3.)

A COMPARATIVE VIEW
OF STATE TAX SYSTEMS

What accounts for differences in tax and revenue policy? Total state-local tax revenues varied from a high of over $500 per person in California and New York to a low of $252 in Arkansas. This means that per capita tax levels of some states are over twice as high as those of other states. Some states rely heavily on their local governments and upon property taxation to supply needed revenue. Some States rely heavily on grants-in-aid. Tax burdens, that is, taxes in relation to personal income, also vary considerably among the states. Available evidence suggests

FIGURE 18–1 The Fifty States Arranged According to Tax Revenue and Median Family Income

Source: Thomas R. Dye, *Politics, Economics, and the Public* (Chicago: Rand McNally & Co., 1966), p. 189. Reproduced by permission.

1	Ala.	11	Hawaii	21	Mass.	31	N.M.	41	S.D.
2	Alaska	12	Idaho	22	Mich.	32	N.Y.	42	Tenn.
3	Ariz.	13	Ill.	23	Minn.	33	N.C.	43	Tex.
4	Ark.	14	Ind.	24	Miss.	34	N.D.	44	Utah
5	Calif.	15	Iowa	25	Mo.	35	Ohio	45	Vt.
6	Colo.	16	Kan.	26	Mont.	36	Okla.	46	Va.
7	Conn.	17	Ky.	27	Neb.	37	Ore.	47	Wash.
8	Del.	18	La.	28	Nev.	38	Pa.	48	W.Va.
9	Fla.	19	Me.	29	N.H.	39	R.I.	49	Wis.
10	Ga.	20	Md.	30	N.J.	40	S.C.	50	Wyo.

that a state's level of economic development is the most important influence on state-local revenue policies.[1]

First of all, let us examine the effect of economic development on levels

[1]Thomas R. Dye, *Politics, Economics, and the Public* (Chicago: Rand McNally & Co., 1966), Chap. 7.

of taxation in the states.[2] There is little doubt that the ability of the states to raise tax revenue is a function of their level of economic development. Figure 18–1 is a scatter diagram showing the closeness of the relationship between tax revenues and median family income among the states. It shows that as family incomes go up, per capital taxes collected by state and local governments also go up.

The concept of tax *burden* generally refers to taxes paid in relation to personal income; because of differences among the states in income levels, states with the highest *levels of taxation* are not necessarily the same states with the highest tax burdens. The total tax burden in a state is measured by "total state and local tax revenues as a percentage of personal income." In 1970 the state-local tax burden averaged 12 percent of personal income in the United States. Among the fifty states, high levels of industrialization usually reduced the burdens of taxation; industrialized states can collect a great deal of tax monies without taking a very large percentage of personal income.[3] Apparently the way to lower the tax burden in a state is to attract industry.

High tax burdens are not necessarily a product of high tax levels, although, of course, there is some relationship between these variables. Yet, high tax levels in an urbanized, industrialized, high-income state may not necessarily be accompanied by a heavy tax burden. It is possible to have low tax levels that, because of the lack of industry and low income levels, may be very burdensome—that is, quite high in relationship to low incomes. In Figure 18–2, all states above the solid horizontal line can be designated as states with high tax levels. In those states in the upper right, high tax levels are accompanied by high tax burdens, but those states in the upper left (Delaware, Nevada, Connecticut, Illinois, and New Jersey) can collect high taxes per capita without imposing high tax burdens; they have sufficient industrial resources or other special tax sources (for example, gambling and entertainment in Nevada) to enable them to collect high per capita taxes without taking a large share of personal income. Even California and New York, which have the highest tax *levels* in the nation, rank below a number of other states in their tax *burdens*, because of their surplus of taxable economic resources. In contrast, states at the lower right (Mississippi, North Dakota, Louisiana and Idaho) are in the unhappy position of having high tax burdens, despite the fact that per capita taxes are low. Their economic resources are so limited that even though per capita taxes and public service levels are low, tax burdens are still quite high.

---

[2]Levels of *revenue* refer simply to amounts of money per person raised from all sources. Levels of *taxation* refer to amounts of money per person raised through taxation and exclude monies from federal grants-in-aid, insurance premiums, rents and charges, and utility and store receipts.

[3]Dye, *Politics, Economics, and the Public,* pp. 188–91.

1 Ala.	11 Hawaii	21 Mass.	31 N.M.	41 S.D.
2 Alaska	12 Idaho	22 Mich.	32 N.Y.	42 Tenn.
3 Ariz.	13 Ill.	23 Minn.	33 N.C.	43 Tex
4 Ark.	14 Ind.	24 Miss.	34 N.D.	44 Utah
5 Calif.	15 Iowa	25 Mo.	35 Ohio	45 Vt.
6 Colo.	16 Kan.	26 Mont.	36 Okla.	46 Va.
7 Conn.	17 Ky.	27 Neb.	37 Ore.	47 Wash.
8 Del.	18 La.	28 Nev.	38 Pa.	48 W.Va.
9 Fla.	19 Me.	29 N.H.	39 R.I.	49 Wis.
10 Ga.	20 Md.	30 N.J.	40 S.C.	50 Wyo.

FIGURE 18–2 The Fifty States Arranged According to Tax Revenues and Tax Burdens

Source: Thomas R. Dye, *Politics, Economics, and the Public* (Chicago: Rand McNally & Co., 1966), p. 190. Reproduced by permission.

Poorer states also differ from richer states in their reliance upon inter-governmental revenues. Federal monies are an important and growing source of revenue for state and local governments. In some program areas, federal grants-in-aid help to overcome economic inequalities among the states, but by no means has federal action eliminated disparities among the states in revenues or the impact of these disparities on state programs.

In earlier chapters, we observed that federal formulas for the distribution of grants-in-aid in many education and welfare programs provided proportionately larger amounts of money to poorer states and communities. The result is that poorer states and communities rely much more heavily upon federal grants-in-aid as sources of revenue.

Another important difference between richer and poorer states is in the degree of decentralization in state and local finance and administration. Local governments tend to play a greater role in the collection of taxes and the provision of public services in urban, high-income states, while state governments collect a greater portion of revenue and provide more services in rural, low-income states. Earlier, we observed that state governments in poorer rural states undertake more direct responsibilities in education, welfare, and highways. Low levels of economic development tend to force decentralization upon these states. Wealthy urban states can afford to let local governments shoulder more responsibilities. This also means, of course, that the property tax—the chief source of income for local governments—is a relatively more important source of revenue in the wealthier urban states, which rely heavily upon their local governments for the provision of public services.

TYPES OF TAXES
AND THE INCIDENCE OF TAXATION

The politics of taxation center about the question of who actually bears the burden or "incidence" of a tax, that is, which income groups must devote the largest proportion of their income to taxes. Taxes that require high-income groups to pay a larger percentage of their incomes in taxes than low-income groups are said to be *progressive,* while taxes that take a larger share of the income of low-income groups are said to be *regressive.*

Economist George Bishop estimates that, in general, state and local tax systems are regressive.[4] Certainly the revenue systems of state and local governments are more regressive than that of the federal government, which relies heavily upon the progressive individual and corporate income tax. This means that, in general, if a particular governmental function is financed through state and local revenue systems rather than federal revenues, it is being financed on a regressive rather than progressive revenue basis. Thus, much of the political debate over "federalism," that is, over which level of government, state or federal, should provide a particular governmental service, concerns the fact that the federal govern-

[4]George A. Bishop, "Tax Burdens by Income Class," *National Tax Journal,* Vol. 14 (1961).

ment tax structure is generally progressive, while the state and local tax structures are generally regressive. If the federal government pays for a particular governmental program, it is being paid out of progressive taxes, whereas if state and local governments pay for a particular governmental program, it is being paid for out of largely regressive taxes. There are many other factors to be considered in the allocation of responsibilities between the states and the federal government, but the incidence of federal and state tax systems should not be overlooked.

According to Bishop, the income group under $2,000 per year was estimated to have paid, in 1958, 11.4 percent of its personal income into state and local taxes, while the income group over $15,000 paid only 5.8 percent of its personal income into these taxes (See Table 18–4.)

Bishop also estimates the incidence of the various types of state and local taxes. *Property taxes* are quite regressive. This conclusion is based on the assumption that the renter actually pays his property taxes through increased rentals levied by the landlord, and the further assumption that high-income groups have more wealth in untaxed forms of property. Since the property tax is the foundation of local tax structures in every state, it is reasonable to conclude that states that rely largely upon local governments for taxes and services are relying more upon regressive tax structures. Yet, in defense of property taxation, it is often argued that no other form of taxation is really feasible for local governments. Local sales and income taxes force individuals and businesses to leave the communities levying them; real estate, on the other hand, is less easy to move about and hide from local tax assessors. Real estate taxes are the only

TABLE 18-4
State and Local Tax Burdens by Income Class

Source	Family Personal Income							
	Under $2,000	$2,000-$3,999	$4,000-$5,999	$6,000-$7,999	$8,000-$9,999	$10,000-$14,999	$15,000-and Over	Total
Individual income	0.5	0.8	0.6	0.2	0.2	0.3	0.7	0.5
Corporation income	0.2	0.2	0.1	0.1	0.2	0.2	0.4	0.2
Excises and sales	4.8	3.9	3.7	3.6	3.5	3.2	2.1	3.3
Estate and gift	—	—	—	—	—	—	0.5	0.1
Property	5.9	4.6	4.1	3.7	3.4	2.8	2.1	3.5
Total, excluding social insurance	11.4	9.5	8.5	7.6	7.3	6.5	5.8	7.6

SOURCE: George A. Bishop, "Tax Burden by Income Class," NATIONAL TAX JOURNAL, 14 (1961), quoted in staff report of the Advisory Commission on Intergovernmental Relations, MEASURES OF STATE AND LOCAL FISCAL CAPACITY AND TAX EFFORT (Washington, D.C.: Government Printing Office, 1962), p. 23.

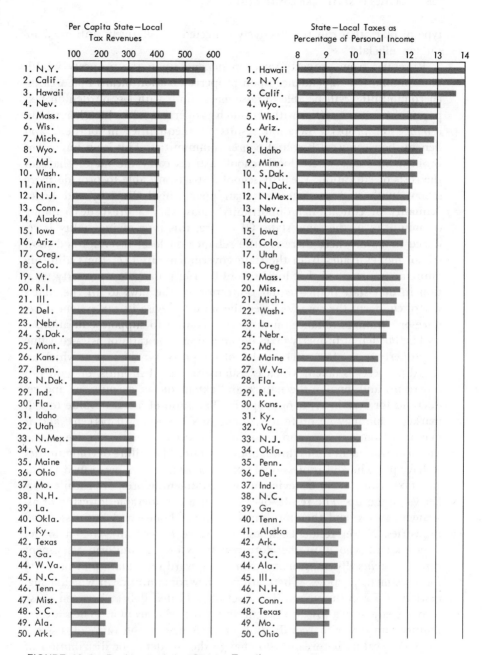

Per Capita State—Local
Tax Revenues

State—Local Taxes as
Percentage of Personal Income

FIGURE 18–3   Rankings of the States: Taxation

type of taxes that can be effectively collected by relatively untrained local tax officials.

Revenues from property taxation depend upon the property wealth of a community. Dependence upon property taxation means that wealthier communities will be able to raise more funds with less burden on taxpayers than communities without much property wealth. In other words, reliance on property taxation results in inequalities in burdens and benefits between wealthier and poorer communities. This is an important problem in states where local school districts carry the major share of the costs of education. Wealthy school districts are able to provide more school funds with less sacrifice than poor school districts, and hence "equality of educational opportunity" may vary a great deal among communities in the same state. Of course, this type of inequality is reduced in states where there is little reliance on local revenues and most school money comes from the state government. In 1971 the California Supreme Court ruled that local school district reliance on property taxation in that state denied equal protection of the laws to all the state's school children; the court ordered the state to revise its tax system to reduce or eliminate reliance on property taxation to support education.

The burden of property taxes depends upon the ratio of assessed value of property to the fair market value of the property; the rate at which assessed property is taxed, which is usually expressed in mills, or tenths of a percent; and, finally, the nature and extent of tax exemptions and reductions for certain types of property. The ratio of assessed value to full market value may be quite low, sometimes less than 10 percent, and it may vary from one community to the next, even in those states requiring uniform assessment ratios throughout the state. The failure of communities to have periodic and professional tax evaluation studies performed means that taxes continue to be levied on old assessment figures, even while market values go up. The result, over time, is a considerable lowering of assessment ratios, and therefore taxes, on older homes and businesses and industries. Newer residents, whose sale price is generally known to tax assessors and who must therefore pay taxes on the uniform assessment ratio, are generally much more favorable toward reevaluation of property for assessment purposes. There are very few communities in which a suggestion of a reevaluation will not set off a heated debate between those who are enjoying a low assessment and those who are not. When a community tampers with reevaluation or a change in the ratio of assessed to market value, it threatens to change the incidence or distribution of tax burdens within a community. If new tax revenues are needed, it is much easier to simply increase the rate or millage to be applied against the assessed value of property. Many communities face state restrictions on maximum tax rates, or they are required to submit any proposed increase in tax rates to the voters in a referendum. These restrictions are usually favored by low-tax forces, which have succeeded in obtaining legislation at the state level that impairs the taxing abilities of local governments.

Some categories of property are exempt from taxation; these usually include properties that are used for nonprofit, charitable, religious, educational, and other public purposes. Occasionally such exemptions are attacked by those who feel that they are, in effect, subsidies to the exempted organizations; this is particularly true regarding exemptions for religious property. Exemptions for educational or public properties sometimes work a hardship on communities in which large public facilities or educational institutions are located. But the exemptions that arouse the greatest controversy are usually those given by state or local governments to new business and industry, in an effort to induce them to locate in the state or community granting the exemption.

State and local *sales and excise taxes* are generally regressive, but not as regressive as property taxes.[5] The regressivity of sales taxation is based upon the assumption that low-income groups must devote most, if not all, of their income to purchases, while high-income groups devote larger shares of their income to savings. Many states exclude some of the necessities of life from sales taxation, such as packaged food bought in supermarkets, in order to reduce the burden of sales taxation on the poor. Yet, on the whole, sales taxation remains more regressive than income taxation.

States generally rely more heavily on sales taxation than on income taxation. However, reliance upon one or the other type of tax varies from state to state. The decision to place primary reliance upon sales or income taxation is one of the most important policy choices facing state government. The yield from both types of taxation can be quite large.

There are several arguments on behalf of sales taxation in the states. The first is that sales taxation is the only major source of revenue left to the states—local governments must rely on property taxes, and the federal government has placed such a heavy tax burden on incomes that taxpayers will not countenance an additional state bite out of their paychecks. Moreover, sales taxes are not as visible as income or property taxes, since sales taxes are paid pennies at a time. Generally, the customer considers the sales tax as part of the price of an item. Taxpayers never add up the total they have paid in sales taxes, so sales taxation appears to be a relatively "painless" form of taxation. In addition, sales taxes insure that low-income groups who benefit from public services will share in the costs of government. Actual hardships for the poor from sales taxes can be reduced by excluding food and other necessities

---

[5]Bishop, "Tax Burdens by Income Class."

from taxation, but the poor will pay taxes when purchasing other consumer items. Finally, sales taxes are useful in reaching mobile populations, that is, tourists, commuters, and transients—persons who derive benefits from a host state but who would not otherwise help pay for these benefits.

In contrast, progressive state *income taxes* are defended on the principle of ability to pay; that is, the theory that high-income groups can afford to pay a larger percentage of their income into taxation at no more of a sacrifice than that required of low-income groups to devote a smaller proportion of their income to taxation. The principle of a graduated income tax based on ability to pay, a principle accepted at the federal level in 1913 with the passage of the Sixteenth Amendment, together with the convenience, economy, and efficiency of income taxes, is generally cited by proponents of income taxation. Sales taxes are more difficult to administer, and some retailers may pocket tax funds unless a state has a considerable force of auditors to oversee sales tax collection.

Occasionally, *state lotteries* or legalized gambling are suggested as an alternative to direct taxation. More than half the states receive income from horse racing, gambling, or lotteries. Nevada leads the way with nearly a quarter of its revenue coming directly from gambling taxes. But only Nevada has generalized legal gambling; most states restrict gambling to pari-mutuel betting on the racetrack. The total revenues raised from such sources, however, make up less than 5 percent of all state-local revenues. Recently New York, New Jersey, and New Hampshire started public lotteries as a means of raising public money. But there are problems involved in this area. First of all, lotteries do not bring in very much money. Second, the administrative costs, including prize money, may run as high as 50 percent of the gross revenue. This compares very unfavorably with the estimated 5 percent cost of collecting income taxes and with the only slightly higher cost of collecting sales taxes. Finally, it seems likely that lotteries are *very* regressive, with low-income groups doing most of the gambling. Perhaps the only justification is that people will gamble anyhow and it is better for the state to reap the benefits than for organized crime to do so.

THE POLITICS OF BUDGETING

Too often we think of budgeting as the dull province of clerks and statisticians. Nothing could be more mistaken. Budgets are political documents which record the struggles of men over "who gets what." The budget is the single most important policy statement of any government. There are few government activities or programs that do not require an expenditure of funds, and no public funds may be spent without budgetary authorization. The budget sets forth government programs, with price tags attached. Determining what goes into a budget, that is, the budgetary process, provides a mechanism for reviewing government programs, assessing their cost, relating them to financial resources, making choices among alternative expenditures, and determining the financial effort that a government will expend on its program. Budgets determine what programs are to be reduced, increased, initiated, or renewed. The size and shape of the budget is a matter of serious contention in the political life of any state or community. Governors, mayors, administrators, legislators, interest groups and citizens all compete to have their policy preferences recorded in the budget. The budget lies at the heart of the political process.

Budget-making authority is formally placed in the hands of the governor. The actual task of preparing the budget is carried out by an agency or official under the supervision of the governor, variously designated as the director of finance, budget director, or secretary of administration of finance. In those states where the governor does not have central control over budget making (generally regarded as "weak" governor states), budget making is often the responsibility of a budget commission. Such commissions are ordinarily composed of a group of state officials—governor, chief budget officer, comptroller, treasurer, attorney general, secretary of state, and perhaps the commissioner of agriculture and superintendent of schools. In addition to these executive officers, often a budget commission will include important legislative leaders, such as the chairmen of the finance and appropriations committees in both houses of the legislature. Most large cities place formal budget-making authority in the hands of the mayor, who in turn relies upon a budget director or finance director to prepare the city's budget under his supervision.

The budgetary process begins with the governor or mayor's office sending to each governmental agency and department a budget request form, accompanied by broad policy directives to agency and department heads about the size and shape of their requests. Very often these budget requests must be made six to twelve months prior to the beginning of the fiscal year for which the requests are made; governmental fiscal years usually run from July 1 to June 30. After all requests have been submitted to the budget office, the serious task of consolidating these many requests begins. Individual department requests are reviewed, revised, and generally scaled down; often departments are given more or less formal hearings on their budget request by the budget director. The budget agency must also make revenue estimates based upon information it obtains from the tax department. Finally, budget requests and revenue estimates must be prepared. A great many decisions may already have been made by the time the budget director submits the tentative budget to the governor or the mayor for his approval. But a governor or a mayor must decide whether his budget is to be balanced or not; whether particular departmental requests should be increased or reduced, in view of the programs and promises important to his administration; whether economies should involve overall "belt tightening" by every agency or merely the elimination of particular programs; or finally, whether he should recommend the raising of new taxes or the incurring of additional debt, and if so, what kinds of taxes or debts should be requested. These decisions may be the most important that a mayor or a governor makes in his term of office, and he generally consults both political and financial advisers—budget and tax experts, party officials, interest group representatives, and legislative leaders. Ordinarily, these difficult decisions must be made before the governor or the mayor presents his budget message to the legislature. This budget message explains and defends the final budget presented by the chief executive to his legislative branch.

The governor's budget generally appears in the lower house of the legislature as an appropriations bill, and it follows the normal path of any bill. It is assigned to a ways and means committee or an appropriations committee, which often holds hearings on the bill and occasionally reshapes and revises the executive budget. After the house committee reports the appropriations bill and it is passed by the lower house, it is then sent to the upper house where it repeats essentially the same steps. How a governor's budget fares in the legislature generally depends upon his general political power, public reactions to his recommendations, the degree of support he receives from department heads, who are often called to testify at legislative budget hearings, his relationships with key legislative leaders, and the effectiveness of interest groups that favor or oppose particular expenditures. After it is passed in identical form by both houses, the final appropriations measure is sent to the governor for his signature. If the governor has an item veto, he can still make significant changes in the budget at that time; however, most governors are obliged to accept the final appropriations measure, which provides basic authority to spend money for the fiscal year. Of course, agencies granted the authority to spend a particular amount are not required to do so, and if the funds are not available, agencies may be forced to spend less than their appropriation. However, no agency may spend more than its appropriation for particular programs.

What forces are actually involved in the budget-making process? First, there is ample evidence that budgeting is a very *conservative* process— that is, if one defines the term conservative to mean preservation of the *status quo*.[6] Invariably the forms provided by the budget office require

[6]For a discussion of the budgetary process at the federal level, see Aaron Wildavsky. *The Politics of the Budgetary Process* (Boston: Little, Brown and Company, 1964).

departments to prepare budget requests alongside of last year's expenditures. Decision makers generally consider last year's expenditures as a base. Consequently, active consideration of budget proposals is generally narrowed to new items or requested increases over last year's base. The attention of governors and legislators, and mayors and councils, is focused on a narrow range of increases or decreases in a budget. A budget is almost never reviewed as a whole every year, in the sense of reconsidering the value of existing programs. Departments are seldom required to defend or explain budget requests that do *not* exceed current appropriations; but requested increases in appropriations require extensive explanation, and they are most subject to downward revision by higher political officials. The "incremental" nature of budgeting creates some interesting informal rules of the budget game. Thomas Anton summarizes some of these budgetary folkways:[7]

1. Spend all of your appropriation. A failure to use up an appropriation indicates that the full amount was unnecessary in the first place, which in turn implies that your budget should be cut next year.
2. Never request a sum less than your current appropriation. It is easier to find ways to spend up to current appropriation levels than it is to explain why you want a reduction. Besides, a reduction indicates your program is not growing and this is an embarrasing admission to most government administrators.
3. Put top priority programs into the basic budget, that is, that part of the budget which is within current appropriation levels. Budget offices, governors and mayors, and legislative bodies will seldom challenge programs which appear to be part of existing operations.
4. Increases that are desired should be made to appear small and should appear to grow out of existing operations. The appearance of a fundamental change in a budget should be avoided.
5. Give the budget office, chief executive, and the legislature something to cut. Normally it is desirable to submit requests for substantial increases in existing programs and many requests for new programs, in order to give higher political authorities something to cut. This enables them to "save" the public untold millions of dollars and justify their claim to promoting "economy" in government. Giving them something to cut also diverts attention away from the basic budget with its vital programs.

Budgeting is very *political*. As Aaron Wildavsky was told by a federal executive, "It's not what's in your estimates, but how good a politician you are that matters.[8] Being a good politician involves (1) the cultivation of a good base of support for one's requests among the public at large and among people served by the agency; (2) the development of interest,

[7]For an excellent description of budgetary politics in a state, see Thomas J. Anton, *The Politics of State Expenditures in Illinois* (Urbana: University of Illinois Press, 1966).

[8]Wildavsky, *Politics of the Budgetary Process*, p. 19.

enthusiasm, and support for one's program among top political figures and legislative leaders; and (3) skill in following strategies that exploit one's opportunities to the maximum. Informing the public and one's clientele of the full benefit of the services they receive from the agency may increase the intensity with which they will support the agency's request. If possible, the agency should inspire its clientele to contact governors, mayors, legislators, and councilmen and help work for the agency's request. This is much more effective than the agency's trying to promote for its own requests.

Finally, as we have already seen, socioeconomic conditions further reduce the alternatives for budgetary action. Very often, local governments *begin* the budgetary process by estimating the amount of revenues that can reasonably be expected from the existing tax base, various service charges, and intergovernmental revenues; this estimate then becomes the ceiling for all budget requests. This practice, together with the conservative tendency of accepting past expenditure levels, seriously curtails policy change. This may be part of the reason why governors and mayors have a difficult time bringing about significant policy changes, and it contributes to the public's view of "politics as usual" and a feeling that nothing can be done, regardless of who is elected.

Budgeting is also quite *fragmented*. In most of the states there is a great deal of constitutional and statutory "earmarking" of revenues. A common example is the earmarking of gasoline tax revenues for highway purposes. This practice fragments the budget and reduces executive control over the allocation of public funds.

Fragmentation also occurs in the consideration of budget requests by the governor and the legislature. In theory, the budget office is supposed to bring together budget requests and fit them into a coherent whole, while at the same time relating them to revenue estimates. But often budget offices do little more than staple together the budget requests of individual departments, and it is very difficult for a governor or a mayor, and almost impossible for a legislature or a council, to view the total policy impact of a budget. Wildavsky explains that the fragmented character of the budgetary process helps to secure agreement to the budget as well as reduce the burden of calculation.[9] Some budgets *must* be agreed upon by the executive and the legislature if the government is going to continue to function at all, and this pressure to agree often means that conflicts over programs must go unresolved in a budget. Calculations are made in small segments, often by legislative subcommittees, and must be accepted by the legislature as a whole. If each subcommittee challenged the result of the others, conflict might be so great that

[9]*Ibid.,* p. 59.

no budget would ever be passed. It is much easier to agree on a small addition or decrease to a single program than it is to compare the worth of one program with that of all others.

Finally, budgeting is *nonprogrammatic*. For reasons that accountants have so far kept to themselves, an agency budget typically lists expenditures under ambigous phrases: "personnel services," "contractual services," "travel," "supplies," "equipment." Needless to say, it is impossible to tell from such a listing exactly what programs the agency is spending its money on. Obviously such a budget obscures policy decision by hiding program behind meaningless phrases. Even if these categories are broken down into line items (for example, under "personnel services," the line item budget might say, "John Doaks, Assistant Administrator, $15,000"), it is still next to impossible to identify the costs of various programs. Reform-oriented administrators have called for budgeting by programs for many years; this would present budgetary requests in terms of end products or program packages, like aid to dependent children, vocational rehabilitation, administration of fair employment practices laws, highway patrolling, and so on. Chief executives generally favor program budgeting because it will give them greater control over the policy. But very often administrative agencies are hostile toward program budgeting; it certainly adds to the cost of bookkeeping, and many agencies feel insecure in describing precisely what it is they do. Wildavsky points out that there are some political functions served by nonprogram budgeting. He notes that

> agreement comes much more readily when the items in dispute can be treated in dollars instead of basic differences in policy. Calculating budgets in monetary increments facilitates bargaining and logrolling. It becomes possible to swap an increase here for a decrease there or for an increase elsewhere without always having to consider the ultimate desirability of the programs blatantly in competition. . . . Party ties might be disruptive of agreement if they focused attention on policy differences between the two political persuasions. . . . Consider by contrast some likely consequences of program budgeting. The practice of focusing attention on programs means that policy implications can hardly be avoided. The gains and the losses for the interests involved become far more evident to all concerned. Conflict is heightened by the stress on the policy differences and increased still further by an inbuilt tendency to an all-or-nothing, "yes" or "no" response to the policy in dispute. The very concept of program packages suggests that the policy in dispute is indivisible, that the appropriate response is to be for or against rather than bargaining for a little more or a little less. Logrolling and bargaining are hindered because it is much easier to trade increments conceived in monetary terms than it is to give in on basic policy differences. Problems of calculation are vastly increased by the necessity, if program budgeting is to have meaning, of evaluating the desirability of every program as compared to all

others, instead of the traditional practice of considering budgeting in relatively independent segments.[10]

Program budgeting also provides the opportunity for the introduction of performance standards in the budgeting process. "Performance budgeting" usually involves the designation of some unit of service, for example, one pupil, one hospital patient, or one welfare recipient, and the establishment of standards of service and costs based upon a single unit of service. A common example of performance budgeting is found in school systems, where pupils are designated as a basic unit of service and standards for numbers of teachers, supplies and materials, auxiliary personnel, building floor space, and many other cost items are calculated on the basis of number of pupils to be served. Thus, standards may allocate teachers on the basis of 1 to 25 students, or a full-time principal for every 250 students, or a psychologist for every 1,000 students, or twenty dollars worth of supplies for every student, and so on. These formulas are used to determine the allocation of resources at budget time. One political consequence of the use of formulas in performance budgeting is the centralization of budgetary decision making. Departments are merely asked to provide the number of pupils or patients or recipients or other units of service they expect to serve in the coming fiscal year. A central staff of budget analysts then determines allocations through the application of formulas to the service estimates provided by the departments. Many departments, accustomed to less bureaucratic procedures, feel that the use of formulas is mechanical and inflexible. But it is not surprising in a large and complex bureaucracy to see the search for equitable patterns in the distribution of resources leading to the use of formulas applied throughout the system. Often, however, once a formula has been established, it is difficult to change or adjust the formula even from one year to the next. H. Thomas James, in a study of educational expenditures in large cities, reported that the traditional inflexibility of formulas could only be adjusted under severe political pressures: "In Chicago, a selected district was provided with extra remedial teachers; in New York the 'more effective school' plan substituted a "saturation' for a 'normal' staffing pattern; in St. Louis a slum district was given an increased allotment of teachers.[11] Performance budgeting places great power in the hands of the staff personnel budget offices who devise the formulas. Performance budgeting is generally favored by economy-minded groups, particularly businessmen who are familiar with the application of unit cost procedures to manufacturing enterprises.

[10]*Ibid.*, pp. 136–38.

[11]For an excellent description of the budgetary process in big-city school systems, see H. Thomas James, *Determinants of Educational Expenditures in Large Cities of the United States* (Stanford, Calif.: Stanford University, School of Education, 1966).

TABLE 18-5

Decisional History of Selected Agency Appropriations in Illinois, 1963

	Last Biennial Appropriation	Budget Request	Budgetary Commission	Governor	Appropriations Bill	General Assembly	Approved
Dept. of Public Aid	$615,707,478	$701,556,483	$-63,433,337	—	$638,123,146	$+1,881,255	$640,004,401
Federal	280,586,446	302,721,006	- 254,716	—	302,466,352		
State	335,121,032	398,835,415	-63,178,621	—	335,656,794		
Supervisor of Public Instruction							
Operating Distribution Grants	51,810,149	77,948,344	-20,988,110	$+ 6,750,000	63,710,234	+4,141,700	67,851,934
Common School Fund	393,396,000	534,250,000	-85,160,000	-16,000,000	433,090,000		433,090,000
University of Illinois	133,741,170	194,387,740	- 4,427,319 / -14,925,200*	-18,968,540*	156,066,681	+4,414,840	160,481,521
Southern Illinois University	41,986,941	102,545,444	- 6,878,475 / -23,950,000*	-16,955,806*	54,761,163	+3,689,154	58,450,317
Teachers College	47,475,140	71,089,029	- 853,756	- 6,071,087*	64,164,186	+ 879,765	65,043,951
Dept. of Mental Health	206,136,237	258,057,410	—	-17,625,000 / -2,538,200*	237,894,210	+9,808,715	247,702,925
Dept. of Public Safety	42,286,783	63,258,383	- 300,000	- 650,000 / -21,533,587*	40,774,746	- 4,030,484	36,744,312
Dept. of Public Works	14,939,056	14,146,390	- 328,820	- 1,585,000*	12,232,070	+5,991,046	18,223,116

* Capital Item

SOURCE: Adapted from Thomas Anton, THE POLITICS OF STATE EXPENDITURES IN ILLINOIS (Urbana: University of Illinois Press, 1966), pp. 266-68.

Thomas Anton has examined the respective roles of the governor, state agencies, budgetary commission, and legislature in the development of the Illinois budget in 1963.[12] Agency budget requests are generally much higher than last year's appropriations. The executive budgetary commission makes heavy cuts into agency requests. The governor makes additional cuts to bring his budget into balance. But the general assembly proceeds to restore many of the cuts in agency requests. The final budget is much higher than last year's appropriations, but much lower than agency requests. (See Table 18–5.)

MONEY, POWER, AND "REVENUE SHARING"

Federal grants-in-aid are money payments made by federal agencies to state and local governments for carrying out programs of interest to the federal government. Federal grant-in-aid programs are established by Congress under its power to "tax and spend for the general welfare." One-sixth of all state-local revenue comes from the federal government in grants-in-aid. We have already described federal grant programs in education, welfare, housing and urban renewal, and highways and mass transit, but there are more than two hundred federal grant-in-aid programs currently in operation, which cover a tremendously wide variety of programs (see Table 2–3 in Chapter 2.) It is true that states and communities administer these programs and generally match federal funds from their own fiscal sources, but federal grants-in-aid usually involve federal intervention in policy making, through minimum standards and "guidelines." Federal agencies retain the right to approve or disapprove grant applications submitted by states and local governments. The federal grant-in-aid system has entailed many problems. Some of these were described in Chapter 2 in our discussion of federalism. The current grant-in-aid structure is a haphazard collection of hundreds of separate programs, each with its own policies, its own requirements and procedures, and its own funding. There are no clear priorities in the federal grant-in-aid system. It is uncoordinated and bureaucratic. Excessive red tape in grant preparation, approval, and funding from Washington creates lengthy program delays and uncertainty. The system restricts the ability of state and local officials to determine their own priorities. The system is unresponsive to the needs of specific communities because guidelines and funding do not take account of local situations.

12Thomas J. Anton, "Roles and Symbols in the Determination of State Expenditures," *Midwest Journal of Political Science*, 11 (February 1967), 27–43.

As a result of widespread dissatisfaction with federal grant-in-aid programs, Congress was persuaded by the Nixon Administration in 1972 to adopt the idea of general revenue sharing—the turnover of a certain amount of federal tax revenues to state and local government with few or no strings attached. The revenue sharing idea had been debated for years inside and outside of Congress before it was incorporated into the State and Local Fiscal Assistance Act of 1972.

Proponents of revenue sharing, including many big-city mayors, argued that the federal government was better at collecting revenue than state or local governments—particularly big cities, with their limited jurisdiction over tax bases. The federal government is not really in competition with anyone for residents or industry, as are state and local governments. The federal individual and corporate income tax is an effective, progressive producer of large amounts of revenue, in contrast to state and local property and sales taxes. Moreover, state and *local* taxable resources are unequally distributed among jurisdictions; federal revenues can help equalize disparities between communities.

Although state and local officials admire the tax collecting capabilities of the federal government, they generally believe that the national government cannot undertake itself to provide basic public services—police and fire protection, garbage disposal and sewage treatment, pollution abatement, public transportation, recreation, libraries, etc. Moreover, difficulties with the haphazard and bureaucratic system of federal grants-in-aid in housing, urban renewal, anti-poverty programs, manpower training, welfare, education, etc.—convinced many governors and mayors that they could do a better job themselves in confronting domestic problems if federal money was made available with no strings attached. In other words, while the federal government is better at collecting revenue, states and communities are better at spending it. Hence, proponents of revenue sharing argued that it combines the best features of each level of government.

Opposition to revenue sharing, as one might expect, is centered in Washington. Congressmen do not like to see a system develop in which they are cast in the unpopular role of tax collector, while state and local officials have all the "fun" of determining how to spend the money. Even conservative congressmen who dislike the centralized bureaucracy in Washington are fearful of separating the spending function from the taxing function. They believe that the decisions to spend money must be accompanied by the burdens of collecting it, or else spending would become irresponsible. They are joined in their opposition to revenue sharing by some liberal congressmen who fear that state and local officials do not share their definition of national purposes and priorities. These congressmen wish to retain the power to control federal funds in Washington. And, of course, the Washington bureaucracy itself, even under a president who supports revenue sharing, is a major source of opposition to the proposal.

The State and Local Fiscal Assistance Act will provide 5 to 10 billion dollars per year for states and communities in shared revenues during the 1970s. This is only about 2 percent of the federal budget, but it will amount to over 5 percent of all state and local government revenue. There are very few restrictions on the use of this money; it may be used for police and fire protection, sewage and garbage disposal, pollution abatement, transportation, parks and recreation, and most other recognized state-local functions. The Act denied the use of these funds for education or welfare, because of the heavy federal support already being given to these areas. This general revenue sharing will not replace any of the established grant-in-aid programs.

Shared revenues are allocated to each state on a formula based on three factors: population, tax effort by state and local governments, and the income level of the population. One-third of the amount allocated to each state may be retained by the state government; but two-thirds are distributed to local governments according to the same factors used to determine the state's allocation. The effect of this formula is to reward poorer states which tax their populations heavily.

An added feature of the Act is that it offers the services of the U.S. Internal Revenue Service (I.R.S.) in collecting *state* income taxes "piggyback" style in conjunction with federal income tax collections. The purpose is to encourage states to use income taxation, to minimize administrative effort in tax collection, and simplify tax matters for the taxpayer. But to be eligible to use the services of IRS, states must first make their own definition of taxable income conform to the federal definition.

Power and money tend to go together in American politics. Power in the federal system has flowed toward Washington over the decades, largely because Washington had the superior taxing powers and therefore the money to deal more effectively with the nation's major domestic problems. Revenue sharing promises to revitalize state and local governments by providing new access to financial resources. If Congress refrains from adding strings over the years to shared revenues (a big "if"), states and communities will acquire both money and power to deal with domestic issues. This is why revenue sharing is potentially a great landmark in American federalism: It offers the hope that states and communities can slow the flow of power to Washington. Of course, the balance of power in American federalism can only be stabilized if states and communities use their new-found money and power wisely and effectively in dealing with the challenges confronting the nation.

Index

DATE DUE